PENNSYLVANIA

A KEYSTONE BOOK

The Pennsylvania State University Press, University Park, Pennsylvania
and The Pennsylvania Historical and Museum Commission, Harrisburg, Pennsylvania

Pennsylvania

A HISTORY *of the* COMMONWEALTH

EDITED BY Randall M. Miller and William Pencak

Library of Congress Cataloging-in-Publication Data

Pennsylvania : a history of the Commonwealth / edited by
Randall M. Miller and William Pencak.
    p.   cm.   — (A keystone book)
ISBN 0-271-02213-2 (cloth : alk. paper)
ISBN 0-271-02214-0 (pbk. : alk. paper)
1. Pennsylvania—History. 2. Pennsylvania—Civilization. I. Miller,
Randall M. II. Pencak, William, 1951– III. Series.
F149.P366 2002
974.8—dc21

                                         2002005457

Pennsylvania Trail of History® is a registered trademark
of the Pennsylvania Historical and Museum Commission.

Published by
THE PENNSYLVANIA STATE UNIVERSITY PRESS,
University Park, PA 16802-1003
and
THE PENNSYLVANIA HISTORICAL AND MUSEUM COMMISSION,
Commonwealth Keystone Building, Plaza Level, 400 North Street,
Harrisburg, PA 17120-0053

Fourth printing, 2017

Book design by REGINA STARACE
Hand lettering by LYNN PALUMBO
Printed by THOMSON-SHORE, INC.

It is the policy of The Pennsylvania State University Press to use
acid-free paper. Publications on uncoated stock satisfy the
minimum requirements of American National Standard for
Information Sciences—Permanence of Paper for Printed Library
Materials, ANSI Z39.48–1992.

To the *People* of the Commonwealth of Pennsylvania

CONTENTS

PART II: WAYS TO PENNSYLVANIA'S PAST

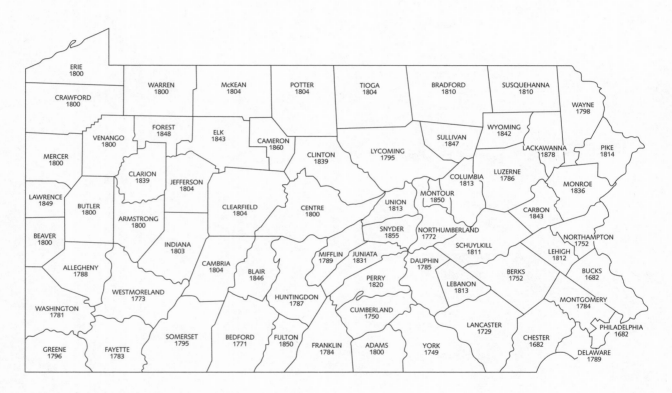

Pennsylvania, showing counties and their date of creation

The Value of Pennsylvania History

George W. Bush won the presidential election of 2000 because the fifty states cast more electoral votes for him, even though more people actually voted for his opponent, Albert A. Gore Jr. The election reminded Americans about a peculiar institution called the electoral college, and an equally peculiar system known as federalism in which each state conducts elections according to distinct laws and procedures. The daily news contains dozens of stories that underline a basic but often overlooked fact of our national experience: what happens in the individual states that make up our nation is of critical importance. Despite the greatly increased power of the national government in Washington, D.C., every state still controls its own destiny—and that of its citizens—in many ways. Whether the issue is utility regulation, abortion rights, welfare reform, education initiatives, or environmental protection, the states serve as "laboratories of democracy" much in the way the founders of the nation envisioned. The history of each state is a narrative that both reflects its own political, social, economic, and cultural traditions and at the same time intersects and shapes the national story.

The history of Pennsylvania, perhaps more than any other state, reveals the complex relationship between state history and national history. From its origins as a colony with a special sense of mission—to show that peoples of diverse religions and nationalities could live in peace—to its emergence as a political and economic power, to its struggle to compete in the global marketplace, Pennsylvania and its history contain almost all the principal elements found in the history of the United States. One way to understand the meaning of Pennsylvania's past is to examine certain places around the state that are recognized for their significance in the entire nation. These icons of state history also illustrate that every chapter of American history has at least a few pages written in Pennsylvania.

Meadowcroft Rockshelter. Human occupation of what we now call Pennsylvania began more than 16,000 years ago. Evidence of the earliest peoples is found at

Meadowcroft Rockshelter in Washington County, a site that is important for its well-preserved artifacts of prehistoric times and that reveals that the region—indeed, the entire North American continent—was inhabited much earlier than previously thought. By the time Europeans moved into Pennsylvania in the mid-seventeenth century, several native groups, such as the Monongahelas and the Eries, had already vacated the area, and Delawares, Susquehannocks, and Senecas lived in small villages like Kittanning, Shamokin, Logstown, and Wyoming. William Penn sought to coexist peacefully with these Native Americans, and the treaty he signed in 1682 instantly became a symbol of a new philosophy and attitude in the New World. Unfortunately, in an action that foreshadowed deteriorating relations between whites and Natives throughout American history, his sons ended a long era of peace and trust with the infamous Walking Purchase of 1737, acquiring through deception a large portion of the northeastern part of the colony.

The Liberty Bell. A popular belief holds that the idea to cast the Liberty Bell in 1751 began as a way to honor the fiftieth anniversary of William Penn's Charter of Privileges, a remarkable constitution that guaranteed religious freedom and defined the political framework of the new colony. In the decades preceding the American Revolution, other colonies followed Pennsylvania's model of religious toleration. During this period, Philadelphia blossomed as a major urban center led by Benjamin Franklin and his colleagues, who created educational, commercial, and social institutions such as the Library Company, the first banks in the British colonies, and the University of Pennsylvania. The Liberty Bell became a symbol of the revolution against Britain and later came to be seen as a touchstone of democracy in a new republic. In the nineteenth century, abolitionists adopted the Liberty Bell as the universal symbol of freedom and justice. Pennsylvania, with the Mason-Dixon Line forming its southern boundary, became a major destination on the Underground Railroad for escaping slaves. In the final decades of the twentieth century, the Liberty Bell has been the centerpiece of Independence National Historic Park in Philadelphia. Enshrined in a specially designed pavilion, it beckons millions of visitors from every corner of the world.

The Forks of the Ohio. In western Pennsylvania the Forks of the Ohio achieved international fame even before it became the site of Pittsburgh, the Commonwealth's second largest city. The strategic importance of that location attracted George Washington to the region on behalf of the Virginia colony, which claimed the region along with Pennsylvania and French Canada. Washington's aggressive push to remove the French and their Indian allies from western Pennsylvania sparked a decade of conflict that spread worldwide. British forces gained control of the Forks of the Ohio in 1758 and established Fort Pitt—an important step contributing to the removal of the French from the North American continent. The city of Pittsburgh grew from this colonial fortification into one of America's greatest industrial centers, the hub of the nation's crucial steel industry. Railroads and warehouses buried the old fort at the Forks in mounds of dirt and coal ash. Remarkably, the old blockhouse of Fort Pitt survived all this development, and the local chapter of the

Daughters of the American Revolution successfully challenged the mighty Pennsylvania Railroad to preserve it. After World War II, Pittsburgh embarked on a "Renaissance" that transformed the blockhouse and fifty acres of industrial blight into a state park and museum commemorating the epic struggles for empire in the eighteenth century.

Amish Farms. Amish farms in Lancaster County reflect both the state's religious heritage and its agricultural heritage. The farms of Pennsylvania, known as "the best poor man's country" in the eighteenth century, earned a reputation for productivity and quality. Places like the Oley Valley in Berks County, where stone bank barns and timbered covered bridges have withstood the challenges of a changing landscape, carry a rich architectural legacy. And the annual State Farm Show in Harrisburg—sixteen acres of indoor displays and attractions—is perhaps the greatest evidence of the variety and vitality of agriculture's place as the state's largest industry. Although the Amish refuse to drive cars or use electric appliances, they actively participate in the Farm Show. Their presence is a reminder of the tradition of religious freedom that made Pennsylvania unique among the American colonies. The Quakers in Philadelphia established this tradition, and William Penn gave voice to this ideal in his writings and policies. Groups that fled persecution in Europe—Moravians, Schwenkfelders, Mennonites, and Harmonists—sought and found refuge and isolation in Pennsylvania. Ironically, these communities of faith have now become some of the state's leading tourist attractions, and they are so popular that commercial development threatens to destroy their integrity and authenticity.

Eastern State Penitentiary. In the nineteenth century, Pennsylvania was a center for a variety of reforms. Concern for individual rights, plus the need for social change, brought about important initiatives in criminal justice, public education, care for the mentally ill, social welfare, and the abolition of slavery. For example, the construction of Eastern State Penitentiary (1829) in Philadelphia introduced a new system of criminal justice that became a model throughout the world. The building itself expressed a new philosophy, that prisoners should be rehabilitated and become "penitent" rather than merely suffer for their crimes. Throughout the nineteenth century and well into the twentieth, Pennsylvanians continued to challenge the status quo. Ida Tarbell, reared in the state's oil region, wrote a pathbreaking study of the Standard Oil Company and exposed the abuses of unregulated capitalism. John Mitchell and Mary Harris "Mother" Jones, well known in the coalfields, led a protracted struggle for the rights of workers to organize. The violence in the anthracite region associated with the Molly Maguires, and the bloody events at Homestead and Lattimer in the 1890s, kept Pennsylvania at the forefront of an epic conflict between management and labor. In the same period, progressives such as Gifford Pinchot, J. Horace McFarland, and Mira Lloyd Dock introduced the concept of conservation and pushed for public improvements to promote health, recreation, and the scenic beauty of cities.

Horseshoe Curve. By the time the Horseshoe Curve near Altoona was completed in 1854, Pennsylvania had emerged as a major hub of transportation and commerce. The roads, canals, bridges, and railroads that crisscrossed the state reflected an engineering daring and genius that literally overpowered its rugged topography. The National Road, the Allegheny Portage Railroad, the Rockville Bridge, and the Tunkhannock Viaduct are just a few of the landmarks associated with the transportation revolution that culminated in 1941 in the first limited-access highway—the Pennsylvania Turnpike—and in many of the milestones of early aviation history. The nation's first modern corporation, the Pennsylvania Railroad, developed into an economic and political force during the latter half of the nineteenth century, employing more than 125,000 workers at its peak. Building and operating the transportation infrastructure required the skills and sacrifice of thousands of workers, many of them immigrants. At one point, nearly every family in Pennsylvania included someone who was "workin' on the railroad." The dramatic decline of railroading in the twentieth century became a case study in corporate mismanagement. Only at museums in Altoona, Strasburg, and Scranton can visitors begin to understand the enormous scope and impact of this vital industry.

Gettysburg Battlefield. The Gettysburg Battlefield represents more than the defining moment in the American Civil War. A century before that conflict, Pennsylvania's strategic importance resulted in decisive military actions that began with the French and Indian War and included major engagements in the Revolutionary War and the War of 1812. Capturing Philadelphia in 1777 became the overarching goal of the British high command and led to battles at Brandywine, Paoli, Fort Mifflin, and Germantown, as well as to George Washington's winter retreat to Valley Forge. In the War of 1812, control of the Great Lakes was a key objective that encouraged the United States to build a small fleet in the remote town of Erie. The naval victory on September 10, 1813, brought fame to Oliver Hazard Perry and his flagship, the *Niagara,* and to his victory message: "We have met the enemy and they are ours." Monuments and memorials to these events stand throughout Pennsylvania. But nowhere is the glory and pain of battle more poignantly remembered than at Gettysburg, where the nation's future literally held in the balance and where Abraham Lincoln spoke in November 1863 and gave new meaning to the national experience.

Drake Well. Pennsylvania's central place in the industrial revolution is evident in so many places, but perhaps Drake Well near Titusville is the most enduring icon of that extraordinary period. The discovery of oil in that Pennsylvania town in 1859, and the commercial exploitation of oil, and later natural gas, triggered a boom that created tremendous wealth—and spectacular failures. An abundance of other natural resources—coal, timber, and iron ore—coupled with entrepreneurial leadership in Philadelphia, Pittsburgh, and several other cities, made Pennsylvania an industrial behemoth for more than a century. Processing industries like textiles, leather, and food, and fabricating plants for steel rails and bridges, locomotives and railroad cars, metal products, and electrical equipment, flourished, attracting a huge number of workers from southern and eastern Europe and the rural South. In 1919 Pennsylvania's major industries employed more than 1.6 million workers. Industry giants like Andrew Carnegie, George Westinghouse, Andrew Mellon, Milton S. Hershey, and Walter Annenberg amassed some of the nation's greatest fortunes, and products like Heinz Ketchup, Hershey's Kisses, Crayola Crayons, Slinkies, and *TV Guide* became national icons of a consumer society. The legacy of discovery and innovation is evident in the twentieth-century milestones in research and technology—for instance, polio vaccine, artificial intelligence, and the computer—that were reached in Pennsylvania's laboratories.

The State Capitol Building. As Pennsylvania approached the pinnacle of its prestige and power as a state, President Theodore Roosevelt came to Harrisburg in 1906 to dedicate the State Capitol, a monument to America's Gilded Age. The art of the Capitol impresses visitors with the significance of Pennsylvania's history and the importance of the several branches of government that labor under its great dome. Completion of this remarkable public building inspired civic leaders in Harrisburg to undertake a series of public works that made the state's capital city a center for the national City Beautiful movement. Over the next thirty years, new buildings in the Capitol Complex reinforced the connections between government, art, history, and progress. Notwithstanding epochal scandals and withering partisanship, the Capitol endures as a unique forum of democracy. In a timeless routine that resembles a staged production, advocates on every issue lobby in its corridors and rally in its ornate rotunda with the murals of Edwin Austin Abbey looming overhead and the Moravian tiles of Henry C. Mercer underfoot. After generations of neglect and careless destruction, a new preservation ethic has saved the artwork of the Capitol and its neighboring buildings. Nearby, an impressive complex housing the State Museum and the State Archives documents and displays the Commonwealth's past.

Fallingwater. If the State Capitol ranks high among Pennsylvania's most dominant public buildings, architect Frank Lloyd Wright's "Fallingwater" (1937) has earned the status of a modern icon and become among the best-known and most admired American buildings of the twentieth century. Wright designed this summer retreat for the Kaufmann family of Pittsburgh to coexist in harmony with its natural setting. In the process, he created a new artistic standard. Several other architectural trends also took shape in Pennsylvania, including Nicholas Biddle's promotion of Greek Revival at Andalusia, Henry Hobson Richardson's Romanesque Allegheny County Courthouse, the rich Victorian gems of Frank Furness, the influential philosophy of Louis I. Kahn, and the witty and controversial postmodernism of Robert Venturi and Denise Scott Brown. Pennsylvania's contribution to the arts extends to literature, painting, and music. Institutions like Carnegie Mellon University, the Curtis Institute of Music, and the venerable Pennsylvania Academy of the Fine Arts offer superb training for the young. The individual achievements of the Calders, the Wyeths, Thomas Eakins, Mary Cassatt, Violet Oakley, John Updike, John O'Hara, James Michener, August Wilson, Marian Anderson, and Andy Warhol demonstrate the state's remarkable artistic range and diversity.

The Huber Breaker. Not far from the ceaseless traffic of Interstate 81 south of

Wilkes-Barre, the Huber Breaker stands as a hulking ruin, a rotting monument to Pennsylvania's industrial past, and to the coal industry in particular. Abandonment and disinvestment, especially in major industries like coal, steel, railroads, and textiles, are the unpleasant realities of the last quarter of the twentieth century, when Pennsylvania became part of America's "rust belt." In the coal mines, the decline was most dramatic. More than 300,000 miners, equally divided in the bituminous and anthracite fields, were at work in 1919, but by the 1980s their numbers had declined by 90 percent. At the Huber Breaker, from 1939 to 1966, as many as 6,000 men processed 700 tons of coal each day. Today, the breaker and dozens of abandoned sites throughout the state form a surreal landscape of iron, steel, and concrete. Occasionally, a plan to recycle these "brownfields" emerges: an industrial park in Homestead; an industrial history museum in Bethlehem; offices and apartments in Phoenixville. Whether this massive infrastructure will rise as part of Pennsylvania's new economy in the twenty-first century remains an unanswered question for the future.

Levittown. Community-building has been a consistent feature of Pennsylvania's history from the time Thomas Holme first surveyed and plotted Penn's "greene country towne" of Philadelphia. The New England–style villages of the northern tier, the Ephrata Cloister and the utopian communities of the Moravians and the Harmonists, and model industrial towns like Vandergrift in Westmoreland County reflected a persistent belief in the benefits of planning and order. A very different kind of community emerged in Levittown (1952) in Bucks County, exemplifying the growth of suburbs that became a major trend in the post–World War II era. Attracted by the promise of guaranteed loans, good schools, and low crime rates, thousands of young families left Pennsylvania's cities. Throughout the second half of the twentieth century, Pennsylvania developed interstate highways, shopping malls, and residential subdivisions to make suburban life attractive. The urban centers could not replace the people and businesses lured away by the promising prospects of the suburbs. Between 1950 and 2000, Philadelphia's population declined by nearly 500,000, from more than 2 million, and Pittsburgh had lost almost half its population, from a high of nearly 700,000. The social and economic challenge of urban blight was a dominant issue throughout this period. By the 1990s, Pennsylvania also faced the consequences of suburban "sprawl"—uncontrolled growth that placed an enormous strain on transportation, schools, water resources, and natural habitats.

Three Mile Island. Like most states in America, Pennsylvania often managed its affairs in reaction to crises and catastrophes. The silent towers of the nuclear power plant at Three Mile Island near Harrisburg became an international symbol of the human and environmental risks inherent in the promise of technology. Although a nuclear meltdown did not occur, the accident there in 1979 focused attention on the issues of corporate responsibility as well as on the regulatory and emergency response role of government. These issues have deep roots in Pennsylvania going back perhaps as far as the Johnstown Flood (1889), the Avondale Mine fire (1869), and the Darr Mine explosion (1907). An estimated 55,000 men lost their lives in the state's coal mines between 1870 and 1999. The Donora smog of 1948 killed twenty-two people. As a result of the Knox Mine disaster in 1959, more than 10 billion gallons of water from the Susquehanna River permanently closed a large portion of the northern anthracite region, killing twelve miners and putting thousands more out of work. This bleak story of death and desolation spawned an aggressive policy of government regulation in the last decades of the twentieth century that included the environmental rights amendment to the state constitution—the first of its kind in the nation. In Harrisburg, state agencies that regulate and protect the environment and manage the state's parks and forests work in a building named for Rachel Carson, a Pennsylvanian whose writings, especially *Silent Spring* (1962), directly led to the modern environmental movement.

This baker's dozen of state icons reflects both the wide range and depth of Pennsylvania's past. The point of this exercise is that we care about the places of Pennsylvania's past—and the people and events of our past—because they define who we are as residents of this state. Pennsylvania's history is at once a source of identity and pride as well as a resource in helping us live and understand our lives. Each place connects us to stories that bear witness to the triumphs and failures of extraordinary and ordinary men and women. We must preserve these places and the stories they represent because they are our collective memory. The loss of memory for any of us is catastrophic. For a society or a state, the impact of such a loss is equally devastating.

Writing a history of a state as complex and diverse as Pennsylvania is, by necessity, a highly impressionistic exercise. A trained historian depends on evidence—written, oral, physical—to reach conclusions about the meaning of events and the significance of people and places. However, the context of the times in which this history is written also has a strong influence on the interpretation of this evidence. This is not a scientific or absolutist endeavor. The historian's authority is constrained by competing opinions of colleagues who also are armed with compelling and often contradictory evidence. Readers of history bring their own collective perspectives and critical faculties to the task of making sense of Pennsylvania's past. Regardless of the point of view of the historian or of the reader, the best history contains a sense of passion, an emotional charge that provokes a response and inspires further research and writing.

The chapters in this book are not the final word on Pennsylvania's history. The authors are scholars who study the past with great intensity and who care deeply about their subjects. If their work encourages further thought and passionate debate on the subject, this will be the greatest measure of success, and the value of Pennsylvania history will be established.

BRENT D. GLASS
Executive Director
Pennsylvania Historical and Museum Commission

March 2002

This book began in 1997 in conversations among Brent Glass, Diane Reed, and others at the Pennsylvania Historical and Museum Commission (PHMC) and Peter J. Potter of The Pennsylvania State University Press on how best to write and present a modern account of Pennsylvania's past. The standard history of the Commonwealth of Pennsylvania by Philip Klein and Ari Hoogenboom was then a quarter-century old in conception and soon to go out of print. Thus the immediate need for a new history. But more than an updated recounting of Pennsylvania's past following the Klein and Hoogenboom emphasis on economy and politics, the dawn of a new century demanded a new kind of state history.

So much had happened over the past generation in redefining the direction and character of historical writing that a simple recasting of the Pennsylvania experience in the Klein and Hoogenboom mold would miss the opportunity to rethink the Commonwealth's past and to write a history drawing on the many new methodologies and materials of the "new history" of the day. Over time, as well, the state had enlarged and enriched its own interpretations of state history through its programs in posting historical markers, developing and managing historic properties, mounting exhibitions and maintaining museums, supporting preservation of historic structures and places, and promoting historic and cultural tourism across the state. The map of "historical Pennsylvania" was becoming ever more crowded with historic sites marking significant events and developments in the state's, and the nation's, history. A new historical narrative to bring together those events and developments became ever more urgent as the panorama of historical imagination broadened and the information on particular places, people, and processes (of migration, manufacture, management, and so much more) thickened. More so, the need for a new history of Pennsylvania invited the prospect of revising not only the history of one state but also the writing of state history everywhere.

Such need and prospect led the PHMC and Penn State Press to engage experts on history, geography, archaeology, architecture, genealogy, folklore and folklife, oral history, photography, art, and literature in roundtable discussions and correspondence on writing a new history of Pennsylvania. From these discussions, and from written proposals by the editors of this book and others on what topics needed to be covered and what themes explored in such a new history, a consensus emerged that the moment demanded a history that embraced "the people" of the Commonwealth of Pennsylvania, in all their variety, as the best way to present a modern, critical history of Pennsylvania as a place and an experience. The discussants, who became the contributors to this book, further agreed that a new history must revisit and remap the many ways Pennsylvania affected and reflected American experience, while discovering and charting the ways Pennsylvania became incorporated into, and in some cases lost in, the larger national narrative.

The contributors to this book also sought to discover when, how, and why Pennsylvania lost its primacy in American thought and experience as the exemplar of "progress." William Penn's "Holy Experiment" sought to build a model society, but Pennsylvania did not become one. The promise of Pennsylvania recast the meaning of Penn's experiment as private gain competed with public good. The profits in farming the land, exploiting its vast resources in coal and timber, and making and moving products were not evenly shared, and the riches of Pennsylvania's religious, political, and economic environments attracted to the area many diverse peoples who did not always agree on what kind of "commonwealth"—by constitution a republic to protect and promote the "common weal," the public good—Pennsylvania should be. If, as historians are wont to point out, Americans are a people of paradox, so too were—and are—Pennsylvanians, as this history reveals.

Thus, no neat linear narrative of progress, unity, and community fits the true story of Pennsylvania, or of America. The contributors recognized all this and determined that tracking the causes and consequences of disagreement and failure was as important as describing and analyzing success. Indeed, trying to understand the more recent problems of deindustrialization, population loss, and social stagnation that especially afflicted Pennsylvania during the last quarter of the twentieth century—and that for a time made it a metaphor for an older America whose day had passed in the postmodern age—was another reason to undertake the new history. Too often, state histories point to the upward trajectories of a state's past rather than grapple with realities of dreams deferred or denied and fortunes lost or never realized. Not so for this history. A new history of Pennsylvania—and any new state history—must be an honest history.

Writing such a history required a double vision, much like putting on Benjamin Franklin's bifocals to see both near and far. Finding the Commonwealth meant looking closely at experiences in Pennsylvania while also plotting Pennsylvania's place in the larger world. Just as another Pennsylvanian, David Rittenhouse, in the eighteenth century had devised a model of the solar system to explain the relationship of the celestial bodies to one another, so the contributors to this book in the twenty-first century needed to fix the state's history in the larger universe of national, and even international, developments over time.

The history of Pennsylvania posed a special problem of perspective and perception because so much of the state's history informed national character and identity. It was no idle boast from state promoters during the 1990s to assert that "America starts here," for in many ways it did. The log cabin, the Pennsylvania rifle, the Conestoga wagon, the turnpike, the steamboat, the petroleum industry, commercial radio, the computer, and so much more had their start in Pennsylvania, which for two centuries became almost synonymous with material progress. Ideas about and practices of religious toleration, political party formation, democratic government, antislavery, communitarian living, social reform, and so much more also had their start in Pennsylvania, which for two centuries was almost synonymous with hopes for human progress. But those inventions, innovations, and ideas did not stay in Pennsylvania and were not always much applied there. They became "American" as they moved outward, claimed and used (and sometimes perverted) by so many people outside Pennsylvania. At the same time, inventions, innovations, and ideas came into Pennsylvania over the centuries. What then was (and is) Pennsylvania in such a process? This book provides no definitive answer so much as it follows and analyzes the process and encourages readers to appreciate how much of America's history is rooted in Pennsylvania.

One problem in approaching Pennsylvania's history is definition. Two questions especially arise. Was (and is) Pennsylvania embodied in its institutions, ideals, individuals—or what? And in a history written about the people of Pennsylvania, who are "the people"? In the fashion of the "new social history," with its emphasis on studying the lives of the "ordinary people," it is common to focus on the everyday lives of the working classes, minorities, women, and others previously shunted aside in the traditional historical narrative of presidents, generals, titans of industry, and "great men" (and a few women) who ruled the public stage. This book very much includes the "masses below," but it also gives the rich and powerful their due. Any less would be neither a history of the people nor a history of the state. To address the problems of defining the state and the people, then, the editors and authors of this book determined to find and present a history that centered its story, or stories, on the ways different peoples occupying and moving across the geographical and cultural "middle ground" of Pennsylvania planted and adapted their values, institutions, technologies, and interests to create and order communities and a commonwealth.

The purpose of this new history of Pennsylvania is not to celebrate the Commonwealth's many virtues (though the contributors find much to admire in Pennsylvania's past, even as they find cause for concerns about promises of progress and a "commonweal" gone awry). Neither the Pennsylvania Historical and Museum Commission nor The Pennsylvania State University Press had any interest in producing a puff piece on the Commonwealth. Nor is the book intended to provide a comprehensive, encyclopedic recounting of all manner of Pennsylvania's history. Rather, the book offers an interpretive history that assesses Pennsylvania history over the centuries, always with an eye to the ways people used and occupied the land, created and built communities, organized work and production, pushed their interests in the public sphere, ordered their private lives, and made and remade Pennsylvania as a place and an idea. It also offers ways to find Pennsylvania's past—in a series of chapters that suggest how different disciplines, methodologies, and perspectives have made and still make possible wider and closer views of that history. The chapters that make up Part II directly encourage readers, the people, to become historians themselves as they consider not only what has been written but also how the historians did so and what else others, such as themselves, might do to gain an understanding of Pennsylvania's past.

The organization of the book bespeaks its purpose. Each of its many elements has its own function, but all are linked together to provide both a history of Pennsylvania and ways to understand that history—or any history—through various sources and perspectives. The two parts might be read separately but are best read in concert. The Foreword and the Introduction suggest why studying Pennsylvania is important and establish a basic framework for considering Pennsylvania's past. The color image sections present numerous images of people, events, and products that have defined Pennsylvania in the public mind. Sidebars focus on particular individuals, events, and processes that illuminate further subjects discussed in the chapters. Tables provide vital statistics on population, religious affiliation, urban growth, gubernatorial elections, and colonial and state governors. The Select Bibliography suggests additional readings and research aids, complementing and supplementing the individual chapter "Sources and Further Reading" sections that address the concerns of each chapter. The many and varied illustrations throughout the book make this a visual as well as a verbal history. They present pictorial and photographic evidence and examples for the arguments in the chapters, as well as additional information on topics that need elaboration and demonstration.

Part I, which provides a history of Pennsylvania from the prehistoric times to the present, contains chapters covering "periods" that roughly demarcate significant clusters of experience and collectively provide the historical narrative. Common themes bind these chapters together: the peopling process (the movement of people into, around, and out from "Pennsylvania"); the ways people defined and defended communities; the means and dynamics of work and production, transportation and communication; the character and content of people's values and interests; and the political cultures that emerged from the kinds of society, economy, and culture formed and sustained in each time period. Chapters treating the periods after European contact with and settlement of Pennsylvania also look at the role of government as an organizing agent in providing the infrastructure that made possible the creation and development of Pennsylvania, bound the regions of the colony/state together, and consciously shaped a common colony/state identity and interest. Each chapter in Part I also points to the connections between developments in Pennsylvania and those in "America," as well as addressing the key themes running throughout the book (religious, racial, and ethnic diversity, for instance). The Epilogue to Part I offers an insightful and critical overview of the meaning of Pennsylvania's past and a speculation on Pennsylvania's future.

The chapters in Part II lay out "Ways to Pennsylvania's Past," each describing a way to discover and understand the world(s) people imagined and made. They suggest the ways certain perspectives, methodologies, and sources inform and illustrate Pennsylvania's history, and how and why such sources have been discovered and utilized to do just that. The chapters frequently reference examples from Part I, thereby encouraging readers to think about how this new history of Pennsylvania was constructed. In that regard, the book does not end with the historical chapters or with the Epilogue to Part I, for the book, taken as a whole through Part II, reminds readers that history is an ongoing process of inquiry and investigation leading to new interpretations.

Finally, a word about the images on the opening page of each component of this book. All are reproductions of some of the nearly four hundred mosaic tiles from Henry Chapman Mercer's Moravian tile floor in the Pennsylvania Capitol building in Harrisburg and are provided courtesy of the Capitol Preservation Committee. Their titles and corresponding tile numbers are listed with the Illustration Credits at the end of this book. In its entirety, the collection of Mercer Moravian tiles at the State Capitol depicts the natural and human history of Pennsylvania. Just as the Mercer tiles in the Capitol building encourage visitors to walk around the Capitol to see, and imagine, the variety and complexity of Pennsylvania and to appreciate its history, the Mercer tiles reproduced herein invite readers to do likewise with this book. We trust that such a tour will prove most enjoyable and instructive both in the Capitol building itself and in this book.

This book is the product of many hands. It was its own experiment in community-building that brought together editors, scholars, researchers, historical agency professionals, and so many others committed to writing a new history of Pennsylvania. Among such individuals none stands taller than Peter J. Potter of The Pennsylvania State University Press. Great editors have vision and vigor, the wisdom to imagine a work, and the skill to realize it. Peter Potter has all that and more. He made this book possible, not only by opening the discussions on the need for a new history, but also by assembling the scholars to design and prepare the book, guiding the work's progress throughout, keeping the project on task and on time, and maintaining a constant conversation with all parties regarding the content and character of the book. And so much more. He rolled up his editor's and historian's sleeves to find illustrations and data, to write many captions and insert key words and phrases in chapters, and to insist that arguments be persuasive and pertinent. And he kept up the enthusiasm for the book throughout. He knew, and made all of us know, that this book promised to remake Pennsylvania history, and indeed all state histories. Any success the book enjoys owes much to Peter Potter's genius.

But he was not alone. Brent Glass stood arm in arm with Peter Potter, the editors, and the authors in not only imagining this history but also in realizing it. Rare it is that someone who directs a major state agency has time to think so deeply and act so forcefully on an idea as has Brent Glass with this book. From conception to completion, he has suggested ways of thinking about state history generally and Pennsylvania particularly that have informed the work, and throughout the reviewing process he insisted only that the historians be true to the facts, honest in the assessments, and clear in the presentation. As his own lucid Foreword to the book attests, he has the historian's eye for seeing the telling detail and the big picture without losing sight of each. So it has been in his support for, and many comments on, this book.

At the PHMC, Diane Reed also has played a vital role in moving thoughts to action. Her special talents in being able to visualize a work, and her knowledge of the state's vast collections in being able to point editors and authors to illustrations and other resources, have made this book substantial in every sense of the word.

Together Glass and Reed realized that a new state history offered the prospect of a new kind of state history. They provided the intellectual, organizational, and financial encouragement to translate hope into reality. By opening the rich resources of the State Archives and other bureaus to the editors and authors, they taught us all much about Pennsylvania and ensured that the book would provide an informed and critical history as well as an informative and engaging one. Also at the PHMC, Linda Ries, Michael Sherbon, Linda Shopes, Louis Waddell, Robert Weible, and so many others suggested topics, sources, and directions, and believed in the project. Their support for this book attests anew to the PHMC's insistence that this be the most modern and meaningful historical interpretation of Pennsylvania history possible.

Also crucial to the book's success was the work of Cherene Holland, Timothy Holsopple, Peggy Hoover, and Jennifer Norton at the Press. Tim Holsopple tracked down sources, especially visual images of all kinds, provided documentation on such sources, and managed a host of support services to keep the project in good order—all with good humor doing sometimes tedious work. Peggy Hoover combed the manuscript carefully in copyediting, smoothing out prose, querying editors and authors on a host of matters of detail and meaning, and making sure all the parts fit together in the end. Cherene Holland and Jennifer Norton kept the book on time despite an impossibly tight schedule, shepherding it through copyediting, design, print, and, ultimately, to the finished product. Regina Starace, a freelance designer for the Press, created a comfortable space for the history to inhabit and made sure that the visual elements of the book coincided with the mission of the project.

In addition to the contributors to the book, numerous scholars in varied fields offered information, provided or pointed to source material, and read critically parts of the book for content and accuracy. The contributors to the book read one another's work as part of the review process, but "outside" support proved most helpful in correcting errors and improving the work. Through discussions at meetings of the Pennsylvania Historical Association, the editors and authors learned much about directions the project might go, topics it might consider, and issues it might raise. Among those providing such insight and encouragement, and also in several instances reading parts of the manuscript or helping to identify sources, were Robert Blackson, Charles Cashdollar, Dennis Downey, John Frantz, Karen Guenther, Carla Mulford, Paul Newman, Rosalind Remer, and Marion Roydhouse. Through discussions organized by the Mid-Atlantic Regional Humanities Center, led especially by Howard Gillette, Philip Scranton, and Morris Vogel, a broader conception of Pennsylvania as part of larger, and sometimes conflicting, regional and national developments matured. Thomas D. Marzik helped in locating a document from Slovak archives. Gloria Kury and Linda Patterson Miller read and improved the chapter on art. Maureen Carothers, a history major at Saint Joseph's University, helped much by fact-checking and gathering source materials. Laura Manifold, a history major at Penn State, was also an efficient fact-checker.

The editors received much assistance from the following libraries and collections in their search for documents and illustrations, corroboration of material presented in the book, writing captions, and other editorial duties (with special thanks to the individuals named): Haverford College, Jordan Rockford and the Historical Society of Pennsylvania, Rebekah A. Johnston and the Historical Society of Western Pennsylvania, Nancy Shedd and the Huntingdon County Historical Society, Valerie Miller and the Library Company of Philadelphia, the Library of Congress, the Pennsylvania Academy of the Fine Arts, The Pennsylvania State University Libraries (especially Sandy Stelts and the rest of the Pattee Library staff), The Pennsylvania State University's Department of Earth and Mineral Sciences and the Steidle Collection, the Philadelphia Museum of Art, the libraries of Saint Joseph's University (especially Christopher Dixon), the State Library of Pennsylvania, the libraries of the University of Pennsylvania, Evan Towle and the Urban Archives at Temple University, Judith Hansen O'Toole and the Westmoreland Museum of American Art, Cristina Neagu and the Worcester College Library, Oxford, and countless others too many to list here but still remembered and appreciated.

And the people of Pennsylvania had their say. The Pennsylvania Humanities Council, led by Joseph Kelly, conducted a series of public forums on what Pennsylvania meant to its citizens. Three such forums, held across the state while the book was in its early stages, proved most instructive in helping the editors think about Pennsylvania and in rendering its history, especially since the people who gathered at the forums suggested variously that Pennsylvania was an idea and a state of mind (especially the idea of "freedom"), a place (though it was many places depending on where the people lived), and a social and political entity (communities of people and a state government providing a measure of unity and coherence amid many contesting local interests). Listening to and learning from the people of Pennsylvania made possible this history about and for the people everywhere.

Why Should We Care About Pennsylvania History?

On television and in the daily papers, unless something extraordinary happens, international and national news appears first, followed by state and local events. This sequence does not exist merely for the convenience of centralized network broadcasting and news services. In the decades following World War II, problems of foreign affairs, war and peace, and military expenditures have been matters of life and death and shaped the career choices of millions who served in the armed forces and in defense-related industries. And since the New Deal, regulation of the economy, federal assistance programs—to the aged, the needy, veterans, schools, students, and industry—and civil rights legislation have affected the lives and pocketbooks of citizens throughout the United States.

For most of American history, however, from the first settlements until well into the twentieth century, the colonies, later the states, and the localities spent more money and set the policies that dominated most people's lives far more than the remote goings-on in London or Washington, D.C. Only the Civil War and World War I provided, between them, a mere six years' preview of the huge expenditures, mobilization of man (and woman) power, and national direction of public life that we have come to take for granted. As a symbol of a vanished small-scale federal government, the president's home and the executive offices were concentrated in the central portion of the White House until 1903. Only then was the West Wing built, because Theodore Roosevelt had six children who were taking up too much space. Around the turn of the twentieth century the federal budget was well under a billion dollars a year—at a time when industries under the control of J. P. Morgan and his partners were valued at $22 billion, one-fourth of the gross national product. Until the Civil War, and occasionally thereafter, citizens referred to "these" rather than "the" United States, to emphasize that regional loyalty came first. It did for Robert E. Lee, who though personally a Unionist insisted on fighting for his "country": Virginia.

Yet, if we examine the catalogs and programs of colleges and high schools throughout the nation, usually only one course on state history is offered—that of the state where the college or high school is located. Colleges sometimes grudgingly provide this course as a "service" to students who want to become high school teachers and who therefore, according to state law, must know their state's history and teach it. But state history is more than a symbol of nostalgia for the "good old days" when states were more prominent. Far more than in any other major industrial nation, states in the United States still shape the fates of their citizens.

The easiest way to sense that states make a difference is to drive through several of them on the interstate highways. The nature of the road surface changes as you cross state lines, indicating different commissioners, contractors, and relative priorities for highway funding in state budgets. Qualities of rest facilities change, and signs appear indicating that certain counties are certified business locations, or that you can now buy fireworks, or that you can access state tourist attractions on the Internet. Fines for speeding and littering vary from less than $100 to $1,000 and thirty days in jail (South Carolina). Some states sell alcoholic beverages in gas stations or supermarkets, while others allow such sales only in hard-to-find state-run stores. Other things that vary from state to state can be the cost and quality of a public education, the amount of assistance to the needy, the legal marriage age, conditions for divorce, inheritance taxes, firearms restrictions, and rules for incorporating and regulating businesses. State and local taxes come in fifty varieties. Some states inflict the death penalty; others do not.

The history of the Commonwealth is one of the nation's most distinctive histories. Founded in 1682, Pennsylvania by 1776 was among the most prosperous of the colonies and arguably "the best poor man's country," as one contemporary put it. On the eve of independence, Philadelphia, with more than 20,000 inhabitants, had surpassed Boston and New York, each of which had more than a half-century head start. As the "Holy Experiment" guided by the Society of Friends, better known as the Quakers, Pennsylvania enjoyed for three-quarters of a century a peace that contributed to spectacular growth in the three leading sectors of economic endeavor—agriculture, commerce, and industry (Pennsylvania led mainland North America in producing iron). Furthermore, only Pennsylvania had a minority of settlers of English descent; Germans and the Scots-Irish, from Northern Ireland, outnumbered the English. The idea of America as a land where diverse peoples could live in something approximating harmony certainly started in Pennsylvania. That is something the equally varied population of New Amsterdam and New York never managed.

Pennsylvania's story is not primarily the tale of great men. In fact, most of the well-known people we associate with Pennsylvania history came from outside the state or left it when they could, often when they became rich or famous. William Penn set the precedent: for only four of the last twenty-six years of his life (1682–84 and 1699–1701) did he live in the province named by King Charles II for his father, Admiral Penn (not for Penn himself). Benjamin Franklin arrived from Boston at the age of sixteen in 1723 and became world-famous as a scientist and author of *Poor Richard's Almanack* (the correct colonial spelling) in Philadelphia. But he became the symbol of America only while living in Europe, in England for most of 1756 to 1774 and in France from 1776 to 1785. Thomas Paine (Tom to his enemies), whose pamphlet *Common Sense,* published in Philadelphia, inspired the United States to declare independence in 1776, was a twenty-nine-year-old former tax collector almost literally just off the boat from England; he left Pennsylvania fifteen years later to join the French Revolution, barely escaped with his life, and retired to New York, where he died in obscurity in 1809. Andrew Carnegie, the man most associated with the Pennsylvania steel industry, was born in Scotland, arrived in America in 1848 at the age of thirteen, and in 1865 moved to New York, which became his principal residence until his death in 1919. (Carnegie's two most famous colleagues, Henry Clay Frick and Charles Schwab, also lived in New York—the former in what is now the Frick Museum at Fifth Avenue and 70th Street, if you want to see some of what Pennsylvania's wealth purchased.) John D. Rockefeller, who organized and profited most from the world's first oil boom in northwestern Pennsylvania, never lived in the state at all. His first headquarters were in Cleveland, which he left for New York City when his Ohio neighbors passed an income tax that applied only to people (or rather the one person) making more than $10 million a year. He ended his ninety-eight-year-long life in Florida. Mary Cassatt, the most famous woman Impressionist painter, left Pennsylvania for Paris. Marian Anderson, the first black singer to perform with the Metropolitan Opera, left her native Philadelphia and attained international fame in Europe before settling in Connecticut.

Most appropriately, Pennsylvania is a "Commonwealth"—officially so designated along with Massachusetts, Virginia, and Kentucky of the fifty states—that is, a society where people ought to work together for the general good. Its history is the story of communities that have persevered, prospered, and perished in astonishing varieties. In the mid-1960s Governor Raymond Shafer still considered Pennsylvania "the vest-pocket edition of the world." Thirty years later, more than 100,000 Pennsylvanians identified with each of fifteen ethnic groups, and more than 1,000,000 with five (German, Irish, Hispanic, African American, and Italian).

Pennsylvania's history is the history of a people who have long been known for their localism and ethnic persistence. Texans will tell you they are from Texas, but Pennsylvanians will tell you they are from Philadelphia or Pottsville or Pequa or Pittsburgh. "We Pennsylvanians," remarked historian Philip Klein, "lack a real sense of identity, because traditionally people's allegiances have centered around their hometown rather than the total entity of the state." Historian John Lukacs has commented that even Philadelphia, which enjoys, if that is the word, the reputation as a somewhat backward, sleepy place that comedian W. C. Fields preferred only slightly to death itself, is best understood as a large number of small, relatively self-contained neighborhoods—

109, to be exact, according to a recent geography text. William Penn encouraged diversity, yet German, Scots-Irish, Quaker, and Welsh communities tended to stick together.

The cultural imprint of these ethnic and religious groups continues to mark much of the state. Philadelphia is still the center of American Quakerism, the hub of numerous "Friends Schools" found throughout the region. And while the Amish and the Mennonites persevere, trying to maintain their identity while marketing themselves as tourist attractions, Pennsylvanians as a whole persevere as well: an astonishing 80 percent of the state's inhabitants were born in Pennsylvania, higher than any other state in the Union. The "Pennsylvania Dutch" southeast, the Eastern European ethnic enclaves in the anthracite northeast and around Pittsburgh, the insular communities in the central, Appalachian mountains of the state, and the quiet yet powerful "old money" Philadelphians of Center City, the "Main Line," and the northern suburbs set the tone for these regions.

Pennsylvanians—who wanted most just to earn a living, practice their diverse religions and folkways, and escape from oppressive conditions in Europe—had the fortune, and at times misfortune, to settle on some of the richest land on the globe. For more than three centuries, German immigrants and their descendants have maintained much of the soil in Berks, York, and Lancaster Counties as among the most productive non-irrigated agricultural regions in the world. During the colonial era, Pennsylvania was the leading producer of raw iron in the British Empire outside the British Isles themselves; in the nineteenth century, two of the world's largest deposits of coal, anthracite and bituminous, were located in northeastern and southwestern Pennsylvania respectively.

Resources by themselves are useless unless transported to where they are needed: hence, Pennsylvania, first in manufacturing for much of the nation's history, was also the nation's leader in transportation. The first paved turnpike in the United States connected Philadelphia and Lancaster as early as the 1790s. John Fitch launched America's first steamboat on the Delaware in 1785, but because it did not lead to regular service we better remember Robert Fulton and the *Clermont,* which followed in New York in 1807. To be sure, New York led the nation in canal construction with the Erie Canal, built from 1817 to 1825, which increased the nation's navigable canal mileage from 28 miles to 395. However, New York has the Mohawk Valley, which permits a relatively flat connection from the Great Lakes via the Hudson River to New York City, while to traverse Pennsylvania one must cross numerous rivers and mountain ranges. Hence the Allegheny Portage Railroad at Johnstown, the Horseshoe Curve at Altoona, the tunnels through the Alleghenies, and the national preeminence of the Pennsylvania Railroad (New York and Baltimore, for instance, still call their major railroad terminals "Pennsylvania Station").

Neither political freedom nor industrial greatness comes easily. As we watch former Communist and present Third World nations struggling to achieve democracy and prosperity, we should not expect too much too fast. Precisely because of Pennsylvania's rich land and commercial/industrial wealth, the state has witnessed some of the fiercest internal struggles over who would possess them in U.S. history. When Quaker rule ended in Pennsylvania in 1756, political conflict between ethnic groups, loyalists and patriots, and Indians and Europeans led to the most violent and radical revolution in America. Pennsylvania's Constitution of 1776 was both the most and the least "democratic" of all the new state charters; it gave the vote to all taxpaying white males *provided* they swore an oath of allegiance to the new, controversial constitution itself, thereby eliminating loyalists, Quakers, and the more conservative revolutionaries who probably constituted a majority of the population. Pennsylvania farmers, feeling overburdened by what claimed to be their national government, launched two major protests against federal taxation that have come to be known as the Whiskey Rebellion (1794) and Fries's Rebellion (1799). The incidents of labor violence in Pennsylvania—in the 1860s and 1870s in the anthracite region, blamed on "the Molly Maguires"; in 1877 throughout the state; in 1892 at Andrew Carnegie's steel plant in Homestead; in the anthracite region again in 1903 (when President Theodore Roosevelt for the first time put the federal government on labor's side); and in the steel towns during the CIO organizing campaigns of the 1930s—rank among the most bloody and famous clashes between workers and management in American history.

Contrary to those who view American industrial growth as the product of industrialists operating without government controls or in opposition to government actions they consider unreasonable or unnecessary, Pennsylvania capitalism would not have been possible without state assistance. During the formative period of its industrial order, the state invested heavily in improvements that no individual or corporation could have undertaken. By the 1840s, Pennsylvania had underwritten turnpikes, banks (which loaned capital in turn to other enterprises), canals, and railroads to the tune of more than $7 million, a sum equal to the cost of building New York's Erie Canal. Legislation—or lack thereof—and law enforcement also provided a favorable climate for business growth: eminent domain granted private property to railroads and roads for right-of-ways; corporate charters guaranteed low or no taxes and limited investors' liability to the amount of stock they held; laws guaranteeing minimum wages, setting maximum hours, and permitting unionization had to be imposed by the national government in the mid-1930s; the State Police joined the National Guard and private forces like the Pinkerton Detective Agency in busting strikes.

Pennsylvania has also been at the forefront of America's deindustrialization. In 1910 Pennsylvania produced half the nation's steel, and less than one-tenth by the 1990s. Employment in the steel industry declined more than 70 percent from 1974 to 2000. Perhaps the quintessential symbol of deindustrialization is the ghost town of Centralia in the anthracite region, whose abandoned buildings sit atop a still unextinguishable mine fire. Philadelphia has lost a quarter of its inhabitants (from just over 2 million to just over 1.5 million since 1950, and Pittsburgh lost more than half (678,000 to 335,000) in the same period.

Yet as of the year 2000 Pennsylvania was coping resourcefully with the problems of transition from a manufacturing economy to a high-tech and service economy. After remaining almost stagnant in the 1980s, Pennsylvania's population rose 3.4 percent in the 1990s, from 11,800,000 to 12,280,000. Metropolitan Philadelphia grew more than 15 percent since 1980, and greater Pittsburgh reversed its decline in the 1990s. Unemployment in Pennsylvania in the mid-1990s hovered just above the national average (5.9 versus 5.6 percent). The state's per family income, at $29,000 in 1984, stood $3,000 below the American mean but had pulled even with the national average by the mid-1990s (coincidentally, the same figure in constant dollars). By the late 1990s fewer Pennsylvanians were below the poverty level (12.5 percent) than in the nation as a whole (14.5 percent). If Pennsylvania does not lead the United States in the "high tech" revolution as it once did in agriculture and heavy manufacturing, its healthy mixture of agriculture, industry, and high tech will cushion the state effectively against future disasters like the collapse of the oil industry in the 1980s or the decline of defense contracts in the 1990s. As we enter the third millennium, Pennsylvania offers previews of two possible futures for the nation: one is found in the squalid streets of North Philadelphia or the boarded-up downtowns of the old steel and coal towns; the other is in the Philadelphia suburbs, the tourist industry of the Poconos, or the high-tech environs of State College.

The book you now hold presents a new vision of state history, one that does justice both to Pennsylvania's distinctiveness and to its impact on the world. The overview provided by the Foreword, the Preface, and the Introduction provides the reader with a framework and rationale for the rest of the book. Where possible, the seven chronological chapters that make up Part I move beyond political and economic history to focus on certain communities and individuals whose odysseys reflect those of people all over the state. The Epilogue to Part I offers an incisively critical look at Pennsylvania's past while peering into the future. By means of these vignettes, and with illustrations that are not simply heads of great men but powerful depictions of the state's history, the authors seek to bring history to life.

A main theme of this book is that history does not leave us. We carry it around in our minds and on our backs. Patterns established on colonial farms, in coal mines, in factories, and on city streets still shape the Pennsylvania in which its people live today. History is neither a bunch of facts nor a fixed, unchanging "thing" to be memorized. It is being re-created by each generation, each community, each individual. While we may admire the film *Gone With the Wind* as a work of art, no longer do people think of slaves as happy servants of friendly masters and mistresses. History is something we all "do" as we evaluate news, make career decisions, participate in politics, and join associations like churches, veterans groups, and organizations that would change the world. Either we make our own history, or we let others make it for us.

We also have a choice whether to write our own history or let it be written for us. The millions of Americans who write about their clubs or churches, write term papers in colleges, or research their ancestors are historians whether they know it or not. Hence, Part II of this book consists of nine chapters that tell how you, the reader, can study the history of Pennsylvania for yourself.

History does not survive only in old documents and books—although that is usually a good place to start. History can be gleaned from church and county records that detail the births, deaths, marriages, land records, criminal activity, and movements of families; it survives in photographs, paintings, furniture, tools, and buildings that tell us how our ancestors dressed, interacted, ate, and slept; it can be discerned in folklore that persists, and it leaps from the pages of such novels as those by John O'Hara or Thomas Bell; it can be reconstructed from interviews with people who may think their lives are only "ordinary" but whose contributions to their workplaces, towns, and families, taken together, constitute history.

In the last analysis, history is about both memory and forgetting. The editors and authors of this book cannot remember everything, nor can we tell the tales of more than 100 million souls who have lived in Pennsylvania since the last ice age in a book of some 600 pages. But, we hope, the seventeen of us can present histor*ies* that remind as many of the Commonwealth's people as possible of their own past. If the story of your particular town cannot be found here, we have tried to ensure that some community with a similar past does appear. We also provide suggestions and tools that will enable you to write your own history—and thereby make ours obsolete as quickly as possible. For the true success of a history book lies in inspiring its readers to go beyond it.

The HISTORY

PART I

The First Pennsylvanians

DANIEL K. RICHTER

The human story of Pennsylvania began long before there was a Pennsylvania, before even the land assumed its modern form. People lived and died, and their societies flourished and declined, for well over 10,000 years before William Penn was born. That is an immensely long time, and so it makes little sense to call Native Americans "the first immigrants." More appropriate metaphors come from Indian origin stories, which speak of supernatural founders who rose up from the ground or fell from the spirit world above to a still-forming earth. It is as if people have lived in Pennsylvania forever.

Scholars usually divide this long human history into three major periods—Paleo-Indian from approximately 10,000 to 8000 B.C., Archaic from 8000 to 1000 B.C., and Woodland from 1000 B.C. to the period of contact with Europe. Each of the latter two epochs is often in turn partitioned into "Early," "Middle," and "Late" subphases. A textbook written thirty years ago would have explained that Paleo-Indians were big-game hunters, that Archaic Indians were hunter-gatherers, and that Woodland Indians were agriculturalists. The picture now appears much more complicated—at the same time both more varied and more uniform across time and space. The Paleo-Indians now seem to have been preceded by much earlier cultures. Meanwhile, the distinctions once thought to distinguish various subphases from Early Archaic through Middle Woodland no longer seem so clear. For thousands of years, it now appears, people adapted in diverse and changing ways to local environmental circumstances, mixing hunting with

TABLE 1.1 PENNSYLVANIA'S NATIVE PAST

Approximate Dates	Major Environmental Events	Cultural Change in the Pennsylvania Region
30,000–22,000 B.C.	Interior continental route from Beringia south ice-free	First migrations from Asia to the Americas
22,000–15,000 B.C.	Pacific coastal route south ice-free, interior route blocked	Migrations continue; South America occupied
15,000 B.C.	Glaciers begin to melt; Beringia submerged	Earliest occupation of Pennsylvania region
10,600 B.C.	Glaciers recede from today's Pennsylvania	Paleo-Indian period
9500 B.C.	Younger Dryas Cooling halts glacial melting	Paleo-Indian period
8000 B.C.	Warming resumes; rivers and coastlines of Pennsylvania region begin to take modern form	Early Archaic period
6500 B.C.	Oak forests predominate	Middle Archaic period
3000 B.C.	Mixed oak and hickory forests	Late Archaic period
1000 B.C.		Early Woodland period
A.D. 0		Middle Woodland period
A.D. 900	"Medieval Optimum" period of global warming begins	Agricultural Revolution; Late Woodland period
A.D. 1350	"Little Ice Age" begins	Late Woodland period
A.D. 1500–1600		First contacts with Europeans
A.D. 1624–1638		Dutch, Swedish, and English colonies established

SOURCES: Jay F. Custer, *Prehistoric Cultures of Eastern Pennsylvania* (Harrisburg: Pennsylvania Historical and Museum Commission, 1996); W. Fred Kinsey, "Eastern Pennsylvania Prehistory: A Review," *Pennsylvania History* 50 (1983), 69–108; E. Willard Miller, ed., *A Geography of Pennsylvania* (University Park: The Pennsylvania State University Press, 1995).

fishing and—perhaps almost always more important—with the gathering of plants. Within this cultural multiplicity, however, there was little direction over time toward any single overarching pattern. Types of stone tools and weapons came and went, pottery was invented, wild grains and semidomesticated crops came to be used in various ways, but the basic population group throughout the area that today is Pennsylvania remained a band of 50 to 150 people who shifted their residences with the seasons and shrewdly exploited whatever resources their local environment offered. Only in the years around A.D. 1000, by the European calendar, did truly transformative changes begin to take place, as an agricultural revolution swept unevenly through eastern North America. The economic, social, and political implications of that agricultural revolution were still working themselves out at the moment Native people first encountered Europeans. As the seventeenth century began, Indian Pennsylvania was in its own way changing at as dizzying a pace as the societies from which the colonizers came.

BEGINNINGS

While occasional ancient travelers from Polynesia, Europe, or elsewhere may have found their way to America and made it their home, there is no doubt that the principal ancestors of Native Americans migrated from Asia across what is now the Bering Strait between 30,000 and 15,000 years ago. With much of the world's water locked up in glacial ice, sea levels were low enough to expose not a mere "land bridge" but an entire subcontinent, Beringia, which spread as much as a thousand miles from north to south. Bands of fishers, hunters, and gatherers did not so much migrate across this vast territory as live on it. Over the course of decades and centuries, they and their descendants gradually shifted their base camps from present-day Siberia to Alaska and ultimately South America. Perhaps they made their way south by foot or by water craft along the Pacific Coast, by routes for which the evidence, like that for Beringia itself, is now submerged. Before 22,000 B.C. and again after 15,000 B.C., an inland passageway on the east side of the Rocky Mountains was also open. Either by that route or by making their way indirectly from points south and west, people filtered into eastern North America.

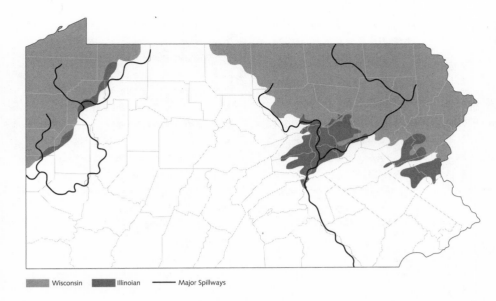

Wisconsin ■ Illinoian —— Major Spillways

Glaciation in Pennsylvania. Pennsylvania's geography and climate did not begin to assume its modern shape until about 10,000 years ago. The darker areas on this map represent the extent of the most recent glaciation at its peak in approximately 16,000 B.C.

At those distant times, the region's climate, vegetation, and landscape bore little resemblance to those of today's Keystone State. During "the Late Pleistocene Maximum," approximately 16,000 B.C., glaciers stretched from what are now the Great Lakes to New England and covered the northern portion of Pennsylvania in twin V's from near present-day Newcastle, to Williamsport, to the Delaware Water Gap. The water trapped in all that ice lowered the sea as much as 300 feet. As a result, the Mid-Atlantic shore lay some 200 miles farther east than it does today, and the Delaware and Chesapeake Bays did not exist; in their places were freshwater river valleys. The extended coastline meant that the portion of Pennsylvania not covered by ice lay well in the interior and had an inhospitably cold climate. Coastal areas would have been more welcoming to human settlement. Thus it is possible that most evidence of the Mid-Atlantic region's earliest population now lies submerged beneath the sea.

Remains from a site approximately thirty miles southwest of Pittsburgh known as the Meadowcroft Rockshelter, however, demonstrate that people did live within the present-day boundaries of Pennsylvania during the closing years of the last ice age. Controversy swirls around the dating of the stone artifacts found there, but with a probable age of between 12,000 and 14,000 years they provide some of the oldest firm evidence of human occupation anywhere south of Alaska. The kinds of tools found at Meadowcroft seem mostly unrelated to hunting and were most probably used for processing fibers, skins, and wood. The people who made them probably did not hunt big game but instead foraged for plants, nuts, berries, and small animals.

BUT HOW DO WE KNOW THAT?

"Writing any history is just pulling a tomcat by its tail across a Brussels carpet," the great American historian Charles A. Beard once said—and he was talking about trying to make sense of the well-documented twentieth century. Pulling a dead mastodon out of a swamp might be a more appropriate image for the task facing a historian trying to piece together the many millennia of Pennsylvania's history before the 1600s, from which no written records of any kind survive. Four basic strategies—all of them imperfect—have to substitute for the usual kinds of documents on which historians rely. First and foremost are insights from archaeology. As explained in Chapter 10, the material remains of past cultures can yield extraordinary insights into the way in which people lived their lives. Stone tools and fragments of broken pottery can be studied for their changes in methods of manufacture, presumed uses, and styles. Traces of pollen and remains of plants and animals can tell us something about the environment in which people lived and the foods they ate. The distinctive marks that cooking hearths, storage pits, refuse dumps, and wooden house posts left in the soil allow us to see how people organized their living spaces and to imagine how they interacted as communities. Graves sometimes reveal how people died and the diseases and dietary deficiencies from which they suffered. The careful ways bodies were prepared for burial yield insights into religious beliefs and (something far too often forgotten until recent years) remind us of the need to treat human remains with the respect they deserve. But in the end, all these forms of evidence raise more questions than they answer. Their interpretation depends not just on such technicalities as Carbon-14 dating but also on sophisticated theory, and

(there is no way around it) sometimes plain guesswork.

To make the story more than mere speculation, at least three other methods need to be employed, each with its own distinctive shortcomings. One is the comparative method of anthropologists who have devised models to predict the ways in which people who make their living in a particular kind of environmental setting—by, for example, hunting and gathering—typically organize their lives and work. Major environmental changes, in particular, tend to be seen as the cause of significant cultural change; a colder or warmer climate or the extinction or arrival of new plant and animal species provide the challenges and opportunities that spark human innovation. But such generalized models can tell us nothing about the historical particulars that distinguished Native Pennsylvanians from other peoples.

So a third method, called "upstreaming," often proves more valuable. Scholars take a cultural pattern for which they *do* have written documentation or firsthand evidence and project it backward in time—"upstream"—to a period for which no such evidence exists. Thus, if we know that a seventeenth-century Native American group lived in a particular kind of housing, and if a fourteenth-century archaeological site shows a pattern of post molds matching that style of housing, we can be fairly confident that people lived in similar dwellings in that earlier period. With slightly less confidence—but quite reasonably—we can also assume that if this kind of house was home to a particular kind of family group in the seventeenth century, it was so in the fourteenth century as well. Similarly, if we know that women were the people who made ceramic pots in the seventeenth century, we assume that was the case in the first century also. But the further back in time we try to upstream, the less confidence we can have. And there is always the danger of assuming that the basic pattern of the human

past is continuity rather than change. How would we ever know if at some distant point in the past a great social revolution led women to take over potmaking from men?

Archaeology, comparative anthropology, and upstreaming all essentially rely on the scholarly perspective of outsiders. The fourth crucial method for trying to make sense of Pennsylvania's deep past draws on the Native Americans' own oral traditions. Yet this too is not as easy as it sounds. No culture's oral traditions convey a literal record of what happened in the distant past. This is not because oral tradition is inherently inaccurate or unreliable—far from it. Instead, we need to consider the *purposes* people have for telling stories about a past they themselves did not directly experience. Almost universally, their point is not to describe what "actually" happened, but to discover something about who they are as a community and what they should do and think in their own present day. To use an example from another culture, Adam and Eve have always had far more to tell Europeans about life in the present than about life in the Garden at the beginning of time. For more on folklore as a way to Pennsylvania's past, see Chapter 11.

THE PALEO-INDIAN PERIOD, C. 10,000 TO 8000 B.C.

By 10,600 B.C. the melting glaciers had retreated from all of present-day Pennsylvania. Between 9500 and 8000 B.C. a colder period that geologists label "the Younger Dryas" halted the process and left much of today's New York State and parts of northern Pennsylvania a frigid and virtually uninhabitable tundra zone. To the south was an ecological patchwork. Lower elevations were covered by stands of fir and spruce. Higher ground tended to be open grasslands roamed by small numbers of megafauna—mastodon, mammoth, muskox, and caribou—and larger populations of deer, elk, and moose. Areas nearer the seacoast (which remained far to the east of its present location)

Paleo-Indian fluted points from the Shoop site. These spearheads, notable for the groove chipped in each side to fit a wooden shaft, are among the few surviving kinds of evidence about the people who lived in what is today Pennsylvania more than 10,000 years ago.

were a mixture of evergreens and leafy forests, wetlands, and open glades. These would have provided a rich variety of animal and plant resources for human inhabitants.

The Paleo-Indians of this era left behind very different kinds of stone artifacts than did the earlier people who camped at Meadowcroft Rockshelter. Most distinctive were the fluted points, two-to-four-inch spearheads with a groove chipped on each side to accommodate a split shaft. Because these and a few stone tools are virtually the only surviving evidence of the Paleo-Indians' existence, it is difficult to say anything definitive about who they were, how they made their living, how their societies were organized, or what differences in languages, beliefs, or customs may have divided them. Yet, far from being the loutish cave dwellers of popular imagination, Paleo-Indians would have needed complex skills to survive in their harsh environment. The varied sites at which their artifacts appear suggest that some camps had specialized purposes—particularly as spots to quarry stone but also for such activities as butchering game—and that others probably were seasonal base camps occupied repeatedly. No evidence of Paleo-Indian clothing or housing has been found, but in their cold environment people must have developed sophisticated ways of using furs and hides to provide both. The bone needles they probably used for sewing these would have long since disappeared along with most other material evidence of their way of life.

While Pennsylvania's Paleo-Indians probably killed the occasional mammoth or mastodon, it is unlikely that they built their lives around the megafauna, which were already on their way to extinction and for which the area provided only a marginal habitat. Using the lance or thrusting spear to which their fluted points were attached, Paleo-Indian hunters would have needed to get very close to large prey, relying more on surprise, traps, and group effort than on brute force. The difficulties that must have been involved suggest that gathering and small game provided a large portion of their diet. Generalized hunter-gatherers of later times in other parts of the world sometimes covered territories of 20,000 square miles or more in their annual rounds.

If the comparison holds, a single band of Paleo-Indians might have traversed half the present state each year as it gathered plants and searched for fish and small mammals.

THE PENNSYLVANIA LANDSCAPE TAKES SHAPE

When global warming resumed about 8000 B.C., the Pennsylvania environment changed dramatically. Massive runoffs of melting glaciers remolded the land, and sea levels rose to create the shoreline we know today. Those of us who spend most of our time indoors and who travel unthinkingly at sixty-five miles an hour on interstate highways regardless of terrain need to appreciate how complicated the state's topography became in the postglacial period, and how profoundly the resulting landscape shaped its human history to the present day.

In that landscape, geographers distinguish seven zones, arranged in bands paralleling the direction of the Mid-Atlantic Coast and the Appalachian Mountains. A thin slice of Atlantic Coastal Plain hugs the west bank of the Delaware River from today's Wilmington, Delaware, through Chester and Philadelphia, to opposite Trenton, New Jersey. For Native people, of course, modern state lines meant nothing, and the much larger lowland of which this is a part—stretching from the Maryland tidewater to the Jersey shore—was all a single region. At the Fall Line where Manayunk and Conshohocken now stand, the gently rolling Piedmont spreads north and west (and south into today's Maryland) until it gives way in turn to the narrow strip of the Triassic Lowland, defined for geologists by the relative youth of its rocks in comparison with those in other regions. Almost invisible to the naked eye, this zone is of great significance for travel and communication. It cuts a wide gap in that formidable continental barrier, the Blue Ridge, creating two separate formations Pennsylvanians today call, in each of their respective localities, "South Mountain."

Beyond, stretching across one-third of the state from its southern midsection to nearly its northeast corner, lies the Ridge and Valley province—parallel ranks of long, narrow sandstone "endless mountains" separated by bands of fertile lowlands. These lowlands include most notably the Great Valley (known at one end as the Cumberland and the other as the Lehigh) and the Wyoming Valley, where now the cities of Scranton and Wilkes-Barre sprawl. This zone ends abruptly at the 1,500-foot escarpment of the Allegheny Front, which defines the

Topographic zones of Pennsylvania. Irrespective of modern political boundaries, geographic divisions shaped the lives of Native Americans and continue to define regional differences in Pennsylvania to the present day.

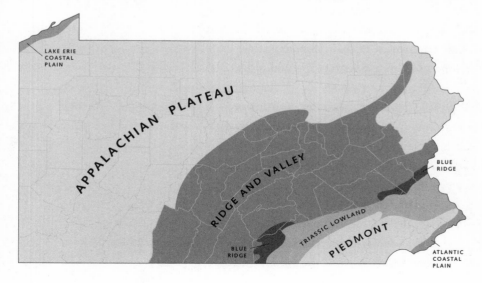

eastern edge of the Appalachian Plateau—rugged uplands that comprise nearly all of the state's northern and western half. There, countless winding streams carve deep hollows that give the appearance of mountains to the contrasting high ground, which actually is of almost uniform elevation, although the retreating glaciers left a somewhat smoother landscape in the north than in the unglaciated southern remainder. Descending from the Appalachian Plateau, the melting ice found a succession of new outlets into what became the Great Lakes. Thus were created the stepped terraces of the narrow Lake Erie Coastal Plain, the last of Pennsylvania's basic topographic zones. Like its counterpart on the Atlantic Coast, this plain is only a portion of a much larger zone stretching into modern neighboring states, in this case the Great Lakes Lowlands of New York and Ohio.

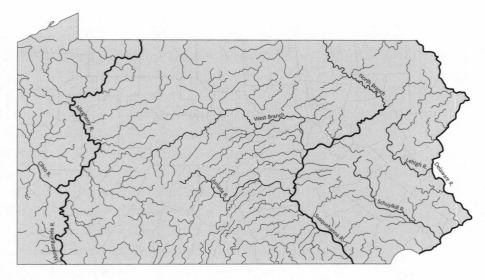

Streams and rivers of Pennsylvania. Three great watersheds—the Delaware, the Susquehanna, and the Allegheny-Monongahela-Ohio—have molded Pennsylvania's human geography since earliest times.

Also crucial in defining Pennsylvania's natural landscape—and perhaps even more significant for its human geography—are three great river systems that punctuate the seven topographic zones. As the glaciers melted, huge volumes of water flowed through what became the Allegheny, Susquehanna, and Delaware watersheds, raising the latter two rivers thirty feet above their current levels. When the meltwaters abated, broad, flat, fertile stream terraces and countless small islands remained as ideal spots for human settlement. As the rivers assumed modern form, they also created other important structural characteristics. The Delaware, with its major tributaries the Lehigh and the Schuylkill, and the Susquehanna, with its North and West branches and its Juniata tributary, each cut through the natural barrier of the Ridge and Valley to provide communication between the newly formed Delaware and Chesapeake Bays and the Great Lakes Lowlands of today's upstate New York. In the region defined by these two river systems, then, the enduring course of human interaction and development would flow from south to north and back again.

By contrast, the southward-flowing Allegheny and its tributaries joined the northward-flowing Monongahela system to form the Ohio, with its broad route westward toward the Mississippi. On the Appalachian Plateau, therefore, the principal natural orientation was south and west, rather than north and east, directions from which it remained relatively inaccessible. While paths from the headwaters of the West Branch of the Susquehanna, and especially the Juniata, provided some access across the plateau to the tributaries of the Allegheny, for the most part the westward-oriented Ohio watershed remained formidably isolated from the southward flowing Susquehanna and Delaware systems.

Or, rather, it was the Susquehanna and Delaware watersheds that were isolated. For centuries, the centers of Native American population and cultural innovation in eastern North America lay in the Ohio and central Mississippi Valleys, and, far beyond them, the great civilizations of Central America. The Susquehanna and Delaware watersheds could communicate with the core only indirectly by way of two regions that were themselves peripheral—the coastal plains of the Great Lakes in the north and the Atlantic Seaboard in the south. The one great relatively level, fertile area of the state—the Piedmont, of which today's Lancaster and York Counties are the heart—stood, most isolated of all, at the point where these two indirect communication routes met. Far from being the keystone, Pennsylvania was on the very edge of the Native American world.

As the land of what became Pennsylvania assumed new forms, its plant and animal population changed. Over the course of several centuries, thick forests spread northward to cover much of the former ecological patchwork. As a result, although the climate warmed, except in floodplains, river valleys, and coastal areas, the variety of food resources that had sustained the Paleo-Indians declined. The megafauna became extinct as their cold grassland habitat disappeared. More important, most of the open spaces and wetlands that had been home to smaller animals and plant resources also were swallowed by the encroaching trees. By no means, however, were all the changes for the worse. The lowering Susquehanna and Delaware river watersheds, for example, became not only travel routes for human beings but also major corridors for migrating ducks, geese, and other waterfowl. These rivers, swarming with freshwater fish throughout the ice-free months of the year, were invaded each spring by huge schools of saltwater herring, shad, and other species headed for spawning sites upstream.

THE ARCHAIC PERIOD, 8000–1000 B.C.

The geographic and ecological transformation of Pennsylvania inspired the new cultural patterns of what is known as the Archaic period. The transformations probably occurred so slowly as to seem imperceptible. Indeed, for many centuries fundamental skills of generalized hunting, fishing, and gathering need hardly to have changed at all. Although locations and specifics of plant and animal species shifted, a basic pattern of scattered coastal, riverine, wetland, and forest-edge points of abundance remained a constant, as did the human methods of exploiting them. Although the traditional archaeological marker of the transition from Paleo-Indian to Archaic is the shift from fluted to notched points (attached to the spear shaft in a new way and designed with barbs that would keep them in place once a blow was struck), no major innovations in the *technology* of stoneworking occurred. Archaic tool kits show great continuity with those of Paleo-Indians.

During the Middle Archaic period, between about 6500 and 3000 B.C., significant environmental changes continued. Modern seasonal variations in temperature took hold, and pine and spruce forests gave way to woods dominated first by hemlock and then by oak. The triumph of oak forests was particularly important because it narrowed the former divide between productive riverine and open environments and impoverished woodlands. In the woods, acorns now provided food for both humans and the animals they hunted. Middle Archaic societies exploited this bounty with new and more varied stone tools, which differed from one another not only chronologically but also geographically.

These patterns suggest that Middle Archaic people were organized as bands of between twenty-five and fifty individuals who worked stone in their own distinctive styles and hunted and gathered in a circumscribed area—most likely a river drainage—of perhaps 500 square miles. Similarities in toolmaking across adjacent areas suggest that such bands might have been affiliated with others in "macrobands" that traded and intermarried. The members of bands and macrobands probably practiced a gendered division of labor. Women were primarily responsible for gathering, and men for hunting and fishing. Both activities required extraordinary knowledge of the landscape and its bounty. Gathering was hardly the random kind of activity its name might seem to imply. Middle Archaic women would have needed an encyclopedic knowledge of wild plants; in some seasons, the fruits and vegetables they harvested may have constituted the bulk of the band's diet. Hunters meanwhile pursued the same kinds of game animals found in Pennsylvania's forests today. Deer, elk, bear, and turkey were significant food sources, but fish, shellfish, and fowl were probably just as important.

In contrast to the scant evidence from the Middle Archaic period, spear points and other stone tools from the Late Archaic period (approximately 3000 to 1000 B.C.) are found almost everywhere in Pennsylvania. The vast majority of relics now resting in backyard gardens, attic cigar boxes, and amateur collections date from this era. The ubiquity of Late Archaic artifacts suggests both the successful adaptation of human societies to every habitable portion of Pennsylvania and the seasonal mobility that allowed still relatively small populations to leave their marks everywhere. But the plethora of material remains also reflect real technological innovations that allowed new types of stone tools to emerge in the second and third millennia before the modern era. The most dramatic of these was the spear-thrower, or atlatl, a shaft of wood approximately two feet long with a handle carved of antler at one end, and a stone weight and antler hook designed to fit into the butt end of a spear at the other. Multiplying the leverage, force, and speed produced by the human arm, the spear-thrower, in combination with barbed, notched points that held fast in the skin of a wounded animal until it dropped of exhaustion, gave hunters a new advantage.

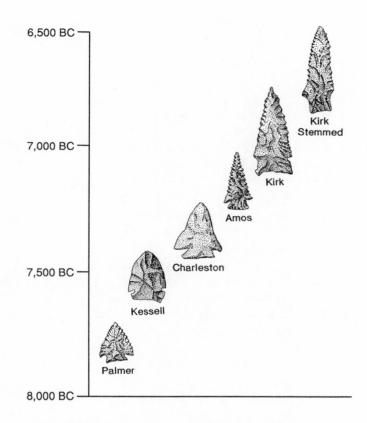

Early Archaic notched point types. As Pennsylvania's modern climate began to take shape, its people developed more efficient stone-hunting technologies. These spear points were designed to stay in place once they struck home. Regional and chronological differences in design provide clues to cultural differences among Native peoples.

ANCIENT HIGHWAYS

Contemporary travelers alert to the occasional roadside historical marker may be aware that many of Pennsylvania's modern highways follow the routes of old Indian paths dating back to the eighteenth century. But many such routes are far older than that.

The southern portion of U.S. Highway 522, for instance, traces a transportation corridor between the Cumberland Valley and the Juniata River that has been in use at least since 6500 B.C. Known in the eighteenth century as the Frankstown Path, since the Archaic period it had been traveled by countless generations of people transporting rhyolite—a volcanic substance used for stone tools—from quarries on South Mountain to points north and west.

After camping at level spots near the quarries to do some preliminary processing and lighten the load, travelers carried the blanks fifty miles or so to seasonal hunting camps in the watershed of Aughwick Creek, where they further worked the stone into spear points and cutting tools. From there, finished products may have been traded far afield by way of the Juniata River valley; such materials particularly turn up on Central Pennsylvania Middle Woodland period sites from late in the first millennium A.D. Artifacts found at the processing spots, the hunting camps, and the overnight stopovers show that people of various cultures occupied these areas repeatedly for thousands of years, until the eve of the Native American encounter with Europeans.

SOURCE: Paul A Raber, "Prehistoric Settlement and Resource Use in the Aughwick Creek Valley and Adjoining Areas of Central Pennsylvania," *Pennsylvania Archaeologist* 65 (March 1995), 1–8.

But more important on a daily basis were more mundane stone artifacts, most of them (like the weights that counterbalanced spear-throwers) made with a time-consuming "ground-stone" technique that used water and grit to shape and polish a rock. Axes, adzes, and other woodworking tools made by this method were common, suggesting that people were making dugout canoes, clearing trees, and cutting firewood on a scale not previously seen. Ground-stone pestles, mortars, and similar devices for processing nuts and other food, along with bowls and cooking pots made of soft soapstone, meanwhile, indicate the use of a wide variety of food resources. Much of that variety resulted from the fact that hickory was joining oak as a predominant species in Pennsylvania's forests. Hickory nuts are more easily processed for food than are acorns; moreover, a mixed oak and hickory forest supports a larger population of deer and small game than one of oak alone. Yet forests were not the only source of abundance. Ground-stone fish-net anchors, platform hearths presumably used to dry the resulting catch, and carefully dug storage pits all testify to a richer diet than in previous centuries and to an ability to accumulate surpluses of food. Such evidence also indicates that Late Archaic people spent a greater portion of the year in a single location.

By the end of the Archaic period, a diverse array of peoples populated all of the state's three major river systems and exploited the natural environment in sophisticated ways. Despite the cultural variety, in light of the enormous stretches of time involved—some 7,000 years—the most striking characteristic of the Archaic period is how slowly its material culture evolved. Only a relatively few locales, inhabited repeatedly across the centuries, provided ideal sites for human subsistence, and technologies for exploiting them changed only gradually. The richest environments were in river valleys, where floodplains provided rich soils for wild plants, where wetlands attracted small game, where migrating fish could be captured on their spawning runs, and where forest edges offered plant fibers, trees small enough to be cut with stone tools, and an array of vegetable foods. By the Late Archaic period, these forest edges were probably managed by periodic controlled fires set by people to encourage new floor growth under the canopy of undamaged larger trees. The courses of streams, too, were modified by the fish-trapping weirs of the Archaic Indians. There was nothing "simple" or "primitive" about such practices, and for the most part life was

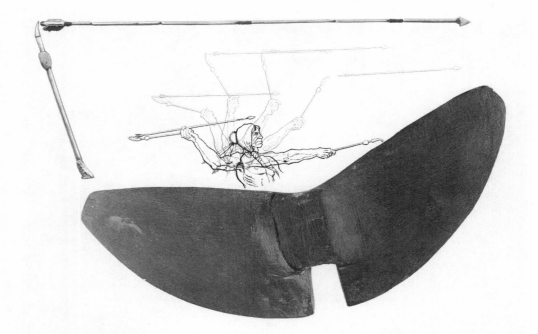

A spear-thrower, or atlatl, with enlargement of ground-stone weight. In the Late Archaic period (c. 3000–1000 B.C.), this hunting technology became common throughout what is today Pennsylvania.

anything but nasty, brutish, and short. Well-adapted material patterns thus endured for millennia, although an infinite variety of human languages, beliefs, and social practices—which leave hardly a trace in the archaeological record—no doubt came and went.

THE EARLY AND MIDDLE WOODLAND PERIODS, 1000 B.C.–A.D. 1000

In the core Ohio Valley and Mississippi Valley regions, the Early Woodland period that began in approximately 1000 B.C., and the Middle Woodland period that followed it from about A.D. 0 to 1000, saw dramatic developments. The great civilizations known as Adena in the Early Woodland period, and Hopewell in the Middle Woodland, developed rich material cultures, built huge earthworks at their ceremonial centers, and, through vast trading networks, spread their influence across much of the continent. Yet Pennsylvania remained on the fringes of these influences. Certainly they touched the Monongahela and Ohio River regions, and Adena funeral practices apparently inspired the builders of a few small burial mounds in the upper Susquehanna and Delaware watersheds. Small-scale trade, both in exotic materials such as copper, shell, and stone ornaments—some of them originating in the heartland—and in more utilitarian items such as raw materials for stone tools, also flourished across Pennsylvania. For the most part, however, Native Pennsylvanians appear to have continued living much as their Late Archaic predecessors had done, while dwelling in slightly larger and more sedentary communities, making more restricted seasonal migrations among fewer locales, and perfecting their exploitation of local resources. In many respects, Pennsylvania's Early and Middle Woodland periods were indistinguishable from the Late Archaic period.

Ground-stone axes, food-processing pestles, and fishing-net sinkers. Painstakingly shaped and polished with water and grit, these items provide evidence of complex patterns of life in the Late Archaic period.

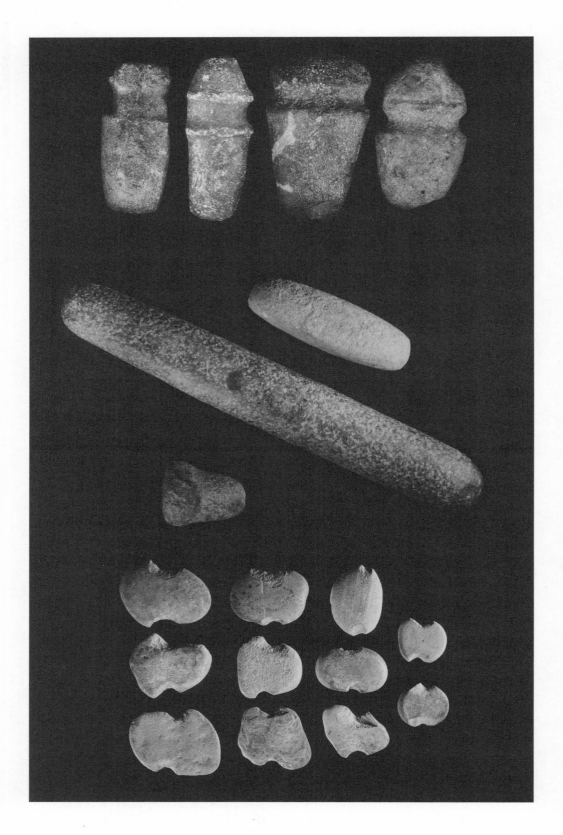

Two innovations deserve attention, however. Both indicate ever-greater food supplies and more sedentary ways of life, and both occurred within the realm of activities associated, in better-documented later times, with women. Everywhere in eastern North America, the characteristic that distinguishes Early Woodland from Late Archaic archaeological sites is the presence of ceramic pottery. Pennsylvanians' first pots were earthenware versions of the straight-sided soapstone bowls used in the Late Archaic period; the women who presumably made them sometimes even used crushed soapstone to temper the clay. With flat bottoms and straight sides and capacities up to several gallons, these vessels were apparently used both for boiling soup and for storing gathered food. By 800 B.C., more structurally sound, round-bottomed forms began to prevail. Either by coiling long filaments of clay or by shaping a single lump of material, potters fashioned rough shapes and then used their hands and wooden paddles wrapped with cord to thin and refine the walls and perfect the vessel's final appearance. This general style of potmaking assumed distinct local variations in the kinds of shell, rock, or grit tempering used to stabilize the clay, in the particular ways in which decorative patterns were etched into a pot's surface, and in the forms a collar did or did not elaborate around its mouth. Capacities varied from a cup or so to many gallons, but pots all tended to be made in a single local style that held for a few decades until it mutated into a related new fashion. The variations are so distinct for time and place that the kinds of pots women made must have carried great significance as symbols of their group identity. Ceramic traditions, much like language and ceremonies, helped define the cultural boundaries of a community.

In the Middle Woodland period, beginning in the first century A.D., the size of the largest ceramic vessels and of storage pits at village sites tended to increase. This phenomenon was probably related to the second important development of the era, the addition of cultivated plants to the wild vegetation that had long been a major part of Native diets. As with much else, the change appears to have come gradually—the line between the careful tending of naturally occurring vegetation and the deliberate cultivation of new varieties is not as clear as one might think—and basic ideas and even seeds probably filtered into Pennsylvania from the centers of Adena and Hopewell innovation. The cultivators almost certainly were women, who, as the principal gatherers, had the necessary expertise with plants to experiment with new crops.

Although it is difficult to find conclusive archaeological evidence, in the Susquehanna and Delaware River watersheds wild rice and grasses of the Chenopodium and Amaranthus families, such as goosefoot and pigweed, almost certainly grew wherever soils and other conditions permitted. The seeds of those plants joined hickory nuts, acorns, and butternuts, along with various roots, as foods ground into flours and eaten in soups and perhaps as bread. Sunflowers, widely cultivated in the Ohio Valley, probably

Birdstone, an exotic item acquired through trade, found on an Early Woodland site in present-day York County. Long-distance trade in such rare and beautiful items is a persistent theme in Pennsylvania's Native past.

Such artifacts as this straight-sided earthenware pot (*left*), patterned after earlier soapstone pots, and this Early Woodland conical ceramic pot (*right*)—used for cooking and storage—allow us to glimpse ways of life 2,000 years ago, when formerly nomadic peoples adopted more settled living patterns.

also joined the list of cultigens. Squashes and pumpkins—among the earliest domesticated plants throughout much of the Americas and grown in today's Illinois by 5000 B.C. and Kentucky by 2300 B.C.—have not been verified for the Susquehanna and Delaware watersheds in this period. Neither has maize, which, while common, was not yet planted on a large scale anywhere in eastern North America. Although all these crops were important to the subsistence of Hopewell peoples in the Ohio Valley, in none of the regions of what would become Pennsylvania do they appear to have been more than an adjunct to the wild plants long relied on. Pennsylvania's Middle Woodland women might better be described as gardeners than as farmers, and gathering remained their principal contribution to their bands' sustenance. The basic rhythms of Pennsylvania Middle Woodland lives continued much as they had for 2,000 years.

THE AGRICULTURAL REVOLUTION AND LATE WOODLAND CULTURES,
A.D. 1000–1500

For many Native people in Pennsylvania, however, these ancient patterns altered profoundly in the years around A.D. 1000. Climatic changes and perhaps major migrations and conquests played an important role, but these were all interwoven with the era's central transformative development: an agricultural revolution that in one way or another touched the lives of all the peoples of eastern North America. As with everything else in the continent's deep past, the origins of the revolution are unclear. Almost certainly, both plants and techniques were imported from Central America, where the bulk of the population had relied on agriculture since at least the first millennium B.C. What made the new crop adaptations possible was a global warming trend known as the Medieval Optimum, commencing in about A.D. 900 and lasting until the mid-1300s. This increase of a few degrees in average annual temperature was the same one that led Norse adventurers to colonize a once-and-future frozen waste and accurately call it "Greenland," while briefly finding the Newfoundland coast a welcoming locale. In the eastern North American heartland, the warm period fostered a great outburst of agricultural creativity, focused on improved varieties of two old crops, squashes and maize, and one new one, beans.

Beans—grown in Central America for thousands of years and in southwestern North America for centuries, but apparently not successfully adapted to the eastern environment until well after A.D. 800—were the key to the new agricultural complex, for only when they joined the diet could Native North Americans successfully rely on corn as their staff of life. Beans are an excellent source of the essential amino acids lysine and tryptophan, both of which are present in corn in such small quantities that the grain's nutritional value on its own is very low. But lysine and tryptophan combine with the principal amino acid in maize, zein, to produce a highly nutritious protein. The two foods together accomplish what neither could do alone.

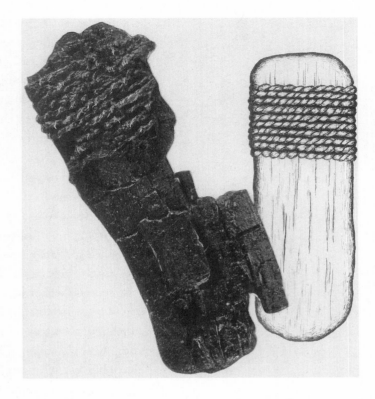

A cord-wrapped potter's paddle with artist's sketch of how it would have looked when new. Native potters used such tools to shape and decorate pottery in styles distinctive to particular communities.

At the same time that farmers were adapting beans to eastern North America, they were also improving strands of maize, particularly by developing a variety known as Northern Flint. With a 90-day growing period, it was ideally suited to the vast stretches of eastern North America where the annual number of frost-free days averaged about 120 days (the margin of error allowed for the inevitable spring and fall cold snaps). In the transitional period when the new breed was evolving, the extended growing seasons of the Medieval Optimum would have made it particularly successful.

Everywhere the new agriculture spread in eastern North America, corn and beans traveled together with squashes. Almost invariably, the three grew not only in the same fields but also in the same hills, for they thrived in a symbiotic relationship. Corn stalks provided a natural pole around which growing bean vines could twine, while, as nitrogen-fixing legumes, the beans replenished modest amounts of a crucial element that corn tended to deplete from the soil. Meanwhile, squashes or pumpkins spread their broad-leaved vines to crowd out weeds and shade the ground, thus retarding evaporation under the hot sun. Together, the trinity of corn, beans, and squash thrived on an agricultural process of impressive simplicity. In easily worked floodplain soils, a digging stick to make a hole in which to plant the seeds, and a hoe to build up a hill around the growing plants, were the only tools necessary. Once the squash vines began to spread, little weeding or other tending was necessary until the crops matured.

The "three sisters" of corn, beans, and squash thus reinforced each other both in the field and in the cooking pot, where they provided a nutritious and abundant diet. In addition to protein compatibility with beans, maize contains a higher proportion of carbohydrates and sugars than other cereal grains; when processed with lime or roasted over an open fire, it also releases substantial niacin. Squashes, baked or boiled, are an excellent source of vitamin C and other nutrients. Supplemented with game and fish, the resulting diet was far superior to anything crooked-boned Europeans—who in the Medieval period toiled so hard for their daily bread, and little else—could imagine. "Their diet is maize, or Indian corn, divers ways prepared: sometimes roasted in the ashes, sometimes beaten and boiled with water, which they call *hominy*," William Penn explained of Native people who still depended on this basic pattern of subsistence in the late seventeenth century. "They also make cakes, not unpleasant to eat: they have likewise several sorts of beans and peas that are good nourishment." The system was as productive as it was nutritious. The average annual corn yield in Late Woodland northeastern North America may have been nearly nineteen bushels an acre. That was roughly equal to what European wheat provided under similar environmental conditions, but European single-crop fields left no room for the prolific beans and squash that Native American techniques also encouraged that acre to produce. Moreover, in good soil one kernel of maize might return as much as 200 kernels at harvest; contemporary European cereals only yielded about fifteen grains for each seed.

Initially, the new crops and their cultivation may simply have joined the repertoire of gathered vegetable foods women had long contributed. But as they became staples that, in many places in eastern North America, contributed 50 to 75 percent of a community's food, they not only encouraged population to expand and villages to become firmly rooted in a single spot, they gave the women who grew them considerable economic and social power. That power derived—like much else in the deep structures of Native American (indeed all human) life—from the ecological setting in which the new agriculture emerged. North America lacked any species that could be domesticated as a source of animal protein, although dogs and the occasional captured bear cub did to some extent play this role. In the absence of equivalents to European hogs, cattle, and goats, hunting and fishing necessarily remained important economic activities. Men had, perforce, to continue ancient patterns of seasonal travels in pursuit of game and migratory fish and fowl, while women became increasingly sedentary in order to tend their crops.

In the core area of the Mississippi and Ohio Valleys, agriculture reached heights of productivity and supported population densities hitherto unimagined. After A.D. 900 a great new agricultural civilization, which scholars label "Mississippian," flourished. The largest and apparently most influential of its many cities and ceremonial centers was

Cahokia, in what is now East St. Louis, Illinois, which at its peak in the twelfth century was home to perhaps 20,000 people, larger than any Euro-American city in British North America before the mid-eighteenth century. Towering 100 feet above a fifty-acre artificial plaza, its main temple mound covered sixteen acres at its base. Surrounding the temple and plaza, at least 100 smaller mounds supported ceremonial structures and covered the accumulated burials of generations of the city's elite residents. Like such other major centers as Coosa and Etowah in present-day Georgia, Moundville in Alabama, and Natchez in Mississippi, Cahokia was a highly stratified society, with a sharp divide between elites and commoners, a specialized artisanry, a widespread trading network, and an elaborate mortuary ceremonialism, to which the burial mounds attest. The Mississippian pattern was probably not so much a single culture or polity as it was a religion, called the Southern Ceremonial Complex or "Southern Cult," whose burial rituals and associated mounds were widely shared across the continental interior.

THE CULTURES OF LATE WOODLAND PENNSYLVANIA

All of that, however, remained in the continental heartland. In considering the ways in which the agricultural revolution may have spread to Pennsylvania's Native American periphery, we need to consider again the shape of the land that determined so much of the region's human past. Cumbersome routes of communication ensured that innovations reached today's Pennsylvania with great difficulty. Moreover, a modern soil map of the state reveals only two regions dominated by the "alfisols" most conducive to cultivation: the Piedmont in the southeast and the unglaciated portion of the Allegheny plateau in the southwest. While the Great Valley and some other sections of the Ridge and Valley region also contain alfisols, in a vast central area covering more than half the map much of the soil today can only support crops with intensive fertilization. The topography of the Appalachian Plateau and the Ridge and Valley region also needs to be considered. With the major exception of the main rivers and a few of their principal tributaries, the countless tiny streams that wind through the landscape provide few of the floodplains best suited for cultivation. And today—although perhaps not during the Medieval Optimum—even in some areas of the plateau with decent soils, the average number of frost-free days dips below the ninety days required for maize, and late and early freezes are common. Only limited areas, therefore, were suited to the new agriculture, and in many of those the conditions were marginal.

The Monongahelas

One such marginal area stretched from present-day Pittsburgh south and west into nearby Maryland, West Virginia, and Ohio. There, from about A.D. 900 onward, people who shared a complex of archaeological traits called "Monongahela" made the best of their region's environmental limitations and came to rely on agriculture for roughly half

Inceptisols   Ultisols   Alfisols

Soil map of Pennsylvania. Inceptisols and especially ultisols require fertilization to sustain agriculture. Alfisols, more suited for farming, predominate only in the southeastern and southwestern portions of the state and in the lowlands of the Ridge and Valley province. As a result, these became the centers of the Native population after the agricultural revolution.

their diet. They lived in villages of perhaps 300 people, usually in upland locations astride watersheds draining in two directions, which allowed their gatherers, fishers, and hunters to complement agriculture with wild plants, freshwater mussels, and game animals, especially white-tailed deer. Whether larger towns exploited the more favorable riverine locations now occupied by Pittsburgh and the Mon Valley steel mill sites may never be known, because urban and industrial development has destroyed so much archaeological evidence. Wherever they were located, Monongahela villages tended to be enclosed in a wooden palisade, with one or sometimes two rings of houses arranged around an open central plaza. Houses were circular, often with a distinctive half-buried storage room extending from one side. Whether the Monongahelas constituted a unified political entity, whether they all spoke the same language, and what relationship they had to later-known tribal groups is one of the many mysteries that comprise the great puzzle of Pennsylvania's Native past.

The Iroquoians

To the north and east, the fertile lands of the Great Lakes Coastal Plain and the valleys of the Finger Lakes and the Mohawk River provided a more hospitable environment for the new agriculture. In the Middle Woodland period, across a broad band of lowlands in today's upstate New York, people associated with a complex of archaeological remains called "Point Peninsula" lived by the same kind of intensive gathering, fishing, and hunting supplemented by gardening as did Native Pennsylvanians in the same period. After A.D. 900, however, villages became larger and clearly based on agriculture, while Point Peninsula artifacts yielded to those known as "Owasco." The people who made these Owasco materials are among the few who can be unequivocally identified as the direct predecessors of any of the Native people of Pennsylvania who later interacted with European colonizers. They were the common ancestors of the Iroquois Five Nations (Mohawks, Oneidas, Onondagas, Cayugas, and Senecas), the Susquehannocks, the Eries, and others who spoke languages of the Iroquoian family.

The longtime assumption among archaeologists was that the Owasco culture evolved directly from Point Peninsula predecessors. Recent reevaluations of the evidence, and especially analyses of Iroquoian languages, now make it seem more likely that Owasco invaders conquered and absorbed the Point Peninsula population, bringing with

them their agricultural ways and a new village-based, matrilineal social organization. Owasco pottery was drastically different from Point Peninsula not only in shape but also in method of manufacture; Owasco pots were fashioned with paddles from a single lump of clay, Point Peninsula ones by the coiling method. With pottery styles everywhere in the Northeast so closely tied to local social identity, this suggests the arrival and dominance of a new group of potters raised in a tradition different from that of earlier inhabitants. Moreover, such Iroquoian languages as Susquehannock, Cayuga, Onondaga, Seneca, Oneida, and Mohawk are so closely related that linguists conclude they must have diverged from each other no later than about A.D. 1000. Both kinds of evidence suggest that a relatively small group spread out through the former Point Peninsula territory and then gradually developed local differences as it mingled with the conquered population.

Artist's reconstruction of a Monongahela village characteristic of the Late Woodland period in what is now southwestern Pennsylvania.

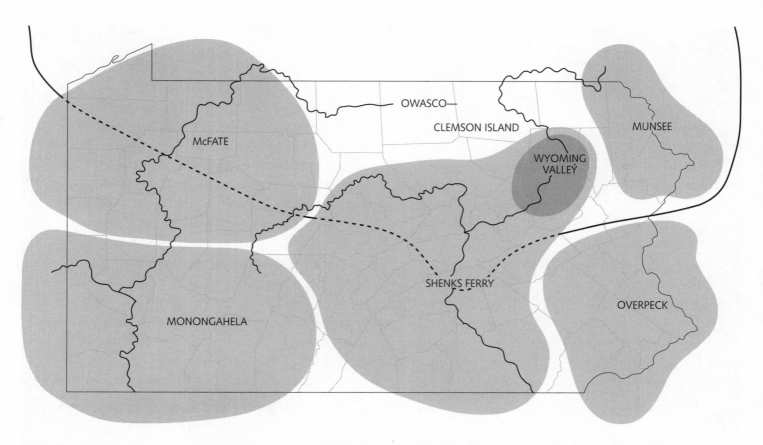

OWASCO—

CLEMSON ISLAND

MUNSEE

McFATE

WYOMING
VALLEY

MONONGAHELA

SHENKS FERRY

OVERPECK

Late Woodland archaeological complexes. Geography, economic patterns, and linguistic differences produced a variegated human landscape on the eve of the Native American encounter with Europeans.

Although the evidence is far from conclusive, the invading agriculturalists probably originated in the upper Susquehanna watershed of Pennsylvania, in villages associated with an archaeological complex called "Clemson Island." The Juniata and the West and North Branches of the Susquehanna River provided numerous broad floodplains and islands well suited to agriculture, and there the basic system that developed in the heartland seems first to have been adapted to the Pennsylvania environment. Little is known about the Clemson Island people—if they *were* a single people, as opposed to diverse groups who shared similar material artifacts—but their culture flourished between A.D. 700 and 1300. Maize dating from the eleventh century has been found on their archaeological sites, and by that time Clemson Island communities no doubt cultivated squash as well; beans probably completed the agricultural trio somewhat later. The population lived in dispersed small hamlets, most probably home only to a single extended family. Some hamlets were accompanied by burial mounds that slowly built up over generations. The mounds—probably ritual centers for a number of hamlets whose leading figures may have been interred there—link the Clemson Island culture not only to Mississippian phenomena but also to contemporaneous patterns in the interior of present-day Virginia.

By about A.D. 1300 the hamlets seem to have been consolidating into larger villages, and mound burials passed out of use. These trends of greater population concentrations accompanied by new burial practices (and so, presumably, new religious beliefs) continued as the Owasco pattern spread northward through the Susquehanna watershed to the Finger Lakes and the Mohawk Valley. Owasco economies relied heavily on corn, beans, and squash and supported communities ranging in size from several hundred to a thousand people. Large main villages were inhabited permanently and often were associated with several nearby smaller hamlets and a variety of seasonally occupied hunting and fishing camps.

Owasco communities seem to have been extremely independent, isolated, and hostile toward outsiders. The small-scale long-distance trade in exotic shells and minerals that had flourished throughout the Middle Woodland period in the Pennsylvania region apparently came to a halt. Warfare was prevalent; we know this not only because village sites became heavily fortified but also because the remains of people buried in Owasco cemeteries frequently show evidence of violent deaths. Reciprocal retaliation produced an ongoing cycle of feuding not easily stopped, a pattern of bloodshed vividly recalled in Iroquois traditions about the dark times before the establishment of their League. Victors adopted those of the vanquished whom they did not kill and incorporated them into their families and villages; this too we know both from Iroquois traditions and from such archaeological evidence as the presence of foreign styles of pottery on Owasco sites.

At least some of the conflicts may have been over territory. Prime hunting grounds and fishing spots—under stress from the larger human populations that agriculture supported—might particularly have become objects of contention for the first time. Out of the violence emerged a gradual consolidation of smaller communities into larger entities, and of large villages into tribal groupings and confederacies across the upper Susquehanna watershed and the Great Lakes Lowlands, from north-central Pennsylvania through upstate New York, southern Ontario, and the St. Lawrence River valley. By the sixteenth century at least two such alliances had been established. One formed in Ontario among the several Huron nations, the other formed in central New York among the Five Nations of the Haudenosaunee, or Iroquois League.

Around the margins of Huron and Iroquois territories other descendants of the Owasco peoples consolidated locally into substantial villages, tribal groupings, and perhaps confederacies, but remained aloof from the two later-documented leagues. Among these were at least two peoples of what would become Pennsylvania: the Susquehannocks and the Eries. As populations consolidated throughout the region, the Iroquoian communities that would become the Onondagas and Cayugas apparently moved gradually northward to the Finger Lakes, while the emergent Susquehannocks moved southward to scattered locations on the North Branch of the Susquehanna, with perhaps a few outposts on the West Branch as well. The Eries, meanwhile, migrated slowly northward through present-day northwestern Pennsylvania to southwestern New York. Their relationships with neighbors farther south in the Allegheny watershed, and with the Monongahelas, are unclear, although the people who made the artifacts of what archaeologists call the "McFate-Quiggle" complex found from the Wyoming Valley westward may have provided the link. At its peak, the total Iroquoian-speaking population of the Great Lakes plain and the Allegheny Plateau may have approached 100,000.

Patterns of Life in Agricultural Native Pennsylvania

Because seventeenth-century European colonists wrote about the descendants of these Iroquoian-speakers more extensively than about any other Native Pennsylvanians, we can infer quite a bit about what life must have been like in the fourteenth- and fifteenth-century villages of not just the Iroquoian area but of anywhere the new agricultural patterns took hold. An Iroquoian town could be home to as few as 300 or as many as 2,000 people. Packed within a perimeter of earthworks and wooden palisades enclosing up to sixteen acres were 30 to 150 buildings, the majority of which were distinctive structures called longhouses. Arranged side by side in parallel rows, they were usually about 20 feet wide and varied in length from 40 to 200 feet. Saplings twisted into the ground at close intervals provided the basic framework for exterior walls and an arched roof. Large sheets of elm bark secured by tree fibers enclosed the framework's sides and most of the rafters, while movable panels covered doorways at each end and rooftop openings that let smoke out and daylight in. Fireplaces were arranged at roughly twenty-foot intervals along a central corridor and were flanked by raised platforms divided into compartments, each of which housed a nuclear family. The fireplaces, and thus heating and cooking facilities, were shared by the two families occupying apartments on opposite sides of the house.

All the families in a longhouse were members of a single lineage traced through the female line. A group of elderly sisters, their daughters, and their grandchildren defined the often-sizable group of kin that shared the longhouse. Men most often, but probably not always, went to live with their wives' families after marriage. Hereditary titles of male authority also descended in the female line, from uncle to nephew, rather than from father to son. More generally within the longhouse, uncles—mothers' brothers— were the principal male role-models and disciplinarians for children. Biological fathers, meanwhile, assumed a close but unauthoritarian role similar to that sometimes played by uncles in patrilineal societies, such as those of Western Europe.

Lineages from several longhouses comprised the local segment of a larger kin group, or clan, believed to be descended from a common mythical ancestor. Typically, three or more clan segments shared a village, and each clan included segments in more than one town. Marriage partners had to be sought outside one's clan, and so people of the various kin groups were tied together by marriage, and every child had parents from two different clans. Thus, in one way or another, everyone in a nation had familial relationships to everyone else. Moreover, kin groups owed each other reciprocal ceremonial obligations, particularly with regard to funeral rites, which "clear-minded" clans conducted for those who mourned.

BEFORE THE GREAT PEACE: IROQUOIS TRADITIONS

When Iroquois leaders codified the oral traditions of the founding of their peace league in the turn-of-the-twentieth-century document known as the Constitution of the Five Nations, they told a story of a chaotic war of all against all in the dark days before the Peacemaker, Deganawidah, brought the Great Law to the Ongwe-oweh, the Real Human Beings:

The Ongwe-oweh had fought long and bravely. So long had they fought that they became lustful for war and many times Endeka-Gakwa, the Sun, came out of the east to find them fighting. It was thus because the Ongwe-oweh were so successful that they said the Sun loved war and gave them power.

All the Ongwe-oweh fought other nations sometimes together and sometimes singly and, ah-gi! ofttimes they fought among themselves. The nation of the Flint had little sympathy for the Nation of the Great Hill, and sometimes they raided one another's settlements. Thus did brothers and Ongwe-oweh fight. The nation of the Sunken Pole fought the Nation of the Flint and hated them, and the Nation of the Sunken Pole was Ongwe.

Because of bitter jealousy and love of bloodshed sometimes towns would send their young men against the young men of another town to practise them in fighting.

Even in his own town a warrior's own neighbor might be his enemy and it was not safe to roam about at night when Soi-ka-Gakwa, our Grandmother, the Moon, was hidden.

Everywhere there was peril and everywhere mourning. Men were ragged with sacrifice and the women scarred with the flints, so everywhere there was misery. Feuds with outer nations, feuds with brother nations, feuds of sister towns and feuds of families and of clans made every warrior a stealthy man who liked to kill.

Then in those days there was no great law. Our founder had not yet come to create peace and give united strength to the Real Men, the Ongwe-oweh.

In those days the Onondagas had no peace. A man's life was valued as nothing. For any slight offence a man or woman was killed by his enemy and in this manner feuds started between families and clans. At night none dared leave their doorways lest they be struck down by an enemy's war club. Such was the condition when there was no Great Law. *

While clearly designed more to convey a moral truth about the ongoing need to follow the Iroquois Great Law than to record historical detail, the story reflects a reality attested by archaeological evidence. The Owasco culture from which the modern Iroquois nations emerged seems to have been almost constantly at war and probably conquered an earlier population in what is now upstate New York. Their internal battles probably divided them into speakers of the various Iroquoian languages, including that of the Susquehannocks of a later-day Pennsylvania, who, for whatever reason and for most of the seventeenth century, refused to heed the Peacemaker's call for unity and remained at war with the Five Nations of the Mohawks, the Oneidas, the Onondagas, the Cayugas, and the Senecas.

*Arthur C. Parker, *Parker on the Iroquois,* ed. William N. Fenton (Syracuse, N.Y.: Syracuse University Press, 1968), book 3, pp. 16–17.

An Iroquoian longhouse, exterior view (*right*), internal floor plan (*opposite page*). Nuclear family units occupied each of the apartments lining the central corridor; each family unit was related through the female line.

Elevation des Cabannes Sauvages

An agricultural Native town was largely a female world. The gendered division of labor and the continued importance of hunting and fishing ensured that, for much of the year, villages would be inhabited primarily by women and their children, who tended the fields while males dispersed to far-flung fowling locations in the spring, and hunting and trapping grounds in the fall and early winter. In the spring and early summer, older men traveled to fishing camps a day or more distant from the village. From spring through fall, warfare also drew young men away to make raids on often-distant enemies. Only in mid- to late winter were most villagers of both sexes at home simultaneously for extended periods.

If the inhabitants of a village changed over time, so too did its location. Despite the efficiency of women's agricultural practices, soil gradually lost its productivity, and new fields had to be opened ever farther from the main town. Meantime, hundreds of people dependent on wood, bark, and vegetable fibers to make everything from houses to baskets had a voracious appetite for trees; together the two trends gradually leveled most nearby forests. Within the village palisades, wood and bark construction materials steadily rotted, while longhouses and storage pits became infested with insects and other pests. After about two decades, therefore, a town site had outlived its usefulness, and a community had to move on to start over in a different location, usually a few miles away.

The Iroquoians and all their neighbors who shared similar subsistence patterns, then, required extensive homelands to support their way of life. At any given time, people needed not only the space occupied by their current town and its surrounding farmland, but also a spot for a new village under construction, sites for future towns, places where former settlements were undergoing a natural process of reclamation, a variety of fishing and fowling camps, and various hunting territories. What would look to later European colonists like empty countryside punctuated by widely scattered villages was in fact an actively used and essential landscape.

That landscape, and nearly everything in it, was considered to be alive with an animating spiritual power. Such "other-than-human persons" as plants, game animals, trees, or the wind could either help people or bring them harm. The "three sisters" of corn, beans, and squash might agree to sustain everyone's life; animals might choose to give themselves as food; winds might restrain themselves to allow a canoe to cross a lake. In return, however, all these spiritual beings demanded respect in the form of offerings of sacred tobacco, the performance of ceremonies, the giving of thanks. If humans neglected their reciprocal obligations and offended these beings, the results could be hunger, sickness, injury, or death. The basic idea was not so much that spirit-beings were inherently good or evil, but that the universe was full of morally neutral forces of unequal power. Some were human, most other-than-human, but all had the potential to be either allies or enemies. To negotiate this complicated maze, human persons had to make alliances—particularly with beings more powerful than themselves. These reciprocal relationships and their ceremonial maintenance, rather than any specific set of dogmas, doctrines, or beliefs about the characteristics of particular spirits, were at the heart of religious experience for Iroquoians and for the neighboring peoples who shared basic patterns of life with them.

In a more material realm, reciprocity similarly shaped ideas about property rights, which rested on need and use rather than on mere possession, and which demanded that in the long run those who gave would also receive. Food, clothing, tools, houses, and land belonged to those individuals or kin groups who needed and made active use of them. Conversely, excess or abandoned property was largely free for the taking, and in times of shortage whatever was available was supposed to be shared by all. This communal ethic encouraged people not so much to accumulate goods but to be in a position to provide them to others. Social status and political authority went not to those who merely *had* the most, but to those who were in a position to *give* the most away. Far from ensuring a utopia of egalitarian bliss, the system encouraged rivalries for influence yet channeled those rivalries into benefits for kin groups and the community as a whole. In this context, economic exchanges generally took the form of gift-giving rather than buying and selling. Exchanges of presents sealed relationships. Competition for authority as well as its exercise rested on the effectiveness with which people could build bonds of reciprocal obligation.

The Lenapes and Their Neighbors

The sweeping changes in land use, gender roles, and social organization wrought by the agricultural revolution came later to the southeastern areas of Pennsylvania that were most isolated from the continental interior. On the fertile Piedmont lands of today's Lancaster County, the dominant Late Woodland cultural pattern was one archaeologists label "Shenk's Ferry," after the site where its distinctive material traits were first categorized. Before A.D. 1300 the Late Woodland people apparently did little farming, and their

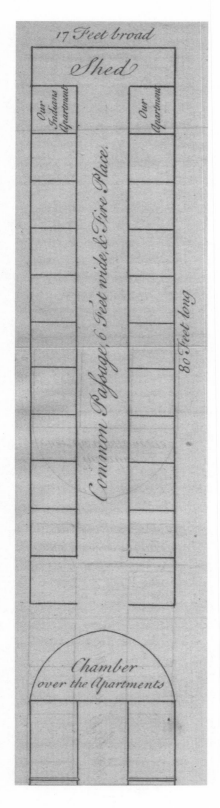

A Susquehannock bark basket lashed with cordage. Stone items are far more likely to survive on archaeological sites, but the vast majority of goods used in everyday life were made of more perishable materials, such as this basket.

settlement pattern involved dispersed hamlets of nuclear families. After that date, larger villages of 500 or more people began to appear, in locations well suited to agriculture, although how heavily their economies depended on crops remains unclear. Covering two to three acres and enclosed by what might better be called peaceful fences than military stockades, these towns consisted of oval-shaped houses arranged in concentric circles; each dwelling was large enough to shelter ten to twelve people, and each had its own storage facilities and associated burials—suggesting that, in contrast to Iroquoian practices, funeral rituals took place at the level of individual families or lineages. Large ceremonial plazas stood at the center of many towns. As with the Monongahelas, the linguistic affiliation of the Shenk's Ferry culture and its relationship to Native groups known in later periods is mysterious.

South and east of the Shenk's Ferry zone lived people whose cultural identity is, by contrast, quite certain. Just as clearly as the Owasco people were progenitors of the Iroquoians, the Late Woodland residents of the lower Delaware Valley who made the artifacts archaeologists identify as the "Overpeck" and "Minguannan" complexes were ancestors of those later known as Lenapes, and their language was surely developing into what would become Unami Delaware. Also as with the Iroquoians, Lenape culture may have resulted from a recent immigration that either displaced or, more likely, incorporated the area's early population. Unami—like most other languages of the Algonquian family spoken on the Mid-Atlantic Coast—seems to have developed from a common source sometime late in the first millennium A.D. The coincidence in time with the similar development of the radically different Iroquoian tongues among those who displaced the Princess Point culture suggests a link between the two phenomena, and that those who entered the Delaware Valley may have been pushed out of today's upstate New York. That something of the sort happened is also suggested by Delaware folklore, but the case is far from proven.

Indeed, there is remarkably little archaeological evidence of pre-sixteenth-century inhabitants of the lower Delaware River watershed, and almost nothing indicating long-term settlement, agriculture, or food storage has been discovered. How this lack of evidence should be interpreted is controversial. To some degree, it is explained by the fact that the now heavily urbanized belt from Wilmington to Trenton was surely the center of Late Woodland Lenape country, and its archaeological record has been almost thoroughly obliterated. The sandy, agriculturally marginal soils of the Atlantic Coastal Plain also would tend to minimize reliance on domesticated crops. As a result, some archaeologists argue that the immediate ancestors of the Lenapes grew no corn at all but instead were gatherers and fishers who lived in small, highly mobile bands that left little permanent mark on the landscape. Others argue on the basis of documented evidence from later periods and comparisons with Algonquian-speaking peoples to the north and south along the Atlantic Coast that the Lenapes camped and fished in the woods during the winter, relocating to clearings and watersides in the spring, where they planted the "three sisters" and gathered wild plants.

North of the Unami-speaking Lenapes, beyond the Delaware Water Gap, lived people who spoke Munsee dialects. The poor soils of much of this region, scoured by glaciers that left little behind but rocks and gravel, and the relatively few archaeological discoveries of crop remains, lead some scholars to argue that gathering, fishing, and hunting continued to be the basis of Munsee subsistence long after the onset of the agricultural revolution elsewhere. Others stress contrary evidence, and in particular the patches of excellent soils that scatter the region. It should also be noted that Munsee-speakers exchanged agricultural products as well as furs with Henry Hudson's crew near Manhattan in 1609. One of Hudson's officers said the Natives had "great store of maize, or Indian wheat," from which they baked "good Bread."

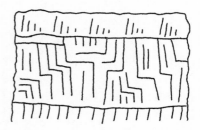

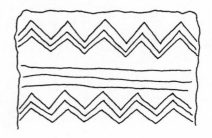

Decorative designs from Overpeck pottery, found in the lower Delaware Valley watershed, show only a few of the many ways in which people of different cultures used pottery decoration to express their identities.

In about 1440, some 500 people of the Shenk's Ferry culture built a new town on a knoll overlooking Conestoga Creek, near present-day Millersville. Within a double row of lightly built fence that would have kept small children in and wild animals out but would not have protected them from any human enemies that might have threatened, they built fifty-six round or oval-shaped houses and an astronomical observatory.

At the center of the town, a complicated set of wooden posts surrounded a large fire pit to define a "woodhenge," the purposes of which were probably similar to, if no less mysterious than, England's ancient Stonehenge. The posts were carefully aligned to the cardinal directions and to track the winter and summer solstices, the movements of the north star, and other significant features of the night sky. The molds left in the ground by several markers show that their placement had been adjusted at least once to track their celestial reference points more accurately. The fireplace at the center of the woodhenge had several times been systematically covered and rekindled, perhaps in a seasonal ritual.

Similar observatories existed 1,000 miles away at the Mississippian city of Cahokia—which was 100 years past its prime when the Shenk's Ferry town was built—and the general layout echoes patterns from the cities of Central America. To suggest any direct link with these models would be mere speculation. But among the Mississippians and throughout much of eastern North America in later times, the sun and its passage through the sky had powerful religious associations. That the sun had similar importance to these Shenk's Ferry people is indicated not only by the alignment of posts in their woodhenge but also by the fact that nearly all the doors of their houses opened eastward toward the dawn. The only certainties are that the Shenk's Ferry people possessed sophisticated knowledge of the heavens and that this knowledge must have

been central to the ritual life of their village.

Deepening the mystery of this Shenk's Ferry town are the apparent absence of a cemetery (had there been one, evidence from elsewhere suggests that its burials would also have faced east), a curious shortage of accumulated garbage, and almost no evidence of rebuilding or repairs to houses or fences. All this suggests that, for all the care taken in building it, the village was only occupied for a year or two. Archaeological sites in other parts of today's Lancaster County show that the Shenk's Ferry culture continued to flourish for more than a century, until its people were presumably conquered by Susquehannock invaders from the north. But what happened to the 500 people who lived and worshiped briefly on this spot, like nearly everything else about the Shenk's Ferry people, may never be known.

SOURCE: Jay F. Custer et al., "Data Recovery Excavations at the Slackwater Site (36LA207), Lancaster County, Pennsylvania," *Pennsylvania Archaeologist* 65 (March 1995), 19–112.

OPPOSITE: Artist's reconstruction of a Shenk's Ferry village. Little is known about the culture of these people, who lived in what is now Lancaster County in the early sixteenth century. These Shenk's Ferry people were apparently conquered by Susquehannocks who invaded from the north after 1575.

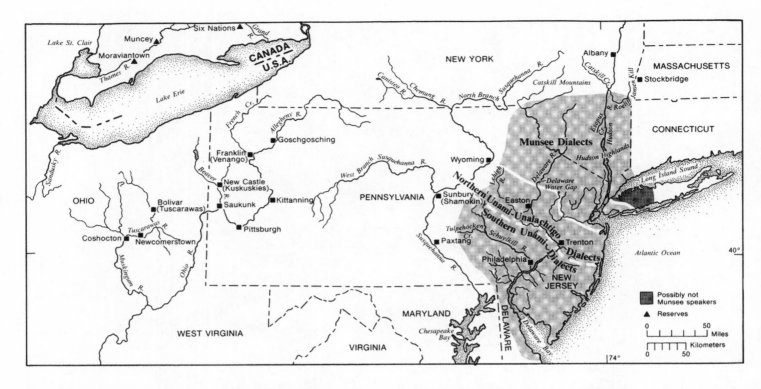

Seventeenth-century territory of the Lenapes (Unami-speakers) and Munsees. In later migrations westward, these peoples would become known collectively as "Delawares."

By the sixteenth century, then, both upper and lower Delaware watersheds appear to have been home to numerous bands of a few dozen to a few hundred people who had participated less thoroughly in the agricultural revolution than other Native Pennsylvanians. These many small communities were for the most part autonomous, but they were united into loose regional political groupings that might best be described not as unified tribes but as collections of peoples who shared strong affinities of marriage, trade, and language with one another. As among their Iroquoian neighbors, kinship was primarily matrilineal. "The children of him that is now king, will not succeed, but his brother by the mother, or the children of his sister, whose sons (and after them the children of her daughters) will reign," explained William Penn a century later. There were many such local "kings," however. No politically unified Lenape, Munsee, or Delaware nations existed.

Farther south, in the Susquehanna–Chesapeake Bay watershed, a variety of groups shared many cultural similarities with the Lenapes and Munsees, although they spoke different Algonquian languages. Those on the eastern shore of Chesapeake Bay came to be known as "Nanticokes," and those on the western shore as "Conoys," after the names of the local groups later most prominent in dealings with European colonists. Among these peoples too there seems to have been scant political centralization, considerable seasonable mobility, and comparatively little agriculture.

Paradoxically, it may have been ecological riches more than ecological impoverishment that explained the continued reliance on ancient gathering, hunting, and fishing patterns on the Atlantic Coastal Plain while the agricultural revolution transformed existence elsewhere. Most people of Western European descent think of farming as a great civilizational advance, the key to the stable food supplies necessary for a secure existence. But anthropologists argue that in the broad sweep of human history people tend to abandon gathering for agriculture out of desperation, not hope. In a varied environment such as a coastal plain, with nearby estuaries and forests, gathering, hunting, and fishing can yield an abundant diet. By contrast, agriculture—even of the productive and healthy variety that swept eastern North America after A.D. 1000— would have brought with it fears of crop failure and crowded, less-sanitary living conditions. It should come as no surprise, then, that the Lenapes, Nanticokes, and Conoys who inhabited the most ecologically abundant region of Pennsylvania continued the basic patterns of life that had succeeded marvelously for millennia, or that, even in the fertile Piedmont, Shenk's Ferry people relied less heavily on farming than did their contemporaries in the harsher environments of the Monongahela and Iroquoian zones.

Impacts of the Little Ice Age

Those environments became still harsher in the middle of the fourteenth century when the Medieval Optimum period came to an abrupt end. Temperatures did not just return to "normal"; they plunged low enough to create a "Little Ice Age" of much cooler and wetter conditions that prevailed until the nineteenth century. The implications for peoples who had tied their destiny to crops and agricultural methods perfected in the earlier warm period were profound. In the Native American heartland, a suddenly overextended system of farming could no longer support the great Mississippian cities. The food crisis was probably a major factor in the emergence of the less densely settled and less politically centralized societies that Europeans later encountered in the region. Among them were the Cherokees, the Creeks, the Chickasaws, and the Choctaws.

In southwestern Pennsylvania the onset of the Little Ice Age evidently forced the Monongahelas to abandon many areas that no longer supported agriculture and to concentrate their settlements south and west of modern Pittsburgh. In their new towns, the projecting half-buried storage rooms that were a distinctive feature of earlier houses became less common, and the formerly open central village plaza tended to be replaced by a large structure ringed by a proliferation of sunken storage rooms arranged like petals. The new pattern suggests that control of scarcer food resources shifted from individual family groups to the village as a whole. In the Iroquoian-speaking zones farther east, meanwhile, the climatic shifts almost certainly intensified the competition for resources that drove the warfare and tribal consolidations of the fourteenth and fifteenth centuries. And, in the more naturally blessed Shenk's Ferry country, it may be no coincidence that agriculture and larger villages apparently took firm root just as the milder conditions that may have supported less-intense gathering and hunting

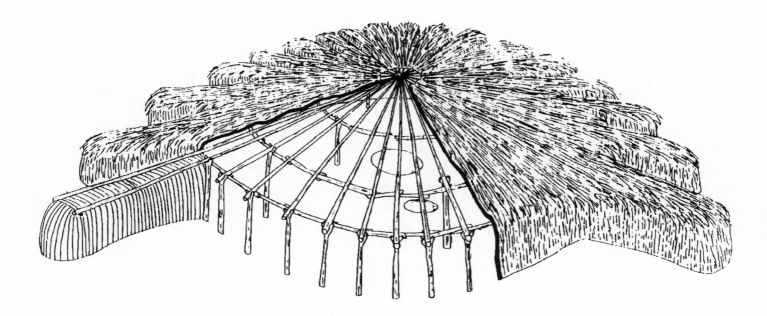

Artist's sketch of the central structure at the Late Monongahela Foley Farm Site, showing multiple storage appendages. The village plan consisted of two concentric rings of circular houses surrounding this so-called petal house. It contained a large fire pit or basin, located in the middle of its floor. One interpretation is that the harsher conditions of the "Little Ice Age" led to more centralized control of food resources. The presence of European-made trade goods on the site indicates the village was occupied around the beginning of the seventeenth century.

economies gave way to the Little Ice Age. Everywhere in what would become Pennsylvania, then, the century or so before the arrival of Europeans was a period of profound and often-stressful change.

NATIVE PENNSYLVANIANS AND THE DISCOVERY OF EUROPE

When Native Pennsylvanians first laid eyes on Europeans is unclear. Some people who may have been Munsee residents of the Delaware Valley observed Giovanni da Verrazzano during his reconnaissance of New York Bay for the French crown in 1524. A party of Susquehannocks met John Smith when he sailed from Jamestown to the head of Chesapeake Bay in 1608. Rumors and stories, at least, of hairy-faced strangers who arrived by water must have made their way to Native communities throughout the sixteenth century. Yet, just as the vast majority of Spaniards did not have to travel with Columbus to feel the effects of his voyages, Pennsylvania Indians did not need to see an English face to feel the transformative impact of contact with a new world.

Viruses from Europe may well have been the first living things to reach interior villages from across the Atlantic. The long isolation of North and South America from Europe, Africa, and Asia and their human, animal, and microbial populations made Indian peoples "virgin soil" for such common eastern hemisphere illnesses as smallpox, measles, and influenza. There is not enough evidence to reach any firm conclusions about when Pennsylvania Natives first died from imported maladies. But it is reasonable to speculate that diseases erupted first in the lower Delaware and Susquehanna watersheds, where Indian travelers from the coast could have spread microbes to people who had not yet directly dealt with Europeans. Farther inland, epidemics probably did not strike until the early 1630s, when smallpox swept New England, the Great Lakes Coastal Plain, and almost certainly the Allegheny Plateau. From that time forward, disease was omnipresent in Pennsylvania Indian life.

Whenever the epidemics began, the devastation they wrought was almost unfathomable. Once viruses hit a given area, population typically declined by 75 to 95 percent over the course of a century or so before reaching a new plateau. Because European observers came to the interior of today's Pennsylvania so late in the process, the vast majority of the deaths went unrecorded in their documents, and most of the Native people who might have preserved oral memories of the carnage failed to survive. One of the few pieces of direct testimony comes from the 1650s, when a Dutch colonist heard Munsee-speaking people "affirm, that . . . before the small pox broke out amongst them, they were ten times as numerous as they now are."

Under such appalling circumstances, Indian communities did not just dramatically shrink; they had to recombine, resettle, and recoalesce into new entities. A village that used to be home to 500 people of various ages and abilities could not continue to function with fifty survivors skewed in their ages, sexes, and skills. Fragments had to join forces, and many formerly heavily populated areas became virtually empty. The people who survived to be known to European colonists as Lenapes, Munsees, or Susquehannocks were products of this ethnic mixing. The descendants of Late Woodland peoples identified only by the names later archaeologists gave them—Monongahelas, Shenk's Ferry, McFate-Quiggle—lived on, if at all, only as submerged elements in other configurations.

In seeking to understand how the human landscape of Pennsylvania was rearranged in the earliest decades when Native Americans discovered the existence of Europe, we also need to consider material goods that crossed the ocean and found their way into Indian communities before Indians ever laid eyes on a Dutch or English person. Passing from hand to hand through traditional forms of exchange, occasional items of European manufacture reached peoples of the Susquehanna watershed by 1550, having filtered northward from Natives who traded with or plundered Spanish and English ships on the shores of Chesapeake Bay and the Outer Banks of today's North Carolina. Somewhat later, the first European goods trickled into the Delaware Valley from various points along the Mid-Atlantic Coast. Difficult communication routes meant that imports may not have arrived in Monongahela country until nearly 1600, and then from the Potomac and Chesapeake rather than from points directly east.

Rare things from across the ocean fit easily into ancient cultural patterns of long-distance commerce in luxury goods, ritual items, and substances believed to embody spiritual power. Accordingly, the European items most likely to be unearthed from sixteenth-century archaeological sites in Pennsylvania are solitary glass beads and fragments of copper, brass, and iron, all of which corresponded in color, texture, and appearance to

A fanciful depiction of a Susquehannock man, from John Smith's map of 1612. Firsthand artistic descriptions of early Native people are rare; it was far more common for European printmakers to recycle a few stock images. This one is based on a painting made on the Outer Banks of today's North Carolina in the 1580s.

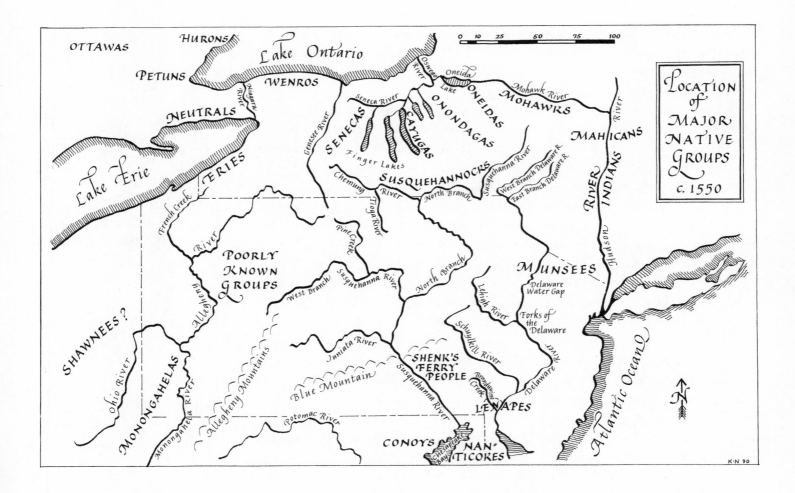

Map showing location of major Native groups, c. 1550.

the sacred shells, chunks of minerals, and pieces of unsmelted copper that Native people had prized for centuries. Indians acquired and used these and other new goods as religious objects and sources of raw materials for Native-style tools, weapons, jewelry, and ritual items. In the period of indirect trade a brass pot or an iron axe head was more likely to be cut up and reprocessed than to be employed as its European manufacturer intended. Before 1600 such items rarely, if ever, reached today's Pennsylvania intact in their original forms.

While the number of such goods was small, the items were evidently valuable enough to provoke violent struggles over access to them. Throughout northeastern North America, archaeological evidence shows that warfare intensified considerably in the late sixteenth century. At bottom, the violence was economically motivated, but struggles over access to valued items did not necessarily involve efforts to corner the market or to become commercial intermediaries between Europeans and rival Indian groups. Cultural patterns of reciprocity and redistribution led leaders (and would-be leaders) to acquire such goods in order to give them away to their followers, rather than to hoard them—at least until the items reached their final redistribution, when members of one clan ritually interred them in the grave of a deceased member of another kin group. If people were dying from strange diseases, this ritual motive for acquiring European goods may even have helped to intensify conflict over access to them. And because one of the ancient patterns of Indian warfare in the Northeast had been the adoption and incorporation of prisoners into the victors' communities, warfare in this period must also be placed in the context of killer epidemics. With people and their labor as perhaps the most valuable resource for disease-ravaged communities, the taking of prisoners was frequently more important than the effort to control trade routes or fur-trapping territories.

But whatever the motives behind warfare, European goods became in their own right vital to military success, because improved weapons were among the most important things acquired by trade. Firearms entered the equation relatively late—probably in the 1630s in Pennsylvania—and initially they were relatively insignificant. Early muskets were notoriously inaccurate, difficult to fire and maintain, and in many ways inferior to a skillfully aimed silent bow and arrow. The more important innovations—indeed, the object of a late sixteenth- and early seventeenth-century Native American arms race—were brass and iron arrowheads. These, like the other items fashioned by Indian craftspeople from the same scraps of kettles used to make jewelry and cutting tools, represented a vast improvement on the flint weapons that those without secure access to trade still had to use. Lighter and far sharper than their predecessors, they traveled farther and truer and could pierce the wooden body armor that had protected warriors from flint points. Meanwhile, sharp bits of copper or brass embedded in war clubs—and later entire hatchets made of iron—made unprecedentedly deadly weapons for hand-to-hand combat.

The Susquehannocks provide a case study in patterns of trade and warfare in the period of indirect contact with Europeans. Their mid-sixteenth-century homeland in the upper Susquehanna watershed left them less favorably situated than their Shenk's Ferry neighbors to the south, who were acquiring—probably from other Indians—small but significant quantities of glass beads and metal from the Chesapeake Bay region. At the same time, however, the Susquehannocks were more advantageously placed than their Onondaga neighbors to the north, who had direct access neither to the Chesapeake nor to alternative sources on the Gulf of St. Lawrence. A complicated rivalry thus apparently pitted the Susquehannocks against the Shenk's Ferry people and against the Onondagas

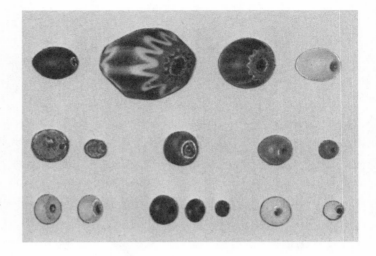

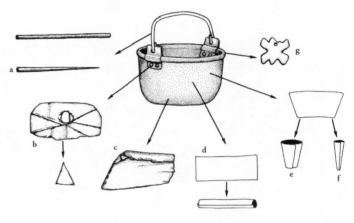

TOP: Early glass beads like these fit easily into ancient patterns of long-distance trade in rare and beautiful items.

BOTTOM: A single brass trade kettle provided raw material for numerous artifacts: the iron handle became an awl (a); the handle lugs became arrowheads and a pendant (b, g); sheet brass from the body became a cutting tool (c) and decorative beads of various shapes (d–f).

Brass objects made by Susquehannocks from pieces of trade kettles. Before about 1630, European metal was primarily used as raw material for Native-produced items.

and perhaps other League Iroquois. Peoples from the Monongahela and Allegheny watersheds may also have been involved. By the time European documents began to record events in the Susquehanna Valley, the Shenk's Ferry people had ceased to exist. Their former homeland was now controlled by the Susquehannocks, all or most of whom—still at war with their northern neighbors—had moved south to a single village in present-day Lancaster County, from which they enjoyed unimpeded access to sources of European goods on the Chesapeake Bay and probably reinforced their numbers with conquered remnants of the people they dispossessed.

The Susquehannock migration occurred at least a generation before any European outposts had been established in the neighborhood of Pennsylvania. Not until 1624 did the Dutch West India Company establish Fort Nassau on the Delaware River at today's Gloucester, New Jersey, and that post would be abandoned between 1627 and 1633. Meantime, in 1630, a Virginia English trader named William Claiborne purchased Kent Island in Chesapeake Bay from the Susquehannocks and began supplying them with unprecedented quantities of imported goods in exchange for furs. In 1634 the arrival of colonists in Maryland (which claimed Kent Island but, because of the Susquehannocks' military might, could not eject the Virginian they protected) added additional sources of trade goods. Then, in 1638, the New Sweden Company established Fort Christina on the site of Wilmington, Delaware, purposely located on the doorstep of the Susquehannocks' country. So began a half-century of rivalry among various European competitors for the Pennsylvania region's Indian commerce, and of Indian rivalries for access to various trading centers and to sources of furs that could be used to purchase imported items. As the struggles intensified, a secure supply of European goods and weapons became vital to Indian survival in their struggles against Native foes.

As metal and other goods became vastly more plentiful beginning in the 1630s, the use of imports as raw material for Native crafts was joined by the wholesale substitution of readily available European items for Native artifacts: brass kettles for clay pots, woolen cloth for animal skins, glass beads for seashells, firearms as frightful adjuncts to bows and metal-tipped arrows. Still, the new items fit into traditional cultural niches and continued to be used in familiar ways, a fact to which European producers quickly adapted by manufacturing varieties of cloth, tools, weapons, and jewelry specifically designed for Indian customers. The substitution of specially made European goods for domestically produced items need not imply the loss of Native craft traditions. While some skills declined—potmaking, for instance, virtually ceased when brass kettles became commonplace—others blossomed. New metal tools allowed both old and new

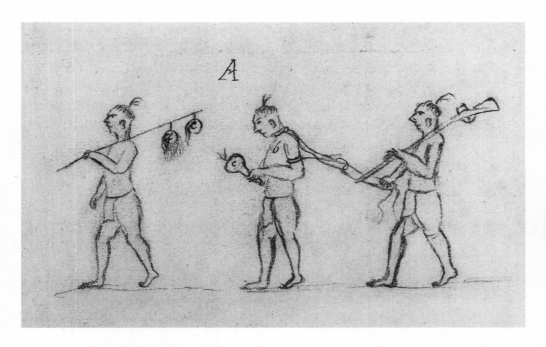

materials to be worked in ways firmly rooted in Native traditions to produce stunning jewelry, combs, and other items. In some ways, the seventeenth century was a golden age of Native material culture.

Much of the new artistic energy went into artifacts associated with the spiritual realm: ritual masks, ceremonial pipes, and, most notably, an entire realm of activities associated with sacred wampum beads. Like other exotic substances, the shells of the whelk and the quahog clam—respectively white and "black" (actually purple) in color—were highly valued in much of eastern North America long before European contact. Seen by inland peoples in particular as gifts from an underwater realm of spirit-beings, the rare early beads came in many sizes and shapes. However, "true wampum"—small tubular beads finely drilled for stringing—became possible only with the introduction of iron tools. In the 1620s, as Dutch traders established their trading settlements in the Hudson and Delaware Valley regions, they discovered a huge market for shell beads and introduced standardized techniques for wampum manufacture to Algonquian peoples of the southern New England coast where whelk and quahog were abundant. By the late 1630s these Indians were churning out the tiny beads by the tens of thousands, to be traded for European manufactures from the Dutch, who would in turn exchange the wampum for furs from peoples farther in the interior. Iroquoian-speakers, in particular, quickly made wampum beads, strings, and belts integral to much of their religious and political life. But Lenapes and Munsees too invested the shell beads with enormous significance. "In case of any wrong or evil fact, be it murder itself," William Penn observed, "they atone by feasts and presents of their wampum, which is proportioned to the quality of the offence or person injured."

ABOVE LEFT: Seventeenth-century Iroquoian warriors returning with a captive. A vast escalation of warfare among natives was one of the major consequences of contact with Europeans in the New World.

ABOVE RIGHT: Brass arrowheads acquired through trade made wooden armor such as that worn by this early seventeenth-century Huron warrior in 1632 obsolete.

UNSETTLEMENT AND RESETTLEMENT IN NATIVE PENNSYLVANIA

With goods such as sacred wampum, newly indispensable tools, and coveted weapons at stake, in the mid-seventeenth century long-simmering military conflicts exploded in an orgy of violence. Native peoples throughout the Northeast competed for access to fur supplies and European markets. Colonial powers contending for control of the trade and lands of the Delaware and Susquehanna watersheds, meanwhile, were almost inevitably pulled into the struggles of their Native trading partners and driven in turn to exploit their Indian connections to preempt territory and seize commercial advantages from European rivals. For all the Natives involved, new weapons made the conflicts unprecedentedly deadly, and the devastation was compounded by simultaneous outbreaks of imported diseases. The mid-century wars did not so much produce winners as survivors. In this grim environment, the peoples most likely to endure were those with the strongest trading ties to Europeans: the Five Nations Iroquois, whose principal trading partners were the Dutch of Fort Orange (later Albany) on the Hudson River, and the Susquehannocks, who could choose on the Chesapeake between traders from Virginia or Maryland, and on the Delaware between the Dutch and the Swedes who, in the short independent lifetime of their colony before 1655, came to command the lion's share of their business.

In their supremely advantageous position, and with apparently firm control of hunting territories throughout the Susquehanna watersheds and points west, the Susquehannocks prospered for a generation. About 1645, at the peak of their power, they relocated to a new, heavily fortified town (at least two cannons

Trade goods unearthed from Susquehannock archaeological sites include, clockwise from left, a rum bottle, glass beads, a spoon, a snuffbox, glass beads and a Swedish ceramic bowl, metal kettles, a flintlock musket mechanism, a metal harpoon, a cut Delft ceramic disk, brass arrowheads, iron axes, a jaw harp, and tobacco pipes.

defended its ramparts) a short distance south of their previous home on the east bank of the Susquehanna, at a place archaeologists now know as the Strickler Site. There between 3,000 and 5,000 people, many of them no doubt adopted war captives, lived in a flourishing economy that was increasingly dependent on trade for weapons, tools, cooking utensils, and countless other everyday goods. From the Susquehannock town, goods also moved northwestward through a trading network that included such Great Lakes Iroquoian people as the Eries, the Neutrals, and the Hurons.

Early Swedish and Dutch colonists, whose knowledge of the interior's geography and inhabitants was extremely sketchy, referred to all the participants in this Susquehannock network as "Minquas," a Delaware word that roughly translates as "Iroquoian-speakers." Colonists sometimes further distinguished between "White Minquas"—by which they meant the Susquehannocks themselves—and a more mysterious western group they called "Black Minquas" because they wore badges of that color. The distinctive presence on southwestern Pennsylvania sites of ornaments made of black coal suggests to many scholars that the Monongahelas may have been those people, but theories abound. The mystery results from the fact that, as communities largely cut off from direct sources of European trade but not from epidemic diseases, inlanders fared worst in the Beaver Wars. Before the seventeenth century's midpoint, the Monongahelas, the Eries, and perhaps other peoples of the western watersheds literally disappeared from the map, and most of the Allegheny, Monongahela, and upper Ohio region was entirely depopulated, the survivors being incorporated into the victorious villages of the Five Nations and perhaps of the Susquehannocks as well.

As the Susquehannocks came to dominate the region's trade, most Lenapes seem to

A HOAX, OR WISHFUL THINKING?

In 1836 an American naturalist named Constantine Samuel Rafinesque announced an amazing discovery. He had been given, he said, an ancient wooden tablet filled with pictographs recording the origins and migrations of the Delaware Indians in minute detail—from their travels across the Bering Strait 3,600 years ago, to their battles with the Moundbuilders, who already lived in the American heartland at that time, to their divergence from other Algonquian-speaking people who settled elsewhere on the Atlantic Coast. All this was explained, Rafinesque said, in transcripts of traditional Lenape songs that went along with what he called the *Walam Olum,* or "painted record."

In 1836 no one had any idea that a massive migration across the Bering Strait would have been impossible 3,600 years ago because the "land bridge" had long been submerged. The prevailing scholarly theory was that the great midwestern mounds we now know were built by the indigenous Adena, Hopewell, and Mississippian cultures were the work of some mysterious, long-gone, non-Indian race. So these parts of Rafinesque's story raised few eyebrows. But many were suspicious of his claim that he had somehow "lost" the original wooden tablets and could only produce a supposed copy in his own handwriting. The language of the songs, too, seemed a little odd to the few white scholars who knew Delaware well enough to try to read it; no one really bothered to ask Native speakers whether the words made sense. Still, at least parts of the story conformed to Delaware folklore as recorded by such respected figures as the late-eighteenth-century Moravian missionary John Heckewelder, and some of the pictographs resembled images found on Indian rock carvings in Pennsylvania and elsewhere.

And so—despite serious doubts by a few scholars—the *Walam Olum* came generally to be accepted. It remains in print to this day, and even some contemporary Lenapes who do not speak Delaware insist that it is an authentic record of Native tradition.

Alas, it is nothing of the kind. Rafinesque may himself have believed his own fictions, but he made the whole thing up. Parts of the *Walam Olum* resemble stories recounted by Heckewelder because the missionary's writings were the source for them. The pictographs resemble the rock carvings because Rafinesque reproduced copies he found in books, while making up others based on Ojibwa and even Chinese and Egyptian models. Native people fluent in Delaware have always found the *Walam Olum* difficult to follow, if not outright gibberish. That is because Rafinesque simply pasted words together from published dictionaries. In fact, a recent analysis of Rafinesque's manuscript by anthropologist David M. Oestreicher clearly shows that the naturalist wrote his English "translation" first and then produced the supposed Delaware original—going so far as to cross out some Delaware words in favor of choices that better fit the English meaning.

The long life of Rafinesque's forgery—and the continued insistence by many readers that it is authentic—is probably best explained by the fact that we all desperately *want* the story to be true. Surely, somewhere, there must be preserved—in human memory if not on paper or wooden tablets—definitive answers to the mysteries of Pennsylvania's Native past. Unfortunately, hopes do not always match reality. The *Walam Olum* is an important cultural document for what it tells us about the triumph of hope over reason, but it tells us nothing about the historical questions it sets out to answer.

OPPOSITE: Page from Rafinesque's *Walam Olum* manuscript, with purported Delaware text in the left column, English in the center, and pictographs on the right.

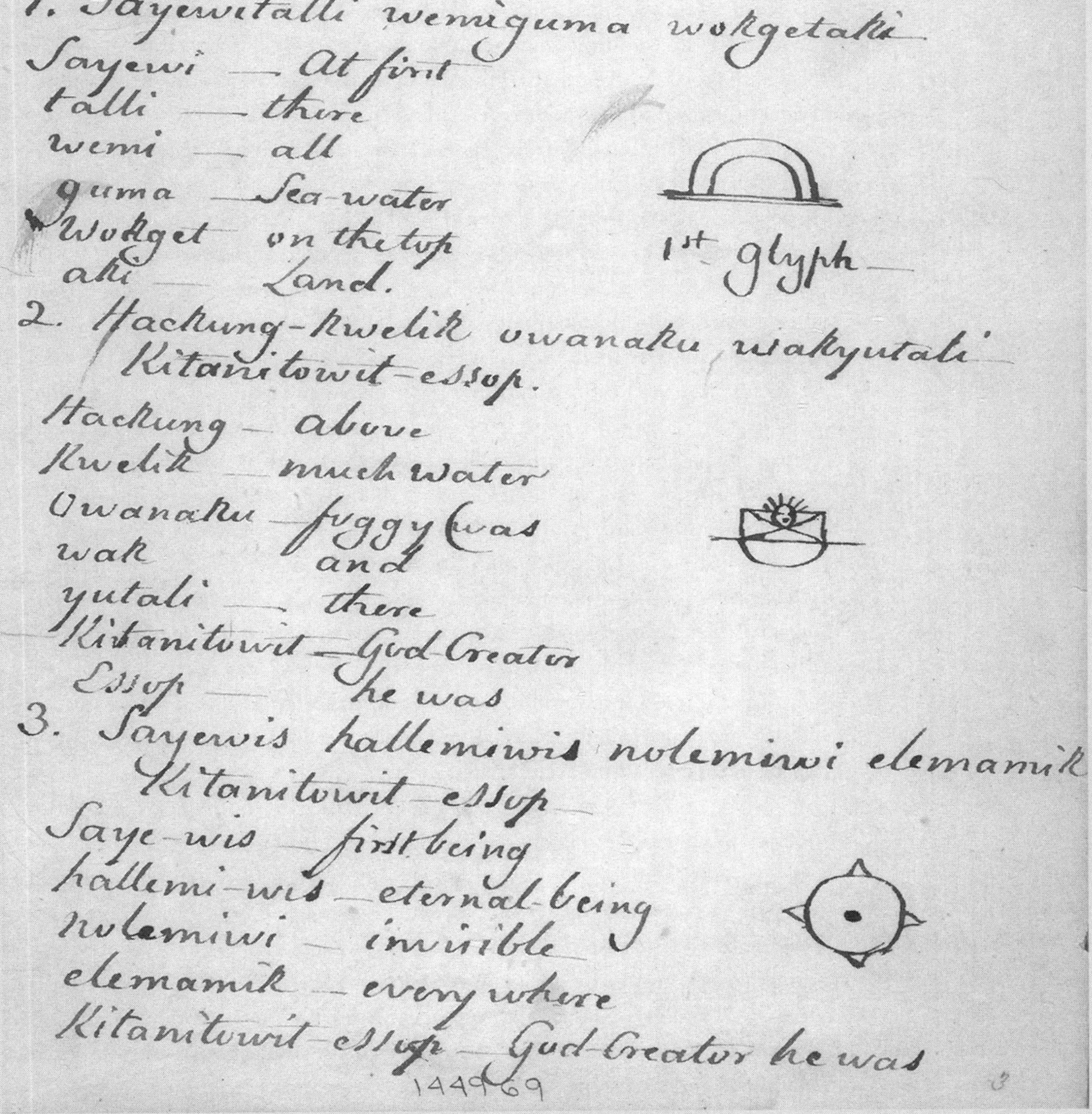

1. Sayewitalli wemiguma wokgetaki

Sayewi — At first
talli — there
wemi — all
guma — Sea-water
Wokget — on the top
aki — Land.

1st glyph —

2. Hackung-kwelik owanaku wakyutali
   Kitanitowit-essop.

Hackung — above
Kwelik — much water
Owanaku — foggy (was
wak — and
yutali — there
Kitanitowit — God Creator
Essop — he was

3. Sayewis hallemiwis nolemiwi elemamik
   Kitanitowit essop

Saye-wis — first being
hallemi-wis — eternal being
nolemiwi — invisible
elemamik — every where
Kitanitowit essop — God Creator he was

144469

have retreated from the west bank of the Delaware to locations in today's state of New Jersey; this may have been a result of a military defeat at the hands of the Susquehannocks in 1634, but the evidence is unclear. In this period too the Lenapes apparently reached a diplomatic accommodation with the Five Nations Iroquois. According to traditions recounted several generations later, they renounced war and accepted a symbolic status as "women" charged with peacemaking among all the region's peoples. If the tradition is an accurate description of events (and many later Delaware leaders vigorously disputed it), the feminine title was rooted in the matrilineal forms of social organization that both Lenapes and Iroquois shared, in which clan mothers indeed controlled vital political decisions about war and peace. Whatever the Lenapes' diplomatic status among their Native neighbors, as the colonial population grew they increasingly relied on the maize agriculture that may not previously have been of much importance to their livelihood—less to feed themselves than to acquire trade goods. Cut off from the prime sources of fur-bearing animals controlled by the Susquehannocks, they instead sold the colonists their crops, along with baskets and other craft items, and, ultimately, plots of their land.

Thus, for the Lenapes, and to a lesser extent the Munsees, the Susquehannocks, and the Iroquois, large-scale participation in trade with Europeans wrought a gradual reversal of precontact economic patterns. For centuries, Indian Pennsylvanians had produced for themselves nearly all the basic needs of their lives and engaged in long-distance trade only to acquire luxury and ritual items. By the late seventeenth century, however, peoples of both the Delaware and the Susquehanna watersheds relied on trade with Europeans for such mundane necessities as clothing, tools, and weapons, while producing luxury and ritual goods at home from domestic or imported materials. Whatever its short-term benefits, in economic terms the trade was inherently biased against Indians, who consumed nonrenewable imports and exported raw materials—furs and hides—while merchants, manufacturers, and financiers located in European imperial centers enriched themselves on accumulated capital.

Within this system, and the brutal inter-Indian conflicts it spawned, Susquehannock dominance of the Pennsylvania region would not last long. In the mid-seventeenth century, war with Native neighbors to the north and south was almost constant—Susquehannock defenders bloodily repulsed a massive Seneca Iroquois assault on their town in 1663, for instance—and epidemics, particularly smallpox in the early 1660s, struck several times. By about 1665, when the usual process of deforestation, housing decay, and soil exhaustion required their town to relocate, its population was declining. Within a decade, most surviving Susquehannocks would be forced to seek refuge, first in Maryland and then with their erstwhile Five Nations Iroquois enemies. The majority were absorbed into Iroquois villages. A few—soon to be known as "Conestogas"—remained in the land their grandparents had conquered from the Shenk's Ferry people.

For the most part, however, by the 1670s the Piedmont, like the Allegheny Plateau, was briefly almost emptied of settled inhabitants, although its ancient pathways and waterways continued to be used heavily by Indian traders and warriors. The long Native history of Pennsylvania had far from come to an end, but its map had been radically redrawn. At the turn of the eighteenth century the almost blank page would be filled again, especially in the areas that for millennia had been population centers. The Indian peoples who reoccupied the Susquehanna, upper Delaware, Monongahela, Allegheny, and Ohio watersheds—Iroquois, Munsees, Lenapes, Nanticokes, Conoys, Conestogas, Shawnees, and other refugees from colonial expansion all over the Mid-Atlantic Coast— had been profoundly reshaped by their previous interactions with the Europeans with whom they struggled for control of a contested landscape. They may have been new-comers to the particular plots of ground on which they settled, but theirs was a history millennia deep in the Pennsylvania past, and their experiences helped to shape all that would follow in the Pennsylvania future.

SOURCES *and* FURTHER READING

Adovasio, J. M. D., et al. "Two Decades of Debate on Meadowcroft Rockshelter." *North American Archaeologist* 19 (1998), 317–41.

Bradley, James W. *Evolution of the Onondaga Iroquois: Accommodating Change, 1500–1655.* Syracuse, N.Y.: Syracuse University Press, 1987.

Caldwell, Joseph R. *Trend and Tradition in the Prehistory of the Eastern United States.* American Anthropological Association Memoir no. 88. Menasha, Wisc., 1958.

Crosby, Alfred W., Jr. *The Columbian Exchange: Biological Consequences of 1492.* Westport, Conn.: Greenwood Publishing Company, 1972.

Custer, Jay F. *Prehistoric Cultures of Eastern Pennsylvania.* Harrisburg: Pennsylvania Historical and Museum Commission, 1996.

Donehoo, George P. *A History of the Indian Villages and Place Names of Pennsylvania.* 1928. Reprint, Lewisburg, Pa.: Wennawoods Publishing, 1998.

Gardner, William M. "Early and Middle Woodland in the Middle Atlantic." In Roger W. Moeller, ed., *Practicing Environmental Archaeology: Methods and Interpretations,* 53–85. Washington, Conn.: American Indian Archaeological Institute, 1982.

Grumet, Robert S. *Historic Contact: Indian People and Colonists in Today's Northeastern United States in the Sixteenth Through Eighteenth Centuries.* Norman: University of Oklahoma Press, 1995.

Hart, John P. "Monongahela Subsistence-Settlement Change: The Late Prehistoric Period in the Lower Upper Ohio River Valley." *Journal of World Prehistory* 7 (1993), 71–120.

Hurt, R. Douglas. *Indian Agriculture in America: Prehistory to the Present.* Lawrence: University Press of Kansas, 1987.

Kent, Barry C. *Discovering Pennsylvania's Archaeological Heritage.* Harrisburg: Pennsylvania Historical and Museum Commission, 1980.

———. *Susquehanna's Indians.* Harrisburg: Pennsylvania Historical and Museum Commission, 1984.

Kinsey, W. Fred. *Archeology in the Upper Delaware Valley.* Harrisburg: Pennsylvania Historical and Museum Commission, 1972.

———. "Eastern Pennsylvania Prehistory: A Review." *Pennsylvania History* 50 (1983), 69–108.

Kraft, Herbert C., ed. *The Lenape: Archaeology, History, and Ethnography.* Newark: New Jersey Historical Society, 1986.

Matlack, Harry A. "Development of the McFate Culture of Northcentral Pennsylvania: The Monongahela–Shenk's Ferry Connection." *Pennsylvania Archaeologist* 62 (September 1992), 66–73.

Miller, Christopher L., and George R. Hamell. "A New Perspective on Indian-White Contact: Cultural Symbols and Colonial Trade." *Journal of American History* 73 (September 1986), 311–28.

Oestreicher, David M. "Unraveling the *Walam Olum.* " *Natural History* 105 (October 1996), 18–25.

Richter, Daniel K. *The Ordeal of the Longhouse: The Peoples of the Iroquois League in the Era of European Colonization.* Chapel Hill: University of North Carolina Press, 1992.

Romanofsky, Anne F. *Vectors of Death: The Archaeology of European Contact.* Albuquerque: University of New Mexico Press, 1987.

Snow, Dean R. *The Iroquois.* New York: Oxford University Press, 1994.

Sturtevant, William C., gen. ed. *Handbook of North American Indians,* vol. 15: *Northeast.* Edited by Bruce G. Trigger. Washington, D.C.: Smithsonian Institution Press, 1978.

Turnbaugh, William A. *Man, Land, and Time: The Cultural Prehistory and Demographic Patterns of North-Central Pennsylvania.* Williamsport, Pa.: Lycoming County Historical Society, 1975.

Wallace, Paul A. W. *Indians in Pennsylvania.* Revised edition. Harrisburg: Pennsylvania Historical and Museum Commission, 1981.

Witthoft, John. *Indian Prehistory of Pennsylvania.* Harrisburg: Pennsylvania Historical and Museum Commission, 1965.

Encounter and Experiment
THE COLONIAL PERIOD

SUSAN E. KLEPP

Numerous towns fronted the river known as the Lenapewihittuck (Fast-Flowing River of the Lenape People) in the early seventeenth century. Despite the traditional look of these longhouses and fields, the pace of change was quickening. News was arriving about strangers to the south who had harassed, displaced, and killed many people. Unusual trade goods were circulating. The shapes and uses were familiar, but the materials were new. These valued goods could be acquired for beaver pelts and given to kin, neighbors, or the dead. The demand for beaver was increasing. Most striking is that disease had become so prevalent that early European phrasebooks noted *n'mechquihn* (I have a cough), *n'daptessi* (I sweat), and *n'matamalsi* (I am sick) as essential terms in the Lenape language. The sick had symptoms never before seen: strange rashes with high fevers or intense chills and stomach cramps. The usual treatments and herbal medicines had no effect, and the majority of the sick died. To the southwest, whole towns had apparently disappeared. The Lenape were wary, and they would not be surprised when the first few strangers finally came to their river.

TWO WORLDS MEET

Dreams of imperial glory and wealth enthralled Western European monarchs in the sixteenth and seventeenth centuries. Spain had garnered and misspent a fortune of gold

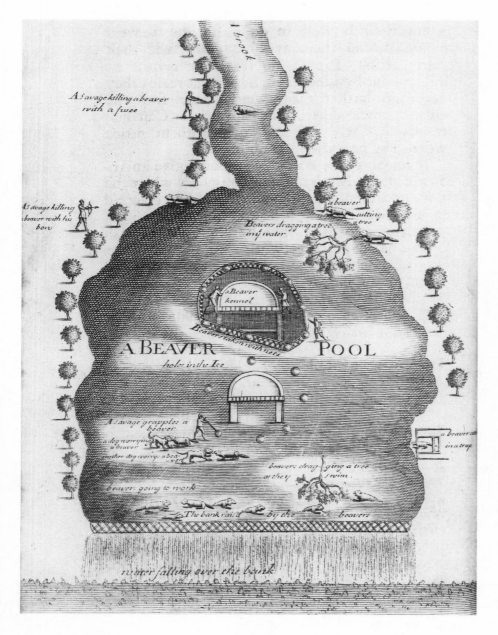

and silver seized from the mines and the forced labor of the Aztecs and Incas. Envious European kings underwrote exploration in hopes of finding comparable riches and similarly vast imperial domains in the Americas. Ignoring Native American history, Europeans considered America a "new world," and if the Lenape, the Iroquois, and other groups would not serve Europe's religious, military, and economic purposes, they would be removed.

Yet the European newcomers shared several characteristics with the original people. Both combined settled agriculture with hunting and fishing; both used fires for clearing land and for light, heat, and cooking. Both viewed their universes in predominantly religious terms. Both employed honor and shame to govern personal behavior. Families raised and educated the next generation, policed individual behavior, and provided housing, food, clothing, and medical care. Both economies also supported specialized political, diplomatic, and religious offices. Neither western Europe nor Eastern Woodlands America was monolithic: significant cultural, linguistic, religious, and political divisions existed in both.

Few Native Americans and fewer Europeans appreciated these similarities. Instead, their common humanity was often less obvious than the economic, political, social, and religious differences separating the two cultures. Eastern Woodland cultures of the Algonquian-speakers and Iroquoian-speakers were based on stone-age technology. Their economy depended on gardening and hunting; strong communal values determined the distribution of resources and labor. Their political systems were based on kinship and might be confederated, tribal, or more localized clan or village societies. Women were influential in both politics and the economy, and the matrilineal line determined descent. Oral tradition, eloquent speech, and the ability to memorize large amounts of information were highly valued. Their religions were based on creation stories and the worship of powerful spirits—some protective, some tricksters.

European cultures, British, Dutch, Swedish, were based on iron-age technology. Their monied economy increasingly centered on international commerce in agricultural products and craft goods. Property was private: a few families controlled enormous wealth, while many were impoverished and servile. Kings claimed absolute rule over vast territories. Men dominated politics, the law, the economy, religion, and the family. Women, whether aristocratic or poor, were considered weak, irrational, and dependent. Europeans depended increasingly on books, newspapers, and written records. The God of European Jews and Christians was considered all-powerful, but many also believed in the devil, in witches, in ghosts, or in other malevolent spiritual beings.

These divergent cultures were the basis for many misunderstandings. Should captives of war be adopted by the victors or returned to the enemy? Did land exist for communal use or for private owners? Did leaders speak for the group or did they command? Did women's opinions matter? Neither the original peoples living on the back of the great turtle (as the Native peoples perceived the continent) nor the Europeans arriving in an uncivilized, unproductive heathen wilderness (as the colonizers perceived it) understood the full extent of the cultural differences. Often, incidental details like skin color or personal ornamentation, or whether travelers wore hard-soled shoes or moccasins, or whether men or women should work in the fields, symbolized Native and European anxieties. Understanding was not impossible, but it proved elusive, particularly in the face of European insistence on land and dominance.

We do not know who the first European to set foot on the territory now known as Pennsylvania was. A few Dutch trappers may have come through the Delaware Water Gap early in the seventeenth century. French explorers may have walked the shores of Lake Erie. Henry Hudson, an Englishman working for the Dutch, noted the existence of a great bay on the Atlantic Coast on August 28, 1609. Sandbars discouraged him from investigating, but his visit established a tenuous Dutch claim to the region. The Dutch named the Lenapewihittuck the South River (Zuydt Revier), incorporating it into the colony of New Netherlands as the counterpart to the North (now Hudson) River where their capital, New Amsterdam (New York City), lay. The English arrived in 1610 and staked their claim by naming the bay and river for Lord De la Warr, governor of Virginia. But because the Delaware River/Zuydt Revier/Lenapewihittuck apparently held no great wealth, neither European nation hurried to act on its claims. A few years later a Dutch sea captain, Cornelius Hendricksen, might have sailed up the river as far as the Schuylkill (Hidden River) River. Then, in 1623 the Dutch established small trading posts and a small fort south and east of what would become Pennsylvania while negotiating with the Lenape for rights to the Schuylkill Valley. These outposts were understaffed and soon abandoned.

OPPOSITE: Drawing showing seventeenth-century beaver-hunting techniques. Men living in the Eastern Woodlands were skillful hunters. Hunting techniques were adapted to a variety of circumstances and incorporated both old and new technologies. In this English print of beaver hunting, the men (labeled as "savages") hunted with dogs, grappling hooks, and nets when beaver ponds were frozen in the winter. In the summer they were confined to the banks of streams and ponds and employed bows and arrows, guns, and traps to kill the beaver, whose pelts were so valuable as trade items.

OPPOSITE: In 1614–15, Dutch Captain Cornelius Hendricksen sailed up the Delaware, perhaps as far as the Schuylkill River. This map by the captain, while inaccurate and difficult to read, is the first to show the area of Pennsylvania in any detail. Delaware Bay is at the bottom, the Susquehanna River is to the left. The map strongly suggests that Hendricksen did not sail as far as the Schuylkill, because that river is not on the map. Yet it is surprising that the forks of the Delaware (the confluence of the Lehigh and Delaware Rivers), or perhaps the juncture of the Lackawanna and Delaware Rivers, are shown, indicating the possibility of earlier Dutch exploration along the southern and eastern Pocono Plateau, coming from the east. Because the branching of the Susquehanna River shows on this map, these unknown explorers may have traveled west and assumed that the Lehigh (or the Lackawanna) and the eastern branch of the Susquehanna were the same river, even though they flow in different directions. They did not come up the Susquehanna, because they portray it emptying into the Delaware Bay and not the Chesapeake. Three groups of Native peoples are indicated. The largest is the Minquas, with four fortified towns on the western shore of the Susquehanna just below its branching, and another large territory north of the Lehigh or Lackawanna. South on the Delaware two Stankekans settlements face each other across the river, and still farther south a settlement of Sauwanew people can be found on the river's eastern bank.

Yet neither the Dutch nor the English were the first colonizers. During the Thirty Years' War (1618–48), Sweden was a military power in northern Europe and chief guardian of the Lutheran faith against both Roman Catholicism and Calvinist Protestantism. A disgruntled Dutch speculator convinced the king of Sweden to authorize a trading company that he hoped would bring Sweden as much wealth as Catholic Spain while also spreading Lutheranism. A corporation founded in 1626 collected large sums from investors, but internal and international events slowed the project. In 1637 the first expedition finally departed in two small ships under the command of Peter Minuit, the former Dutch governor at New Amsterdam. After an arduous journey, they sailed up the Svenske Rivier (Swedish/Delaware/South/Fast-Flowing Lenape River) in mid-March 1638. The forty men—soldiers and servants—were to purchase lands from the "wild nations" and seek their conversion to Swedish standards of behavior and religion. Already aware that there was no gold, colonial officials were instructed to collect beaver pelts and grow tobacco and raise silkworms. They were to search out valuable woods and minerals and to judge the quality of local grapes for winemaking. New Sweden was intended to be an immediate source of profit to investors, not a self-sufficient colony of permanent settlers. It was doomed to failure. The beaver were of poor quality because their fur was not as lustrous as those in colder climates, and the Delaware Valley never became a major source of wine, tobacco, or silk.

Peter Minuit negotiated a treaty with five local Lenape chiefs—Mattahorn, Mitatsemint, Eru Packen, Mohomen, and Chiton—on April 8, 1638. The content of that treaty was variously remembered. The Swedish authorities claimed to have negotiated rights to sixty-seven miles of frontage on the Delaware River, centered at Minquas Kill just below Fort Christina (Wilmington, Delaware) and extending west "as far as the setting sun." But several decades later three Swedish witnesses remembered a much smaller grant measured by the distance of a cannonball shot from Fort Christina. In addition, an early nineteenth-century metaphorical account of these earliest contacts aptly describes the expansive demands of the Europeans and the misrepresentations they employed at treaty negotiations. The Seneca Chief, Cornplanter, recalled: "The great man wanted only a little, little, land, on which to raise greens for his soup, just as much as a bullock's hide would cover. Here we first might have observed their deceitful spirit. The bullock's hide was cut up into little strips, and did not cover, indeed, but encircled a very large piece of land." When Governor Johan Printz wrote that the Lenape "trust us in no wise and we trust them still less," both sides had their reasons. European notions of private personal property were alien to the Lenape, who could authorize the use of the land but not its sale. The Swedes also expected exclusive alliances, while the Lenape, recognizing their technological disadvantages and aware of distant warfare, continued to negotiate with all parties for their own protection—Swedes, Dutch, English, Susquehannocks, Minquas, and others. The Swedes regarded Lenape diplomacy as treachery.

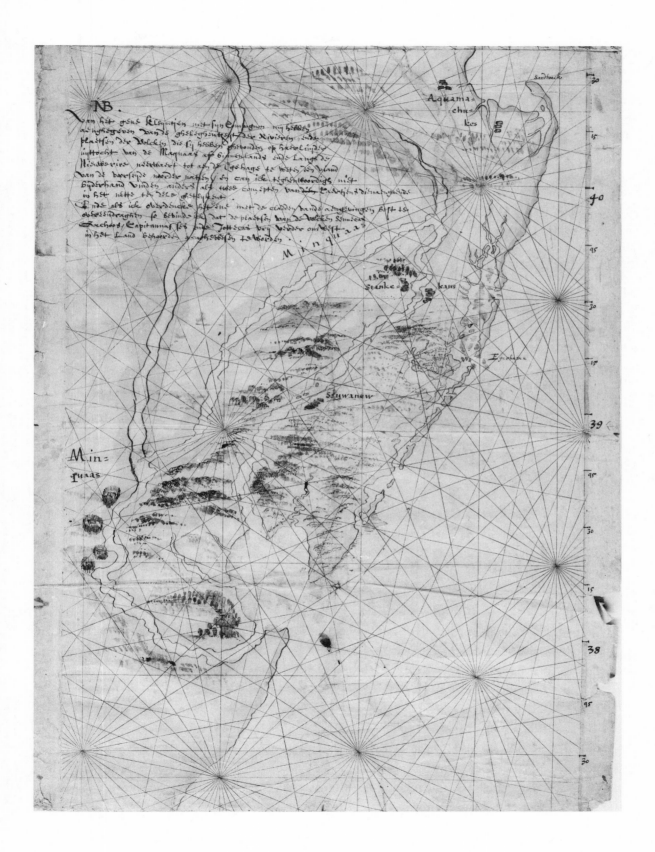

Two views of the Lenape. The first (*left*), perhaps more imaginative than realistic, is based on a description given to an artist in Sweden in the late seventeenth century; the artist had never been to America. The second (*right*) was sketched in the late eighteenth or early nineteenth century when the Lenape had adopted some European items: sleeved garments, buttons, and what look like rifles. Except for the feathered headdress, colonists on the frontier would have dressed in a similar fashion, imitating Native leggings and moccasins.

Despite the Europeans' aggressive seizure of additional land, relations were remarkably peaceful. Printz was reminded by the Swedish crown to treat the Lenape well. He generally did—signing treaties and negotiating after the occasional killings of settlers. Surviving Swedish sources claim that these few killings were unprovoked, but five took place in March 1643 and 1644, at a point in each year when food supplies were low. European settlers may have been poaching on Lenape hunting grounds. In any event, the Swedes began no wars of revenge for the killings. New Sweden's stance, less aggressive than other colonies, did not reflect understanding, toleration, or belief in human equality. Printz had a foul temper, and Europeans were certain that their culture and religion were superior to those of "savages." Military restraint was necessary because the colony was weak. Fewer than 110 men were available in 1644, and not all were fit for service. At its peak the colony numbered only a few hundred men, women, and children while several thousand Lenape lived in the region. Had the colony been more successful, its early history might well have been as bloody as those of other colonies. Printz thought that with 200 additional soldiers he could "break the necks of every one in the river." Fortunately for William Penn, he never got his wish.

New Sweden lasted only a few decades, but it became a cultural hearth. Colonists combined Northern European and Native American traditions to create a culture of market-orientated maize and wheat production, extensive rather than intensive farming, supplemental hunting and fishing, frequent migration, and log construction of buildings. These practices would continue to evolve and spread as later generations of settlers moved throughout the United States.

New Sweden grew to claim land on both sides of the Delaware River, including territories now within the states of Delaware, New Jersey, and Pennsylvania. The river was not a dividing line on a map but the center of a system of interconnected waterways that connected scattered farmsteads. It linked a series of small forts designed for protection and for holding church services. Rudimentary administrative and commercial centers at Fort Christina and at Tinicum Island (modern Essington, Delaware County, Pennsylvania) were barely maintained through twelve expeditions from Sweden between 1638 and 1656. Two expeditions never arrived, while the last docked after the Dutch conquered the colony. Because of the sporadic traffic between the mother country and its fledgling colony, the settlement remained underdeveloped and understaffed. Supporting even this small imperial outpost with soldiers, tools, ammunition, clothing, livestock, bricks, and other necessities was expensive and complex. The corporation soon learned that the chances for profit were remote, and investors lost interest in assisting the colony.

Swedish authorities insisted that to maximize profits settlers should be "good men, fewer women and fewest children." The scarcity of women, the absence of basic amenities, and the impossibility of family life caused many servants and soldiers to run away to other colonies or to return to Sweden. In 1644, after six years, only 143 inhabitants lived in New Sweden, three-quarters of them men. Of the 200 souls present in 1654, approximately 130 flocked to the ship that had just deposited some 200 new arrivals and returned home to Sweden. Governors complained about shortages of food and clothing, caused in part by planting too much tobacco (with little success) and too few edible crops. Men had to do "things which belong to the women," in addition to their regular tasks of military service, field work, hunting, and fishing. They were forced to transgress customary gender roles "to look after the garden and the cattle, to spin and to weave . . . , to keep the nets and the seines in order, to make malt, to brew the ale, to bake, to cook the food, to milk the cows, [and] to make the cheese and butter." In the near absence of women's economic contributions, life was precarious, arduous, and uncomfortable. Even when more women arrived, they left the care of cattle to men, shocking a later Swedish visitor. He was convinced that the "women-folks" had nothing better to do than "roast themselves by the kitchen-fire," although the list of remaining chores would indicate otherwise. This change was just one sign that European practices would have to be adapted to a new and different environment.

Governor Johan Printz. This portrait shows the governor's massive girth and imperious look. He weighed 400 pounds and was dubbed "the big tub" by Native Americans.

The comparatively few settlers of New Sweden anticipated the later development of the region in their diverse ethnic, racial, and social origins. Large numbers of Finns were recruited, with smaller numbers of Swedes, Dutch, German, and Polish migrants and at least one enslaved Angolan. There were convicts serving out their sentences, bound laborers, conscripted soldiers, volunteers, artisans, missionaries, officers, gentlefolk, and the occasional aristocrat. Language, religion, and political authority served to tie these disparate people into a semblance of a colony. Swedish became the dominant language, and Swedish clergymen promoted the Lutheran religion. The royally appointed military governors ruled without being hampered by constitutions, legislatures, newspapers, or a voting public. The court had powers of life and death. Yet the people were not passive. They petitioned the governors over various contentious issues. In 1653 one-quarter of the male population signed a document accusing Governor Johan Printz of failing to protect the colony, of restraint of trade, and of personally profiting from his position. Printz tried and executed one opponent, but instead of suppressing the discontent the execution caused the gover-

nor's own soldiers to threaten to kill him at the nearest opportunity. Printz soon fled the colony. Royal authority would be difficult to enforce in the New World.

Despite the small number of adventurers, they did not congregate in villages. They established scattered farmsteads along the banks of the Delaware and its tributaries, with the most densely populated area at Upland (Chester, Delaware County). Swedish, Dutch, and German settlers generally preferred to acquire the already cleared fields of the Lenape and to build substantial houses and barns and carefully fence fields, orchards, and pastures. The Finns and some Swedes practiced a distinctly Northern European agricultural life developed in the deep forests of northern Scandinavia. They burned away the underbrush and then girdled the trees so that they died. Wheat, rye, or other grains were planted between the dead trees and stumps. The settlers soon learned to grow maize, squash, and beans from the Indians. The trees provided logs that were notched by axes at the ends and turned into houses, stables, and granaries. Horses, cattle, sheep, and pigs were allowed to forage in the woods. The most meticulous farmers built flimsy shelters to protect livestock from winter storms, but most provided no shelter at all. Fields were fenced, but to keep the animals out of the grains and gardens, not to tend and control the livestock.

The interiors of the log houses were as crude as the exteriors, with little more than an open fireplace, a table, a bench or two, and some bedsteads in the corners. They were not necessarily permanent structures. Farmers moved when the soil became less fertile, or when the game and fish that supplemented the harvest gave out. Settlers from more temperate, pastoral areas in Sweden, England, and Germany were appalled at the untidiness of the landscape, the foraging livestock, the crudeness of the houses, the lack of substantial outbuildings, and the absence of roads. They accused the woodland farmers of laziness or of having degenerated into "savages." But in fact these methods were ideally suited for the topography of the eastern half of North America. Subsequent immigrants, particularly the Scots-Irish, adopted them. The accusations of frontier laziness persisted, however, even after log cabins entered into the mythology of America when Abraham Lincoln and others in the mid-nineteenth century made these cabins a proud symbol of their humble origins and democratic intentions.

SOME CONSEQUENCES OF EUROPEAN COLONIZATION

Even the small number of Europeans in the Delaware Valley caused environmental change in an area that had been isolated for thousands of years. Animals intentionally brought and shipped by settlers from Europe—such as horses, cattle, pigs, and sheep—were accompanied by rats and mice, houseflies, horseflies, lice, and other pests. Intermixed with imported wheat, rye, and barley seeds were the seeds of dandelion, plantain, daisy, and other weeds. Outside their usual ecological niches European weeds and pests spread rapidly. Some plants that were brought to Pennsylvania were beneficial. The Native people prized the peaches grown by the Swedes and planted peach trees throughout the region, so that by the 1680s newly arriving Europeans assumed that peaches were native to America because the fruit trees were found well past the bounds of colonial settlement. Not all transplantations were so benign, however. One Swede noted that when the colonists first arrived American grasses were abundant, but that "as soon as the country has been settled, the grass has died out from the roots, so that scarcely anything but black earth is left in the forests." Whether it was close cropping by farm animals, or new species of rodents, worms, parasites, or microbes that killed the grasses, the environment had been altered.

American species of animals were of interest to the European newcomers both out of scientific curiosity and for potential profit. When the newcomers asked the Lenape for the names of plants, animals, and places, the Europeans often misunderstood. In this case, the Algonquian word *arakun* was turned into "a raccoon." Europeans also named new species by looking for parallels with familiar Old World creatures. The small, short-legged, white-striped mammal reminded colonists of ferrets back home, so it was originally called the American polecat. Only later was the Algonquian word adopted: skunk.

TWO ARRIVALS IN NEW SWEDEN, 1639

The Europeans' New World has been mythologized as a land of opportunity, and so it was, for some.

Peter Gunnarsson Rambo, born in a small town near Gothenburg, Sweden, in 1612, sailed to New Sweden at the age of twenty-seven. He carried a box of seeds—apple, rye, barley, and other tree and garden seeds—for a European-style farm. Rambo worked as a lowly farmhand on a three-year contract, but he was fortunate. He was not a bound laborer or a conscripted soldier, but an independent wage earner. He earned ten guilders a month, sent part of his wages home to his father, and saved the rest. Unlike most of his fellow servants, he chose to remain in New Sweden at the end of his contract. He acquired land in Kingsessing, now West Philadelphia, and in November 1644 he became a freeman: a citizen entitled to certain privileges, including officeholding. With land and freedom ensured, he married Britta Mattsdotter, who had emigrated from Finland. By 1669 the couple had also acquired a 300-acre plantation in Passyunk, now South Philadelphia, where they raised four sons and three daughters.

While Rambo never learned to write and could not even sign his own name, he could probably read. He was one of the Swedish settlers who put his mark on the petition opposing abuses by Governor Johan Printz. He served as an adviser to the next governor and as justice of the peace for twenty-nine years under Swedish, Dutch, and English rule. A prominent and moderately wealthy member of a growing community, he lived to see his sons become large landholders and his daughters marry well. Like their father, the sons could not write their names. Rambo valued education, even though he, his children, and his thirty-seven grandchildren lacked book-

Spread of the Surname Rambo, 1725–1825

IMPLANTMENT OF SURNAME IN 17TH CENTURY

● SURNAME PRESENT IN COUNTY BEFORE 1775

• SURNAME PRESENT IN COUNTY, 1775–1825

▲ TOPONYM CONTAINING SURNAME

⟵ KNOWN OR PRESUMED MAJOR ROUTES OF DIFFUSION

0   100   200 miles
0   150   300 kilometers

learning. In 1692 he joined other leading residents in petitioning the Swedish king to send ministers and schoolbooks to the former colony. At the same time, he dictated a letter to his sister in Sweden expressing his regret that money he had sent her had miscarried but highlighting his pride that his children were "well provided for and live in plenty . . . in a very splendid fruitful land." He died in 1698. Rambo's life was a model of upward mobility in a new world, and the surname is still common in Pennsylvania. It achieved

national renown in the 1970s as the name of the hero of the novel *First Blood* by David Morrell, who earned his doctorate from The Pennsylvania State University, and in a series of action films starring Sylvester Stallone, who grew up in southeastern Pennsylvania.

Anthoni Swartz was born in Angola in West Central Africa, but when and exactly where is unknown. Like many of his countrymen, he was probably captured in a slave raid and sold to a Portuguese merchant. That merchant

may have sold him to a Dutch or English ship captain who in turn sold him to the Swedes. It was unlikely that Swartz would ever be freed or that he could have a settled family life. He was chattel, legally equivalent to livestock and under the control of his master. Even his given name had been supplied either by one of his owners or by the Catholic priest who baptized him in Angola. Like many caught in this international traffic in human beings, he undoubtedly became multilingual and able to speak not only his native language but also Portuguese, Swedish, and perhaps Dutch and English, and eventually Lenape as well. He arrived in New Sweden in 1639, as did Peter Rambo, but he had little of the good fortune of his fellow passenger. Swartz first lived at Fort Christina, where he was the sole African and the sole slave in an alien society. Within a few years he was moved to Tinicum, where he cut hay for the cattle and followed the governor in a little sloop, indicating not only his agricultural and navigational skills but also his servile status. He worked with three other men, all Swedish servants.

Before 1654, Swartz was identified in the colonial records by first name alone, an indication that even as an adult he was considered dependent and inferior, like a child. By 1654 he had won one mark of respect: he had acquired a surname. He was Anthoni Swartz (in English, Anthony Black). A Lars Swartz is listed next in that year's record. Could this have been his son, free because his mother was a free woman? Or was this man another, unrelated African, or even a dark-haired Swede? The records do not say. That same year, Anthoni Swartz made several purchases from the company store in his own name, but although he may have earned some money as well as a surname he was still identified as "the slave." The 1654 list is the last mention of both Lars and Anthoni Swartz. Their anonymity and lack of opportunity were quite typical of later experiences of servants and slaves in Pennsylvania.

Some species disappeared early in the settlement process. The European demand for beaver hats led to the unintentional depletion of the beaver during the seventeenth century. The extermination of the local wolf population, accomplished by about 1700, was the deliberate result of bounties paid for wolf scalps by colonial governments. Europeans firmly believed in the wolves' fabled reputation as predators of human flesh, although the Native peoples might have disabused them of this folklore had they been willing to listen. The environment was being enriched by new varieties of plants and animals, threatened by parasitic species, and degraded as some native species died out.

It was the importation of microbial agents, however, that was most devastating in the seventeenth century. Smallpox, measles, influenza, amoebic dysentery, whooping cough, malaria, and more arrived from Europe. Africa supplied yellow fever, dengue fever,* yaws,** and a few other diseases by way of the Caribbean trade. The first recorded epidemic in the Delaware Valley occurred in 1642 when a "great sickness" spread among the colonists. The next year, 15 of the 135 male inhabitants died in July and August alone, perhaps of amoebic dysentery or yellow fever. The survivors, Printz noted, "have no longer any desire to remain here." These epidemics probably spread among the Lenape as well. In 1654 a "plague" broke out on board a ship sailing to New Sweden, killing more than 100 of the 350 passengers. Typhus spread by body lice was the probable culprit. As soon as the ship landed, the disease spread to local residents. The Lenape wanted to send two medicine men to the ship to take the spirit away, but the Swedes refused, saying that if the Lenape would trust in the Christian God they would not get sick. However, because Christians were the first victims of the disease the Lenape were skeptical, and did not convert. In 1658 an "ardent prevailing fever" and scurvy afflicted residents, and in 1659 and 1661 there were outbreaks of smallpox. While the records highlight the sufferings of the colonists, the Native peoples of the Delaware River valley, of the Susquehanna region, and of the Ohio River systems suffered the most. Sheltered from the disease cycles of the Old World, they lacked immunity to these imported germs. Disease, more than weaponry, weakened the hold of the Native peoples on their homelands.

But the Swedes had even more difficulty holding on to their colony. Its weakness encouraged the Dutch to encroach from the north, and the English from the south. During the 1650s the Dutch again laid claim to the region, and encouraged settlement with a small military presence. In 1654 the new Swedish governor captured a small Dutch fort just south of Fort Christina. The Dutch responded in 1655 with a force of several hundred soldiers and sailors against a few score Swedes. The Swedes capitulated without a fight, humiliated by being paraded out of their fort "with musketballs in their mouths," presumably to indicate their symbolic deaths. New Sweden vanished forever, but it had bequeathed a legacy of uneasy peace in the Delaware Valley that allowed Quaker pacifism to flourish into the next century.

Despite some initial plundering of Swedish farms, Dutch rule was not harsh. Recognizing Swedish customs, the Dutch divided their territory at the Delaware River

*An infectious, viral, mosquito-borne eruptive fever, also known as breakbone fever, causing severe illness but rarely fatal.

**A contagious disease of the tropics caused by a spirochetal bacterium related to the syphilis Trepanoma, but not spread venereally, whose most obvious sign is skin lesions of the extremities; also known as frambesia.

and allowed the Swedes on the west bank to maintain their own officers and court system. The boundaries of the future state were being created based on administrative convenience, not on the economic and ecological functions of the river system. The period of Dutch control had little lasting impact on the area, and when the English conquered New Netherlands in 1664 there was little change until William Penn arrived in 1682. The Swedish community outlasted the Swedish colony, and in fact grew because of continued immigration and high birth rates. The settlers began to thrive economically, shifting from tobacco production to wheat and rye. In 1697 the king of Sweden sent a Lutheran minister and 400 religious and children's books to a Swedish community that numbered nearly 1,000 individuals. The Swedish government supported a mission in Pennsylvania until 1831, considering it for more than a century as a primitive place where inhabitants and immigrants alike needed the assistance of a civilized nation.

This late nineteenth-century re-creation of Penn's landing shows the dense woods of the Delaware River valley in 1682, the joy and the weakness of the passengers after two months at sea, the signs of existing European settlement in the presence of Swedish residents, and a log cabin.

As European territories along the Delaware River changed hands, equally important changes were occurring among the Lenape, the Iroquois, and the Susquehannocks. The wars, economic changes, and migrations of peoples, described in the previous chapter, weakened and distracted these nations as European immigration surged. The hostilities particularly devastated western groups in the Ohio River valley. The Eries, the Monongahelas, and others disappeared; located too far west to have acquired the metallurgy and firearms that had strengthened the Susquehannocks and the Iroquois, they may also have suffered their first devastating epidemics. The Eries provide one example. In 1634 "Queen" Gegosasa permitted the Eries to join the Massassaugues in attacking some Senecas in revenge and in mourning for a murder. A mourning war channeled the grief of the survivors and was intended to be brief. In this case, however, the Erie warriors suffered heavy casualties. New economic rivalries turned a single incident designed to maintain honor and assuage grief into a twenty-year struggle. By 1654 Gegosasa sued for peace, but negotiations collapsed and war broke out with renewed violence. According to tradition, Gegosasa died in battle with many of her people, an epidemic swept through their villages, and any remaining Eries were absorbed by other groups, leaving only their name on the landscape. Now the Iroquois nominally controlled the Erie territory. In the absence of any significant population in the area, however, Shawnee people began moving into the newly depopulated lands, and French explorers mapping the Great Lakes began to look with interest on the western territory.

Meanwhile, the English initiated a new kind of colonial venture. Based on the massive

ARMEGOT PRINTZ: ESTATE MANAGER, POLITICAL NEGOTIATOR, WOMAN

Armegot Printz.

European customs were based on complex social, political, and judicial systems that could not be easily replicated in smaller, more primitive settlements. For some, colonial life was liberating because it might provide a chance to cast aside repressive roles. For others, weakened authority encouraged unruliness and was subversive of civil order. Armegot Printz was not the subordinate, meek-and-mild ideal of womanhood that both church and state promoted. Some historians have seen her as overbearing, irritable, and self-willed; others as a precursor of the liberated woman.

Armegot Printz was born around 1627 in Sweden, the eldest of five daughters. Unlike most women (and men) at the time, she had learned to read and write. Her father, the fierce-tempered, 400-pound Johan Printz, was the longest-serving governor of New Sweden. They arrived in New Sweden in early 1643, followed by Count Johan Papagoja, Printz's deputy. The men determined that an arranged marriage between the governor's daughter and the governor's assistant would be advantageous. The problem was that sixteen-year-old Armegot Printz absolutely refused. For two years she resisted pressure by her father, by Papagoja, by the church, and by the crown, but shortly after receiving a letter from the Swedish queen urging that the marriage take place, she capitulated. They had five children, but the marriage was not a success.

When her husband and her father returned to Sweden in 1654, Printz remained in America, perhaps with her three daughters. She soon dropped her married name and reverted to her maiden name—a sign of her independence. She negotiated ownership of her father's plantation on Tinicum Island after its seizure during the Dutch invasion of the colony and, with a few servants, raised cattle, hogs, grain, and corn and distilled her own liquor. She negotiated a reduced tax rate for herself, built a new house in Upland (Chester), and pursued a complex series of legal actions against the purchasers of her estate that included a voyage to Amsterdam. In 1669 she was involved in an attempt to overthrow Dutch rule led by a man called the Long Finn. Although he was deported, she suffered no consequences; she was too powerful and too well-connected. A shortage of servants and her advancing age seem to have forced her to move back to Sweden in 1676.

In retrospect, Armegot Printz was neither a shrew (she had good reason to resist) nor a proto-feminist (she did not, as far as we know, seek rights for all women), but an aristocrat whose superior social status on the far edge of two empires allowed her to separate from an uncongenial husband and run her own affairs. She was able to maintain her independence for more than two decades.

movement of peoples overseas and the establishment of permanent, self-supporting, economically complex communities, they encountered a substantially weakened Lenape presence in the east, and dislocations among the Iroquois and Shawnee in the west. The numeric balances in the east were about to be reversed in favor of the Europeans, but the Native peoples were still powerful, having honed their diplomatic and military skills over the course of the seventeenth century.

THE FOUNDING OF PENNSYLVANIA

The territory that Europeans were slow to exploit in the seventeenth century was by the mid-eighteenth century "one of the most considerable of [England's] *American Colonies*," because "none has thrived more, nor is more rich and populous." Philadelphia soon became one of the largest cities in the British Empire. It boasted wide streets, weekly newspapers, handsome churches, a statehouse with large clocks on the tower, a new academy, libraries, markets, two yearly fairs, a growing population, and, by the 1750s, a hospital and, soon after, a medical school. Small towns and individual farms dotted Philadelphia's hinterland and were tied to the city by newspapers, commercial transactions, religious organizations, and sometimes by politics. By the early 1760s Pennsylvania had the first English settlements west of the Appalachians at Fort Pitt. Events in England had brought this dramatic shift in the territory's fate.

TABLE 2.1 **ESTIMATED POPULATION OF PENNSYLVANIA AND SELECTED TOWNS, 1680–1780** (excluding Native Americans)

Year	Pennsylvania	Philadelphia	Germantown	Lancaster	Pittsburgh
1680	680	0	0	—	—
1690	11,450	2,031	147	—	—
1700	17,950	3,220	220	—	—
1710	24,450	4,415	248	—	—
1720	30,962	5,940	279	—	—
1730	51,707	7,500	310	Unknown	—
1740	85,637	8,720	372	960	—
1750	119,666	12,736	785	1,912	—
1760	183,703	18,756	1,562	2,839	201
1770	240,057	28,802	2,152	2,832	c. 100
1780	327,305	36,946	2,411	3,637	c. 150

SOURCES: U.S. Bureau of the Census, *Historical Statistics of the United States, Colonial Times to 1970, Bicentennial Edition*, 2 vols. (Washington, D.C.: U.S. Government Printing Office, 1975), 2:1168, tables Z1–19; P. M. G. Harris, "The Demographic Development of Colonial Philadelphia in Some Comparative Perspective," in *The Demographic History of the Philadelphia Region, 1600–1860*, ed. Susan E. Klepp (Philadelphia: American Philosophical Society, 1989), 274; Stephanie Grauman Wolf, *Urban Village: Population, Community, and Family Structure in Germantown, Pennsylvania, 1683–1800* (Princeton: Princeton University Press, 1976), 43; Jerome H. Wood, *Conestoga Crossroads: Lancaster, Pennsylvania, 1730–1790* (Harrisburg: Pennsylvania Historical and Museum Commission, 1979), 47; "An Early Record of Pittsburgh," *Pennsylvania Magazine of History and Biography* 2 (1878), 305; William H. Egle, *An Illustrated History of the Commonwealth of Pennsylvania*, 2 vols. (Philadelphia: Gardner, 1880), 1:322.

NOTE: When Robert Thomas Malthus wanted evidence of the unrestrained reproductive capacities of human beings, he turned to Benjamin Franklin's analysis of Pennsylvania. Franklin guessed quite accurately that the population doubled every generation. In the eighteenth century most of the colony's growth did in fact come from births, not immigration. Women who married early and lived to age fifty averaged seven to nine children, although by the end of the colonial period Quakers and Philadelphians were beginning to have fewer children.

Pennsylvanians' life expectancy at birth was about forty years in the countryside, twenty-eight years for free persons in the city, but only eighteen years for urban slaves. If Pennsylvanians survived the many diseases of infancy and childhood to celebrate their twentieth birthday, they might expect to live another fifteen to forty years, depending on their location and economic status, but roughly half of city children and one-third of rural children did not live to see their twentieth birthday.

"The Quaker Meeting," mezzotint from a painting by Egbert van Heemskeerk, late seventeenth century. Although intended as caricature, it captures the Quaker practices that so shocked outsiders, particularly the woman preaching and gesticulating while standing on a box.

In seventeenth-century England, political and religious strife arose as economic and cultural change transformed town and country. The economy was becoming commercialized, and merchants, shopkeepers, and some artisans were rising in importance. London and other towns boomed, markets expanded, and overseas trade opened up financial and intellectual possibilities, while the old landed aristocracy was losing some of its influence. These changes, however, were less perceptible than the dissension over religion. Roman Catholics, Anglicans, Puritans, Presbyterians, Ranters, Diggers, Muggletonians, Anabaptists, and others struggled for supremacy or for simple survival as civil war engulfed Britain. Between 1640 and 1660 a Puritan minority dominated England, only to find that without competent leadership for their Commonwealth the majority accepted a return to monarchy and the Anglican Church.

In reaction to the Puritans' belief in a harsh, judgmental God, there arose in England a small group whose members called themselves "Friends" and who were referred to by their enemies as "Quakers," although the Friends adopted that name as well. The Quakers taught that every human being had "the light of Christ within," later referred to as the "inner light," and that the loving deity had planted a seed of salvation inside every person. These beliefs led Quakers to become pacifists, because if all individuals have a divine light within them, then killing such a person would be a sacrilege. For the same reason, Quakers also believed in the basic spiritual equality of all people. This belief did not initially prevent Quakers from buying and selling slaves just as their neighbors did. Spiritual equality was not understood to result in civil equality. Quakers rejected theology, rituals, professional clergy, and other institutional, hierarchical, or coercive practices because they thought that, with a minimum of guidance, anyone could find truth by searching the light within. And because they believed the material world, like the human will, was distracting and corrupting in the search for truth, Friends advocated plain speech, dress, and housing.

These were the radical beliefs of people of moderate means and little prominence. Many aspects of Quaker practices were shocking to the English. For instance, Quaker beliefs offended social conventions of female subordination and were counter to Paul's biblical injunction that women were to keep silence in the church. In addition, Quaker women preached both indoors and out, traveled without their husbands, ran their own meetings, and collected and spent money for their own projects. Furthermore, Quakers disavowed the doctrine of original sin, believing instead that children were born innocent, and they were also early advocates of an affectionate and egalitarian family life. At a time when many seventeenth-century English people believed that children were little sinners who needed strict discipline, William Penn, like other Quakers, urged parents to "Love [their children] with Wisdom, Correct them with Affection: Never strike in Passion, and suit the Correction to their Age." Quakers also refused to pay taxes to support war, and, when arrested, refused to doff their hats to the judge. Many were jailed for breaking laws, contempt of court, and disturbing the peace.

At the end of the seventeenth century, Quakers, although less assertive than they had been earlier, were still a thorn in the side of English authorities. As in Europe generally, such dissenting religions were at best mistrusted and at worst actively persecuted. One unusual Quaker developed a refuge for persecuted Friends and other dissenters. William Penn was born in 1644. While most Quakers were small farmers and shopkeepers, Penn was the eldest son of a wealthy and prominent father. Rebellious as a young man, he was expelled from Oxford University at the age of seventeen and was a convert to Quakerism at age twenty-two. Both incidents infuriated his father, an admiral in the English navy. The Quaker faith allowed Penn to continue to rebel against religious and social orthodoxies, yet he remained a product of his upbringing, enjoying the privileges and comforts of wealth and high status. He married twice, both times for money as well as for love; he had large country estates and town houses in both the Old World and the New; and he rode in carriages and dressed in fine clothing. Penn's unique combination

The only two known likenesses of William Penn. The first (*above left*) shows young William Penn in armor. This eighteenth-century portrait is one of several copies from a lost original believed by many to depict Penn at the age of twenty-two in 1666, the year before he became a Quaker. (Some scholars think the portrait is of Penn's father, also named William.) The young Penn wanted to be a soldier, and, the legend goes, he was wearing a sword as a symbol of his gentlemanly social status when he first met George Fox, a founder of the Friends. When he asked Fox if he could continue to wear his sword, Fox answered, "Wear it as long as thou canst." The next time the two met, Penn had no sword. Penn sat for no more portraits, for Quakers believed it was vain to pay such attention to one's image. The second likeness (*above right*) is a sketch by Francis Place from the 1690s and was probably drawn informally without Penn's knowledge.

of a radical faith, great wealth, and aristocratic connections made Pennsylvania possible.

William Penn was looking for a place where his co-religionists could establish a "Holy Experiment," a place to experience Quaker precepts. He was also looking to make money. Penn must have been enormously persuasive. After only ten months of negotiation, King Charles II granted him 45,000 acres on the Delaware River to settle a debt owed to Penn's father's estate. The grant was named "Pennsylvania"—in honor of Penn's father, not, as Penn was careful to point out, for himself. Thanks to Penn's persistent solicitations, some 600 investors bought shares in this new venture, and between 1682 and 1684 some 4,000 emigrants joined Penn in founding the colony of Pennsylvania; fifty ships set sail for Pennsylvania in 1682–83 alone. His early revenues from land sales were above £9,000 (well over $1 million in the year 2000), yet by 1685 Penn was heading toward bankruptcy. He had spent money freely, aided some migrants, paid the Lenape for several land purchases, built a town house and a country house for himself, bought slaves and servants to wait on his family, mismanaged tax collection for the colony, and speculated in shop goods like hosiery and horse collars. In his first two years in Pennsylvania he spent £10,000. Penn returned to England in 1684 to look after his financial interests and to try, in vain, to preserve his title to three counties that were also claimed by the Calvert family of Maryland. These counties eventually became the separate colony of Delaware.

One of William Penn's first actions in Pennsylvania was to sign treaties with the local Lenape for access to land. These documents were lost within a few decades, perhaps because later Pennsylvanians did not want to follow Penn's example. Penn's agents and, later, Penn's sons were not so scrupulous. And as peaceful as Penn's intentions were, in reality the Lenape were being dispossessed. They began moving southwest to Brandywine Creek, east into New Jersey, or north to the forks of the Delaware, where they joined newly combined Lenape and Munsee bands who called themselves Delawares.

Penn was able to maintain peaceful relations with the Native people in part because of his careful negotiations and in part because of the dislocations throughout the territory at the end of the Beaver Wars. The previously successful Susquehannocks left the middle Susquehanna Valley after 1675 to travel south to Maryland for protection from the Iroquois. But they failed to find peace. Caught once again in warfare, the survivors disbanded and became refugees, moving frequently and forming villages with people from other decimated towns and tribes; one such group was the Conestoga. Other dispossessed people flocked to the depopulated central, northern, and western sections of Pennsylvania—Shawnee from unknown origins, and Nanticokes, Conoys, and Tuscaroras from the south. The territory was in upheaval.

The Beaver Wars ended with the Iroquois as the winners, but it was a costly victory. Suffering from loss of population and fighting strength, they were anxious to appear stronger than they were. Like the remnant Delaware, Conestoga, and other newly formed groups, the Iroquois too had adopted many strangers who spoke different languages and had different customs. In order to retain their strength, a "Covenant Chain" of diplomatic alliances was formed to tie the Iroquois and the Delaware, the Conestoga, and other refugee people living throughout Pennsylvania to the English government in New York. Relations between the new European arrivals and the Native people were temporarily peaceful, both because of William Penn's diplomacy and because of western military and diplomatic developments over which he had little control or even knowledge. It was an increasingly volatile situation.

GOVERNING PENNSYLVANIA

According to the crown, Pennsylvania was to be a feudal estate, the personal property of the Penn family. William Penn and his heirs would appoint the governors and collect the quit-rents (land tax). Their official title was "the True and Absolute Proprietary of Pennsylvania." Yet England had a House of Commons elected by substantial landowners, and Englishmen had certain rights, including a right to be tried by a jury of their peers. Colonists expected similar privileges. These checks on absolute authority had generally been expanding before the creation of Pennsylvania, and the Glorious Revolution of 1688, the Declaration of Rights of 1689, and John Locke's *Treatises on Government* (1690) only strengthened Anglo-American opposition to arbitrary rule. Penn's huge

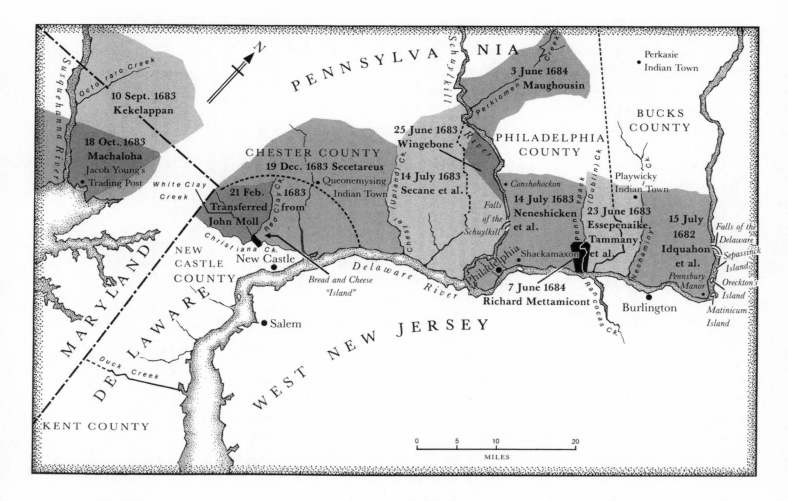

On the map:

PENNSYLVANIA

Susquehanna River

Octoraro Creek

10 Sept. 1683
Kekelappan

18 Oct. 1683
Machaloha
Jacob Young's
Trading Post

White Clay Creek

CHESTER COUNTY
19 Dec. 1683 Secetareus

21 Feb. 1683
Transferred from
John Moll

Red Clay Ck.

Christiana Ck.

New Castle

NEW CASTLE COUNTY

Bread and Cheese "Island"

Queonemysing Indian Town

25 June 1683
Wingebone

14 July 1683
Secane et al.

Chester Ck. (Upland) Ck.

Schuylkill River

Perkiomen Creek

3 June 1684
Maughousin

PHILADELPHIA COUNTY

Conshohocken

Falls of the Schuylkill

14 July 1683
Neneshicken et al.

Philadelphia

Shackamaxon

7 June 1684
Richard Mettamicont

Pennypack (Dublin) Ck.

23 June 1683
Essepenaike
Tammany et al.

Neshaminy

Rancocas Ck.

Perkasie
Indian Town

BUCKS COUNTY

Playwicky
Indian Town

15 July 1682
Idquahon et al.

Pennsbury Manor

Burlington

Falls of the Delaware

Sepassinck Island

Oreckton's Island

Matinicum Island

Delaware River

Salem

DELAWARE

MARYLAND

Duck Creek

KENT COUNTY

WEST NEW JERSEY

N

0   5   10   20
MILES

William Penn's purchases from specific Lenape chiefs, 1682–84. This map shows that Penn acquired land in numerous small parcels rather than all at once—in contrast to the romantic image of Penn's treaty with the Indians painted by Benjamin West.

estate had to adopt some of the characteristics of an English-style government. In addition, the Quakers who dominated the legislature in Pennsylvania were divided, contentious, and not inclined to endorse automatically Penn's rather elitist wishes. So the first frame of government proposed by Penn in 1683 was quickly discarded by the Assembly, despite the ten revisions it had undergone before submission. A second charter, calling for fewer elected officials and greater protection of property rights, was passed the following year. In 1693 Penn had his colony taken away. It was restored in 1695, after he was acquitted of treasonable associations for his friendship with the deposed king, James II. This resulted in two more governments. Finally, in 1701, Penn reluctantly signed the Charter of Privileges that remained the constitution of the colony until the American Revolution.

The Charter of Privileges gave the voters much more power than Penn had originally intended. No upper house represented the wealthiest inhabitants. The single-house Assembly was elected annually. Men owning fifty acres or who had estates worth at least fifty British pounds could vote—which included most free men in the countryside but only a small proportion, perhaps 10 percent, in Philadelphia and other towns. The Assembly could initiate legislation and conduct its own affairs, but the proprietor or his governor retained the right to veto legislation. The first article of this charter, like its predecessors, was pathbreaking for its time: it guaranteed freedom of religion to the inhabitants of Pennsylvania.

Pennsylvanians needed a legal code as well as constitutions. Quaker assemblymen had to combine the ideals of the Holy Experiment with English legal traditions. Particularly in domestic relations and in the criminal code, Pennsylvania legislators tried to institute more enlightened and moral policies in accordance with both the latest theories of legal reform and their version of Christian belief. Major revisions or additions to the legal code in 1682, 1683, 1693, 1700, 1705, and 1718 indicate the contentiousness of the issues involved.

The marriage laws were one area of legal innovation and frequent revision. The English law that permitted girls of twelve and boys of fourteen to run away and marry even when their fathers objected was unpopular, and Quakers especially insisted on carefully supervised marriages. Pennsylvania legislators therefore sought to give parents more control over their children. In 1682 Pennsylvania law simply stated that parents must always give approval before marriage, but because the parents of many young adults in Pennsylvania resided overseas, this proved unworkable. The next year the Assembly passed "An Act to prevent Clandestine, Loose and unseemly proceedings in this Province, . . . regarding Marriage" stating that "the parents and guardians shall, if possible, be first consulted." It was possible to send letters overseas, but an answer might take a year to arrive, a delay that could lead to more loose and unseemly behavior, so in 1684 legislators required that "parents and guardians shall, if conveniently can, first be consulted." But this was considered too lenient. After 1700 parents had to be given one month's notice of an upcoming marriage, and from 1729 they had to provide a certificate of consent if they lived in the province and their children were under the age of twenty-one or still dependents. This law remained in effect until the middle of the nineteenth century.

Protection of the slave system required sharp legal distinctions based on race even with respect to family life. Legal marriages or independent family life for slaves would have interfered with a master's ability to sell enslaved husbands, wives, and children. Even when

CHARTER OF PRIVILEGES, ARTICLE ONE, 1701

Article One, The Pennsylvania Charter of Privileges, 1701, granted freedom of conscience to all Christians and Jews and provided for the separation of church and state by forbidding the use of taxes to support religious bodies. It opened up officeholding to all male Christians.

> *That no Person inhabiting in this Province or Territories, who shall confess and acknowledge One almighty God, the Creator, Upholder and Ruler of the World; and profess to live quietly under the Civil Government, shall be molested or prejudiced because of his Conscientious Persuasion or Practice, nor be compelled to maintain any religious Worship, contrary to his Mind.*
>
> *All Persons who profess to believe in Jesus Christ, the Saviour, shall be capable to serve this Government in any Capacity, he solemnly promising Allegiance to the King and Fidelity to the Proprietary and Governor, and taking the Attests as now established.*

The definition of religion excluded Native American belief systems entirely and barred Jews and nonbelievers from holding any office in the government. Defective by early twenty-first-century standards, this experiment in overcoming nearly two centuries of religious hatred on the part of Roman Catholics, Lutherans, Calvinists, Anglicans, Anabaptists, and other Christian sects was one of William Penn's greatest achievements.

The simplicity and plainness promoted by early Quakers was challenged by the lure of worldly goods, particularly when some Quaker families acquired great wealth in the eighteenth century. This blue silk quilt, inscribed "Drawn by Sarah Smith Stitched by Hannah Callender and Catharine Smith in Testimony of their Friendship 10 mo. 5th [day] 1761," was faced with expensive cloth, and the skills that went into making it were the result of years of instruction in embroidery and quilting. Only the wealthy had the time and resources to produce such works of art. For the backing of this quilt, however, the three cousins chose a simple cotton cloth.

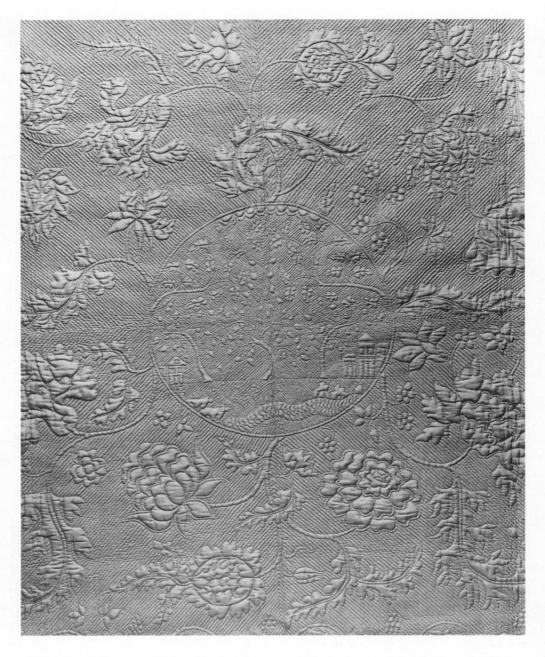

enslaved couples married in church, their marriages had no legal standing. After 1725, interracial marriages or liaisons were also banned. The white transgressors could be sold as servants for seven years, free Negroes were enslaved, and the children of mixed unions were to be taken from their parents and sold for thirty-one years. The legislators' goal of strengthening family ties and trying to protect minor children did not apply to slaves.

Revisions of the criminal code were equally troublesome. Pennsylvania tried to eliminate the vengeful European reliance on the death penalty; Quakers hoped to reform criminals, not execute them. William Penn wrote: "It were an happy Day if Men could bound and qualifie their Resentments with Charity to the Offender: For then our Anger would be without Sin and better convict and edifie the Guilty which alone can make it lawful." The Assembly restricted the death penalty and introduced noncapital, alternative punishments that included incarceration, disfigurement, whipping, and branding. A convict's spouse was allowed a divorce in cases of adultery, bigamy, and bestiality. In many cases punishments were increased for second offenses on the grounds that the possibility of yet harsher penalties would make first-time offenders think twice about committing another crime. For example, a first-time rapist was whipped, imprisoned for seven years, and heavily fined by the law of 1700; after a second offense he was castrated.

TABLE 2.2 **ESTIMATED ARRIVALS THROUGH THE PORT OF PHILADELPHIA, 1720–1769**

Decade	From the Caribbean & Africa	From Ireland	From Amsterdam
1720	135	—	2,956
1730	454	3,811	13,006
1740	256	6,035	20,850
1750	283	6,944	30,374
1760	1,148	9,221	8,058

SOURCES: Darold D. Wax, "The Negro Slave Trade in Colonial Pennsylvania" (Ph.D. diss., University of Washington, 1962), 46; Marianne S. Wokeck, *Trade in Strangers: The Beginnings of Mass Migration to North America* (University Park: The Pennsylvania State University Press, 1999), 45–46, 172–73.

NOTE: Mass migration began in the 1720s with German-speaking and some French-speaking people arriving in Amsterdam from scores of small villages located near the Rhine River. They were packed into ships and sent overseas, most often to Pennsylvania. Migration from Ireland began a decade later. The slave trade rose and fell with the supply of other migrants, rising particularly in the early 1760s when the Seven Years' War prevented commerce between continental Europe and the colonies. Unfortunately, no records were kept of the large migration from Great Britain, except for scattered listings of indentured servants, but it was sizable.

Concern for the offender's reform did not cross racial boundaries. A black man who raped a white woman was executed. For an attempted rape, not a crime for white men under any circumstance, he was castrated. The same law made the conviction of white men for the rape of a black female virtually impossible by barring the testimony of a black person against a white. Enslaved Pennsylvanians were tried in a separate court system without a jury of their peers and without any right of appeal. The property rights of the master rather than impartial justice dominated these courts.

Economic investments in a slave system, a mobile population of recent immigrants, religious diversity, English precedent, and Quaker idealism all affected the evolution of a legal code in the colony. In 1718 the British Privy Council overturned many of Pennsylvania's most radical criminal laws as inconsistent with English law. They were replaced by the traditional punishment of hanging with the possibility of leniency. Pennsylvania legal practice continued to move toward the British model in the late colonial period, when the Revolution would bring another period of legal innovation, much of it likewise concerned with the reformation of the criminal offender and with questions of race.

THE GROWTH OF PENNSYLVANIA: ETHNICITIES

When William Penn returned to England in 1684 he spent much of his time recruiting settlers for Pennsylvania. He traveled through England, Ireland, and Holland proclaiming Pennsylvania's geographic advantages and its guaranteed freedom of conscience to Quakers and allied Protestants. He did not return to the colony until 1699. Pennsylvania politics remained contentious, and the Quakers were often sharply divided over religion and politics. Penn's finances were still precarious. By 1701 he was back in England, with his debts mounting as he defended various legal challenges to his proprietorship. While he eventually won these legal cases, he spent nine months in prison for debt in 1708 and

An unusual attempt to attract attention to Pennsylvania and denigrate non-Quaker ventures can be seen on these playing cards. The nine of diamonds reads "Come all ye Saints that would for little Buy / Great Tracts of Land, and care not where they lye, / Deal with your Quaking Friends, they're Men of Light, / The Spirit hates Deceit and Scorns to Bite [cheat]." The eight of diamonds predicts murder and mayhem for settlers in French Acadia (Nova Scotia).

then tried to sell the colony in 1712. That same year he was incapacitated after suffering two severe strokes. Hannah Callowhill Penn, his second wife, became the de facto colonial governor until her husband's death in 1718. As sole executor of the estate, her heavy responsibilities continued until her death in 1726. This fourteen-year stewardship was as close as Pennsylvania has come in 300 years to having a woman governor.

Despite Penn's personal difficulties, his colony grew. English, Scottish, Scots-Irish, Welsh, and Irish Quakers risked six to twelve weeks at sea in leaky vessels to immigrate to this ethnically diverse colony. Migrants, even those debarking from a single port, came from different national, regional, local, religious, social, and economic backgrounds and usually did not perceive of themselves as a group. Their old ethnic or national identities were challenged by new experiences. New arrivals reacted in many ways to the mix of peoples in Pennsylvania. Some acculturated to English or Quaker ways in language and manners, changing their names, adopting the English language, and intermarrying. Georg Bachofen became George Bakeoven, Magdalena Eschman became Lena Ashman, Schmidt became Smith, and Göstaffsson eventually became Justis. A Frenchman found it remarkable that a man he knew had an English grandfather, a Dutch wife, and children who had each married spouses of different backgrounds.

Some immigrants invented new ethnic identities in the New World. Pennsylvania Germans developed a group identity more than a century before their European colinguists united to create the state of Germany. Whites began to see their common interests four centuries before there was a European Union. Other immigrants idealized their homeland as a separate, or even superior, national inheritance. Exclusive and elitist city organizations like the St. Andrews Society (Scottish), the Deutschen Gesellschaft von Pennsylvanien (German), the Society of the Friendly Sons of St. Patrick (Irish), and the Society of the Sons of St. George (English) combined a sense of belonging with charitable aid to new immigrants.

Ethnic identities were especially strong where discrimination was present: among German-speaking people who lived in predominantly German communities, among Scots-Irish farmers in the west who lacked clear titles to their land, or among those in the north and west who were underrepresented in the legislature. Ethnicity was a potent political force in Pennsylvania, particularly near the frontier. Neither class interests nor political ideology developed as a way of organizing political opposition, except in Philadelphia. Ethnicity and religion organized local interests and provided a sense of community among recently settled strangers.

The largest group of non-English immigrants departed from the German-speaking principalities, dukedoms, and kingdoms along the Rhine River. Their homelands suffered French invasions, feudal restraints, and a devastated economy. Before 1720 only small numbers of immigrants came, but as soon as transporting immigrants became a profitable business, tens of thousands were carried to Pennsylvania. In Philadelphia the Germans soon became bilingual; in York, Lancaster, Berks, and Northampton Counties,

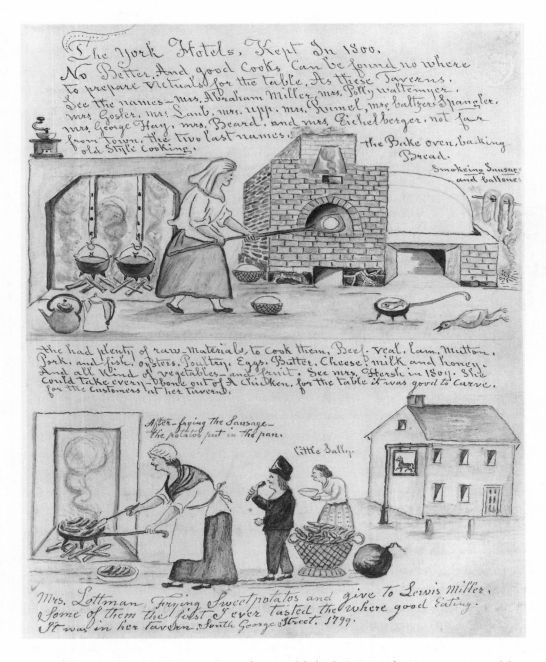

The York Hotels, Kept In 1800.
No Better. And good Cooks can be found no where to prepare Victuals for the table, As these Taverns. See the names – mrs. Abraham Miller, mrs. Polly waltemyer, mrs. Goster, mrs. Lamb, mrs. Upp, mrs. Rummel, mrs. baltzers Spangler, mrs. George Hay, mrs. Beard, and mrs. Eichelberger. not far from town, the two last names, old Style cooking.

the Bake oven, baking Bread.

Smokeing Sausage and ballones

they had plenty of raw–Materials, to cook them, Beef. veal. Lam, Mutton, Pork. and fish, oysters, Poultry. Eggs. Butter, Cheese, milk and honey, And all Kind of vegetables–and fruit. See mrs. Hersh in 1809. She could take every–bone out of A Chicken, for the table it was good to Carve, for the Customers at her tavern.

After frying the Sausage– the potatos put in the pan.

Little Sally.

Mrs. Lottman frying Sweetpotatos and give to Lewis miller, some of them the first I ever tasted the where good Eating. It was in her tavern South George Street. 1799.

Women's work during the colonial era was backbreaking, essential, and usually unpaid. Tavern-keeping, because it involved many traditional female tasks, was one of the few occupations open to women, especially widows. In this drawing by Lewis Miller, a York tavern-keeper juggles several tasks simultaneously: grinding coffee, brewing tea and coffee, simmering two stews or joints of meat, baking bread, frying a fish, plucking a chicken, and smoking sausage and baloney. In addition, fires had to be tended and customers waited on. Not shown are butter-churning, egg-collecting, cheese-making, honey-gathering, oyster-shucking, beer-brewing, and such other chores as keeping accounts and dealing with suppliers. Miller's drawing is from a later time (c. 1800), but it depicts a world that would have been familiar to women in the colonial era.

and in northern Bucks County, they often established German-language communities, some of which preserved their linguistic identity into the twentieth century. These German immigrants were noted, and sometimes feared, for their devotion to work and their patient accumulation of assets. Their houses had distinct floor plans, they used stoves for heating and cooking instead of the open fireplaces used by other Europeans, and they built substantial barns for their livestock. Their farmsteads often stood out because of their neat utilitarian design and air of quiet prosperity.

Separate and mixed ethnic identities could be found in Pennsylvania furniture as well as in marriages. These three chairs—in English style, Dutch or German style, and hybrid style— would probably have been made to the specifications of the buyer. Ethnic background helped to determine what purchasers saw as fashionable or comfortable, but so too did the tastes of their neighbors.

*Anglo-German, from the German word *deutsch,* meaning "German."

German-speaking people from Württemberg, the Palatinate, Würzburg, Bavaria, Hesse-Cassel, Brandenburg, or Switzerland came from separate, sovereign states that differed in government, religion, and customs. Most were Lutheran or Reformed (German Calvinists), others were Anabaptists, Roman Catholics, or members of pietistic sects. Yet once in predominantly English-speaking Pennsylvania, the differences between German-speaking people appeared less substantial than their non-Englishness. Germans found similarities that transcended the politics and localisms of the Europe. By the end of the colonial period, the colony possessed a Pennsylvania Dutch ethnic culture and a German identity that did not exist in Europe. Expressed through architecture, literature, language, and the decorative arts, particularly in rural areas, Pennsylvania Dutch* culture helped to distinguish German settlements from English settlements.

The Scots-Irish, often simply called "the Irish" in the colonial period, were lowland Scots, mostly Presbyterian, who had migrated to northern Ireland in the seventeenth century as part of the English attempt to strengthen control over Ireland. The Scots had long-term leases on land owned by English landlords, but the leases expired after 1717. Rents were raised, and many farmers were displaced. By the 1720s large numbers migrated to Pennsylvania. Those who settled in Philadelphia and its immediate hinterland tended to blend into the larger society, as did those who came with some financial resources. While some Scots-Irish were as somber as any Quaker or New England Puritan, and some were Quaker, others were assertive, proud, and festive. This boisterous culture became emblematic of frontier society. Scots-Irish settlers and their neighbors

This early nineteenth-century drawing recalls Philadelphia fifty years earlier. The London Coffee House was a meeting place for merchants where news about commodities, sales, and prices was circulated. A slave auction with the human merchandise stripped for inspection by potential buyers is also portrayed. The survival of African customs in the city can be seen in the woman carrying a basket of fish on her head.

in rural areas celebrated weddings, for example, with horse races, drinking contests, fiddle-playing, and lively dances, while the newlyweds were teased with sexually explicit jests. These parties might last several days and end with construction of a new house for the young married couple. Many of the Scots-Irish on the edge of colonial settlements adapted the log construction of the Finns and the Swedes to the low, one-story houses of the Scottish lowlands and Ireland. They also borrowed clothing styles from the Native people, with both women and men wearing moccasins, and men decked out in loose shirts and leggings. Whether boisterous or restrained, however, few Scots-Irish Presbyterians were pacifist or pro-Quaker.

The major migration streams from the Rhine and from Ireland were joined by smaller numbers of Welsh, French Huguenots (Calvinists), Jews from the Spanish Empire, German and Irish Catholics, and others. These migrants remained mobile in the New World, frequently moving between townships and counties to find land, safety, or co-religionists. Pennsylvanians were not constrained by provincial boundaries; many moved southwest into the Great Valley of Virginia, for instance, or into the Ohio country, for the same reasons that they came to Pennsylvania. Daniel Boone, whose stories of his adventures would shape Americans' images of the frontier, was born in Berks County in 1732 and then moved with his parents to North Carolina in 1750. (His parents had themselves relocated from Bucks County.) As a married man, Boone continued the tradition of restless mobility by moving to Kentucky and later to Missouri. As the family moved, it shed its English Quaker identity and adopted a mix of practices most often associated with the Scots-Irish.

A DELAWARE PROPHET

During the late eighteenth or early nineteenth centuries, the Rev. John Heckewelder, a Moravian missionary to the Delawares and the Iroquois, recorded this speech. The last large groups of Native people were being harried out of Pennsylvania and into the Ohio Territory.

Look here! See what we have lost by neglect and disobedience; by being remiss in the expression of our gratitude to the great Spirit, for what he has bestowed upon us; by neglecting to make to him sufficient sacrifices; by looking upon a people of a different colour from our own, who had come across a great lake, as if they were a part of ourselves; by suffering them to sit down by our side, and looking at them with indifference, while they were not only taking our country from us, but this (pointing to the spot [on his map]), this, our own avenue, leading into those beautiful regions which were destined for us [central and southeastern Pennsylvania]. Such is the sad condition to which we are reduced. What is now to be done, and what remedy is to be applied? I will tell you, my friends. Hear what the great Spirit has ordered me to tell you! You are to make sacrifices, in the manner that I shall direct; to put off entirely from yourselves the customs which you have adopted since the white people came among us; you are to return to that former happy state, in which we lived in peace and plenty, before these strangers came to disturb us, and above all, you must abstain from drinking their deadly beson, which they have forced on us for the sake of increasing their gains and diminishing our numbers. Then will the great Spirit give success to our arms; then he will give us strength to conquer our enemies, to drive them from hence, and recover the passage to the heavenly regions which they have taken from us.

The ethnic and religious differences among immigrants helped shape emerging political alliances in late colonial Pennsylvania. Most Germans in the better-protected hinterlands, and pietistic pacifist German sectarians, tended to ally themselves with the Quakers and the legislature. They sought to avoid open warfare and to advance westward slowly and deliberately. Frontiersmen, most obviously the poorer Scots-Irish, allied with Anglicans and the non-Quaker proprietors. They supported a more militant and aggressive stance against the Native Americans and sought to expand European control of western territory as rapidly as possible. Cultural differences, beliefs in pacifism or militarism, and anxieties about control of the land, about the presence of Native Americans, and about regional representation in the Assembly divided Pennsylvanians and were expressed as ethnic or religious differences.

Enslaved people were not voluntary immigrants to Pennsylvania, yet they represented another source of ethnic diversity. Most had ancestors from West Africa: Mandinka, Fulbe, Jola, Serer, Wolof, and Bambara from the Senegambia region; Vai, Mende, Kpelle, and Kru from the Windward Coast; Ashanti and Fanti from the Gold Coast; and Ibo and Ibibio from Benin and Biafra. A smaller number had come from Central Africa: Kongo, Tio, and Matamba. The skills of these involuntary migrants were diverse. Most were agriculturalists, some were herders, and a few had been townspeople. Some were Muslim, some were Roman Catholic, and the majority followed local religions that combined monotheism with animism. Most had worked on Caribbean sugar plantations, and many had been born there and had learned English before being shipped to the mainland; they were creoles. Yet early in the eighteenth century there were enough African-born slaves to gather in separate groups in Philadelphia to celebrate their various national heritages.

The meeting of people from such widely different cultures led to new identities based on skin color instead of nationality. No longer did Europeans describe themselves as dark if they had black hair, or as brown if they worked outdoors, or as ruddy, which had been considered a sign of health. Nor did they stress the political, ethnic, and religious rivalries of the Old World. They were beginning to define themselves as whites. A slowly developing white racial identity helped to unite Europeans from a variety of political, religious, and linguistic backgrounds and to distinguish themselves from "savages" and slaves. Even as ethnic and religious rivalries shaped Pennsylvania history, an ideal of toleration accepted a certain amount of diversity in people of European ancestry.

Native Americans and African Americans, excluded from citizenship and from these new forms of American identity, each discovered similarities in their experiences with "whites" that could surmount older national and linguistic divisions. A pan-Indian movement led by the Delaware prophet Neolin united various tribes in the Ohio region and contributed to Pontiac's Rebellion and other uprisings against European influence in the 1760s. An African American cultural tradition, developing underground in the colonial period, emerged after 1780 with the gradual abolition of slavery in Pennsylvania. Separate black churches, cultural societies, and charities gave institutional form to a developing African American identity that refuted white prejudices. Pennsylvania became the first modern pluralistic society where ethnic and religious diversity existed in an atmosphere that encouraged, if it did not always achieve, toleration for those of European descent and at the same time created shared experiences of cultural distinctiveness, exclusion, and exploitation for those of Native American and African backgrounds.

Immigrants and their American-born children filled the land. By 1760 they had occupied all of southeastern Pennsylvania and the lower reaches of the Susquehanna River basin. They crossed the Blue (or Endless) Mountain and pushed north and west into the valleys beyond. No single ethnic group had a majority. In Lancaster County in the 1750s, the Scots-Irish were the largest group, 35 percent of the population; then came the Germans and English, each with 25 percent, while the remainder were Welsh and other nationalities. Only a few were of African descent. The majority of arrivals in Pennsylvania after 1720 believed that war might be necessary to protect their interests and honor. As pacifist influence faded, particularly at the edges of European settlement, so too did the relatively benevolent treatment of the Native people. The settlement of Lenape at the Brandywine River lasted barely fifty years; Provincial Secretary James Logan allowed European settlers to grab the entire valley by the 1720s. Groups located north of the Blue Mountain were somewhat better protected against intrusion, but the colonists demanded more land. William Penn's sons, Thomas and John, hastened the process. They had renounced their father's faith, but they retained his poor financial skills. Like their father, they hoped to increase their income through land sales and collection of quit-rents, but worried because by the 1730s there were squatters from New York and elsewhere settling in the Lehigh Valley and along the upper reaches of the Delaware River. In addition, William Allen and other wealthy and influential land speculators were anxious to purchase land in northern Pennsylvania. Here was a chance to profit.

To get this land, the Penns found an old, incomplete draft treaty from 1686. Never

TABLE 2.3 **NUMBER OF TOWNS FOUNDED IN SOUTHEASTERN PENNSYLVANIA, 1681–1775**

Before 1700	8
1700–1740	3
1741–1765	46
1766–1775	56

SOURCE: James T. Lemon, *The Best Poor Man's Country: A Geographical Study of Early Southeastern Pennsylvania* (Baltimore: Johns Hopkins University Press, 1972), 123.

NOTE: The dates that towns were founded provide evidence of the pace of Pennsylvania's growth, how and where Pennsylvania expanded. Few towns were created in the first several decades of the eighteenth century. Then, in the wake of the Walking Purchase and during the Seven Years' War, town foundings increased dramatically as both central and northern Pennsylvania were conquered and colonized. Still, many of the outlying towns grew slowly because of warfare in the 1750s and thereafter. In the 1760s, Lancaster stagnated and Pittsburgh shrank. (See Table 2.1.)

The Lenape lost most of the Lehigh Valley to William Penn's sons through the infamous Walking Purchase of 1737. The treaty, shown here, was signed on August 25, 1737, after the Penns convinced Lenape chiefs of their obligations to an invalid treaty from 1686. The signatures of provincial officials, starting with James Logan, can be seen on the lower left side. Manawkyhickon, Lapowinsa, Tishcohan, and Nutimas made their marks on the far right.

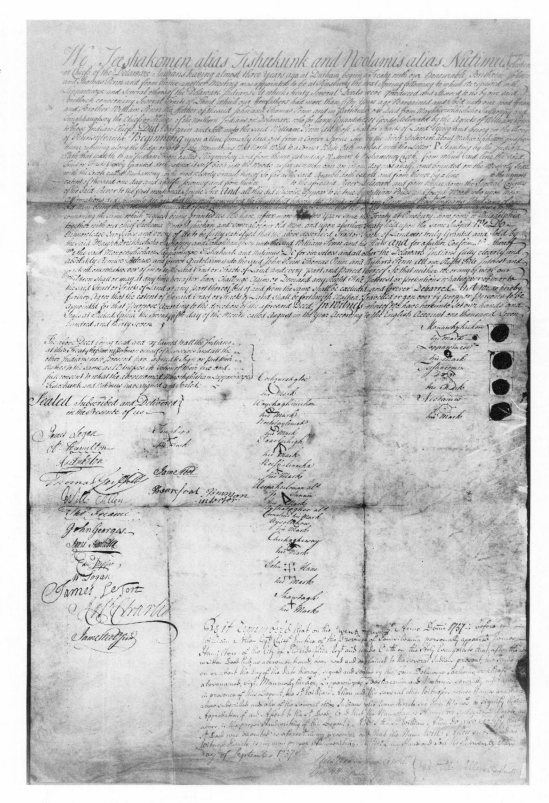

implemented, it would have granted Pennsylvania additional Lenape lands north along the Delaware River as far as a man could walk in a day and a half. The new proprietors pretended that this was a valid treaty. As early as 1735, the Penns authorized a trial walk and prepared a path veering far to the northwest. In 1737 the Penns convinced Manawkyhickon, Lapowinsa, Tishcohan, and Nutimas, four Delaware chiefs living north of colonial settlement, of their obligations under the treaty. The walk began at 6:00 A.M. on September 19. The walking party consisted of three "walkers," plus the sheriff of Bucks County, provincial surveyors, and three representatives of the Delawares: John Cumbush, Joe Tuneam, and Tuneam's brother-in-law Tom. But only the provincial officials, mounted on horseback, could keep up with the "walkers" as they hustled and sprinted along the path. Then one of the "walkers" dropped out, and another suffered a stroke and died soon after. The Delaware contingent also fell behind, complaining bitterly about the fraud, but the third "walker," a young man named Edward Marshall, and one provincial official persisted. In the end Marshall covered some sixty-five miles in a day and a half, starting from (to use the modern place-names) Wrightstown in Bucks County and ending near the town of Jim Thorpe in Carbon County. This bit of chicanery added 750,000 acres to the Penn estates.

Settling those lands would not be easy. While the Delaware leaders felt honor-bound to respect the results, anger rankled among individual Delawares in the region, particularly among young men. Edward Marshall's later life was one example of developments in the region. He and his family took advantage of the new territorial acquisition and settled in Mount Bethel, near Easton. In one of the revenge raids by a roving band of dispossessed Native Americans in the 1750s, Marshall's wife and a son were killed. Marshall came to hate all nonwhites, bragging about killing more than twenty "Indians" on sight without ever bothering to find out whether they were hostile or not. Warfare in the west, which had been only occasional before the 1750s, became endemic during the Seven Years' War and the Revolution. For his own safety, Marshall eventually moved to Tinicum, where he died peacefully in his own bed—something that fewer and fewer Delaware people had the chance to do.

Through much of the eighteenth century there were Pennsylvanians who straddled the large ethnic and cultural divides between Native Americans and colonists. Some go-betweens were personally ambitious for fame and power, including most colonial officials and Delaware Chief Teedyuscung in his later career. Others were concerned with justice. Conrad

Major land transfers between the Native nations and colonial and federal authorities. The Purchase of 1754 originally included most of the land west of the Susquehanna, but this huge grant was reduced in 1758 as part of a peace agreement between the British Crown and the Delawares and the Iroquois.

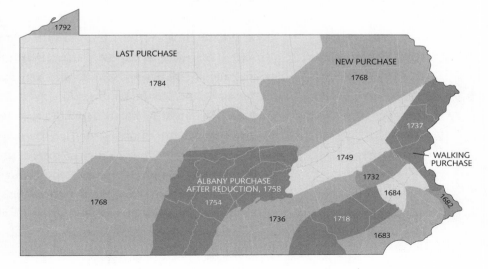

Weiser had lived with the Iroquois as an adolescent and understood both cultural traditions, even if he preferred European ways. Isabella Couc, also known as Madame Montour, had both Native and European ancestry. She spoke several European, Iroquoian, and Algonquian languages and often translated at treaty conferences. Her son, Andrew Montour, was also influential, in part because he had kin in French Canada and among the Oneida, the Delaware, the Conoy, and the Miami. His connections and loyalty to Pennsylvania made him a valued go-between, but colonists never quite trusted his motivations. Christianized Delawares, including Tunda (Moses) Tatamy and Isaac Stille, worked for peace between the two cultures, as did a few Moravian and Presbyterian missionaries and some Quaker activists. A few Europeans were adopted after capture in war raids and preferred to stay with their adoptive families. Mary Jemison is the best known. Captured near Gettysburg in 1758 and adopted by the Seneca, she would participate in treaty-making in her old age. Such people proved that a degree of understanding was possible through negotiation and acceptance, even if it was enormously difficult both culturally and politically. Go-betweens kept the peace in Pennsylvania until the 1750s, but both sides were becoming impatient with negotiation, distrustful of treaties, and emboldened by the possibilities of a military solution.

THE GROWTH OF PENNSYLVANIA: RELIGION

Religion as well as ethnicity brought diversity to colonial Pennsylvania. Lutherans, Reformed (German Calvinists), Presbyterians, Anglicans, Roman Catholics, Jews, and other religious groups formed congregations that were centers of their communities. Many denominations had been state-sponsored in the Old World and had to adjust to being self-supporting. Churches established schools, engaged in missionary activities, and learned to live with neighbors of different faiths. The congregations provided much of the colony's charitable aid. Henry Melchior Muhlenberg helped Lutherans develop a denominational status as one faith among many. He organized and monitored congregations across the colony, baptized adults and children, listened to problems, and offered instruction. Baptist, Presbyterian, Anglican, Reformed, Methodist, and other churches also developed systems of governance while expanding the numbers of congregations. Some denominations splintered as leaders or parishioners questioned traditional ways. William and Gilbert Tennent criticized the power of "Presbyterian bishops" and embraced a more emotional and revivalist approach to salvation. They founded a "Log College" in Neshaminy to train ministers for a revitalized church, one of the first breakaway denominations. Anglicans and Roman Catholics worked, unsuccessfully in the colonial period, to obtain American bishops—efforts that succeeded only in the 1780s when the Anglicans formed the separatist Episcopal Church and Roman Catholics were released from the control of the vicar apostolic in London. Churches had to adjust to both religious diversity and colonial status.

Pennsylvania became a refuge for people whose beliefs diverged from the established churches of Europe. From Germany came the "Society of the Woman in the Wilderness," or the "Chapter of Perfection." Elaborating on a passage from the biblical Book of Revelation, they predicted the second coming of Christ would occur in the wilderness in 1694. What could be more like a wilderness than seventeenth-century Pennsylvania? They were somewhat disappointed when 1694 came and went without any particular sign, but for more than a decade afterward several of the faithful continued to live in celibacy on the banks of Wissahickon Creek, searching the stars for portents from God and hoping for the end of the world.

Conrad Beissel was a mystic and the charismatic, creative, and choleric founder of the Society of Solitary Brethren, an offshoot of the German Baptist Brethren. In 1732 he founded a religious commune at Ephrata that combined medieval characteristics such as monastic celibacy, book illumination, the composition of religious choral music, and highly ritualized daily activities with what were at the time "high-tech" operations like milling, the mass printing of books, and clockmaking. The Ephrata Cloister, which eventually contained eleven large buildings, housed men and women in separate quarters. Those in the cloisters dressed in white robes, worked in the gardens, and slept on wooden benches with a wooden block for a pillow. Married couples lived on nearby farms. At its peak more than 300 people lived at the settlement. Over time, Beissel became domineering, verbally abusing any opponents, real and imaginary, and in some cases destroying their work or expelling them from the commune, which in the case of mill operators who were excluded led to a series of lawsuits in the 1760s that divided the community. Beissel's relationships with some women were also suspect. After Beissel's death in 1768, all but a handful of followers left, and although too few in number to carry on the cloister as in Beissel's lifetime, some Sabbatarian Brethren lived at Ephrata until 1934. A related group at Snow Hill disbanded only in 1998, and a third settlement survives near Salemville in Bedford County.

More successful were the Moravians, or the Unum Fratrum, founded in the fifteenth century in Bohemia and Moravia (now the Czech Republic). Revitalized under the leadership of Count Nicholas von Zinzendorf, Moravians arrived in Pennsylvania in 1741, first founding the towns of Bethlehem and Nazareth. The members formed "Choirs," age-and sex-segregated residential groups designed to wean individuals from kin and unite them with their fellow believers in order to achieve salvation. Like the Quakers, the Moravians were pacifists and promoted gendered

Johannes Kelpius, a mystic who was interested in the occult and in botany, lived with his followers on Wissahickon Creek from 1694 to his death in 1708. He was one of the many pietist, communitarian, or free-thinking groups who left an intolerant Old World for the congenial religious climate of Pennsylvania.

Depictions of two Ephrata Cloister sisters and a brother in their white habits, from illustrated manuscripts produced at the settlement. Men and women in the cloisters lived in separate quarters and devoted themselves to a monastic life devoid of many comforts but filled with music. Married couples lived on nearby farms.

equality, but, unlike the Quakers, they mistrusted the nuclear family. Marriages, when they occurred, were arranged. Children stayed with their parents only until eighteen months of age and then joined the Choir that fitted their age, condition, and sex. All slept in dormitories, ate in the Choir building, and worked with other members of their particular Choir. The days, weeks, and year were filled with religious celebration. This system began to moderate after 1760, but it was not officially abandoned in favor of nuclear families and the private ownership of property until 1817. Moravians were active missionaries and founded towns for Native peoples while working to convert them to Christianity and western ways.

Pennsylvania's religious diversity was compounded in the three decades after the 1730s when a reforming impulse known as the Great Awakening transformed many Protestant sects. Spread through open-air camp meetings led by traveling preachers or lay ministers, the revivalists stressed conversion or rebirth through a direct, heartfelt apprehension of God's grace. They mistrusted the old church hierarchies and favored a brotherhood and sisterhood of believers who would teach each other through Bible study and prayer. Many believed in universal salvation and actively proselytized among the downtrodden, including slaves. The black and white converts formed some of the first integrated groups in America, although white racism too often surfaced despite a theology of equality. The Presbyterians split into Old Light and New Light congregations, the Baptists flourished, and Methodism spread. At roughly the same time, the

Quakers turned inward, fearing that political power and growing wealth had turned the Society of Friends from its spiritual mission. They discouraged converts, disowned less-committed members, withdrew from direct participation in politics, and turned to social reform: hospitals, schools, support for Native peoples, and antislavery activism.

Hannah Harkum was one of many teenagers swept up by the Great Awakening. She was entranced by the Rev. George Whitefield's heartrending preaching and promises of universal salvation, and she went to hear him at every opportunity, even walking twenty miles to Neshaminy with crowds of other young Philadelphians. In her old age she was appalled at this freedom of action among young people, believing it was far too likely to end in worldly temptation. But she had not wavered even after being thrown out of her father's house for her religious rebelliousness. With her sister, she supported herself as a seamstress in a small rented room and soon married another young enthusiast. She and her husband devoted the rest of their long lives to their church and their shop.

The emotional exhortations of the Great Awakening could affect even the resistant. Benjamin Franklin came with a skeptical mind to hear Whitefield, and by the end of the sermon he had emptied his pockets into the collection plate. The Great Awakening, and to a lesser extent the reformation of Quakerism, contained strong undercurrents of equality, social reform, and antiauthoritarianism. All could be saved, and even the un-educated could be moved to preach or lead Bible-study groups. Enslaved people were admitted into full membership in the awakened churches, particularly among Baptist

The Moravian Community at Nazareth in 1761, by Nicholas Garrison. The ordered life of the Moravians is revealed in the neatly arranged fields and the Manor House, on the left. The town had been founded only twenty-one years earlier.

In the eighteenth century, there existed what literary critic Daniel B. Shea has memorably called "a Pennsylvania of the soul." Freedom of conscience and the variety of faiths made a physical and moral space for Pennsylvanians to experiment with different religions. Elizabeth Ashbridge was one of many immigrants who created a new sense of self by exploring many faiths and ultimately discovering her own spiritual truth. She did not find material success in Pennsylvania, but she eventually found spiritual fulfillment after a long and harrowing quest.

Elizabeth Ashbridge was born in Cheshire, England, in 1713 and brought up Anglican. She "sometimes wept with Sorrow, that I was not a boy that I might have been [a minister,] believing them all Good Men and beloved of God." But her youthful spiritual yearnings were secondary to her enjoyment of a merry life: she loved to sing and dance and considered becoming an actress. She ran away from home at the age of fourteen and married a poor stocking-weaver. Her husband died just six months later, leaving her a young widow, disowned by her father, with no home, no money, and few friends.

Ashbridge settled briefly with Irish kin and toyed with converting to Catholicism. To escape her dependence on family, she boarded a ship headed, she thought, for Philadelphia and opportunity, but she was deceived. The captain forced her to sign an indenture, and she was sold as a bound servant in New York City. Like many other servant women, she was overworked, ill-clad, and sexually harassed by her master. This mistreatment by a professed staunch Anglican brought her spiritual dissatisfactions to the fore. She married as soon as her servitude ended, but she "had got released from one cruel Servitude" and "into another, and this for Life." Her second husband was an abusive drunkard.

Her spiritual longings grew greater and more desperate as the couple wandered from place to place throughout the northern colonies. Ashbridge investigated the Presbyterians, the Lutherans, and other religious groups, but was increasingly drawn to the Quakers. Conversion to the Quaker faith entailed much soul-searching and despair, and increasingly violent opposition from her husband. Eventually she gave up the singing, dancing, and fine clothing that she had so loved. She adopted a Quaker style of life and overcame a strong aversion to women preachers. Her husband left her for the army. But in the end, he refused to take up arms against his fellow man and died of the military punishments inflicted on him for his disobedience—even he had seen the "light."

Elizabeth Ashbridge became a noted Quaker minister and elder, selected by the Goshen Monthly Meeting in Chester County to travel to other meetings in Pennsylvania and abroad. She married a third time, and her new husband, Aaron Ashbridge, fully supported her ministry. She, and many others with liberty of conscience, ultimately found contentment.

BELOW: Great Awakening camp meeting on the Schuylkill River. This print shows Baptists meeting in the woods for a full-immersion adult baptism in the river.

and Methodists. True believers, even the lowly, could form their own churches. These experiences would help prepare the way for the Revolution's overthrow of established authorities.

There was a saying that Pennsylvania was heaven for farmers and artisans but hell for preachers and officials. Many ministers, used to established churches, found themselves unable to discipline their flocks in Pennsylvania. No church courts had coercive powers, and ministers' salaries depended on the goodwill of their congregations. Church members could leave the church, move to another congregation, or form new congregations.

Many Pennsylvanians reasoned that the existence of so many religions, each claiming divine sanction, proved that none was valid. While individuals and groups of many persuasions found spiritual fulfillment, the jumble of beliefs, rituals, and social arrangements was troubling, confusing, or absurd to others. In Philadelphia most inhabitants did not belong to any church, and the countryside was often no better—as traveling missionaries discovered, decrying the heathenism of the backwoods settlers.

Pennsylvania began as a Quaker colony. Pietistic German-speaking Protestants with similar beliefs soon joined them—Mennonites, Moravians, Brethren, and Amish—and French-speaking Huguenots. But not only the religiously oppressed came. Adherents of established religions arrived as well: Anglicans from England, Presbyterians from Scotland and Ireland, and German-speaking Lutherans, Reformed Calvinists, and Roman Catholics migrated. The "Quaker" colony soon became a misnomer. In 1699 approximately 947 Friends lived in Philadelphia, along with 550 Anglicans, and 969 Presbyterians, Baptists, and others. In addition, there were 213 enslaved Africans, few of whom were baptized as Christian. While the surrounding counties had larger numbers of Friends, they too would soon lose their majority. Only in the Assembly did Quaker domination persist through the colonial period.

Even ethnic churches were in fact mixed. The Swedish Lutherans in Philadelphia, Montgomery, and Chester Counties took a census of member families in the 1780s, the only record of ethnic identities in the seventeenth or eighteenth century. Barely half the 174 adults considered themselves Swedes. One-quarter reported being English, German, or Irish. The remainder called themselves Scottish, Dutch, African, French, Negro, or Welsh. The only American was the sixteen-year-old son of African parents. Many families included non-Lutherans: there were eight Quakers, six Methodists, two Roman Catholics, plus one Presbyterian, one Huguenot, and one Anabaptist—and not all the nominal Lutherans attended church or had their children baptized. Diversity and toleration of other European ethnic and religious groups came to be widely shared values in Pennsylvania. Colonists who wanted to enjoy Pennsylvania's liberties discovered that they had to extend that privilege to others.

The religious diversity modified sacraments and holidays. Some Pennsylvanians stopped baptizing infants, arguing that Quaker children did well enough without the rite. The practice of naming godparents declined because parents often did not know or did not trust their neighbors. By the mid-eighteenth century, most engaged couples rejected the church-controlled reading of banns in favor of the more private marriage license. Holiday celebrations, including Christmas, changed. The Quakers refused to acknowledge the day as special, which apparently influenced other Protestant denominations to do the same. In Philadelphia, only the Roman Catholics still decorated their churches with laurel branches and candles and performed special music. Anglicans rang church bells on Christmas Eve and fired guns into the air the next morning, but otherwise had no special celebration. The Old World Lutheran customs of special breads, Christmas Eve porridge, and Christmas music had disappeared by the middle of the eighteenth century. And in rural New Hanover Township, the Rev. Henry Melchior Muhlenberg was in tears upon finding that good Lutherans were celebrating Christmas like their neighbors (who were probably Scots-Irish), with tippling, fiddling, dancing, and similar "abominations." By the early nineteenth century, one of the German Christmas traditions did start to become widespread. The custom of having a decorated Christmas tree, lit with candles and surrounded by gifts, spread from Pennsylvania throughout the United States. Borrowed rites and practices were other effects of religious freedom.

THE GROWTH OF PENNSYLVANIA: IDEAS AND PRACTICES

Formal religion was only one way of understanding the world. Magic and superstitious beliefs were widespread in Pennsylvania as well. While William Penn merely required two accused witches to post bonds for their good behavior, not all Pennsylvanians were so sure that the devil was not abroad. Almanacs provided astrological charts and predictions about the future, about the best time to plant and harvest, about auspicious signs for weaning a baby. Sailors' wives watched to see whether a seagull flew over their house, a sign that an overseas traveler was about to return. Still, superstitions were on the wane. In the 1740s John Coates insisted that the way to cure someone's bleeding nose was to catch the patient's blood in a handkerchief and put it under someone else's arm. That person should then walk six to eight miles away from the victim and touch the blood with vitriol—and the distant nose would be cured by sympathetic magic. His sister, Hannah Coates Paschall, crossed this recipe out of her medical book by the 1760s, preferring to conduct her own medical experiments based on personal observation or to consult the authoritative medical books she found at the Library Company of Philadelphia. The library, bookstores, the College of Philadelphia and its medical school, and the appearance of weekly newspapers were evidence of the colony's increasing sophistication.

Ministers were prominent in Pennsylvania's intellectual life. Many combined scientific curiosity and religious faith, believing that the natural world revealed God's laws. The city's Anglican ministers recorded and published the annual number of baptisms

and burials to study local health conditions. A Presbyterian minister, John King, produced an even more elaborate, twenty-year study of conditions in West Conococheague (Mercersberg) in Cumberland (later Franklin) County. Peter Kalm, a Swedish minister and scientist, published one of the first books on local plants and animals. Henry Melchior Muhlenberg was particularly interested in medicine but commented on all aspects of life in the colonies.

Scientific and enlightened ideas increasingly shaped the intellectual life of the province. The Junto, originally a workingmen's discussion group that by twists and turns became the American Philosophical Society, sought to expand useful knowledge through the meetings where formal papers on controversial topics were presented and their merits tested through reasoned debate. Some Pennsylvanians became famous for their investigations. Benjamin Franklin attained transatlantic renown for his theoretical and practical investigations of electricity. Botanists John and William Bartram and William Young (Wilhelm Jung) achieved fame for collecting and describing the plant species of the New World. Anthony Benezet's radical humanitarianism and studies of Africa helped shape the international campaign against slavery. In the arts, Benjamin West was hailed for his historical paintings, considered the highest form of art at the time. In all these cases, however, London, not Philadelphia, conferred honor, renown, and patronage on these men. Pennsylvania was merely provincial; the capital was in England.

Pennsylvania imported many of its ideas from England. Republican, liberal, and proto-democratic ideas about individualism, self-interest, liberty, progress, limited government, and natural rights, so important to the Revolution, came from English, Scottish, French, and Italian books, magazines, pamphlets. Novels, plays, and histories brought

The FLYING MACHINE.

This is to give NOTICE to the PUBLIC, THAT the FLYING MACHINE, kept by JOHN BARNHILL, in Elm street, near Vine-street, Philadelphia; and JOHN MASHEREW, at the Blazing star, performs the Journey from Philadelphia to New-York in two days, and from thence to Philadelphia in two days also; a circumstance greatly to the advantage of the traveller, as there is no water carriage, and consequently nothing to impede the Journey. It has already been performed to the general satisfaction of many genteel people. They set off from Philadelphia and New-York on Mondays and Thursdays, punctually at Sunrise, and change their passengers at Prince Town, and return to Philadelphia and New York the following days: passengers paying ten shillings to Princeton, and ten shillings to Powles's Hook opposite to New-York, ferriage free, and three-pence each mile any distance between. Gentlemen and Ladies who are pleased to favour us with their custom, may depend on due attendance and civil usage, by their humble servants,

§ JOHN BARNHILL and JOHN MASHEREW.

By the end of the colonial period, links between colonies were growing stronger, and there was demand for regularly scheduled coaches between Philadelphia and New York City. As this 1767 notice shows, punctuality, speed, convenience, and comfort were increasingly valued as the economy expanded.

models of independent, sympathetic heroes and heroines. Locally produced poems, essays, and letters circulated at tea tables and taverns and increasingly appeared in local publications. Women's writings were rarely published, although they were collected in commonplace books for perusal among friends and as textbooks in girls' schools. These colonial writings helped spread enlightened ideas about gentility, the uses of reason, and the cultivation of empathy, sympathy, and heightened sensibility and came to identify an American set of interests among readers.

Growing curiosity about native species of plants and animals did not protect them. Progress was still defined as the creation of a European-style landscape. Clear-cutting of the forests in southeastern Pennsylvania meant that by the end of the colonial period firewood was scarce and expensive. Charities provided fuel to the poor, but many suffered during the coldest months. Franklin's innovative stove conserved firewood by heating more efficiently. Clear-cutting also seems to have increased flooding and soil erosion around the capital city and threatened many bird species. Killing birds was a popular sport for boys, and for a brief period caged cardinals were the rage in England and thousands were caught and sold overseas. Privies polluted the wells in Philadelphia, resulting in the spread of dysentery and other septic diseases. Runoff from farmyards seeped into the water supply in the country and brought worsening health conditions. At the Susquehanna River and its tributaries, "wars" broke out as those who depended on the abundant shad fought both against those who overfished by stretching seines across the waterways, and against the millers whose dams prevented the return of the fish in the spring. Such enemies to the fishermen found their nets cut and their dams destroyed. The Assembly passed legislation supporting the free movement of fish as an economic right, not an ecological priority.

Scientific ideas and the example of other cultures began to modify some behaviors by mid-century. Europeans began to take an unprecedented interest in cleanliness both on farms and in the city, because one theory of disease blamed sickness on "putrefaction" or "bad air." Farmers dug garbage pits instead of flinging refuse and offal out the nearest door or window, and in Philadelphia pigs were regularly run through the city streets to eat garbage, the major streets were paved and guttered, city water pumps were provided, and swamps were drained, all in an effort to reduce the very high death rates. A hospital and a quarantine station were built to control the spread of disease, save lives, and train doctors. Quinine proved to be an effective treatment against malaria, and smallpox inoculation revealed the possibilities unleashed by scientific experimentation. By observing

1. The Governours House
2. Quakers Meeting
3. The Market House
4. Where the Ships are built
5. Coopers Ferry
6. The Island
7. Society Hill
8. Wickacove
9. The Sweeds Church
10. Part of Gloster

and testing the inoculation practices of Turks and West Africans, Europeans and colonists learned how to provide immunity against an ancient scourge. Epidemics diminished in frequency and ferocity by the second half of the eighteenth century; more children survived, and fewer had scarred faces. Progress was possible.

THE GROWTH OF PENNSYLVANIA: THE WEALTHY, THE MIDDLING SORT, AND THOSE WHO LABORED

At the top of colonial society was the great merchant who provided the commercial links between the backcountry, the port city, the province, the empire, and the Atlantic trading world. The largest mercantile establishments had strong ties to English and Scottish commercial houses and frequently cemented their financial arrangements with religious links and, where possible, with marriage. They also had close ties to the sugar islands in the Caribbean, trading legally with the English colonies and illegally with French, Spanish, and Dutch colonies. Merchants made loans, gave advances, and speculated in crops, goods, and bound laborers. They were the bankers, distributors, marketers,

"The Prospect of Philadelphia from Wickacove, exactly delineated by G. Wood" (1735). Although somewhat fanciful, this is the only surviving depiction of Philadelphia c. 1730. It highlights the acquisition of civilized life, defined by European standards, in a colony not quite fifty years old. A powerful executive government is shown symbolically by a governor's house that overlooks the town. Organized religion is represented in the Quaker Meeting House and the Swedish Church. Commerce can be seen in the Market House, at the hill where the Society of Traders met, and in the large ships safely at anchor. Manufacturing appears in the shipyard, while the crowded housing, with gables, spires, and banners, indicates an urban style of life that would have been familiar to Londoners and others in the Old World.

Few pictures of the "middling sort" exist for the colonial period. This sketch of David Dove, a schoolmaster and sometime professor at the College of Philadelphia, shows him on his way to work. Drawing by Benjamin West.

wholesalers, and retailers of their time. Their agents might take flour to Jamaica, bring sugar up to Boston, and carry dried cod back to Philadelphia. Then they might sail to Antigua with flour and cod to trade for rum, ship the rum to Cape Castle in exchange for ivory, then take the ivory to Bristol to exchange for Bibles, magazines, cloth, and furniture, and home again. Timber was sent to Madeira, where the ship would be partially loaded with wine, then stop at Whidow to haggle for slaves, then on to Charleston to sell the slaves and pick up rice or indigo, and then back home to Philadelphia. These varied goods then went out to individual customers, smaller merchants, and shopkeepers throughout the province. The goal was to profit at each stage of these complex transactions, but it was highly risky business. Intense competition, bad weather, leaky ships, pirates, frequent wars, rapacious officials, and business cycles of boom and bust brought down many merchant houses.

The great merchants, as well as some lawyers and large landowners, lived lavishly on profits and credit. Henry Drinker, of the mercantile firm Drinker & James, built a large three-story mansion in Philadelphia run by seven household servants and owned a country residence with a tenant family in residence. As a Quaker, he was relatively restrained. Anglican and Presbyterian merchants built their houses with elaborately decorated rooms designed for sumptuous entertainments. They lined the walls of their mansions with family portraits, dined on fine imported china, served multiple courses of food on silver platters, and dressed in the latest ostentatious fashions; outside were formal gardens filled with statuary. These wealthy Philadelphians invested heavily in real estate, particularly in the western part of Pennsylvania; Drinker owned $100,000 worth of property in the 1770s. The influence of these wealthy individuals spread far beyond the city, but their power and opulence could not match that of the English aristocracy. The local elite, no matter how rich, were still provincials and mere commoners, and many came to resent their inferior status within the British Empire.

Independent farmers were the largest single category of Pennsylvanians. They and the crafts men and women of the towns made up the bulk of the "middling sort"—the people midway between the wealthy and the impoverished and dependent. Their values— hard work, thrift, order, and sincerity—were widely endorsed if not always practiced. Sentiments like "A Penny sav'd is Twopence clear, A pin a day is a Groat [four cents] a Year, Save & have" made almanacs the best-selling reading material in the province.

The average farm family in late colonial Chester and Lancaster Counties owned 125 acres. There were seven head of cattle, three or four horses, eight pigs, ten sheep, some chickens, and a hive or two of bees. Fifty-three acres were under plow, in hay meadow, or in orchards. Another twenty acres were pastureland. Three acres were devoted to the house, barns, springhouse, and corncribs, while the remainder was woodlot, providing lumber, fuel, and foraging for cattle and pigs. The family, often with the assistance of a slave, servant, tenant family, or hired help, harvested 300 bushels of grains, dressed 450 pounds of pork and beef, made cheese, butter, beer, and grew vegetables, fruit, flax, and

WILLIAM ALLEN

William Allen was a major power in early Pennsylvania. His financial success was tied to the many political offices he held, and his political power came from his personal connections with other influential individuals both in Pennsylvania and abroad.

William Allen was born in Philadelphia in 1704, the only son of wealthy Presbyterian, Scots-Irish parents. Like other wealthy colonials, he was sent to England to finish his education, first at Middle Temple, where he supposedly studied law, later at Cambridge University for a liberal education, and finally in a gentlemanly tour of the continent undertaken in order to broaden his connections. As was common, he spent most of his time in revelry and riot with other young gentlemen and never learned the law. A lack of legal expertise was no drawback to his political or judicial career, however, once he inherited his father's fortune in 1725. His position was enhanced through marriage: Margaret Hamilton's brother was deputy governor. Ties to the proprietors were strengthened in 1766 when his daughter Ann married John Penn, grandson of the founder. Allen expanded his inheritance through international mercantile activities, including the slave trade. He invested heavily in land—most speculatively in areas held by Native peoples—and in capital-intensive industries like iron forges.

Allen was both extravagant and generous. He built a luxurious estate at Mount Airy modeled after the country estates of British gentlemen. He contributed money to the major projects of early Philadelphia: the building of the statehouse, the hospital, the college and other schools, and charities. He supported many talented men and expected their loyalty. He served in multiple government positions, often simultaneously—on the

Governor's Council, in the Assembly, as mayor of Philadelphia, and as chief justice of Pennsylvania. There was little concern about checks and balances in the colony, and wealthy gentlemen expected to both consolidate their influence and enhance their wealth through public office.

Allen supported the initial protests against British policy in the 1760s but balked at war in 1775; his wealth and influence were tied to the British Empire. He died in 1780,

much of his fortune gone and his children living in England. He was little remembered by later Pennsylvanians, who expected greater limits on government officials.

ABOVE: Portrait of William Allen by Robert Feke, c. 1750.

Letter Press Printer.

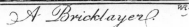

A Bricklayer.

A Cooper.

ABOVE AND OPPOSITE: Occupations as represented in an 1807 Philadelphia publication from an earlier English edition. A well-dressed printer acts as a compositor, while his journeyman does the laborious work at the press. Bricklayers were among the many artisans in great demand during these years of rapid growth in Pennsylvania. Coopers produced the barrels that carried flour, ship biscuit, shad, and other products to local and international markets. Farm wives or the wives of cottagers spun wool and linen whenever possible; cloth was both necessary and expensive. The merchant inspects his cargo and orders an unskilled laborer to move a barrel, while his clerk or apprentice keeps records; a few women owned their own ships in the towns. A milliner was expected to keep abreast of the latest styles in hats and to have a good supply of feathers and ribbons. Urban life offered more opportunities for women.

tobacco every year. But these were not the self-sufficient farmers of nineteenth-century urban romantics. This average farm family sold about 55 bushels of wheat, 200 pounds of meat, plus flaxseed, hay, and other products and purchased cloth, shoes, hats, salt and spices, almanacs, Bibles and prayerbooks, hardware, tools, and more. They were enmeshed in complex credit/debtor relations with the local storekeeper, the miller, and urban shopkeepers and merchants. Farmers paid for the services of laborers, blacksmiths, harnessmakers, weavers, tailors, schoolmasters, midwives, physicians, and other specialists. On top of this they paid taxes. Farmers were deeply involved in local and transatlantic markets. As early as 1693, Peter Gunnarsson Rambo noted that his prosperity derived from trade with the Caribbean "islands [which] are fed by us with the land's goods, with grain, flour and beer."

By the late colonial period, Pennsylvania was the breadbasket of the British Empire. The colony shipped flour and ship biscuit to Europe, Africa, and the Caribbean. Flourmills dotted the countryside. Typically owned by several wealthy investors, ownership and management were separate. Managers supervised the wage workers and the slaves who ran the machinery, and worked with commission agents who secured supplies of wheat and sales of flour. The mills ran on waterpower, and ingenious eighteenth-century Pennsylvanians made several technological breakthroughs that increased efficiency. Oliver Evans's conveyors and elevators were major laborsaving innovations in the Brandywine mills. The mills supported a growing number of

Spinner.

A Merchant.

Milliner.

subsidiary industries: bakers, brewers, ship chandlers, barrelmakers, forges, teamsters, and shipbuilders. Flour and related products were mass-produced for consumers at home and abroad. The flour industry anticipated many of the features associated with early nineteenth-century industrialization, except that production typically took place in the countryside, not in the city.

Iron forges at Reading and other places were as sophisticated as the mills, but skilled artisans working in their own shops made most products. These men, and some women, were the urban "middling sort." Shoes, saddles, looking glasses, highboys, tea tables, wigs, and other products were bespoke—that is, made specifically to a customer's order. Colonial artisans faced a shortage of labor and currency, an uncertain supply of raw materials, a developing market, and competition from imported English goods, which often were cheaper and more skillfully made. Shoemakers, tailors, weavers, and others producing cheaper goods frequently lived on the verge of destitution. Still, many skilled producers could live comfortably, and a minority became moderately wealthy. There was a demand for luxury goods, for housing, and for products that supported the shipping industry. Cities and towns expanded because of artisans. Lancaster, the first inland town of any size in British North America, had in 1751 some 254 artisans at work, greatly outnumbering the town's 87 wagoners, 59 merchants and shopkeepers, and 20 lawyers and doctors.

The promise of economic independence enticed most immigrants to Pennsylvania. The earliest migrants often wrote home, and those letters, read aloud and passed from

Servants and slaves made up a significant percentage of new immigrants to America in the eighteenth century. *Top:* a 1729 issue of the *Pennsylvania Gazette* notifies Philadelphians of the arrival of the ship *Boneta* with servants for sale. *Bottom:* the *American Weekly Mercury* (Philadelphia) advertises slaves for sale in 1738. The African man, woman, and child are pictured as round and happy-go-lucky, signaling to purchasers that they are healthy, well fed, and easy to manage. They are portrayed as exotic, primitive creatures dressed in large leaves rather than in the richly dyed clothes and straw hats that were in fact worn in West Africa. Portraying Africans as so very different from European standards helped justify enslavement.

hand to hand, encouraged others to migrate too, often settling near their old neighbors. Durs Thommen migrated from Neiderdorf in 1736, and then wrote back warning those at home that the trip was expensive and difficult and that immigrants were exploited. But he had acquired 435 acres, two houses and barns, full granaries, and "believe it or not," he added, "6 horses, 2 colts, [and] 15 cattle." There were few taxes and "abundant liberties in just about all matters." News encouraged migration, especially when heard amid military conscription, economic depression, and/or overpopulation in the German states, Scotland, Ireland, and elsewhere. For those who arrived free and with cash, this was "the best poor man's country" in the empire. Benjamin Franklin ran away from his master, purloined a friend's money, which he admitted was one of his "great errata," and by creating a reputation for hard work and supporting ingenious projects, he achieved fame as a printer, writer, scientist, and politician. Franklin's autobiography overturned the older idea that men should honorably fulfill whatever station in life they were allotted. He celebrated a new masculine ideal: the self-made man, who by his wits and willpower and work habits would rise to the top. Andrew Carnegie was just one of many later Americans who recounted the story of his career in a similar fashion.

Comparatively few individuals who had opportunities in Europe made the dangerous ocean voyage to America. Strapped for cash, immigrants sold their belongings, accepted aid from religious groups, borrowed from family and friends, and often sold themselves as "voluntary slaves." About one-third of all immigrants to Pennsylvania were indentured servants—individuals, mostly young men, who sold themselves for three to seven years to finance their transportation to the New World. Early in the colony's existence, these servants could reasonably expect to become landowners after their contracts expired. Later, opportunity dwindled and land was no longer a reward for service. William Moraley was an unemployed journeyman watchmaker in London when he sold himself in 1729 for five years. Only rarely did he work at his craft in the New World, however. He recalled: "Sometimes I have acted the Blacksmith; at other times, I have work'd in the Water, stark naked, among Water Snakes. Sometimes I was a Cow Hunter in the Woods, and sometimes I got Drunk for Joy that my Work was ended." He served out most of his term but ended his stay in the Delaware Valley as poor as he began. More and more Pennsylvanians ended their servitude without resources. They joined the ranks of the cottagers and wage laborers of the countryside and the working poor of the city.

Indentured servants at least had a contract stipulating the length of their service. German-speaking immigrants who sailed down the Rhine River to Amsterdam often found themselves hundreds of miles from home, stripped of their savings by toll collectors, found themselves hundreds of miles from home, stripped of their savings by toll collectors, unscrupulous boat captains, and others. They became redemptioners, who hoped to find relatives or friends in Pennsylvania to redeem them by paying the captain for their passage. If not, they were sold for what the market would bear. Children, in particular, were sold for long terms, and it sometimes happened that husbands, wives, and children were separated. German newspapers carried advertisements of family members looking for one another years after being sold apart. Redemptioners, like indentured servants and slaves, were valuable commodities with few rights. One young German girl with an additional three years to serve was jailed by her master in 1762 for running away. He authorized her to be sold only "to the frontier district where it is not likely that one finds a neighbor who will conspire with a servant against his fulfilling his obligation."

A Loft Wife went away, on the 29th Day of March, in the Year of our Lord 1765, Rachel Middleton, the Wife of Richard Middleton, Shoemaker, of Concord, Chester County; she went away with an intent to go for England, but she has been heard of to remain in these Parts still; she is a Woman of about 50 Years of Age, was born in Pescoat, in Lancashire, her maiden Name was Pickering, and her first Husband's Name Holland. If the said Rachel will return within two Months from the Date hereof, she shall be kindly received by her Husband, and six Children, as usual, and have Money to take her over to England. †

November 24, 1766.

WHEREAS Lætitia, the Wife of William Thompson, of Ashton Township, Chester County, did, on the sixth Day of October last, elope from her said Husband, and has since come privately, and in a clandestine Manner caused the Servants to plunder his House; this therefore is to forewarn all Persons from trusting her on my Account, for I will pay no Debts of her contracting from the Date hereof. ‡ WILLIAM THOMPSON.

In 1730s America it became a commonplace that people were either free or not free. If you had white skin, you were free and a full citizen. But in colonial Pennsylvania, as elsewhere in the colonies, white skin meant superiority to African and Native peoples but did not always equal freedom or independence. Many whites were indentured servants or redemptioners as liable to sale and whipping as slaves. Many boys and a few girls were apprenticed in their teens for four to seven years. Apprentices, like servants, were under the authority of their masters. Poor children could be sold as servants as soon as they were weaned, although they were not considered very valuable at so young an age. In some areas, the poor, the aged, and the disabled were auctioned off to the lowest bidder, the person who promised to maintain these unfortunates at the lowest cost to taxpayers. This system lasted into the twentieth century in some parts of Pennsylvania. In the larger cities the sick and abandoned were incarcerated in poorhouses or workhouses. Married women, whether rich or poor, were by law *femes covert*— that is, once married they ceased to exist for legal purposes, because their identity was covered by their husbands' legal authority. Wives' bodies, property, wages, children, choice of residence, and political allegiance belonged to their husbands.

Other Pennsylvanians were nominally free but were denied political rights because they were not landowners. Rural cottagers (called inmates in the tax records) were given a house and allowed a few acres on which to grow crops, but the families were bound by contract to provide weeks of labor planting and harvesting crops, or making cheese, weaving, or doing other domestic labor for the landowner. They could not vote. Wage earners and independent artisans in the city were also free but usually lacked the wherewithal to own property and qualify to vote. There was a range of statuses: free, bound, dependent, disenfranchised. Pennsylvania newspapers were filled with advertisements for

Divorce was nearly impossible in colonial Pennsylvania, but this does not necessarily mean marriages were stable. Men abandoned their wives with impunity. Wives could flee abusive husbands, although that was against the law. Hoping to retrieve their wives, husbands often alerted the community by running newspaper advertisements, such as these from the *Pennsylvania Gazette*. A frequent feature of such ads was the refusal to pay any debts, thus making it impossible for women to survive on their own. A few wives publicly refuted their husbands' interpretations of events.

resorted to riots to get their point across, and the Overseers of the Poor had to deal with absconders from the workhouse and with impoverished mothers who stole their children away from their assigned masters.

The most demeaned individuals were enslaved Africans. In Pennsylvania, enslaved people worked on farms and enslaved men manned the mills and forges dotting the countryside. In the cities and towns these women, men, and children were craftspeople, seamstresses, caterers, sailors, teamsters, and more, providing a variety of products and services. A few practiced medicine based on African botanical knowledge. Everywhere enslaved women cooked, cleaned, and tended babies as colonists took advantage of the substantially higher standards of cleanliness maintained in African societies. Slaves either worked for their masters or were hired out by the day or by the season.

In the northern colonies, slavery was not nearly as common as it was in the southern colonies, in part because in the north other sources of labor were available: wage workers, indentured servants, redemptioners, and local children. In Chester County in 1760, the 3,281 landowners could utilize the labor of 4,208 unmarried, landless adolescents and adult whites, of 833 cottagers and their families, of 149 indentured white servants, and of 231 slaves. In Philadelphia in 1750 there were 1,429 indentured servants and 787 slaves in a labor force totaling 4,129. Except when wars cut off European migration, indentured or waged servants were a cheaper source of labor. At an average price of £45, an adult slave in Pennsylvania would have to serve for eleven years to match the £4 per year average cost of an indentured servant, and high death rates—50 percent higher for blacks than for whites—made slaves a risky investment. Inadequate clothing, housing, and food contributed to ill health among slaves, while unfamiliar diseases like pleurisy, influenza, tuberculosis, and measles shortened their lives. Slavery was not usually the most rational economic choice, although for most of the colonial period owning slaves did confer some prestige on owners. Access to slave traders influenced slaveholding patterns too. Philadelphia had a supply of slaves from the Caribbean trade, and south-central Pennsylvanians acquired slaves from Maryland and Virginia, but most colonists lived farther from the centers of the slave trade and held fewer slaves.

As in the southern colonies, slavery in Pennsylvania was for life, passed to the next generation based on the status of the mother, and was assumed to be the condition of any person with dark skin unless she or he had documented proof of freedom. Whereas most other forms of bound labor were temporary, slavery was permanent. Rigid legal and social boundaries based on skin color separated Africans from others. Enslaved Pennsylvanians were beaten, fed the worst food, clothed scantily, and given the lowliest sleeping quarters. Benjamin Lay, an early abolitionist, castigated Philadelphia Quakers for their hypocrisy in keeping their slaves "Starved with Hunger, perish[ing] with Cold, [so that they] rot as they go, for want of every thing that is necessary for an Humane Creature; so that Dogs and Cats are much better taken care for, and yet some have had the Confidence, or rather Impudence, to say their Slaves or Negroes live as well as themselves."

The Quakers disowned Lay for his aggressive antislavery stance. Olaudah Equiano recalled the deprivations he experienced as the slave of Robert King, a Philadelphia Quaker. King was accounted a "good" master since he used the threat of sale more often than physical punishment to force obedience. Still, Equiano remembered that he "often went hungry" and was relieved to be resold. Enslaved Africans in Pennsylvania experienced physical conditions as bad or nearly as bad as southern slaves. In one respect their lives were worse. Few northern slaveowners owned more than two or three slaves, most owned one. Compared with slaves on southern plantations, enslaved Pennsylvanians suffered from social and familial isolation. They had less opportunity to form families or to live with family members, nor could they easily develop a semiautonomous community centered around a slave quarter.

The majority of whites developed racial ideas that asserted the inferiority of African people, based first on ignorance about African religions and cultures and later on equally specious biological grounds. Enslaved Pennsylvanians argued, at least among themselves, that they were not meant to be slaves any more than other men and women, so these slaves protested by absconding from their masters, making free with forbidden food, drink, and clothing, shirking work, and keeping their own counsel. When one slave, known to us only as Peter, absconded from on board ship in 1762, his master knew that he would "pretend that he is free" and that free Negroes in the city would help conceal him. A few whites also challenged the slave system. Anthony Benezet of Philadelphia published an influential series of pamphlets against slavery. A handful of slaveowners left wills freeing their slaves, but usually required them to work as indentured servants for a period of years before becoming completely free. At the end of the colonial period there were about 6,000 enslaved people in Pennsylvania and only a few hundred freed men and women. It was not until the revolutionary period that conditions were ripe for substantial change.

By the end of the colonial period a growing number of wealthy Pennsylvanians shared in the benefits of empire. But at the same time Pennsylvania had an increasing number of sailors and tailors, the unskilled, the widowed, the disabled, the pregnant and abandoned, and the elderly. These unfortunates worked at whatever jobs they could find or made work by gleaning after the harvests, catching fish, gathering oysters, or hawking pins or jam or hot soup in

ALICE

Portrait of Alice, 1803.

Few enslaved individuals left accounts of their lives. "Alice" (c. 1686–1802) received some attention from historically minded Pennsylvanians in the early nineteenth century because she lived to well over 100 years old with her memories of her youth still sharp. She had a reputation for unimpeachable honesty and was an important source of information on the earliest days of the colony.

Alice's parents were from Barbados, but she was born in Philadelphia and spent her first ten years there. Constant work began in childhood. Her master then moved her to Dunk's Ferry at Bristol in Bucks County, where she spent most of her life tending the ferry that crossed the Delaware River to New Jersey. Although she was illiterate, her master entrusted her with collecting the fees as well as managing the boats. Her last master finally excused her from work, but she would not be idle, and fished for her supper even when blind in her old age. When she had a chance, she would return to Philadelphia to attend Christ Church. One of her memories was of lighting William Penn's pipe as a girl.

Early historians collected Alice's many memories of old buildings and famous men, re-creating the founding years of the Commonwealth, but they did not think it important to discover the fate of her parents, the date of her emancipation, or whether she married or had a family.

The Province of Pennsylvania in 1730. In the
115 years since Cornelius Hendricksen's map,
English place-names have become dominant,
and the rivers and bays are better mapped
although still imperfectly drawn. A road connects New York City and Philadelphia, but
boats carried passengers as much of the way as
possible. Native peoples have been pushed to
the margins of the map, a fortified Susquehannock town is noted on the eastern bank of the
Susquehanna River, a Mohawk settlement is situated near the headwaters of the Delaware
River, and Iroquois dominate the northwest.
Other settlements of Native people did exist in
1730, but their presence is not acknowledged
on this map of the western edge of the British
Empire. The map also makes clear that colonists
still know little of the geography outside the
Delaware, Hudson, and eastern Susquehanna
River valleys.

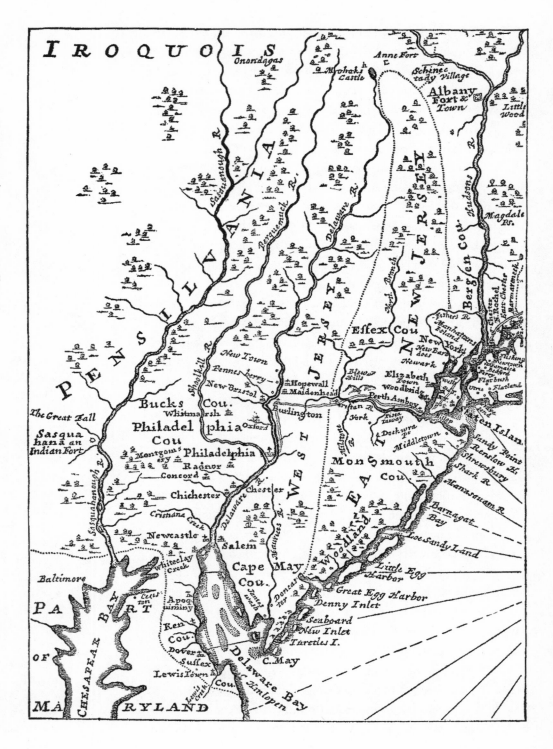

THE GERMANTOWN PROTEST, 1688

"The Germantown Protest," 1688, the first abolitionist petition in American history, was written by four German-speaking Quakers and submitted to the Yearly Meeting, the chief deliberative body among Quakers. No action was taken, and it would be nearly ninety years before the Quakers were convinced that slavery violated their beliefs. The arguments advanced here would continue to be used in the fight against the slave system—a struggle that took another century in Pennsylvania and another 170 years in the country as a whole. The spelling and punctuation have been modernized, and the passage is slightly abbreviated.

These are the reasons why we are against the traffic in men's bodies: Is there any[one] that would be done or handled in this manner? to be sold or made a slave for all the time of his life? How fearful and fainthearted are many on the sea when they see a strange vessel, being afraid it should be a Turk, and they should be taken and sold for slaves in Turkey. Now is this better than Turks do? yea it is worse for them who say they are Christians for we hear that the most part of such Negroes are brought here against their will and consent, and that many of them are stolen.

Now though they are black, we cannot conceive there is more liberty to have them as slaves, as it is to have white ones. There is a saying that we shall do to all men, like as we will be done to ourselves; making no difference of what generation, descent, or color they are. And those who steal or rob men and those who buy or purchase them, are they not all alike? Here [in Pennsylvania] is liberty of conscience, which is right and reasonable, here ought to be likewise liberty of the body, except of evil doers which is another case. And we, who know that men must not commit adultery, some do commit

adultery in others, separating wives from their husbands, and giving them to others and some sell the children of those poor creatures to other men. Oh, do consider well these things, you who will do it, if you would be done in this manner: and if it is done according to Christianity? We contradict and are against this traffic in men's bodies. And we who profess that it is not lawful to steal, must likewise avoid to purchase such things as are stolen, but rather help to stop this robbing and stealing if possible and such men ought to be delivered out of the hands of the robbers and set free [here] as well as in Europe. Then is Pennsylvania to have a good report.

If once these slaves (which they say are so wicked and stubborn) should join themselves [together and] fight for their freedom and handle their masters and mistresses as [slaves]; will these masters and mistresses take the sword at hand and war against these poor slaves? Or have these Negroes not as much right to fight for their freedom, as you have to keep them slaves?

These were noble sentiments, but only four men—Garret Hendricks, Derick op de Graeff, Francis Daniell Pastorius, and Abraham op den Graef—endorsed the petition. Four years earlier, scores of Pennsylvanians had eagerly purchased 150 people shipped directly from Africa—so anxious to acquire a permanent labor force that most of the hard cash in the colony left with the emptied ship. Antislavery arguments convinced only a tiny minority before the Revolution, and even then won the grudging support of a bare majority of the voters.

Benjamin Lay was odd in his appearance, eccentric in his behavior and manner of living, and aggressive in his attacks on slavery. He was disowned by the Quakers for his accusations of Quaker hypocrisy in keeping slaves.

the streets. They lived in the alleys of Philadelphia or on small lots in the countryside in one- or two-story, ramshackle houses measuring twelve feet by twelve feet, sharing that space with boarders, and hoping to be able to afford food and firewood. They were often sick, and many of their children died young from inadequate food in barely heated households. Social and economic divisions were widening as the colony matured.

In many ways Pennsylvania's colonial culture came to an end in 1754. A great war for empire between England, France, their colonies, the majority of the Iroquois, the Delaware, and other tribes would bring an end both to peace and to direct Quaker control of the government. Imperial control would threaten the colony's autonomy, and Pennsylvania would move reluctantly toward revolution as the struggle over proprietary control versus royal control became moot. For Native Americans this was the beginning of a thirty-year war for economic and political autonomy. By 1755 Pennsylvania had its first state militia, and by 1756 it had appropriated some money for the defense of the colony, but given the size of the territory and the reluctance to raise taxes, it was not enough. Bloodshed, resentments, heightened racism, and ethnic and geographic divisions were one legacy of the war that fed into the turmoil of the Revolutionary War. Confidence in Pennsylvania's ability to govern itself, impatience with policies made overseas, and an awareness of the similarities among the thirteen colonies also helped pave the way to revolution, especially when combined with an awakened, novel, and enlightened language of liberty, equality, reason, and rights—for whites.

On August 30, 1773, Sallie Eve, an Anglican and the daughter of a formerly prosperous ship captain and merchant, noted in her diary: "Yesterday [Mr. John Penn] made a public entery into Town with a large train, but I have heard say since that there was but one out [of] the whole but what was depentant on him, and that was Hoffman the sugar baker. I rather would have had as many indepentant sweeps, cobblers or barbers in my train and should of thought myself twenty times more honourd, then by depentant Gentry." Sallie Eve scorned a government based on the inherited privileges of superior gentlemen and their compliant, deferential political appointees. In sharp contrast is her revolutionary vision of herself as the governor, freely chosen by those commoners who, like herself, did not yet qualify to vote. Politicians, she thought, should work to gain the "hearts of the people"; anything else was contemptible. Her vision of the province would have shocked William Penn and his descendants. Pennsylvania had developed into a religiously, culturally, racially, socially, and intellectually diverse colony with an ideal of toleration and liberty for those of European descent. Politically, colonial Pennsylvania represented white, male, Protestant eastern landowners, the British crown, and a feudal proprietorship. Reconciling the two Pennsylvanias as Sallie Eve imagined was a process that would begin two years after she wrote but that has hardly ended yet.

Bodle, Wayne. "Themes and Directions in the Middle Colonies Historiography, 1980–1994," *William and Mary Quarterly,* 3rd ser., 51 (July 1994), 355–88.

Cremers, Estelle. *Reading Furnace, 1736.* Elverson, Pa.: Reading Furnace Press, 1986.

Dunn, Richard S., and Mary Maples Dunn, eds. *The World of William Penn.* Philadelphia: University of Pennsylvania Press, 1986.

Eldridge, Larry D., ed. *Women and Freedom in Early America.* New York: New York University Press, 1997.

Fischer, David Hackett. *Albion's Seed: Four British Folkways in America.* New York: Oxford University Press, 1989.

Fogelman, Aaron Spenser. *Hopeful Journeys: German Immigration, Settlement, and Political Culture in Colonial America, 1717–1775.* Philadelphia: University of Pennsylvania Press, 1996.

Freeman, Sabina Shields, and Margaret L. Tempas. *Erie History—The Women's Story.* Erie, Pa.: Benet Press, 1982.

Frost, J. William. *A Perfect Freedom: Religious Liberty in Pennsylvania.* New York: Cambridge University Press, 1990.

Higginbotham, A. Leon, Jr. *In the Matter of Color: Race and the American Legal Process, the Colonial Period.* New York: Oxford University Press, 1978.

Hoffecker, Carol E., et al., eds. *New Sweden in America.* Newark: University of Delaware Press, 1995.

Horle, Craig W., Joseph S. Foster, Jeffrey L. Scheib, et al., eds. *Lawmaking and Legislators in Pennsylvania: A Biographical Dictionary.* Vol. 2: *1710–1756.* Philadelphia: University of Pennsylvania Press, 1997.

Horle, Craig W., Marianne S. Wokeck, et al., eds. *Lawmaking and Legislators in Pennsylvania: A Biographical Dictionary.* Vol. 1: *1682–1709.* Philadelphia: University of Pennsylvania Press, 1991.

Hutchins, Catherine E., ed. *Shaping a National Culture: The Philadelphia Experience, 1750–1800.* Winterthur, Del.: Winterthur Museum, 1994.

Illick, Joseph E. *Colonial Pennsylvania: A History.* New York: Scribner's, 1976.

Jordan, Terry T., and Matti Kaups. *The American Backwoods Frontier: An Ethnic and Ecological Interpretation.* Baltimore: Johns Hopkins University Press, 1989.

Kelley, Joseph J. *Pennsylvania: The Colonial Years, 1681–1776.* Garden City, N.Y.: Doubleday, 1980.

Klepp, Susan E. *"The Swift Progress of Population": A Documentary and Bibliographic Study of Philadelphia's Growth, 1642–1859.* Philadelphia: American Philosophical Society, 1991.

Klepp, Susan E., and Billy G. Smith, eds. *The Infortunate: The Voyage and Adventures of William Moraley, an Indentured Servant.* University Park: The Pennsylvania State University Press, 1992.

Lemon, James T. *The Best Poor Man's Country: A Geographical Study of Early Southeastern Pennsylvania.* Baltimore: Johns Hopkins University Press, 1972.

Levy, Barry. *Quakers and the American Family: British Settlement in the Delaware Valley.* New York: Oxford University Press, 1988.

Merrell, James H. *Into the American Woods: Negotiators on the Pennsylvania Frontier.* New York: W. W. Norton, 1999.

Salinger, Sharon V. *"To Serve Well and Faithfully": Labor and Indentured Servants in Pennsylvania, 1682–1800.* New York: Cambridge University Press, 1987.

Schwartz, Sally. *"A Mixed Multitude": The Struggle for Toleration in Colonial Pennsylvania.* New York: New York University Press, 1989.

Shea, Daniel B. "Introduction to 'Some Account of the Fore Part of the Life of Elizabeth Ashbridge.'" In *Journeys in New Worlds: Early American Women's Narratives,* ed. William L. Andrews, 117–46. Madison: University of Wisconsin Press, 1990.

Simler, Lucy. "The Landless Worker: An Index of Economic and Social Change in Chester County, Pennsylvania, 1750–1820." *Pennsylvania Magazine of History and Biography* 114 (April 1990), 163–99.

Smaby, Beverly Prior. *The Transformation of Moravian Bethlehem: From Communal Mission to Family Economy.* Philadelphia: University of Pennsylvania Press, 1988.

Soderlund, Jean R. *Quakers and Slavery: A Divided Spirit.* Princeton: Princeton University Press, 1985.

———. "Women in Eighteenth-Century Pennsylvania: Toward a Model of Diversity," *Pennsylvania Magazine of History and Biography.* 115 (April 1991), 163–84.

Wokeck, Marianne S. *Trade in Strangers: The Beginnings of Mass Migration to North America.* University Park: The Pennsylvania State University Press, 1999.

Wolf, Stephanie Grauman. *Urban Village: Population, Community, and Family Structure in Germantown, Pennsylvania, 1683–1800.* Princeton: Princeton University Press, 1976.

Wood, Jerome H. *Conestoga Crossroads: Lancaster, Pennsylvania, 1730–1790.* Harrisburg: Pennsylvania Historical and Museum Commission, 1979.

Wulf, Karin. *Not All Wives: Gender, Marriage, and Urban Culture in Colonial Philadelphia.* Ithaca: Cornell University Press, 1999.

Zuckerman, Michael, ed. *Friends and Neighbors: Group Life in America's First Plural Society.* Philadelphia: Temple University Press, 1982.

The Promise of Revolution
1750–1800

WILLIAM PENCAK

During the fifty years of war, revolution, and nation-building between 1750 and 1800, Pennsylvania symbolized America, and, for much of the world, Benjamin Franklin symbolized Pennsylvania. In the 1750s Americans pointed to Franklin's scientific work on electricity as proof that America could produce geniuses equal to those whom Europe had produced. Serving in Britain as the agent of several colonies in the 1760s and 1770s, Franklin in effect spoke for all his compatriots as the colonial crisis worsened. When he went to Paris to negotiate the alliance of the fledgling United States with France in 1778, he donned a fur cap to hide his scalp condition, but the French interpreted this unusual headgear as the symbol of a supposedly uncorrupted new nation. The philosopher Voltaire embraced Franklin and praised him as the scientist who stole lightning from the sky and the scepter from tyrants like King George III of England.

In literature too, Pennsylvania came to symbolize America. Perhaps most well known is the French immigrant Michel Guillaume de Crèvecoeur (1735–1812), who, taking the persona of a farmer from Carlisle, drew on his own experience to write *Letters from an American Farmer* (1782). Crèvecoeur showed how "the American . . . a new man" (or woman, for he named his daughter "America") could rise from "idleness, servile dependence, penury, and useless labor" in Europe to "ample subsistence" on the Pennsylvania frontier. Crèvecoeur's work, still in print more than two centuries later, was

Two sides of Benjamin Franklin. The portrait (*right*), painted by Mason Chamberlain in 1763, shows Franklin as the internationally famous scientist measuring the effects of positive and negative electrical charges on his apparatus. In the background a lightning rod protects one house during a storm, while an unprotected house crumbles to the ground when struck by lightning. Reproduced widely in mezzotint, the portrait shows how the American public viewed Franklin. By contrast, the second image (*above*), a terra-cotta medallion from France, shows Franklin as he chose to represent himself in Europe—the unspoiled natural man in a fur cap. Franklin understood the diplomatic advantages he could gain when negotiating for the United States in France, whereas in North America Franklin frequently had himself painted as a gentleman in a fancy coat with a wig, to show how a poor boy had made good.

the first to synthesize the central tenets of the American dream—that a mixture of diverse peoples could govern themselves in peace, tolerate one another's religions, and achieve prosperity through diligent and honest work.

Less well known is that a disillusioned Crèvecoeur returned to Europe during the Revolution. A second book by Crèvecoeur, which remained unpublished until 1925 and is rarely read, is titled *Sketches of Eighteenth-Century Life* and depicts Pennsylvania's revolutionary age as "a fatal era," its people "torn with internal divisions." He specifically wrote this book to refute in advance "the journals, memoirs, and elaborate essays which shall not fail hereafter to commemorate the heroes who have made their appearance on the new American stage." Instead, focusing on the brutal frontier war of the Wyoming Valley, Crèvecoeur hoped to paint "more humble but perhaps not less interesting" scenes of "sorrow and affliction."

Between 1750 and 1800, war, revolution, and economic crises wracked Pennsylvania. Previously, Quaker and proprietary rule had effectively maintained peace and ensured prosperity, but Pennsylvania's existing government was unprepared to fight wars and mobilize its people for revolutionary political action. The Commonwealth suffered exceptional turmoil in this violent half-century. In 1754 the French and Indian War began on its western frontier. The French surrendered in 1763, but almost immediately thereafter an unprecedented coalition of Indian nations led by Pontiac attacked Pennsylvania. Then the British government decided the colonies should help pay for their own defense and confine most of their trade to the British Empire. Afflicted by economic hardship, and angered that Parliament had taken away their right to tax themselves, Pennsylvanians protested along with their fellow colonists. Philadelphia, British North America's largest and most centrally located city, became the site where Congress adopted the Declaration of Independence, and then the first capital of the new nation.

The eight-year war required to establish a new nation did not solve Pennsylvania's problems. Other states continued to dispute its boundaries, and Native Americans fought for their lands until the 1790s. When conservative patriots as well as loyalists opposed the state's radical Constitution of 1776, two parties emerged. The Republicans (later Federalists) hoped that an elite of wealth and intellect could direct a government that promoted commerce and industry. Constitutionalists (later Anti-Federalists) favored local rights and were suspicious both of elite rule and of the high cost of economic development. Party rivalry continued as Philadelphia played host to the Constitutional Convention in 1787.

But consensus that the United States needed an effective national government did not produce agreement on what policies it should pursue. The Federalists soon split, many joining Anti-Federalists to form the Democratic-Republican Party, which opposed the national bank, taxes, and seemingly pro-British foreign policy supported by President George Washington's administration. Partisan strife, which was especially fierce in Pennsylvania, culminated in the Whiskey Rebellion of 1794 and Fries's Rebellion of 1799, incidents that produced some of the mere handful of indictments for treason in American history. Only in 1800, with the political defeat of the Federalists and the triumph of the Democratic-Republicans, did Pennsylvania regain the stability it had enjoyed during the years before 1750.

The commercial/elitist/Federalist and agricultural/populist/Anti-Federalist/Democratic-Republican visions of Pennsylvania came to symbolize two ideals of the new nation that emerged after the Revolution. Both models were satirized in the first comic novel written in the United States. Hugh Henry Brackenridge (1748–1816), a western

Pennsylvania legislator and judge, spent the last quarter-century of his life writing *Modern Chivalry.* In that book, upper-class Captain Farrago is a mock Don Quixote who uses Enlightenment ideas to manipulate his dim-witted Sancho Panza-like servant, Teague O'Reagan. Farrago talks O'Reagan out of election to the legislature, membership in the American Philosophical Society, ordination as a Presbyterian minister, and even becoming an Indian chief: "Let it never be said, that you quitted an honest livelihood, the taking care of my horse, to follow the new fangled whims of the time, and to be a statesman." Brackenridge exposed the underside of America's national mythology: if the founding fathers were philosophers and statesmen, they employed their abilities to keep ordinary folk in line. And if the Revolution opened new doors for the masses, it also revealed that their abilities did not always match their aspirations. As we traverse Pennsylvania's fast-paced, complex revolutionary era, we need to keep Crèvecoeur's darker side and Brackenridge's satire in mind.

THE TWO FACES OF REVOLUTIONARY PENNSYLVANIA: PHILADELPHIA AS A CASE STUDY

Nowhere did the divisions of revolutionary Pennsylvania stand out more clearly than in Philadelphia. In the land's "most beautiful" city "you will find more well-educated men, more knowledge of politics, and literature, and more political and learned societies than anywhere else in the United States," commented Jacques-Pierre Brissot de Warville, a future leader in the French Revolution who visited during the 1780s. Yet the city also endured the sort of poverty, crime, and disease that today can be found in the Third World.

With more than 20,000 inhabitants by the time of the American Revolution, Philadelphia had outstripped Boston and New York, each of which had more than a half-century head start. By modern standards the city was tiny. Population in the 1770s was concentrated between Vine Street on the north and Cedar (now South) Street, between the Delaware River on the east and Seventh Street on the west. By 1800 the western limit of thick settlement was Tenth Street. Cows belonging to town inhabitants were driven to pasture near Broad Street. Unlike Boston and New York, much of central Philadelphia was built of brick rather than wood, and thus it was spared the catastrophic fires that destroyed almost all the prerevolutionary buildings in those other two cities. To this day, you can wander south from Independence Hall down Third or Fourth Street and understand why in 1765 an English visitor considered Philadelphia "a great and noble city."

At the apex of Philadelphia society were such families as the Shippens, the Allens, the Logans, and the Galloways, an economic, cultural, and political elite comprising Quakers, Anglicans, and Presbyterians who in general socialized amicably despite political and religious differences. The men were government officials and merchants who specialized in trading Pennsylvania's ample surpluses of grain to the West Indies and importing both luxury items and household goods from Britain. The women—notably

Francis Hopkinson in conversation with Elizabeth Graeme (later Fergusson). Hopkinson, a well-known poet and composer, and Graeme, a poet, exemplified the genteel society that flourished in Philadelphia's environs in the mid-eighteenth century. Women played an important role in intellectual and artistic exchanges. Drawing by Benjamin West.

Susanna Wright, Milcah Martha Moore, Elizabeth Graeme Fergusson, and Hannah Griffitts—ensured that elite get-togethers were intellectually as well as socially stimulating. Presiding over American equivalents of the famous Parisian literary "salons," their fascinating but privately circulated diaries, poems, essays, and personal letters are only now being rediscovered. Many of these soirees occurred in the pleasant mansions, such as Strawberry Hill or Lemon Hill, that still overlook the Schuylkill River and grace Germantown Avenue. Here, in respectful imitation of the British gentry, the wealthy had established country estates and gardens that permitted them to escape the city's bustle and summer heat.

Christ Church (Anglican/Episcopal), the tallest building in the American colonies. Benjamin Franklin is buried at the northwest corner of the burying ground of this still-functioning Episcopal church.

While not all of the elite worshiped at the Anglican (Episcopal) churches—Christ Church, located at Third and Mulberry (now Arch) Street, and St. Peter's Church several blocks to the south—more and more of them did. The tallest building in prerevolutionary British North America at 196 feet, Christ Church exemplified local wealth and a colonial upper class that was becoming increasingly anglicized, refined, and conscious of its importance. Quakers, on the other hand, numbered one-fourth of the city's population in 1750, but only one-seventh a quarter-century later.

Philadelphia's elite was public-spirited, after a fashion. To be sure, its members enjoyed themselves at the Dancing Assembly (whose annual ball still takes place at the Academy of Music), numerous fishing clubs, and the Tammany Society, where members played at being Indians. But they also founded the first medical school in the colonies in 1765, fire companies, and several libraries. They liberally supported the American Philosophical Society, modeled on the London's Royal Society and founded in 1769, where scientists and thinkers exchanged ideas with groups of European intellectuals and published their transactions.

What is not obvious is that the public the elite benefited was largely themselves. The Philosophical Society disputed the claims of Europeans that America was inferior to the Old World and incapable of producing first-rate minds. The Society publicized its members' own achievements, especially those of Benjamin Franklin, as their prime exhibit. Fees charged by both the College of Philadelphia and the Library Company closed these associations to the aspiring middle-class youth for whom Franklin had intended them. Under Provost William Smith, the nonsectarian college founded in 1749 came under the control of the Church of England. People belonged to fire companies by invitation, and needed to turn out only when a member's property was in danger. Their main tasks were to put out the blaze and save a building's contents from looters. And while ordinary medical care was generally affordable, smallpox inoculation, which saved the lives of most people who received it, cost two weeks' wages for a laboring man.

Yet while wealthy Philadelphians have left us most of the buildings, furniture, and documents that survive from the revolutionary era, they were only a tiny, albeit influential, minority in both the city and the province. Few of the flimsy wooden structures that crowded the alleys behind the sturdy brick houses and filled the Northern Liberties (part of which was known as "Helltown") and Southwark—poor neighborhoods that sprawled along the Delaware just outside the city limits—survive. At any given time, one-quarter to half of all taxpayers paid only a poll tax, meaning they possessed almost no wealth, while the top 5 percent of the population held between 40 and 50 percent of the taxable wealth. Of twenty typical Philadelphia men, three or four were servants or slaves, six were sailors or unskilled laborers, seven were artisans (of whom a majority were poorly paid apprentices and journeymen), one was in trade or services (barber, clerk, porter, or the like), one was a shopkeeper, one a merchant, and one a government official or professional man (lawyer, doctor, clergy). At best, one-quarter of the population belonged to the "middling" or "better" sort, to use the language of the time, while more than half could barely afford a place to live and a plain diet.

By the time of the Revolution, the city had given up taking care of its numerous

Philadelphia's John Bartram owned the most famous garden in early America. He exhibited here the plants he gathered from his extensive travels, and he helped make Philadelphia the new nation's scientific center. Bartram's house and garden in West Philadelphia still stand and may be visited.

The diverse economic and racial nature of early Philadelphia is depicted in this print from about 1799. The Quaker couple probably lived in a house similar to the one in the background.

poor. A public almshouse, which rarely held 100 people before the French and Indian War, was replaced in 1768 by the privately funded Bettering House, where the able-bodied worked at spinning and cobbling to earn their keep. More than 600 people passed through its doors each year. Another 350 were treated annually at the Pennsylvania Hospital for the Sick Poor, founded in 1751. Philadelphia's annual birth rate was 45 per 1,000 population (about one child annually per five adult women), and its death rate was 35 per thousand, both of which exceed the birth and death rates for Ethiopia in the year 2000. (The contemporary figures for Philadelphia are 18 births and 12 deaths per thousand.) Late eighteenth-century Philadelphia's crime rate also resembled that of the present-day Third World. Slaves, servants, and the poor were defendants in most of the thousand-odd cases that were reaching the courts annually by the 1790s. Philadelphia's homicide rate for the eighteenth century was twice as high as notoriously unsafe London.

But all of Pennsylvania was more statistically prone to crime than the British capital. Many crimes, especially assaults, burglaries, and cases of disorderly conduct, were committed by the propertyless and frequently homeless laborers who cannot be traced except on court records. One such person visited the wealthy widow Elizabeth Drinker on August 30, 1794: "A dismal looking object came to our back door this forenoon to ask charity. Our young people were frightened by his appearance. . . . [I] desired him to go quickly off, and shut the gate after him . . . as I thought there was a likelihood he would scare many, and have the dogs set on him." Drinker observed far more "ill looking vagrants about the country than in the city," for Philadelphia typically sentenced homeless beggars to one month's hard labor.

How can we account for this increasing poverty and violence? In both city and countryside, Pennsylvania's labor relations were undergoing a fundamental change, fully comparable to the deindustrialization of the late twentieth century. The land of opportunity young Benjamin Franklin had found in 1723 was fast disappearing. By 1755 in Philadelphia, two-fifths of all workers were indentured servants, slaves, or apprentices—people who lived with masters in a family unit and in return for food, clothing, and shelter provided labor. While masters could be cruel and exploitative, they owed their dependents protection, support, and frequently education, in return for labor and loyalty. By 1775 the number of dependent laborers had fallen to 10 percent. Economic hard times for much of the revolutionary era made it more profitable for the wealthy to hire temporary workers and discharge them when business was slow. Cash exchanges replaced paternal oversight as workers lived less often with their employers and more often in increasingly impoverished neighborhoods.

In the countryside too, many people sought the few jobs and competed for increasingly scarce land. Contrary to the myth that early America offered land in abundance, by the 1750s nearly all Pennsylvania's good farm acreage—south and east of a mountainous frontier still occupied by Native Americans—was claimed, and most of it was being farmed. Middle-class families produced on average five or six offspring, requiring that farms be subdivided and children move on. These native-born Pennsylvanians then competed with thousands of immigrants, driven out of Europe by poverty and religious persecution and lured by Pennsylvania propagandists—including Franklin and beginning with William Penn himself—who assured them that land was plentiful and cheap. But the colonial land of opportunity was fast filling up. By the end of the eighteenth century, half the people in eastern Pennsylvania worked on someone else's land.

Nowhere could the contrasts between the two Pennsylvanias be seen more vividly than in the summers of 1776 and 1787. While the Continental Congress debated human liberty and equality, a Philadelphia crowd stoned a suspected witch to death. "Hunger during the want of the last year has made the common people unruly," a wealthy Quaker merchant noted. Had he not recorded this event in his diary, and had the diary not survived, we would have no knowledge of an incident that otherwise went unrecorded and unpunished. Eleven years later, while the Constitutional Convention was hoping to "ensure domestic tranquility" through "a more perfect union," another accused witch, who died of her injuries, was paraded by a crowd through the city as bystanders "hooted and pelted her." A "gentleman" who tried to protect her was "greatly insulted." If elite culture was enlightened and rationalist, the lower orders clung to a premodern worldview, which still appears in more favorable and watered-down guise in the ethnic and religious loyalties and celebrations of folk culture for which Pennsylvania is noted. Such stories of the lives of the lower and middling sort remind us that suffering, injustice, and violence accompanied revolutionary Pennsylvania's rise to become the "keystone of the democratic" arch. And democracy and elitism have always coexisted uneasily in both a state and a nation that remain imperfect experiments.

THE COLLAPSE OF THE HOLY EXPERIMENT

From 1682 until 1754, Pennsylvania prospered without fighting a war, maintaining an army, or enforcing conformity to an established church. William Penn's "Holy Experiment," under which diverse peoples would live together in peace, attracted

Advertisements for runaway slaves in the *Pennsylvania Journal*, 1765. Black slaves were not the only people fleeing; indentured servants ran away too, and rewards were posted in the newspapers. Note that the text states that "Will" has part of his right ear cut off. Whether this reflects mistreatment, the dangerous nature of his work, ritual scarification, an accident, or disease remains unknown.

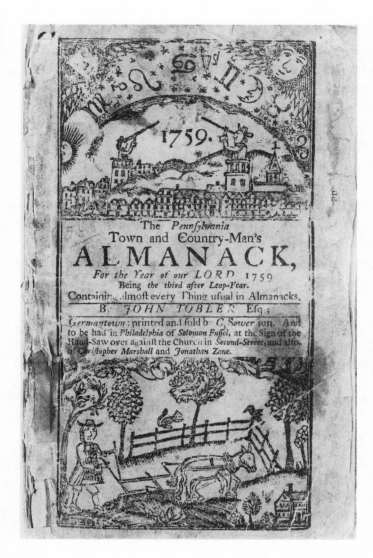

The Pennsylvania Town and Country-Man's Almanack, by John Tobler (1758). Almanacs were the most widely read works—other than the Bible—in colonial America. The leading German printer in colonial America, Christopher Saur, also published works in English from his Germantown press. This cover depicts both urban and rural prosperity in early Pennsylvania. Philadelphia astrologers are scanning the heavens in hopes of predicting the future.

Moravians and Mennonites from Europe; Indians such as the Seneca and Tuscarora, who had moved north after being displaced in the Carolinas; and, in greatest number, Scots-Irish and German Lutheran and Reformed (Calvinist) immigrants, who would, respectively, comprise about one-fourth and one-third of the province's population (most of the rest being of English descent) by the time of the Revolution. But in Pennsylvania's attractiveness lay its fatal flaw.

While many of the Germans were welcomed by fellow Germans in the new land, the Scots-Irish had nowhere to go. By the 1750s Pennsylvania had in effect closed its frontier. The colonial government cooperated with the Iroquois so the two could share power and limit settlement. Treaties relocated the Delawares and the Shawnees from eastern Pennsylvania to the Wyoming and Juniata Valleys, where they would protect the Iroquois from encroachments of whites. To placate the Iroquois, Pennsylvania authorities in turn burned the cabins and fields of whites who squatted in the Juniata Valley. Behind Pennsylvania's benevolence toward the Indians lay an ulterior motive: Philadelphia-area leaders hoped to restrict settlement to areas they could control and tax. Nevertheless, the Scots-Irish poured into the west. Conrad Weiser, who had mediated between colonists and Indians for decades, retired. He was angry at the "rudeness, lawlessness, and ignorance" of the backcountry inhabitants who "curse and damn the Indians and call them murdering dogs into their faces."

Despite sporadic frontier violence, war came to Pennsylvania only indirectly. Both French Canada and Virginia claimed the Ohio Valley, including what is now southwestern Pennsylvania. In 1749 France sent 2,000 Canadians south to secure the region with a series of forts extending from Lake Erie to the present site of Pittsburgh, where they built Fort Duquesne. Four years later, Virginia countered with a small force under George Washington, who after two skirmishes was forced to surrender his post, Fort Necessity, in July 1754.

Washington's expedition was a turning point in history. For the first time, the British used a remote American frontier conflict as a pretext to launch a major war. Thus, a twenty-two-year-old Virginia militia colonel unwittingly initiated the French and Indian War—more accurately termed the "Great War for the Empire" by historian Lawrence Henry Gipson. Extending beyond western Pennsylvania and beyond America, this nine-year war for global supremacy between France and Britain was also fought in Europe, Asia, Africa, and the Caribbean.

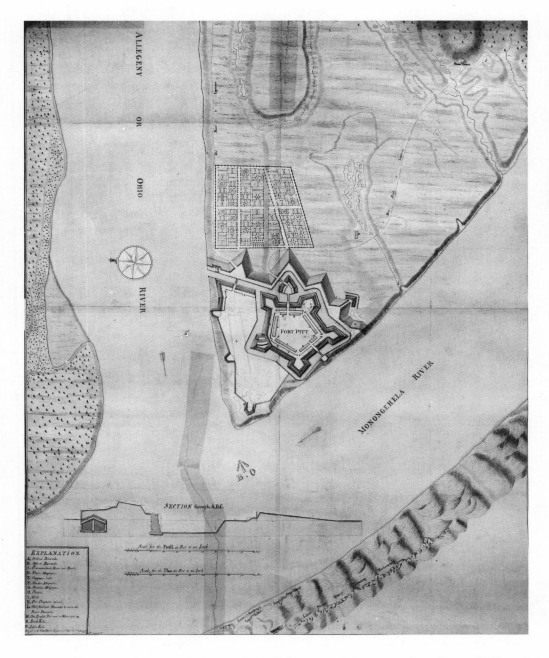

This plan of Fort Pitt, drawn in 1761, three years after the English occupied the fort, shows that, like its French predecessor Fort Duquesne, it was built according to the model designed by Louis XIV's chief engineer, Sébastien le Prestre de Vauban. The moats, interior walls, and star-shaped defenses were designed to withstand heavy siege. Capturing Fort Duquesne consumed much of the Pennsylvania and British war effort in the French and Indian War. The map also shows the early beginnings of the town of Pittsburgh in the shadow of the fort. The remains of Fort Pitt are found at Point State Park in Pittsburgh.

Pacifist Pennsylvania stayed out of the fighting even in 1755, when General Edward Braddock arrived to capture Fort Duquesne. Braddock landed his 1,400 regulars in Williamsburg, where, joined by Colonel George Washington and the Virginia militia, they hacked a road through forests and mountains for several hundred miles. Just south of Fort Duquesne, on July 9, a small French and Indian force ambushed Braddock. Half the British army, including Braddock, was killed or wounded. Washington led the other half back to Virginia.

War finally came to Pennsylvania when Braddock's defeat inspired the Shawnees and Delawares, now aided by the French, to try to regain the lands from which the Iroquois and Pennsylvania had expelled them. Led by chiefs known to the colonists as Jacobs and Chingas, they burned the scattered homesteads and small towns that dotted the Pennsylvania landscape, killing or capturing some 3,000 colonists in a little over a year. By November 1755, Provincial Secretary Richard Peters reported: "Almost all the women and children over Susquehanna have left their habitations, and the roads are full of starved, naked, and indigent multitudes." Raiding parties came to within a few miles of Bethlehem and Reading, which became centers for refugees who had lost everything they owned.

This catastrophic rolling back of the frontiers transformed Pennsylvania's political system. In April 1756 seven pacifist Quaker deputies, including the party's leader, Israel Pemberton, resigned from the Assembly. This action allowed the remaining legislators to mobilize Pennsylvania for war for the first time. When the Quakers prefaced their leave-taking by saying, "The present situation of public affairs calls upon us for service in a military way, which after mature deliberation we cannot comply with," they were admitting that Penn's "Holy Experiment" had collapsed.

When Pennsylvania finally joined the fray, its contribution to the war proved vigorous, extensive, and eventually effective. Beginning in 1756, the province established a string of some forty forts from the Delaware Water Gap, over the Blue Mountain, across the Susquehanna, and into the Juniata Valley. Forts operated as focal points to shelter refugees and draw Indian attacks away from farms and toward the garrisons. When forts failed to deter further raids, Pennsylvania launched an expedition under Lieutenant-Colonel John Armstrong that on September 8, 1756, surprised and defeated the Delawares at their principal camp near Fort Duquesne. Chief Jacobs "refused to surrender when the house was even on fire over his head. And when the flame grew too violent for him, he rushed out into the body of our men flourishing his tomahawk, and told them he was born a soldier and would not die a slave."

Pennsylvania also contributed 2,700 volunteers and four battalions of "Royal Americans" who joined the British army that made the final push against Fort Duquesne. Beginning in July 1758 from Carlisle, Pennsylvania, rather than Williamsburg, Virginia, General John Forbes ordered the road that still bears his name cut across numerous mountain ranges. The army did not reach the French stronghold until November 1758; then it found an attack was not necessary after all. Deserted by their Indian allies—whom the British had reconciled that October at the Treaty of Easton with promises not to permit settlement west of the Appalachians—the French destroyed their own fort. Fort Pitt, the future Pittsburgh, rose in its stead.

As with so many wars throughout history, victory for the British and the Americans created more problems than it solved. Despite the Treaty of Easton, settlers returned to the Juniata Valley and to Cumberland County, then comprising the entire southwest of the province. In response, a leader of the Ottawas residing at Detroit, Pontiac, launched

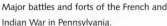

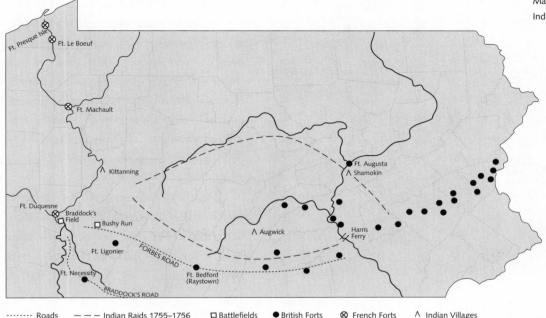

Ft. Presque Isle
Ft. Le Boeuf
Ft. Machault
∧ Kittanning
Ft. Duquesne
⊗ Braddock's Field
□ Bushy Run
Ft. Ligonier
Ft. Necessity
FORBES ROAD
Ft. Bedford (Raystown)
BRADDOCK'S ROAD
∧ Augwick
● Ft. Augusta
∧ Shamokin
Harris Ferry

-------- Roads   — — — Indian Raids 1755–1756   □ Battlefields   ● British Forts   ⊗ French Forts   ∧ Indian Villages

a war that historians later demeaned as a "conspiracy." But it was much more than that. Pontiac forged the first federation among various Indian nations, the model for Tecumseh's "confederacy" during the War of 1812. Pontiac's religious leader, Neolin, gained support by preaching that whites were innately evil and that Indians who remained true to their traditional ways were destined for Paradise. He thereby turned whites' views of the Natives against themselves. Before Pontiac's Rebellion, political allegiances among different groups of Indians and whites mattered more than racial division between peoples. Once the French were eliminated, racist attitudes among frontier people became more pronounced: they regarded all Native people as enemies and redefined them as "red."

Under Pontiac's onslaught, the Pennsylvania frontiers reeled once again, and once again the British and the colonials united to save them. In May 1763, with Fort Pitt under siege, Colonel Henry Bouquet embarked from Carlisle with a hastily assembled force of 400 volunteers. To assist the expedition, he approved distributing blankets infected with smallpox to the Indians. This tactic revealed the willingness of the British to use any means to conquer the west. Ambushed on August 5 at Bushy Run near Fort Pitt, Bouquet's outnumbered force turned the bags of flour they had brought to feed the beseiged troops into barricades. Then, innovating a light infantry formation for which he is credited in histories of the British army, Bouquet lured the Indians to attack his center while men held in reserve charged the enemy's flanks with bayonets and drove them from the field. The following year, 1764, Bouquet achieved yet another temporary peace on the frontier by marching a force through the Ohio

Political cartoons from the debate over the Paxton Boys, 1764, the first cartoons to appear in colonial Pennsylvania. In the first, Benjamin Franklin stands at the right as Pennsylvanians fight among themselves. Israel Pemberton, leader of the Quakers, is satirized for his friendliness toward the Indians as he embraces an Indian woman on the left. The second shows the Quakers as a burden to a Pennsylvania society wracked by warfare.

country, avoiding ambushes, and forcing the Indians to free prisoners while delivering hostages to the whites. Bouquet's own fate was ironic, considering his willingness to start an epidemic among the Indians. Promoted to brigadier general and placed in charge of the newly conquered province of Florida, he died of yellow fever nine days after assuming command.

Marches through Indian country could at best deter raids; they could not halt them. Whites retaliated in kind. During the hiatus between Bouquet's campaigns of 1763 and 1764, the "Paxton Boys," who had settled near present-day Harrisburg, took action on their own. They believed that peaceful Indians converted by the Moravians were harboring an enemy in their settlement in Conestoga, near Lancaster. On December 14, 1763, about fifty men entered Conestoga and "without the least reason and provocation . . . barbarously killed" six unarmed Indians. Fourteen Indians survived the massacre, but the whites followed them to Lancaster, where they too were slaughtered. At this point, the government decided to shelter friendly Indians in Philadelphia. Undeterred, the Paxton Boys marched on the capital, along the way "running the muzzles of their guns through windows, swearing and hallooing, attacking men without the least provocation, dragging them by the hair to the ground, and pretending to scalp them," scientist David Rittenhouse observed. On February 5, 1764, armed Philadelphia volunteers, hastily mobilized under Franklin's command, met the Paxton Boys at Germantown and persuaded them to submit their grievances to the government instead of trying to overthrow it. They finally dispersed.

In the wake of the Paxton Boys' march, an unprecedented sixty-three political pamphlets and ten political cartoons—the first in America—spewed forth from the presses of Philadelphia. Some attacked the "Piss-brute-arians" (Presbyterians) who killed helpless

Indians when they could find no hostiles to fight. Others damned Proprietor John Penn for neglecting frontier defense because he refused to approve money bills that taxed his lands. Still others condemned the Quakers, who would not fight Indians but mustered against their compatriots, and another set criticized the Pennsylvania Germans as ignorant dupes of the Quaker Party, which they invariably supported. An elegant Quaker was pictorially depicted seducing an Indian woman—literally sleeping with the enemy. Another main target was Benjamin Franklin, who was accused not only of scheming to replace the proprietor with a royal government (true) but also of plotting to become governor himself (questionable). What the pamphlets as a whole revealed was widespread disgust with all participants in an elitist, eastern government that had ruled peaceably for three-quarters of a century before 1755 only to collapse into impotence and mutual recriminations almost overnight when called on to defend itself. The pamphlets of 1764 show Pennsylvania's great internal revolution of 1776 in embryo.

THE REVOLUTION APPROACHES

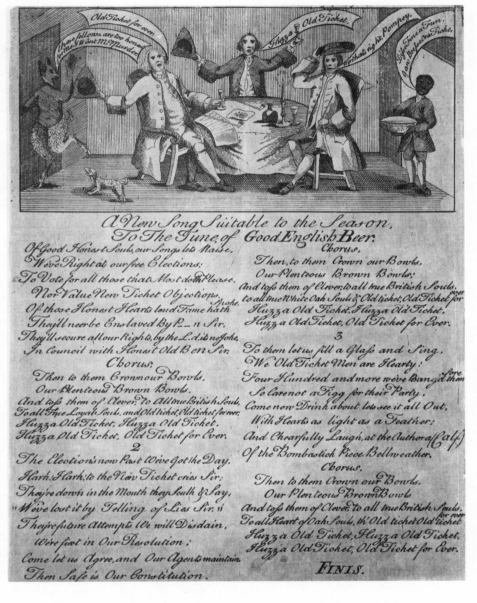

This political cartoon from the 1760s urged voters to continue the Quaker "old Ticket" in power, making the point that Quaker rule was as healthy for Pennsylvania as good English beer was for the British people. Note the well-dressed slave at right.

In the years leading up to the American Revolution, the Quaker Party and the Proprietary Party were swept aside. Pennsylvania's situation was unique: as other colonial elites were mobilizing to resist British taxes and trade regulations, the Quakers were courting royal favor to replace the Penn family, which had refused to pay taxes. The Penns were also currying favor at court, insisting that the Quakers had refused to fight the enemy. Unlike the Massachusetts House of Representatives or the Virginia House of Burgesses, Pennsylvania's Assembly, dominated by the Quaker Party and wealthy property holders from the old counties of Bucks, Chester, and Philadelphia, never endorsed either resistance or independence. In consequence, disgruntled members of both parties joined

Americans throughout the colonies regarded the Stamp Act of 1765 as signaling "dreadful, dismal, doleful, dolorous, and dollar-less" times ahead, as the caption accompanying this image claims. The British were astonished, because all the money would stay in America to defend the frontier. Furthermore, several colonies had passed stamp taxes of their own.

with Pennsylvanians hitherto excluded from political power, not only to oppose the British but also to create a Pennsylvania that was more responsive to popular needs. Pennsylvania exemplifies historian Carl Becker's point that the American Revolution was fought both to achieve home rule from Britain and to determine who was to rule at home.

Philadelphia workers joined with professional men and people from the newer counties to lead Pennsylvania's dual revolution against provincial and British authority. They had good reasons. Philadelphia was struck by a severe postwar depression swelled by an influx of immigrants and demobilized soldiers. As early as 1764 a doctor who worked among the poor said, "Tradesmen begin to grow clamorous for want of employment [and] our city is full of sailors who cannot procure berths. Who knows what the united resentments of these two numerous people may accomplish." People west of the Delaware Valley remembered the province's reluctance to defend them. Like the colonies vis-à-vis the British, they were taxed and ruled without representation.

Pennsylvania lagged behind other colonies in resisting the British. Its first organized opposition to the new policies of the taxation and trade regulation arose from a "half and half" party, so dubbed by its enemies because it drew strength from the dissatisfied in both the Quaker Party and the Proprietary Party. Its members preferred the label "Whigs," to identify with British politicians who defended popular and Parliamentary rights against a strong monarchy. Their leader was Philadelphia lawyer John Dickinson, who condemned the "prudent, peaceful, dutiful, and submissive behavior of this province" as opposed to the "hot-headed proceedings" of Massachusetts and New York. His most famous pamphlet was the 1767 *Letters of a Pennsylvania Farmer,* whose clever title was designed to take the city's political case to the colony's overwhelming majority in rural areas. Dickinson's was the first well-publicized pamphlet that denied all British authority to tax the colonies in any manner whatsoever. Once Parliament had its foot in the door, he wrote, "the several colonial legislatures would . . . before long fall into disuse" and "nothing would be left for them to do, higher than to frame by-laws for the empounding of cattle or the yoking of hogs."

But the "half and half Whigs" were moderates themselves. In 1765 they limited their protests against the Stamp Act—which placed a tax on all colonial legal documents and newspapers—to polite requests that Parliament repeal the law. Although they included Philadelphia merchants injured by Britain's stricter enforcement of trade regulations, the merchants refused for two years to join in the Non-Importation Agreement that their New York and Boston counterparts adopted in 1767 to protest the new Townshend Act duties on tea, glass, paint, and paper. Philadelphia's merchants caved in only when pressured by tradespeople, artisans, and laborers who joined sailors and shipbuilders to form the first independent working-class body of the Revolution in any city or colony.

In Pennsylvania, the conservatism of both Proprietary and Quaker elites opened a wedge for a radical lower- and middle-class movement to appear. Beginning in 1770 artisans successfully ran for city office. Obscure men who made their political fortunes

Timothy Matlack, by Charles Willson Peale, c. 1826.

Son of a Quaker brewer and merchant, and son-in-law of a Quaker preacher, Timothy Matlack seemed destined for respectable society. However, the Philadelphia Quaker Monthly Meeting disowned him in July 1765 for his bad debts, gambling, and general way of life. Matlack abhorred gentility and associated freely with blacks and "the lower sort." He loved the rough-and-tumble sporting culture: horse racing, bull-baiting, and especially cock-fighting. The 1770 intercolonial match between his bird and one belonging to the wealthy James Delancey of New York symbolically expressed the class tensions brewing in colonial cities. Matlack was instrumental in forming the Society of Free Quakers in 1781, composed of those "fighting Quakers" disowned by the Meeting for taking up arms in the cause of independence. And he was not above doing some fighting on his own: he caned two Quakers who criticized his son for taking up arms.

Matlack was one of the leaders who overthrew the Pennsylvania Assembly in the mid-1770s and installed Pennsylvania's radical government. His guiding principle was "All men are born free and equal," and he urged the abolition of slavery. As clerk to Charles Thomson, secretary of the Continental Congress, he is the most likely person to have prepared the final parchment draft of the Declaration of Independence. Matlack vehemently defended the 1776 Pennsylvania constitution he helped to write under the pseudonym "T.G." (for "Tiberius Gracchus," the Roman tribune who had hoped to distribute the property of the wealthy to the poor). His opponents called him "Tim Gaff."

Matlack, like Thomas Paine, was one of the few radicals of 1776 who also favored banking to aid commercial and industrial development. He joined the board of directors of the Bank of North America, which had been established by the opposition Republicans in 1781, but his new allies did not appreciate his change of heart. The State Assembly, now dominated by the Republicans (soon to be Federalists), called him an "upstart," a "demagogue," and a "villain" and charged him with mismanaging funds, although he was ultimately cleared.

After a brief stay in New York, Matlack returned to Philadelphia, held a variety of state offices, and married again in Christ Church. In 1799 he retired to Lancaster, where he tended his gardens and orchards, but the threat of a Federalist comeback as the War of 1812 approached caused him to move back to the city. Matlack again threw himself into the political fray as one of the "warmest Democrats," serving as alderman from 1813 to 1818 and prothonotary (keeper of public records) from 1817 to 1822. Only at the age of eighty-six did he finally retire to Holmesburg. Matlack's portrait, which may be viewed at the Gallery at Independence Hall National Historic Park, was painted in great old age and depicts him in a workingman's or liberty cap smoking a pipe. His desire to be remembered this way, unlike most leading citizens of the time, who were painted in formal clothes, calls attention to his lifelong identification with the common man.

through grassroots activism included Charles Thomson, a merchant of humble origins who was later praised as "the Sam Adams of Philadelphia"; David Rittenhouse, an aspiring astronomer; Charles Willson Peale, a young artist; Dr. Thomas Young, a New Yorker who had arrived via Boston; James Cannon, a mathematics professor at the College of Philadelphia; physicians Benjamin Rush and James Hutchinson; Timothy Matlack, an indebted shopkeeper noted for his fighting cocks; and political exile Thomas Paine, a fired British tax collector and former corsetmaker who joined the protests as soon as he landed in 1775. Unlike the merchants, lawyers, and estate owners who dominated the provincial government, these young men (mostly born in the 1740s) were either college-educated or self-taught intellectuals who wrote pamphlets and harangued crowds of workers with whom they socialized in the city's numerous taverns. They transformed the city's "crowd," the people in the streets, from a nonpolitical entity that had rioted only occasionally in times of emergency into a political body that mobilized at regular meetings in defiance of the government.

Until mid-1774, Pennsylvania's resistance was confined to Philadelphia. But when Governor John Penn refused to summon the Assembly to select delegates to the First Continental Congress—which was to debate the colonies' joint response to the Coercive Acts, passed by Britain to punish Boston for the "Tea Party"—Committees of Correspondence formed to select the delegates instead. Although jointly composed of radicals and moderates, as opposition to the Coercive Acts was almost unanimous, Philadelphia's working people first organized these Committees outside the structure of government and called for forming more of them throughout Pennsylvania.

After Congress convened in September 1774, Pennsylvania's radicals began a successful two-year campaign to overturn the province's conservative government. To encourage the radicals and prod the laggard elite, Congress turned down the Assembly's offer to meet in its chamber. Congress preferred instead to meet in Carpenters Hall, because, John Adams wrote, that location "was highly agreeable to the mechanics and citizens in general, but mortifying in the last degree to Joseph Galloway," the longtime Speaker of the Pennsylvania Assembly who led a fusion of Quaker and Proprietary forces into the "Tory" or "loyalist" camp. Congress then authorized the extralegal Committees of Associators forming throughout Pennsylvania to enforce the Continental Association to boycott commerce with the British. In May 1775, when the Assembly and the proprietor refused to act when war broke out at Lexington and Concord, these same Associators organized a militia system to send volunteers to fight with the newly created Continental Army. Lancaster, Berks, and York Counties each immediately sent a regiment to Massachusetts. At the same time, the militia itself, represented in Philadelphia and elsewhere by a Committee of Privates, issued broadsides and petitions, collected supplies, silenced loyalists, and in general educated people about the Revolution.

Insisting that commitment to the Revolution, rather than wealth, family, or education, ought to be the basis of political power, the Privates demanded that a reluctant

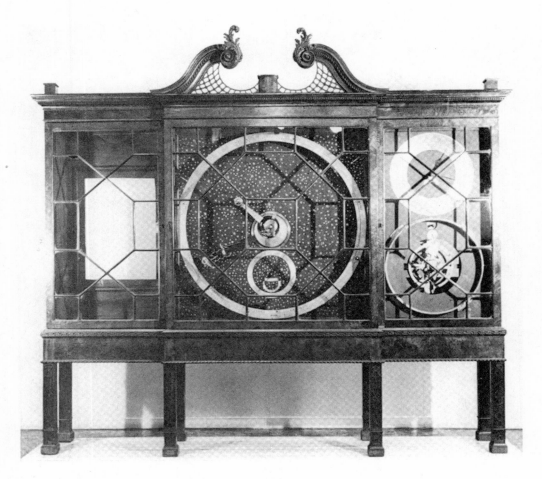

Eighteenth-century thinkers viewed the universe as a clocklike machine and believed society and politics could similarly be regulated by scientific laws. The classic example is the orrery, the first planetarium, designed by David Rittenhouse, which can still be viewed at the University of Pennsylvania Museum. Built between 1767 and 1771, this mechanical device with moving parts accurately showed the elliptical paths of the seven visible planets around the sun and permitted reproduction of solar eclipses and phases of the moon. Originally a clockmaker, Rittenhouse taught himself the necessary mathematics, physics, and astronomy required to build this intricate device, which stands as a monument to the ingenuity and hard work of an American "mechanic." Americans resented that the device was named after a British nobleman (the Earl of Orrery), who developed a later model, rather than after Rittenhouse.

Pennsylvania elite move toward independence, allow all soldiers to vote, permit the election of military officers by their men, and impose heavy penalties on those who refused to participate in the Revolution—notably pacifist Quakers. The city radicals criticized their own elite for the same reason that Americans fought the British: "Our great merchants [are] making immense fortunes at the expense of the people" and would "soon have the whole wealth of the province in their hands, and then the people will be nearly in the condition that the East India Company have reduced the natives of Bengal to." They demanded that the province "put all on that equal footing which the common danger and the common interest required." The wealthy in turn denounced the "damned riff-raff, dirty, mutinous, and disaffected" as "a number of violent, wrongheaded people of the inferior sort." Nowhere in America were the rhetoric and politics of class so pronounced as in Pennsylvania, as nowhere else had the elite so overwhelmingly resisted the Revolution.

Ultimately it required Congress itself to overthrow a Pennsylvania Assembly that refused to budge. By 1776 the movement for independence was growing, inspired in large part by Thomas Paine's pamphlet *Common Sense,* published in Philadelphia, which

The Pennsylvania Constitution of 1776 produced the fiercest internal political strife in the new nation. This political cartoon shows artisans or workers defending the constitution against wealthy members of the elite.

denounced monarchy in general, George III as the "royal brute," and Britain as a "monster," not a "mother," country. He called for an independent America "to begin the world anew" and serve as "an asylum for mankind," as Pennsylvania had been for himself and so many others. In May, for Pennsylvania's benefit, Congress adopted John Adams's resolution that "where no government sufficient to the exigencies of affairs existed" the people should themselves adopt one "best conducive to their happiness and safety." Seizing the moment, the leader of the Committee of Privates, James Cannon, declared that the Pennsylvania Assembly "have abdicated the government, and by their acts of detestable cowardice have laid the Provincial Conference under the necessity of taking instant charge of affairs." Calling for a convention in June, the radicals declared the Assembly dissolved and permitted only those who repudiated allegiance to the crown and swore they believed in the Holy Trinity to vote for representatives who would write the state's constitution—thereby eliminating most Quakers and much of the population in the three older counties. The Assembly, which to the last repudiated independence, quietly went out of existence in the fall of 1776.

By the time Congress proclaimed independence, Pennsylvania politics were in turmoil. Franklin's old allies in the Quaker Party, such as Joseph Galloway, had become loyalists; and so had his old foe, Chief Justice William Allen, who led the proprietary faction. Franklin, on the other hand, emerged as the grand old man of the radicals and first president of the Commonwealth of Pennsylvania. He had learned from the Stamp Act riots—directed against his own house, which his wife Deborah had defended while he was in England—that his fellow countrymen would not tolerate acceptance of British policies they could not prevent. And Franklin had been humiliated and virtually forced out of England in 1774 for conveying the private letters of Massachusetts Governor Thomas Hutchinson to his Boston opponents. For his part, John Dickinson led a moderate faction in favor of military resistance but opposed to independence. He is famous for remarking, "Before we are prepared to build the new house, why should we pull down the old one, and expose ourselves to all the inclemencies of the season?" The Quaker Meeting continued to expel members who participated in the war, begetting a group of "Fighting Quakers," which included Matlack and Hutchinson. Proprietor John Penn tried to remain neutral, and he did such a good job of it that in the nineteenth century the federal government compensated his descendants for the confiscation of his estates during the Revolution.

About all that can be said concisely about Pennsylvania in 1776 is that, apart from many loyalists and neutrals, two groups crystallized. The radicals, or Constitutionalists, implemented a revolutionary state government, while the moderates, or Republicans, opposed the Commonwealth's constitution and its redistribution of power down the social ladder and to the western parts of the state. Until the moderates (by then known as Federalists) triumphed in 1790, Pennsylvania's 1776 constitution stood at the center of the most tumultuous state politics in the new nation. Observing the scene, John Adams exclaimed: "Good God! The people of Pennsylvania in seven years will be glad to petition the Crown of Britain for reconciliation in order to be delivered from the tyranny of their new constitution." They did not go that far, but Pennsylvania's radicals offered a populist alternative to the elite rule that had characterized the colony in the past and that would return to the state in the mid-1780s.

THE REVOLUTION WITHIN PENNSYLVANIA

Historians have sometimes praised Pennsylvania's 1776 constitution as the most democratic of those adopted by the new states. To be sure, it had democratic features; free taxpayers (including blacks) and their sons over the age of twenty-one were eligible to vote, and representation was now weighted in favor of the more radical western counties. An enlarged Assembly was chosen annually and had to take its laws back to the people, except in emergency cases, before final approval the next year. In the nation's first experiment in rotation in office, representatives could serve for only four years out of seven, to hinder them from aggrandizing power. The only check on the Assembly came from a Council of Censors, which could call attention to abuses and recommend changes in the constitution. A president was just that—he presided over the Assembly.

While the American colonies fought for liberty and independence against Great Britain, many people struggled for their personal rights against the new revolutionary government. Isaac Klinkerfuss, a Hessian peasant, was forced to serve in America by the greedy Duke of Hesse, who sold his subjects as mercenaries to fight for the British. One of many Germans captured in October 1777 at the Battle of Saratoga, Klinkerfuss escaped. Upon arriving in Pennsylvania, he ran afoul of Dr. Andrew Ledlie of Easton, who was district commissioner for prisoners. Ledlie blackmailed Klinkerfuss as a "deserter" who could be detained until the two sides agreed to an exchange of prisoners. Threatening to send Klinkerfuss to jail or to a camp for prisoners of war, Ledlie extorted labor and money from the unfortunate veteran. When Klinkerfuss, a skilled stonemason, balked at quarrying 300 or 400 loads of stone, Ledlie imprisoned him and proceeded to beat him "in a very cruel manner, making as it is said, a hole in his head." To add insult to injury, Ledlie claimed that Klinkerfuss owed him money for curing him of a venereal disease.

Ledlie's behavior enraged Robert Levers, head of the Northampton County Associators, who claimed that the Congressional Board of War, under whose authority Ledlie acted, had no right to jail anyone in Pennsylvania. "So far from enforcing an order for the confinement of the Hessian prisoners of war, I have pitied them in their state of vassalage," Levers wrote to Pennsylvania's Governor William Moore. As Mrs. Klinkerfuss was preparing to take Levers's case to Philadelphia, Ledlie finally gave up and freed her husband.

Klinkerfuss moved to New Jersey, where he became a prominent citizen of Sussex County. As with hundreds of German prisoners

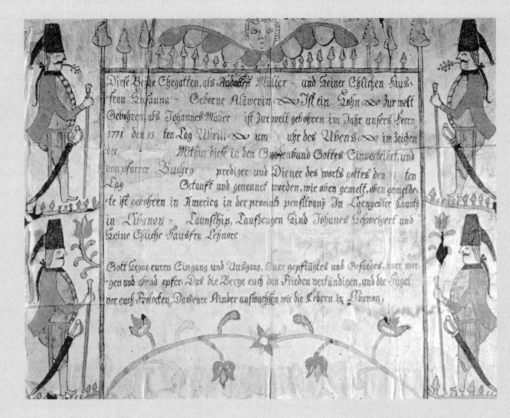

of war—many of them loosely detained near Reading and Bethlehem, where they were permitted to wander about and earn their keep to fill the wartime labor shortage—Klinkerfuss's story had a happy ending. After escaping the clutches of a war profiteer and a tyrannical revolutionary government official, this European peasant became an American citizen.

ABOVE: This certificate of birth and baptism employs the Fraktur script and decoration typical of Pennsylvania German legal documents. It depicts four Hessian soldiers with their characteristic pigtails.

Yet in one important way, Pennsylvania's constitution was very undemocratic. Participation in politics required a "Test Oath" affirming loyalty to the constitution, which disfranchised Quakers, neutrals, and loyalists. The extreme concentration of power in the hands of a popularly elected Assembly also aroused fears from moderate revolutionaries, who complained that the constitution installed "the most unbounded liberty and yet no kind of barrier to prevent its degenerating into licentiousness." They considered it to be an "absurd and foolish doctrine [that] was too successfully propagated among the unthinking *many*—that men of property, however much they might have at stake, men of experience and knowledge, however well they might have acquitted themselves in former trusts, were carefully to be avoided."

To deal with its many opponents, the new government employed what were known as Committees of Safety and Committees of Associators throughout the state to enforce its edicts. To their credit, they kept General George Washington and the Continental Army supplied with food, clothing, and munitions, even if the price was sometimes too high, the quantity too low, and the delivery too slow. Farmers from the interior ensured that the army did not starve at Valley Forge during the winter of 1777–78. Despite many discomforts, Valley Forge, located on high bluffs twenty-two miles northwest of Philadelphia on the Schuylkill River, proved to be an ideal location for Washington and his troops to receive supplies, remain immune from British attacks, and subdue the considerable loyalist sentiment in Bucks and Chester Counties. But as the war dragged on, more force and less persuasion were required to collect taxes, raise troops, and obtain supplies, as paper money became almost worthless.

Between 1776 and 1782, when the Republicans swept into power, supporters of the Constitution of 1776 gradually went over to the opposition. James Cannon, a principal author of the document, disapproved of the Test Oath. He claimed that only "fools, blockheads, [and] self-righteous and zealous bigots" determined to "keep some of the best and most valuable men out of government" supported the oath. Neither Thomas Paine, a Deist, nor Timothy Matlack, a disowned Quaker, approved of it either. Benjamin Rush, appalled by the militia and mechanics in the streets who rounded up supplies and suspected loyalists, found the one-house legislature "big with tyranny." He was soon condemning the new Assembly as "our state dung cart with all its dirty content." Matlack and Paine later joined leading Republicans like Robert Morris in organizing the Bank of North America to fund the army and stimulate commerce. David Rittenhouse left politics to continue his scientific work. Charles Willson Peale became the new nation's most famous artist and began its first museum in Philadelphia in 1786.

Support for the 1776 state constitution varied by region. Philadelphia, Bucks, and Chester Counties had dominated the colonial Assembly, to which they elected conservative Anglicans and Quakers. The Delaware Valley contained many loyalists and neutrals and in general supported the Revolution reluctantly. (One exception was Chester's General "Mad Anthony" Wayne.) Except for Philadelphia workers and a small minority

Military action in the American Revolution came to Pennsylvania only at the very end of 1776. Chased across New Jersey by British columns led by General Lord Charles Cornwallis, General Washington regrouped his scattered forces at the end of December. The day after Christmas, he crossed the Delaware River from Pennsylvania into New Jersey, at the site now known as Washington Crossing Historic Park. The general's four-pronged force surprised and surrounded the Hessian garrison at Trenton and forced more than 1,000 troops to surrender. By defeating another British force at Princeton, New Jersey, on January 2, 1777, Washington restored morale and preserved an army that had been badly mauled in and around New York City in August and September.

The remainder of 1777 provided mixed results for American forces in Pennsylvania. British Commander-in-Chief General Sir

William Howe resolved to take part of his large army, which was occupying New York, and head for Philadelphia, where he hoped (in vain) that the region's numerous loyalists and neutrals would flock to his standards. Howe did not reach Pennsylvania until early September, however, squandering most of the year's campaigning weather. (Large armies could not maneuver in winter because they might be trapped in snowstorms.) It seems incredible today that to reach Philadelphia, only ninety miles away, Howe transported the British soldiers from New York into the Atlantic Ocean, around the eastern shore of Maryland, and up Chesapeake Bay. But he had no choice: a strung-out column of more than 10,000 soldiers could have been ambushed in New Jersey, and patriot Forts Mifflin and Mercer and *chevaux-de-frise* (underwater defenses that could rip holes in ship bottoms) blocked the Delaware River.

ABOVE: "The Battle of Germantown," by Xavier della Gatta, 1782 (detail). The Chew Mansion, "Cliveden," which is much larger than it appears here, survives today as a museum and is the site of annual battle reenactments in Germantown.

Howe's army finally met Washington's on September 10 at Brandywine Creek. Washington defended the likely crossings, but repeating the same maneuver that had proven so disastrous for the revolutionaries at the Battle of Long Island, Howe sent a column around the Americans far to the right, catching Washington between the two forces and inflicting 1,200 casualties.

Washington's forces, however, withdrew in good order. Later in September, Howe began to occupy Philadelphia and fortify it against possible attacks. With the British now divided throughout the region and not expecting the defeated Americans to attempt

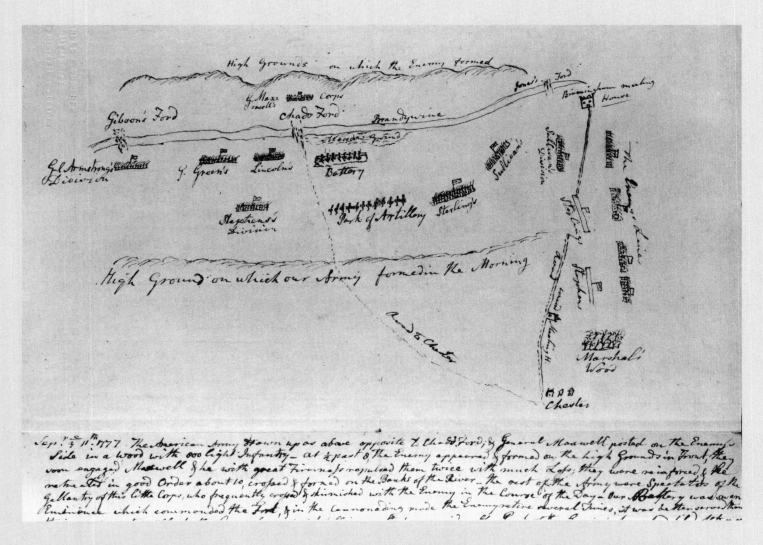

a major assault, Washington saw a chance to attack their principal camp at Germantown. He used the same plan he had at Trenton: on October 4, four columns would attack at dawn, surprising the British, with good fortune surrounding them, and forcing Howe to surrender the main British army in the colonies. It might have worked except for a dense fog that caused general confusion, and when the air finally cleared, the Americans spent too much time attacking a small British force entrenched in the mansion of Benjamin Chew. This enabled the British to regroup and repulse the Americans. But the Americans withdrew intact and in high spirits.

Along with the surrender of British General John Burgoyne at Saratoga, New York, on October 17, Germantown impressed the French that the American army was a viable fighting force and that declaring war on the British was a good proposition. Washington's army, however, centering its winter quarters at Valley Forge so as to block British access to the rich Pennsylvania countryside (in fact, American troops guarded a region stretching into Delaware and New Jersey), did not learn until the following spring that their sacrifices had paid off.

ABOVE: The Battle of Brandywine, September 11, 1777, as depicted by George Weedon of Virginia. Weedon sketched the line of Washington's troops before the battle and later that day wrote a brief account of the battle below his drawing.

Charles Willson Peale, "A Representation of the Figures exhibited and paraded through the Streets of Philadelphia" (1780). Benedict Arnold commanded the American troops in Philadelphia from 1778 to 1779. He consorted with former loyalists and married the young Peggy Shippen, from a loyalist family. When news of his treason reached Philadelphia, a two-faced Arnold was paraded in the streets and burned in effigy. The scene in the background shows Arnold fleeing West Point to the safety of the British fleet. This print also shows how lower- and middle-class Philadelphians took to the streets to express their views and entered political life during the revolutionary period.

of the upper class, those city merchants and prosperous commercial farmers from the surrounding region who supported the Revolution were moderates. Loyalists, termed "bandits" by revolutionaries, included James Fitzpatrick of Chester County, and the Doan "gang" of Bucks waged guerrilla warfare much like their patriot counterpart, the "Swamp Fox" Francis Marion of South Carolina. In the three old counties, as a result of the Test Oaths, a minority composed mostly of Scots-Irish Presbyterian and German Reformed landowners seized control of the Revolution.

Regardless of their residence, the Revolution was especially empowering for Pennsylvania Germans. Before the Revolution they had followed the lead of the Quaker Party without actively seeking political office. During the war, although the Moravians, Mennonites, and other small sects joined the pacifist Quakers in refusing to take sides, members of the Lutheran and Reformed churches—the vast majority of Germans—joined enthusiastically in the struggle. Prominent German American revolutionaries included David Rittenhouse, the Continental Army's Surgeon General Dr. Bodo Otto of Reading, and the brothers Muhlenberg, who left Lutheran pulpits—Peter to serve as a general, Frederick to be a member of Congress. "In Pennsylvania, our chief reliance is upon the Germans," Charles Thomson commented with only moderate exaggeration.

However, as elsewhere in the new nation, the British attempt to capitalize on loyalist sentiment in the Delaware Valley backfired. During the British occupation of Philadelphia in 1777–78, Sir William Howe's redcoats made enemies even among the favorably disposed. Many revolutionaries fled before their arrival, and the patriots in turn had already shipped off the most important loyalists and Quaker merchants to a prison camp in Winchester, Virginia. On both sides of the political fence, women had to head the households of their absent husbands. Elizabeth Drinker heard daily "of enormities of one kind or other being committed by those from whom we ought to find protection."

Obliged to feed and quarter high-living officers and obstreperous troops, Philadelphia women expressed disgust at the "shameful scene of dissipation" that culminated at the Meschianza, an elaborate farewell party held on May 18, 1778, for General William Howe. Howe was recalled to Britain to answer charges that after defeating the rebel army he settled comfortably into winter quarters, failing to pursue Washington's army, which was being trained by Prussian drillmaster "Baron" Von Steuben only twenty-two miles away on the uncomfortable but defensible heights of Valley Forge. At the farewell, officers dressed up as medieval knights held a mock tournament as Philadelphia belles appeared as maidens from a Turkish harem. Some former slaves, lured to British lines with promises of freedom, play-acted their former servitude.

Things did not improve for the city when the revolutionaries arrived on June 18, only fifteen minutes after the last British troops evacuated Philadelphia. Now wives of prominent loyalists lost their homes. The patriots arrested 638 men on charges of treason—although only 7 were executed and 121 lost their property. Loyalist poet Hannah Griffitts commented, "In the . . . scene of desolation, the British and American armies may each take their part, share and share alike." By May 1779 the Philadelphia militia ordered food prices fixed to combat a vicious circle of price rises and currency depreciation. Broadsides throughout the city proclaimed: "By the living God, we have turned out the enemy and we will not be eaten up by monopolizers and forestallers." Soldiers searched warehouses, jailed suspected loyalists, and blamed a "combination" of those who were "getting rich by sucking the blood" of their fellow citizens for what they termed a pretended scarcity. But given increasingly worthless Continental money, farmers sold their produce elsewhere—where possible, for British gold in New York. Despite its lackluster support for the Revolution, the Delaware Valley prospered during and after the war as farmers and millers supplied an increasing demand for flour among loyalists and the British army and in the West Indies, especially in rapidly growing Saint Domingue (Haiti) and Cuba.

Militia price-fixing prompted Philadelphia's greatest riot of the Revolution. On October 4, 1779, troops seized four suspected profiteers and then marched on the house of James Wilson. Although he had signed the Declaration of Independence, Wilson was a moderate with loyalist friends. Hearing the crowd coming, Wilson gathered twenty sympathetic men and barricaded himself in what became known as "Fort Wilson." Radical leader Charles Willson Peale tried to persuade the attackers to disperse, but instead they brought up a cannon when they could not break down Wilson's doors. Only the arrival of the Light Horse Regiment, led by the state's Constitutionalist President Joseph Reed and Timothy Matlack, ended the affair. When it was over, six or

ELIZABETH DRINKER, 1735–1807

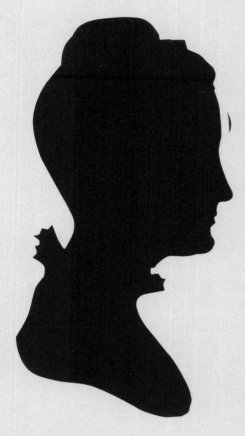

Silhouette of Elizabeth Drinker. Because many Quakers believed portraits were signs of vanity, only this graceful silhouette provides an idea of what Drinker looked like.

For forty-nine years, from 1758 until her death, Elizabeth Sandwith Drinker, wife of prominent Quaker merchant Henry Drinker of Philadelphia, kept a diary. In the years before the Revolution her entries are short and reflect the time and care she lavished on her five surviving children (she bore nine in all). But as with so many Americans, the Revolution forced her into the public realm against her will. In September 1777 Henry Drinker refused to sign a loyalty oath to the new government and was one of twenty Quakers banished to Winchester, Virginia. The following March, Elizabeth joined three other wives in pleading for his release before George Washington and the Pennsylvania state government. Her month-long journey may have aided her husband's release in April. During the Revolution, Drinker expressed frequent loyalist sympathies, complaining of "the tyrannical conduct of the present wicked rulers" (September 9, 1777). Of the revolutionary Tom Paine she later (December 16, 1796) wrote: "A better, more thorough past agent, the Old one [Satan] cannot have, I think, than this same T.P. The wise, the virtuous and informed see through him; but the ignorant, the weak, and the vicious readily fall into his snare."

Drinker's range of reading was astonishing. She had mixed feelings about Mary Wollstonecraft's *A Vindication of the Rights of Women:* "In very many of her sentiments, she . . . speaks my mind, [but] . . . I am not for quite so much independence" (April 22, 1796). Confucius, however, gave her pure pleasure: "If there were such men in that day, what ought to be expected in this more enlightened age!" (May 28, 1795).

Drinker was conservative, but her views on slavery changed with the times. She had always been protective and generous toward her slaves and servants, taking in homeless blacks (December 6, 1794) and having her neighbors ("Dutch folk") arrested for beating her servant "Black Tom" when he threw a stone at their vicious dog (May 23–24, 1782). In one of her last diary entries, Drinker was visited by Judy, a slave that she and her sister had sold fifty-one years earlier when "there was nothing against the keeping or selling negroes." They later regretted their action and tried unsuccessfully twice to buy Judy back at a substantial loss in order to free her. Yet the Drinkers' arguments may have had some effect, for Elizabeth notes that Judy's master freed her when he died (October 12, 1807). In this entry as in many others, Drinker's diary provides a telling anecdote that humanizes the study of race relations, politics, and the life of women in early Pennsylvania.

Esther DeBerdt Reed. The wife of the president of the Commonwealth of Pennsylvania, Esther Reed raised money from Pennsylvania women to aid a bankrupt national government in 1780. Her portrait reflects the appearance of an elegant woman of the day but belies her radicalism. Reed's effort to mobilize women to raise money for the Continental Army was the most significant attempt to organize American women thus far—and this female activity troubled General Washington, although he was glad to receive the money.

THE ALLIES. — *Par nobile fratrum!*

A 1780 cartoon criticizes the British use of Indians during the Revolution. King George III shares a feast of his former subjects with cannibals and a dog, while a bishop approves of the grisly behavior. Indians were not cannibals. Behind the bishop is a slave carrying scalping knives, crucifixes, and tomahawks. This propaganda piece thus recognizes that many slaves ran away from colonial masters to fight for the British and their own freedom.

seven people had been killed, and between fourteen and seventeen were wounded. Fort Wilson marked a turning point: radical leaders were forced to acknowledge that the new constitution was leading to the very disorder their opponents had predicted.

Little internal disorder hindered the revolutionary ardor of Pennsylvania's settled central region—Lancaster, Berks, York, Cumberland, and Northampton Counties—which overwhelmingly joined the Philadelphia lower orders to support the state constitution. Here the iron foundries made guns for the Continental Army, the fertile soil grew its grain and supplied its livestock, and thousands of soldiers, including the famous Pennsylvania riflemen, enlisted in the army for long periods.

The interior counties prospered during the Revolution, but because so many of their men were away in the army, stay-at-homes grew rich from government contracts while soldiers returned laden with worthless money and promissory notes. Lancaster—source of the superb Pennsylvania rifles (sometimes misnamed Kentucky rifles)—was the largest inland town in British North America, with some 4,500 inhabitants. The poorest 60 percent of taxpayers held one-third of Lancaster's wealth in 1751 but only 13 percent in 1788. York, the temporary national capital when the British occupied Philadelphia, also developed a more pronounced class structure. Artisans, farmers, and munitions makers took what payments they could from the elite refugees, while condemning them for holding balls and performing plays—the same grievances the people of Philadelphia had against the occupying British. Congressmen in turn denounced York as a "horrid scene of extortion," "the most inhospitable scandalous place," and, in the words of Benjamin Rush, "the damndest hole in the world."

The Pennsylvania rifle was famous for its accuracy in an age when muskets were notoriously cumbersome and unreliable and not likely to hit a target more than 100 yards away. The Pennsylvania rifle was accurate to 300 yards and proved effective in hunting small game. In western parts of the early republic, the Pennsylvania rifle was sometimes called the Kentucky rifle. The one shown here features a hand-carved, curly maple stock with engraved brass inlays and is a fine example of the work of the early Pennsylvania gunsmith. It is attributed to Frederick Sell, of Littlestown, Adams County, and dates to about 1810.

As the war dragged on, Pennsylvanians increasingly refused or were unable to pay their state taxes. The state filed thousands of lawsuits against delinquents in the 1780s, and as a result courts ordered sold the lands and goods of between 12 and 40 percent of the taxpayers in any given county. The people responded by forming covenants against their own revolutionary government, that they would not buy confiscated property and that they would intimidate anyone who did. They also blockaded narrow passes on roads to prevent the removal of their goods or the arrival of government officials. Some imaginative resisters piled a small mountain of manure on a road in Westmoreland County, forcing the authorities to bear with the stench as they tore it down.

Tax resistance exhibited the state's impotence and the Constitutionalist leadership's remoteness from the people as the war ended. Only a minority of inhabitants ever took the Test Oath required to participate in political life. Even after the oath was abolished in 1786, only about one-quarter of all eligible Pennsylvanians voted for delegates to the Constitutional Convention in 1787 and the First Congress in 1788. Most people remained outside the political system, becoming actively involved only when government threatened their immediate interests, usually by imposing taxes they considered excessive.

It was survival, not taxation, that was the main problem on Pennsylvania's frontiers. The Revolution was just another complication in struggles that began before and continued after the war. Beginning in the 1750s, Yankees from overcrowded Connecticut journeyed through New York and into the fertile Wyoming Valley to the north fork of the Susquehanna. On April 19, 1763, they burned the principal Indian settlement at Wyoming and killed its leader, Teedyuscung, to whom Pennsylvania had granted the right to live in the valley. Captain Bull, Teedyuscung's son, in turn burned out the Connecticut intruders that October in the easternmost action of Pontiac's Rebellion.

The Iroquois feared Connecticut occupation of the Wyoming Valley, because that valley was the main corridor through which whites could approach their stronghold in northwestern New York. Thus in 1768, at the Treaty of Fort Stanwix (now Rome, New York), they invited the less-hostile Pennsylvanians to settle the valley instead. From 1769 to 1784, Connecticut and Pennsylvania settlers fought the Yankee-Pennamite War. Many of the Paxton Boys aided the Yankees; during the Revolution, the Pennsylvanians accepted the assistance of Tory guerrilla leader John Butler and loyalist Iroquois. On July 3, 1778, the famous "Wyoming Massacre" took place: 500 Indians and loyalists

PENNSYLVANIA INDIANS AND THE REVOLUTION: CORNPLANTER AND HANDSOME LAKE

Before the American Revolution, the vast frontier bordering the Great Lakes on the north and the Gulf of Mexico on the south, the Appalachians on the east, and the Mississippi River on the west was the scene of complex interactions among Native Americans, Spaniards, French, British, colonists, and mixtures among them in which skin color did not distinguish friend from foe. But because most Indians sided with the British during the Revolution, in the hope of saving their lands from the voracious colonists, a new mentality emerged with only two sides: "whites" had to oppose the "redskins" and either expel or exterminate them.

The Iroquois, of whom most favored the British, were unable to negotiate their fate in the new republic. Cornplanter (*Ki-on-twog-ky*), son of a Seneca woman and a Dutch trader from Albany, New York, fought for the British during the Revolution, then made peace with the Americans. In 1791 he persuaded the Iroquois to cede the "Erie Triangle" in northwestern Pennsylvania to the state so it could have an outlet to the Great Lakes. The Iroquois received $5,000 from Pennsylvania, which then paid the federal government $150,000 to clear the area of federal land titles. For his efforts Cornplanter received a medal from President Washington and land on the Allegheny River just south of the New York border. He brought in Quaker missionaries, established schools, and tried to persuade his people to raise crops and cattle. However, whites were more interested in exploiting the Iroquois. As a result, many Iroquois became dependent on white trade goods, including alcohol, and became despondent.

Cornplanter's half-brother Handsome Lake (Skaniadariyo) rescued his people. In 1799, having led an aimless and unhappy existence,

ABOVE: *Cornplanter, Ki-on-twog-ky*, by F. Bartoli, 1796.

Handsome Lake experienced a series of mystical visions while near death from illness. Messengers from the Creator appeared to him and taught him the Gaiwiio, or "Good News": Indians were to give up liquor, adultery, and quarreling among themselves; they were instead to be proud of their heritage and not imitate the white people. Jesus Christ had given up on the immoral whites and their perverted Christianity, and now the Indians would enjoy Jesus' favor if they adhered to his teachings as interpreted by Handsome Lake. Until his death in 1815, Handsome Lake preached his "New Religion" to the Iroquois in New York and Pennsylvania. Cornplanter, before he died in his mid-eighties in

1836, took up Handsome Lake's teachings, closed the missions, and destroyed the medal Washington had given him.

Even after two centuries many Iroquois continue to follow the path of Handsome Lake, whose religion offered such a strong sense of identity that the New York Iroquois still maintain self-respect and a measure of independence within the United States. But no Iroquois settlement remains in Pennsylvania. In 1964 the Seneca reservation containing Cornplanter's town was flooded to become part of the Kinzua Dam Reservoir. The story of this final dispossession is in Chapter 7.

The new coat of arms for Philadelphia, designed in 1789, expressed postrevolutionary optimism that commerce and agriculture would produce peace and plenty tempered by justice. Pregnant women symbolize the fertile land, whose population was doubling every twenty or thirty years. This is an 1821 Thomas Sully painting of the coat of arms.

surrounded Forty Fort, near present-day Wilkes-Barre. Within half an hour, 227 of the 400 Connecticut militia who marched out to meet them were killed in an ambush.

Because the Connecticut people, like most New Englanders, were staunch revolutionaries, the Pennsylvanians became identified with the loyalists; for both groups, however, the Revolution was secondary to acquiring possession of the Wyoming Valley. As late as 1784, Pennsylvania militia were driving out Yankees. In 1787 Congress ruled that the territory in fact belonged to Pennsylvania, but it granted the Connecticut people their private land. Exactly which land was theirs, however, took another two decades to decide.

Western Pennsylvanians faced equal tribulation. On the eve of the Revolution, Virginia's governor Lord Dunmore sent an expedition against the Indians still occupying the area and formed three Virginia counties. Pennsylvania responded by establishing Westmoreland County in 1773, but had almost no authority in the area. Nevertheless, in 1779 Virginia agreed to a boundary extending the Mason-Dixon Line—the 233-mile border surveyed between 1764 and 1768 to separate Maryland and Pennsylvania—another 84 miles to the present western border of the state, the five degrees longitude from the Delaware River that William Penn's Charter had stipulated. The region's Virginia settlers, however, were less compliant. Armed mobs prevented the boundary from being surveyed until 1784.

Shawnee and Delaware Indians were even more troublesome than the Virginians. Hanna's Town, the county seat of newly formed Washington County, was burned by Indians in 1782. It was never resettled. That same year, frontier men massacred ninety peaceful Christian Delaware Indians at Gnadenhutten in the Ohio Valley in the infamous "squaw campaign"; in retaliation, the expedition's leader was tortured to death after his capture. Federal troops sent in 1784 to secure the west quarreled with local inhabitants and their officers, who tried to prevent their drunken brawls. Too weak to confront the Indians, the small force instead burned the dwellings of whites whose extended settlements threatened to provoke Indian attacks. As late as 1791, attacks occurred on the outskirts of Pittsburgh; only with the Battle of Fallen Timbers in 1795 in present-day Ohio was the far western portion of the state finally secure.

Wracked by small-scale yet persistent and devastating warfare, both the northern and the western frontiers were lucky to survive during the revolutionary era. Visiting the Wyoming Valley in 1786, Timothy Pickering commented: "I did not imagine such general apparent wretchedness could be found in the United States." This matched a description of the west: "The country . . . is very poor in everything but its soil. . . . Money we have not nor any practicable way of making it."

In sum, Pennsylvania's Constitutionalist government failed to keep order, pay debts, maintain the value of currency, win the allegiance of perhaps half the inhabitants, and protect the frontiers. The increasingly successful moderates, or Republicans, led by a circle of Philadelphia merchants centering on Robert Morris and including James Wilson and a more conservative Benjamin Rush, directed these charges against both the state and the weak national government of the Articles of Confederation, under which Congress conducted the Revolution based on the voluntary cooperation of the states. Federal and state impotence merged strikingly in the inability of either government to control the mutinous behavior of Pennsylvania soldiers. On New Year's Day 1781 several hundred Pennsylvanians in the Continental Army, their courage bolstered with liquor, killed and wounded several officers when informed they had enlisted in the army not just for three years, as they had thought, but for the duration of the war. They disbanded only when Joseph Reed promised them amnesty and offered to discharge anyone claiming to have served three years. In June 1783 several hundred Pennsylvania soldiers encamped at Lancaster, impatient to be paid, marched on Philadelphia, surrounded the Continental Congress, and insulted the delegates. Congress, to escape future threats, departed for Trenton, then Princeton, and finally New York City. For too many Pennsylvanians, what had begun as an experiment in participatory democracy had turned into an exercise in military despotism.

CONSTRUCTING MODERN PENNSYLVANIA

As Pennsylvania recovered from the Revolution, the state's boosters transformed its image as well as its economy. They reenvisioned William Penn's rural, pacifist refuge instead as a commercial and industrial powerhouse at the center of a dynamic American nation. Urging that the national capital be placed in Philadelphia, Benjamin Rush bragged: "Here the people are natives of America and visibly interested in its prosperity. Manufactures and human improvements of every kind flourish."

Rush had accurately described the situation. Between 1780 and 1800 the Republican Pennsylvanians, who generally became Federalists by the mid-1780s, developed numerous plans and institutions to restore prosperity along with elite authority. They created banks, formed societies to further economic development and social reform, undertook new commercial and industrial ventures, and altered the state government. Most important of all, Pennsylvania Federalists were instrumental in joining with their like-minded countrymen to frame the United States Constitution.

Banking in Pennsylvania arose out of the Continental Army's shortage of funds. On July 17, 1780, ninety-two Philadelphia merchants had raised £315,000 in Pennsylvania currency and established the Bank of Pennsylvania, the first in the United States, to assist the army. It was soon supplanted by the Bank of North America, chartered by Congress in December 1781. Robert Morris, superintendent of finance for the national

JOHN FITCH (1743–1798) AND THE FIRST STEAMBOAT

Credit for inventing the steamboat has frequently been misattributed to Robert Fulton of Lancaster County, who built the *Clermont* in New York, but most evidence points to Pennsylvania's John Fitch as the first to develop this machine. His invention, first viewed on August 22, 1787, by delegates to the Constitutional Convention and their fellow citizens on the shores of the Delaware River, appeared during a period of economic optimism in which the state sponsored banks and roads while private associations formed to place Pennsylvania at the forefront of the new nation's economic development. Fitch's steamboat used an engine of the sort designed by James Watt that propelled six oars on each side. In 1789 Fitch and his partner Henry Voight developed a new boat with a double-acting engine and rear paddle. By 1790 their third boat was operating a packet service between Philadelphia and Burlington and Trenton in New Jersey. It logged 2,000 miles at eight miles an hour before it went out of business.

Another contender for the invention was Maryland's James Rumsey, whose model appeared a month after Fitch's. For about six years, Fitch and Rumsey disputed which boat was the best before the American Philosophical Society, various state legislatures, and the Continental Congress, then took their respective plans to Europe in the hope of receiving the acclaim denied them in their native land. Their squabble was a major reason the federal government passed its Patent Act in 1790; the Patent Office refused to take sides and granted the two men their patents on the same day.

Competition with Rumsey was only one of John Fitch's problems. Born in Goshen, Lancaster County, Fitch worked without much

Plan of M.ʳ Fitch's Steam Boat.

ABOVE: America's first working, but not profitable, steamboat.

success as a farmer, surveyor, seaman, brass-button-maker, clockmaker, silversmith, and gunsmith before serving as a militia lieutenant in the Revolution. He married in 1767, then abandoned his wife and child within a year. In 1782 Indians friendly to the British captured him while he was surveying in the Ohio Valley, where he was also a land speculator. They turned Fitch over to the British at Detroit, who released him in New York City on Christmas Day 1782.

Fitch then moved to Bucks County, Pennsylvania, which served as his base for more trips westward and fund-raising for his steamboat experiments. After his trip to Europe in 1793–94, he took up residence in Bardstown, Kentucky, hoping to claim land he had surveyed a decade earlier, but the settlers only ridiculed him. He turned to drink and opium pills, and in 1798 he took an overdose and left the "damn wicked world" he had castigated in his autobiography for failing to appreciate "one of the greatest and most useful arts that was ever introduced." One can only guess how many casualties like John Fitch paved Pennsylvania's path to progress. Unlike the success stories of the Franklins and the Fultons, those of the Fitches rarely come to light.

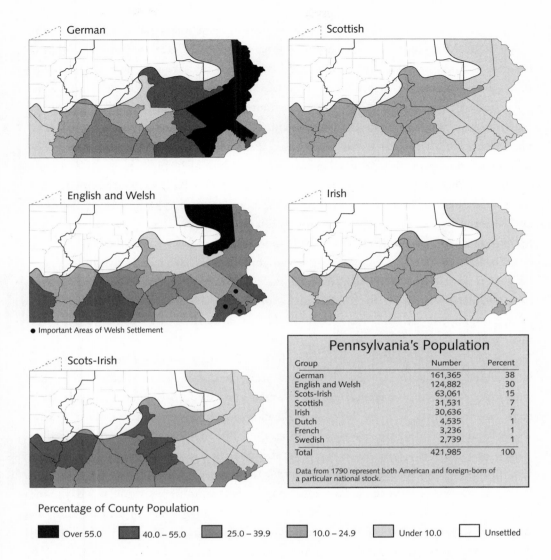

German

Scottish

English and Welsh

● Important Areas of Welsh Settlement

Irish

Scots-Irish

Nationality groups in Pennsylvania in 1790, as percentage of population.

Pennsylvania's Population

Group	Number	Percent
German	161,365	38
English and Welsh	124,882	30
Scots-Irish	63,061	15
Scottish	31,531	7
Irish	30,636	7
Dutch	4,535	1
French	3,236	1
Swedish	2,739	1
Total	421,985	100

Data from 1790 represent both American and foreign-born of a particular national stock.

Percentage of County Population

■ Over 55.0 ■ 40.0 – 55.0 ■ 25.0 – 39.9 ■ 10.0 – 24.9 □ Under 10.0 □ Unsettled

government, was the power behind both banks, but able Philadelphians helped him. Haym Salomon, a Jewish refugee from British prisons in New York, negotiated the loans from Holland that provided some solid backing for the oceans of inflated paper currency flooding the nation. Thomas Willing, Morris's patron and business partner, became president of the bank and prepared for his role as president of the First Bank of the United States, founded as part of Secretary of the Treasury Alexander Hamilton's financial program to stabilize the nation's finances in 1790. Tench Coxe, a third Morris associate, became Hamilton's assistant secretary.

Earlier, Coxe had founded the Society for the Encouragement of Manufacturers while the Constitutional Convention was sitting in 1787. He hoped that Pennsylvanians would spin cotton into cloth, thereby encouraging development of this crop in the southern states and competing with Britain as a manufacturing power. The next year,

Pennsylvania passed a law forbidding the exportation of industrial machinery or the emigration of artisans who could use it. At the same time, Coxe's Society was offering bounties to those who violated the identical British law and brought new technology to Pennsylvania. Coxe also wrote treatises explaining how a well-run bank could concentrate the capital of diverse individuals to facilitate large-scale economic projects beyond their reach. It was Coxe who actually provided the first draft of the national financial plan that bears Hamilton's name. Coxe based his draft plan for a national banking system on the success of Philadelphia's banks and their investment policies.

One of the many investments funded by Pennsylvania's Bank of North America was the Philadelphia & Lancaster Turnpike Company. Begun in 1792 by Morris, Willing, and Willing's son-in-law, U.S. Senator William Bingham, that company built the nation's first road of macadam or crushed stone that extended beyond the limits of one city. Completed in 1794, it cost $465,000 to connect two towns sixty-five miles apart. Despite nine tollgates, America's first turnpike cut farmers' transportation costs by two-thirds. Other Philadelphia firsts were the nation's first stock exchange (1791), first insurance company (1792), and first steamboat (1787), only the last of which failed to be profitable.

During the two decades after the Revolution, Philadelphia added manufacturing to its commercial economy. By 1800 it was leading the nation in textile production, metal-working, carpentry, and leather goods. Women and children worked alongside their men, and frequently without them, to make clothing. In a competitive situation made worse by the arrival of thousands of immigrants, Philadelphia's workers organized to protest low wages and long hours. The first strike in American history was called by the Franklin Typographical Society in June 1786, the nation's earliest approximation of a labor union: printers refused to work for less than their customary six dollars a day. Nine years later, cabinetmakers and chairmakers issued a *Book of Prices* in a futile effort to keep their wages up. One observer noted in 1791: "Many [are] willing to work, but [are] destitute and starving for want of employ." Hostile judges made matters worse: in 1805, following a strike by the cordwainers (shoemakers) of Philadelphia, the state Supreme Court declared that workers' organizations were unconstitutional conspiracies that devalued employers' property, which amounted to theft.

Religion contributed mightily to Pennsylvanians' feelings of class consciousness. In postrevolutionary Pennsylvania, Baptist, Methodist, Roman Catholic, and Universalist churches rose in numbers as membership in Quaker Meetings and Episcopal churches fell proportionately. All the rising denominations had large numbers of working people in their congregations. Meanwhile, the more elite and longer-established religions ensured their survival through national organizations.

TABLE 3.1 **RELIGIOUS CONGREGATIONS IN PENNSYLVANIA, 1775**

Lutheran	142
German Reformed	126
Presbyterian	112
Quaker	64
Mennonite	64
Baptist	24
Anglican (Episcopal)	24
Moravian	13
Roman Catholic	11
Methodist	7
Jewish	2

SOURCE: Lester Cappon, *Atlas of Early American History: The Revolutionary Era, 1760–1790* (Princeton: Princeton University Press, 1976).

Philadelphia's William White became the first bishop of the Protestant Episcopal Church in America, which came into existence in 1785 at a meeting in Philadelphia. The body's new constitution separated it from the Church of England. Four years later, Presbyterians from throughout the nation also met in Philadelphia to declare their independence from the Church of Scotland. As the Scots-Irish continued to pour into the west, their churches proliferated; the Presbyterian synod of Pittsburgh was established in 1802.

During the early republic, religion became increasingly important as a means to promote moral values, for Pennsylvanians were concerned about how the increasing poverty accompanying economic growth bred disorder. They therefore sought to rehabilitate rather than merely punish criminals. In 1786 whipping gave way to public labor, such as construction work and street cleaning. Prison reformers were determined that "by dint of hard labour" miscreants would "acquire such a spirit of industry and sobriety" that they would regain "that place in the community which their misdemeanours had forfeited." Prisoners with shaved heads wearing uniforms were to serve as examples both to deter vice and to symbolize their moral reclamation. This plan failed: people joked with the convicts, bought them liquor, and helped them escape. In 1790 the state replaced public labor with indoor confinement in the Walnut Street prison, where the labor continued to be hard but was performed in private. Executions too, which had been the scene of elaborate public spectacles, also moved indoors when the large crowds began frequently to express sympathy for the convicted and brawled among themselves, instead of reflecting on the consequences of criminal behavior. Pennsylvania pioneered the new nation's criminal justice system, which rejected mere punishment of the body as insufficient and replaced it with rehabilitation that conditioned criminals' minds to voluntarily accept the social order. Visits by clergy and other religious people were an important part of the criminals' new regimen.

In the transforming years of the late eighteenth century, women played a key role in stabilizing and shaping the character of Pennsylvania and the new nation. Revolutionaries expected women to become "republican mothers," teaching their children, future citizens, the virtuous behavior and Christian morality required for popular self-government to survive. Numerous female academies, many of them academically equal to the colleges for men, dedicated themselves to the goal Rush advocated in an address to the Young Ladies' Academy of Philadelphia: "There have been few great or good men who have not been blessed with wise and prudent mothers." If Pennsylvania's women failed in their duties, the state would "probably too soon follow

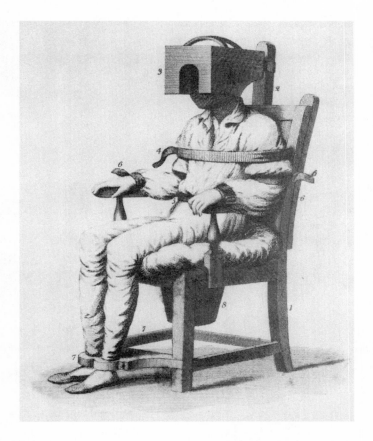

Benjamin Rush's restraining device for calming violent mentally ill patients. Concerned with healing rather than consigning the mentally ill to jails and institutions, Benjamin Rush and the Philadelphia Hospital argued for treating the mentally ill as sick people who with proper care might be responsible members of society. Rush took such ideas to prison reform too, believing in rehabilitation rather than punishment alone for criminals.

Two perspectives on women's role in the new republic, shown in engravings from the frontispiece of *Columbian Magazine, or Monthly Miscellany*—the "proper" role of women in the new republic, at least as male educational theorists conceived it. *Left:* 1787: "Columbia" appears as a mother leading two children to the goddess of wisdom. The pedestal is inscribed "Independence, the reward of Wisdom, Fortitude, and Perseverance." *Right:* 1792: Militant women influenced by Mary Wollstonecraft claiming equality, a position that rarely met with favor from women, and even less so from men of the day, who termed them "fiery Frenchified dames."

the footsteps of the nations of Europe in manners and vices [with] idleness, ignorance, and profligacy—drunkenness, immorality, and the decline of religion." On women's shoulders Rush placed the burden of keeping men in line.

Revolutionary circumstances compelled women to provide more than moral support: in addition to running their households, they had to defend their property in the absence of their husbands. During the occupation by the Continental Army, loyalist wives remained alone in Philadelphia in a futile effort to retain the family property. Joseph Galloway's wife, Grace, claiming she had done no wrong, had to be literally dragged from her doorway by Charles Willson Peale before her house and furnishings could be confiscated. Some Quaker women had more luck: they successfully pleaded with General Washington to return their exiled husbands from Winchester, Virginia. Some loyalist wives were believed to be enough of a threat to order that they were sent to British lines in New York. One of them, Jane Bartram, insisted on returning to Philadelphia because she, unlike her estranged husband Alexander, was a patriot. She later became the first woman to be divorced in Pennsylvania under its first law permitting this in 1785. Bartram not only kept her ceramics shop operating under the patriots, but also persuaded the British to grant her part of her husband's compensation for wartime losses at the hands of the revolutionaries.

Some women wanted to do more than serve as the behind-the-scenes foundation for men's rise to greatness. As Pamela Mason, a sixteen-year-old student at the Young Ladies'

Richard Allen's Bethel Church, being moved into place by teams of horses in 1794, is dwarfed by the imposing Walnut Street Prison constructed four years earlier. The church, shown in the foreground, left, began in a blacksmith shop. By 1800, some 1,000 people had been incarcerated in the prison, about one-third of them African Americans. Engraving by William Birch.

Academy, publicly proclaimed in 1793 in a speech before the Philadelphia elite, "Our high and mighty Lords"—that is, men—had "early seized the sceptre and the sword; with these they gave laws to society; they denied women the advantage of a liberal education; and forbade them to exercise their talents." Mason anticipated that the republic would transform the role of women in history. She urged her sisters "by suitable education, [to] qualify ourselves for those high departments" of church and civic office, and then "they will open before us." If the gates remained shut during the late eighteenth century, women turned the mission men had given them, to become republican educators, into an opportunity to insist on the right to republican citizenship. As groups termed "Democratic Societies" emerged to support the French Revolution, some women began to call themselves "Citess," as the female equivalent of "Citizen," and took to the streets in processions and protests to voice their support for republican France and its American friends.

Blacks as well as women began to develop an independent identity in revolutionary Pennsylvania. Before the war, most were slaves and lived with their masters either on farms, at iron plantations, or in city houses. They seldom married, and they had few children. Heroic efforts by abolitionist Anthony Benezet convinced the Quaker meeting to condemn slavery in 1758, but in the decade before the Revolution whites freed only 18 of nearly 1,000 slaves in Philadelphia.

During the War of Independence, Americans had to come to terms with their own Declaration of Independence, "that all men are created equal," and some seconded the indictment of British writer Dr. Samuel Johnson, who wondered why "the loudest yelps for liberty come from the drivers of negroes." Led by Benjamin Franklin and Benjamin Rush, the Pennsylvania Abolition Society became the nation's most energetic antislavery organization. In 1780 Pennsylvania became the first state to begin the gradual abolition of slavery. Although the law stipulated that only those slaves who thereafter attained the age of twenty-eight would become free, and those who previously had reached that age would remain enslaved, by 1800 all but 55 of Philadelphia's more than 6,500 blacks were free. Cheaper immigrant labor as well as conscience encouraged manumission.

Between 1780 and 1800, Philadelphia blacks created their own community. Their numbers swelled as freed and escaping slaves moved north to the first free state. They abandoned demeaning slave names, such as Cuffee and Cato and Ben and Joe, and became Benjamin, Joseph, Absalom, or Elijah (many chose biblical names) and added surnames, which rarely matched those of their masters. Denied the use of white schools, they began their own. The first African American churches, located near South Street, became the core of America's first thriving, middle-class black community.

Yet growth also brought problems. Whereas Philadelphia blacks had been noted for their law-abiding behavior (in 1790 there were only five in the Walnut Street prison), by 1800 they numbered one-third of more than 120 inmates admitted each year, although most were accused of petty larceny and were not convicted. Beginning in 1793, illiterate and unskilled blacks arrived with their former masters as refugees from the revolution in Haiti. Having little choice but to become indentured servants or casual laborers, they appeared frequently among those accused of theft, disorderly conduct, or prostitution. American blacks could be troublesome as well: in 1794 President Washington had his manservant committed to jail for sixteen days for being "frequently drunk, neglecting his duty, and otherwise misbehaving." African American civic and religious leaders attempted to police their own ranks by forming a Society for the Prevention of Vice and Immorality in 1809. As with the white community, an African American elite (in this case, middle-class shopkeepers and professional people) attempted both to uplift and to control a poor and potentially dangerous majority.

For their part, white Philadelphia merchants and their allies forged civic institutions to safeguard their investments and secure their hold on political power. In 1789 the Philadelphia Corporation that had governed the city from 1701 to 1776, when it was replaced by a town meeting, reappeared. Only real-estate owners could vote for the aldermen, who elected the mayor, a right laborers and mariners had gained during the Revolution. A new state constitution of 1790 did not revoke the broad suffrage of 1776, but it did abolish rotation in office and the Council of Censors, restore the Senate, and give a much-strengthened governor power to appoint hundreds of officials, from the attorney general and the secretary of the Commonwealth to local justices of the peace.

FOUNDING PENNSYLVANIA'S FIRST BLACK CHURCHES: RICHARD ALLEN AND ABSALOM JONES

Richard Allen (1760–1831) and Absalom Jones (1746–1818) were instrumental in establishing a strong, religious black community in Philadelphia. Both were born into slavery, worked to purchase their freedom, and became ministers. They founded the first two "African" (as early black Philadelphia congregations were called) churches in the northern states.

Born in Delaware, Richard Allen was permitted by his master to travel throughout the middle states with Methodist circuit-riding minister Freeborn Garretson. Allen learned to preach while earning his freedom as a wood-cutter and wagon driver. By 1786 he was in Philadelphia, where St. George's Methodist Church offered him its use for blacks—at 5:00 A.M. on Sunday mornings. There Allen met Absalom Jones, also born in Delaware, who at age sixteen had been taken by his master to live in Philadelphia. In 1787 the two men organized the Free African Society, the first black self-help association in America.

Allen and Jones, however, came to a parting of the ways. Black Methodists had helped build and pay for the expansion of St. George's. During the first service in the new structure, in the middle of a prayer, Jones and other blacks were forcibly removed from the seats they had always occupied, and ordered to an upstairs gallery. Instead, they all walked out and began holding interdenominational services for blacks who had experienced similar segregation in other congregations. More and more blacks turned to the Episcopal church, where many had worshiped with their former masters and where they had been married, baptized, and for the most part treated cordially. The first African church in Philadelphia was thus St. Thomas Episcopal Church, founded in 1794. But Allen stayed

ABOVE: Leaders of the Philadelphia African American community and founders of the first black churches in the northern states: Richard Allen (*left*) and Absalom Jones, portrait by Raphaelle Peale (*right*).

with the Methodists: the African Methodist Episcopal Church, "Mother Bethel," began later the same year and remains at the heart of Philadelphia's black community. Allen is buried in the basement of the present structure, the third to stand on the original site at Sixth and Lombard Streets. Within a year, 40 percent of the city's blacks were attending one of the two African churches, where they were not segregated and otherwise subordinated to whites.

Despite their parting of the ways, Allen and Jones joined in petitioning Congress to abolish the Fugitive Slave Act of 1793, which permitted masters to pursue runaways across state lines. During the War of 1812 they together recruited 2,500 blacks to defend Philadelphia should the British attack it. The year before he died, in 1830, Allen presided at his church over the first national convention of blacks in the United States; the meeting was instrumental in persuading blacks to reject schemes to colonize them in Africa and to insist instead on freedom in the United States.

On the national level, Pennsylvania Republicans were at the forefront of the movement to strengthen the national government. Benjamin Franklin, at the age of eighty-one, not only lent his tremendous prestige to the Constitutional Convention but also calmed down its members when they were on the verge of bolting. He closed the proceedings with a speech publicized throughout the colonies, ending: "I doubt . . . whether any other Convention we can obtain may be able to make a better Constitution." James Wilson, one of the more influential delegates, argued successfully for a broad citizenship open to immigrants on the basis of Pennsylvania's own experience: "It was perhaps the youngest (except Georgia) settlement on the Atlantic; yet it was at least among the foremost in population and prosperity. . . . Almost all the general officers of the Pennsylvania line (of the late army) were foreigners. And no complaint had ever been made against their fidelity or merit. Three of the deputies to the convention [from Pennsylvania—Robert Morris, James Fitzsimons, and himself] were also not natives." Neither the federal Constitution nor the Pennsylvania Constitution of 1790 imposed any religious requirement for officeholding or voting, thus effectively reenfranchising Quakers and loyalists and enfranchising for the first time Roman Catholics and the handful of Jews in the state, most of whom had been fervent revolutionaries.

Pennsylvania was also the second state, and the first major state, to ratify the U.S. Constitution. The backbone of the old Quaker Party—Quakers, Anglicans, and German Lutherans—supported it, while most Scots-Irish Presbyterians and German Reformed, who had dominated the Constitutionalists and shared a strong local religious self-government, were opposed. But although most Pennsylvanians who voted were in favor of ratification, the state convention required to ratify almost never met. While the Republicans—who adopted the name "Federalists," as had the Constitution's supporters throughout the nation—had a comfortable majority in the state's Assembly, they were two short of the two-thirds quorum required if the Assembly were officially to meet. For this reason, Anti-Federalists tried to prevent the Assembly from calling a state ratifying convention simply by not showing up. But acting on a summons from the Assembly's speaker to "require the members absenting themselves to attend," a pro-Federalist crowd found two Anti-Federalists residing at a boardinghouse and dragged them through the streets to the Assembly chamber, which the Federalists refused to let them leave. With this bit of skulduggery, Pennsylvania Federalists kept the movement for the Constitution alive, as none of the other large states so quickly and enthusiastically endorsed it.

Ironically, the national Federalists undid their party's political achievement in Pennsylvania, which was to unite diverse groups by compromising differences among them. Consisting primarily of New Englanders and southern planters from relatively homogeneous societies, out-of-state Federalists who came to the nation's capital were uncomfortable with Philadelphia's ethnic diversity and raucous political scene. Discomfort turned to disgust in 1793, when the city's many new Irish and British immigrants, who almost unanimously supported the French Revolution, joined with

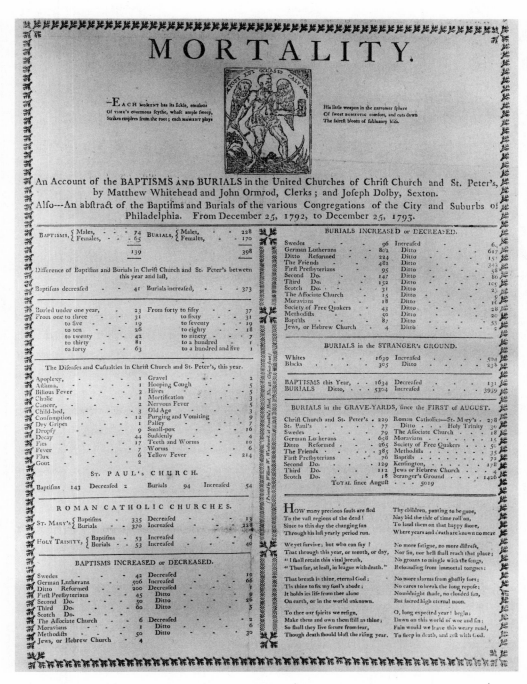

Broadside, Mortality Bill, Yellow Fever Epidemic, 1793. Between Christmas 1792 and Christmas 1793, deaths far outnumbered births in Philadelphia. The epidemic struck repeatedly each summer until 1798, and eight summers in all until the final outbreak of 1805.

native-born citizens of diverse classes to form "Democratic Societies." Cross-class organizations where artisans linked up with merchants and professionals, these societies' members sported Jacobin "liberty hats" or wore red-white-and-blue cockades in their headgear to proclaim their opposition to a Federalist Party that hated the French Revolution and sympathized with British efforts to suppress it. Stylistically too, the

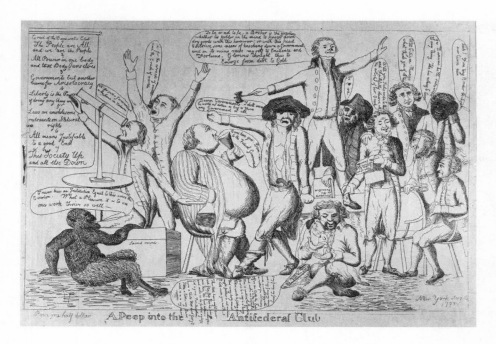

"A Peep into the Antifederal Club." This Federalist cartoon criticizing the motley nature of the Democratic Societies may be the first pictorial slander of "un-American" groups in the new republic. Israel Israel is probably the tall man speaking, calling himself a broker or exchanger of currency, the occupation of several Jews in Philadelphia at the time (although Israel himself was not Jewish). Blacks are present along with a German drunkard, people wearing costumes depicting the French Revolution, a Pennsylvania printer funded by Edmond Gênet, the French Minister to the United States, and other ne'er-do-wells.

Federalists were offensive. Both at the President's mansion and at the "Republican Court" hosted by Anne Willing Bingham, wife of Pennsylvania's Federalist Senator William Bingham, elaborate parties and rituals limited to the elite created suspicions that the "Anglomaniac" Federalists were engaged in "the rapid march of our government toward monarchy." So wrote Benjamin Franklin Bache, Franklin's grandson and heir and editor of the Democratic *Philadelphia Aurora,* the principal newspaper to oppose the Washington administration's policies.

The Federalists in turn regarded these "self-created" Democratic Societies, which soon appeared throughout Pennsylvania and much of the nation, as nothing short of revolutionary. John Fenno, editor of the *Gazette of the United States,* described their campaigns against Federalist candidates and policies as a "system of organized treason." Instead of representing "the people," the Federalists claimed, these societies were instigated by "a detestable banditti of foreign invaders." This charge had some truth to it, as pro-French radicals from the British Isles who had fled to Pennsylvania were prominent in the opposition. Most notable among these was the English scientist Joseph Priestley, the discoverer of oxygen and a Unitarian theologian who had moved to Northumberland County. And Pennsylvania was such a powerful magnet for refugees that even aristocrats escaping from the French Revolution came there as well. Some hopeful monarchists built the town of Azilum at Towanda, where they constructed a house for Marie Antoinette in the hope she would escape to America as well.

The Pennsylvania elite's claim to superior public spirit rang hollow, however, after it deserted Philadelphia en masse during the worst health crisis in early American history. Swampy ground along the city's rivers, and poor sanitation, created "reservoirs of putrid excrements" that were "truly pestilential." The pestilence itself came in 1793, when French refugees from a Haiti in revolution brought yellow fever with them. Between 4,000 and 5,000 people died that year, one-tenth of the city's population. Forty percent of the population, including President George Washington and most of the federal government, fled. The fever struck eight times until 1805. The year 1798 was the worst year: only 20 percent of the city's nearly 60,000 inhabitants remained in town, and of these 4,000 died, including *Aurora* editor Bache. Philadelphian Charles Brockden Brown (1771–1810), the first American who tried to earn his living as a novelist, discussed the

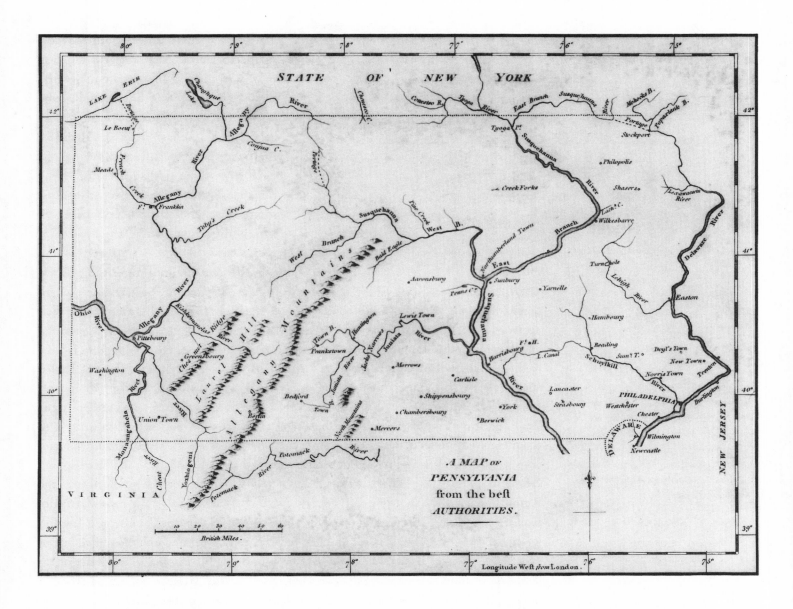

A MAP OF
PENSYLVANIA
from the beſt
AUTHORITIES.

epidemic in his novel *Arthur Mervyn*. He used a mansion, "Bush-hill," to symbolize the different impact of the plague on different classes: "While the upper rooms of this building are filled with the sick and the dying, the lower apartments are the scene of carousals and mirth."

While the elite fled, underprivileged people sought out dangerous public service as nurses of the sick, to prove they were worthy citizens deserving of equal rights. Black Philadelphians were initially told by their friend and principal physician Benjamin Rush that they were immune to the epidemic. But even when they began to die, blacks continued their work with the afflicted. Nevertheless, they were still obliged to refute charges by whites that they took advantage of the epidemic to charge excessive rates.

"A Map of Pennsylvania from the best Authorities," by Jedidiah Morse. The Mason-Dixon Line now appears on this 1794 map, but the Erie Triangle added in 1792 does not. Pennsylvania's boundaries reached their present limits, with minor exceptions. Towns, mostly commercial centers where agricultural and rurally manufactured goods were exchanged, replace the forts of Hutchings's 1757 map. Note the portages at the northeast and northwest corners, indicating that commerce had already penetrated the most remote parts of the state.

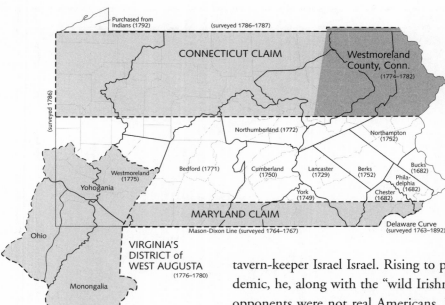

The evolution of Pennsylvania's boundaries (1682–1892). Had the claims of Maryland, Virginia (whose three land companies are depicted), and Connecticut been recognized, Pennsylvania would have been less than half its present size and lost much of the natural resources of iron, lumber, and coal that made it an industrial powerhouse.

The Rev. Richard Allen rebutted these slanders, claiming that if blacks did earn money from their life-threatening work, they thereby were worthy Americans who hoped to improve their lot through honest labor. In the last analysis, much like African American soldiers during the Civil War, black Philadelphians during the 1790s earned the respect of at least some whites and strengthened their own community by assuming the most dangerous tasks.

Also remaining to nurse the sick was tavern-keeper Israel Israel. Rising to prominence in the Democratic Society after the epidemic, he, along with the "wild Irishmen," bore the brunt of Federalist attacks that their opponents were not real Americans. Israel became the main target of the first extended anti-Semitic political campaign in the United States. Earlier, George Washington and the founding fathers had praised the Jews for their patriotism, but by 1793 their Federalist successors began to insist that only native-born Christians could be real Americans. Editor John Fenno suggested, for instance, that "the children of Israel, or rather of Israel Israel" go live in the wilderness like their biblical ancestors if they were dissatisfied with the present government. Ironically, despite his name, Israel was an Episcopalian who later converted to Universalism, although his father had been Jewish. Fellow Philadelphian Benjamin Nones, who in fact was Jewish and who had served heroically in the Revolutionary War, ably refuted Federalist charges that he was unfit for citizenship. Condemning the "illiberal buffoonery" of his opponents, he "gloried" in being a Jew and a Republican and claimed: "In republics we have rights; in monarchies we live but to experience wrongs." Israel was finally elected sheriff of Philadelphia in the Jeffersonian landslide of 1800, the year Republican Governor Thomas McKean appointed Nones a notary public, which gave him the right to approve citizenship applications.

Political strife in the 1790s was so intense that it led to personal violence. Israel assaulted Fenno with an umbrella when the *Gazette* published an article claiming that, having formerly been a Jew (untrue), Israel "was now an ugly Christian." When Bache's *Aurora* criticized President John Adams's construction of an American navy for use against the French in 1797 to prevent attacks on American ships trading with Britain (the "Quasi-War"), Clement Humphreys, son of the contractor building the frigate *United States* at the Philadelphia docks, led a gang of workers who beat up Bache. Opponents of the navy had earlier threatened to burn the ship. A Federalist mob of thirty also chased after the *Aurora*'s next editor, William Duane, who escaped by fleeing over the city's housetops.

Tax collectors in western Pennsylvania were tarred and feathered by the populace. This nineteenth-century print depicts the fate of John Neville, whose house was also burned to the ground.

In the countryside, political violence was even more serious. In 1791 Congress passed an excise tax of 25 percent on the value of distilled whiskey, which provided western Pennsylvania farmers with much of their income because it was unprofitable to ship solid corn across Pennsylvania's mountainous terrain. In 1798 a "Direct Tax" on lands and houses, the latter assessed by the number of windows, followed. The federal government appointed the worst people imaginable to collect these taxes in Pennsylvania. The principal collector of the liquor tax was John Neville, a Virginia aristocrat who lived in Westmoreland County and related poorly to the frontier people around him. Federal Marshal David Lenox detonated the Whiskey Rebellion in July 1794 when he ordered tax protesters to appear for trial in distant Philadelphia rather than in nearby sympathetic Pittsburgh. Five years later, in Northampton and Bucks Counties, President Adams selected Quakers and former Tories to collect money from German American Revolutionary War veterans, thereby provoking Fries's Rebellion.

The Whiskey Rebellion followed two years of sporadic tax resistance to the excise. Protests proceeded much like those against the Stamp Act before the Revolutionary War. Tax collectors, like stamp masters, were given the opportunity to resign. Liberty poles sprang up throughout western Pennsylvania as masked men with blackened faces tarred and feathered collectors. When Neville refused to quit his post in July 1794, some 600 men from the Mingo Creek Democratic Society burned his house near Pittsburgh. Earlier, they had made "threats that they would not leave a house standing in Allegheny County owned by a person complying with the law." Although the westerners condemned the "watermelon" army led by President Washington and Alexander Hamilton, they did not resist the formidable force of some 7,500 men who marched throughout western Pennsylvania. At least five protesters and one government supporter were killed in the rebellion, four of them in the battle at Neville's house. President Washington pardoned the twenty-four obscure men his army had captured.

Fries's Rebellion of 1799 was named after John Fries, an auctioneer of Welsh descent. He encouraged the mostly German-speaking "rebels" in Northampton, Bucks, and to a lesser degree Montgomery and Berks Counties to resist paying the new federal tax. At first the inhabitants poured hot water on the collectors, then assaulted them and destroyed their records. When a federal court ordered twenty-three ringleaders arrested, a crowd led by Fries marched on the Sun Tavern, where they were confined (it still stands in Bethlehem) and freed them on March 7. At the request of President Adams the Philadelphia militia marched out, captured the leading protesters, and tracked down Fries himself by following his dog "Whiskey" into a swamp where Fries was hiding. Tried for treason and sentenced to death, Fries was pardoned by Adams. The President believed Fries and his followers were guilty only of "riot and rescue," not of making war against the government, as Adams's arch-Federalist advisers insisted.

Adams was correct, for neither the "Whiskey" nor the "Fries" incident was a "rebellion" in the conventional sense. They were cases of traditional Pennsylvania tax resistance, as the state's Republican U.S. Senator William Maclay noted: "The Legislature of Pennsylvania had been obliged to wink at the violation of her excise laws in the western parts of the State ever since the Revolution," for they "could not be enforced by collectors or civil officers of any kind, be they ever so numerous." Nor were the Democratic Societies' "Jacobins" engaged in "treasonable combinations . . . subversive of the Constitution itself." Out-of-state Federalists had yet to understand that Pennsylvania had already established broad-based, popularly organized political organizations, which most of the nation would only learn to tolerate during the era of Jacksonian Democracy.

As they were putting down Fries's Rebellion, the Federalists added to their unpopularity by attempting to silence their critics through the Alien and Sedition Acts, passed by Congress in 1798. These allowed the President to deport or imprison aliens he termed undesirable, and permitted the opposition press to be prosecuted for "seditious libel." In large part these laws were directed at the *Philadelphia Aurora,* the Democrats' leading national organ. Benjamin Franklin Bache, grandson of the famous Benjamin, and his successor as editor of the *Aurora,* William Duane, were two of the seventeen men indicted for sedition. Thomas Cooper, editor of the *Sunbury & Northumberland Gazette,* which worked closely with the Philadelphia paper, was a third. Bache died of yellow fever while free on bail awaiting trial; Duane was acquitted. Only Cooper was fined $400 and served six months in jail, of which he made the most by continuing his attacks with essays that prominently identified his residence as the "PHILADELPHIA PRISON."

The main victim of the Alien and Sedition Acts, however, was the Federalist Party

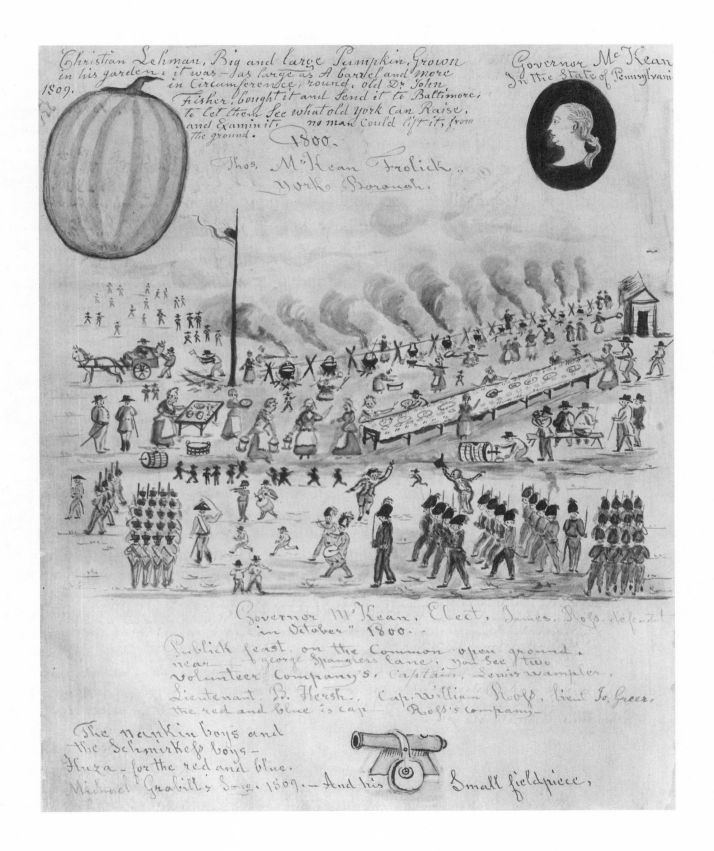

itself. To voters the party seemed prepared to eliminate all opposition through both law and force. Pennsylvania, a state dominated by Federalists from 1786 until the early 1790s, cast thirteen electoral votes for Jefferson and two for Adams in 1796, and all fifteen for Jefferson in 1800. Thomas Mifflin, governor from 1790 to 1799, like President Washington, had tried to remain aloof from the partisanship that sprang up around him. Best described as a moderate Federalist, Mifflin distributed patronage widely, appointing the able Republican Westmoreland County lawyer Alexander Dallas, for instance, as secretary of the Commonwealth. He had refused to order the state militia (which Washington then nationalized) to put down the Whiskey Rebellion. Mifflin was elected overwhelmingly three times until he stepped down. When he was succeeded in 1799 by Republican Thomas McKean, who narrowly defeated his Federalist opponent, the margin of victory was provided by defecting Federalists of German descent in those areas that had supported Fries's Rebellion. Soon thereafter the Pennsylvania Federalists almost went out of existence: by 1802 they held no seats in the state's U.S. Congressional delegation and the state senate, and only nine of eighty-six seats in the legislature.

Also disappearing from Pennsylvania was the national capital: in 1800 the federal establishment left Philadelphia for a handful of unfinished buildings in a swamp along the Potomac River. The year before, the state government had left Philadelphia for Lancaster, and ultimately relocated to its present site in Harrisburg in 1811. The census of 1800 showed that New York had replaced Philadelphia as the nation's largest city. After the turbulent half-century from 1750 to 1800, Pennsylvania would never again be at the center of national politics or suffer so many repeated crises. Wars between nations or between the Native peoples and whites would never again be fought on Pennsylvania soil. But like the nation itself, the Pennsylvania that had emerged by 1800 was beginning to solve its problems. It was fiscally sound, economically progressive, and politically stable. It stood at the forefront of American industry, although New York had seized the trophy for shipping, importing, and exporting as commerce shifted increasingly from the Philadelphia-dominated West Indies grain trade and more toward Europe, better handled through New York's ocean port.

In the early nineteenth century, Pennsylvania's economically ambitious state government, directed by a Federalist elite in the 1780s and 1790s, was democratized, embraced by citizens throughout the state who could not build roads, canals, railroads, or factories fast enough. Albert Gallatin, a Swiss-born Democratic-Republican who lived in Fayette County and served as U.S. secretary of the treasury from 1801 to 1813 under Presidents Jefferson and Madison, symbolized Pennsylvania's post-1800 enthusiasm for commercial growth regardless of section or party. Originally an Anti-Federalist, Gallatin opposed Hamilton's financial system to the extent that the Federalists blamed him for the Whiskey Rebellion. In contrast to Hamilton's belief that a federal debt ensured that wealthy men would support the government, Gallatin eliminated the national debt and achieved a surplus. Nevertheless, by 1807 he too was urging that the federal government aid commercial development, for the good of the entire nation. Gallatin proposed that the federal government assist states and private companies in constructing a nationwide system of roads and canals. "No other operation within the power of government," he argued, "can more effectively tend to strengthen and perpetuate that union which secures external independence, domestic trade, and internal liberty." Although not adopted, his plan anticipated later federal aid for railroads and highways.

Gallatin's devotion to government-supported economic expansion followed the lead of Pennsylvania's Governor Thomas Mifflin, who in his 1789 inaugural address exhorted the legislature "to persevere in improvements of every kind." Aware that Pennsylvania was the keystone in the nation's political arch, Pennsylvanians were also aware that their state's prosperity was critical for American economic development. "Consider Pennsylvania . . . as a natural avenue from the shores of the Atlantic to the vast regions of the western territory," Mifflin urged. And he correctly predicted: "Imagination can hardly paint the magnitude of the scene which demands our industry, nor hope exaggerate the richness of the reward which solicits our enjoyment." How those "improvements" would proceed and who would enjoy "the richness of the reward" have been the central questions of Pennsylvania history ever since.

SOURCES *and* FURTHER READING

Anderson, Fred. *Crucible of War: The Seven Years' War and the Fate of Empire in British North America, 1754–1766.* New York: Alfred A. Knopf, 2000.

Bridenbaugh, Carl, and Jessica Bridenbaugh. *Rebels and Gentlemen: Philadelphia in the Age of Franklin.* Second edition. New York: Oxford University Press, 1968. First edition published in 1942.

Brunhouse, Robert L. *The Counter-Revolution in Pennsylvania, 1776–1790.* Harrisburg: Pennsylvania Historical and Museum Commission, 1942.

Crane, Elaine Forman, ed. *The Diary of Elizabeth Drinker.* 3 vols. Boston: Northeastern University Press, 1982–86.

Doerflinger, Thomas M. *A Vigorous Spirit of Enterprise: Merchants and Economic Development in Revolutionary Philadelphia.* Chapel Hill: University of North Carolina Press, 1987.

Estes, J. Worth, and Billy G. Smith, eds. *A Melancholy Scene of Devastation: The Public Response to the Philadelphia Yellow Fever Epidemic of 1793.* Canton, Mass.: For the Philadelphia College of Physicians and Surgeons and the Library Company of Philadelphia, 1997.

Foner, Eric. *Tom Paine and Revolutionary America.* New York: Oxford University Press, 1976.

Fox, Francis S. *Sweet Land of Liberty: The Ordeal of the American Revolution in Northampton County, Pennsylvania.* University Park: The Pennsylvania State University Press, 2000.

Frantz, John B., and William Pencak, eds. *Beyond Philadelphia: The American Revolution in the Pennsylvania Hinterland.* University Park: The Pennsylvania State University Press, 1998.

Harper, R. Eugene. *The Transformation of Western Pennsylvania, 1770–1800.* Pittsburgh: University of Pittsburgh Press, 1991.

Hawke, David Freeman. *Benjamin Rush, Revolutionary Gadfly.* Indianapolis: Bobbs-Merrill, 1971.

Ireland, Owen S. *Religion, Ethnicity, and Politics: Ratifying the Constitution in Pennsylvania.* University Park: The Pennsylvania State University Press, 1995.

Mancall, Peter. *Valley of Opportunity: Economic Culture Along the Upper Susquehanna, 1700–1800.* Ithaca: Cornell University Press, 1991.

Meranze, Michael. *Laboratories of Virtue: Punishment, Revolution, and Authority in Philadelphia, 1760–1835.* Chapel Hill: University of North Carolina Press, 1996.

Nash, Gary B. *Forging Freedom: The Formation of Philadelphia's Black Community, 1720–1840.* Cambridge, Mass.: Harvard University Press, 1990.

Pennsylvania History, special issues: Pennsylvania at War (1754–1765), Spring 1995; Pennsylvania Loyalists, Summer 1995; Fries's Rebellion, Winter 2000.

Roeber, A. G. *Palatines, Liberty, and Property: German Lutherans in Colonial British America.* Baltimore: Johns Hopkins University Press, 1993.

Rosswurm, Steven. *Arms, Country, and Class: The Philadelphia Militia and the "Lower Sort" During the American Revolution, 1775–1783.* New Brunswick, N.J.: Rutgers University Press, 1987.

Ryerson, Richard A. *The Revolution Is Now Begun: The Radical Committees of Philadelphia, 1765–1776.* Philadelphia: University of Pennsylvania Press, 1978.

Schultz, Ronald. *The Politics of Class: Philadelphia Artisans and the Republic of Labor, 1720–1830.* New York: Oxford University Press, 1993.

Slaughter, Thomas P. *The Whiskey Rebellion: Frontier Epilogue to the American Revolution.* New York: Oxford University Press, 1986.

Smith, Billy G. *The "Lower Sort": Philadelphia's Laboring People, 1750–1800.* Ithaca: Cornell University Press, 1990.

Thompson, Peter. *Rum, Punch, and Revolution: Tavern-Going and Public Life in Eighteenth-Century Philadelphia.* Philadelphia: University of Pennsylvania Press, 1999.

Tise, Larry, ed. *Benjamin Franklin and Women.* University Park: The Pennsylvania State University Press, 2000.

Ver Steeg, Clarence L. *Robert Morris: Revolutionary Financier, With an Analysis of His Earlier Career.* New York: Octagon Books, 1972.

Wright, Esmond, ed. *Benjamin Franklin: His Life as He Wrote It.* Cambridge, Mass.: Harvard University Press, 1989.

Building Democratic Communities
1800–1850

EMMA LAPSANSKY

"Americans are constantly driven to engage in commerce and industry. Their origin . . . social condition, their political institutions, and even the region they inhabit urge them irresistibly in this direction. Their present condition, then, is that of an almost exclusively manufacturing and commercial association, placed in the midst of a new and boundless country, which their principal object is to explore for purposes of profit." So wrote Alexis de Tocqueville in response to his visit to America in 1831–32.

When he recorded his impressions in *Democracy in America,* the French visitor included this analysis in his several volumes of sensitive comments about who Americans were, and what kind of society they were creating. Though he spent only nine months in the United States, Tocqueville's visit was inspired by his desire to explore the prison system of the new democracy. Thus, he spent much of his time in Pennsylvania, where an innovative prison system was an integral part of the new way that Americans envisioned "community."

Tocqueville did not stay long enough to see beneath the surface to the underpinnings of American democracy, but his insightful first impressions were heavily influenced by what he observed in the nation's second most populous state. Nineteenth-century Pennsylvania was playing an important part in the prosperity of the Union. Since 1800, immigration and natural increase in population had brought Pennsylvania to surpass Virginia; only New York had more residents. As Tocqueville had described the nation, so did his description reflect Pennsylvania: industrial and commercial, "boundless," and seemingly waiting to be exploited "for purposes of profit."

The state was well positioned for this. By the 1830s its regions and towns were accessible to one another and linked to the world beyond by a sophisticated system of roads, canals, mail routes, and commercial connections. A geographic and cultural gateway from Europe into the New World, and an advantageously located entry-point into the American West; an experimental laboratory for testing out new ways to define and discipline a "community"; a way station of hope and freedom for desperate African American fugitives from slavery; an incubator of political and ideological innovation for scientists and financiers, photographers and inventors, artists and religious visionaries, philosophers and industrialists, and for myriad other special-interest constituencies of American society—the "Keystone State" was justly proud of its central place in the structure of America, if also a bit uneasy about maintaining its centrality. Home to the country's first enduring lending library and to one of the nation's first historical societies, Pennsylvania also claimed leadership in shaping Americans' notions of identity and would eventually identify itself as "the birthplace of a nation."

Tocqueville was very aware that he had stepped into the middle of a social and economic revolution that had grown out of the aftershocks of an American Revolution that had in many ways disconnected the New World from the Old World. The new political system taking shape opened the way for a new democracy—while simultaneously setting the stage for accompanying political and social tensions. Pennsylvania reflected and affected critical aspects of the new nation's contours. The revolution Tocqueville saw, in progress for more than a generation, was the prelude to a bustling industrial hub that would reach its peak in the latter half of the nineteenth century.

GATEWAY TO A NEW WORLD

In 1809 Samuel Martin, an English immigrant, opened a textile mill in Frankford, near Philadelphia. In 1816 Isaac English started a pottery nearby. Next came an umbrella-frame shop and a metallurgy shop, where a young apprentice named Matthias Baldwin learned his trade. To be sure, manufacturing was not new in Frankford, where there had been a gristmill, and other industries, for several generations. But in the early nineteenth century something different was in the air.

Ninety miles to the west, in Harrisburg, the Pennsylvania legislature authorized a toll bridge across the Susquehanna River. By 1812 the Harrisburg Bridge Company was hard at work raising money to build the two-thirds-of-a-mile span that would bring Cumberland County—just west of Harrisburg—under the influence of urban development. Skeptics thought it could not be done, but by 1817 the bridge was in operation; in just four years the construction debt was retired.

Two hundred miles still farther west, where the Allegheny and the Monongahela

Built by Theodore Burr, 1812–17, Harrisburg's "Old Camelback Bridge" displayed state-of-the-art technology. The bridge carried traffic until a flood destroyed it in 1902. Charles Dickens, who visited the bridge in 1842, was fascinated: "We crossed the Susquehanna river by a wooden bridge, roofed and covered in on all sides, and nearly a mile in length. It was profoundly dark, perplexed with great beams, crossing and recrossing at *every* possible angle, and through the broad chinks and crevices in the floor the rapid river gleamed far down below like a legion of eyes. . . . I have often dreamed of toiling through such places and as often argued, even at the time, 'this cannot be reality'" (from *American Notes*).

Rivers meet to form the Ohio River, coal mining and the growth of the iron furnace started by Charles Anschutz led the few thousand residents of the area to incorporate Pittsburgh in 1816. Within the next few decades, these fledgling cities would be linked by a transportation system and an intertwined economy that fanned the flames of industry and commerce and began to cement the unity of the state.

In 1800 Pennsylvania had had only a handful of urban centers, the major ones being Philadelphia, a bustling city and suburban area of almost 68,000 to the east, and Pittsburgh, 300 miles west in Allegheny County, with its 3,000 residents. These two urban centers were the hub of activity in Pennsylvania. More than 70 percent of the state's 810,000 residents were clustered in the dozen counties within a 100-mile radius of Philadelphia and the half-dozen counties within fifty miles of Pittsburgh. By contrast, the more than 2,500-square-mile area of the Wyoming Valley in the northeast corner of the state was home to fewer than 5,000 residents. By 1850 Philadelphia County—soon to be consolidated so that the city and county were one—had more than 400,000 people in a state of some 2.3 million residents. Pittsburgh had grown almost tenfold, to encompass more than 25,000 people.

After 1800 the new Pennsylvania burgeoned. But the old one did not fare so well: Native Americans—Susquehannocks, Delaware, the Erie, and the Lenape peoples—were pushed into the northwest quadrant of the state, bordering on New York. By 1850 they had become part of the forced migration into New York and as far west as Oklahoma, leaving behind them only place-names adopted by those who took over their land.

This 1843 painting by Russell Smith shows Pittsburgh from the salt works at Saw Mill Run. Selling salt was an important and profitable business of the day. Even in this early scene one can see the industrial presence that eventually earned Pittsburgh the name "Smoky City."

Viewed by themselves, the changes in Frankford were unremarkable: history is, after all, about change. But seen in the context of similar changes across the state, the growth in Frankford, Harrisburg, and Pittsburgh, as well as Lancaster, Allentown, and Erie, signaled an important transition in Pennsylvania's economic, demographic, and social landscape. In the early nineteenth century, Pennsylvania joined New York in plunging the young country headlong into modern capitalism. Those few who could get there first and grab an early fortune became the owners, and everyone else either worked for these early-comers or moved on to try to make their own fortunes elsewhere. With factories and canals, banks, and new efficient fuels, and especially the railroad, Pennsylvanians were the standard-bearers of a modern era. The state government itself would work hand in hand with the private financiers to shape the way that industrial production, and the control and exchange of money, would be defined.

TABLE 4.1 **POPULATION OF SELECTED PENNSYLVANIA URBAN COMMUNITIES, 1800–1850**

	1800	1810	1820	1830	1840	1850
Philadelphia	41,220	53,722	63,082	80,462	93,665	121,376
Phila. County*	81,009	111,210	137,097	188,792	258,031	408,762
Pittsburgh	1,565	4,768	7,248	12,568	21,115	46,601
Harrisburg	—	2,287	2,990	4,312	5,980	7,834
Lancaster	4,292	5,405	6,633	7,704	8,417	12,364
Erie	81	304	635	1,465	3,412	5,858

SOURCES: Campbell Gibson, "Population of the 100 Largest Cities and Other Urban Places in the United States: 1790–1990," in Population Division Working Papers no. 27 (Washington, D.C.: U.S. Bureau of the Census, 1998); David J. Cuff et al., eds., *The Atlas of Pennsylvania* (Philadelphia: Temple University Press, 1989).

*Philadelphia County became the City of Philadelphia in 1854.

Who were the Pennsylvanians behind the changes? What motivated their ambitions and their dreams? What was the foundation on which they built them? In 1800 the majority had been born in America, though their ancestors hailed from a wide variety of origins—England, Germany, France, Spain, Poland, Africa, and the West Indies, among others. But that would soon change, and the variety of backgrounds and heritages would become broader and much more complex. In 1800 most Pennsylvanians were farmers. Almost 90 percent of the state's residents were engaged in small-scale, family-based agriculture. That too soon began to change as urban areas offered a myriad of ways to make a living or to make a fortune. Wheat and corn, cattle and sheep, dominated the vast cultivated landscape of the state. Isolated rural families, far from cities and markets, made tools and clothing at home and built their dreams out of what they could grow on the land or manufacture with hand tools or in small mills or factories. But although most farmers were still using manual methods and traditional tools, the cast-iron plow, machines that sowed grain, and scientific strategies for maximizing the land's production were soon to come. And over the horizon were factories that aggregated dozens of workers into manufacturing hubs.

The commercial success in eastern Pennsylvania was mirrored by similar developments in the western part of the state. In 1815 Pittsburgh's fledgling economy was just beginning to hit its stride. Before 1800, ships regularly left Philadelphia for China and Spain, France and England. And by 1803 western Pennsylvania had joined the party. In that year a Pittsburgh-built sailing ship embarked for Liverpool with a cargo of cotton it loaded during a stop on the Mississippi River. Soon a parade of Pittsburgh products made transatlantic crossings, navigating the thousands of miles along the Ohio and Mississippi Rivers and out through the Gulf of Mexico to the Atlantic. Boatyards such as that of James Berthoud & Company were, by that year, also turning out hundreds of boats to carry local freight and passengers down the Ohio and the Mississippi. The next step in Pittsburgh's manufacturing development was the steam engine. Oliver Evans built a steam gristmill in 1809. In 1811 the 450-ton-capacity *New Orleans,* commissioned by Nicholas Roosevelt, a partner of steam-engine developer Robert Fulton, steamed from Pittsburgh to Louisville, Kentucky, in only sixty-four hours. The industry of such

Into the dynamic economy of Pennsylvania, by 1820, came Constantine Pinchot. Having sided with the losing faction in France's Napoleonic wars, Pinchot fled with his family to find—and to make—a New World.

Purchasing a 400-acre farm in Milford, Pennsylvania, near the Delaware River Water Gap, Pinchot, like many a new immigrant, had ambitious dreams about this new world. He leased his land out and then set up a store to distribute his tenants' produce to a broad market in New Jersey, central New York, and northeastern Pennsylvania, and farther afield to the ports of New York City and Philadelphia. In return he brought to the area's farmers the finished goods he purchased in the cities. Lumber and grain went out from his storehouse; clothing and tools and sophisticated housewares from the cities flowed—through Pinchot hands—into Pike County and beyond into the backcountry of Pennsylvania and New York. Pinchot used his profits wisely: he purchased more land. By 1826 he was the largest landholder in Pike County and had modeled an attractive life possibility for his heirs. In building his economic empire, Constantine Pinchot also inaugurated a dynasty that typified a few dozen families whose members would appear and reappear as part of the economic, political, social, and cultural story of their state. Like wheat carried on the wind, Pinchot's own human "seedlings" would seem to be everywhere.

After Constantine Pinchot's death, his son, Cyrille, left his mother to tend to things at home while he traveled through New York, Pennsylvania, Michigan, and Wisconsin, speculating in land for himself and serving as agent to help other French immigrants purchase land. Cyrille Pinchot saw land primarily as a source of timber. He quickly stripped his

holdings bare, floated the lumber downriver to New York, Baltimore, and Philadelphia, and then moved on to new territory. And he was a man in the right place at the right time: lumber translated into—among other things—wagons and canal boats and railroad ties, which in turn provided transportation to carry lumber for homes in the burgeoning cities, which in turn generated a need for coal, which then generated a need for more railroad ties and canal boats and wagons, and

ABOVE: Cyrille C. D. Pinchot with Edgar Pinchot's daughter Lucy (c. 1865), exemplifying the Victorian ideal of family affection.

provided a market for inventors who could provide tools for more efficient lumbering. All this activity stimulated new town growth, with ever-widening circles of economic possibility—and the political opportunity that came with it. Like his father, Cyrille Pinchot was an astute businessman who invested heavily in stagecoach lines and railroad construction—and in land. He was even a manager in the turnpike company that connected Milford to New York's Finger Lake Region and to Pennsylvania's northern anthracite coal fields.

By the 1840s Cyrille Pinchot, like his father, had become a wealthy and influential man. From his father he had learned to be alert to local dynamics that would affect his fortunes. So when a rival transportation company obtained a state charter to build a railroad bridge that would connect New Jersey to New York at a site eight miles north of Milford, he leapt into action. Such a bridge would undercut Milford's monopoly on travel through the region. Pinchot called on political contacts in the legislature—men whose attention and respect he had garnered through his economic influence—and was successful in getting the bridge relocated. He had won the battle, but in the end he lost the war: the railroad planners chose a slightly different route that bypassed Pennsylvania, and the bridge became superfluous.

Pinchot had been right to be concerned. By 1850 Milford's star had dimmed. Ambitious young people left the town in droves: off to Chicago, to New York City, even just eight miles away to Port Jervis, New York, which became the region's railroad hub. Two of Cyrille's own sons left home for New York City. The elder son, Edgar, following in the family tradition, set up a wholesale grocery outlet, moving produce from the backcountry out into national and international markets. A younger son, James, used his family connections and political skills to create a complex set of connections through which to regularize lumber sales and establish a solid network to corner the market on land sales

to German immigrants. Using these connections, he also established a wholesale business in wallpaper, curtains, and shades, supplied both by New York and Pennsylvania factories (in which he owned shares) and by imports from England.

Fortunately for the Pinchot family, large landholdings that could be profitably farmed, and the broad range of commercial ventures, allowed them to absorb setbacks without great hardship. Thus did three generations of French entrepreneurs create and consolidate their Pennsylvania fortunes, adjusting their strategies with changes in the economic and political moods of their world.

ABOVE: The old Pinchot store, which became a center of commerce in Milford in the 1820s and 1830s, tying the ports of New York City and Philadelphia to the backcountry of Pennsylvania and New York.

In the years after the American Revolution, Pennsylvania thrived on the export of wheat to the West Indies and Europe. Production increased greatly after 1785, when Oliver Evans invented the automated gristmill, shown here in Evans's 1795 diagram. The mill received grain from wagons or ships and, using water-power and gravity, moved it through the grinding process into barrels without human interven-tion. Numbers show the movement of the grain.

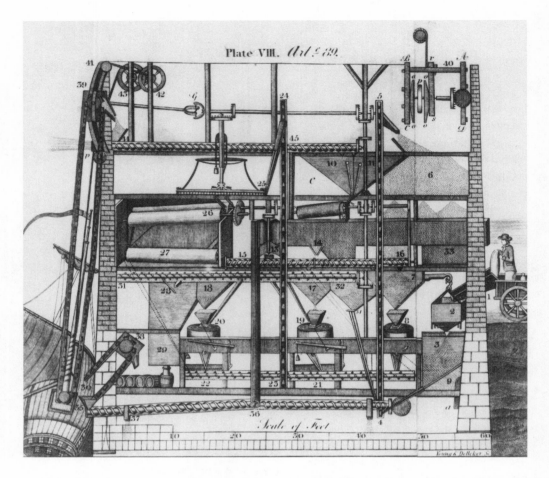

Plate VIII. *Art.º 89.*

innovators was matched by other industrious western Pennsylvanians. Glass works, iron foundries, metal, leather, wood, and textile production were established sectors of Pittsburgh's economy in the first decade of the nineteenth century.

In this first decade of the nineteenth century, Pittsburgh experienced an economic dynamic that would be repeated numerous times in Pennsylvania's history. In 1802 both iron production and textile production were flourishing parts of Pittsburgh's economy. Eight years later the city's gross production had increased by 30 percent, but while iron production had almost doubled, textile production had *decreased* by more than 60 per-cent. The diversity of the economy meant that even while one sector declined, another arose, in the same locale, to take its place. Thus, through the early part of the century, Pennsylvania communities often were able to offset losses in one sector of the economy with gains in another.

Pittsburgh's economy was off to a promising start. What brought it to maturity was a war. In fact, the War of 1812 marked a watershed for Pennsylvania as a whole. But Pittsburgh's strategic position meant that the war gave this city an exceptional boost. Located directly in line with one of the few convenient crossings of the Appalachian

Mountains, Pittsburgh became the easy choice for inland transport when it became too dangerous to ship goods on the Atlantic Ocean from New Orleans to Philadelphia. Instead, cotton, hemp, sugar, and other products from the South were sent north via the Mississippi and Ohio Rivers, then east by land to Philadelphia. Iron foundries in adjacent Fayette and Westmoreland Counties turned out cannons and shells, tools and cooking equipment, liquor and tobacco, and shoes, to supply Commodore Oliver Hazard Perry on Lake Erie and Andrew Jackson's troops in New Orleans.

From a vigorous but isolated outpost, Pittsburgh was rapidly being transformed into a center of influence. By 1816, when Pittsburgh was incorporated as a city, it had a population of more than 6,000, three banks, a theater, eight churches, a courthouse, and a jail—and two bridges to bring people into the city or to send them on their way west. Other areas of Pennsylvania also received a boost from the 1812 war effort. Fort Mifflin, on the Delaware River in Philadelphia, became a launching site for American naval campaigns, and Delaware River shipyards were busy supplying and repairing the United States naval fleet.

The job of provisioning the military energized the activity in the Frankford Arsenal in northern Philadelphia County. Before the war, the Frankford Arsenal, like its counterparts in Pittsburgh and in Harper's Ferry, Virginia, was mostly engaged in buying, inspecting, repairing, and storing weapons and powder produced by local private manufacturers. During and after the war, its responsibilities broadened. Over succeeding decades the Frankford Arsenal took the lead in testing and manufacturing gunpowder and ammunition, and in developing innovations in small arms. The same was true of the Allegheny Arsenal near Pittsburgh, where a steam-powered ship, the *Western Engineer,* was built, making its maiden voyage in 1819.

Meanwhile, in the northwest corner of the state, Erie also was reshaped by wartime activity. It had been the point of origination for Captain Oliver Hazard Perry's dramatic naval attack on British forces, in the fall of 1813, that left the United States in control of Lake Erie. Perry's campaign had mustered hundreds of soldiers from all over the state— including dozens of African Americans. Many of these young men remained in the Lake Erie region, where they also began to build an industrial economy.

If the War of 1812 provided a focus for some of the state's industrial development, it had a similar effect on the political alignment of Pennsylvanians. In taking office for his second term as governor, Jeffersonian-Democrat Simon Snyder proclaimed his position as a "friend of the people" and a "foe to lordly aristocrats." His leadership signaled the end of the Federalist Party in Pennsylvania. The son of a German immigrant, Snyder espoused a position of democratic egalitarianism that presaged the power of wage-workers who would soon demand inclusion in the political process. So too did the relocation of the state capital from Lancaster to Harrisburg in 1812, where it was perceived to be less under the control of the state's eastern aristocrats and more amenable to the influence of residents in the middle and western parts of the state. In addition to the

ERIE AND THE WAR OF 1812

On June 17, 1812, the United States declared war on England. Pennsylvania's heavily Republican congressional delegation voted in favor of war, joining a group of "war hawk" congressmen, mostly from the South and West. At the start of the conflict, few would have given the Americans much of a chance against England's vaunted Royal Navy, but one of the surprises of the war was that Americans generally fared better on water than on land, thanks in large part to a fleet of ships built in the northwestern corner of Pennsylvania. Beginning in the fall of 1812 and continuing throughout the long Erie winter, men and supplies poured in from Pittsburgh, Philadelphia, New Jersey, and Washington, D.C. By the summer of 1813, the Americans had constructed a fleet of ships and recruited enough seamen to mount a fighting force.

Although the Americans failed to achieve their main military objective of the war—to take Canada from the British—Oliver Hazard Perry's dramatic victory in 1813 over British forces at Put-in-Bay on Lake Erie gave the United States control of the Great Lakes, which for the time eliminated the British threat on the northwestern frontier. British officers had underestimated the capability and resolve of American forces, which included farmers, African Americans, and other "common people" recruited for the defense.

After the war, many of the men who came to Erie as soldiers, sailors, and shipbuilders remained in the region, building an economy based on manufacturing, shipping, and agriculture. By mid-century the advent of canals and then railroads integrated Erie into the transportation network of Pennsylvania, and access to the Great Lakes extended Pennsylvania's reach into the developing midwestern region. By the end of the century Erie had become a leading center for commercial freshwater fishing, thanks to the invention of the fishing steam tugboat.

TOP: The decisive moment of the Battle of Lake Erie: Perry's transfer from his own ship, the *Lawrence,* to the *Niagara.* Although romanticized, this painting depicts three African Americans as part of the American force.

BOTTOM: Erie celebrated the Perry Centennial in 1913. Here the centennial parade navigates down State Street. The float bears replicas of a grain elevator and Perry's flagship, the *Niagara.*

relocation of the capital, and the demise of the Federalists, one other important innovation defined the new face of Pennsylvania politics: in 1817 Pennsylvania became the first state to use the device of a nominating convention. Consisting of delegates from each county rather than representatives from the legislature, the convention gave the people from various parts of the state a greater voice in choosing a candidate. In offering broad participation in its political workings, Pennsylvania set the example that other states would follow. In this era Pennsylvania also became firmly wed to the Jacksonian Democratic Party of the "common man." The War of 1812 also foreshadowed the coming of ethnic and regional politics to Pennsylvania. Beginning with Snyder, the state was for many years led by a coalition of Scots-Irish legislators from the western part of the state, and Pennsylvania German governors from the state's eastern region.

Thus, though virtually untouched by any battles, Pennsylvania's economy, demography, and political development were significantly affected by the war. In the years following the war, other demographic changes also played into important economic change. We have seen that the sons of Cyrille Pinchot were dislocated in these years, but they were not the only ones. By the early decades of the nineteenth century, the number of Pennsylvania farmers' sons exceeded the available farmland. Landless and disfranchised, young men often drifted to the cities of Philadelphia and Lancaster, Columbia, Harrisburg, Pittsburgh, and Erie, loosening the controls of family connections, swelling the labor force, and adding to the cacophony of cultures. Such social forces fed urban unrest in antebellum America.

The Pinchots were immigrants who arrived in America with big dreams and plenty of energy. They were able to turn these attributes into tidy profits, building their empire amid the small farmers, lumbermen, and roadbuilders whose labor made their dreams possible. The intertwining stories of such settlers are a dramatic and colorful example of the phenomenon that shaped Pennsylvania in the years before Tocqueville's visit. European immigration, economic ambition, and strong family and ethnic ties that often could be parlayed into political connections were part of the story. This immigrant story also highlights the complex partnerships between private plans for exploiting the state's varied resources and the state legislature's desire to maintain economic supremacy among neighboring states. Often powerful men like Pinchot, who had private ambitions, could enlist allies in the legislature to use state policy to further those ambitions.

Shifting transportation routes; economic and political ambitions; new ways of acquiring, defining, and exchanging wealth; the movement of young men from countryside to city—these are the dynamics that defined Pennsylvania in the first decades of the nineteenth century. In a physical way, Pennsylvania became a gateway. Philadelphia and Pittsburgh, in particular, served as portals through which one might enter the United States from many parts of the world, and through which a person could enter a new world of economic opportunity. But the physical aspects of the Commonwealth were only part of the story.

Fourth of July in Centre Square (1812) by John Lewis Krimmel. Commemorating national events was an important part of community life. This Fourth of July celebration in Philadelphia took place in the shadow of the pump house of the city's waterworks, which brought water from the Schuylkill River and delivered it through wooden pipes to hydrants along the city streets. The pump house, completed in 1800 and from the classical design of Benjamin Henry Latrobe, was capped by a white marble dome.

NEW MEANINGS OF COMMUNITY

The new dynamics of the early nineteenth century reflected and stimulated new ways for people to relate to one another. Pennsylvania's population, increasing at a rate of about 30 percent in each decade after 1800, seemed to call for a reconsideration of the machinery of public life. Financial institutions and political parties, government structures and social organizations, now joined churches, schools, labor unions, and neighborhoods as ways for individuals to shape a public and private identity.

Among the most notable of the new structures were the local and regional banks. Economic expansion requires a financial intermediary to provide a standardized medium of exchange, and to make loans to finance construction of roads and ships and canals. Hence, the establishment of banks heralded economic and industrial development. Beginning in 1791, both the Bank of the United States and the state bank had been centered in Philadelphia. In 1802 a branch of the Bank of the United States was organized in Pittsburgh—it was the first bank west of the Allegheny Mountains. And therewith began the proliferation. By 1809 the Pennsylvania legislature authorized the Bank of Pennsylvania to establish more branches in Harrisburg, Easton, Lancaster, and Reading. Then in 1811 the charter of the Bank of the United States expired, leaving only the Bank of Pennsylvania (of which the state itself held one-third of the assets), the Bank of Philadelphia, and, shortly thereafter, Stephen Girard's bank in Philadelphia, financed by his own fortune. That the Bank of Philadelphia opened branches in Columbia (York County) and in the county seats of Dauphin County (Harrisburg), Washington County (Washington), and Luzerne County (Wilkes-Barre) suggests the growing economies in various regions of the state. By 1819 there was the Philadelphia Saving Fund Society, and a few years later a similar savings bank opened in Pittsburgh. The Bank of the United States, its charter renewed in 1816, now had a panoply of teammates and competitors.

As the War of 1812 gave shape to Pennsylvania, it also highlighted some of the ongoing tensions between the state's regions. By the end of the war, there were forty-one local banks in the state, each supported by a shareholder community of local residents who decided how, and to whom, loans would be made. This economic infrastructure financed much of the transportation network across the state, and loan decisions were based on the clear and simple expedient of local loyalties. Often political maneuvering brought the legislature into the negotiations, as in the case of the construction of the "main line" of transportation network of the Columbia Railroad (82 miles from Philadelphia to Columbia), the Eastern Division Canal (171 miles from Columbia to Hollidaysburg), the Allegheny Portage Railroad (37 miles from Hollidaysburg over the mountains to Johnstown), and the 104-mile Western Division Canal from Johnstown to Pittsburgh. This expensive and complicated system, the result of Philadelphia lobbying, was opened in the mid-1830s, a decade after New York's Erie Canal. It came much too late to regain the commercial lead that had been lost to New York several decades before, but it still effectively kept Pennsylvania's economy firmly in the number-two position.

Pennsylvanians were well aware that they were losing their position of leadership in the national economy, but they were too engulfed in their intrastate regional suspicions to work cooperatively to stem the tide. The banks in the large cities—particularly Philadelphia—often devised schemes to undercut the local banks. Between these maneuvers and the economic Panic of 1819, nearly one-third of the local banks had failed by 1820. Undaunted, however, Pennsylvania banks began immediately reorganizing. Within a decade, there was again a flourishing climate for financial institutions. Economic depressions in the 1830s and 1840s punctuated rises and falls in the number of banks, but though the industry remained strong it also—like much else in the state—remained parochial.

Negroes in Front of Bank of Pennsylvania (1812). This street scene, painted by Russian Consul Pavel Svinin, captures two realities that were soon to disappear. The Bank of Pennsylvania, chartered in 1791, had helped put the state firmly in the center of the American economy, but it would close by the mid-1830s. Also by the 1830s the black wood sawyers who made a steady living in the early nineteenth century would be marginalized when coal replaced wood as the preferred fuel.

Student laborers at the new state agricultural college, a forerunner of Penn State University, in 1855. These young men, standing with the plows that were part of their workday, were not at work on their families' farms. Instead, they were learning their trade under the tutelage of "professionals" at the state's new facility for instructing young men in the skills of "modern farming."

Pennsylvania's financial institutions were closely allied with the political networks of the state, as many of the leaders in one sector were leaders in both. At the local and state level, Pennsylvania entered the 1820s as a firmly Democratic state. As one historian has described it, "lacking an opposition party of strength, leaders of the Democratic-Republican Party battled liked cats and dogs among themselves." Through the 1840s, though, state politics was dominated by farmers and those who thought of the state as an agrarian stronghold. Wary of urban sophisticates, rural Pennsylvanians, like their counterparts in other states, tried to keep a safe distance from urban corruption. Across the southern tier of the state, from Philadelphia through Lancaster County and Allegheny County, an industrial world was growing, and similar developments were taking place along the northeast sections. But as late as 1840 most sections of Pennsylvania were still rural. Young people still learned how to farm from their parents, who taught them by example and by passing on the family lore. In Potter County, farmers were still building log cabins. Even access to such necessities as gristmills and county officials required miles of travel over poor roads. Soon many young men and women, frustrated by the isolation, would be lured by the cash wages and stimulation of the cities.

But even as many young people were leaving the farm for urban life, state legislators sought to reaffirm the value of agriculture by making its practice more systematic and by providing professional consultants and printed guidelines to increase the efficiency of farm production. Charged with county-wide oversight, volunteer agricultural societies were chartered by the state and enjoined to encourage farmers to adopt modern methods of production, to maximize the output of milk, butter, and cheese in the southeastern counties, and to streamline sheep and wool cultivation in Washington and Greene Counties in the southwest. In all areas, crop rotation and other soil conservation methods were advised. The state legislature even authorized the founding of a state college to promote agricultural education.

If the legislature sought to offer guidance about farming, it also hoped to redesign the state constitution to keep pace with the modern world. In 1838 Pennsylvania adopted a new constitution. Like many of the older states, Pennsylvania had been looking to discourage its residents from abandoning the eastern seaboard states for the more liberal

The Conestoga wagon originated in Lancaster County's Conestoga River valley in the early eighteenth century to carry furs, farm produce, and freight to the Philadelphia market. The rugged wagon soon became synonymous with Pennsylvania transportation, and evolutions of it made the long trek across the Overland and other trails westward in the nineteenth century. The Conestoga wagon's heyday was from the 1820s into the 1850s, before the railroad crossed the Appalachians.

franchise available in the new western states. After the 1803 Louisiana Purchase opened a beckoning west to easterners, one of Pennsylvania's most important exports had been its people. Across the rivers into Ohio and Kentucky, and farther west into the Northwest Territory, many Pennsylvanians joined the trek to new lands, and from England, Ireland, and northern Europe immigrants passed through the state, traveling to the less restrictive territories of the West.

Like its neighboring states to the north and south, Pennsylvania assembled a committee to rewrite the state constitution, in part shaped by changing demography. Wage-earning young men, annoyed by their exclusion from the franchise, had been agitating for the right to vote. A political leadership that was increasingly responsive to the prevailing mood of Jacksonian "common man" Democrats shared this desire for reform. When Pennsylvania called together its 133 delegates, however, the composition of the state's population was evident: more than one-third were farmers, and another forty were lawyers. Wage-earning urban working-class men were seeking a political voice, but they were not yet providing leadership of their own. Nevertheless, the interests of Pennsylvania's workers were heard. After deliberating for several years and considering petitions from many different constituencies, the state adopted a constitution that reflected a regional manifestation of the national mood.

In general, Americans wanted to curb executive authority, and they wanted a bigger say in how their affairs were run. Pennsylvanians were no exception. The Constitution of 1838 limited a governor's service to six years out of any nine-year period (the 1790 constitution had allowed nine years of service out of any twelve). It crimped the governor's power to appoint public officials; more offices were made directly answerable to the electorate. Justices in the state Supreme Court were no longer appointed for life, but for a term of fifteen years. Yet despite the rhetoric, the electorate was not significantly expanded. The attempt to remove the taxpayer qualification for voting was defeated, and because there was no income tax, "taxpayer" remained synonymous with "property holder."

But the new constitution did make a clear statement about who was to be excluded from Pennsylvania's political community. Consistent with national practice, women were excluded from the franchise. And in a reversal of Pennsylvania's liberal leadership two generations before, when it had taken the bold step of abolishing racial slavery, the legislature specifically denied the franchise to its black population. Anticipating this probability, African Americans and their allies had gathered evidence to show that black Pennsylvanians had been responsible citizens and that they had earned the rights of full citizenship. They presented the legislature with statistics showing the contributions of the state's black residents—recounting their property-ownership, literacy, church membership, business leadership, and service in the nation's defense. But their lobbying was in vain. From 1838 until after the Civil War, black Pennsylvanians were barred from the polls. And Pennsylvania's women citizens, like most American women, would wait until the twentieth century to be counted as full members of the state's political community.

In terms of democratic leadership, this was a low point in Pennsylvania's history. In economic terms, however, the new political climate brought hope and stability. Into office came Governor David Rittenhouse Porter, whose administration institutionalized what would be a long-standing tradition of fiscal responsibility and a balanced budget. And out of the Pennsylvania of the next two decades came politicians who brought some national recognition to the state: George Mifflin Dallas, elected as James K. Polk's vice-president in the 1844 presidential election; and U.S. Congressman David Wilmot, whose 1846 proposal to ban slavery in new territories in the West won approval in the House before being defeated in the Senate.

James Buchanan, the Mercersburg-born lawyer who had distinguished himself as a Federalist in the state legislature in the early nineteenth century, had also gone to Washington, D.C., in the 1820s, serving in the House of Representatives and then, in 1832, as ambassador to Russia. From this position he was elected to the U.S. Senate. A loyal Democrat with an ambiguous rhetoric that denounced both slavery *and* the agitation of abolitionists, Buchanan was serving as ambassador to England during much of the most heated antislavery debate in Congress of the early 1850s, in which his colleague, Thaddeus Stevens, was an outspoken leader of the abolitionist position. Returning to America in 1856, Buchanan was an ideal presidential candidate, bringing to this role a

Pennsylvanian's understanding of diverse constituencies and political contention—and a deep sympathy for the slave South. He built his cabinet out of both northerners and southerners and tried, without success, to keep both sides loyal to the Union.

Wilmot, Buchanan, and Stevens were anomalies. Throughout the early decades of the nineteenth century, Pennsylvanians, despite the economic leadership of the state, did not become leaders in national politics. Historian E. Digby Baltzell has speculated that the strong influence of Quaker leadership in the state set a tone of private reform rather than political involvement. Such an explanation, however, does not help us understand why non-Quaker Pennsylvanians did not step

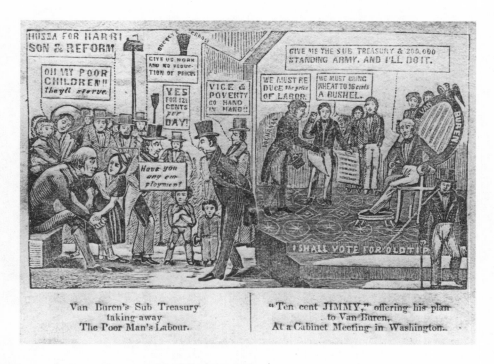

Van Buren's Sub Treasury taking away The Poor Man's Labour.

"Ten cent JIMMY," offering his plan to Van Buren, At a Cabinet Meeting in Washington.

"Ten Cent Jimmy," political cartoon from 1840. If one of the roles of political candidates is to provide fodder for pundits, James Buchanan performed it as well as any. In this cartoon, Buchanan, then a U.S. Senator from Pennsylvania, is shown presenting to President Martin Van Buren his plan to reduce the costs of labor, thereby saving starving workers and their families. The 1837 depression and the concurrent appearance of a nascent labor movement left both local and national politicians struggling to envision solutions.

into the national political limelight. Other historians have suggested that Pennsylvania's business and commercial leaders—the logical participants in national politics—allowed themselves to become too immersed in their own local or regional affairs to pay much attention to a larger national perspective. Still others argue that maintaining a coalition among such a broad regional, ethnic, and religious diversity required so much compromising and solicitation of interest groups that it was impossible to create enough unity to fashion a platform for a national campaign.

To be sure, not all Pennsylvania leaders were idle or self-centered. Such influential Pennsylvanians as Thomas P. Cope in Philadelphia or Cyrille Pinchot in Milford were very active in their local communities. Cope, an importing merchant with an international network of connections, founded a Board of Trade in Philadelphia to oversee the business of the port; provided a mail service between Philadelphia and Liverpool; used some of his own funds to help finance the Chesapeake & Delaware Canal; and helped lead the lobby to petition both the state and federal governments for roads, railroads, and canals. He argued in favor of the Philadelphia waterworks, housed in a neoclassical building that still adorns the Schuylkill River, and he donated funds to purchase private estates around the reservoir to protect the city's water supply. Cope also helped found a public library and manage Philadelphia's almshouse, and he gave money to support the Institute for Colored Youth. In 1838 Cope was a delegate to the 1838 state constitutional convention and he served briefly in the state legislature. But when asked to run for U.S. Congress, he declined.

In Milford, Cyrille Pinchot's career was similar. Throughout his life, he kept in close

East King Street, Lancaster. On the busy streets of Lancaster in the 1850s, James Buchanan's law office occupied the second floor of the building in the center of the picture. Carriages, congestion, and the "news depot" suggest the bustling quality of this industrial city.

touch with his contacts in the state legislature, using these connections not only to further his private ambitions but also to help guide the development of transportation routes in northern Pennsylvania. He assisted in settling Indian claims to western lands, and he served as a manager of the Milford & Oswego Turnpike. But Pinchot did not take a seat in Harrisburg or in Washington, D.C. In Harrisburg, the families of banker Thomas Elder and ironmaster Jacob Haldeman followed a similar path of responsibility for local community affairs, but as one historian described it, "men of substance were [only] expected to serve brief stints in local or county office." Though often well educated at cosmopolitan institutions like Yale or Princeton, Pennsylvania's outstanding businessmen did not go on to represent their state in federal government positions.

While legislators and local leaders pondered the boundaries of their public responsibilities, wage-workers clustered in the growing number of cities and towns. In Pittsburgh and Lancaster, in Columbia and Allentown and Bethlehem, in Philadelphia, Lancaster, and Erie, urban design and cosmopolitan residents shaped new communities. Most of the new urban places took their cue from the city plans of Philadelphia and Pittsburgh. Straight streets—often named for local trees—laid out in a rectangular grid and lined with row houses intermingled with stores, factories, and banks were a common pattern across the state that was carried into Ohio, Illinois, and Indiana by Pennsylvanians migrating westward.

The typical city was located on a waterway, its center oriented to maximize the port connection. Most often influential citizens had their residences in the center of town, convenient to the pulse of commerce and industry. Neighborhood segregation by class— if it existed at all—was subtle: affluent owners lived in spacious houses on wider streets that backed up to smaller, more crowded residences for servants and laborers on narrower streets. Lacking public transportation, both owners and workers lived near their work-places. Shop owners lived above their stores, blacksmith shops and livery stables had to be convenient to patrons, bakers lived where potential customers could easily locate them, and all services needed to be accessible in inclement weather. Services of question-able value or of ill repute—theaters, gambling halls, and houses of prostitution—often were relegated to the edges of town, where were often clustered, also, the most disrep-utable of urban newcomers, marginal workers, or drifters displaced by economic misfor-tune. Such was the profile of most early nineteenth-century industrial American cities.

Pennsylvania cities, however, with their diverse economies and concomitant popula-tions of diverse ethnic and racial background, had an added dimension of complexity. Thousands of new immigrants, separated from the discipline of family and community, staffed the shipbuilding industry in Pittsburgh and the coal yards in Columbia. From Ireland and Germany, from the slave South, and from France and England, Scandinavia, and Italy, Pennsylvania's urban communities were by 1850 divided along the fault-lines of ethnicity, race, and class.

The fracturing of Pennsylvania's communities was gradual, as may be illustrated by the slow growth of Italian communities in Philadelphia and Pittsburgh. In 1800 Philadelphia had only about one hundred people who were identified as being of Italian background, and about 2,000 African Americans. Pittsburgh and Harrisburg had even smaller numbers. After the War of 1812, however, these populations burgeoned—but unevenly. In Philadelphia the black population increased by one-third during the 1820s, reaching 15,000 by 1830. The Italian population grew slowly, still at a total of fewer than 200 in 1850. The Irish population, however, rose quickly through the 1830s and 1840s, reaching more than 70,000 by 1850. Pittsburgh's growth over the same half-century shows a similar profile, with few Irish and Italian immigrants at first, but by 1850, when the U.S. Census began to take note of national origin, Irish, German, and French immi-grants were approaching one-third of the Pittsburgh area's population.

Many of the cities' newcomers arrived with few work skills, and just as those skills—

TABLE 4.2 PHILADELPHIA COUNTY POPULATION BY HERITAGE

	Irish-born	German-born	English-born	African American	Jewish[a]	Total	Increase per Decade
1800	—	—	—	2,000	—	67,787	—
1840	—	—	—	19,833	—	258,037	—
1850	72,312	22,750	17,500	19,761[b]	3,000	408,672	63%

SOURCE: Wilbur Zelinsky, "Ethnic Geography," in E. Willard Miller, ed., *A Geography of Pennsylvania* (University Park: The Pennsylvania State University Press, 1995), 113–31.

[a] For this column, the number is an estimate, and most came from southern Germany, Alsace, and Poland.
[b] Race riots in the 1840s are believed to have contributed to the decline.

textile work, for example—were being taken over by mechanical tools. Searching for a better life, many immigrants found a landing place that was only slightly more hospitable than the famine and joblessness they had left behind.

Thus the workplace became a meeting-ground—and a source of contention—for immigrants from a variety of backgrounds. The lives of workers both skilled and unskilled were economically precarious. Always at the mercy of economic downturns and the whims of employers, workers lived their lives cheek-by-jowl with competitors from differing religious, racial, and/or ethnic backgrounds. In these circumstances, it took little to spark a flame of resentment from white against black, Protestant against Catholic, German against Irish. As the century wore on, no occupation was immune to erosion. Black woodcutters were supplanted by better-capitalized white coal dealers. Local Irish hand-loom weavers were pushed aside by the mechanized power-loom textile mills that supplied inexpensive cloth to foreign markets. German glass blowers, Irish and German shoemakers, local tailors—all felt the pressure of modern machines.

Religion, often an important aspect of ethnic identity, played a part in the rise of urban tensions. The establishment of a particular church or congregation was often an indicator of the ethnic character of a community. Frankford, for example, was a Quaker community in the late seventeenth century, and soon thereafter the appearance of an Episcopal church signified the dilution of Quaker control. By the early nineteenth century a Baptist church suggested the presence of nonelite white workers, and the new African Methodist Episcopal church signaled the presence of an organized black community. With the entrance of Irish workers into the calico, wool, and chemical industries, the Catholic Church also caught hold in the increasingly mixed religious setting of Frankford. In fact, by 1830, Catholics across the state had grown in number from a few thousand in 1800 to more than 10,000—centered mostly in the urban centers of Philadelphia, Pittsburgh, and Erie.

Native-born Americans extended the newcomers a lukewarm and ambivalent welcome. On the one hand, Pennsylvanians were glad to have much-needed labor to pull coal from the earth, to lay track for railroads, to provide labor for factories and mills. Still, the culture and life of these new immigrants annoyed and distressed those already here. A man named Joe Barker was arrested and jailed in 1849 when a riot erupted while he was delivering an anti-Catholic tirade on a street corner in Pittsburgh. That he was elected mayor while he was in prison on this charge says something about how his behavior was regarded by the electorate. Pennsylvania, despite its claim to democracy, reflected the nativist mood of the country and contributed its share of support to the "American" or "Know-Nothing" Party. Rampant nativism and anti-Catholicism swept the nation in the 1840s and early 1850s. Why the violence was so prevalent in Philadelphia, when New York and Boston had much larger Irish Catholic and German Catholic populations—and an equal amount of expressed anti-immigrant sentiment—has never been clearly understood. Perhaps the size of the foreign populations of New York and Boston was sufficient to discourage attempting to mob them.

TABLE 4.3 **REPRESENTATIVE RELIGIOUS AFFILIATIONS, PENNSYLVANIA, 1850**
(members as percentage of population)

	Pennsylvania	U.S.
Presbyterian	15.57	8.94
Methodist	14.77	18.67
Lutheran	11.31	2.30
Baptist	5.56	14.00
German Reformed	4.57	0.68
Roman Catholic	3.86	2.87
Episcopal	2.92	2.77
Quaker	2.65	1.23
Moravian	1.42	0.47
Mennonite	1.03	0.13
Jewish	0.13	0.07

SOURCE: David Cuff et al., eds., *The Atlas of Pennsylvania* (Philadelphia: Temple University Press, 1989).

Partisan politics, legal and illegal, covertly practiced, and overtly violent, was the by-product of this mix. The exclusion of African Americans from the franchise, anti-Catholic riots in several cities, and attacks on the persons and property of African Americans were integral parts of antebellum Pennsylvania's story. In the heat of ethnic or racial hatred, the line between comradeship and warfare, or between criminal and law-enforcer, often was blurred. Young men frequently banded together with others of their same religious or ethnic background to form private fire-fighting companies designed to provide quick assistance to anyone in their group who was in need of aid. But it was not uncommon for gangs of alienated young men to torch the homes or shops of individuals from rival fire companies, and then lie in wait for the fire company when it responded, to prevent them from extinguishing the fire. Catholics were taunted on the streets. African Americans were kidnapped and sold into slavery. Street crime was rampant, and any man or woman could be dragged from the sidewalks and robbed. In all such cases there were reports that law-enforcement officials sometimes either stood idly by or joined in the fray.

As factories replaced independent artisans, new wage-workers felt acutely the capitalist reordering of the methods and rhythms of production. Workers saw their incomes decline and were sharply aware of being made to submit to the discipline of schedules set by factory owners. A dramatic rise in alcohol-related deaths was further evidence of the deterioration of the lot of urban workers in the 1830s. So too was the nascent development of a labor movement both in cities and in smaller communities. These were workers whose immigrant experiences were considerably different from those of the Pinchot family; seeing their individual power waning, they began to imagine a safety in numbers.

By the end of the 1840s this community-consciousness was flowering. In Pittsburgh and Philadelphia, labor solidarity led to dramatic action. As early as 1828 Philadelphia's short-lived newspaper the *Mechanic's Free Press* touted the importance of the Working Men's Party. This organization demanded abolition of imprisonment for debt, a free public

RELIGIOUS DIVERSITY IN PENNSYLVANIA

In 1850 Pennsylvania was the nation's most religiously diverse state, not only embracing the widest number of religions but also encompassing a strangely skewed representation of particular denominations, which appear as considerably higher or lower than the national average. Of nine major religions, only Episcopalians were close to the national average.

Beginning with William Penn's Quaker system of religious tolerance—"a haven for those low in the world"—Pennsylvania retained a unique religious profile, one that supported ecumenism and tolerated the associated conflict. By the middle of the eighteenth century, Jewish residents in Philadelphia had established Mikveh Israel Synagogue, and a network of committed families—including the Gratz family—kept that organization vibrant. Meanwhile, German and Swiss immigrants brought their Old Order Amish Anabaptist traditions to settle in farm communities in Lancaster County and other areas of southeastern Pennsylvania. Their belief in the redemptive power of humility, simplicity, and noncompetitiveness, and in maintaining and protecting community traditions, has allowed this small sect to remain intact over several centuries.

Bishop Francis Asbury's ambitious "Methodist plan" of itinerant preaching and camp meetings was also well suited to the Pennsylvania of the early nineteenth century. Though Asbury complained about both urban and rural Pennsylvanians, he spent three decades using the camp meeting to create a strong Methodist network in the isolated towns of central Pennsylvania.

Early nineteenth-century Pennsylvania was also the birthplace of two denominations. Richard Allen's African Methodist Episcopal Church, founded in postrevolutionary Philadelphia, separated into its own governance by 1816; and, living in the Susquehanna County community of Oakland, Joseph Smith married Emma Hale and spent the years from 1827 to 1830 developing his Mormon theology, before Methodist disapproval induced him to move north into New York, and then west into Ohio by 1831.

Pennsylvania's religious individuality often corresponded with political or social radicalism as well. Quakers embraced antislavery as part of their religious faith, and, under the leadership of William Furness, so did many Unitarians. In both cases, such political positions led to friction within the denominations as well as with those outside the religious community.

ABOVE: St. Thomas African Episcopal Church in Philadelphia.

OPPOSITE: Denominational variety continued to mark the religious landscape in Pennsylvania in the early nineteenth century. Churchgoing became a more regular affair and, especially in rural Pennsylvania, a time of social gathering as well as worship. The establishment of meetinghouses, schools, and seminaries by different religious groups brought religious worship and more formal religious practices and discipline to the backcountry. The spread of churches also fueled religious revivals, which convulsed Pennsylvania several times before the Civil War. Its numerous seminaries and religious publishing houses also helped Pennsylvania exercise a powerful, if contested, influence on American religious thought and observance.

ABOVE: American Friends going to Meeting in summer.

LEFT: Camp meeting, 1830.

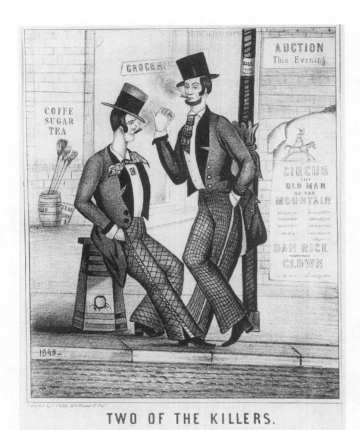

TWO OF THE KILLERS.

Broadside of "Two of the Killers." An 1852 visitor to Philadelphia described the myriad gangs of young men with names such as "Flayers," "Killers," and "Gumballs."

school system, and tighter regulation of alcohol sales. In Pittsburgh in 1836, fourteen artisan groups created a confederated Pittsburgh Central Labor Union, hoping that their combined strength could stem the tide of decline in their wages and working conditions. Through the 1840s Pittsburgh's cotton mill and iron mill laborers tried labor strikes to make their point. Many of these workers were immigrants, and their demands suggested a growing sense of both solidarity and oppression, and evidence of what they hoped for their heirs. Economic depressions diluted their solidarity, and racial/ethnic tensions, always an undercurrent, often triumphed over labor loyalties. Hence, the effectiveness of such organizations remained limited.

Although it would be decades before a durable workers' movement finally took hold in Pennsylvania, workers' consciousness of being a separate constituency with a special agenda was born in the early years of Pennsylvania's industrial age. Mining accidents and coal dust that could suffocate were issues that galvanized workers. Low wages and being cheated at the company stores added insult to injury. In 1842 workers in the anthracite town of Minersville walked off the job, demanding higher wages and fairer policies in the company store. They marched to nearby Pottsville, hoping to strengthen their numbers with more recruits, but instead they were set on by the militia. In another part of Schuylkill County, in 1846, a union claiming 5,000 members sent a list of demands to the coal-mine owners who employed them. When the owners responded by shutting down the mines, the union action was suspended, only to be renewed as the Bates Union in 1849.

For many generations, a handful of small schools had provided private education for those who could afford it. But wage earners were acutely aware that without literacy their children were at the mercy of employers. So they agitated for public education. At the same time, the legislators also recognized the value of an informed populace. The state's Free School Act of 1834 led to the establishment of some 3,000 public elementary schools by 1840, a number that mushroomed to more than 10,000 by 1850. Most of these schools educated students only to the elementary level. But broader education was also on the horizon. Western University opened in Pittsburgh in 1830 (and is presently the University of Pittsburgh), as did the state-sponsored Farmers' High School, which would grow into Pennsylvania State College (now The Pennsylvania State University).

Farther west, in Titusville, Venango County, along the Allegheny River, local speculators had taken over Indian land in 1818 and had built a blast furnace, a mill, and a foundry. Known as the Oil Creek Furnace because of the area's petroleum-tainted water,

SEEDS OF MODERN LIFE

The same technology that threatened the jobs of manual laborers brought leisure and new ways of life to the middle and upper classes. For urban people of means, the task of learning the "good life" became more complex, but the tools for managing that learning became more accessible. Beginning in the 1830s, scheduled public transportation, in the form of horse-drawn trolleys, provided a relatively comfortable commute for those who could afford it. Now neighborhoods could begin to be segregated by class, as professional men left their homes for offices in the city, leaving their homes in the hands of their wives. The wives, in turn, took on a new set of roles, as indoor plumbing, central heating, and other modern conveniences freed them to intellectualize their household routines. "How-to" books and periodicals prescribed the characteristics of the ideal woman in her ideal home: pious, thrifty, and delicate, the protector of family morality, middle- and upper-class women were to be protected from the crassness of the urban scramble so that they could maintain an atmosphere of gentility in their homes.

Women's publications—of which Philadelphia was an important center—taught the idealizing of children's innocence, the deifying of chastity and temperance, and the redeeming beauty of death. Stylized "rural" cemeteries, accessible by trolleys, became the fashion for a Sunday picnic, while romanticized renditions of funerary art became a preferred style for architectural detail and home decoration. As the new techniques of printing and lithography made specialized publications more accessible and affordable, upper-class women increasingly took their identities from published templates.

WALKING DRESSES OF THE THIRTIES
Leg o' Mutton Sleeves, Scoop Bonnets, and Crinolines
From *Godey's Lady's Book*, October, 1835

LEFT: When the Philadelphia-based *Godey's Lady's Book* began publication in the early 1830s, sophisticated urban homemakers used it to help design and manage the "modern" lifestyle, where women's role came to be defined as creating a "haven in a heartless world" for men, who went out to work and returned home for comfort and moral regeneration. Godey's images were the first "fashion plates."

BELOW: View from Laurel Hill Cemetery. The bustle of city life could be offset by a soothing stroll in the repose of parklike cemeteries, such as Laurel Hill, pictured here with its undulating walkways and elegant sculptures.

it remained in business for more than forty years. Soon a post office was opened, and mail was received from Franklin one day a week. By 1859 the discovery that petroleum could be used for heating-fuel had turned this valley into a boomtown. Like other burgeoning industrial towns, Titusville attracted an immigrant labor force. And like other industrial towns, Titusville experienced alienated workers and outbreaks of violence.

Still, for all the economic difficulty and interpersonal conflict, Pennsylvania's workers remained, and remain today, remarkably loyal. Fertile soil, beautiful vistas and a temperate climate, multiple industries, and—in spite of the tensions—a high degree of tolerance for cultural diversity have led a majority of native-born Pennsylvanians to stay in the state where they were born. In the area of community life also, Tocqueville had caught the spirit of Pennsylvania: "Political institutions, and even the region they inhabit urge them [Americans] irresistibly in . . . [the] direction [of commerce and industry]." But the community life of Pennsylvania's cities and hubs was complex. It was formed by immigrants who came to play their part in coaxing the riches from the land, but layered over by new workers—some who came to stay, many who were just passing through.

CANALS AND RAILROADS: A BRIGHT PATH TO NEW FORTUNES?

In 1834 Harriet Martineau traveled from her home in England to visit the young nation. Like Tocqueville, she spent a significant part of her visit in Pennsylvania. In her account of that visit, she focused on the Pennsylvania transportation system: the turnpikes, the canals, and the new railroad from Columbia to Philadelphia, the first such structure anywhere in the world built by a state government. Like Tocqueville, Martineau had caught a central thread in the tapestry of Pennsylvania's revolution. The thousands of miles of transportation system—important for the construction jobs it created as well as for the commerce and communication network it facilitated—were the foundation of the state's economy.

This transportation network opened up the regions west and north of Philadelphia's sphere of influence. The Lancaster Turnpike, connecting Philadelphia to Lancaster, had been opened in 1794. The first of the nation's roadways to use macadam-like paving, it was the precursor of the more than 200 turnpike companies chartered by the state legislature to build more than 3,000 miles of roads by 1830. Pushing west, by 1804 the turnpike had reached Pittsburgh: the eastern and western extremes of the state were now linked. Within three decades Pennsylvania's northeastern and western borders were settled by farmers, miners, and manufacturers, and the thirteen counties in the north-central and northwest region of the state were also experiencing staggering population growth. New county names appeared on the map: McKean and Potter, Cambria and Tioga, Erie and Crawford and Mercer—each new designation reflected the filling in of the geographic puzzle.

The observant traveler would quickly notice that Pennsylvania's riches were not the

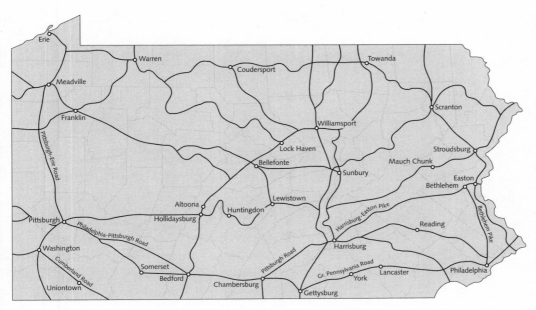

sort to attract the impatient. It was not easy to get rich quick in Pennsylvania. There was no gold and no silver, and precious few pelts that could be carted off to another place and sold for fortunes. Rock quarries and fertile land, coal and iron and, later, petroleum—Pennsylvania's treasures—yielded up their wealth only to those who would settle down among them. Those in search of quick wealth did not stay long. But some, like the Pinchot family, did settle.

The varieties of cultures and peoples brought with them various skills and preferences. Some were accustomed to dairy farming; they could flourish here. Others brought a tradition of shipbuilding; there was a place for them here too. Still others were clever with machines, happiest when working with textiles, or preferred the satisfaction of shaping stone or cutting lumber or milling grain. Pennsylvania's diverse treasures could satisfy these multivariate competencies and desires. The regional economy might not be glamorous or exciting or a place to turn a quick buck. But there was plenty of good farmland, creating the backbone for an economy that was sturdy, durable, and flexible— and able to ride the winds of change.

In Reading and in Lancaster in the east, and in the Great Lakes town of Erie, the manufacture of agricultural tools and machinery joined the hum of lumber-milling and the processing of grain into flour. By 1800 Pennsylvania led the nation in the production of flour, and it was a leader also in distilling grain into beer and whiskey—especially in the isolated western areas, where it was more cost-effective to ship valuable liquid alcohol than the heavier, more perishable grain that would bring a lower price in the marketplace. Along the waterways and turnpikes, the wagon-makers' shops became the precursors of the modern auto service station. Here haulers could purchase new transportation or make repairs to ailing wagons. The wagon-makers' subspecialty, leather-

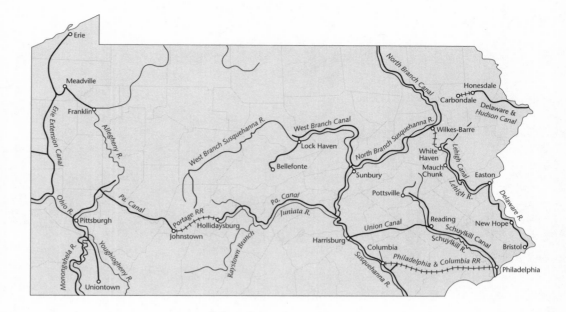

tanning, flourished because it could nestle comfortably between a steady supply of hides from nearby farm animals and a market hungry for leather goods. Similarly, abundant anthracite coal in the valley forty miles northwest of Reading in Schuylkill County was a natural partner for the iron furnace that opened in Pottsville in 1836.

Anthracite coal was crucial to the early nineteenth-century Pennsylvania economy. From along the Lehigh River, in Lehigh County, the Schuylkill Canal had, by 1825, connected Pottsville with the Schuylkill River, which brought freight south to Reading and on to Philadelphia. Two years later the Union Canal connected Reading to another important coal center at Middletown, on the Susquehanna River near Harrisburg. In 1844 the town of Erie was linked to the state canal system. Section by section, isolated Pennsylvania counties were brought into the transportation orbit, with the Susquehanna & Tidewater Canal, opened in 1840, symbolizing the interconnectedness of state and region. That new canal linked the Susquehanna Valley, through Columbia, into Havre de Grace, Maryland, and the ports of Baltimore and beyond. Through these routes anthracite coal left Pennsylvania for England, Russia, central Europe, and Asia. The Old World may have exhausted its fuel, but Pennsylvania's supply seemed—to use Tocqueville's word—"boundless."

By the 1830s, fuel production had joined boat and wagon construction as a major part of the state's economy, both for powering industries and for sale to other locales to power *their* industries. Pennsylvania had abundant supplies of what the world needed. But getting the supplies to those who needed them was the challenge. The state, although mountainous, was rippled with rivers and lakes; all that was needed was to link those waterways so that people and freight could be connected. In the early decades of the nineteenth century, Pennsylvanians met those challenges. A network of canals was

An early view of Mauch Chunk (now Jim Thorpe) after the completion of the Lehigh Canal. Anthracite coal was delivered by wagon on rails to the dock and then transported downriver by boat. Note the lock at bottom right.

the beginning of a solution. Dozens of small companies engineered waterways that enabled their private owners to transport products from local areas to central distribution points. The first iron-hulled steamer, launched near Harrisburg in 1825, was the harbinger of a fleet of 100 such iron barges that carried freight along the Lehigh River by 1840. The Schuylkill Navigation Company brought out coal from Pottsville, and the Lehigh Canal Company carried coal from its parent company, the Lehigh Coal & Navigation Company. The Delaware & Hudson Company loaded coal from Carbondale and delivered it to New York and Pennsylvania. Water traffic had become a powerful, if limited, solution to expediting travel in Pennsylvania.

But canals were an imperfect solution to moving freight and people. They were expensive to build and maintain, they covered relatively short distances, they could not

The canal boat *Little Freddie* tied up at the Delaware Aqueduct, Lackawaxen. Many canal boats were family-owned, with the family living on the boat.

William Frick's Boat Yard at Highspire. Building canal boats was a large industry. This yard built boats for the privately operated Schuylkill Canal.

be constructed across mountains, and they were subject to the rhythms of climate: frozen and impassable for many months out of each year. The Lehigh Canal, for instance, required at least fifty dams and locks, which were swept away by a flood in 1862. True, the canals had more than cut in half the cost of bringing lumber from Williamsport to eastern ports, and, after 1840, the canals brought out mountains of bituminous coal, which was easier to mine than anthracite, from the westernmost counties of from the westernmost counties of the state. But surely there must be a better way. And by the 1840s Pennsylvanians were on their way to embracing it.

As the mid-century state legislature sought to regulate education and agriculture, it also entered into the development of the state's infrastructure. In 1834, the same year that the legislature authorized public schools, it appropriated funds to assist with building the Philadelphia & Columbia Railroad, to transport coal along the eighty-mile stretch from Columbia's coal mines to the Delaware River. The legislature saw its charge as nurturing the growth of the state's many economic structures, and the transportation network was key to that growth.

At the end of the 1820s, the state legislature had taken it upon itself to encourage canal-building; shortly thereafter, railroad planning was incorporated into the plan for some 700 miles of transportation network. The first railroads had been primitive; the "trains," drawn by horses, were simply wagons placed on rails to reduce friction and thereby increase possible speed. The next step was to increase speed by using gravity. In 1827

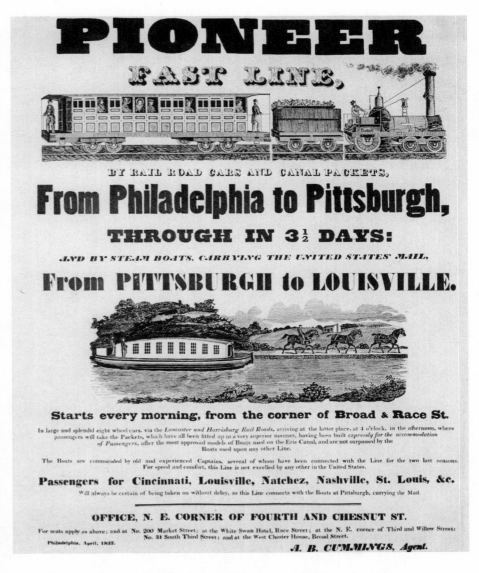

An 1837 broadside advertisement showed combined rail and canal service from Philadelphia to Pittsburgh in three and a half days.

the railroad that carried anthracite coal from Mauch Chunk's coal mines in Carbon County to the Lehigh River used this method. In 1829 steam power brought real independence to railroad design, when it was used to bring coal from Carbondale to Wyoming County southeast across the Wayne County line into Honesdale, where it could be transferred to the Delaware River.

Passenger rail travel, and the subsidiary industries to support it, caught on quickly too. The Philadelphia-Germantown-Norristown line began, after 1832, to redesign neighborhood patterns, introducing a way for the wealthy to commute between Philadelphia workplaces and suburban homes. Between 1836 and 1846 many new lines were added: the Lehigh & Susquehanna line linked Wilkes-Barre, 100 miles north of Philadelphia, with the Lehigh River; the Philadelphia & Reading Railroad stretched

more than 100 miles, connecting Pottsville, Reading, Pottstown, and Philadelphia; and York gained a railroad connection across the Maryland border to Baltimore. Within a few years, many of these short spurs were joined together under the umbrella of the Pennsylvania Railroad. Matthias Baldwin—the young man who had learned metallurgy in Frankford—turned his talent to making locomotives, building more than 1,000 rail cars between 1830 and 1850. Furnishing railroad cars also gave furniture makers, textile manufacturers, and glassmakers access to new markets for their wares. By 1850 a traveler who left Europe and went west to Philadelphia could then cross the 300 miles to Pittsburgh, the "gateway to the west," along the way encountering farmers and industrialists, coal and sheep, canals and quarries, and taverns, each at the hub of an orbit of influence that might stretch through Maryland into the south, up through New York on the north, or beyond Pittsburgh into Ohio on the west.

Railroads invigorated the fuel industry, redesigned urban neighborhood patterns, and opened the way for new manufactures. They also brought profound changes in agricultural systems. Beginning in the 1820s, cowboys had rounded up beef cattle fattened in Ohio's pastures and herded them east, through Pittsburgh, to slaughterhouses in Harrisburg. Upward of 100,000 cattle a year, and the thousands of drovers who managed them, crossed through the state: the cattle resting and grazing in local fields, the drovers drinking in the local taverns. By 1850 the railroad began to change all this: rail cars transported cattle, cowboys had to find new employment, and tavern owners that were not near railway stations found themselves without patrons.

Private financiers, such as the Pinchot family, and public servants in the legislature shared the enthusiasm—and the cost—for creating this intricate and far-reaching network of communication. They wanted to ensure Pennsylvania's centrality in the nation's economy. Even before New York's legislature, in 1817, embarked on its 362-mile Erie Canal, linking New York City's Hudson River with the Great Lakes, Philadelphians were aware that their supremacy in shipping was in jeopardy. By the time the Erie Canal opened in 1825, both Baltimore and New York had usurped Philadelphia's place as the premier exporter of flour. In both imports and exports, New York outstripped Philadelphia three to one. Philadelphia businessmen banded together in 1824 to try to stem the tide. Their new organization, the Pennsylvania Society for the Promotion of Internal Improvements, was clear about the desperation of its mission: "A large proportion of . . . trade has been withdrawn from this city, and the present exertions are calculated not merely to regain what is lost. The struggle assumes a more serious aspect. It is to retain what is left."

Complacent and unobservant, Philadelphia's business leaders were taken by surprise when Baltimore and New York bested them in the marketplace. After all, their own economy had *seemed* to be thriving. In the 1820s more than 500 ships passed through their port each year, carrying whale oil from Massachusetts, tobacco from the South, rum from the West Indies, fine woods from South America, and excellent liquors from France and Scotland, as well as an infinite array of luxuries from China. Philadelphia

OPPOSITE: On December 10, 1852, the first train from Philadelphia pulled into Pittsburgh. Now the trip between Pennsylvania's eastern and western hub cities took only fifteen hours. Unlike canals and turnpikes, the railroad was largely able to overcome problems of seasonal weather barriers. For passengers, it eliminated the need to change carriers.

merchants had long been aware that the value of their imports was beginning to exceed that of their exports, but because business was brisk and the hotels were filled with tourists, they had been slow to recognize that they might have to take aggressive action.

In the 1830s, Pennsylvania's economy was staging a rear-guard defense. The broad diversity of the state's natural resources was in its favor, but there was also plenty of reason for concern, for Pennsylvania had some significant handicaps. First of all, the ambitious construction of railroads and canals had been largely haphazard, driven more by which entrepreneurs could get their voices heard in the legislature than by any long-range strategy for development. Much of the system consisted of short spurs between two discrete destinations—it was not a broad, integrated plan. Parts of the network linked the state with areas of Maryland and New York but did not provide easy access to the emerging lucrative markets in the American West. For the most part, the Pennsylvania transport system worked best for moving freight from the state's hinterlands to the port of Philadelphia. But Philadelphia, the state's largest port, was on a waterway that was frozen for several months of each year: the Delaware River. Several times during the decade of the 1830s alone, commerce came to a virtual standstill as boats awaited the spring thaw. Laborers were out of work, and merchants took their trade to New York. By late 1830s, when the city council authorized funds to build a boat to break up the ice floes, the city had lost its edge, and it would never be regained.

Pennsylvania seemed destined to be innovative in some areas, tradition-bound in others. The state had been a leader in providing funds for turnpike development, yet had come late—and timidly—to the idea of supporting its ambitious "main line" rail/canal system to link the east and west. The legislature had led the way in opening a political voice for a broad swath of white male voters, but had denied the vote to African Americans and women. By 1834, when economic subsidy for the canal/rail project of linking Philadelphia to Pittsburgh was approved, renowned engineer William Strickland had returned from a tour of Europe convinced that the day of the canal was over and that railroads would soon replace them. By the 1830s, Pennsylvania was dependent on the export of coal for its economic livelihood, but for several more decades the state's residents remained wedded to wood as the preferred fuel for their own home use. And though the State House in Philadelphia introduced natural-gas lighting as a novelty in 1816, not until 1836 did the city establish Pennsylvania's first municipal gas works— bringing up the rear behind New York, Baltimore, and Boston.

A conservative mind-set was not the only hindrance to Pennsylvania's reclaiming dominance in America's economy. Another significant factor in Pennsylvania's economy was the leadership of one of its most influential citizens, Nicholas Biddle, who headed the Bank of the United States from 1823 until its demise in 1838. Biddle's experience with the politics of the Bank left many Pennsylvanians cynical about financial institutions.

Graduating young, with honors, from Princeton in 1801, the fifteen-year-old Nicholas Biddle was a rising star in the early nineteenth century. He was smart, urbane,

For many years Harrisburg had languished as nothing more than a pass-through between Philadelphia and Pittsburgh. Even the presence of the State Capitol did not ignite a spark in this sleepy outpost. The railroad, however, did what the government alone could not: it brought Harrisburg alive. The Cumberland Valley Railroad made Harrisburg a hub by which Carlisle and Chambersburg, small villages a few miles to the southwest, could become satellites of the capital. These connections soon provided a link through western Maryland and into Virginia and Baltimore, adding a new vector to Pennsylvania's economy.

From a population of just over 4,000 in 1830, Harrisburg mushroomed to become an industrial center with more than 7,000 residents by 1850. The opening of a municipal waterworks in 1843, followed by a gas works and a Pennsylvania Railroad station in 1849, ensured that the new cotton mills and railmaking industry would usher in a new energy.

ABOVE: With the arrival of the railroad, Harrisburg became more accessible to visitors, many of whom came on government-related business. This lithograph depicts the 1855 inauguration of Governor James Pollock at the old Capitol building, completed in 1822. Pollock, the Whig candidate, was also endorsed by Free-Soil Democrats and Know-Nothings.

Cartoon satirizing Nicholas Biddle and the Bank War. While Biddle had grand visions of what might be accomplished with good banking foundations, not everyone agreed. Satirists were quick to take advantage of the tension between financiers like Biddle and such men as Andrew Jackson, who had more economically conservative ideas and viewed banks and bankers as taking advantage of laboring people. Bare-knuckle prizefighting was one of the principal spectator sports in the early republic; the number of rounds had no limit. Both sides in the Bank War also took an all-or-nothing approach to the issue, as this cartoon predicts.

and well connected, a man whom one contemporary described as "representing the money power of the country . . . [which] . . . combined with his personal qualities, his manners [and] talents, . . . gave him a degree of influence among the monied and educated classes equaled only by that of General Jackson with the populace." By 1810 Biddle had traveled widely in Europe and had established close friendships with Thomas Jefferson, James Monroe, and John Quincy Adams. In the 1820s, when President Monroe called on Biddle for leadership of the Bank of the United States, Biddle brought to the task his expressed desire for "achieving results." He also brought with him his belief that liberal credit and good transportation networks were keys to helping the nation grow. Deeply concerned about stabilizing Philadelphia's declining commerce, he was involved in planning several of Pennsylvania's railroad projects, and at lavish parties in his home he entertained Pennsylvania's business leaders. Through the 1820s, when coal shipments from the Lehigh area stimulated the development of wharves along the Schuylkill River, and more than 100 new textile mills at Manayunk (near Philadelphia) took on nearly 10,000 weavers, spoolers, and dyers, Biddle was pleased to be at the hub of the credit that made it all possible.

In the early 1830s Biddle's dreams began to go sour. In a controversy with President Jackson over the standard of currency—Jackson favored hard money, Biddle believed that carefully controlled paper currency was a better idea—Biddle became embroiled in a political standoff that ended with Jackson overriding Congress in 1832 and refusing to renew the Bank's charter, which would expire in 1836. In preparation for the dissolution of the Bank, Biddle began limiting credit and closing branches, policies that were perceived by many as arbitrary and vindictive, especially because Biddle's concern for protecting the relationship between Pennsylvania cotton mills and southern cotton led him to continue to extend credit to internal improvement projects in both Pennsylvania and the South. At the end of the 1830s, when economic depression led many states—including Pennsylvania—to suspend interest payments on money borrowed from the Bank of the United States, Biddle became the object of bitter recriminations. For many years, the memory of these events would influence Pennsylvania entrepreneurs to be conservative in their economic choices.

Despite such setbacks, the Pennsylvania economy hummed along through the early nineteenth century. New discoveries and technologies—coal and oil and steam and railroads—layered fresh initiatives on the sturdy agricultural foundation that had long sustained the state. Even the Panic of 1837 did not seriously disrupt the growth of internal improvements—roads, canals, public works, building construction, and industrial development. By 1850 the Philadelphia area's 2,000,000 residents had a modern water distribution system and hundreds of miles of paved streets, and Philadelphia was about to combine the surrounding municipalities to create a municipality coterminous with the 127-square-mile Philadelphia County. And while Pittsburgh's population had increased almost sixfold in one generation, smaller cities like Harrisburg, Lancaster, and York had also grown from mere villages to urban places. Public-private economic partnership had reshaped the landscape in dramatic and prosperous ways. Even though, as in the South, Pennsylvania's transportation network was uneven—too many rail lines in some portions of the state, too few connections to other areas, and too much investment in canals that would soon be outmoded—the idea of government-subsidized roads and bridges was to prove a great boon to the state's growth. Huge expanses of the state were still sparsely populated, still without cities or manufactures, but soon government support helped the modern world reach these areas too. Pennsylvania would move to blend in many of its people and places, but like the nation of which it was a part, Pennsylvania struggled long and hard with the problem of tension among its diverse inhabitants.

THE PRICE OF DIVERSITY: RACIAL, ETHNIC, AND RELIGIOUS TENSIONS

In 1837 Martin Delany and Lewis Woodson, former slaves from Virginia, were living in Pittsburgh. Together they dreamed of and tried to plan for a better world for their African American compatriots. A decade younger than Woodson, Delany was Woodson's student and protégé. Part of a community of some 500 black residents in Pittsburgh, they were acutely aware of their responsibilities to their peers—both the free and those still enslaved. Literate men, they dedicated themselves to educating other black residents, encouraging them to read the black press—in a few years Delany would start his own newspaper, *The Mystery*—and to think deeply about the options and possibilities for black Americans. The two leaders were active in Pittsburgh's independent African American church community (Woodson was a minister), and they put before their community a series of options. Should black Americans continue trying to gain the rights of full citizens? Did antiblack sentiment rampant across the North, and the removal of the African American franchise from the Pennsylvania's constitution, suggest that this strategy was doomed to failure? Perhaps it was best to follow the example of Woodson's father, who was living in an all-black settlement in rural Ohio. Maybe it would be best to find a way to leave the United States altogether and establish a home in Canada or in West Africa.

"Abroad," by H. Harrison after Edward W. Clay, c. 1833. Caricaturists were fond of ridiculing the "aspirings" of African Americans, shown here as this couple appears in public dressed "above their station in life."

In 1840 Delany and Woodson were among the most articulate of Pennsylvania's 47,000 African Americans, but their concerns were those of all black Americans: the short-term problem of agitating to end slavery in the South, and the longer-range question of how to build black communities. While contemplating long-term options, it was clear that Allegheny County's African American residents had an immediate assignment: to assist fugitive slaves from the South. Through the 1830s and 1840s Delany remained in Pittsburgh, taking an active part in western Pennsylvania's branch of the "Vigilance Committees," a network of black reformers radiating out from William Still in Philadelphia, William Whipper in Columbia, and numerous other black activists in towns and villages across the state. These committees kept up a steady dialogue about antislavery strategies, ranging from emigration to boycotts of slave-produced goods. They also formed the backbone of the Underground Railroad, a clandestine network of black and white abolitionists whose goal was to help runaway slaves find safe havens.

In 1820 Columbia, just thirty miles north of the Maryland-Pennsylvania border and a few miles west of Lancaster, counted 288 free black residents and 64 slaves among its population of 1,100. The town, which included a large population of Scots-Irish heritage, had been founded by the Wright family, who were abolitionist Quakers. In the 1820s and 1830s the Wrights welcomed freed slaves to this labor-starved region and provided leadership for the Columbia Abolition Society.

A pillar of Columbia's black community was Stephen Smith, who had purchased his freedom in 1816—the year Constantine Pinchot set sail from France. Like Pinchot, Smith began to make his fortune in real estate and lumber, and by 1830 he was a wealthy man in a town where the African American population had grown to more than 20 percent of the town's 2,000 residents. In the next few years white workers in Columbia petitioned the town government to limit the growth of the black population, lest they flood the labor market and thereby reduce employment opportunities and depress the wages of white workers. When the municipal government was unresponsive, local white residents took matters into their own hands, lashing out with mob attacks on the black community. These riots, which occurred in 1834, echoed similar expressions of racial resentment in cities across Pennsylvania, New York, Ohio, and Maryland. Where the local legislature had refused, the citizens' direct action succeeded. Some African Americans fled the city; others who might have moved into the city chose other destinations.

Evidence of white resistance to African Americans' progress came from many parts of the state but especially from Philadelphia, which was home to the largest and best-situated concentration of the North's free black population. Philadelphia had long been a haven for African Americans, as its proximity to the slave South, and its strongly abolitionist Quaker community, made it a natural stopping place for fugitive slaves. But Philadelphians were not united in offering sanctuary to black refugees. Through the 1820s, as the African American population approached 15,000, resistance rose to what one observer described as African Americans' "aspirings and little vanities." Their "aspirings" were indeed noticeable. By the 1840s a small but well-settled black middle class had established a firm hold on an urbane life. They owned some $600,000 worth of real estate and supported almost two dozen churches and dozens of philanthropic and intellectual organizations. They had their own insurance companies, libraries, loan associations, labor unions, and fraternities. Though representing less than 10 percent of the city's total population, these bustling black residents were highly visible. But their place in the city's economy was always precarious. Low-skilled African Americans had had a virtual monopoly on the poorly paid but steady work of wood-sawyering, chimney-sweeping, hauling, laundering, and food service. When the 1830s brought Irish immigrants who competed for those jobs, the stage was set for racial/economic violence.

FRANK JOHNSON.

Published at the Arch St. Gallery of the Daguerreotype, Philadelphia.

PRINTED BY WAGNER & M¢GUIGAN

Musician and composer Frank Johnson (1792–1844) performed with his band at upper-class events for whites in both American and European cities. This lithograph is by another talented member of Philadelphia's African American community, Robert Douglass Jr.

Violence against Philadelphia African Americans was frequent and brutal. In the summer of 1834, for example, a three-day riot resulted in the destruction of an African American church and the injury of numerous black residents. One observer described the cause: "An opinion prevails, among white laborers, that certain portions of our community prefer to employ colored people . . . to the employment of white people; and in consequence of this preference, many whites who are willing and able to work, are left without employment." In Columbia, that same summer, a similar attack also destroyed a black church and injured black residents.

In Philadelphia, occupational competition was one factor in racial tension, but there were other aspects. Though the overwhelming majority of Philadelphia's population was probably opposed to abolition (because the local economy and social life had close ties to the cotton-producing South), the city was a locus of abolitionist activity. The American Anti-Slavery Society was founded there in 1833. So too was the Philadelphia Female Anti-Slavery Society (1833) and the Pennsylvania Anti-Slavery Society (1837). In 1835 a group of rioters had seized a shipment of antislavery pamphlets, shredded them, and disposed of them in the Delaware River, but the abolitionist community remained

The California House race riot of 1849, depicted here, was one in a series of violent uprisings in Philadelphia during the 1830s and 1840s that pitted blacks against whites.

undaunted. Unable to obtain meeting space in local accommodations, they built their own meeting place, Pennsylvania Hall.

White resistance was swift and powerful. The hall was completed in May 1838. The following week, when black and white friends were seen there arm in arm, a crowd gathered and torched the building, burning it to the ground. Local authorities stood passively by as street-brawling ensued, and congregants barely escaped with their lives. A few years later, the Flying Horse Tavern, owned by a mixed-race couple, was subjected to a similar attack. In both cases the cry of "amalgamation" (intermingling of the races) accompanied the uprising.

By 1840 the proportion of African American residents in Pennsylvania cities and towns began to level off or decline. In Columbia the Wright family, sobered by white workers' angry outbursts and no longer concerned about a labor shortage, began to encourage free black people to relocate to Africa. Few took this suggestion, but many did emigrate to Ontario, where the government offered sanctuary to the refugees. Stephen Smith refused to leave the commercial empire he had painstakingly constructed, but the Columbia where he had made his fortune was no longer the hospitable home he had known. Thereafter, he spent a great deal of his time in the larger and more stable Philadelphia black community, where there were broader opportunities for economic success (Smith teamed up with William Still in a coal business), companionship (he also joined Philadelphia's black social clubs), and political action (Smith was active in the battle for restoring the franchise to black Pennsylvanians). For this Philadelphia community Smith would, in his will, endow a community home for elderly African Americans.

Pennsylvania was for several reasons an important link in the Underground

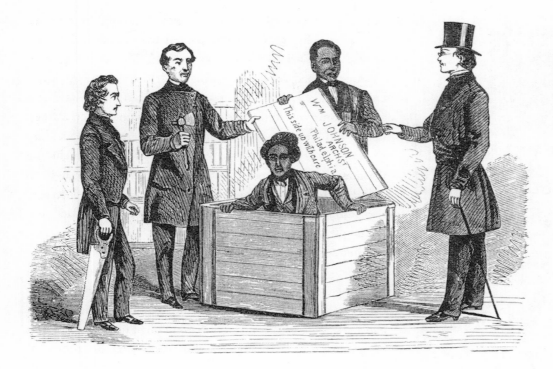

Henry "Box" Brown was a slave who traveled from Richmond, Virginia, to Philadelphia packed inside a two-foot-square crate. This image was created around the year 1854 to raise public awareness of the plight of runaways and the successes of the Underground Railroad. In fact, Brown's daring feat had been carried out some years before.

Railroad. First, its 200-mile-long border with Maryland, and easy access to the Potomac and Susquehanna Rivers and the tangle of waterways and railways that connected the state to Richmond, Baltimore, and the Chesapeake region, made it an obvious exit-point from the South. Finally, by 1800 Pennsylvania was home to more than 16,000 African Americans, and by 1830 that number had tripled, making the state a logical place for a fugitive to expect to find a community with which to blend in. Philadelphia was just such a location. But so too were Columbia, Lancaster, Erie, and Pittsburgh. In these cities a runaway slave could expect the kind of protection that was given to a fugitive named Briscoe when slave catchers caught up with him in Allegheny County, near Pittsburgh. The Vigilance Committee confronted the hunters, rescued Briscoe, and sent him on his way north.

The Fugitive Slave Law, which required federal marshals and local residents to assist with recapturing runaway slaves and was passed in the U.S. Congress in September 1850, caused the Vigilance Committees to reallocate their energies. While this Underground Railroad network continued to help settle people in Philadelphia, Harrisburg, Columbia, and other towns, more of their focus was shifted to helping people move across the border into Canada, out of the jurisdiction of federal marshals. Sometimes, however, the black communities exploded in rebellion, such as that which rescued Briscoe, and occasionally these communities resorted to armed confrontation.

One notable incident occurred in Christiana, near Lancaster, in 1851. A Maryland fugitive named Joshua Kite, who had begun to make a life for himself in the two years

MOTHERS LOOK OUT FOR YOUR CHILDREN!
ARTISANS, MECHANICS, CITIZENS!
When you leave your family in health, must you be hurried home to mourn a
DREADFUL CASUALITY!
PHILADELPHIANS, your RIGHTS are being invaded! regardless of your interests, or the LIVES OF YOUR LITTLE ONES. THE CAMDEN AND AMBOY, with the assistance of other companies without a Charter, and in VIOLATION OF LAW, as decreed by your Courts, are laying a
LOCOMOTIVE RAIL ROAD!
Through your most Beautiful Streets, to the RUIN of your TRADE, annihilation of your RIGHTS, and regardless of your PROSPERITY and COMFORT. Will you permit this! or do you consent to be a
SUBURB OF NEW YORK!!
Rails are now being laid on BROAD STREET to CONNECT the TRENTON RAIL ROAD with the WILMINGTON and BALTIMORE ROAD, under the pretence of constructing a City Passenger Railway from the Navy Yard to Fairmount!!! This is done under the auspices of the CAMDEN AND AMBOY MONOPOLY!
RALLY PEOPLE in the Majesty of your Strength and forbid THIS
OUTRAGE!

Railroads penetrating urban places brought goods and people but also danger, and they disrupted neighborhoods with their intrusion of noise, dirt, and speeding trains. Antirailroad riots broke out in such places as the Kensington section of Philadelphia, where local residents complained bitterly of the risk of fire caused by hot cinders from coal-powered steam engines spraying onto their houses, or by train wrecks, which threatened the safety of local residents. Many of these were Irish hand-loom weavers dislocated from their cottage-industry jobs by the introduction of power mills; they also resented the threat railroads presented to workers' local monopolies.

since he had escaped from slavery, was discovered by his master's spies. The master, accompanied by federal authorities, arrived in Christiana to claim Kite. But the Vigilance Committee had advance warning, and by the time the slave-hunting party arrived, Kite was ensconced in a makeshift fort at the home of committee member William Parker. Parker, Kite, and several others—including a machete-wielding woman—held off the attack, killing several people (including the master) and wounding others. The rebels were brought to trial, but the local residents, in protest against federal intervention into local affairs, refused to convict them. Local black residents, pleased with their victory, passed the story on to their children, who have kept it alive over many generations.

The issues raised by the "Christiana Riot" reoccurred in various guises all across Pennsylvania: issues of what communities felt they could or could not—or would or would not—allow residents to do; issues of who might exercise what kinds of authority. In Philadelphia, ethnic and religious confrontations occurred throughout the 1830s and 1840s, as the city's Irish population increased dramatically. Many of the new immigrants were unskilled factory or dock workers, many were from southern Ireland, and most were Catholic. In the Kensington district of Philadelphia, they shared a neighborhood with Northern Irish skilled weavers, who were mostly Protestant. Believing that the rising number of Catholics signified a papist conspiracy to seize control of the United States, a coalition of Protestants formed a Union of Protestant Associations and began distributing anti-Catholic literature. They were encouraged by the Native American Party, a nativist political organization formed to contest Catholic "invasion." When, in the early 1840s, Bishop Francis Kenrick requested that Catholic children in public schools be allowed to use the Catholic Bible, the stage was set for conflict.

In May 1844 a group of Irish Catholic men heckled a meeting of nativists in Kensington. The nativists retaliated by burning several Irish Catholic churches and homes. Before the dust had settled on this, another anti-Catholic riot, elsewhere in Philadelphia a few weeks later, caused extensive property damage. These incidents required widespread use of militia, and dozens of deaths resulted from these battles over neighborhoods, religion, and authority.

Like labor disputes and the conflicts over racial boundaries, the Protestant/Catholic, nativist/immigrant, skilled/unskilled worker conflicts were manifested general apprehension about the stability of society and the future of Pennsylvania. The unrest was widespread. Swept up in the ferment of reform, Pennsylvania women were among the leaders of the early nineteenth-century movement for woman's rights. Here again Quaker culture provided an atmosphere in which a women's crusade could be nurtured. Quaker tradition had long promoted the equality of women. While not every Quaker supported women's independence, enough Quaker women traveled and preached that most Quakers were not surprised to see women holding forth in public.

Pennsylvania woman's rights leaders included Jane Grey Swisshelm in Pittsburgh and Lucretia Mott in Philadelphia, a white antislavery advocate who quickly saw the incongruity in protesting injustices against African Americans while women themselves were denied full citizenship rights. In 1833 Mott was one of the handful of women who founded the Philadelphia Female Anti-Slavery Society. Mott's colleagues in drafting the charter of the Society included African American teachers Margaretta Forten and Sarah Mapps Douglass. The Society sent numerous petitions to state and federal officials, calling attention to the dual injustices of racial and gender disfranchisement. The group also raised funds to support the work of the Vigilance Committees. But not until World War I did Pennsylvania's legislature adopt an attitude sympathetic to enfranchising women.

In the 1850s Pennsylvanians were open to an influx of varied people and liberal ideas. But they were uncertain about how deeply and consistently they could embrace these ideas and remain politically, economically, and socially at peace. Social protest and social reform could be tolerated, but only to the degree that they did not interfere with a stable work force or threaten industrial growth. Columbia's African American residents had learned all-too-clearly that when the labor shortage disappeared, so too did the enthusiasm white residents had for their plight. In response, legislatures would mandate larger, more formal, and more professional police forces to maintain social and political peace.

Contemporary printers of newspapers and other media found that the drama of street-rioting sold publications. This pamphlet, "embellished with ten engravings," fed and was fed by public anxiety about ethnic conflict.

A PRISM FOR IDENTITY

In 1828 John Fanning Watson, chronicler of Philadelphia's history, rode out to look at Valley Forge, the rural location where George Washington had camped with his troops during the Revolutionary War. What Watson saw was a lime quarry and a thriving textile mill. Two years earlier, the Friendly Association for Mutual Interests had also taken an interest in the site. There had been a plan afoot to turn the area into a cooperative community village modeled after European socialist economic experiments. William Maclure of Philadelphia had been a leader in another scheme to memorialize this site where Washington and his Continental Army had, according to popular accounts, nearly starved and frozen to death during the bitter winter of 1778, while the British army celebrated in the warm houses of Philadelphia.

Maclure's vision of Valley Forge as an experimental community never caught on, but in the year that Watson took notice of the hallowed ground, a Fourth of July celebration was held there, and references to Washington's army encampment were included in the commemoratory presentations. But then once again Pennsylvanians turned their atten-

Crazy Nora, a painting in oil by William E. Winner, c. 1860–65, depicts Irish-born Honora Power (d. 1867). Power suffered a mental breakdown following the anti-Catholic riots in Philadelphia and for a time survived on public charity. She was one of the many "street" figures who fascinated and occasioned comment from visitors to Philadelphia, but her life was in fact representative of the vagaries of urban life for many immigrants and members of the working classes.

tions elsewhere, and industry continued to claim the site. In the early decades of the nineteenth century, Americans found themselves drawn to the task of creating an identity that defined their separateness from Europe. Identifying places and ways to highlight the nation's story was one way to do this. Historical consciousness was in the wind, and John Fanning Watson was not the only one to notice. In the early nineteenth century, many Pennsylvanians were looking at Valley Forge, at the Old State House in Philadelphia, and at a number of other sites and ways to heighten their image as the social, political, and economic "birthplace of a nation."

In the decade preceding Watson's pilgrimage, Pennsylvania leaders had begun to take notice of the region's history. They had renovated the State House, where the Declaration of Independence was signed. They had reclaimed the city squares laid out by William Penn that had been allowed to decay as cemeteries for the poor—landscaping and renaming them in honor of eighteenth-century local heroes William Logan, George Washington, and David Rittenhouse. In Philadelphia the self-conscious remodeling had begun with the preparations for the 1824 visit of the Marquis de Lafayette—his first visit to the city since he had come to help Americans win their Revolution more than four decades earlier. The Historical Society of Pennsylvania, organized in Philadelphia that same year, took seriously its mission to collect and protect the state's heritage. So too did the historical society organized in Pittsburgh only a decade later. Similar image-building institutions proliferated. In Philadelphia the Academy of Natural Sciences, established in 1816, envisioned a mission of promoting Philadelphia's image as a locus of scientific inquiry; the organization's charter prohibited discussion of politics or religion. Under William Maclure's leadership, it began assembling a library and specimens illustrating aspects of astronomy, geology, and meteorology. Libraries and voluntary reading societies proliferated wherever a group could gather with a few books.

But the seed of self-consciousness had been planted. Voluntary associations across the state took up the cause of rescuing and interpreting Pennsylvania's cultural identity, and interpreters of the state's history emphasized its leadership in shaping American traditions. They put the focus on Pennsylvanians as political innovators; after all, the Pennsylvania Constitution of 1790 was the model for Kentucky's 1792 constitution. And they reminded their compatriots that the "Pennsylvania system" of nominating governors by conventions of delegates from across the state had caught on in many other states, and that Andrew Jackson was the first President of the United States nominated by this system.

State boosters also cited other areas of innovation. The Library Company of Philadelphia, the first continuously operating lending library in America, was held up as an indication of what could be accomplished by cooperative civic responsibility. In Philadelphia, in 1824, the Franklin Institute, established "to promote the mechanic arts," sought to promote modern technology, encourage manufacturing innovation, and establish communication with like-minded people in other parts of the United States and Europe. In Pittsburgh Stephen Foster wrote songs celebrating American people and places, and by 1846 this twenty-one-year-old musician had published more than 200 songs.

Not content only to be leaders in manufacturing, Pennsylvania's urban areas trumpeted their importance through their architecture and town planning. Ambitious architects, lured by the wealth and the building boom in Pennsylvania cities, competed to display their talents. British architect Benjamin Henry Latrobe, who had come to the United States at the turn of the nineteenth century, trained several architects who then spent much of their careers in Pennsylvania. Among the most influential of Latrobe's students was William Strickland, an accomplished engineer and illustrator as well as a master of early nineteenth-century Greek Revival style. Nicholas Biddle, who had become enamored of Greek architecture while he was in Europe, probably was instrumental in helping Strickland get the contract for the Second Bank of the United States, which still stands on Chestnut Street in Philadelphia. Among Latrobe's students was also John Haviland, whose design for the dramatic, fortress-like Eastern State Penitentiary, near Philadelphia, was the main reason for Tocqueville's visit to the United States. Haviland's work in Philadelphia, including several museums, churches, and charitable institutions, soon led to a career in New York as well.

A fourth member of the early nineteenth-century Philadelphia architectural giants was Thomas U. Walter. As urban Americans tried to keep abreast of the demands of urban life, public charity (orphanages, work houses for widows, homes for the aged, hospitals and special schools) added to the already brisk demand for new buildings. Many of these buildings were massive in conception—designed to do a big job, and to do it with flair. Such an example was Girard College, a school for orphaned boys from Philadelphia. Walter was delighted to be the winner in the brisk competition for the Girard College design, and the resulting project was lavish and elegant.

Impressive too was Walter's county prison, built at Moyamensing in 1833. The work of Latrobe, Strickland, Haviland, and Walter dominated the grand buildings of Philadelphia and gave new energy to the classic design of the Philadelphia row house. Their ideas were copied in smaller towns by local builders, who also aspired to help their communities advance Pennsylvania's economic stature.

Redesigned prisons and philanthropic institutions were but one aspect of a general social ferment. Across the western world, the mood of the early nineteenth century was to bring order out of chaotic urban life. It was a mood marked by social reform and by a

Eastern State Penitentiary. Originally named Cherry Hill, for its commanding view of the environs, this experiment in social rehabilitation was located just north of Philadelphia. Its design, heavily influenced by Quaker ideas of the value of silent prayer, included individual sky-lit, monastery-like cells that were meant to encourage transgressors to contemplate and pray for salvation. Outdoor exercise yards and useful manual labor were also part of the plan for preparing repentant prisoners to return to their communities. That it soon became clear that solitary confinement was counterproductive in rehabilitating criminals did not detract from the majesty of the design. Eastern was a major tourist destination for Europeans in the years before the Civil War.

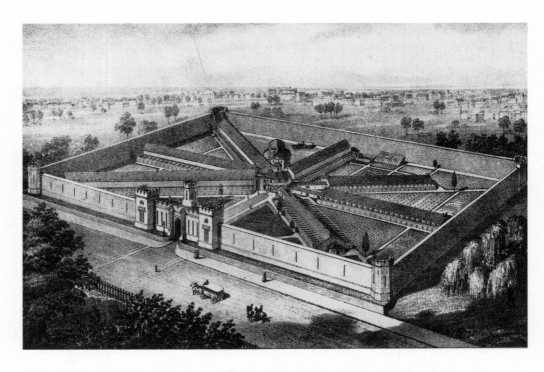

Western State Penitentiary. In 1818 the state legislature voted for "a penitentiary on the principle of solitary confinement of convicts" at Allegheny. The building took eight years to complete. Although much less celebrated than Eastern State Penitentiary, the Allegheny penitentiary also reflected the state's interest in prison reform, with an emphasis on rehabilitation rather than only punishment of inmates.

desire to seek improvements in community life, to reduce suffering, to create "rational" systems for understanding and guiding human interaction. Some reformers tried to make prisons more humane; abolitionists were convinced that ending slavery would improve society; religious reformers were sure that reshaping religious practices would bring about social salvation; and followers of such idealists as French philosopher Charles Fourier made various attempts to shape communal experiments. No longer subjects of a monarch, Americans now experimented with ways to create an identity and to define what it might mean to be a "citizen."

The Oneida Community in New York, and Brook Farm in Massachusetts, are the best known of such cooperative communities, but Pennsylvania also had its share of such experiments. One Pennsylvania community in Pike County, Sylvania Phalanx, in which *New York Tribune* editor Horace Greeley played a leading role, was part of this network of agrarian-handicraft movements. Founded in 1842, Sylvania lasted less than a decade. In Butler County, George Rapp helped lead a group of German Pietists to establish a community built on "divine economy." Renewed in the twentieth century as a living museum known as Old Economy Village, the 3,000-acre community was focused around arts, crafts, and silkmaking. But the community also invested in railroads and oil fields. Evergreen Hamlet, near Pittsburgh, was conceived by lawyer William Shinn. Designed around an eighty-five-acre plot of ground, it was to be home to sixteen families and to offer the "advantages of country at a moderate cost" but with the social advantages of city life. Begun in 1851, Evergreen built only four houses before it dissolved in 1866.

There was innovation in every arena, and in this period the tools for capturing the visual romance of Pennsylvania's past and present became more sophisticated also. In the 1820s several skilled lithographers turned the energy of this new craft to illustrating the city's buildings and vistas. In 1839 Philadelphia's Franklin Institute published a translation of Frenchman Louis Daguerre's description of how to create a visual image, and shortly thereafter the *Pittsburgh Daily Gazette* followed suit; within months, Pennsylvanians were experimenting with the technique. Over the next decade Pittsburgh dentist W. M. Wright and Philadelphians Marcus Aurelius Root and John Fries Frazer advertised their ability to make "accurate miniatures of themselves and their friends." So too did Miss A. Smith and African American John Ball enter the trade in the Pittsburgh area. Increasingly it became possible to publicize an image that would inform, inspire, and unify Pennsylvania's communities.

But deciding what symbols would best typify Pennsylvania was not a simple matter. In 1844 there was yet another attempt to recognize the importance of Valley Forge as a historically important site. This time it was Daniel Webster, holding a political rally there, that brought Isaac Pennypacker of Phoenixville to undertake the mission of rescuing what he referred to as a "neglected" location of historical significance. This was the year when the Fairmount Park Commission began purchasing private estates along the Schuylkill River in order to gain control over the region's water supply. As with canals and railroads, public and private goals seemed to merge.

THE DIVERSITY OF THE HUB

By 1850 almost one-quarter of Pennsylvania's 2,000,000 residents lived in urban places.

BURGEONING CITY LIFE:
PERILS AND PASTIMES

The romantic side of city life was that it was dynamic, stimulating, and exciting. But urban places were also filled with epidemics, crowded streets and traffic accidents, fires that could ravage whole neighborhoods, and the seamy life of saloons and drunkenness. All this reminded city-dwellers that something must be done to make city life less threatening. Various reformers had diverse ideas about what that "something" should be.

CLOCKWISE FROM TOP: "Great Conflagration at Pittsburgh, Pa., April 10 1845." The great fire destroyed many of the city's buildings and the Monongahela Bridge, which reportedly burned in eight minutes.

Lager Beer Saloon, by Christian Schuessele, a German immigrant who later became head of the Pennsylvania Academy of the Fine Arts.

"Trotting Cracks of Philadelphia Returning from the Race at Point Breeze Park."

Philadelphia and Pittsburgh, the two largest industrial centers, accounted for more than 50 percent of the state's manufacturing revenue, with Pittsburgh surpassing Philadelphia in technological sophistication. A diversity of people—Scots-Irish and African American, German and Irish, Methodist, Lutheran, and Catholic—worked in a wide variety of industries: iron and textiles, chemicals and meatpacking, glassmaking and petroleum processing, bootmaking and sugar-refining, manufacturing of rifles and rope and scientific instruments, farming, and mining. Though settlement in the state was clustered into regions separated by mountainous terrain, trains and canals and wagon traffic and mail routes kept the regions from becoming completely isolated from one another, or from the state leadership in Harrisburg.

Perhaps Columbia was as good a measure as any of the diversity of a "typical" Pennsylvania town. In 1850 more than 10 percent of its 4,000-person population had been born outside the United States, and of that number more than half were from Germany and another one-third were from Ireland. More than 20 percent of Columbia's residents were of African American heritage; more than half that number were from slave states, and a significant number were of mixed-race heritage. The town's economy was a combination of industry and transportation technology. Its geographic location, at a hub between major cities, the hinterlands of Pennsylvania, and the nearby connection to Maryland, ensured that it would have a central place in the state's economy. By 1850, having lived through violence and unrest that resulted from the friction of divergent peoples, cultures, and economies struggling to create community out of disparate and discordant histories, Columbia had come to an uneasy—and frequently broken—truce with its variety of people.

By 1850 Pennsylvanians of many backgrounds had spent more than two generations amassing a shared experience through which to explain to themselves who they were. Visitors like Alexis de Tocqueville, who described Pennsylvanians with an outsider's eye, helped Pennsylvania citizens clarify new ways to see themselves. The world that Tocqueville had described as "driven to commerce and industry" was poised for the next big leap into the modern world.

SOURCES *and* FURTHER READING

Blumin, Stuart M. *The Emergence of the Middle Class: Social Experience in the American City, 1760–1900.* New York: Cambridge University Press, 1989.

Bruggeman, Seth C. "Pennsylvania Boatbuilding: Charting a State Tradition." *Pennsylvania History* 65 (Spring 1998), 170–89.

Caric, Ric Northrup. "'To Drown the Ills That Discompose the Mind': Care, Leisure, and Identity Among Philadelphia Artisans and Workers, 1785–1840." *Pennsylvania History* 64 (Autumn 1997), 465–89.

Clark, Dennis. *The Irish in Philadelphia.* Philadelphia: Temple University Press, 1973.

Dubofsky, Melvyn. "The Origins of the Labor Movement in the United States: Themes from the Nineteenth Century." *Pennsylvania History* 58 (October 1991), 269–77.

Eggert, Gerald G. *Harrisburg Industrializes: The Coming of Factories to an American Community.* University Park: The Pennsylvania State University Press, 1993.

———. "'Two Steps Forward, a Step-and-a-Half Back': Harrisburg's African American Community in the Nineteenth Century." *Pennsylvania History* 58 (January 1991), 136.

Farley, James J. *Making Arms in the Machine Age: Philadelphia's Frankford Arsenal, 1816–1870.* University Park: The Pennsylvania State University Press, 1994.

Juliani, Richard N. *Building Little Italy: Philadelphia's Italians Before Mass Migration.* University Park: The Pennsylvania State University Press, 1998.

Light, Dale B. *Rome and the New Republic: Conflict and Community in Philadelphia Catholicism Between the Revolution and the Civil War.* Notre Dame, Ind.: University of Notre Dame Press, 1996.

Lorant, Stefan. *Pittsburgh: The Story of an American City.* New York: Doubleday, 1964.

Majewski, John. *A House Dividing: Economic Development in Pennsylvania and Virginia Before the Civil War.* Cambridge: Cambridge University Press, 2000.

Miller, Char. "All in the Family: The Pinchots of Milford." *Pennsylvania History* 66 (Spring 1999), 117–42.

Reimherr, Otto, ed. *Quest for Faith, Quest for Freedom: Aspects of Pennsylvania's Religious Experience.* Selinsgrove, Pa.: Susquehannna University Press, 1987.

Ruby, Jay. *The World of Francis Cooper: Nineteenth-Century Pennsylvania Photographer.* University Park: The Pennsylvania State University Press, 1999.

Shirk, Willis L. "Testing the Limits of Tolerance: Blacks and the Social Order in Columbia, Pennsylvania, 1800–1851." *Pennsylvania History* 60 (January 1993), 35–50.

Smith, Eric Ledell. "The End of Black Voting Rights in Pennsylvania: African Americans and the Pennsylvania Constitutional Convention of 1837–1838." *Pennsylvania History* 65 (Summer 1998), 279–99.

Toll, Jean Barth, and Mildred Gillam, eds. *Invisible Philadelphia.* Philadelphia: Atwater Kent Museum, 1998.

Treese, Lorett. *Valley Forge: Making and Remaking a National Symbol.* University Park: The Pennsylvania State University Press, 1995.

Warner, Sam Bass. *The Private City: Philadelphia in Three Periods of Its Growth.* Philadelphia: University of Pennsylvania Press, 1968.

Weprich, Thomas M. "Pioneer Photographers in Pittsburgh, Pennsylvania." *Pennsylvania History* 64 (Spring 1997), 193–203.

Winch, Julie. *The Elite of Our People: Joseph Willson's Sketches of Black Upper-Class Life in Antebellum Philadelphia.* University Park: The Pennsylvania State University Press, 2000.

———. *Philadelphia's Black Elite: Activism, Accommodation, and the Struggle for Autonomy, 1787–1848.* Philadelphia: Temple University Press, 1988.

Civil Wars: 1850–1900

WALTER LICHT

July 3, 1863, 3:00 in the afternoon. Division commander George E. Pickett finally receives his orders to lead 14,000 Confederate troops across a three-quarter-mile stretch of rolling Pennsylvania farmland just west of the town of Gettysburg. For two days, southern forces under General Robert E. Lee had failed through bloody assaults at the flanks to break a Union troop high-ground hold along Cemetery Ridge. Lee's daring, massive attack on the North now rests on Pickett's charge into the center of the Union line. Within half an hour, the assault will be completely repelled, 7,000 Confederate soldiers summarily losing their lives. Lee would retreat the next day to the south, on the defensive again facing a continued multifront Yankee invasion. On Pennsylvania farms-turned-battlefield, the tide of the Civil War forever shifted with a toll of more than 50,000 Northern and Southern troops killed or wounded in three days of fighting. President Abraham Lincoln would come to deliver his famous eulogy address at Gettysburg on November 19.

July 21, 1877. A crowd of 6,000 men and women gather at a railroad crossing in the city of Pittsburgh to block freight trains of the Pennsylvania Railroad. On the rail cars are state militia brought in from Philadelphia at the request of Thomas Scott, president of the railroad. Two days earlier, railway workers on the line had joined a nationwide strike to protest severe wage reductions, and local militia had refused to protect company property and take up arms against their neighbors. As community supporters of

Detail from Peter F. Rothermel's massive oil painting *The Battle of Gettysburg: Pickett's Charge* (1870). Rothermel focuses on numerous individuals locked in mortal combat, thereby showing personal heroism as a persistent feature of battle despite the terrible bloodshed fostered by modern technologies of warfare during the Civil War. This painting, 32 feet wide by 16 feet high, is on view at The State Museum of Pennsylvania.

RIGHT: During the 1877 railroad strike, two square miles of downtown Pittsburgh were destroyed and more than forty people were shot. Even though it was a nationwide strike, the greatest loss of life, limb, and property occurred along the tracks of the Pennsylvania Railroad in and around Pittsburgh.

the railway workers assembled to prevent train movements, the Philadelphia troops fired into the crowd, killing twenty and wounding seventy more. Word of the massacre quickly spread, and the people of Pittsburgh took to the streets, looting and setting fires to the property of the Pennsylvania Railroad. By late evening a red glow lit up the city, and daybreak revealed the stations, shops, and rolling stock of the Pennsylvania Railroad reduced to embers and rubble. Pittsburgh remained a battlefield for two more days before order was restored.

July 6, 1892. Three hundred private police from the Pinkerton National Detective Agency are secreted on covered barges to Homestead, Pennsylvania. Henry Frick, general manager of the Homestead steelworks owned by iron and steel magnate Andrew Carnegie, has purchased their services. In June, Frick and Carnegie had determined to expunge the Amalgamated Association of Iron, Steel & Tin Workers, the strongest union of skilled workers in the nation, from their mill. To that end, Frick had refused all dealings with the union and built fortifications around the plant, instructing guards to block entry of Amalgamated members. The Pinkerton guards were there to shore up the defense. Their landing, however, met with armed resistance. As the covered barges

This lithograph depicts scenes from the Homestead Strike of 1892: the Pinkerton detectives attacking the factory workers from a barge on the Monongahela, the role of women in supporting the strike, and the bloody outcome.

neared the Homestead works, striking workers attacked, pelting the Pinkertons with stones and bricks and firing guns. Open warfare ensued, lasting for hours and leading to the death of nine steelworkers and seven Pinkerton guards. Order would be restored only with the arrival of state militia. In the weeks to follow there would be a dramatic assassination attempt on Frick, but ultimately he and Carnegie prevailed as they gradually succeeded in operating their mill with nonunion workers. Gathering national and international attention, the battle at Homestead emerged as an epic confrontation between capital and labor.

Conflict was a hallmark of Pennsylvania's history in the last half of the nineteenth century. Virtually all the great national crises of the latter part of the century unfolded on Pennsylvania soil. Before 1876, sectional tensions, slavery, southern secession, civil war, emancipation, and the restoration of the Union transfixed Americans. Industrial capitalist development, the rise of the corporation, the boom-and-bust cycles of the economy, and the concomitant tensions between capital and labor dominated attention and concerns thereafter. Pennsylvanians were centrally entwined in this shifting fractious history. Ethnic and racial hostilities, the growth of cities, and urban machine politics and corruption made for further divisiveness. Peace did not prevail in Pennsylvania between 1850 and 1900.

THE DIVIDED POLITICS OF THE 1850S, THE CIVIL WAR, AND ITS AFTERMATH

When Robert E. Lee formulated his daring attack on the North in May 1863 he had several ends in mind: to lure northern troops away from besieged southern battlefields, to seize enemy food and military supplies, and to discredit Republican Party leaders while strengthening the hands of northern Democrats who now openly petitioned for a peace settlement with the Confederacy. In invading Pennsylvania, Lee entered a state that held great promise for his latter political objectives. Divisiveness had marked Pennsylvania politics in the decade before the war, and as Lee prepared his troops for the assault on the North, Democrats in the Commonwealth were increasingly questioning the Republican-managed Union cause, especially emancipation as a war aim, and calling for granting concessions to the South and for a negotiated truce.

Flux and confusion had marked Pennsylvania politics in the 1850s. The Democrats maintained a steady but shaky bare majority lead in the state, the party buffeted by internal divisions and evolving challenges from without. At the outset of the decade, Pennsylvania Whigs represented the chief opposition, but within a few years the Whig Party all but disappeared from the state's political scene. Into the breach stepped the quixotic Know-Nothings, a nativist insurgency that had immediate impact but peaked politically in two years' time. The newly formed Republican Party then picked up the pieces of the opposition to the Democrats and began to forge a political force that would see the election of a Republican governor in 1860 and the Electoral College votes of the state awarded to Abraham Lincoln, ensuring his presidential victory. While Pennsylvanians were stirred by such national questions as the tariff and the extension of slavery, local concerns and tensions greatly contributed to the heated and shifting politics of the 1850s.

Until the end of the decade, the Democratic Party generally held sway in Pennsylvania. Between 1840 and 1856, four of the six men elected governor were Democrats; Democrats enjoyed majorities in the state's legislature; and in three of the five presidential elections of the period, Pennsylvanians supported Democratic Party candidates. The Democrats successfully appealed to Pennsylvania with a mélange of often-contradictory messages. The party claimed to represent the common people; opposed privilege, state-charted monopolies, and centralized, invasive government; advocated measures to improve the lot of workers; and recruited immigrants into the political system. Democrats also took pro-South positions, supporting federal compromises that allowed for the extension of slavery, and defending fugitive slave laws. Attacking abolitionists as agitators who exacerbated tensions between the North and South, these Democratic leaders further raised fears of emancipation, of granting rights to African Americans, and of the potential mass migration of blacks from the South to Pennsylvania.

Democratic Party strongholds tended to be in the northern and eastern counties of the state. Several fault lines jeopardized the party's greater success. Party officials had to soft-pedal the tariff question, placing them at odds with their southern counterparts; protection of industry and manufacturing jobs was a popular cause in Pennsylvania. The strong Irish Catholic presence in the party, and the party's avoidance of the temperance issue, generated nativist votes for the opposition. Finally, the party's defense of the South and its condoning of the extension of slavery produced ongoing defections of leaders and the rank and file. David Wilmot, for example, who gained national prominence by sponsoring a measure in Congress dubbed the Wilmot Proviso, to prohibit slavery in territories annexed through war with Mexico, parted company with his fellow Pennsylvania Democrats in the late 1840s. Emerging as a leading spokesman for "free soil," the nonextension of slavery, he later helped establish the Republican Party in Pennsylvania.

The fluctuating fortunes of the Democrats are well illustrated in the life of James Buchanan, the only Pennsylvanian (and the only bachelor) to become President of the United States. Born in Mercersburg in 1791, Buchanan prospered as a lawyer in his young adulthood and then entered public life, serving in the Pennsylvania legislature, the U.S. House of Representatives, and the U.S. Senate from 1834 to 1845. In Congress, Buchanan often sided with the South in sectional controversies, regularly denouncing abolitionists. He unsuccessfully sought the Democratic Party presidential nomination three times, but after holding various diplomatic posts he captured his party's endorsement and the presidency in 1856.

As President, Buchanan presided over the fracturing and decline of the Democratic Party both nationally and in his home state. With a strict view that the U.S. Constitution protected private property—including slaves—he moved against such party leaders as Stephen Douglas, who upheld the principle of popular sovereignty in determining whether slavery would be allowed in newly organized western territories. Buchanan's endorsement of a new state constitution for Kansas permitting slavery that had been enacted without popular approval not only drove a wedge in the party that would see both a southern and a northern Democrat campaign for the presidency in 1860, but also gained votes for candidates who were opposed to any extension of the institution. Buchanan's inaction in the face of a severe economic downturn in 1857 proved equally disastrous to his party's fortunes and contributed to the Democrats' loss of a majority position in the state. After he left the presidency amid the secession crisis of early 1861, Buchanan retired to his beloved estate, "Wheatland," outside Lancaster.

Abraham Lincoln would not have been elected President in November 1860 had the Democrats maintained leverage in Pennsylvania. Lincoln's capture of the state's electoral votes also rested on a consolidated and effective opposition. By the early 1850s the opposing role, appeal, and viability of the Whig Party in Pennsylvania had dissipated. With a leadership largely of well-bred, moralistic, Protestant upper-class men, the party counted few adherents in working-class wards, and particularly among immigrants. While the Democrats sponsored legislation limiting workday hours, Whigs boosted prohibitions on the manufacture and sale of alcoholic beverages. Moreover, the Whig defense of high tariffs and job protection did not lure workers to the fold, as Pennsylvania Democrats generally did not toe to their party's historic opposition to taxes on imported goods. While Pennsylvania Whigs also held definite (though varying) antislavery views, their alliance with southern Whigs prevented them from developing

Never before or after was such a large cohort of Pennsylvania politicians as prominent and influential nationally as during the period directly before, during, and after the Civil War. Congressmen Wilmot, Cameron, Kelley, and Stevens distinguished themselves in opposition to the institution of slavery and for the rights of freed slaves. James Buchanan, the only Pennsylvanian ever to become President, sided with the South in sectional controversies.

CLOCKWISE FROM TOP RIGHT: President James Buchanan, David Wilmot, Thaddeus Stevens, Simon Cameron, William Kelley

Charles Willson Peale, *The Artist in His Museum*, 1822.

CLOCKWISE FROM RIGHT: Peter Cooper, *The South East Prospect of the City of Philadelphia*, c. 1720.

Edward Hicks, *The Peaceable Kingdom,* 1826. This painting is one of many by Hicks that incorporates Benjamin West's popular image of Penn's Treaty with the Indians.

The Charter of Pennsylvania, March 4, 1681.

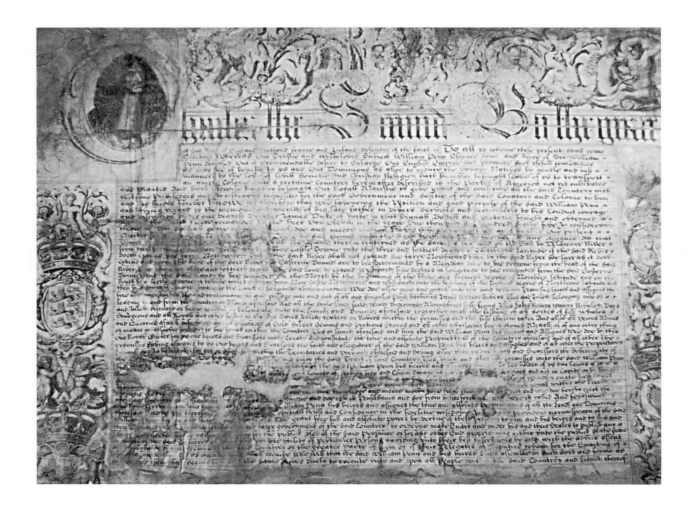

of The City of
ooper Painter

The leopard with the harmless kid laid down
And not one savage beast was seen to frown

The wolf did with the lambkin dwell in peace
His grim carnivorous nature there did cease

The lion with the fatling on did move
A little child was leading them in love;

When the great PENN his famous treaty made
With indian chiefs beneath the Elm-tree's shade.

John Valentine Haidt, *The First Fruits*,
c. 1755–60. Haidt, a Moravian who came to
Bethlehem in 1754, was rare among colonial
American painters in treating mainly religious
subjects. This painting, showing early converts
(or "first fruits") from various cultures, reflects
the Moravian emphasis on missionary work,
which extended to Africa and Asia as well as
the Americas.

Gustavus Hesselius painted these portraits of
the Delaware chieftains Tishcohan and
Lapowinsa on a commission from John and
Thomas Penn during the time of the Walking
Purchase treaty, c. 1735–37.

John Singleton Copley, *Portrait of Mr. and Mrs. Thomas Mifflin (Sarah Morris)*, 1773. Prominent early Americans often had such husband-wife portraits painted when they were married and displayed them prominently in their homes. Thomas Mifflin was the first elected governor of Pennsylvania under the Federal Constitution, from 1789 to 1799, and retained the support of most of the population despite the decade's fierce political struggles.

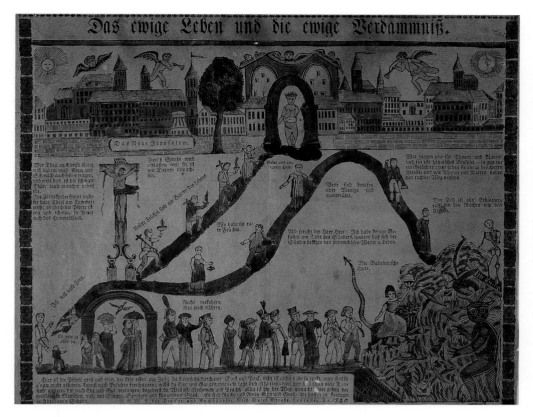

CLOCKWISE FROM LEFT: Hand-colored printed broadside from Lancaster, c. 1820, featuring the Fraktur script and decoration popular among Pennsylvania Germans. This particular broadside, copied from a European original and entitled "Eternal Life and Eternal Damnation," offered pious admonition to the faithful in Lutheran and Reformed congregations.

Linton Park, *Flax Scutching Bee,* 1885. Park, from present-day Marion Center, first exhibited this painting at the 1885 Indiana County Fair.

John Lewis Krimmel, *Election Day at the State House,* 1815. Scenes of public celebrations were a favorite of Krimmel, a German immigrant who worked in Philadelphia from 1809 to 1822.

John Trumbull, *Declaration of Independence in Congress, at the Independence Hall, Philadelphia, July 4, 1776.* This is one of four large paintings that Trumbull completed for the rotunda of the U.S. Capitol, where it was installed in 1819.

ABOVE: George Inness, *The Lackawanna Valley,* 1855. Commissioned by the Delaware, Lackawanna, and Western Railroad, Inness's painting is perhaps the most famous nineteenth-century American landscape to juxtapose sublime nature and industrial advance.

RIGHT: George Hetzel, *Two Young Fishermen in Summer Landscape,* 1867. Hetzel was one of a number of artists who, during the years of the industrial revolution, found solace in the beauty of Pennsylvania's rural landscapes.

antislavery as the defining and sustaining issue of the party. Holding on, but heading toward extinction, the Whigs disappeared with the emergence of the Know-Nothing and Republican insurgencies.

When nativists joined the nationwide secret fraternal Order of the Star Spangled Banner, founded in 1849, they pledged to say "I know nothing" when asked about the organization. The first lodge of the order appeared in Pennsylvania in 1852, and by 1854 Pennsylvania Know-Nothings, under the aegis of the newly formed American Party, triumphantly entered the public arena, severely cutting into the Whig vote and scaring Democrats, while championing immigration restriction and temperance and specifically attacking Catholic institutions and candidates. The appeal of the Know-Nothings lay in more than simple fear of immigrants. In pointing to the hierarchical principles and practices of the Catholic Church and the hold that Catholic priests presumably had on parishioners, Know-Nothings presented themselves as antiauthoritarian and the defenders of democratic republican traditions and institutions. In linking political corruption to the immigrant vote and championing temperance, they also claimed to be the upholders of moral reform and order. The Know-Nothings ascended rapidly in Pennsylvania politics—building on the first upsurges of nativism in the 1840s—but did not remain an independent force for long with their limited platform. Rather than disappearing, they folded into a broader anti–Democratic Party alliance put together by leaders of the new Republican Party, a party established in opposition to any extension of slavery.

David Wilmot played a leading role in the founding of the national Republican Party at a convention in Pittsburgh in February 1856 (the party held its first presidential nominating convention several months later in Philadelphia). Its chosen candidate, John C. Frémont, however, fared poorly in Pennsylvania, recording there his lowest percentage of votes in a northern state. Pennsylvania Republicans faced the challenge of building a strong base. Within four years, they would succeed by uniting Free Soilers, former Whigs, disaffected Democrats, and Know-Nothings. The political failings of James Buchanan, and his insensitivity to the plight of his fellow Pennsylvanians affected by the economic downturn of 1857, worked to their great advantage as well.

The principled stand of Republicans against the extension of slavery provided a new home for such Free Soilers as David Wilmot. Abolitionists, a tiny minority in the state, also joined—but with resignation, certainly not encouraged by the expressed antipathies of Republicans for African Americans. Republican support of positive government activity to promote both economic development and moral order—they supported high tariffs as well as temperance—similarly lured former Whigs to the banner. For Democrats dissatisfied with their party's varied defense of slavery or the growing strong immigrant Catholic presence in the ranks, the Republicans appeared as a tolerable alternative. In representing themselves as the true defenders of the republic in the face of similarly despotic conspiratorial challenges from the slaveholding elite and Catholic

Political gatherings in nineteenth-century Philadelphia invariably attracted crowds. Here, a depiction of the first Republican Convention in Philadelphia, 1856.

Church authorities, the Republicans effectively appealed to Know-Nothings.

The Republicans' ability to cut across and merge these different constituencies is highlighted in the career of a third nationally prominent Pennsylvania politician of the era, and archrival to James Buchanan: Simon Cameron. Cameron embodied the various strands of the party. Born in Lancaster in 1799, he made his first mark as a newspaper publisher and then entered politics, where he would be in the limelight through a long career, largely and unfortunately for the charges of corruption that repeatedly surrounded him. Cameron cast his lot first with the Democrats, but not with the mainstream of the party. He became a strong advocate of tariffs and government-sponsored internal improvements and a foe of James Buchanan. Without Buchanan's support, he won a seat in the U.S. Senate in 1845 but served only one term. In 1854 he renounced his Democratic Party allegiance and joined the Know-Nothings, unsuccessfully running again for the Senate on the American Party ticket, campaigning on a platform to lengthen the naturalization process for immigrants. Two years later he switched to the Republican Party, and under that party's banner he was elected to a second senatorial term. Cameron worked hard to strengthen the Republican Party organization in Pennsylvania and secure Abraham Lincoln's election, and for his service Lincoln awarded him the post of secretary of war. New charges of corruption forced the President to drop Cameron from his inner circle, however, and after holding an ambassadorship Cameron returned for a third term in the Senate representing Pennsylvania. There he joined other Republicans in supporting a radical reconstruction for the South after the defeat of the Confederacy.

Simon Cameron personified not only the Republican fusion but also the very flux of politics in Pennsylvania during the 1850s. National issues, such as slavery and the tariff, divided and mobilized Pennsylvanians, but local ethnic and religious hostilities and the vicissitudes of the economy shaped political arrangements and realignments as well. The decade ultimately saw the emergence of a consolidated opposition to the Democrats and the casting of the critical Electoral College votes of the Commonwealth of Pennsylvania for Abraham Lincoln.

The election of Abraham Lincoln in November 1860 set in motion a series of decisions and events that led to the outbreak of war between the North and South in April 1861. Within months of the election, political leaders in seven southern states declared their entities independent of the United States and then in February 1861 joined together to form the Confederacy. Pennsylvanians did not receive news of the South's secession with overall alarm or immediate calls to arms to stem the treachery. At least until April 12, 1861, with the Confederate bombardment of Fort Sumter in Charleston's harbor,

widespread sentiment existed in Pennsylvania for granting concessions to the South and an amicable return to unity.

Among those advising caution, opinions varied; some advocated actual support for secession and formal recognition of the Confederacy, others suggested compromises—such as a constitutional amendment guaranteeing slavery where it existed—that would encourage the secessionists to reverse their course and return to the fold. Only with the assault on Fort Sumter did Pennsylvanians rally to preserve the Union with force. Pro-South, anti–Republican Party views receded with the initial enthusiasm for the battle, but a vocal antiwar movement surfaced within two years.

Upward of 360,000 men enlisted in Pennsylvania regiments during the four years of bloody fighting, but because men signed on for discrete periods and frequently reenlisted, the actual number who fought was far fewer. Still, Pennsylvanians formed 248 Union battalions that saw service in all the war zones and critical engagements. More than 33,000 were killed in battle or mortally wounded. Included in the ranks of the Pennsylvanians

"The Capitol Grounds at Harrisburg Turned into a Camp," from *Harper's Weekly,* October 4, 1862. Tens of thousands of Pennsylvanians volunteered to defend the Union cause and the Commonwealth and trained in camps throughout the state. Yet resistance to enlistment and the drafting of soldiers was also widespread.

"United States Soldiers at Camp William Penn" (1864), by P. S. Duval. Based on Duval's chromolithograph "Come and Join Us Brothers" (1863), this became the most famous Civil War recruiting poster for African Americans. It featured black soldiers stationed at Camp William Penn outside Philadelphia. They were commanded by white officers, as were all black soldiers during the war, but their determined gaze bespoke their resolve to save the Union and end slavery. Opposition to enlisting black troops in Pennsylvania did not let up until after Lee's invasion in 1863. When black soldiers training at Camp William Penn were denied access to local streetcars on their way to and from home, an Equal Rights League emerged within Philadelphia's black community to protest segregated public facilities.

mobilized against the Confederacy were 8,600 African Americans, organized belatedly in all-black troops with white officers after intensive lobbying by abolitionist forces. Pennsylvania also supplied military leaders of varying ability and success for the Union army, notably Generals George B. McClellan, George G. Meade, Winfield S. Hancock, John F. Reynolds, John W. Geary, and John F. Hartranft. Admiral David D. Porter, who directed western river campaigns, hailed from Pennsylvania. Lincoln's secretaries of war—first Simon Cameron, then Edwin M. Stanton—were proud Pennsylvanians too.

On the home front, workers in Philadelphia's textile mills produced wool blankets for soldiers and cloth to be sewn into uniforms in the city's garment shops and homes. Philadelphia's vast metalwork firms issued locomotives and critical supplies of rifles and cannons for the war effort. Along the Delaware River, workers constructed vessels that enabled the North to maintain a blockade of southern ports. Fleets for Ohio and Mississippi River campaigns were similarly built in Pittsburgh, where iron mills also operated around the clock producing iron to be cast and forged into rifles and cannons. The Fort Pitt Works alone supplied 1,200 cannons during the war, 15 percent of the total manufactured in the North. From the anthracite coal fields of the east and the bituminous of the west came coal to fuel locomotives and produce iron. Agricultural regions of the state similarly yielded foodstuffs to sustain Union soldiers.

These sizable and indispensable contributions of Pennsylvania in providing military and food supplies rested on the firm agricultural and industrial base that the state had established before the war. Railroads provide another example of the ways in which the previous achievements of Pennsylvanians greatly assisted the Union war effort. Pennsylvania's rail carriers were able effectively to move troops and supplies in one of the first military uses of railroads in history. The building of the railroads before the war also had required development of financial institutions and markets, particularly for the issuance and circulation of bonds. Established banking houses had appeared in Philadelphia in the antebellum period. Jay Cooke, a Philadelphia investment banker who had pioneered in the marketing of railroad bonds, served as the chief agent for the federal government in the sale of war bonds, raising critical funds to pay for the war effort (and for which he received handsome commissions).

During the Civil War, Pennsylvania communities kept up with the war through letters and reports from the men they sent off to fight, but especially through the press. Major newspapers stationed correspondents with the northern armies to report the doings of the troops, and wire services provided reports from the front. Here, on June 9, 1862, the *Pittsburgh Dispatch* office advertises its report from the Battle of Fair Oaks and a naval engagement at Memphis. Posting war news not only sold newspapers but also brought people to newspaper offices, telegraph and train stations, and other places to find out what happened to their "boys."

The noneconomic contributions of Pennsylvanians to the Union cause were also significant, and again the continuity with the past is notable. Pennsylvanians, particularly women, were engaged in organizing and participating in charitable, religious, and civic groups, and once the war began they volunteered their services for that cause too, preparing bandages, sewing uniforms and quilts, collecting medical supplies, sending food and refreshments to the front, providing meals and lodging to troops on furlough, and serving as nurses in army camps and hospitals. In addition, Philadelphia volunteers staged a fair attracting 400,000 visitors, raising $1.2 million for the relief efforts of the

Women at the Pennsylvania Academy of the Fine Arts for the 1864 Philadelphia Sanitary Commission Fair, the largest of numerous such events in the North held throughout the war. Flags were among the items sold to benefit the Commission, which provided nurses and medical care for the troops. The fairs also charged admission for people to view old and specially commissioned works of art. The Philadelphia event was so successful that it inspired both the Philadelphia Centennial Exhibition of 1876 and the Philadelphia Museum of Art.

U.S. Sanitary Commission, a national private organization that emerged to coordinate the outpouring of service work. Pennsylvanians lent their labors and spare time to the Union cause never at remove from the gruesome fighting. Dead and wounded soldiers regularly passed through the state; jerrybuilt mobilization centers and hospitals appeared in Philadelphia and elsewhere.

The war too always threatened to spill into Pennsylvania, especially as key battles ensued directly below the state's southern border. Confederate troops entered en masse in the great confrontation at Gettysburg, but two alarming, smaller invasions also occurred. On October 9, 1862, some 1,800 Confederate cavalry crossed into the state with orders to destroy a key railroad bridge just north of Chambersburg. They succeeded in seizing arms and ammunition and burning a railroad depot and machine shop, but not in dismantling the bridge. A year after the epic assault on Gettysburg, in early June 1864, another Confederate brigade of 2,600 men marched into Chambersburg, this time demanding a sizable monetary ransom. When local leaders refused to pay, the Confederates set fire to the town. Union troops then chased the raiders back into Maryland.

Threats of raids, actual invasions, and eventual war-weariness provided fuel for Pennsylvanians who strongly opposed the war but who at the outset had tactfully retreated in the face of general enthusiasm for Lincoln's campaign to nullify the secession of the South and restore the Union. By the time of off-year elections in November 1862, antiwar adherents had determined that the time was right to resurface openly and argue their case. Leaders of the antiwar movement included Democratic Party politicians and a set of prominent Philadelphia businessmen and professionals who had strong family, commercial, and ideological ties to the South. Their opponents called them "Copperheads," snakes who attacked without warning, but they soon proudly donned the label. Copperheads called for an immediate peace settlement with slavery maintained, assailed wartime censorship measures and prosecution of dissenters (some of them would be jailed for their outward disloyalty), opposed conscription laws and increased taxation, venomously attacked abolitionists and Lincoln, and reserved their harshest criticism for the Emancipation Proclamation. Lincoln's announced freeing of the slaves, they predicted, would produce a massive exodus of blacks from the South to Pennsylvania, where they would rape and pillage and fill charitable poorhouses.

The depth of support for the antiwar position is difficult to measure, but antiwar Democrats barely lost in state and local elections in 1862 and 1864; they received strong votes in immigrant farm and labor communities, where antipathy for the Republicans prevailed for ethnic and class reasons. Political divisions in the state were particularly evident in the presidential election of 1864. Abraham Lincoln eked out a narrow victory to capture Pennsylvania's Electoral College votes over favorite son General George B. McClellan, who ran on a Democratic Party platform that called for a negotiated end to the war. Pennsylvania soldiers casting their ballots on the battlefield provided the margin of victory for Lincoln's reelection.

The Confederate destruction of Chambersburg in 1864. The refusal of townspeople to provide money and supplies to the desperate "rebel" raiders pointed up the dangers of a border war.

Pennsylvanians also opposed the Union effort in more personal ways. More than 2,000 left the state to enlist in the army of the Confederacy. The expatriates included young men who had strong family connections in the South and who had been educated in southern military academies. A shortage of volunteers led to the institution of a federal military draft in July 1863, but conscription failed to meet the needs of the army; the draft law allowed men to buy themselves out of service or to provide substitutes. In Pennsylvania, conscription only yielded 21,000 new recruits. Of several hundred men drafted in Venango County, for example, ninety paid the commutation fee, thirty furnished substitutes, 20 percent failed to report, and practically all the rest were exempted for medical reasons. Outright obstruction of the draft occurred too. All over the state, troops were regularly called to protect enrollment stations; arrest of antiwar activists counseling resistance to the draft, and of mothers and wives simply blocking the enlistment of sons and husbands, often followed.

The most serious antidraft incidents in Pennsylvania unfolded in the anthracite region. Immigrant Irish coal miners saw little reason to give their lives to a Republican Party–led war to preserve the Union or challenge slavery, especially as they engaged in ongoing labor disputes with Protestant mine owners allied to the party. In one episode, in Tremont, Schuylkill County, riots broke out when 1,000 miners attempted to block a train transporting inductees; in another, an official of a coal-mining company in Carbon County was murdered in his home because he had allegedly supplied information about his employees to draft officials. Other outbreaks of violence convinced federal authorities to move troops into the region to restore order; the soldiers guarded draft offices, but also the mines to quell disruptions by disgruntled workers. In this way, the kinds of internal civil wars that marked Pennsylvania in the 1850s—involving class, ethnic, and political differences—persisted during the nation's great ordeal of the War Between the States.

Robert E. Lee's surrender at Appomattox on April 9, 1865, effectively ended the war, but not the political conflict. The nation remained divided for more than a decade over the terms of the peace: how were the seceding states to be brought back to the Union, how were the leaders of the defeated rebellion to be treated, and most important, what kind of political, civil, and economic rights were to be guaranteed to the freed slaves. The debate engaged Pennsylvanians, and they divided as earlier along different lines. Democrats generally supported a quick restoration of the southern states without undue political burdens on former Confederates, but with slavery abolished; Republicans advocated some kind of reform of the ways and institutions of the southern states. During this critical dialogue, two Pennsylvanians achieved national prominence for their staunch advocacy of a radical reconstruction of the South, William Kelley and Thaddeus Stevens.

Elected to the U.S. House of Representatives from Philadelphia in 1860, William Kelley served there for thirty years until his death. For his leading support of high tariffs and protection particularly of Pennsylvania's iron industry, Kelley earned the nickname "Pig Iron Kelley." Kelley reserved his greatest advocacy and oratory for attacks on slavery and for defense of African Americans. He staunchly championed the arming of black troops during the Civil War, the creation of a Freedmen's Bureau to provide relief services to emancipated slaves, and the guaranteeing of suffrage to black males. In Pennsylvania he forcefully argued against segregation practices and laws. William Kelley also left a great legacy to his state and nation in the person of his daughter, Florence Kelley. Born in Philadelphia in 1859, she became a prominent social reformer—a relentless advocate for woman's suffrage, settlement houses, and protective laws for workers and consumers.

Thaddeus Stevens emerged as one of the most radical politicians of his day. Elected to the U.S. House of Representatives from Lancaster County in 1848, he delivered frequent speeches attacking the "slave power"—the control of Congress by southern slaveholders. In Pennsylvania, Stevens provided legal assistance to fugitive slaves. During the Civil War, he constantly criticized Lincoln's moderation, demanding the mobilization of black troops. After the war, he called for a military occupation of the defeated South, the disempowering of the planter elite, and, most notably, a program of land redistribution that would have provided forty-acre farmsteads for former slaves and their families.

The advocacy of Kelley and Stevens led to a brief flowering of democracy in the South after the war. They oversaw congressional passage of military Reconstruction acts that enabled the creation of new state governments in the South where African Americans openly participated in political decision-making. That Reconstruction failed in the South due to southern white intransigence and violence does not diminish the importance of two Pennsylvania radicals envisioning not only a "new South" but also a new role for blacks in public life.

The disputed presidential election of 1876 signaled the close of Reconstruction. Pennsylvania had a hand in that process too, with Thomas Scott, president of the Pennsylvania Railroad, playing a key behind-the-scenes role in the so-called Compromise of 1877 that gave the Republican presidential candidate the election in exchange for concessions to white conservative Democrats in the South and the promise of federal subsidies for railroad development, among several aspects of a complicated political deal.

The same Scott was in the public eye just six months later, when as president of the Pennsylvania line he refused to negotiate with striking railroad workers and then used his great influence to have state militia placed on his trains. These troops at the seeming beck and call of Scott fired into protesting crowds on the night of July 21, 1877, in Pittsburgh, setting off several days of rage. Thomas Scott thus symbolically strode between two eras in U.S. and Pennsylvania history: a time when Americans divided on interrelated issues of sectional power and economic policy and of slavery, religion, secession, civil war, and reconstruction, and an age marked by extraordinary capitalist development and extreme conflict between business and labor.

GETTYSBURG: CONTESTED HALLOWED GROUND

"The second battle of Gettysburg is not over," proclaimed one protester. Tempers flared at meetings called in the spring of 1998 to challenge a decision by the National Park Service to demolish the Cyclorama Building at the battlefield, to make way for a new commercialized visitor center built and managed by a private developer. Various groups stepped forward to voice their opposition. Merchants from the town of Gettysburg feared losing their share of tourist dollars. Scholars and others decried the new complex as the latest defiling of sacred historical grounds.

Protesters of the 1990s may have declared the fight over the Cyclorama Building the second battle of Gettysburg, but in fact controversy has surrounded the battlefield as a historical landmark since Pickett's failed charge and the withdrawal of Confederate troops. The very landscape of the memorial, as well as notions of what is to be memorialized, has been in continuing dispute. Within months of the Union victory, local groups emerged to buy parcels of private farmland on which the troops fought in order to create a permanent, untouched public space where future generations could honor the Northern victory and the dead. But there were limited means for purchasing property, so large sections of the battlefield remained in private hands. In 1895 Congress established a national park out of the fields that were preserved, and allocated funds for additional land purchases, but to this day private homes and businesses and commercial thoroughfares and highways are jarringly interspersed in the original battlefield.

Such infringement of private enterprise on public visual space has sparked repeated protests. In the 1890s the proposal to build a railroad through a historic key battle point that remained outside the national park drew anger and lawsuits, and was ultimately blocked. Similarly, a 307-foot observation tower constructed in 1973 by a private concessionaire rankled critics for more than a quarter-century before it was dismantled in the year 2000. Housing developments built at the edges of the preserved battlefield breed ongoing zoning disputes.

The original preservers of the battlefield imagined a place to mark the great Union victory and honor the fallen soldiers, but when Reconstruction ended Gettysburg emerged as a symbolic venue to achieve reconciliation between the North and the South. William Kelley and Thaddeus Stevens of Pennsylvania never convinced their compatriots that the Civil War and its immediate aftermath were about slavery and the rights and well-being of former slaves. Weary and wary of more tension, northerners and southerners began shaking hands after the compromise settling the disputed presidential election of 1876. At Gettysburg, surviving Union and Confederate troops literally would embrace. Preservers of the battlefield organized the first reunions in the early 1880s, and in 1887 the custom of reenacting Pickett's charge on July 3 began with veterans from both sides participating and saluting one another. Federal officials institutionalized the reunions and battle re-enactments in the 1890s, and on the fiftieth anniversary of the great battle, roughly 56,000 Civil War veterans joined in events furthering reconciliation. In 1917 the state of Virginia erected an equestrian statue of General Robert E. Lee on the grounds, and other southern states soon erected stone memorials alongside northern ones to honor local battalions.

Slavery and racial matters remained conspicuously and deliberately absent from the exhibitions, monuments, and pageantry of Gettysburg. At the centennial celebration of the battle in 1963, however, amid civil rights protests and with racial divides in the nation no longer submergible, the history represented at the national park came under serious question. Is Gettysburg a place to portray a military battle where equally honorable men from both sides valiantly fought? Or is it a site that should articulate the issues that brought the combatants together in early July 1863? Park planners, curators, and educators face these questions now, and their job of interpretation is made no easier as public-private disputes continue to have an impact on the landscape. Gettysburg remains contested terrain.

During the second half of the nineteenth century, the population of Pennsylvania increased dramatically. In 1850 census enumerators totaled 2.3 million people in the state; in 1900 the count stood at 6.3 million. The population of Philadelphia more than tripled in the same fifty-year period to 1.3 million, the city remaining second to New York in population size. Pittsburgh's population grew at an even faster seven-fold pace, from 46,601 to 321,616. Immigrants from northern Europe and, late in the century, from southern and eastern Europe contributed to the growth.

A dramatic expansion in economic output marked Pennsylvania in the last half of the nineteenth century. In 1850 more than 21,000 manufacturing firms in the state produced $155 million worth of goods; fifty years later more than 52,000 companies manufactured products whose worth topped $1.8 billion, a twelvefold increase. While representing 8 percent of the nation's population, Pennsylvanians contributed more than 14 percent of the nation's total industrial product. Pennsylvania vied with New York State for economic leadership, and Philadelphia and New York City in the last half of the nineteenth century alternated between first and second place as the nation's leading industrial cities.

The economic progress of Pennsylvania can be measured in developmental terms too. A glance at the state's economic map as of 1850 provides hints of a fuller maturation with flurried manufacturing activity in the southeast and southwest corners, start-up mining enterprises in the eastern anthracite coal area, and canal and early railroad connections beginning to link the whole. The map fifty years later reveals advanced transportation ties and three highly developed and productive regional economies, each marked by dense labor, material, and capital resource utilization and intense interconnected entrepreneurial activity: the light-manufacture center of Philadelphia, the anthracite mining area of the northeastern part of the state, and the heavy-industry hub of Pittsburgh.

By the time of the Civil War, Philadelphia had emerged as the premier manufacturing city in the nation, but no single invention, business owner, event, or circumstance can be designated as a prime mover. Thousands of individual initiatives contributed to a steady mushrooming of varied enterprise. At least four features characterized Philadelphia's industrial structure. The first was product diversity. Instead of one kind of product, a vast array of goods poured from the city's work sites: cotton and silk cloth, hosiery, lace, hats, plain and tailored garments, shoes, tools, machines, saws, lumber, furniture, chemicals, drugs, glass, jewelry, books, bricks and tiles, and more.

A diversity of work settings was a complementary feature. Philadelphia workers toiled in factory buildings, operating water- and steam-powered machinery; in smaller manufactories with hand- and foot-driven machines; in artisans' shops, where craft practices and standards persisted into the twentieth century; and in sweatshops and homes.

OPPOSITE: Members of the Philadelphia Brigade Association and Pickett's Division Association shake hands during the fiftieth anniversary of the Battle of Gettysburg in 1913. The Gettysburg battlefield served as a place of reconciliation where the issues dividing the North and South were submerged.

Rows of large circular-saw grinding machines at the Disston Saw Works in Tacony. Disston saws were prized for their craftsmanship and durability.

Single goods could be manufactured in diverse workplaces—hats, for example, were produced in factories as well as craft shops—but single goods might pass through several settings during the complete production process. In textiles, for example, a fiber might be cleaned and carded in a home, spun in a mill, woven in an artisan shop, and dyed or printed in a small manufactory.

Specialization was a third component of Philadelphia's industrial system. Firms either concentrated on one aspect of product fabrication or produced small batches of custom items to the specifications of particular customers. Philadelphia manufacturers prospered by operating in niche markets and not by achieving economies of scale. The small to medium-sized family-owned-and-managed business was an allied fourth critical feature. Philadelphia boasted only a handful of large, corporately owned and bureaucratically administered enterprises.

Diversified products and work settings, specialization, and proprietorships marked Philadelphia's developed industrial structure in the second half of the nineteenth century. A number of factors contributed to Philadelphia's particular economic history. An abundance of skilled labor allowed for custom production. Known as a craft center, the city attracted new generations of skilled immigrant workers and potential small-scale specialty manufacturers, perpetuating the process. The absence of major waterfalls initially limited the building of large-scale, fully mechanized factories. Philadelphia custom producers further chose not to compete with major firms in other cities who manufactured cheap, standardized goods; the small size of such producers provided a flexibility that allowed them to shift into new product lines and profit in specialty markets. Because few companies engaged in all aspects of production, the city's manufacturers also provided one another with orders, creating a community of enterprise—a regional economy. Finally, Philadelphia's Quaker commercial elite tended to invest their savings in additional trade, banking, canal and railroad construction, and mining, rather than in local industry. This meant that capital for manufacturing within the city was scarce and created a vacuum that enterprising native-born and immigrant skilled workers could fill with their small-to-medium-sized custom manufactories.

A few Philadelphia stories can illustrate developments. William Horstmann, a skilled silk weaver, immigrated to Philadelphia in 1814 from Germany and with borrowed funds from relatives started a small business producing silk tassels, ribbons, labels, and threads. By the late nineteenth century his sons were operating a business that was the nation's leading supplier of specialty silk items. Henry Disston arrived in the United States in 1833 and, relying on the knowledge and skills of fellow immigrants from Sheffield, England, Disston started producing high-grade Sheffield steel for the manufacture of finely cut, durable saws with beautifully fashioned wooden handles. He greatly expanded his business after the Civil War, as Disston's crafted saws became the standard of superior quality in the industry.

Born in nearby New Jersey, Matthias Baldwin established his famed Baldwin Locomotive Works in the early 1830s, an atypical Philadelphia firm for its huge size. The company grew in the second half of the century to be one of the world's greatest manufacturers of locomotives—selling internationally—yet the firm remained a specialty producer, efficiently constructing one-of-a-kind engines, according to the specifications and needs of the large number of railroads that became its customers. The fine products fabricated in Philadelphia's manufactories were showcased at the great Centennial Exposition of 1876, and Philadelphia served most fittingly as the site for that paean to American industrial progress and prowess.

The Philadelphia specialty production system determined to a great extent who came to live and work in the city. Light industrial jobs in textiles and the garment industry provided employment for children and women who by the late nineteenth century comprised a sizable proportion of the city's labor force. The production of custom goods required skilled workers as well, and Philadelphia continued particularly to attract British- and German-born weavers, loom fixers, patternmakers, molders, and machinists.

The erecting shop at the Baldwin Locomotive Works in Philadelphia. Baldwin was the largest manufacturer of locomotives in the world. It built locomotives to order rather than through mass production, and relied on highly skilled workers. This scene from the late 1860s depicts the metal-parts makers and assemblers

President Ulysses S. Grant and Emperor Dom Pedro of Brazil turned the valves, the vented steam powered the giant cylinders of the 56-ton Corliss engine, and beltways and shafts rotated, setting in motion 800 separate machines. Thus culminated the opening-day festivities of the nation's great Centennial Exhibition in Philadelphia's Fairmount Park on May 10, 1876. More than 180,000 guests cheered the events, and in the next six months 10 million visitors streamed through the extensive fairgrounds, dazzled by displays of world cultures and the latest technological inventions.

Two hundred buildings; the twenty-one-and-a-half-acre main exhibition hall, the largest building ever constructed; an internal railway system; fifty nations contributing displays—the Centennial Exhibition, created to honor the nation's 100 years of independence, was conceived and executed on a grand scale. Visitors could see demonstrations of Alexander Graham Bell's newly invented telephone, among other wizardry. Specially spotlighted were the fine products fabricated by Philadelphia's specialty manufacturers. The Japanese hall and exhibits drew particular attention and would influence American art and architecture for decades.

But there was a definite western imperial cast to the total exhibition, with Europe and the United States appearing as the apex of progress and civilization. In spite of organized efforts, African Americans did not succeed in gaining a place at the fair or having a permanent statue of Richard Allen, Philadelphia's early black religious and civic leader, dedicated on the fairgrounds. White activist women, who had been essential in raising funds for the exhibition, overcame the objections of exhibition planners and raised $30,000 on their own accounts to see to the building of a controversial Women's Pavilion. The pavilion displayed women's contributions to the arts, crafts, home production, and industry and served as a forum to boost the cause of woman's suffrage.

ABOVE: President Ulysses S. Grant was joined by Brazil's Emperor Pedro II to open the Philadelphia Centennial Exhibition on May 10, 1876. Crowds gathered that day outside Memorial Hall, the Exhibition's main building, which was filled with the latest in technological wonders. The building still stands in Fairmount Park.

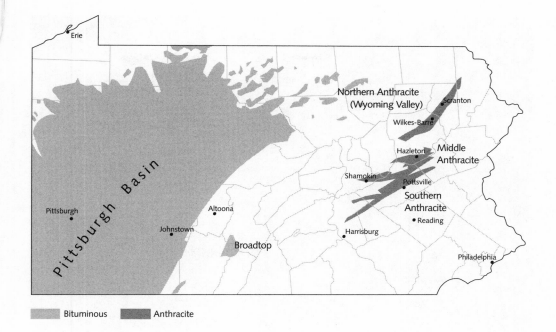

Coal regions of Pennsylvania.

Bituminous   Anthracite

Male immigrants without craft experience, particularly those from southern and eastern Europe, had a more difficult time finding regular work in the city. For this reason, the anthracite coal fields northwest of Philadelphia, and the steel mills of Pittsburgh, provided better opportunities and attracted these men in greater numbers.

Below the surface of a five-county region beginning some fifty miles north and west of Philadelphia lay 95 percent of the nation's supply of anthracite coal. Anthracite is a hard coal, almost pure carbon and difficult to ignite, but once lit it burns slowly and extremely hot; it was the perfect fuel for powering the steam engines of American industrialization and heating the homes of the nation's growing urban population. As early as the third decade of the nineteenth century, investors from Philadelphia were already betting on the value of anthracite. They sponsored first canal and then railroad construction to expedite the transport of coal from the region to manufacturing centers. Small-scale operators followed, quickly (and hazardously) digging mine shafts.

The second half of the nineteenth century saw the greater development of Pennsylvania's anthracite region. Major rail companies, most notably the Philadelphia & Reading Railroad, began purchasing enormous tracts of land in the area to monopolize claims to the anthracite coal. Huge mining operations then opened either directly managed by the railroads or through leases. Consolidation of ownership and production facilitated the building of extensive deep-pit mines and the mass excavation of anthracite.

The mining of anthracite required much and varied labor power, including construction crews, who drilled through rock, excavated shafts and underground gangways, and shored up and maintained the labyrinth of tunnels dug hundreds of feet below the surface; the coal miners, who worked on the basis of per-tonnage contracts and with their

Mules worked alongside men in anthracite mines. This mule had labored below ground for twenty-eight years when this photograph was taken. Gangways often ran for miles, requiring extensive underground hauling systems.

helpers detonated and picked at coal seams to free large blocks of the valuable anthracite; the haulers and hoisters, who transported the coal out of the mines; the men and boys who worked in breakers, where the coal was crushed, cleaned, and screened into small pieces for sale to industrial and residential customers; and the host of supervisors who managed the works. In the second half of the nineteenth century, a succession of immigrants came to northeastern Pennsylvania from England, Ireland, and Wales, and then from southern and eastern Europe, to form the anthracite labor force, numbering 140,000 strong by 1900. They resided in large and small cities, such as Wilkes-Barre, Scranton, and Pottsville, which emerged as transportation and commercial centers of the five-county regional economy, as well as in mine company towns and small mine-patch communities.

Danger and economic uncertainty marked the lives of the anthracite miners and their families. Hastily constructed facilities to draw quick profits, natural cave-ins, and the buildup of explosive methane gas produced frequent and catastrophic disasters. The worst tragedy of the period occurred in Avondale on September 6, 1869, when a mine fire killed 108 men and boys trapped 300 feet below ground. Through breathing coal dust on a regular basis, anthracite miners also suffered ultimately fatal respiratory diseases.

Uncertain and exploitative working circumstances compounded the physical perils Pennsylvania anthracite miners faced in the late nineteenth century. Demand for coal

Miners' housing was poor, and their villages were surrounded by coal-slag heaps that polluted the environment. Land sometimes subsided because of mine tunnels dug too close to the earth's surface, as shown here near Hazleton.

fluctuated widely, and employment and income slackened periodically. In company towns, miners and their families also found themselves in constant debt as the high prices of tools, food, clothing, and other goods charged at isolated company stores were deducted from the earnings of the miners. Company managers also set low per-tonnage rates of return and controlled the critical weighing of the coal, systematically bilking the miners. The exploitation and arduousness and perils of the labor caused one anthracite miner to have the following words chiseled on his gravestone:

> Fourty years I worked with pick and drill
> Down in the mines against my will
> The Coal King's slave, but now it's passed
> Thanks be to God I am free at last.

Grievances festered, and the anthracite region of northeastern Pennsylvania witnessed ongoing violent confrontations between the independent-minded coal miners

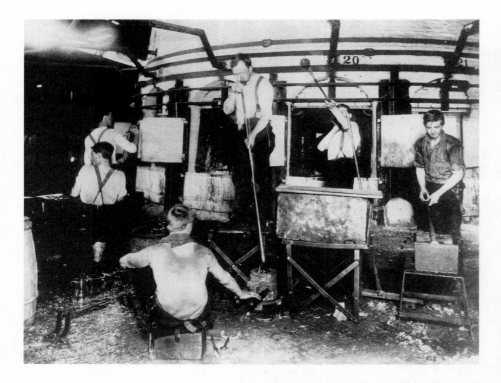

and the mine bosses. In their battles with their employers, the miners sought union recognition; a sliding scale of compensation, where the per-tonnage compensation rates rose and fell with the price of coal in the marketplace; and implementation of union work rules, including union oversight of the weighing of the mined coal.

Labor conflict and employment opportunities for unskilled immigrants also characterized Pennsylvania's third great hub of economic activity, Pittsburgh. With nearby rich deposits of coal, iron ore, and other minerals, and water transport and railroad linkages in all directions, Pittsburgh was primed for success. By the onset of the Civil War, the city had already become the leading glass-producing center in the nation, accounting for 50 percent of the nation's output. Glass and rail transport remained key endeavors after the war, but the city's new fame would be based on iron and steel manufacture. By the turn of the twentieth century, with the city accounting for one-sixth of the nation's production of iron and steel, Pittsburgh and steel became synonymous.

The picture of Pittsburgh in the mind's eye is of sprawling steelworks, powerful corporations, and masses of workers, but reality is more complicated. By the 1880s numerous ironworks had been established in the city and in surrounding communities in Allegheny County, usually proprietorships with 200 to 300 employees. Iron-mill owners generally left the management of their works to skilled ironworkers, who supervised teams of men whom they often hired directly. Skilled puddlers oversaw the difficult mixing and heating of the ore; rollers oversaw the shaping of the molten iron into ingots, sheets, and rails; molders were in charge of the preparation of casts; and forgers supervised the hammering of large iron components into shape. Mill owners reached per-ton and per-piece

TOP: Glassblowing was an important industry in nineteenth-century Pittsburgh, requiring highly skilled workers.

BOTTOM: The Heinz Company pioneered in promoting brand loyalty by advertising the order and hygiene of its production.

"Making Steel at Pittsburgh: The Bessemers at Work," a famous wood engraving from an 1886 *Harper's Weekly.* The image, of Carnegie steelworks, suggests the heat, noise, and scale in making steel. The highly automated Bessemer process eliminated the jobs of puddlers and other skilled, unionized workers, whose control of the work process pitted them against steel-company executives in dramatic confrontations in Pennsylvania in the late nineteenth century.

Pennsylvania's transportation infrastructure linked the state's mines, farms, and factories to the national market. This photograph of Pittsburgh in the 1890s shows the busy mix of steamboats, barges, roads, and railroads—a combination of old and new that gave Pennsylvania a competitive advantage in the great economic expansion of the period.

agreements with these skilled workers, and as these craftsmen organized into unions, arrangements began to be negotiated on a collective basis. Ironworkers and steelworkers achieved agreements that eluded anthracite miners in the period.

The hold of the iron craftsmen on production came under attack on many fronts in the late 1880s. A general move toward greater production of versatile steel—and in Bessemer converters—eliminated the skills of the puddlers. Business consolidations occurred, reducing competition and also allowing for investments in new capital-intensive technologies. Mechanical moving devices and other automated processes further reduced needs for certain skills. New corporate enterprises also began to hire newly arrived immigrants from southern and eastern Europe at low wages to tend to the new machinery, and these new workers were being supervised by salaried bureaucrats.

Finally, and most important, steel executives deliberately moved to break the power of the strong craft unions in the industry. The defeat of the unions in a series of dramatic strikes in the late 1880s and early 1890s boosted managerial control over operations. The violent, monumental Homestead Strike of July 1892 capped developments. In a decade's time the vast operations of Andrew Carnegie and other steelworks would be combined under the aegis of financier J. P. Morgan into the business behemoth United States Steel Corporation, based in Pittsburgh. This giant steel-producer—corporately owned, bureaucratically managed, mechanized, and automated—emerged only after a long, unfolding history and amid great conflict.

Extraordinary business figures and corporations distinguish Pittsburgh's regional economic history. Andrew Carnegie had a looming presence. Carnegie and his family left desperate circumstances in Scotland and immigrated to the United States in 1848, settling in Pittsburgh. Securing a position as a telegraph operator on the Pennsylvania Railroad, the young Carnegie had the good fortune to come under the tutelage of Thomas Scott, who taught him managerial skills, saw to his rise on the Pennsylvania, and gave him advice on investing in the stock market. After the Civil War, Carnegie became convinced that great opportunities lay ahead in iron and steel production, and with money his investments earned he took the first steps toward establishing the Carnegie Steel Company. Innovating with new technologies, particularly the Bessemer converter, and paying great attention to administration and efficiency, his firm quickly emerged as the most profitable in the industry, making even more expansion and modernization possible.

To fully integrate his operations, Carnegie bought iron-ore reserves, established transportation facilities, and invited Henry Frick, who owned huge bituminous coal fields in western Pennsylvania and coke smelters, to join his company. In the 1890s, however, tensions grew between Carnegie and Frick, particularly over the handling of the Homestead Strike, and Carnegie determined to sell his holdings. He received $250 million when J. P. Morgan founded the U.S. Steel Corporation, and with these earnings Carnegie began a second career as the world's most important philanthropist.

George Westinghouse emerged as a leading industrial figure in the late nineteenth century through his inventive genius more than through his investments or business acumen. Westinghouse moved to Pittsburgh at an early age, and at twenty-one received his first patent, for a rotary steam engine. Four years later, in 1869, he invented a device that made him world famous: an air brake for trains, to replace hand-turned brakes. After establishing a company to manufacture new braking systems, Westinghouse began to experiment with electrical railroad switches and signals. His inventions single-handedly reduced the great perils of early railroad transport. Ever inventive, during the decades of the 1880s Westinghouse received 134 additional patents, but he turned his greatest attention to the new and expanding field of electrical generation and use. Then he founded the Westinghouse Electric Company to manufacture electric generators and appliances, and gambled on producing goods based on alternating current (AC).

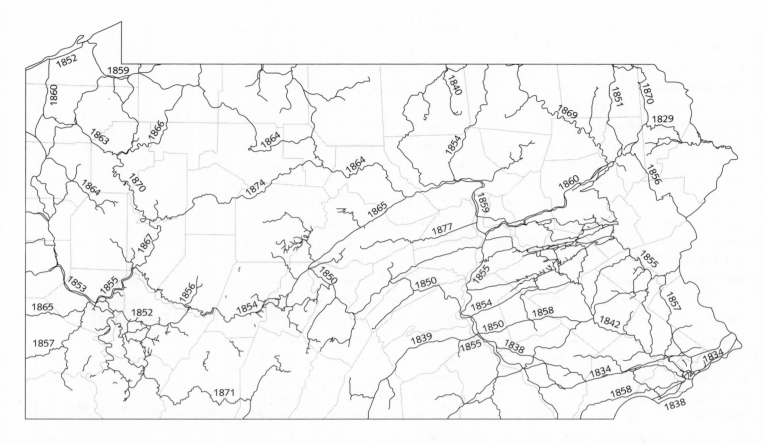

Railroad network of Pennsylvania, 1880, with dates selected routes opened.

Building concerns on the order of Carnegie Steel, U.S. Steel Corporation, and Westinghouse Electric required enormous capital investments, and local sources of financing played a critical part. The Mellon family of Pittsburgh became principal backers of many of the large industrial ventures of the period. Thomas Mellon, after a long judicial career, opened a private bank in 1870. A year later, he loaned the young Henry Frick $10,000 to purchase coalfields and build coke ovens. Mellon, and later his sons, soon became intimately involved in the financial affairs of Frick's, Carnegie's, and Westinghouse's enterprises. Andrew Mellon, who served as U.S. secretary of the treasury in the 1920s, assumed leadership of the family bank in the 1880s, and in a key move he supported another young inventor, Charles M. Hall, who patented an electrolytic process for recovering aluminum from bauxite ores. This investment led to the formation of the Pittsburgh-based Aluminum Company of America (ALCOA), which gained and maintained a monopoly position in the industry for the next half-century. The Mellons spread their wings to back critical oil explorations in other parts of the nation and the world, but the bank remained a critical force in the economic development of Pittsburgh and Pennsylvania.

Although the family-owned and -operated firm (and the small partnership) were the hallmarks of Philadelphia industry, the corporately owned and bureaucratically

PENNSYLVANIA AND INNOVATIONS IN BUSINESS MANAGEMENT

As the Commonwealth led in corporate development, Pennsylvanians contributed greatly to managerial innovations. J. Edgar Thomson, for example, who was born in Springfield, Pennsylvania, in 1808, rose to the presidency of the Pennsylvania Railroad in the 1850s after planning and overseeing the line's construction. Managing a railroad as extensive as the Pennsylvania created new challenges, and in 1858 Thomson published a scheme that became a model for the administration of large-scale enterprises. He divided the line into divisions and appointed divisional officers to supervise the daily transport and maintenance of facilities. At the same time, he created a central office of managers who set overall standards and procedures and engaged in long-range planning. Thomson further instituted a system of reports and accounting that allowed for coordination among levels of management.

If J. Edgar Thomson attended to macro-management, Frederick Winslow Taylor gained worldwide fame and notoriety in focusing on the micro-supervision of work. Taylor was born in Philadelphia in 1856 of parents who were Quakers and active abolitionists. Instead of pursuing academic studies, Taylor became a machinist's apprentice and then foreman at the Midvale Steel Company in Philadelphia. There he began a series of experiments aimed at increasing productivity. Although he introduced a range of managerial reforms and technologies, Taylor is most famous for his time-and-motion studies—his efforts to break work into detailed, easily supervised tasks, catalog them, establish expected rates for completing jobs, and structure incentive schemes to boost output. "Scientific management," a system of control that "de-skills" labor, was thus born.

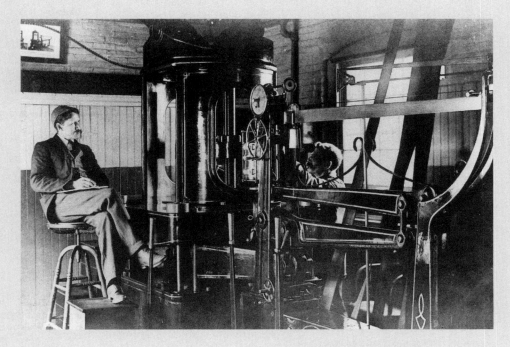

Taylor became a consultant to many firms and promoted his methods through speeches and writings. One of his favorite stories and examples involved a coal shoveller whom he dubbed Schmidt who worked for the Bethlehem Steel Corporation in Bethlehem. Schmidt seemingly exhibited all the behaviors and traits that irked Taylor, from ignorance and sluggishness to intransigence. Taylor studied Schmidt at work and then determined the most efficient technique of wielding a shovel, optimum shovel loads, necessary rest times, the best design for a shovel, and a piece-rate incentive payment system. According to Taylor, his scrutiny and reengineering of the work process transformed Schmidt and his fellow coal shovellers into highly productive, and engaged, workers.

Taylor gained great publicity with such stories, but the impact of so-called Taylorism was mixed as both supervisors and workers protested against his interventions, and firms discovered that the cataloging of tasks had become unwieldy because the market forced constant changes in product lines and production arrangements. De-skilling, in fact, proved counterproductive. At the same time that Taylor advocated an impersonal and technical approach to labor management, another Philadelphian, John Wanamaker, introduced in his grand department store pioneering benefit programs that fostered employee diligence and loyalty through positive means.

ABOVE: A "scientific manager," unidentified but most likely Frederick Winslow Taylor, cataloging the work of a testing machine operator at the Midvale Steel Company in Philadelphia in the mid-1880s. Taylor developed his time-and-motion-study approach to the management of labor at Midvale.

Philadelphia was a major shipbuilding center from colonial days until after World War II. In the late nineteenth century, large shipyards, such as William Cramp & Sons, seen here, dominated the Delaware River waterfront. The battleship *Maine* and other naval carriers were the most famous Cramp products of the time, but just as important were the many thousands of tons of merchant vessels built in Philadelphia shipyards to serve the vast Atlantic commerce that flowed through Pennsylvania and beyond. The river also supported recreation, especially boating.

administered enterprise became the signature of Pittsburgh. Various factors contributed to the rise of big business in the late nineteenth century in the United States: the nationwide system of railroads increased competition and forced firms to expand to control directly both the accessing of raw materials and the merchandising of products; anti-monopoly politics and laws prohibited collusive practices among firms but ironically fostered mergers; investment bankers further encouraged acquisitions and mergers with the profits to be made in the underwriting of such ventures; and, when well managed, large concerns could achieve economies of scale and scope that eliminated competition, especially with the adoption of expensive new technologies. Whatever the particular reasons, in the history of the emergence of the corporation Pennsylvania occupied center stage. In fact, in addition to the businesses of Carnegie and Westinghouse, Pennsylvania housed by far the largest and most powerful corporation of the age, the famed Pennsylvania Railroad.

In 1846 a group of Philadelphia merchants received a state charter to build a railroad linking Philadelphia and Pittsburgh. With railroad construction proceeding apace in neighboring states, these merchants feared that western commerce would be diverted to Baltimore and New York City. Under the leadership of J. Edgar Thomson, construction of the main line of the Pennsylvania Railroad was completed in the 1850s. By the end of the Civil War the company was the largest corporation in the world in terms of capitalization, revenues, profits, and employment. Thomson's chief lieutenant, Thomas Scott, then ushered in a period of even greater expansion, in which connections to the original line were established north and south of Philadelphia along the Atlantic Seaboard, north of Pittsburgh to Erie, and west of Pittsburgh through the Midwest to Chicago. By the turn of the twentieth century, the Pennsylvania's operations east of Pittsburgh alone comprised 3,715 miles of track with 46,000 employees.

The story of the Pennsylvania Railroad brings to the fore again Thomas Scott, a ubiquitous but shadowy figure who had an enormous impact on the nation's and the state's economic and political history. (Scott left no personal papers and remains elusive and enigmatic to biographers.) Born in 1823 in Louden, the son of a humble innkeeper, Scott rose from a lowly position on the Pennsylvania Railroad eventually to be its president. Along the way he tutored Andrew Carnegie; worked under Secretary of War Simon Cameron during the Civil War to coordinate railroad movements of Union troops and supplies; effectively controlled the Pennsylvania state legislature to secure bills favorable to his vast expansion plans

ABOVE: Men using a steam thresher to fill a granary in Somerset County. The late nineteenth century was a time of transition for Pennsylvania farmers as they had access to a growing array of agricultural machines to aid them in their work. Machinery boosted efficiency, but also the capital costs of farming; cooperative purchases of machines became common in Pennsylvania and elsewhere in the late nineteenth century, as farmers organized into granges and other alliances.

LEFT: The lumber industry in Pennsylvania, 1880.

for the Pennsylvania Railroad; helped engineer the national Compromise of 1877 that ended Reconstruction and placed Rutherford B. Hayes in the White House; and presided during the great railroad strikes of July 1877, as railroad workers and their community supporters vented their anger at the threatening economic and political powers of the likes of Scott and his company.

With the entrepreneuralism of Carnegie, Frick, Scott, Westinghouse, and other leading businessmen, the economic prominence of Pennsylvania in the late nineteenth

White Pine   Hemlock   Both

The rains began in the late afternoon of May 30, 1889. Eight inches fell in the next twenty-four hours, raising fears of another flood among the citizens of the small but burgeoning western Pennsylvania river-basin industrial city of Johnstown. Great concern focused on the South Fork Dam, holding back Lake Conemaugh in the mountains upstream. Built in the 1840s as a reservoir in the soon abandoned Pennsylvania canal system, the lake area had been purchased by Andrew Carnegie, Henry Frick, Andrew Mellon, and other wealthy associates to establish a private resort, the South Fork Fishing and Hunting Club. The organization had made repairs to the dam in 1879, but subsequent warnings of potential problems went unheeded. On May 31 at three o'clock in the afternoon, with the lake swollen, tragedy beyond imagination struck as the dam broke. A thirty-six-foot-high wall of water flowed down the Conemaugh River at fifty miles an hour, wiping out neighboring villages and then plunging into Johnstown, destroying major sections of that city. Amid the debris of washed-away bridges, track, houses, and businesses, rescue crews exhumed a staggering 2,209 dead, one-ninth of the city's population.

Americans from all walks of life responded to news of the great Johnstown flood with extraordinary charity. Wealthy individuals, corporations, benevolent associations, school-children, and church members contributed more than $3.6 million for disaster relief. Within a day's time, the citizens of Pittsburgh were able to transport 1,000 blankets, and trains bearing carloads of lumber, furniture, and foodstuffs arrived soon after from communities around the nation—a 20,000-pound donation of ham from the city of Cincinnati alone. Hundreds of volunteers also traveled to Johnstown to help clear debris, provide nursing services, and rebuild homes and businesses. The outpouring of munificence is an important part of the story of the Great Flood.

Johnstown deserves more than passing mention in any industrial history of Pennsylvania, for the city housed the Cambria Iron Works, the first steel company in the nation to innovate with Bessemer converters, and a major producer of rails. Yet Johnstown is remembered primarily for the Great Flood of 1889—the Cambria Iron Works sustained more than $18 million dollars of damage on May 31—one of the greatest disasters in American history. Whether the flood was natural or the result of neglect remained a matter of contention. With the labor battles of the period and class antagonisms severe, accusations percolated for years that the true blame rested with the corporate barons of the South Fork Fishing and Hunting Club. They had enjoyed their lakeside retreat high up on the mountain, but their negligence brought disaster to the working people of the city downstream.

TOP: On May 31, 1889, the South Fork Dam broke, pouring 20 million tons of water from Lake Conemaugh down the Conemaugh River, wiping out villages and destroying major sections of Johnstown.

BOTTOM: This postcard advertised the Johnstown Flood attraction at New York's Coney Island. Amusement parks across the nation offered people the chance to experience vicariously the thrills of industrial life—such as riding in dark tunnels or on roller coasters—without the consequences.

century seemingly rested on the state's good fortune in having such men reside in the state. With all due respect to the accomplishments of these extraordinary figures, a great man explanation is insufficient. The actual history is much more complicated. A strong base for economic progress had already been established during the antebellum period. Natural resource advantages, population expansion, widening market activity, urbanization, intraregional mushrooming of enterprise, and other impersonal forces contributed mightily to developments. Moreover, Philadelphia emerged as a major manufacturing center with a system of small-to-medium-sized specialty production. The ascendance of the anthracite region required the hard toil and sacrifices of the anthracite miners, and

Much of Pennsylvania was covered with trees more than 100 feet tall before the lumber boom of the late nineteenth century, which centered in Pennsylvania. Rail lines were run to improvised lumber camps, like the one depicted here in Clinton County, where migrant loggers felled forests with great efficiency. Today the state's forests are almost entirely second, third, or fourth growth.

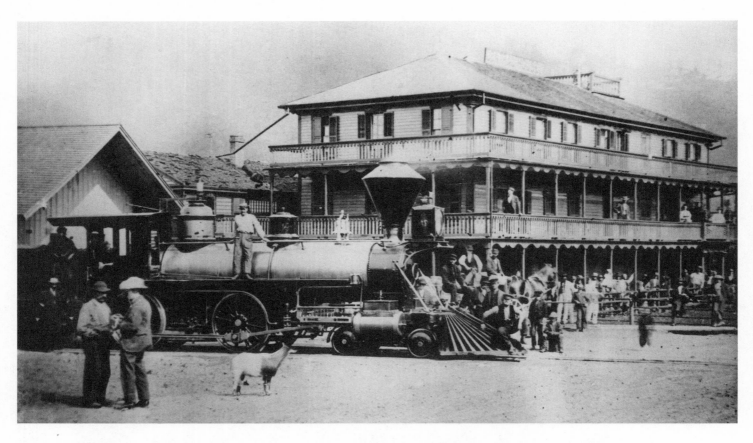

A train pulls into Petroleum Centre in 1873. By this time the peak of the oil boom was over, but the town was still a busy commercial center with twenty-four scheduled rail stops each day. Behind the engine, people pose outside Central House, one of the town's several hotels, where two years earlier President Grant had attended a reception as he campaigned through the Oil Creek valley.

Pennsylvania workers everywhere served as the backbone of the state's progress.

Finally, a focus on the notable titans of industry misses the very diversity of economic activity in the state. The wide range of endeavor is particularly apparent within the vast portions of the state lying between Pennsylvania's three advanced regional economies. A line of small industrial centers emerged across the southern tier of the state in the late nineteenth century, including the machine-shop and textile city of Reading; the iron and steel works of the Steelton-Harrisburg area and, farther west, of Johnstown; the bituminous coal mining communities throughout the southwest counties; and the mammoth repair complex of the Pennsylvania Railroad in Altoona. (Another major steel center was established in the northeast city of Bethlehem late in the century.) Along the Delaware River from Philadelphia south to Chester, the state could also boast of the nation's largest complex of shipbuilding firms. Pennsylvania similarly led the way in glassmaking, the smelting of nonferrous metals, such as zinc, and the tanning of leathers and production of leather goods.

While Pennsylvania lost its prominence in agriculture with the opening up and rapid development of farming in the prairie states and the Far West after the Civil War, its farmers continued to grow wheat, potatoes, tobacco, hay, and fruits and vegetables in sizable quantities. Unable to compete with western ranchers, Pennsylvania farmers also

Like the lumber industry, the oil boom in northwestern Pennsylvania also led to rapidly constructed shantytowns and a denuded landscape. Here in 1865 the Shoe & Leather Petroleum Company's makeshift office in the middle of a field of derricks at Pioneer Run exemplifies the way quick profits rather than long-term development characterized the oil industry in Pennsylvania.

switched from cattle raising to dairy production. The forests, however, particularly in the central northern counties, allowed Pennsylvania to remain the nation's leading producer of lumber, and a modern sawmill industry developed in and around the city of Williamsport. A rich base of natural resources had always favored Pennsylvanians and allowed for diverse enterprise—be that timber, iron ore, soft and hard coal, or the fertile earth of the state. But the discovery of one more natural resource in the late nineteenth century almost led to even greater economic advancement and the creation of a fourth thriving regional economy.

On August 27, 1859, Edwin L. Drake, after two years of failed efforts, struck oil in Titusville, in the northwestern part of the state. No one at the time could even imagine the variety of products that could be distilled from the oil, or their uses, but after Drake's discovery sufficient interest in the liquid black gold for the lighting of streets, homes, and workplaces spurred a rush of drilling and refining ventures. A prosperous regional economy akin to that of the anthracite counties was expected, with major oil companies operating in the field and a metropolitan transport, financial, and retail center—perhaps Erie—emerging to serve the industry and the area's potential swelling population. Circumstances, however, conspired against such a possibility.

Once again, Thomas Scott of the Pennsylvania Railroad enters the picture, this time joined by an equally powerful figure of the period but not a Pennsylvanian: John D. Rockefeller. Rockefeller was in the process of forming his Standard Oil Company, which

Thousands of industrial accidents occurred every year in late nineteenth-century Pennsylvania. For those that resulted in death, sometimes the employer might compensate the family with small payments, but ethnic churches and fraternal societies were the principal source of both financial and emotional support. Here a funeral in the Pennsylvania anthracite region is held with an empty casket, indicating that the body of the deceased was not recovered.

would soon command the transportation, refining, and merchandising of oil throughout the nation. Scott wanted his railroad to achieve a lion's share of the business of transporting oil in tank cars and pipe lines; Rockefeller sought to dominate the refining of oil and sales in urban centers. Together the two magnates colluded in setting transport rates that drove local refiners out of business and forced local drilling companies to sell crude oil to them at low prices. Oil issued from the earth of northwestern Pennsylvania, but it did not stimulate regional development. Oil discoveries in more productive fields, first in Ohio and then in Texas and Oklahoma, ultimately doomed Pennsylvania's place in the industry, although as late as 1900 the state still produced 60 percent of the nation's oil supply.

Pennsylvania thus held a principal place in the industrial capitalist development of the United States in the second half of the nineteenth century. It supplied coal, iron, steel, machinery, railroad transport (and then electricity and oil) for the nation's economic modernization. Continuity and change marked developments within the state. Agricultural production expanded and shifted, diversity remained a hallmark of Pennsylvania manufacture, and three distinctive, nascent regional economies fully matured. Pennsylvania was also home to the great innovations in technology and business practices of the times. The progress of the age, however, did not bring general prosperity. For the men and women whose hard work had placed Pennsylvania in the economic forefront, insecurity and a life of barely making ends meet characterized their daily lives.

HARD TIMES AND PROTEST

Economic crises accompanied economic progress. In the late nineteenth century, Pennsylvanians suffered through three major economic tailspins: a great depression between 1873 and 1879, a serious recession from 1884 to 1886, and another precipitous depression between 1893 and 1897. Unemployment in Philadelphia and Pittsburgh, and in the anthracite region, ranged between 30 and 40 percent of the labor force during these particularly bleak times. In the absence of government measures to pattern growth and development, and with the failure of businessmen to self-regulate, cycles of intense speculation and investment leading to overconstruction, overproduction,

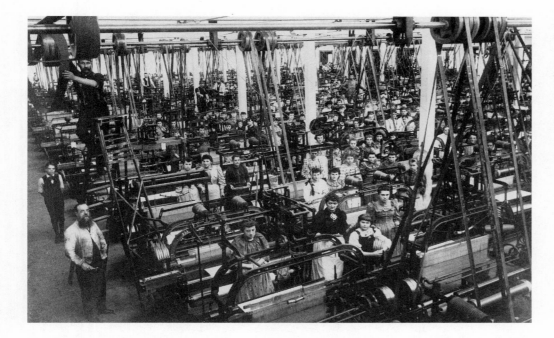

Teenage and young adult women workers predominated in certain industries that did not require heavy labor, such as silk weaving. The Keystone Silk Mill in Emmaus is representative of the towns between Pennsylvania's three major economic regions in which one industry or company often served as the single source of employment. Note the male supervisors and the man fixing the overhead belt; the segmentation of jobs by gender was the absolute norm.

ruinous competition, and falling profits, and then retrenchments, were inherent and recurrent during the period.

Pennsylvania workers, however, faced uncertain prospects not just during the calamitous downturns but also in relatively good times. Normal seasonal shifts in demand, constantly fluctuating business circumstances, the need to retool (especially for specialty producers), and even bad weather meant that employers frequently closed shop and furloughed their employees for months at a time. As a result, workers alternated between periods of intense and slack work, and even in the steel industry, where the plants operated on a more regular basis, steelworkers could expect to lose about a month's worth of work and income. Underemployment wreaked havoc on family budgets. The ever-present and pressing threat of accidental injuries and fatalities on the job made matters worse, but even in the absence of tragedy, low wages and irregular employment meant that few households in the late nineteenth century could survive on one paycheck. With wives and older daughters needed for child care and home production, the burden of being family breadwinners fell to boys and younger girls in the family.

In 1848 Pennsylvania became the first state in the nation to prohibit child labor in factories and mines; later laws provided policing mechanisms and made school attendance mandatory. Legal restrictions, however, did not prevent child labor, as the laws were flagrantly ignored. Over the course of the late nineteenth century the percentages of young people at work and not at home or in school actually grew. Youngsters twelve to fifteen years old came to represent more than 15 percent of the total Philadelphia work force by the year 1900, and boys under the age of fourteen constituted more than 10 percent of those laboring in anthracite mines and breakers. The income of children

William Henry Mills worked in the Whitsett Mine in Fayette County, c. 1900. Originally from Roanoke, Virginia, Mills moved northward very early in the "Great Migration" that brought millions of African Americans from the South to industrial centers in the North in the first half of the twentieth century. Only small numbers of blacks found employment in Pennsylvania mines and manufactories. Discriminatory hiring practices prevented them from establishing the family and personal networks of the kind that helped white workers, both native-born and immigrant, find jobs.

was essential for family survival in many households. In Philadelphia, children contributed to between one-third and one-half of total family income. Among anthracite mining families, children furnished at least 50 percent of family financial resources. In Pittsburgh, where steelworkers received higher and more regular pay, and where there were fewer light industrial opportunities for child labor, children's contributions to family income were generally less critical.

Women too served as economic bulwarks of the family in the face of the uncertain earnings of adult male breadwinners. Single adult women made up nearly one-third of Philadelphia's industrial work force, representing clear majorities of employees in textiles, garments, and hat and paper making; in the anthracite region, they staffed silk mills, and in

Pittsburgh they came to represent 18 percent of the city's labor force by 1900. Throughout the state, single adult women also served in great numbers as paid domestic servants. In entering into gainful employment outside the home before marriage, young women in their late teens and early twenties contributed significantly to household income.

White married women entered the work force only in the most desperate of circumstances, normally if their husbands died or they had few children of working age. Before 1900 less than 5 percent of all married white women in Pennsylvania earned wages on a regular basis, but their unpaid labor in the home substantially subsidized the family economy. Working-class women spent their days endlessly sewing and mending clothing, cleaning, laundering, fetching water, shopping, cooking, engaging in child care, tending gardens, canning foods, managing boarders, laboring on piecework, and hawking and scavenging on the streets. The taking in of lodgers and piecework were especially important sources of income. In Philadelphia in the late nineteenth century, boarders could be found in more than one in six of all households, contributing to as much as 15 percent of total family income. In the apparels trade in Philadelphia and Pittsburgh, about 40 percent of the labor involved in garment production—including attaching collars and sewing buttons—occurred in homes on a putting-out basis. Thousands of homemakers in these cities thereby earned extra income for their families. Dollar values can be affixed to the tasks assumed by Pennsylvania housewives in the late nineteenth century, and the sum price of goods and services provided is twice as great as the income they could have earned in paid employment outside the home, and near their husbands' total wages.

The low rate of labor force participation of married women in the nineteenth century in Pennsylvania applied only to white women. Black married women faced drastically different circumstances; in Philadelphia, for example, one-fourth of them toiled outside the home, largely in commercial laundries and as domestic servants. They thus worked a double shift, supplementing their unpaid labor in the household with paid employment, out of necessity to sustain their families. Married black women joined the labor force in great numbers because their husbands and children faced blatant discrimination in the job market.

The African American population in Pennsylvania grew to 2.5 percent of the total by 1900, although blacks comprised 5 percent of the population in Philadelphia and Pittsburgh. In both cities most industrial firms made a practice of not employing black adult males or black youngsters, even at the lowest level of positions. Company managers denied jobs to blacks on the basis of their own prejudices or under pressure from organized white workers who feared loss of employment and lower wages if blacks were hired. The frequent use of blacks as strikebreakers generated further hostility among Pennsylvania white workers. Black males thus found themselves relegated to the least desirable of jobs; 60 percent were in domestic service positions, another 30 percent in common day labor, such as hauling and carting. Even the 10 percent of black males in the state who had received trade training and were skilled workers could find jobs only in black-owned businesses serving the black community. Employment prospects for adult black males in Pennsylvania actually deteriorated in the last half of the nineteenth century.

Unlike their white counterparts, African American youngsters also faced severe discrimination in employment and thus could not help their families. As W. E. B. Du Bois noted in his classic sociological survey *The Philadelphia Negro,* published in 1899, "[The] absence of child labor . . . is not voluntary on the part of the Negro but due to restricted opportunity." Black children, however, did not idle away at home, but rather attended school in great numbers and stayed longer than young whites who left to take employment.

Hard times generated great working-class grievance and protest in Pennsylvania in the late nineteenth century, but largely involving white workers and their employers. Black workers, denied access to industrial jobs, entry to meetings and demonstrations, and membership in labor organizations, remained at a distance from these battlefronts; their occasional presence as strikebreakers destroyed any chances for solidarity.

White workers in Pennsylvania engaged in some of the monumental labor battles of the late nineteenth century—the great railroad strikes of July 1877 and the Homestead Strike of 1892. Focusing on the epic confrontations, however, obscures the very prevalence of strike activity throughout the period. In the last two decades of the century, authorities reported the outbreak of no less than 4,000 work stoppages in the state, involving close to 25,000 firms and 1.7 million workers. On average, the strikes lasted thirty-seven days. Workers walked off their jobs seeking higher wages. They also demanded shorter workdays (six days a week, twelve hours a day was the norm in Pennsylvania during the period), union recognition, safer working conditions, controls on hiring and layoffs, an end to the capricious decision-making of foremen, and the installation of union-determined work rules. Striking workers also enlisted community support, particularly in battles with the state's major corporations, and enjoyed some successes. Sixty percent of the strikes ended with the workers achieving at least some of their demands.

Many strikes during the period had a definite spontaneous quality, involving neither known labor leaders nor unions. In fact, close to 50 percent of the work stoppages recorded in Pennsylvania in the last two decades of the nineteenth century were categorized by authorities as grassroots insurgencies, a mark of the depths of local community grievances and common interests. A strong tradition of building working-class organizations, however, persisted in the Commonwealth. As the state during the antebellum period gave rise to the nation's first trade unions, central trade councils, and workers' newspapers and parties, Pennsylvania in the last half of the century remained the birthplace and center of labor organization.

In 1866 in Philadelphia, William Sylvis and Jonathan Fincher founded the National Labor Union (NLU), the nation's first national federation of trade unions. Sylvis, a Philadelphia iron molder, had risen to prominence as the articulate leader of a newly formed national union of molders. Fincher, a Philadelphia machinist, turned his talents

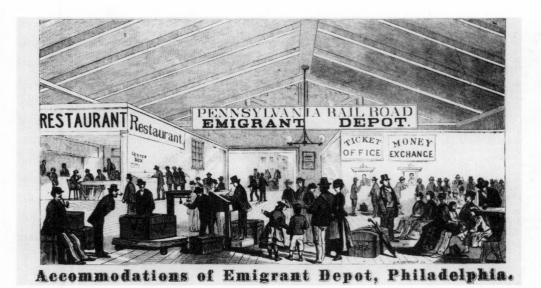

Accommodations of Emigrant Depot, Philadelphia.

Although most immigrants to Pennsylvania came through New York City during the late nineteenth century, Philadelphia continued to be a busy port of entry as well. The Pennsylvania Railroad handled much of this traffic, and in the 1870s it built this two-story Emigrant Depot on its wharves at Washington Avenue to receive newcomers. There immigrants passed through customs, purchased their train tickets, and boarded the railroad en route to jobs and homes elsewhere in the state. Immigrants represented between 13 and 16 percent of the state's population in the second half of the nineteenth century, but 25 to 30 percent of the inhabitants of Philadelphia, the anthracite region, and Pittsburgh. Immigrants and their offspring made major marks on Pennsylvania with the small specialty businesses and ethnic communities, associations, and churches they created; the hard labor they provided in the factories and mines of the state; and their presence in the contentious electoral politics and labor conflict of the period.

toward writing and began publishing *Fincher's Trade Review*, which became in the 1860s the most influential and largest selling labor news weekly in the county. The NLU quickly launched campaigns on behalf of the eight-hour workday and the building of so-called producers' cooperatives or worker-owned businesses. (Sylvis spoke of the cooperatives as "the true remedy for the evils of society . . . [breaking] the present system of centralization, monopoly, and extortion . . . [allowing] ourselves the wealth we have been so long creating for others.") The National Labor Union maintained a visible presence but failed to survive the depression of 1873 and internal fractures. From its ashes, however, rose another federation of unions having an even greater impact: the Knights of Labor.

Uriah Stevens and James Wright, skilled garment cutters, founded the Noble and Holy Order of the Knights of Labor in Philadelphia in 1869 as a secret organization. Little is known about the organization until 1878, when the order went public and grew dramatically under the leadership of Terence Powderly, a teetotalling Catholic machinist from Scranton and at the time the city's mayor. The Knights developed as an amorphous federation of skilled craft unions, factory and neighborhood groups of workers, city and statewide labor assemblies, and reform associations. The message of the Knights was equally protean. Their official stand was in favor of abandonment of the wage labor system, but Knights officials openly repudiated socialism, renounced strikes, and remained ambivalent about politics. Knights leaders also upheld the vision of building a Cooperative Commonwealth, but Knights adherents established few producers' cooperatives. The order remained open to the enrollment of all workers regardless of skill, sex, or race, and while unprecedented strides were made in organizing women and African Americans, gender and racial divisions marked its history. In spite of the many contradictions, workers throughout the nation got swept up in a broad social movement, and with several successful Knights-led strikes in the mid-1880s, membership in the organization swelled nationally to 750,000.

PINKERTON'S NATIONAL DETECTIVE AGENCY.
We never sleep.

ALLAN PINKERTON, Principal.
Geo. H. Bangs, Genl Supt.

LIST OF FUGITIVE MOLLIE MAGUIRES, 1879.

WILLIAM LOVE.—Murderer of Thos. Gwyther, at Girardville, Pa., August 14th, 1875. Is a miner and boatman; 26 years old; 5 ft. 9 in. high; medium build; weighs about 150 lbs.; light complexion; grey eyes; yellow hair; light mustache; has a scar from burn on left side of neck under chin, and coal marks on hands; thin and sharp features; generally dresses well. Lived at Girardville, Schuylkill Co., Pa.

THOMAS HURLEY.—Murderer of Gomer Jamas, August 14th, 1875. Is a miner; 25 years old; 5 ft. 8 in. high; well built; weighs about 160 lbs.; sandy complexion and hair; small piercing eyes; smooth face; sharp features; large hands and feet; wears black hat and dark clothes; lived at Shenandoah, Schuylkill Co., Pa.

MICHAEL DOYLE.—Murderer of Thomas Sanger and Wm. Uren, September 1st, 1875. Is a miner; 25 years old; 5 ft. 5 in. high; medium built; dark complexion; black hair and eyes; full round face and head; smooth face and boyish looking generally; wears a cap. Lived at Shenandoah.

JAMES, ALIAS FRIDAY O'DONNELL.—Murderer of Sanger and Uren, is 26 years old; 5 ft. 10½ in. high; slim built; fair complexion; smooth face; dark eyes; brown hair; generally wears a cap; dresses well; is a miner and lived at Wiggan's Patch, Pa.

JAMES McALLISTER.—Murderer of Sanger and Uren, is 27 years old; 5 ft. 8 in. high; stout built; florid complexion; full broad face, somewhat freckled; light hair and moustache; wears a cap and dark clothes, lived at Wiggan's Patch, Pa.

JOHN, ALIAS HUMPTY FLYNN.—Murderer of Thomas Devine, October 11th, 1875, and Geo. K. Smith, at Audenreid, November 5th, 1863. Is 53 years old; 5 ft. 7 or 8 in. high; heavy built; sandy hair and complexion; smooth face; large nose; round shouldered and almost humpbacked. Is a miner and lived at New Philadelphia, Schuylkill Co., Pa.

JERRY KANE.—Charged with conspiracy to murder. Is 38 years old; 5 ft. 7 in. high; dark complexion; short brown hair; sharp features; sunken eyes; roman nose; coal marks on face and hands; wears black slouch hat; has coarse gruff voice. Is a miner and lived at Mount Laffee, Pa.

FRANK KEENAN.—Charged with conspiracy to murder. Is 31 years old; 5 ft. 7 in. high; dark complexion; black hair, inclined to curl and parted in the middle; sharp features; slender but compactly built; wears a cap and dark clothes. Is a miner and lived at Forrestville, Pa.

WILLIAM GAVIN.—Charged with conspiracy to murder. Is 42 years old; 5 ft. 8 in. high; sandy hair and complexion; stout built; red chin whiskers; face badly pock-marked; has but one eye; large nose; formerly lived at Big Mine Run, Pa. Is a miner. Wears a cap and dark clothes.

JOHN REAGAN.—Murderer of Patrick Burns at Tuscarora, April 15th, 1870. About 5 ft. 10 or 11 in. high; 40 years old; small goatee; stoop shouldered; dark hair, cut short; coal marks on hands and face; has a swinging walk; wears shirt collar open at the neck.

THOMAS O'NEILL.—Murderer of Patrick Burns, at Tuscarora, April 15th, 1870. About 5 ft. 9 in. high; 35 years old; light hair; very florid complexion; red moustache and think red goatee; stoop shouldered; walks with a kind of a jerk; think has some shot marks on back of neck and wounded in right thigh.

PATRICK B. GALLAGHER, ALIAS PUG NOSE PAT.—Murderer of George K. Smith, at Audenreid, November 5th, 1863. About 5 ft. 8 in. high; medium built; dark complexion and hair; latter inclined to curl; turned up nose; thick lips; wears a frown on his countenance; large coal cut across the temple; from 32 to 35 years old; has been shot in the thigh.

Information may be sent to me at either of the above offices,

ALLAN PINKERTON.

Pinkerton "Wanted" poster for Molly Maguires. Deputized by state and local governments to break strikes, the Pinkerton Detective Agency functioned as an expanded police force in the years before the Pennsylvania State Police was formed (partly in response to Pinkerton brutality). This list of "fugitives" was issued two years after twenty alleged Mollies were hung for insurrectionary activity; a Pinkerton spy who provided testimony was somewhat of an agent provocateur.

The Knights had a particularly strong presence in Pennsylvania, with 95,000 members in the state. Knights unions operated in mining and iron and steelworks communities, but thrived especially in Philadelphia among textile workers. Fifty thousand men and women in the textile industry joined the organization and engaged in an outburst of strikes in 1886 that closed the mills of the city. In these and other confrontations, Powderly and other Knights leaders warned local Knights against striking. While this did not deter work stoppages, divisions between the rank and file and officers of the order on policies and tactics contributed to the disintegration of the organization in Pennsylvania and elsewhere by the late 1890s (businessmen also launched effective counteroffensives to still the movement).

Labor organizing in Pennsylvania in the late nineteenth century took its most enduring and dramatic form in the anthracite region. In 1868 John Siney founded the Workmen's Benevolent Association (WBA) in the area, and the union was able to achieve the first collective-bargaining agreement in the industry. In the mid-1870s, however, Franklin B. Gowen, president of the Philadelphia & Reading Railroad, which dominated in both the mining and transport of anthracite, determined to eliminate the WBA. Collaborating with other mining company owners, Gowen successfully withstood a major strike in 1875 that nullified all contracts with the union. Victory enabled Gowen also to clamp down on the guerrilla warfare that percolated in the region for years involving a clandestine order of Irish miners, the legendary Molly Maguires.

Irish immigrants came to work in the anthracite mines in great numbers in the 1850s. They brought with them traditions of secret revenge against their exploiters—English landlords—and in Pennsylvania their wrath would be directed toward their English and Welsh overseers in the mines in a mix of ethnic and class antagonism. During the Civil War, bands of Irish miners murdered a mine superintendent and foreman who colluded in the drafting of miners into military service. Other mine managers suffered similar fates after the war, and the legend of the Molly Maguires grew. Zealous to stamp out the insurrectionaries, Franklin Gowen enlisted the help of the Pinkerton Detective Agency, and, along with his own Coal and Iron Police (in the face of the Mollies and other labor agitators, Pennsylvania state legislators had enacted laws that allowed coal companies to form their own militias), he had the group infiltrated. Pinkerton agent James McParlan ultimately provided testimony that led

Immigrant miners marched toward Lattimer, near Hazleton, on September 10, 1897, hoping to convince miners there to join the nationwide campaign of the United Mine Workers of America. The Lattimer Massacre ensued.

to the conviction and hanging of twenty men. Ten were executed on June 21, 1877, which became known as the "Day of the Rope." The guilt of the condemned and the actual existence of an organization of Molly Maguires have remained disputed matters.

After the defeat of the Workmen's Benevolent Association and the hanging of the Mollies, labor organizing stalled in the anthracite region until the late 1890s, when anthracite miners joined the nationwide campaigns of the United Mine Workers of America (UMW), a union founded in 1890. After gaining a strong foothold in bituminous coal areas of western Pennsylvania through successful strikes and collective bargaining, UMW organizers moved into the anthracite region. This led in 1897 to one of the bloodiest confrontations of the period.

On Friday, September 10, 1897, some 400 miners, recent immigrants from southern and eastern Europe, marched under the banner of the United Mine Workers toward the small coal-patch town of Lattimer; they hoped to convince miners there to join their walkout against the Lehigh & Wilkes-Barre Coal Company. Company executives had received assurances from local law enforcement officers that the protest would be quelled. At 3:45 in the afternoon, Sheriff James L. Martin, with a force of 150 police behind him, walked to the head of the marchers' column and ordered them to disperse. He then grabbed at the American flag held by the lead marcher, and in the scuffle that ensued the assembled police fired into the crowd. Nineteen unarmed miners lay dead in the road and thirty-six others lay seriously wounded, in what became known as the Lattimer Massacre.

The families of the killed and wounded received some solace in the next five years. In 1900 the United Mine Workers, under the leadership of John Mitchell, engaged in a five-week strike of 90,000 anthracite miners that produced significant gains in wages, benefits, and working conditions. Two years later, 150,000 anthracite miners joined a five-month strike whose crippling effect on the nation's economy required the intervention of U.S. President Theodore Roosevelt. Victory in the great Anthracite Coal Strike of 1902 ushered in a new age of industrial relations involving settlement of disputes by boards of coal company executives, union officials, and government arbitrators.

Hard times, uncertain employment, perilous working conditions, arbitrary management, and growing senses of dependency in the face of the rise of the corporation generated civil wars in Pennsylvania in the last decades of the nineteenth century. Labor protest and organizing in the period raised awareness of the insecurities wrought by an unfettered market economy and served as a prelude to calls for and the enactment of measures regulating business and employment practices in the opening decades of the twentieth century.

THE MIDDLE CLASS AND POLITICS IN THE GILDED AGE

Between the great magnates and accumulators of wealth of the age, and the working people of Pennsylvania, stood a burgeoning population of middle-class Pennsylvanians. Their swelling ranks in the late nineteenth century included small-town bankers, merchants, and manufacturers; their small business counterparts in metropolitan areas; lawyers, doctors, and other professionals; educators; white-collar office and sales clerks; and the most highly skilled and well-off of workers, the so-called aristocrats of labor. Perched in the middle, these citizens of the state had torn loyalties and identities. Fearing and decrying the violent assaults on property and management by striking workers, with their own independence threatened by large-scale business, they also sympathized with labor protests aimed at corporate power.

Though buffeted by the economic storms of the period, middle-class families enjoyed a modicum of security thanks to the relatively stable positions and incomes of the fathers of these households. The children of professionals and mill owners could stay in school. In Philadelphia and Pittsburgh, the daughters of skilled workers attended commercial course degree programs in the new girls' high schools opening up at the turn of the century, on their way to clerical jobs in downtown office buildings. Office work represented a step upward socially, although many young women would learn that laboring behind the desk—typing and addressing letters, filing, and taking dictation, under strict supervision—could be as demeaning, routinized, and exploitative as jobs in the factories. As offices expanded in the late nineteenth century with the growth of corporations, they became mechanized, feminized, and administered according to the principles of scientific management promoted by the likes of Philadelphian Frederick Winslow Taylor.

JOHN WANAMAKER AND HIS EMPORIUM

John Wanamaker envisioned what we would now call a modern shopping mall. Born in Philadelphia in 1838, Wanamaker entered the retail trade when he opened a men's clothing store in 1861. As his business expanded, he invited other Philadelphia storekeepers to join him in a daring plan: to establish a grand emporium of separate stores in a former Pennsylvania Railroad depot in the heart of the city. When other merchants shied away from such an enterprise, Wanamaker moved ahead on his own, opening an awe-inspiring department store overflowing with varied wares in 1876—just in time to draw the throngs attending the Centennial Exhibition.

Not just a pioneer in the concept of the department store, Wanamaker also led businessmen in the use of advertising and sales promotions, electric lighting in workplaces, and the engendering of loyalty among employees through positive means. Wanamaker offered his store workers fringe benefits and educational and social programs that anticipated modern personnel practices by decades.

Wanamaker led the way also in spreading a consumerist ethos. By flourishing a cornucopia of wares—from fashionable clothing to perfumes, draperies, furniture, and dishes—in his alluring window displays, sumptuous showrooms, and newspaper advertisements, he effectively created new desires among Philadelphians, who under his tutelage would become consumers by habit. His well-mannered and well-adorned young female sales clerks served as agents of his revolution. Wanamaker preferred young women who spoke proper English and whose appearance and manner reflected familiarity with the goods of a more comfortable life. They became models to be aspired to; working-

class immigrant girls, who blended into the crowds promenading wide-eyed through the store, could only dream of becoming Wanamaker sales clerks, but with wages they were allowed to keep after contributing to family income, they could purchase some of the trappings of a more glamorous life.

In addition to creating his world-renowned emporium, John Wanamaker also entered the political realm, serving as U.S. Postmaster General and launching reform crusades against the entrenched Republican leadership in Pennsylvania. He somewhat humbled the likes of Matthew Quay and Boies Penrose, but he lost in efforts to gain senatorial and gubernatorial nominations of the Republican Party. To the day he died, in 1922, John Wanamaker was a deeply religious man and a great patron of churches and religious charitable organizations.

ABOVE: Wanamaker's department store used fixed prices, well-lighted displays, and informed salespeople to make shopping easy. Consumption was becoming a measure of success for women and men. With its restaurants, men's smoking room, variety of departments, and location at the junction of railroads, the department store became a place where different classes converged. Every city of any size in Pennsylvania had its own department store, which often extended its influence to the countryside with mail-order catalogs.

Still, for young women from working-class backgrounds and neighborhoods, working downtown in clerical jobs had its definite attractions, including being able to browse in department stores during lunch breaks and go out after hours to downtown entertainment spots. The daughters of the upper middle class had greater options. They could pursue higher education at new women's colleges, such as Bryn Mawr, and at state "normal schools," which trained teachers. The opening decades of the twentieth century would thus see in Pennsylvania the first generation of high school and college educated young women assuming their places in white-collar and professional employment and civic affairs—and making greater demands for enfranchisement in the process.

While the middle class could not match, and even disdained, the conspicuous consumption of the business tycoons of the period—with their town mansions, country estates, and opulent parties—the middle class of Pennsylvania did enjoy certain luxuries and new levels of comfort. In Philadelphia and Pittsburgh they could purchase three-story stately Victorian homes built by developers in outlying bucolic neighborhoods and so-called streetcar suburbs, away from the industrial cores of the cities. They could further afford to appoint their homes with proper furnishings and to hire servants. The middle class in the late nineteenth century particularly delighted in browsing and shopping in the great new emporiums of the age, the most famous and spectacular of which was John Wanamaker's department store in downtown Philadelphia.

Members of the middle class could also participate in the new high culture of the period. Reputable symphonies and symphony halls were established in both Philadelphia and Pittsburgh late in the century, and opera houses graced small towns throughout the state. Two renowned art museums were created in Philadelphia: the Pennsylvania Academy of the Fine Arts and the Philadelphia Museum of Art. The great American

Sarah Reed

The history of Pennsylvania in the last half of the nineteenth century has a masculine tenor—it is about men at war, male titans of industry, and workers on strike. But for the early industrial period in Pennsylvania—before 1850—a figure such as Rebecca Lukens can be cited as a great builder of enterprise. Inheriting her husband's iron mill in Coatesville at his death in 1825, the firm under her administration, before her own passing in 1854, grew and became a major producer of iron and steel that thrives to this day. There is no equivalent to Rebecca Lukens to join the pantheon of late nineteenth-century Pennsylvania business leaders.

Women may not have been in the limelight, but they anchored the state of Pennsylvania between 1850 and 1900. They served on the home front during the Civil War; subsidized the family economy through their unpaid work in the home; provided labor in mills, stores, and offices; and as teachers, nurses, and doctors they schooled Pennsylvania children and cared for the sick. Women were also the bulwarks of their communities, building and sustaining what today would be called "nongovernmental organizations," the cornerstones of civic society. In rural townships, small cities, and urban centers, women created and administered a wealth of religious, educational, charitable, and recreational institutions.

A good example is Sarah Reed of Erie. The great-granddaughter of one of the earliest settlers of that city, Reed was born in 1838. In her twenties as a member of the Ladies' Aid Society, she ministered to battle-injured soldiers on hospital troop trains passing through Erie. Moved by her Civil War service, Reed then helped raise $10,000 for construction of a monument to honor the men of Erie

who had given their lives for the Union cause. Reed also became a charter member and leader of more than twenty-five societies, including the Woman's Christian Temperance Union, the Women's Auxiliary of St. Paul's Episcopal Church, the Young Women's Christian Association, the Daughters of the American Revolution, the Needlework Guild, and the Erie Art Club. She sponsored literary salons in her home (and wrote children's books in her spare time) and began an education program for secretaries that evolved into Erie's first women's business club. Most important, in 1871 she helped found the first welfare agency in Erie, the Erie Association for Improving the Conditions of the Poor and a Home for the Friendless. For forty-four years she served as president of this association, which offered relief to Erie's dispossessed, and shelter for its wayward children. Unlike many of her civic-minded fellow women, Reed lived long enough to see ratification of the Nineteenth Amendment to the U.S. Constitution in 1920, which granted women the franchise and formal citizenship. Characteristically, although she was in her eighties and nineties, she threw herself into mainstream politics through leadership in the League of Women Voters and the Erie Council of Republican Women.

painter Thomas Eakins, a Philadelphia native, taught at the former, and his paintings of rowers on the Schuylkill River emblazoned a scenic and serene image of the city. Among Eakins's prize Philadelphia-born pupils was Henry Ossawa Tanner, who became the leading African American painter of his generation. The nation's most prominent female artist of the period, Mary Cassatt, also studied at the Academy; born in Allegheny City (Pittsburgh) and sister of Alexander J. Cassatt, president of the Pennsylvania Railroad late in the century, her career as the nation's leading Impressionist painter flourished while she was living in Paris.

When not consumers of relative luxuries or the arts, Pennsylvanians of middling status also filled their leisure hours with rich associational activities—as members of churches, fraternal orders, temperance societies, and political reform leagues. Women remained core participants in these organizations. The civic engagement of the Commonwealth's middle class in the late nineteenth century marked African American communities too. In Philadelphia, notably, a leadership group of black clergymen, professionals, and proprietors emerged to establish and sustain black churches and cultural institutions, including libraries and educational societies. Philadelphia's black middle class also mobilized to protest infringements on civil rights. In 1864 they organized demonstrations to demand an end to the practice of denying blacks access to public transportation, and in 1867 they succeeded in petitioning for passage of a state law that required railroad and streetcar companies in Pennsylvania to carry all passengers without regard to race. Leading the fight was Octavius V. Catto, a schoolteacher. Four years later, Catto became a martyred figure in Philadelphia's black community when he was killed on Election Day 1871, during riots aimed at keeping black males from voting after passage of the Fifteenth Amendment to the U.S. Constitution.

During the Reconstruction period the black middle class struggled to gain unimpeded access to and a place in Pennsylvania politics, a battle that would continue for another 100 years. For the white middle class, the political system of the Commonwealth generated concern and warranted scorn, for it was in vast need of cleansing. Scandals and corruption abounded in the late nineteenth century as the state's political kingpins performed legislative services for the corporate elite while at the same time building their power on patronage and working-class votes. Newspaper headlines told the story and raised the anxieties of the white middle class.

In Philadelphia, construction began in 1874 on a mammoth French Renaissance

"THE GREAT SUPREME."

Thomas Nast, the great political cartoonist of the late nineteenth century, drew caustic caricatures of the immigrant ward bosses of America's cities. Nast was a campaigner for civil service reform and routing out corruption, and his cartoons were also infused with anti-immigrant sentiment. Here he depicts James McManes, Philadelphia's leading political boss, wielding a whip against both the poor and the wealthy as money is slipped into his hands in return for the jobs, favors, and contracts he provided as he lorded over the city's gas works.

Frank Kelly shot and killed Octavius Catto in Philadelphia on Election Day 1871. Kelly had joined other whites that day in roaming through the city's African American neighborhoods, making sure that no adult black male would exercise his newly achieved constitutional right to vote. Whether he targeted Catto as a rising, magnetic leader of Philadelphia's African American community is unknown, but Kelly and other known white assailants responsible for killings and assaults in the Election Day riots never stood trial.

Had Octavius Catto not been murdered at the age of thirty-one, he probably would today have a prominent place in American history textbooks. The son of a leading black minister in Philadelphia, Catto had received a strong education at the Institute for Colored Youth, a school established by Philadelphia Quakers to provide learning for black teenagers denied entry to the city's one public high school. After graduation, he joined the faculty of the Institute, where he became an inspiring teacher and advocate for the education of African Americans.

During the Civil War, Catto joined others in petitioning for the formation of black troops; eventually he enlisted and became a junior officer, but he saw no battlefield action. When black soldiers were denied access to local streetcars on their way to and from Camp William Penn, a major training ground for black soldiers on the outskirts of Philadelphia, he became a leader of the Equal Rights League, which demanded an end to segregated public facilities. As chief lobbyist, he succeeded in his efforts to get state legislation banning discrimination on streetcars passed in 1867. In the late 1860s, Catto became a national spokesperson for enfranchisement and civil rights of African Americans,

ABOVE: Octavius Catto

and a representative for blacks in the inner circles of the Republican Party. On Election Day 1871, Philadelphia's African American community gained a martyr who has been remembered by blacks in the city for generations.

city hall at the intersection of Broad and Market Streets that would not be completed until the 1890s. Budgeted at $10 million, the cost escalated to $25 million as contractors connected to the city's political machine pocketed great profits. "King" James McManes, Philadelphia's leading political boss, aptly earned his moniker as he lorded over the city's gas works; McManes amassed a fortune through kickbacks he received controlling and dispensing 5,000 jobs and lucrative contracts. In Harrisburg, the state's political boss of bosses, Matthew Quay, sat as head of the Commonwealth's treasury. Money seeped out of the state's coffers during his and his handpicked successor's reign, to pay for political campaigns and Quay's private investment schemes. Until very late in his political career, Quay successfully deflected criticism and attacks on his machinations, and often with devilish quips. For example, he attributed his staying power to adhering to the following definition of politics: "The art of taking money from the few and votes from the many under the pretext of protecting one from the other."

Urban population growth and the expansion of public services, particularly in cities, allowed for the great political scandals of the day. The political bosses had funds, business, and jobs to distribute in return for fealty and the vote. In burgeoning immigrant, working-class city wards, the machine provided valuable social services, including charity and employment assistance at a time when public support hardly existed and the middle class disdained any responsibility for the "huddled masses." Certainly, the ability of corporate executives to buy legislative favors contributed to the corruption of politics that horrified the proper middle class. The pervasiveness of shady politics in Pennsylvania, however, was due in no small part to the effective one-party rule that prevailed in the state after the Civil War.

The Republican Party, with few exceptions, completely dominated the political landscape of Pennsylvania after 1865. While the Democrats could occasionally don the hat of reformers, pledging to root out the corrupters and their practices, even if they had the will—which was improbable given the party's own dynamics—the Democrats definitely never had the might to effect change. The Republicans held the sword of Copperheadism and treachery (as well as panderers to the Irish and intemperance) over them for generations, and also built an unbeatable machine to get out the vote on election days. The well-heeled and well-oiled Republican organization made sure that the Electoral College votes of Pennsylvania were registered for Republican Party presidential candidates in every presidential election from the end of the Civil War through 1900. Eight of the ten governors elected during the period were Republicans, and with Republican control of the state legislature the Commonwealth, before the direct election of senators, sent Republican senators to the U.S. Senate without fail. In fact, four of Pennsylvania's most powerful political figures, exerting great influence both locally and nationally, held U.S. senatorial seats sequentially from 1867 to 1921: Simon Cameron; his son, Donald; Matthew Quay; and Boies Penrose.

Pennsylvania had the distinction nationally of having a strong Republican Party

Horse-drawn wagons and carriages compete with an electric trolley car in downtown Philadelphia in 1897. It was a changing, congested, and complicated world that Pennsylvanians inhabited as they entered the twentieth century.

machine. In other states, Democrats created boss-led organizations tied to immigrant, working-class votes (Tammany Hall in New York City is archetypal). The peculiar connection of the Pennsylvania Democrats to Copperheadism made for a different history in the state. Equally important was the determination of such men as Cameron, Quay, and Penrose to establish and command a political juggernaut. They willfully used public funds, kickbacks, and corporate donations to finance campaigns (and enhance their own wealth), and with an estimated 20,000 federal, state, and local patronage jobs in their control they assembled an army of political faithful and ward heelers. The Republicans succeeded too by holding rural areas of the state and the votes of Protestant workers in cities. The only Democratic strongholds remained in Irish wards in Philadelphia, in the anthracite region, and in non-Protestant immigrant rural communities.

In the absence of an effective opposition, the Republican bosses could rule. Reform groups appeared, such as the Committee of One Hundred in Philadelphia in the early 1880s, an organization comprised of middle-class professionals and educators that championed civil service reform and measures to limit the license of ward politicians. The politicos, however, easily defrayed or manipulated the petitions of the reformers. Matthew Quay, for example, supported the recommendations of the Committee of One Hundred for charter change in Philadelphia that curtailed the patronage powers of the machine—but he did this only to humble his chief rival, James McManes. Department store owner John Wanamaker similarly headed a reform crusade in the 1890s to cleanse the Republican Party, but Boies Penrose easily defused his campaign.

As Pennsylvanians greeted the twentieth century, they had grounds to be weary— and wary. In the second half of the nineteenth century, they had directly faced war, economic depressions, the jolting rise of the corporation, intense labor strife, ongoing political turmoil and corruption, ethnic and racial divides, and the growth of cities and immigrant populations. Rather than sag under the weight of these developments, Pennsylvanians in the first decades of the new century joined a myriad of groups to demand reform of the social, political, and economic institutions of the Commonwealth and the nation—all in response to the great transformations of the previous decades.

Convergence, not consistency, marked these efforts. Labor advocates pushed for state regulation of working conditions, for worker compensation laws, and for protecting the rights of workers to organize. Consumer groups sought restrictions on the collusive and deceitful practices of businessmen. Middle-class reformers petitioned to curb political corruption and to bring social and physical order to cities. Corporate leaders themselves pressed for measures that would stabilize the economy. Coalitions formed to see certain reforms implemented. Yet in Pennsylvania the reform impulse was shaped and constricted in the opening decades of the twentieth century by the entrenched one-party political system set in place by Republicans in the bygone politics of national and internal civil wars.

SOURCES and FURTHER READING

Aurand, Harold. *From the Molly Maguires to the United Mine Workers: The Social Ecology of an Industrial Union, 1869–1897*. Philadelphia: Temple University Press, 1971.

Baltzell, E. Digby. *Philadelphia Gentlemen: The Making of a National Upper Class*. Glencoe: The Free Press, 1958.

Black, Brian. *Petrolia: The Landscape of America's First Oil Boom*. Baltimore: Johns Hopkins University Press, 2000.

Blair, William A., and William Pencak, eds. *Making and Remaking Pennsylvania's Civil War*. University Park: The Pennsylvania State University Press, 2000.

Blatz, Perry. *Democratic Miners: Work and Labor Relations in the Anthracite Coal Industry, 1875–1925*. Albany: State University of New York Press, 1994.

Bodnar, John. *Immigration and Industrialization: Ethnicity in an American Mill Town, 1870–1940*. Pittsburgh: University of Pittsburgh Press, 1977.

Brody, David. *Steelworkers in America: The Nonunion Era.* Cambridge, Mass.: Harvard University Press, 1960.

Bruce, Robert V. *1877: Year of Violence.* Indianapolis: Bobbs-Merrill, 1959.

Couvares, Francis G. *The Remaking of Pittsburgh: Class and Culture in an Industrializing City, 1877–1919.* Albany: State University of New York Press, 1984.

Davenport, Walter. *Power and Glory: The Life of Boies Penrose.* New York: G. Putnam's Sons, 1931.

DeVault, Ileen D. *Sons and Daughters of Labor: Class and Clerical Work in Turn-of-the-Century Pittsburgh.* Ithaca: Cornell University Press, 1990.

Du Bois, W. E. B. *The Philadelphia Negro: A Social Study.* 1899. Reprint edition with Introduction by Elijah Anderson, Philadelphia: University of Pennsylvania Press, 1996.

Dusinberre, William. *Civil War Issues in Philadelphia, 1856–1865.* Philadelphia: University of Pennsylvania Press, 1965.

Eggert, Gerald G. *Harrisburg Industrializes: The Coming of Factories to an American Community.* University Park: The Pennsylvania State University Press, 1993.

Gallman, J. Matthew. *Mastering Wartime: A Social History of Philadelphia During the Civil War.* Cambridge: Cambridge University Press, 1992.

Golab, Caroline. *Immigrant Destinations.* Philadelphia: Temple University Press, 1977.

Greene, Victor R. *The Slavic Community on Strike: Immigrant Labor in Pennsylvania.* Notre Dame: University of Notre Dame Press, 1968.

Higginbotham, Sanford, William A. Hunter, and Donald H. Kent. *Pennsylvania and the Civil War: A Handbook.* Harrisburg: Pennsylvania Historical and Museum Commission, 1961.

Holt, Michael Fitzgibbon. *Forging a Majority: The Formation of the Republican Party in Pittsburgh, 1848–1860.* Pittsburgh: University of Pittsburgh Press, 1990.

Kehl, James A. *Boss Rule in the Gilded Age: Matt Quay of Pittsburgh.* Pittsburgh: University of Pittsburgh Press, 1981.

Kenny, Kevin. *Making Sense of the Molly Maguires.* New York: Oxford University Press, 1998.

Klein, Philip S. *President James Buchanan: A Biography.* University Park: The Pennsylvania State University Press, 1962.

Kleinberg, S. J. *The Shadow of the Mills: Working-Class Families in Pittsburgh, 1870–1907.* Pittsburgh: University of Pittsburgh Press, 1989.

Koskoff, David E. *The Mellons: The Chronicle of America's Richest Family.* New York: Thomas Y. Crowell Co., 1978.

Krause, Paul. *The Battle for Homestead: Politics, Culture, and Steel, 1880–1892.* Pittsburgh: University of Pittsburgh Press, 1992.

Lane, Roger. *Roots of Violence in Black Philadelphia, 1860–1900.* New York: Cambridge University Press, 1986.

Licht, Walter. *Getting Work: Philadelphia, 1840–1950.* Cambridge, Mass.; Harvard University Press, 1992.

———. *Industrializing America: The Nineteenth Century.* Baltimore: Johns Hopkins University Press, 1995.

Livesay, Harold C. *Andrew Carnegie and the Rise of Big Business.* Boston: Little, Brown, 1975.

McCullough, David G. *The Johnstown Flood.* New York: Simon & Schuster, 1968.

Miller, Donald L., and Richard E. Sharpless. *The Kingdom of Coal: Work, Enterprise, and Ethnic Communities in the Mine Fields.* Philadelphia: University of Pennsylvania Press, 1985.

Nelson, Daniel T. *Frederick W. Taylor and the Rise of Scientific Management.* Madison: University of Wisconsin Press, 1980.

Scranton, Philip. *Proprietary Capitalism: The Textile Manufacture at Philadelphia, 1800–1885.* New York: Cambridge University Press, 1983.

Shankman, Arnold M. *The Pennsylvania Antiwar Movement, 1861–1865.* Rutherford, N.J.: Fairleigh Dickinson University Press, 1980.

Silcox, Harry C. *A Place to Live and Work: The Henry Disston Saw Works and the Tacony Community of Philadelphia.* University Park: The Pennsylvania State University Press, 1994.

———. *Politics from the Bottom Up: The Life of Irishman William McMullen, 1824–1901.* Philadelphia: Balch Institute Press, 1989.

Thomas Eakins, *The Gross Clinic*, 1875. Eakins painted this dramatic work shortly after taking anatomy courses at Jefferson Medical College in Philadelphia, where he attended surgical lectures and clinics presided over by Professor Samuel D. Gross. The work was much maligned in its day for its bloody realism.

Thaddeus Mortimer Fowler, bird's-eye view of Wilkes-Barre, 1899. Hailed as "the most prolific of all American viewmakers," Fowler created more than 240 views of cities, boroughs, and villages (even a college campus) from across the Keystone State.

Two of the twenty-four stained-glass windows by William B. Van Ingen that grace the House and Senate Chambers of the Pennsylvania State Capitol. These, from the House, depict *Liberty* and *Commerce*.

Edwin Austin Abbey, *The Camp of the American Army of Valley Forge, February 1778.* Originally painted for the Senate Chamber, it was moved to the north wall of the House Chamber when Abbey died in 1911. Violet Oakley completed Abbey's commission.

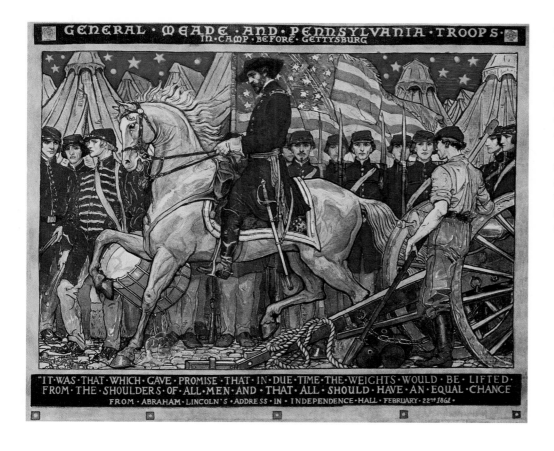

ABOVE: *Penn's Vision* is one of thirteen murals painted by Violet Oakley as part of the frieze *The Founding of the State of Liberty Spiritual* in the Governor's Reception Room of the State Capitol. According to Oakley, Penn's desire was to "bring out of Captivity all those who were oppressed for conscience' sake, whatever their creed or belief."

LEFT: *General Meade and Pennsylvania Troops in Camp Before Gettysburg,* a painting from Violet Oakley's series *The Creation and Preservation of the Union* in the Senate Chamber.

Mary Cassatt, *Mother and Two Children*, 1901. This painting, originally intended for the ladies' parlor at the Capitol, was sold privately and eventually ended up at the Westmoreland Museum of American Art.

Jacob Lawrence, *They arrived in Pittsburgh, one of the great industrial centers of the North, in large numbers*, 1940–41. This panel painting is no. 45 in Lawrence's epic *Migration* series, which depicts the "great migration" of African Americans who left the rural South for the "promised land" of the industrial North in the first half of the twentieth century.

Charles Demuth, *In the Province (Lancaster)*, 1920. Demuth's "view" of the architecture of industry in his native Lancaster. He created most of his art in the small second-floor studio of his King Street home in Lancaster, which today is the Demuth Museum.

Reforming the Commonwealth
1900–1950

DAVID R. CONTOSTA

CHAPTER 6

Pennsylvanians were delighted to learn in 1906 that their new capitol building in Harrisburg, erected to replace the structure that had burned nine years before, was finished one year ahead of time and supposedly within the $4 million budgeted. In retrospect, the massive Renaissance Revival building seems entirely fitting for a commonwealth that had become an industrial empire—and whose government would assume more and more power over the lives of its citizens during the first half of the twentieth century, particularly during and after the Depression of the 1930s. The lines of the State Capitol also blended well with the other projects recently launched in Harrisburg as part of a nationwide "City Beautiful" movement.

Various forces had given rise to the City Beautiful movement in Harrisburg during the early twentieth century, as they had elsewhere in the United States. These included a desire to provide open space for densely packed urban-dwellers, to increase property values in aesthetically enhanced areas of the city, to construct boulevards for the freer flow of traffic, to inject an element of nature into the artificial metropolis, to create scenic vistas that would elevate the human spirit, and to convey a sense of order that might help to tame the chaotic city. Although the roots of this movement lay well back in the nineteenth century, the 1893 Columbian Exposition in Chicago, with its white neoclassical buildings, scenic lagoon, grand boulevards, and overall sense of order, had been a powerful catalyst for the City Beautiful idea.

In Harrisburg, most of the inspiration for city beautification came from J. Horace McFarland and Mira Lloyd Dock, who is notable as one of a growing number of American women who were challenging traditional notions of male leadership. Dock came from a prominent and prosperous Harrisburg family. A botanist by training, she was a devoted conservationist who had acquainted herself with the leading theories of landscape architecture. In addition to a desire to save forests and other aspects of the rural landscape, McFarland and Dock believed that natural scenery should be brought into Harrisburg itself for all to experience and enjoy. As an expression of this idea, she wanted to clean up the capital's filthy streets, develop parkland along the despoiled Susquehanna River banks, and ensure that the city would have a pure supply of drinking water.

In 1898 Dock helped to found the Civic Club of Harrisburg as a vehicle for realizing her plans. Through lectures in other forums, she enlisted the support of the local press and elected officials. Dock was an extremely effective speaker who often illustrated her remarks with lantern slides. One newspaper reported about Dock: "Her vivid description of the roughness, slime and filth we create for ourselves caused applause and then the hush of full comprehension." The results of Dock's and McFarland's efforts were an extensive boulevard system and several graceful bridges in the neoclassical style, the paving of numerous streets, purification of the water supply, and intercepting sewers that kept raw waste from polluting the Susquehanna and its local tributaries. But most impressive were the beautifully landscaped parks along the river that converged with a park constructed on the new State Capitol grounds.

Yet appearances could be deceptive. The public soon learned that the new Capitol had actually cost $13 million, the additional amount having been squandered on lavish decorations and furnishings at scandalously inflated prices. For example, one contractor charged $2,500 for a chandelier that should have cost less than $200. There were also kickbacks and graft that involved several dozen state officeholders and the Capitol's architect himself, Joseph M. Huston of Philadelphia. In that regard, Harrisburg's "progress" symbolized the state's character, for across Pennsylvania public improvements too often came with political corruption.

Despite earnest efforts to clean up politics, Pennsylvania's reformers achieved only limited gains against entrenched political machines in the state's largest cities and in the state capital itself during the early years of the twentieth century, though they did succeed in achieving a number of social and economic reforms. At the same time, few could have predicted—in Harrisburg or elsewhere in the Commonwealth—that Pennsylvania was reaching the peak of its industrial might and would soon begin losing some of its economic and strategic advantages. This assumption—that the basic forces shaping the Keystone State would remain more or less constant, despite certain reforms—was especially evident between 1900 and 1929, before the Great Depression and then World War II brought wave after wave of change.

(OPPOSITE)

TOP LEFT: The Pennsylvania State Capitol at Harrisburg, following the destructive fire of 1897.

TOP RIGHT: The new Pennsylvania State Capitol under construction, April 1, 1904.

BOTTOM: President Theodore Roosevelt dedicating the new State Capitol building, October 4, 1906.

TABLE 6.1 POPULATION OF PENNSYLVANIA, PHILADELPHIA, AND PITTSBURGH, 1900–1950			
	Pennsylvania	Philadelphia	Pittsburgh
1900	6,302,000	1,294,000	322,000
1910	7,665,000	1,549,000	534,000
1920	8,720,000	1,824,000	588,000
1930	9,631,000	1,951,000	670,000
1940	9,900,000	1,931,000	672,000
1950	10,498,000	2,072,000	677,000

SOURCE: U.S. Bureau of the Census.

At the beginning of the twentieth century the Commonwealth of Pennsylvania was known throughout the nation for its industrial might. For the state's 6.3 million inhabitants in 1900, this industry was a source of pride, and it provided a good standard of living for many. Yet the exploitation of workers was the cause of much misery. Pennsylvania's industries also contributed greatly to urban blight and to devastation of the natural environment.

In 1900 Pennsylvania ranked second, just behind New York, in the value of its manufacturing. By 1919 it employed 12.4 percent of all manufacturing workers in the United States, compared with New York's 14 percent. In two industries especially, steel and textiles, Pennsylvania led the nation, producing 15 percent of the nation's textiles during the early twentieth century and more than half its iron and steel. Pennsylvania manufacturers as a whole employed about 25 percent of the state's work force, as of 1919, or 1,135,837 workers.

Manufacturing took place at many locations throughout the Commonwealth, but the two most important were at opposite ends of the state, in Philadelphia and Pittsburgh. Philadelphia, as from the beginning of the industrial revolution in Pennsylvania, continued to lead the way in both the value and the volume of manufacturing. Its manufacturing was also the most diverse in the state. While Philadelphia remained the nation's most important center for shipbuilding, locomotives, and textiles, it also poured forth a steady stream of other finished goods, from machine tools, saws, and watches to carpets, umbrellas, and soap.

But it was Pittsburgh, with its gigantic steel mills and mighty forges, that captured the nation's imagination when it came to sheer industrial might. In addition to the city itself, several towns and small cities in southwestern Pennsylvania, such as Homestead, Duquesne, Aliquippa, and McKeesport, were known for their iron and steel industries.

Andrew Carnegie remained the most important player in this vast operation as the twentieth century began. In 1900 the Carnegie Steel Company produced 25 to 30 percent of the nation's steel, half the armor plate for its ships, and 30 percent of the nation's rails. But Carnegie, who turned sixty-five in 1900, had long wanted to retire from active business, and the following year he sold his company to the investment banker, J. P. Morgan, who merged it with several other steel manufacturers to create the massive United States Steel Corporation, the first billion-dollar corporation in American history. The fact that the merger had been arranged through a New York banker demonstrated just how much the Pennsylvania economy was becoming enmeshed in a national system of capital markets. By the time of the merger, Carnegie had left the Pittsburgh scene and was living either in his New York City mansion or in a castle in his native Scotland. He would spend the rest of his life giving more than $350 million to various philanthropies, including the famous Carnegie libraries.

VIOLET OAKLEY, CAPITOL MURALIST

When the architect of Pennsylvania's new Capitol, Joseph Huston, announced in 1902 that he had commissioned artist Violet Oakley to execute thirteen murals for the governor's reception room, many in the art world were surprised. Up to this time, mural painting had been the almost exclusive preserve of male artists. But Oakley's work in the Capitol made her one of Pennsylvania's most successful artists.

Oakley was born in 1874 in Bergen Heights, New Jersey, into a family with a great love of art and travel that later moved to Philadelphia. Essentially a late-Victorian artist, Oakley believed that art should uplift the public both morally and spiritually. This is evident in the murals she painted for the Governor's Reception Room in the State Capitol, for which she chose a historical narrative of the role William Penn, and Pennsylvania itself, played in the cause of religious freedom.

In 1911 Oakley received a commission to complete the largely unfinished murals for the state senate chamber and the state supreme court, which had been assigned to Edwin Austin Abbey before his death. In these works Oakley gave full rein to her abilities as an illustrator. The murals in the senate chamber (1911–20) depict important scenes in the creation and preservation of the American union. Her theme in the supreme court chamber (1917–27) is the victory of law over force, again with a sequence of historical panels. Her other works include a large series of portraits of the delegates and other dignitaries at the League of Nations installed at League headquarters in Geneva, Switzerland (1927–30).

Oakley was a lifelong advocate of world peace and believed that art like hers could help to achieve it. Although even the out-break of World War II did not destroy her optimism, her artistic style was, by then, falling out of favor. During the last years of her life, she worked in relative obscurity at her studio in Philadelphia, where she resided with her longtime companion and fellow artist, Edith Emerson.

ABOVE: Violet Oakley at "Cogslea," her home and studio in Philadelphia, c. 1914, with a portion of her 44-foot-wide mural *International Unity and Understanding,* eventually installed in the state senate chamber (see Chapter 14).

This cartoon ridicules Andrew Carnegie's library-building campaign, depicting him as a child playing with familiar wood alphabet blocks. After selling his Homestead steelworks to J. P. Morgan for a king's ransom, Carnegie invested in philanthropy as part of his "Gospel of Wealth" belief that the wealthy should encourage people to improve. Carnegie underwrote library construction as a way to help workers help themselves through education. Such libraries also served as community and recreation centers. Critics, though, wondered how much exhausted workers would benefit from such facilities.

Besides its steel empire, Pittsburgh and vicinity were home to a variety of enterprises established or otherwise fostered by the Mellon family. By 1900 the leader of this family was Andrew W. Mellon, who in 1902 incorporated the old T. Mellon & Sons Bank as the Mellon National Bank, with himself as president. The bank went on to finance several large corporations, including the Carborundum Company, Gulf Oil, and the Aluminum Company of America (ALCOA). Mellon later served as U.S. secretary of the treasury—under Presidents Harding, Coolidge, and Hoover—and played a prominent part in trying to manage Pennsylvania's Republican Party. Many economic historians have blamed Mellon's fiscal policies as secretary of the treasury, which included steep tax reductions for the wealthy, for contributing to the Great Depression of the 1930s.

Another important Pittsburgh entrepreneur was Henry J. Heinz. The H. J. Heinz Company, with its famous "57 varieties," had been established in 1888 and by 1900 was the largest maker of pickles, vinegar, and ketchup in the United States. Headquartered in Pittsburgh, the company had factories in six other states and sales agencies throughout the world. Three-quarters of a century later, a family descendant, John Heinz III, would be a U.S. senator from Pennsylvania.

The Westinghouse Electric Company continued to grow as a major industrial component in the Pittsburgh economy. Founded in 1886 by George Westinghouse, it manufactured a variety of electrical devices and pioneered a number of new inventions, including alternating current, steam turbines for generating electricity, and electric power for railroads. In 1920 Westinghouse launched the first radio broadcasting station in the world, KDKA in Pittsburgh.

Essential to fueling Pennsylvania's vast manufacturing establishments was coal, which in the Pittsburgh area meant soft bituminous coal. Production of bituminous coal reached a peak of 177,217,000 tons in 1918 and employed nearly 200,000 miners. Bituminous coal from Fayette and Westmoreland Counties was particularly well suited to the rendering of coke—a nearly pure carbon fuel used in making steel and created by burning off various impurities.

Northeastern Pennsylvania continued to extract hard anthracite coal. In the early twentieth century, anthracite was reaching its peak demand as a home-heating fuel because of its even, constant heat and minimum amount of smoke, ash, and sulfur content. Because the anthracite mines were often very deep and because owners neglected or refused to adopt safety measures, mining was particularly dangerous in these coalfields. There were numerous explosions, fires, and cave-ins, with many resultant injuries and deaths. In 1911 nearly 700 of the 175,000 anthracite miners then employed lost their lives digging anthracite coal.

Many children labored in the anthracite industry as breaker boys, and some were as young as eight years old, though it was illegal for them to work under the age of twelve. The boys had to straddle chutes on the wooden breakers and pick out slate and other impurities as the coal came sliding by. The dust was often so thick that the boys could

The telecommunications revolution got a kick-start in Pittsburgh when radio station KDKA began regular broadcasts in the early 1920s. The station was the first to broadcast election results from the 1920 presidential election, and by 1922 such entertainers as Will Rogers, seen here, came to KDKA studios to perform "live" for the station's growing listening audience. Through radio, and later television, cities like Pittsburgh also extended their reach outward (once electricity came to the farms), reinforcing the urban imperialism of department-store catalogs, advertisements, and newspapers that promised to bring city culture and goods to the countryside.

not see beyond their own outstretched arms and had to wear handkerchiefs over their noses and mouths to keep from choking on coal dust. A large proportion of them chewed tobacco to help absorb the dust that constantly infiltrated their mouths and throats. Since the breaker boys were forbidden to wear gloves, because it would loosen their grip on the chunks of coal churning past them, badly cut and mangled hands were common. And because they were not in school, the breaker boys had little prospect of escaping from a miner's life. In compensation for their labors, the boys might receive forty or fifty cents a day.

Miners organized to fight long working hours, low wages, and dangerous conditions by forming unions. The first truly effective national union for miners—to which many in Pennsylvania belonged—was the United Mine Workers, founded in 1890. Headed by John Mitchell until 1908, and later by John L. Lewis, the United Mine Workers became a major force in the coal industry. In a speech that Mitchell gave in Philadelphia in 1902, he spoke about the hard life of miners and what he hoped to do for them in the future: "The present miner has had his day. He has been oppressed and ground down; but there is another generation coming up, a generation of little children prematurely doomed to the whirl of the mill and the noise and the blackness of the breaker. It is for these children that we are fighting. We have not underestimated the strength of our opponents; we have not overestimated our own power of resistance."

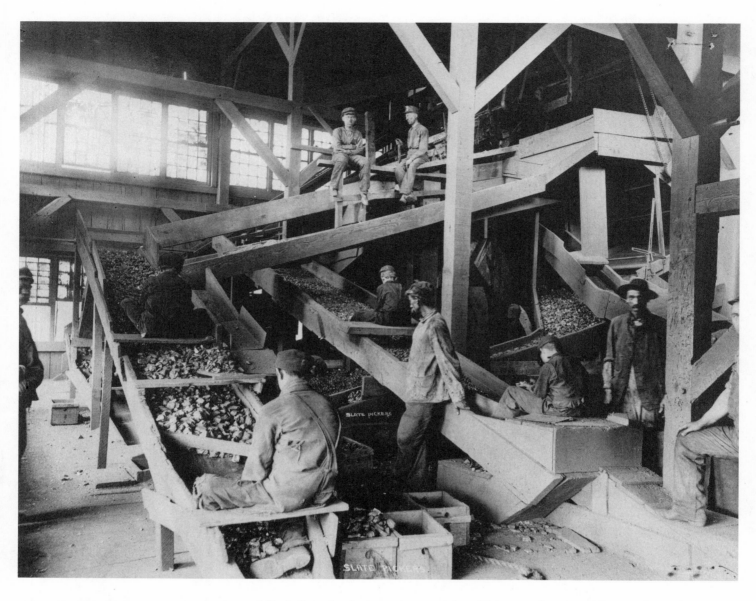

Breaker boys picking slate out of coal. Photo by John Horgan Jr., who was hired by the Hudson Coal Company, a subsidiary of the Delaware & Hudson Coal Company, to photograph its various operations and holdings.

Mitchell spoke during a protracted and bitter anthracite strike. At that time miners' earnings averaged less than $300 a year. Just a year earlier, 441 miners had been killed in accidents. Responding to these conditions, 150,000 miners struck the anthracite fields in May 1902. The mine owners, charging that the work stoppage was an attack on property rights, arranged for 3,000 coal and iron police and deputized 1,000 other men. This proved unnecessary, though, because the miners were orderly and peaceful throughout the five-month strike. Fortunately, the union had raised large sums of money, which it used to pay miners for the duration of the strike.

The union obtained an unwitting ally—at least in the realm of public opinion—in George F. Baer, whose outrageous statements about the power and prerogatives of the

Miners and their families being ejected from coal company housing in the Hazleton area during the strike of 1902. Because coal companies owned the housing, they regarded the strikers as trespassers on their property, and evictions were common during the six-month coal strike.

coal companies elicited much sympathy for the miners. Baer was president of the Philadelphia & Reading Railroad, which owned a number of anthracite mines and hauled much of the coal to market. In answer to an appeal to end the 1902 strike Baer responded, "The rights and interests of the laboring man will be protected and cared for—not by the labor agitators, but by the Christian men to whom God has given control of the property rights of the country." Such talk, in which Baer insisted that God himself had given the owners control over the mines and the lives of the miners, likewise disgusted President Theodore Roosevelt, who used his influence to arrange for arbitration. In early 1903 the arbiters awarded the anthracite miners a 10 percent pay increase and an eight- or nine-hour day, depending on their responsibilities, and forbade company discrimination against union members.

Not all workers in Pennsylvania were ruthlessly exploited, or their communities recklessly endangered. Those employed by the Hershey Chocolate Company in Hershey, some ten miles east of Harrisburg, knew few of the horrors of many other workers in the state. Their paternalistic employer was Milton S. Hershey, who in 1903 had returned to the area where he had been born to set up a factory for making milk chocolate. Although most of his workers rented their dwellings at modest rates from the company, Hershey made provisions for his workers to buy their houses on generous terms through a trust company he established. There were no real-estate taxes, and utilities were virtually free. Hershey provided his workers with insurance against sickness, accident, or death and offered a good retirement plan. He built all the local schools, as well as a junior college that residents of Hershey could attend tuition free.

Hershey also established a park for his employees that by the time of his death in 1945 had become a full-fledged amusement park with a dance pavilion, swimming pool,

Payday at the Olyphant Colliery in Lackawanna County, 1915. Workers regarded payday as a festive occasion and dressed up in
their Sunday best, often bringing their families
along. In 1915 the colliery employed 1,988
workers and produced 946,000 tons of coal.

rides, and landscaped gardens. The childless Hershey and his wife, Catherine Sweeney
Hershey, established the Milton Hershey School in 1909 for orphaned children and later
for those from broken or poor families. They left their entire, large estate, including their
majority stock holdings in the Hershey Chocolate Company, to the school as a permanent
endowment that was worth over $5 billion at the beginning of the twenty-first century.

Yet Milton Hershey's paternalism could be overbearing at times. He was known to
tour the town in his Cadillac convertible, chauffeur at the wheel, taking note of front
yards that were not neatly manicured or houses whose occupants had neglected some
detail of maintenance. Several times he even hired private detectives to discover who was
littering the grounds of his beautiful park or who was engaging in other kinds of behav-

ior that he disapproved. And in a small company town like Hershey, it was impossible to escape from being thrown together with fellow employees after hours, whether one liked them or not. As Marlene Hubbard, a former employee, remembered the situation, "You had to get along with everybody. If you didn't like your co-workers, that was just tough. You couldn't get away from them; they were your neighbors and your fellow churchgoers. You couldn't go anywhere without seeing somebody you worked with or worked for."

Many of those who worked in Pennsylvania's mines, factories, and mills were immigrants. As of 1920 the foreign-born population of the state was 1.4 million, or 16 percent of the whole, and many others were the children of immigrants. During the early twentieth century the great majority of these newcomers were the so-called new immigrants, who came from southern, central, and eastern Europe, as opposed to the old immigrants who had come primarily from northern and western Europe in the period before 1890.

The new immigrants, like those who had come before them, commonly settled in certain towns and cities—and even in specific neighborhoods—for a number of reasons. These included their work experiences back in the "old country," the kinds of jobs available in various parts of Pennsylvania, the competition for such jobs with other immigrant groups and even the native-born, and encouragement from family members or compatriots who had already settled in a particular part of the state. Many single Italian men, for example, went to Philadelphia because of the numerous unskilled jobs available: constructing public works or building and maintaining the vast Pennsylvania Railroad network. Because these Italian workers were without wives and children, they were willing to report to widely scattered job locations, where employment lasted for anywhere from a few days to several months. Assembling these men, and acting as their interpreters—and in some cases functioning as their paymasters in the immigrants' first years in America—was the padrone, an Italian immigrant himself, or the son of Italian immigrants, who already knew his way around the new country.

Many, if not most, of these unmarried Italian immigrants came to the United States with no intention of staying for good. Their dream was to save money while in America and then return to their homeland, where they would be able to enjoy a higher standard

The Pennsylvania State Constabulary (later the State Police) were the first such police force in the nation. Their commanding appearance and frequent presence at coalfields and steel towns during strikes earned them the nickname "Black Hussars" among eastern European immigrants. This photograph shows troopers on horseback in Bethlehem during the 1910 strike at Bethlehem Steel.

CHARLES C. BALDI AND THE CREATION OF AN ITALIAN AMERICAN COMMUNITY

By 1905 the Philadelphia Italian community was the second largest in the nation. It also was entering an important transitional phase, as large numbers of Italian immigrants began to settle in the area, marry and have families (or bring families over from the "old country"), found churches, and form mutual-aid and other ethnic associations. Many of the Italian immigrants coming to Pennsylvania in the late nineteenth and early twentieth centuries were young men, "sojourners" who came to America looking for work with no intention of staying. Enough such men found not only work but also enough opportunity in Pennsylvania to remain. They clustered in work and in places where others from their home regions had first come, and with familiar sounds and food to sustain them, laid the basis for community. Philadelphia was such a place.

The formation of any immigrant/ethnic community required leaders to help newcomers both in adapting to their new world and at the same time holding on to identities and interests from the world left behind. Charles C. Baldi played such a role in building the Italian community in Philadelphia. In many ways his life story reflects the process whereby immigrants from several regions in Italy became Italian Americans in Philadelphia, and why Philadelphia became such a powerful magnet for Italians during this period.

Baldi first came to Philadelphia in 1877, when the city had only a few hundred Italians. Although he had immigrated with his father and brother, he found little to hold him in America, so he returned to Italy. Unable to find steady work there, he returned to Philadelphia in the mid-1880s and hired on as a labor recruiter, or padrone, with a railroad company in the anthracite coal region that employed large numbers of Italian immi-

grants. He parlayed his knowledge of the railroad and the coal business into his own venture—a coal company in Philadelphia that catered to Italians there. In alliance with other family members, Baldi became involved in banking, real estate, labor contracting and travel, undertaking, and fruit merchandising. He also began *L'Opinione,* Philadelphia's first Italian American daily, in 1906, and helped organize, and sometimes led, several mutual-aid associations.

Baldi promoted ethnic pride and adaptation to American ways. One of his great achievements was organizing the city's Columbus Day celebration in 1892 and turning Christopher Columbus into an "American" hero. Baldi's financial success, his prominence in the larger Philadelphia community, and his advocacy for Italian American interests and culture provided an Italian American success story that others might emulate. By the 1920s, though,

younger Italians were chafing at Baldi's politics, his increasingly fascist leanings, and his authoritarian manner, and by the time of his death in 1931 the Philadelphia Italian community no longer needed a Baldi to negotiate for it. Now that Italians had their own churches, clubs, and businesses, they had a place staked out in the city, and differences of regional origin that earlier had separated the immigrant generation were giving way to a common Italian American identity. In numbers there was strength. Still, Baldi's funeral procession, with more than 100 Italian fraternal organizations in the cortege, bespoke the respect Italians had for Baldi and the collective institutional strength of the community.

of living than before. In fact, an estimated one-half of all the Italians who came to the United States seeking work eventually returned to Italy. In contrast, virtually all the Jews who came from Russia—and most Jews in the early twentieth century were from Russia or from Russian-controlled Poland—had fled with their families from persecution and death and had no intention of ever returning home.

In addition to settling in Pennsylvania's larger cities, a good many immigrants during the early decades of the century went to smaller industrial towns in the state. One such place was Steelton, located immediately south of Harrisburg, where the Pennsylvania Steel Company had opened its plant in 1867. Because the town and its steel industry were relatively new, this was a place where recent immigrants with families confronted little competition for unskilled jobs from earlier immigrant groups. By 1910 there were 14,000 people living in Steelton, 4,600 of them foreign-born. Many of these were Slavic immigrants, including Croats, Serbs, Bulgarians, and Slovenians.

These groups established their own national churches and fraternal societies. In addition to providing such social entertainment as dances and musical performances, these societies assisted their members financially in times of sickness and other hardship, defended their particular group from criticism by the native-born population or the local press, and mediated in conflicts with other ethnic groups in town. Several of the societies fielded athletic teams for children and offered classes in the English language. These organizations also eased the pain of removing to a strange land by helping immigrants keep the language, customs, and memories of the old country alive. One might also conjecture that such groups kept workers from cooperating with one another across ethnic and linguistic lines to form effective unions, and thereby inadvertently served the interests of their employers. In time, the descendants of these immigrants lost the ability to speak their ancestral tongue, became fluent in English, and allowed their ethnic organizations to atrophy or collapse altogether.

Another smaller city that attracted large numbers of immigrants was Clifton Heights in Chester County. There, owners of textile mills recruited hundreds of Polish peasants, often financing their passage, which the immigrants were then expected to pay back from future wages. In addition to work at the mills, Clifton Heights offered Polish-language schools and churches, along with stores that sold items familiar to Polish immigrants. Children born to these Polish immigrant parents, even though they became American citizens at birth, continued to identify with the old homeland. One woman who had been born in Clifton Heights to Polish parents tried to put this dual identification into words: "I'm an American citizen because I was born here, but my people were immigrants. But you see, Americans, they don't know another nationality. They have only one nationality, that's it."

Although the married women in the Polish community of Clifton Heights had to quit the mills while their children were very young, they typically returned to work as soon as one of the older children was able to look after younger siblings. Because wages

Immigrants brought technical skills and genius, along with willing hands and strong backs, to America and added numerous inventions and innovations to the industrial workplace and everyday life. The revolution in communications in late nineteenth- and early twentieth-century America attracted several immigrant inventors who tried to find ways to speed information with electricity. Among them was a young Slovak Catholic priest, Father Jozef Murgas, who devised a wireless telegraphy system that was tested in 1905 in Wilkes-Barre. Murgas tried to market this and other inventions, but after a storm destroyed his equipment his company failed. The honor of inventing a practical wireless went to Guglielmo Marconi of Italy, but Slovak Americans continued to give Murgas the credit. Shown here is a stamp issued by the Slovak Republic in 1939 commemorating Murgas. The radio tower, which stood near his church, is depicted on the right.

were low in the mills, wives had to work whenever possible in order to maintain a very basic standard of living for the family. This was in contrast to native-born middle-class families in urban areas, where the ideal was still a breadwinning husband with the wife remaining at home and out of the work force.

For the approximately one million Pennsylvanians who lived on farms at the beginning of the twentieth century, life was far different from living in the state's industrial centers. Although farmers worked long hours, those who owned land were at least their own bosses and could take much satisfaction in what they and their families had accomplished. Such satisfaction was not shared by tenant farmers and farm laborers, however, whose livelihoods and working conditions were more precarious. Tenants and farm laborers did not own the land, did not build up any equity over the years, and suffered from a lower social status than landowners. Tenants had to pay rent to landlords regardless of conditions, like the weather, over which they had no control, and they could never be sure of renewing their leases on reasonable terms.

A host of mechanical devices made agricultural work easier than in the past, though most of these were drawn and powered by horses during the first decades of the century; such implements included cultivators, mowers, rakes, bailers, grain drills, corn huskers, and grain threshers. Increasingly, threshing machines were powered by steam engines that resembled small locomotives. Itinerant threshers could drive their engines, mounted on wide cleated wheels, from farm to farm along dusty rural roads.

Although grain farmers in the Keystone State had a growing list of implements to assist them, it had become more and more difficult for Pennsylvania farmers to compete with the large and efficient grain producers in the midwestern and plains states—the new "breadbasket" of America. As a result, farmers increasingly turned to dairy and poultry farming, but some specialized in fruit and vegetable cultivation. Erie County in the northwest corner of the state, along the shores of Lake Erie, was particularly suited for fruits, including grapes. In Lancaster County and adjoining areas, tobacco became an important cash crop.

To promote more scientific and efficient agriculture and to find new ways to use the soil, the state supported agricultural extension stations and set up experimental farms, and The Pennsylvania State College expanded its agricultural research programs. The heavy public investment in agriculture ensured that it would always have a place in the state's economy, though the higher cost of machinery, fertilizers, and other improvements threatened small farmers, and market forces continued to erode profits for many.

PROGRESSIVISM: TRIALS AND CONTRADICTIONS

Despite great social and economic diversity, Pennsylvania remained a one-party state during the first three decades of the twentieth century. The Republicans were in firm control, as they had been since the Civil War. Yet the state Republican Party became

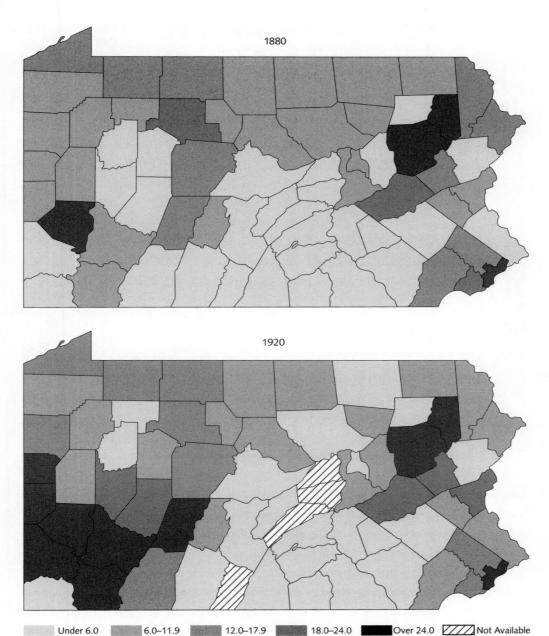

1880

1920

Pennsylvania's foreign-born as percentage of county population, 1880 and 1920.

Under 6.0   6.0–11.9   12.0–17.9   18.0–24.0   Over 24.0   Not Available

divided between those who were content merely to win elective office and make few demands for change, and more reform-minded Republicans, whom historians would later include in the category of "Progressives."

The so-called Progressive Movement was a complex national phenomenon that continues to defy the best efforts of historians to define it. Yet the handy concept of a Progressive era or movement, having to do with a welter of reforms and reformers during the first decades of the twentieth century, has become so familiar and so useful that

Mikolai Koval is laid to rest with his Greek Catholic Union hat and ribbon at St. Mary's Rusyn Greek Catholic Church in Johnstown. Koval was killed in a mill accident on May 9, 1916. Ribbons on lapels denote fellow members of Koval's fraternal lodge. Such lodges in immigrant communities often used dues to pay death benefits to families and offered immigrants social and cultural support.

historians are unlikely to abandon it anytime soon. Despite difficulties in making any sweeping generalizations, it seems safe to say that virtually all Progressive reformers (whether Republicans, Democrats, or independents) agreed that the United States faced serious problems resulting from the rapid industrialization and urbanization of the last several decades. Political corruption, business monopolies, the erosion of democracy in general, the exploitation of workers—and the poverty, ignorance, and disease that afflicted large segments of the urban population in particular—were all issues the Progressives focused on. These reformers were mostly optimistic about the possibility of making "progress" against even the most serious problems—a basic reason for their being called "Progressives." Many were also motivated by religious convictions—and especially by the social teachings of Jesus, collectively known at the time as the Social Gospel.

Yet there was much disagreement and even contradictions within the movement. For example, some Progressives believed that public exposure of problems through investigative reporting and sociological surveys was sufficient to promote private solutions without government intrusion. As time went on, an increasing number of Progressives—

though by no means all—looked to the states and the federal government for answers to the most pressing problems. At the root of these differences about government intervention were conflicting views of public authority as opposed to private rights and individual enterprise. Many Progressives also held contradictory views of past and present: sometimes extolling modern science and technology as tools for investigation and reform, the very same Progressives could lament the passing of a simpler, preindustrial era and call for a return to certain virtues that they associated with farms, small towns, and pride in individual craftsmanship.

It is not surprising that Pennsylvania's Progressives believed the larger cities needed their attention most. Pittsburgh came to mind first as a city in need of massive reform in almost every area. In article after article in the national press, Pittsburgh emerged as the prime example of a dirty and polluted industrial city whose economic and political leaders put profits ahead of all else. Yet as late as 1900 many of Pittsburgh's boosters continued to see their city's blighted and blackened streets and frequent smog as symbols of well-being. In 1901 an article that appeared in the *Atlantic Monthly* waxed eloquent over Pittsburgh's reputation for grime produced by its abundant use of coal: "One . . . cannot fail to recognize the prime mover in this intense industrial drama. . . . The housetops and hillsides wear its colors, and numberless columns, like gigantic organ pipes, breathe forth graceful plumes of black and white. The city and its environs bear testimony to the sovereignty of Coal."

Such images did not impress the muckraking journalist Lincoln Steffens, who described Pittsburgh in 1903 as "hell with the lid off." Some years later the acerbic commentator H. L. Mencken found Pittsburgh "a scene so dreadfully hideous, so intolerably bleak and forlorn that it reduced the whole aspiration of man to a macabre and depressing joke." Other observers of the Steel City likened its workers to beasts of burden or to mere cogs in the machinery that turned its mighty mills. In 1907 local critics, including Alice B. Montgomery, chief probation officer of the Allegheny Juvenile Court, and William H. Matthews, head of the Kingsley settlement house, enlisted the New York Charity Organization Society to undertake an ambitious study of conditions in its city. Supported by a large grant from the newly established Russell Sage Foundation, several dozen researchers descended on Pittsburgh. Their efforts turned into the most massive study of this type ever undertaken in the United States to that time, with many of the researchers going on to considerable renown in the field of sociology.

This poster for a meeting of the Cloak and Skirt Makers Union on August 20, 1917, was printed in English, Yiddish, and Italian to appeal to workers of the different ethnic backgrounds in the garment trades and to urge all the workers to unite. Ethnic differences often undermined attempts to organize workers, because employers were able to play different groups off against one another.

Mechanical devices were making life easier in agriculture, but many were still drawn and powered by horses well into the twentieth century, as in this photograph from Millmont in Union County.

In the six volumes of reports that resulted, published between 1909 and 1914 and titled *The Pittsburgh Survey*, the researchers emphasized again and again the impressive organization of corporate Pittsburgh and the nearly complete control that it gave the corporations over the city and its people. Mill and factory owners could force their employees to work long hours for little pay, undo attempts to form labor unions, poison the environment with contemptuous abandon, and undermine local government and civic activism. Overwork, particularly in the steel mills where men toiled twelve hours a day for six days a week, wrecked workers' health and destroyed their family life. Women fared even worse in local industry, where they were paid half as much as men. More than 500 workers a year, the survey pointed out, suffered fatal industrial accidents in Pittsburgh, and as many more died from diseases like typhoid fever that were the direct consequences of poor sanitation and unfiltered water. The survey also found that much of the

Boiling apple butter at the Jodon home at Forest Hill, Union County, c. 1922. This was a familiar autumn activity in rural Pennsylvania, providing an opportunity to socialize while working.

BOTTOM LEFT: Students compete in a dairy exposition at Penn State's stock-judging pavilion, 1948.

BOTTOM RIGHT: Barn raising in rural Pennsylvania continued into the twentieth century as a community-building enterprise, but with strict division of labor by sex.

IDA M. TARBELL, PENNSYLVANIA'S MUCKRAKER

Pennsylvania's Ida M. Tarbell (1857–1944) offers a prime example of the importance of women in the Progressive Movement and of the central role that investigative journalism played in this era of reform. Born in Erie County, Tarbell had witnessed how John D. Rockefeller's Standard Oil Trust destroyed her father's independent oil business in Titusville, Pennsylvania, where the first oil well in the United States had been drilled in 1859. After earning a reputation as a successful researcher and writer, Tarbell accepted an assignment by the crusading *McClure's Magazine* to write a serialized exposé of Standard Oil, and especially of the ruthless methods Rockefeller employed to control much of the oil market in the United States.

Tarbell's *History of the Standard Oil Company*, which began appearing in *McClure's* during 1903, was a sensation that later had a major influence on the U.S. Supreme Court when it ordered the dissolution of the Standard Oil Trust in 1911. This and several other investigative works won Tarbell a reputation as the nation's most effective muckraker, a term of disparagement that President Theodore Roosevelt, ironically a Progressive himself, had applied to journalists who seemed interested only in raking through the muck in order to reveal the worst aspects of American life. In fact, muckrakers were reformers whose lurid descriptions of social wrongs and political corruption were intended to stir the conscience and focus public attention on issues.

Miss Tarbell Has the Distinction.

ABOVE: Ida Tarbell's muckraking articles on John D. Rockefeller's Standard Oil Trust showed the power of the new investigative journalism that thrived on controversy and exposés of the rich and powerful in business, labor, and politics. This cartoon shows Tarbell smoking out Rockefeller with muckraking "truths."

housing in the city was unfit for human habitation; this was particularly true of recent immigrants, who crowded into dank cellars where they suffered and died from respiratory and other illnesses.

Behind most of this misery, insisted Paul U. Kellogg, the editor of the published survey, was rampant greed "with little of the milk of human kindness." But he cautioned readers not to blame Pittsburgh alone, as if it were a mere "scapegoat city." Rather, he insisted, Pittsburgh was "the capital of a district representative of untrammeled industrial development which . . . is rampantly American." The way out of this alarming set of circumstances, Kellogg and the researchers advised, was for the community to organize itself as thoroughly and effectively as the corporations. Only then could Pittsburgh fight to clean up the environment, provide decent housing for all, improve wages, secure safer workplaces, and generate more open space.

Many Pittsburghers, and especially the more well-to-do, reacted to the survey reports with "feelings of mingled humiliation and indignation." The local press rallied as soon as the first reports appeared, publishing a series of upbeat articles about the city and condemning the survey for ignoring the "good news" about Pittsburgh. The Chamber of Commerce swung into action with its own study of economic conditions in 1911 that emphasized the more positive aspects of Pittsburgh. Local politicians for the most part ignored the survey; during the mayoral elections, which took place in 1909, neither candidate mentioned it. Such inaction in the face of overwhelming evidence of serious problems in Pittsburgh showed that the collection of data and the issuance of reports were not enough, by themselves, to bring about reform. Only the social and political will of community leaders, backed by public opinion, could achieve real and lasting changes.

Cleaning up political corruption in the Keystone State proved just as difficult as tackling Pittsburgh's numerous problems. Standing in the way was the well-entrenched Republican machine, headed in the early twentieth century by Boies Penrose, a gigantic and self-indulgent man who stood six feet four inches tall and weighed 350 pounds, whose nickname was "Big Grizzly." As described by historian John Lukacs, "his enormous body was dominated by a mountain of a belly. His lips bit down on a face that was frozen darkly with severity and contempt. In spite of his English ancestry, . . . Penrose bore a resemblance to someone like German Field-Marshall Ludendorff in mufti." Though a machine politician of grotesque physique, Penrose was a Harvard graduate from an upper-class Philadelphia family.

In his political beliefs, Penrose was a thoroughgoing reactionary who believed that the state should be greatly limited in its power over individuals and economic enterprises. He opposed votes for women (then known as woman's suffrage), the income tax, primary elections, direct election of U.S. senators, and labor unions. A chief goal was to keep Pennsylvania's Republican Party in power and to hold on to his own seat in the U.S. Senate, which he first won in 1896 and kept for the next twenty-four years.

Ironically, this sometimes required compromises with Progressive elements within his own party. Accordingly, in 1907 Penrose supported a legislative investigation into the overspending and corruption surrounding the new State Capitol. He also backed mildly reform-minded governors: Edwin S. Stuart, who prosecuted the Capitol grafters; and John K. Tener, whose administration obtained direct primary elections for Pennsylvania, a state highway system, and a revised school code and established the state Public Service Commission and the state Department of Labor and Industry.

When Penrose died in 1921, no one in Pennsylvania was powerful enough to take his place as boss of the state's Republican Party. As a result, a shifting coalition of regional party chiefs emerged, including Philadelphia's Vare brothers (Edwin, George, and William); Joseph R. Grundy, who hailed from the town of Bristol and who was president of the Pennsylvania Manufacturers Association; and the Mellon interests in Pittsburgh.

The Progressives in politics had a difficult time battling the party bosses. The disdain that many felt for strong partisanship—and even for party organizations—left them at a disadvantage when it came to challenging statewide or municipal machines. And although their moral denunciations of machine politics sometimes brought temporary victories, words were no substitute for consistent organizational efforts. The machines also stayed in power because of the easy and familiar access they gave to their urban constituents, and the many services the machines performed for them, from fixing problems with the police to dropping off food and fuel in times of distress.

The fragmentation of the Republican machine after Penrose's death allowed Pennsylvania's best-known Progressive, Republican Gifford Pinchot, to become governor of the Commonwealth from 1923 to 1927 (and again from 1931 to 1935). Ironically, there were certain similarities between Pinchot and Boies Penrose. Like Penrose, Pinchot enjoyed the freedom of inherited wealth. Indeed, he lived grandly at his family's country seat at Milford in northeastern Pennsylvania, a large stone house in the French chateau style named Grey Towers that had been designed by Richard Morris Hunt. Like Penrose too, Pinchot was a graduate of an Ivy League college (but Yale instead of Harvard), had a tremendous desire for political power, and was not above cutting political deals in order to win public office. The two men were also similar in that they loathed one another. Pinchot once wrote Penrose calling him "the most perfect living representative of the

A tall and hulking Boies Penrose stands before a parade float that includes a replica of the Liberty Bell.

OPPOSITE: Smog-induced darkness in downtown Pittsburgh, c. 1945, where pollution from the steel mills was so severe that streetlights were often needed during daylight hours. Cleaning up Pittsburgh's air through smoke control became a major incentive in the Pittsburgh Renaissance, but it took the decline of steelmaking after World War II to finish the job.

Cornelia Pinchot waving to a crowd of miners in Uniontown in 1934 after addressing them at the celebration of the thirty-sixth anniversary of the eight-hour day in the mine fields. Following her speech, rioting broke out among several hundred miners.

worst type of politics in America." Penrose did not deign to answer, but on another occasion said of his critic: "Pin-Shot seems to me about as important as a cheap side show outside the fence of a county fair, like the tattooed man or the cigarette fiend." In other ways too they appeared as polar opposites. The tall, slender, and athletic Pinchot bore no physical resemblance to Penrose, and his desire was to use public office to bring about extensive and lasting reforms.

By the time Pinchot won the governorship of Pennsylvania he was already well known. With the moral support and financial backing of his family, he had become the first professional forester born in the United States, and as chief forester under President Theodore Roosevelt he had made large strides in the cause of conservation. Then, as Pennsylvania's commissioner of forestry in the early 1920s, Pinchot had done much to expand the size of state-owned forests, to assist in the replanting of privately owned lands, and to control forest fires.

During his initial term as governor, Pinchot pushed through a new state administrative code that provided for a formal budgetary system and that grouped some 139 agencies under fifteen departments, each headed by a member of the governor's cabinet. The code also provided for the standardization of positions and pay within the state civil service.

Pinchot failed in his efforts to curb private electric utility companies, which he accused of using a monopolistic position to charge outrageous prices at the expense of consumers who had no other alternatives, and of refusing to extend electricity into sparsely settled areas because the effort would not be lucrative enough for the companies. Pinchot's idea was to create one state-controlled monopoly that, he reasoned, would charge fairer rates and bring electricity to rural citizens. In the end, however, the governor was no match for the resourceful lobbyists the power companies sent to Harrisburg. On the electric utility question, as on many others, Pinchot showed himself to be a Progressive in the tradition of his former "boss" Theodore Roosevelt, who had become more and more convinced of the need for extensive government control of the economy.

Equally reform-minded was Pinchot's wife, Cornelia Bryce Pinchot. The daughter of a wealthy, socially prominent, politically active New York family, Cornelia Bryce had been a reformer before she met and married Gifford Pinchot in 1914. While still single, she had worked to end child labor and had demanded better pay and working conditions for women. As secretary of Pennsylvania's Woman's Suffrage Association in 1918 and 1919, she had helped to secure ratification of the Nineteenth Amendment to the U.S. Constitution in the Keystone State, which granted women the right to vote. Later she was an outspoken advocate of birth control. Like her husband, she was a strong supporter of the prohibition of alcoholic beverages, which had become the law of the land following the Eighteenth Amendment in 1919, and made numerous speeches calling for strict enforcement of Prohibition legislation. In 1928 she sought, unsuccessfully, the Republican nomination for U.S. Congress from her home district in northeastern Pennsylvania.

Women like Cornelia Pinchot who had sought the vote faced some powerful opponents in Pennsylvania. These included the political machines, which feared that women voters were likely to be too independent and too favorable toward the Progressive movement; and the manufacturers and vendors of alcoholic beverages, who believed that women, already strongly identified with the Prohibition cause, would seek legislation to ban alcohol altogether. More conservative religious leaders also opposed votes for women, insisting that God had designated separate spheres for men and women that did not include voting or political activism for "the fairer sex." Supporters of woman's suffrage, on the other hand, increasingly included most Progressives, many prohibitionists, and a growing number of well-educated women.

Even while campaigning for the vote, women supplied most of the inspiration and effort for creating and sustaining urban settlement houses. These were generally large dwellings in poor immigrant neighborhoods where young women (and some young men) just out of college lived for several years. There they made studies of working conditions and helped their neighbors to organize labor unions and other pressure groups, and they often sponsored an array of educational and social activities that might include instruction in prenatal care and child nutrition, drama clubs, and summer camps for youth. The best known of these settlement houses in Pennsylvania were Pittsburgh's Kingsley House and Philadelphia's College Settlement.

The settlement houses were the forerunners of professional social work. By the second and third decades of the twentieth century, many women in the settlements enrolled in formal social-work programs at urban universities. One such woman was Elsa Ueland, who spent a half-dozen years at a New York City settlement house, where, in addition to working with individuals and families in an Italian immigrant neighborhood, she marched for women's right to vote, picketed sweatshops that were exploiting women garment workers, and helped to conduct a survey of vocational guidance in the city's schools. In 1916 she moved to the Philadelphia area, where she became the president of

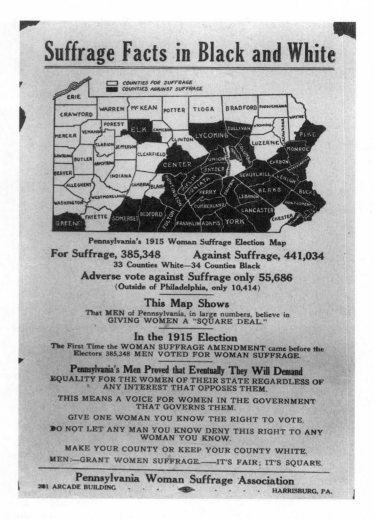

Contemporary broadside showing the results of the 1915 suffrage referendum, which was defeated. The counties in black voted against giving women the right to vote. The voting reflected the values different ethnic and religious groups attached to women's participation in public life, as well as the areas where suffragists were well organized to make their case.

SUFFRAGE COMES TO PENNSYLVANIA

Pennsylvania had an active suffrage movement led by such Progressive figures as Anna Elizabeth Dickinson, Lavinia Lloyd Dock, Florence Kelley, Jane Grey Cannon Swisshelm, and Cornelia Bryce Pinchot. These women and the others who joined them were committed to securing for women the right to vote in local, state, and national elections.

Suffragists faced powerful opponents in Pennsylvania. Conservative religious leaders saw women's votes as a threat to male dominance in the church as well as in the home. Brewers and distillers also came out against votes for women, given that so many women were vocal supporters of Prohibition. Political machines, which often received powerful support from the brewers and distillers, and who generally opposed reform, were another formidable obstacle to woman's suffrage. And many women in Pennsylvania opposed, or were indifferent to, the suffragists' appeals, favoring instead a reform effort to "clean" the ballot and replace the politics of interests with one of issues. For immigrants and working-class people, personal politics meant some access to, or protection from, government, and the Protestant cast and language of the suffrage movement made some immigrants and working-class people suspicious of the reformers' motives.

In 1915 a referendum on woman's suffrage went down to defeat in Pennsylvania, with 385,348 in favor and 441,034 against. The issue generally garnered more support in the northern and western parts of the state, where the reformers were well organized, than in the central and eastern portions, where ethnic and religious opposition to woman's suffrage was strong. Not until the Nineteenth Amendment to the U.S. Constitution in 1920, which Pennsylvania ratified,

did women win the right to vote. With ballot in hand, though, women did not vote much differently from men, and woman's suffrage did not bring the promised moral order to state politics or kill the boss-run machines. Also, Pennsylvania lagged behind other states in electing women to statewide offices.

ABOVE: Suffragette marches were common in towns throughout America during the years before ratification of the Nineteenth Amendment in 1920. This march occurred in Centre County along Allegheny Street in Bellefonte, c. 1913. Leading the way with the "Votes for Women" banner is Bellefonte resident Anna Keichline, Pennsylvania's first registered woman architect. Men watch from the sidewalk, some with arms firmly crossed in seeming disapproval.

LEFT: An advertisement against woman's suffrage that appeared in the *Pittsburgh Post* the day before Pennsylvania's 1915 referendum on the vote.

Carlisle Indian School Shoemaking Shop. The Carlisle Indian Industrial School, established in 1879, provided the national model in the campaign by the federal government and social reformers to transform Native Americans into self-supporting "Americans" through specific vocational education (such as shoemaking, shown here) at nonreservation boarding schools. At Carlisle and the other schools, Native Americans were taught Christian ways and work habits intended to fit them for life in the dominant society. The schools had mixed success, and enrollment declined after 1905, but Carlisle Indian School remained in the public eye because of its famous "graduate" Jim Thorpe.

the newly established Carson College for Orphan Girls (later known as the Carson Valley School), located just beyond the Philadelphia city limits in the village of Flourtown. Besides continuing her interests in women's issues, Ueland was determined that her orphans would grow up to be capable and independent young women, able to understand the practical world as well as any man. Accordingly, she told an interviewer in 1919:

> It has been my idea always that the average woman is unnecessarily helpless. She has no knowledge of tools and mechanics. Whether or not she has any actual need for this knowledge, she should know about it. It is, to my mind, part of the foundation of a broad economic understanding of how the world progresses and how cities and industries are built. The lack of such simple, fundamental information explains why many women find it difficult to understand problems of finance and industry and construction.

One way Ueland conveyed such practical knowledge of the world was through a progressive system of education at the orphanage. While connected to the larger Progressive movement, progressive educators, led by philosopher John Dewey, were attempting to break down the physical and psychological barriers between the world of school and the world of work, and to emphasize "learning through doing" by combining book-work with field trips and manual activities. Thus, when the orphanage decided to erect two new buildings, Ueland had the children visit both a quarry where the stone was being taken out of the ground and a sawmill where the lumber was being cut into beams and boards for the new structures. She also had them look over the architectural plans, visit the construction sites and talk to the workers, and even help pour some of the concrete steps. And like many Progressives, Ueland believed that early twentieth-century children suffered from a lack of contact with nature and with traditional craft techniques. Consequently, her orphans took many hikes in the woods, helped grow and preserve vegetables, and engaged in a variety of crafts—from pottery and weaving to making natural dyes and fashioning crude musical instruments.

Word of what Ueland had achieved soon began to spread. She was much in demand as a speaker before professional and civic organizations east of the Mississippi, and her orphanage was the subject of numerous articles in periodicals with a national circulation. Ueland herself contributed a number of pieces to newspapers, magazines, and professional journals of the day. She was an outspoken advocate for women's right to vote and remained a supporter of women's issues, including the Equal Rights Amendment, until her death in 1980.

WAR, MORAL "REVOLT," AND SOCIAL REACTION

Many Progressives in Pennsylvania and in the nation at large, including Elsa Ueland, wanted to believe that humans were achieving some sort of moral progress. Accordingly, they were horrified at the outbreak of war in Europe during the summer of 1914 and vowed that the United States should stay out of the conflict at all costs (though most Progressives supported the war once the United States entered it in 1917). Pennsylvanians of German ancestry joined in hoping that the nation could remain neutral. In January 1915, members of the American Neutrality League of Philadelphia, made up principally of German Americans, staged a massive rally at the Academy of Music, where Pennsylvania's Governor Martin Brumbaugh presided amid the singing of patriotic German songs and denunciations of Great Britain. Once the United States entered the war, the great majority of German Americans either rallied to the cause or kept quiet about their views. Even so, there remained in Philadelphia strong suspicions against all things German. The city's board of education ended the teaching of German in the public schools, and the Philadelphia Orchestra stopped playing music by German composers. Germans and German institutions in the city also suffered physical attacks, which came to a peak in the spring of 1918.

World War I was just one of several national or international events that affected the Keystone State during the first half of the twentieth century. Among its most noticeable consequences was a great stimulus to Pennsylvania industries. In the Pittsburgh area some 250 war plants employing more than a half-million men and women operated around the clock for six or seven days a week. Pittsburgh mills turned out 80 percent of all the steel used by the U.S. Army for arms and ammunition, while mines in southwestern Pennsylvania provided 75 percent of the coal consumed by munitions manufacturers during the war. But perhaps the most impressive industrial operation in Pennsylvania during the war was construction of the world's largest shipyard on Philadelphia's Hog Island in the Delaware River. Undertaken by the Emergency Fleet Corporation and led by Charles M. Schwab of Bethlehem Steel, the yard boasted fifty shipways and seven large piers that stretched for two and a half miles along the river. Although huge, the yard did not manage to deliver its first vessel until after the war had ended in November 1918.

About 371,000 Pennsylvanians served in World War I. The most famous unit from the Keystone State was the Twenty-Eighth Division, whose actions at the front in France during the spring and summer of 1918 gave much needed relief to British and French troops and helped to turn the momentum against the Germans.

For Americans—and for Pennsylvanians, who suffered relatively few casualties—the most deadly consequence of the war was the worldwide influenza epidemic. This plague hit Pennsylvania very hard in October 1918, not long before the armistice was signed. The toll from this epidemic was higher in Philadelphia than in any other city in the United States, with some 13,000 residents dying from the flu, 700 of them in one day. Undertakers and gravediggers were so overwhelmed that hundreds of victims had to be hastily lowered into mass graves until they could be disinterred and given proper burials.

As in other parts of the United States, the patriotic crusades during World War I, and the campaigns against opponents of the war—both real and imagined—touched off a new wave of intolerance in Pennsylvania that outlasted the war itself. The large numbers of African Americans who migrated to the North for wartime jobs also led to a heightened racism. This "great migration," as it was called, would continue for the next several decades, as black southerners continued the trek northward to Pennsylvania and to other states to escape racism and poverty in the South and, they hoped, to find greater opportunities and better lives in the "promised land" of the urban North. But blacks did not find a ready welcome there. Jobs beckoned, but whites resented the black influx.

One of the worst racial incidents occurred in Philadelphia in June and July of 1918. Tensions in the city had been exacerbated by a 58 percent increase, between 1910 and 1920, in the number of blacks living in Philadelphia, from 84,459 to 134,229. Most of them had arrived from the South in the most recent few years in order to get jobs in the manufacturing boom that followed the outbreak of war in Europe in 1914. Traditionally segregated sections of the city, by custom rather than by law, soon become overcrowded, forcing blacks to move into neighborhoods that were all, or largely, white.

Trouble began on June 29, 1918, when white neighbors in the 2500 block of Pine Street attacked the homes of two black families. Several other racial incidents occurred in late July, with rioting breaking out on July 28, 29, and 30. Four persons were killed and several hundred were injured. Although whites had initiated the violence, most of those arrested were black. G. Grant Williams, of the *Philadelphia Tribune,* the principal African American newspaper in the city, blamed these arrests largely on the failure of Philadelphia police to protect the property of black citizens, thereby forcing them to protect themselves. This led him to ask of the city's mayor, Thomas B. Smith, in an editorial: "Is it not lawful, Mr. Mayor, for a man to protect his home if anyone attempts to damage it? Why then do your police arrest a colored man or woman for protecting their home? . . . The colored people of Philadelphia are law-abiding citizens and ask your protection, and if you don't protect them, they shall and will defend themselves."

In response, a group of black clergy and prominent lay supporters founded the Colored Protective Association. In the months that followed, the association collected funds for legal counsel for blacks who had been arrested and led a campaign to expose police brutality. In both areas the group met with at least moderate success.

Because of continuing violence and discrimination against African Americans, two black state representatives introduced an equal rights bill in Harrisburg in 1921. One of them, John C. Asbury, a Republican from Philadelphia, spoke to the chamber at Easter time, asking his colleagues to remember that Christ had died to redeem all mankind— "not white men, brown men or even yellow men or black men, but all men." The measure passed in the House but failed to muster the necessary votes in the Senate. The state was not yet ready to grant equal citizenship to all its people.

While African American legislators continued to be a rarity in Harrisburg, black communities in Pennsylvania assisted themselves through a range of institutions. None was more important than the black churches, the largest denomination being the African Methodist Episcopal (AME) Church, founded in Philadelphia during the nineteenth century. Besides offering spiritual comfort and hope, the black churches served as social gathering places and centers where information was exchanged about housing, jobs, and educational opportunities. Some of the churches established insurance societies and building and loan associations. They also dispensed charity to families suffering from sickness, unemployment, or other kinds of distress.

Storefront churches also sprang up wherever large numbers of black migrants settled. In them, blacks often preached and worshiped in a more charismatic style than was deemed "proper" in the more established churches, such as Mother Bethel in Philadelphia. Also competing for attention and money, among the newcomers especially, was Marcus Garvey and his United Negro Improvement Association, which urged blacks to patronize their own businesses and, through Garvey's shipping line, to go "back to Africa." Garvey's movement enjoyed a large following in Philadelphia during the 1920s, but scandals and the failure of his company dampened enthusiasm for his program. These did not, however, discourage blacks from looking to their own institutions to make their way in Pennsylvania.

African American newspapers, such as the *Philadelphia Tribune,* kept their readers

informed of sporting events, reported stories and issues of interest to the black community, and exposed racism. There were also thousands of businesses run by African Americans in Pennsylvania, including banks. One of the most successful of these banks was established by Philadelphia's Wright family in 1920 and incorporated six years later as the Citizens & Southern Bank & Trust Company of Philadelphia. Meanwhile Richard Wright Jr., an officer of this bank, played an instrumental role in founding the National Negro Bankers Association.

Woogie Harris performing at the Crawford Grill in Pittsburgh's Hill District. The Crawford Grill on Wylie Avenue was one of the Hill's many black-owned businesses and entertainment establishments. After its opening in 1931, it quickly attracted an interracial crowd that over the years came to hear such black musicians as Billy Eckstine, Johnny Mathis, and Dizzy Gillespie, who often showed up for late-night sessions after their downtown performances. Woogie Harris, owner of the nearby Crystal Barber Shop, was one of the Hill's best-known businessmen and one of Pittsburgh's first African American millionaires. Many blacks counted on Harris for business loans when they were denied loans by white-owned banks.

Even as black communities formed in Philadelphia, Pittsburgh, and elsewhere, they divided over religion, class, and "culture," with newcomers from the South bringing their own "country" styles in music, folkways, and speech that both fascinated and appalled the older black communities. In time, cultural differences among blacks, as with immigrants, blurred in the city. Racial segregation in housing and jobs also reminded blacks of all backgrounds that they needed to stand together. There was no other way.

African Americans continued to come into Pennsylvania during the 1920s, especially after the severe immigration restriction legislation passed by the U.S. Congress in 1921 and 1924 cut off foreign unskilled labor. In this nationwide atmosphere of antiforeign (and antiblack) sentiment, the Ku Klux Klan emerged as a powerful force in Pennsylvania. The Klan had been founded in the South just after the Civil War as a white supremacist organization that terrorized the recently emancipated slaves, and was revived in Atlanta, Georgia, in 1915. In addition to acting on their prejudice against African Americans, the resurrected Klan castigated Jews, Catholics, and "foreigners" and railed against the immoralities and corruption of modern urban America.

"DISGRACED AND DISHONORED": THE COATESVILLE LYNCHING

Addressing the hideous murder of an African American man named Zachariah Walker in Coatesville on August 13, 1911, Pennsylvania Governor John Tener declared that Pennsylvania had been "disgraced and her fair name dishonored." This event and the reactions to it dramatize the sometimes violent side of the state's diversity.

Coatesville, located some thirty miles west of Philadelphia, had recently undergone tremendous changes. Thanks to booming steel mills, the town's population had gone from 3,680 in 1890 to 11,084 in 1910, a threefold increase. Many newcomers were African Americans who had left the South for better jobs and for the improved racial conditions in the North. But old-stock white residents in town often resented these newcomers and frequently complained of a rise in crime and in behavior that they saw as inconsistent with white, middle-class norms.

The lynching victim, Zachariah Walker, had been drinking all day on Saturday, August 12. Stumbling along a darkened road, he shot his pistol into the air twice. This alerted Edgar Rice, a coal and iron policeman from the Worth Brothers Steel Company and a well-respected citizen of the town. Rice accosted Walker and, during the ensuing struggle, Walker shot and killed Rice, later insisting that he had acted only in self-defense. Walker fled but was apprehended the next morning, whereupon he shot himself in the jaw in an unsuccessful attempt to commit suicide.

A mob of about 2,000 residents, enraged at Officer Rice's death, stormed the hospital where Walker lay wounded and dragged him to a field outside town. There they built a huge fire and thrust Walker into the inferno,

ABOVE: Crowd gathered at the site of the Coatesville lynching.

despite repeated pleas of self-defense. According to one witness, Walker's screams could be heard a half-mile away.

Newspaper reaction across the North was united in outrage, but most residents of Coatesville believed that justice had been done. At the same time, they put blacks on notice that further breaches of racial etiquette would not be tolerated. In 1913 the Pennsylvania legislature took up a bill to make lynching a crime, but an antilynching measure would not pass for another decade, when Governor Gifford Pinchot signed one into law in 1923.

An estimated quarter-million Pennsylvanians were members of the Klan during its peak in the 1920s. The largest concentrations of Klan lodges, or "klaverns," as they were called, were in southwestern Pennsylvania—that is, in Allegheny and surrounding counties, with somewhat smaller concentrations in Philadelphia and southeastern Pennsylvania. The Klan also attracted many in the anthracite district of northeast Pennsylvania, including Luzerne, Carbon, Lehigh, and Schuylkill Counties. Although most Klan rallies were peaceful, fighting between Klan members and those who opposed them did turn violent on several occasions. One death occurred at Carnegie, just outside Pittsburgh, in 1923; and there were four deaths at Lilly, in Cambria County near Altoona, also in 1923. By the late 1920s the Klan had begun to decline in Pennsylvania, as well as in the nation at large, because of scandals and internal dissension among leaders, and continued reports of Klan-induced violence.

One source of Klan denouncements was the revolution in manners and morals during the "Roaring Twenties," which was actually a multifaceted phenomenon with roots that extended back into the prewar period. This social revolt manifested itself most noticeably in the behavior and dress of some of the more daring young women of the period, who were known as "flappers"—a reference to the unbuckled boots they wore, which flapped as women walked. Flappers "bobbed" their hair short and wore short, shapeless dresses that minimized the female form, as part of an effort to appear "boyish" in this first era when women had won the vote and were claiming rights and opportunities equal to those of men. Flappers also smoked in public, drank illegal alcohol in the "speakeasies" of this Prohibition decade, and drove automobiles at breakneck speed. They danced to the tunes of jazz bands or of the popular music played on the radio, a technological marvel that was spreading across the nation and bringing the "hot sounds" of jazz and the commercial blandishments of Philadelphia, Pittsburgh, and other cities into small towns. They imitated the gestures and clothing styles they saw in motion pictures, another irresistible technology of the early twentieth century. Even young people who were not flappers, or who did not participate directly in the cultural rebellion that the flappers represented, imbibed some elements of this youth culture.

Many conservative mothers and fathers who had been born in the late Victorian period joined religious leaders and other moral preceptors in denouncing such behavior, but to little avail. The Dress Reform Committee in Philadelphia, for example, designed a loose-fitting, long-sleeved "moral gown" to save America's youth from eternal damnation. Although endorsed by ministers from fifteen denominations, the gown, like so much else that smacked of the old Victorian code, found few takers among the "smart set." Not until the Great Depression did hemlines fall. Yet for all the ballyhoo about the revolution in manners and morals and the new sounds and styles of the "jazz age," many Pennsylvanians were hardly affected. Rural areas without electricity still moved to the rhythms of the seasons and awoke early to the daily chores of farm life, and in many eastern, central, and southern European immigrant/ethnic communities, the toll of

The Martha Washington Kamp No. 1 American Krusaders paraded in the Frankford section of Philadelphia on July 4, 1927. During its heyday, Ku Klux Klan members marched unabashedly without hooded masks to demonstrate the Klan's power and to show who "true believers" really were. The Klan had surprising strength in Pennsylvania and even recruited with modest success in cities.

church bells and the authority of fathers and priests counted more than the latest dance craze. Shop girls in the department stores saw, and sold, the latest fashions, but few working-class people had time to dance the night away.

The struggle to enforce Prohibition in Pennsylvania also reflected cultural divisions within the state—between urban centers and many ethnic groups who saw Prohibition as an illegitimate intrusion into their private lives and economic interests, and more rural areas, where native-born Protestants were more likely to support the ban on alcohol. Governor Pinchot, who like many Progressives believed that alcohol was at the root of numerous social evils, pressed for vigorous enforcement of the Eighteenth Amendment in Pennsylvania. But the legislature refused to pass two of his three enforcement proposals and failed to fund the one item of enforcement legislation that did make it through.

Pinchot's difficulty with enforcing Prohibition in Pennsylvania was nowhere more evident than in Philadelphia. There, Major General Smedley D. Butler, on leave from the U.S. Marines and serving as the city's director of public safety in 1924 and 1925, launched a crusade against bootleggers and illegal dispensers of alcohol. Butler boarded up nearly 1,000 speakeasies in just one week, discovered liquor being transported in condensed-milk cans and other unlikely places, and even raided several debutante parties in search of illicit "hootch." But magistrates often refused to convict those arrested by Butler's men, and policemen on the beat, who owed their jobs to the Vare brothers' Republican machine, generally ignored violations of the Prohibition laws. Less than two years after his appointment as public safety director in Philadelphia, Butler was fired at the behest of the Vare machine. The city remained one of the "wettest" in the United States, with breweries operating in open defiance of the law, and suppliers of alcohol selling their wares with little or no fear of legal consequences.

PENNSYLVANIA AND THE GREAT DEPRESSION

As the debate over Prohibition continued, the stock market crash of October 1929 sent powerful signals throughout the nation that the economy was in deep trouble. By the end of 1930, the United States was in the midst of a major economic depression. In addition to the untold suffering visited on Pennsylvanians by the decade of hard times that followed, the Great Depression brought many social and economic reforms to the Keystone State and restored a viable two-party system in Pennsylvania. The depression in particular allowed reformers who favored an enhanced role for state government to press forward with their agenda. Once again, forces operating outside the borders of the state would have a powerful impact on Pennsylvanians.

In reality, the Pennsylvania economy had not performed well during the boom of the 1920s, thereby indicating to the few people who had a keen sense of measurement and comparison that the state might be losing its advantages as an industrial power. For example, manufacturing jobs had peaked in Pennsylvania during World War I at 1,135,000, where they stayed, on average, throughout the 1920s. The state's coal industry also stagnated and then slumped. One big reason for this downturn was the new "by-product" method of making coke from bituminous coal that was less wasteful than the old "beehive process" carried out in the Pittsburgh region, and particularly in and around Connellsville. The newer method allowed by-products extracted from coal, in the process of making coke, to be used profitably for a variety of hydrocarbon products, such as explosives, coal-tar dyes, and medicines. But the by-products had to be used near where they were extracted—which might mean any number of places around the United States that produced steel, not necessarily in the coal regions of western Pennsylvania. The demand for coal, and especially anthracite coal, as a heating fuel also began to decline in the 1920s, when Americans started to switch to cleaner and more convenient fuels, such as oil and natural gas, a trend that accelerated over the years. The state's textile industry, concentrated in the Philadelphia area, also suffered during the decade before the depression as manufacturers relocated in the southern states, where nonunion wages were 25 to 60 percent lower, and as some clothing styles moved toward synthetic fibers like rayon and later nylon.

As these areas of the Pennsylvania economy declined, other regions of the United States, most notably the upper Midwest, experienced great growth. The automobile industry, centered in and around Detroit, Michigan, was a prime example. Ironically, the Duryea brothers, who had built the first successful automobile in America, had produced cars in the Reading area until 1914. But Pennsylvania capitalists and entrepreneurs simply did not have the foresight to move into the auto industry in a large way, even though the state held great potential for such an enterprise, with its steel mills, its large supply of both skilled and unskilled workers, and an impressive market for motor cars. Part of the problem was a lack of imagination in a state that had prospered under a regime of coal, steel, and railroads and where so much capital was tied up in those sectors of the economy.

Perhaps another factor contributing to the decline of Pennsylvania industry was a more highly stratified social system, especially in the Philadelphia area, than in the upper Midwest, where social lines were less finely drawn. Henry Disston II, in reflecting on the eventual decline of his family's saw-manufacturing plant in the Tacony section of Philadelphia, believed that the family practice of placing sons, nephews, or socially respectable friends into the firm, regardless of their competence or commitment to the enterprise, was partly responsible for the company's distress. He also believed that many other Philadelphia firms that relied on this "old boy" method of recruiting managers and executives fell into the same trap.

In his book *The Protestant Establishment,* Philadelphia-born sociologist and historian E. Digby Baltzell explores this theme of an essentially moribund upper class that had once combined social prominence with actual merit in business and the professions. By refusing to admit the newly capable and successful into their ranks, Baltzell argues, the old socioeconomic establishment in Pennsylvania doomed itself and many of its enterprises to stagnation and failure. In a later book, *Puritan Boston and Quaker Philadelphia,* he contrasted the intellectual vitality and public spirit of the Boston elite with the family-oriented and conservative Philadelphia upper class.

For a variety of reasons, then, Pennsylvania was experiencing declines in a number of its industries even before the Great Depression of the 1930s began. But the dislocations of that earlier decade paled in comparison with those of the 1930s. During the worst months of the depression, in the winter of 1933, nearly 1.4 million Pennsylvanians, or 37.1 percent of the work force, were unemployed. Per capita personal income had slid from $775 in 1929 to $421 in 1933, while industrial production was about half what it had been in 1929. Some Pittsburghers who had lost their homes or apartments turned to living in packing boxes. In Philadelphia, desperate men and women begged for leftover food scraps or resorted to subsisting on dandelion greens, and Philadelphia hospitals reported a number of deaths from starvation. Furthermore, at a time when it was assumed (though not always true) that men were the principal supporters of their families, women were particularly likely to lose their jobs.

In many areas of the state, private organizations, along with new charitable networks that emerged in the face of the crisis, strove mightily to provide relief for the unemployed. Perhaps the most ambitious of these was Philadelphia's Committee for Unemployment Relief, founded in November 1930 and headed by Horatio Gates Lloyd, a partner in Drexel & Company, an investment banking house affiliated with J. P. Morgan in New York. Essentially conservative in outlook, and assuming that the Depression would be short-lived, the committee initially raised $4 million in private donations, which it supplemented with another $3 million from the City of Philadelphia. In order to make this fund last as long as possible, the committee at first concentrated on filling weekly grocery orders, ranging from $1.50 for two adults to $5.00 for a family of six. The committee also distributed small amounts of coal, and secondhand clothing and shoes, to the needy. There was no attempt to pay the rent of unemployed workers.

Later, in addition to handing out direct relief, the committee created a "make-work" program that tried to provide jobs for all categories of unemployed, much like the Works Progress Administration (WPA) later created by the federal government. The unskilled were put to work clearing rubbish and boarding up vacant houses, while others worked for the city's Fairmount Park Commission to clear out dead wood and to construct new drives and walkways. The Philadelphia chapter of the Institute of Architects used out-of-work architects and draftsmen, who were paid by the Committee for Unemployment Relief, to undertake a survey of landmarks from the colonial period. The committee engaged jobless actors, actresses, and musicians to perform in local settlement houses, playgrounds, hospitals, and other institutions. In order to aid those who appeared to be in temporary need, the committee also made small loans. In addition, it operated shelters for the homeless and provided a breakfast program, through the schools, for children in need.

During 1931 and 1932 the Committee for Unemployment Relief continued to raise additional funds from both private and public sources, but by April 1932 it found itself overwhelmed by the gravity of the situation and by the realization that additional money would be difficult if not impossible to obtain. In June 1932 the committee voted to disband itself rather than mislead families into thinking that continued help was available. Despite the nationwide praise heaped on the committee, including kind words from

President Herbert Hoover, who preferred nongovernment solutions to the Great Depression, Philadelphia's experiment in private relief did not have the resources to cope with the mounting crisis.

Without doubt the economic emergency helped Gifford Pinchot to win the governorship of Pennsylvania a second time in 1930. Once elected, Pinchot again attacked the utility companies. The state legislature refused to give the governor a powerful regulatory commission that could set utility rates, but he did gain control of the already existing Public Service Commission by making his own appointments to it.

The deepening depression convinced Pinchot that both the state and federal governments had to step in with unprecedented assistance. Though Pinchot convened several special sessions of the legislature to request relief funds for the unemployed, the conservative lawmakers came up with very little. He also turned to President Franklin Roosevelt's New Deal, which ended up paying most of Pennsylvania's relief costs. Only when the federal administration threatened to cut off funds, in 1934, unless the state shared some of the burden, did the legislature come through with $20 million.

Having promised to "get farmers out of the mud," Pinchot convinced state lawmakers to assume, from the townships, the responsibility for some 20,000 miles of rural roads, and then embarked on an extensive road-building program. The roads, as completed, were narrow and tended to follow the contours of the land, with little or no grading, but they did improve farmers' access to markets. The road-building project used as little machinery as possible, in order to provide employment for manual laborers.

Meanwhile, Pinchot had been pressing for a cluster of laws that would benefit labor: mandatory unemployment insurance, minimum wages for women and minors, maximum hours for all workers, prohibition of child labor, and old-age pensions. The legislature did pass laws for old-age assistance, as well as pensions for the blind, but not the rest of the governor's legislative proposals. Pinchot also sympathized with striking coal miners in 1933 and ordered the National Guard, which he had sent in to restore order, to be strictly neutral and not side with either the strikers or the mining companies. Finally, Pinchot did whatever he could to oppose discrimination, appointing more women, blacks, Catholics, and Jews to state positions than any of his predecessors. From the time that Franklin Roosevelt was elected President in 1932, Pinchot warmly supported him and his New Deal

A "Hooverville" in Depression-era Pittsburgh, which stretched from 11th to 17th Street. Such shantytowns cropped up in many cities as displaced workers and families evicted from housing desperately sought shelter. Denizens called these makeshift camps "Hoovervilles," mocking President Herbert Hoover's limited effort to help the unemployed.

As the Depression deepened, churches did not wait for government to provide relief. Catholic charities and churches, for example, opened soup kitchens, job centers, and other places to aid desperate families who were without work or savings. Father James Cox, pictured here in 1932, brought food directly to the unemployed in "Shantytown," Pittsburgh. But relief was not the only issue. In 1932 Father Cox led a large protest march to Washington, D.C., both to galvanize workers to stand together for economic and social justice and to make sure the downtrodden would be heard.

policies, and even considered switching to the Democratic Party in 1934, with the idea of running for the U.S. Senate once his term in Harrisburg was over.

Although Pinchot had been a popular Republican governor, Pennsylvania voters in 1934, disenchanted with a Republican Party that disparaged the New Deal and its relief efforts, elected George H. Earle III of Philadelphia the state's first Democratic governor since the 1890s. That same year Joseph F. Guffey, from the Pittsburgh area, became the state's first Democrat in the U.S. Senate since the 1870s, winning by more than 10,000 votes. Twenty-four of the state's thirty-four-member U.S. congressional delegation were also Democrats as a result of the 1936 election. President Roosevelt carried Pennsylvania that year too, something he had failed to do four years earlier. In addition, Democrats gained control of the Pennsylvania House by a margin of 116 to 90. They did not win the state senate, however, because only half the seats were up for reelection that year.

George H. Earle III modeled his governorship after the New Deal program of President Franklin Roosevelt, a man he much admired. Because of this association, Earle's administration was known as the "Little New Deal." Nevertheless, during Earle's first two years in office the Republican state senate blocked many of his proposals. It even refused to pass legislation that would have given Pennsylvania $250 million in federal funds for relief and public works. However, the Senate did join with the House in revising the state's "blue laws," passed in 1794, to allow local option for Sunday sporting events and the showing of motion pictures (which had been forbidden on the Sabbath throughout Pennsylvania by law). It also enacted an Equal Rights Act that prohibited racial discrimination in hotels, restaurants, and places of public amusement within the state.

In 1936, with Roosevelt and the Democratic Party winning smashing victories nationwide, Pennsylvania voters gave Earle a two-thirds majority in the state senate that now cooperated with the already Democratic house to pass numerous reforms. During this period Pennsylvania's Little New Deal secured a host of new laws and programs. Benefiting labor were improved workmen's compensation, prohibition of imported strikebreakers, state minimum-wage and maximum-hour legislation, the outlawing of company unions, and the right to join unions and bargain collectively. The Earle admin-

CHATHAM VILLAGE AND THE LIMITS OF PRIVATE HOUSING

During the 1920s, inflationary pressures and a modest wage scale in Pittsburgh made an already critical housing shortage even worse. In 1928 the Buhl Foundation, funded by department-store owner Henry Buhl Jr., who had died the year before, set out to demonstrate that low-cost housing could be built under private auspices while yielding modest profit.

The foundation called its development Chatham Village, in honor of Pittsburgh's namesake, William Pitt, who became the First Earl of Chatham. The development was in the Mount Washington area, about a mile and a half southeast of downtown and thus within easy commuting distance. Planning consultants Clarence Stein and Henry Wright agreed that this was a good location but concluded it would be impossible to build single-dwelling homes within the income range ($2,000 to $2,500) established by the foundation. They therefore recommended a series of row houses, all in a simple but attractive red-brick, Georgian Revival style, designed by the firm of Ingham & Boyd. The houses would be rented rather than, as planned originally, sold. Altogether the Buhl Foundation constructed about 200 units in Chatham Village, the first group in 1931–32 and a second in 1935–36.

The Buhl Foundation trumpeted the success of Chatham Village as proof that limited-dividend housing had proven itself on a large scale. But as critics pointed out, all the tenants in Chatham Village were middle-class, allowing them to conclude that the experiment had done nothing to meet the need for true low-cost housing for working-class families. Those who believed that public action was necessary to address the housing needs of the least well-off, and especially during the

ABOVE: Chatham Village, Pittsburgh's model housing project.

Great Depression, pointed to Chatham Village as proof that private capitalism could not meet the state's housing needs. This would remain largely true until the post–World War II period, when mass-produced housing like that in Levittown, Bucks County, showed that the private sector was capable of delivering modest-priced housing for working- and lower-middle-class families.

istration also secured millions of federal dollars for enormous public works programs that built dams, schools, post offices, bridges, playgrounds, parks, and highways, including the pioneering Pennsylvania Turnpike.

Earle's victory as governor, and the election of numerous Democrats from Pennsylvania to state and national office in the mid-1930s, signaled a revival of the two-party system in the Commonwealth. The Democrats were particularly successful in the larger cities, which had been hurt most by the Depression and where more people benefited from New Deal measures. Especially surprising was the return of a viable Democratic Party in Philadelphia. For years it had been a joke, with the Republicans paying the rent for the Democratic headquarters in order to maintain the pretense of an opposition party. Under the direction of John B. Kelly, a wealthy contractor and father of the future Princess Grace of Monaco, and Matthew H. McCloskey Jr., likewise a successful contractor, Philadelphia's Democratic Party began to thrive with the assistance of New Deal patronage and the conclusion of many local voters that the Republicans were out of touch with their needs. However, it took another decade and a half before the Democrats were strong enough to take over City Hall in Philadelphia.

The transformation of politics in the Pittsburgh area was no less dramatic. As in Philadelphia, the Republicans had controlled the city and surrounding Allegheny County for decades. In Allegheny County steel towns, Republican mayors and councils had invariably sided with mill owners and had not hesitated to use the local police to arrest and beat up workers who tried to organize unions. Roosevelt's New Deal, in combination with Governor Earle's Little New Deal, emboldened steelworkers to form unions. "Revolution up and down the river!" cried Pittsburgh's weekly magazine, *The Bulletin Index*. The Steel Workers' Organizing Committee (SWOC) did more than win better wages and hours. By 1936, rank-and-file union leaders like Elmer Malloy of Duquesne, Paul Normile in Aliquippa, and Philip V. Carl in Ambridge won election on the Democratic ticket. They protected workers' rights and forbade local police to intimidate workers or to engage in strikebreaking. In one community after another—including Homestead, where local police had joined in brutally putting down the famous Homestead Strike four decades earlier—the Democrats took control of local government. These large Democratic majorities in Allegheny County, as well as in the city of Pittsburgh itself, turned out to be permanent, at least for the remainder of the twentieth century, and were as important in securing workers' rights as the unions themselves.

Although not as powerful as in the past, Pennsylvania's Republican organization was far from moribund. Fighting among Democrats during the 1938 gubernatorial primary and a nationwide recession that year (following Roosevelt's cutbacks in spending) helped the more unified Republicans to elect their candidate, Arthur H. James. During the campaign, James denounced Roosevelt's New Deal, vowed to "make a bonfire of all the laws passed by the 1937 legislature," promised to reduce what he called confiscatory taxes levied by the Democrats, and claimed that he would revive business in Pennsylvania, and

at the same time assured people that anyone who really wanted to work would have a job.

Many Pennsylvania Republicans had joined party members nationwide in blasting the New Deal for inconsistent and unscientific experimentation, in addition to its invasion of states' rights. One such Republican critic in Pennsylvania was State Senator George Woodward from Philadelphia, a Progressive Republican who had long advocated greater efficiency in government. The United States, Woodward accordingly complained in 1936, was "now witnessing a series of laboratory experiments of trial and error fostered by after-luncheon declarations pleasing to the company gathered around the table with the coffee and cigarettes, but quite disastrous to the hard world of office hours and balanced budgets." Two years earlier he had asked his fellow senators, "Let us all become stand-patters on state sovereignty." Fittingly, Woodward's grandfather, George W. Woodward, was a fierce states' rights Democrat during the Civil War who had run unsuccessfully for governor of Pennsylvania in 1863.

Governor Gifford Pinchot at a groundbreaking ceremony for a new road in York, one of many throughout the state that came to be called "Pinchot roads."

Among the federal New Deal programs that had a large, enduring impact on Pennsylvania was the Civilian Conservation Corps (CCC), which enrolled more than 190,000 young men from the state. The CCC reforestation, forest fire and erosion control, road construction, and clearing and improving of state park sites reshaped the Pennsylvania landscape and fashioned an "outdoors" that was more accessible to many people. Pennsylvanians still enjoy some of the cabins, campsites, and other facilities built by the Corps. The CCC also did historical restorations at such places as Fort Necessity and Gettysburg. This 1936 photograph shows a Corps team planting trees on Little Round Top at Gettysburg National Military Park.

OPPOSITE TOP: When the Pennsylvania Turnpike opened in 1940, motorists lined up at the interchanges waiting for the gates to open at midnight. The same scene was repeated when the Philadelphia and Western Extensions opened in the 1950s. Here C. C. Schleicher of Wilkinsburg, heading east, is the first motorist through the Pittsburgh interchange of the Western Extension at 12:01 A.M., August 7, 1951. The large crowds belied the gloomy forecast of naysayers who predicted that people would not pay to use a toll road.

OPPOSITE BOTTOM: An early promotional map of the Pennsylvania Turnpike.

Yet once back in office the Republicans made little headway in reducing taxes or immediately improving the business climate of the state. Nor did the legislature "roll back" the Little New Deal. Although Governor James's three successors would likewise be Republicans, they too failed to take state government back to where it had been before the Great Depression. Instead, Pennsylvania Republicans even extended some of the reform programs enacted by Democrats during the 1930s, such as increased workmen's compensation and increased funding for public health.

In addition to restoring a two-party system in Pennsylvania, the Depression and the New Deal gave organized labor in the state, as elsewhere in the nation, its first widespread opportunity to stand up against the power of concentrated capital. Section 7a of the National Industrial Recovery Act (NIRA) of 1933 and the National Labor Relations Act (or Wagner Act) of 1935, which replaced the NIRA after the U.S. Supreme Court declared it unconstitutional, gave federal protection to union-organizing and collective bargaining. These provisions were reinforced by Pennsylvania's Little Wagner Act of 1937, which created a state Labor Relations Board. This state law also protected workers' rights to organize and to engage in collective bargaining, in addition to prohibiting various unfair labor practices.

One of the greatest labor successes under these new provisions was the organization of steelworkers in Pennsylvania. Taking the lead was John L. Lewis, president of the United Mine Workers. When the American Federation of Labor, largely a coalition of craft unions, failed to organize the steel industry, Lewis formed the Congress of Industrial Organizations (CIO) in 1936. A year later, U.S. Steel, fearing the effects of a crippling strike, agreed to recognize the United Steelworkers of America. So-called Little

THE PENNSYLVANIA TURNPIKE

An important legacy of the Depression era was the Pennsylvania Turnpike. Before the turnpike opened, people driving across the state found the existing routes over the mountains slow, dangerous, and inconvenient. This difficulty in breaching the mountain barrier was an old one in Pennsylvania that had been solved for several generations by the Pennsylvania Railroad, but now, with the motor age in full force, a new solution had to be found.

Surveyors agreed that the incomplete and long-abandoned South Pennsylvania Railroad route would be suitable for a limited, double-lane, divided highway over the mountains, and in 1937 the legislature in Harrisburg established a Pennsylvania Turnpike Commission. President Franklin D. Roosevelt offered his assistance and ordered the Reconstruction Finance Corporation (RFC) to underwrite a bond issue for $35 million. Another $29.1 million came from the federal Public Works Administration (PWA) as an outright grant.

The original stretch of turnpike, which opened in October 1940, was 160 miles long and ran from Middlesex, some eighteen miles west of Harrisburg, to Irwin, approximately twenty-four miles east of Pittsburgh. This meant that an automobile trip from Harrisburg to Pittsburgh, which had taken five and a half to six hours, could be completed by turnpike in about half the time.

The turnpike was immensely popular from the beginning. Soon after World War II the commission completed the toll highway through to both the eastern and western boundaries of the state for a total of 327 miles and had ambitious plans for various extension routes. As the first of its kind in the nation, the turnpike provided many of the ideas, as well as much of the impetus, for the massive interstate highway system that Congress authorized in 1956, just a decade and a half after the turnpike opened.

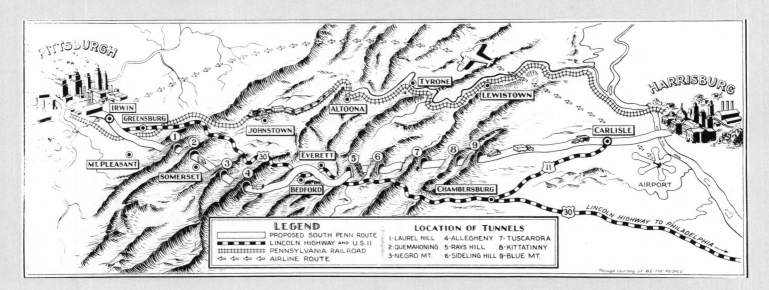

RIGHT AND OPPOSITE: Several major floods inundated Pennsylvania communities during the twentieth century, destroying millions of dollars of property, costing lives, and taxing public and private relief. In 1936, floods swamped central and western Pennsylvania, as shown in St. Patrick's Day pictures of Pittsburgh (*right*) and Harrisburg (*opposite page*). In Pittsburgh the waters rose as high as 46 feet, knocking down power lines, setting fires, and fouling the water supply. Fears of looting and epidemic disease led the governor to send in the National Guard and state police to keep order. Volunteers provided makeshift craft to get people and supplies about and to clean up the city after the water subsided, but private efforts alone could not do the job of recovery. Such natural disasters during the Depression heightened the call for more organized and regular public regulation of basic services. Pennsylvania passed the Flood Control and Pure Streams Act in 1937, enabling the construction of small dams across the state to prevent flooding and soil erosion and protect streams from pollution due to soil run-off.

Steel, made up of such smaller companies as Bethlehem and Republic, held out until 1941, but they too gave in and recognized the union. The days when Pennsylvania's most powerful captains of industry could unilaterally dictate wages and working conditions were over.

WAR AGAIN

Despite all the efforts to end severe unemployment by various government programs, it was the American rearmament in anticipation of World War II, and then the nation's direct participation in that war after December 1941, that finally ended the Great Depression in Pennsylvania and elsewhere in the United States. Instead of facing massive unemployment, the state now faced the prospect of not having enough workers. Once again, it was external decisions and events that played a large part in shaping the lives of Pennsylvania citizens.

As in World War I, Pennsylvania's industries contributed greatly to the war. The steel mills in Pittsburgh and vicinity again ran around the clock to supply war needs, producing 95 million tons of this essential metal. Pittsburgh's Westinghouse Corporation developed a wakeless, electrically powered torpedo that did not produce the telltale stream of

bubbles that had characterized earlier submarine torpedoes. The Hershey Chocolate Company produced the favorite D-ration bar for troops in the field. In Butler, the Bantam Car Company developed the world-famous Jeep, while Mack Truck of Allentown made heavy trucks and half-tracks for the military.

Philadelphia, with its many and varied industries, turned out a flood of war materiel. The Philadelphia Navy Yard produced fifty warships of various kinds and fitted out or repaired numerous other vessels. A total of more than 1,200 vessels passed through the facility. Because of the city's still-substantial textile industry, the Philadelphia Quartermaster's Depot became the army's center for the procurement of uniforms. The Frankford Arsenal, also in Philadelphia, poured forth streams of small-

arms ammunition and trained workers to go into new munitions plants. The city's Baldwin Locomotive Works made tanks, as well as continuing to manufacture locomotives. The Disston Saw Works took up the manufacture of armor plate.

In order to fill the demand for labor at a time when much of the male work force was in the military, thousands of Pennsylvania women took jobs. By 1943 they numbered one-fourth of those in war-related civilian employment. Many of them were married—in contrast to earlier in the century, when it was primarily single women who entered the industrial or professional work force. These new married workers set an important example for their daughters, many of whom would insist on having both a career and a family.

The war brought many other changes to civilian life in Pennsylvania. In order to conserve rubber, the federal government limited highway speeds to thirty-five miles an hour. Gasoline was rationed in amounts depending on need, but most drivers received only three gallons a week. Commuters formed car pools or switched to public transportation; families doubled up for the few pleasure trips that were possible with what little fuel they could obtain.

Other scarce items—such as meat, coffee, sugar, and shoes—were rationed. Local rationing boards distributed booklets of stamps each month to residents in their

Salvage drive in State College, 1942. Salvage drives for the war effort—where citizens pulled together to collect rubber, metal, paper, and other materials that could be recycled—took place throughout Pennsylvania and the nation. Centre County ranked eighth in the state during this 1942 drive, collecting 220 pounds of scrap per capita.

districts, and consumers had to surrender the appropriate stamps, along with the purchase price, when buying rationed commodities. Other products simply disappeared from the market; nylon stockings, for instance, fell victim to the need for thousands of parachutes. Still other products were altered or abbreviated; skirts and dresses were made shorter in order to save cloth, while the men's popular double-breasted, wide-lapel jacket gave way to more streamlined models, and trouser cuffs were eliminated in the name of economy. Some Pennsylvanians purchased scarce goods from illegal sources—the "black market"—but widespread patriotism and general support for the war kept such activity to a minimum.

Yet patriotism was not enough to prevent a strike by transit workers in August 1944 that threatened to disrupt Philadelphia's wartime production. The federal Fair Employment Practices Commission had ordered the Philadelphia Transportation Company to hire and train blacks to work as conductors and motormen on its buses and trolleys. On August 1, the day the first black trainees were to start work, the transit union struck, leading to a complete shutdown of trolleys, subways, and buses at a time when many employees depended on public transportation to get to work. After transit workers refused to return to their jobs, President Roosevelt sent a detachment of 5,000 troops into Philadelphia to run the transit system if necessary. The Roosevelt administration told strikers that if they continued to stay off the job, they would lose their draft deferments, be barred from any other defense work, and be denied unemployment compensation. The workers complied on the deadline of August 6 and returned to their jobs.

James Stewart, the first African American to be trained as a motorman, pays close attention to instructions given by William Poisell, then the Philadelphia Transportation Company's chief instructor, on the practice track at Third Street and Wyoming Avenue on July 31, 1944. The next day, when Stewart and other African Americans were to begin working as motormen and conductors, the transit union struck in opposition to a recent ruling forcing the PTC to hire and train blacks to work on their buses and trolleys. Intervention by the federal government sent the PTC back to work within five days and kept armed soldiers on the trolleys and buses as a precaution against further disruptions in service.

As a precaution against violence or further disruption of service, armed soldiers rode on all transit vehicles until calm was restored.

More than 1,000,000 men and women from Pennsylvania served in the military during World War II. These included some of the most important high-ranking officers in the services: General of the Army George C. Marshall, a native of Uniontown; the Commander of the Army Air Corps, General Henry "Hap" Arnold of Gladwyne; and Admiral Harold R. Starke of Wilkes-Barre, Chief of Naval Operations. Pennsylvania's Twenty-Eighth Division again distinguished itself by standing up against the Germans' last great offensive at the Battle of the Bulge in Belgium, during December 1944.

SOCIETY AND CULTURE

In a state with a population as large and diverse as Pennsylvania's, social life and cultural offerings were broad and varied. How Pennsylvanians spent their leisure time and interacted with one another was often a function of income and social class. In Philadelphia and Pittsburgh, for example, socially prominent families held elaborate "coming-out" parties for daughters who were just turning eighteen. Mary Wickham Porcher Bond (1898–1997), a Philadelphia debutante, recalled one of the more elaborate coming-out balls in 1916: "It was on the roof garden of the Bellevue Hotel. The scene was a hunt, and the waiters had to dress in hunt clothes. And they had live horses! They had stalls up there with straw in them and we could lean over a fence . . . and pat the horses. I always wondered how they got the horses up there in the Bellevue elevators."

As a writer under the pen name Mary Fanning Wickham, Bond later ridiculed certain upper-class ways. This she did in her novel *Device and Desire* (1949), about a disputed will in a wealthy Philadelphia family. In a second novel, *The Petrified Gesture* (1950), she wrote about the social intricacies of the close familial ties between Philadelphia and Charleston, South Carolina. The little-known phenomenon of families from different regions and cities intermarrying over generations had its origins in the colonial period, when Philadelphia merchants, bankers, and insurance agents did extensive business with Charlestonians. Their families subsequently intermarried over the generations, a practice that continued well into the twentieth century. Bond, who descended from seventeenth-century French Huguenots in Charleston, was herself a product of this phenomenon.

Most urban-dwellers would never expect to attend a "coming-out" party. Middle-class men continued to frequent a number of lodges, some more prestigious than others, such as the International Order of Odd Fellows, Woodmen of the World, and the Benevolent Protective Order of Elks. As Civil War veterans died off in large numbers during the early twentieth century, their fraternal organization, the Grand Army of the Republic (GAR), began to fade as a lodge and veterans advocacy group. In the aftermath of World War I, veterans of that conflict established the American Legion, with numerous "posts" throughout Pennsylvania. Unlike the GAR, the Legion ensured its survival by inviting veterans of future wars into its membership. Still other lodges were ethnic in character, including the Ancient Order of Hibernians (Irish) and the Sons of Italy. Free Masonry continued to appeal to many upwardly mobile men, while the Knights of Columbus provided an alternative for Catholic men, who were forbidden by the church to join secret societies, like the Masons.

Middle-class women joined church auxiliaries and assisted in numerous volunteer activities. A variety of women's clubs became advocates for social and educational reform, while at the same time giving women the opportunity to research and discuss literature and current events and to assume a variety of leadership positions. Many middle-class and upper-class women also became interested in lineage societies, such as the Daughters of the American Revolution and the Society of Colonial Dames. Although these societies did much important work in restoring and maintaining historic sites and structures, many women were attracted to them because membership, which required proof of colonial American ancestors, indicated social respectability and upper-class aspirations.

Working-class men congregated in neighborhood saloons and billiard halls, while their wives sought out one another for conversation on front stoops or in neighborhood stores. By the 1920s, men and women of numerous backgrounds could enjoy movies

OWEN WISTER AND THE WILD WEST

Among the outraged critics of early twentieth-century political corruption in Pennsylvania was Owen Wister (1860–1938), one of the nation's most successful writers and a member of Philadelphia's upper-upper class. While castigating the corrupt politicians themselves, he also admonished the citizens of Pennsylvania for creating conditions in which such corruption could take root and flourish. In his unfinished novel, *Romney,* Wister blamed this atmosphere on the complacency, stupidity, and cowardice of the average Pennsylvania voter. But even more culpable were the better-off citizens of the state. "Well-to-do, at ease, with no wish but to be left undisturbed," he wrote, "the traditional [Pennsylvanian] shrinks from revolt."

At the time that Wister was taking Pennsylvanians to task for their acceptance of corruption, he was already well known for his 1902 novel, *The Virginian,* in which Wister popularized the romantic cowboy hero more than any other American writer. Several movie versions of *The Virginian* subsequently appeared, and later the novel was the basis for a long-running television series of the same name.

With his cowboy hero, Wister believed he had found a perfect counterpoise to the spoiled easterner, of the sort too often found in and around Philadelphia. Though sometimes rough, his cowboy was a natural gentleman who offered the Anglo-Saxon race its last chance at courage, adventure, and self-sufficiency. Wister could only hope that some of this spirit could yet inspire well-to-do Pennsylvanians—and their counterparts elsewhere in the nation—to shed their mantle of contentment and fight for political honesty, but he was none too hopeful.

It is a great irony that Pennsylvania, one of the original thirteen colonies, should have produced an important contribution to the cowboy legend. If nothing else, Wister is a testament to the state's important role in fashioning a wider American culture.

ABOVE: Owen Wister in the early 1890s, during a period when he made several extended trips to the West.

and, late in the decade, radio entertainment. Another favorite pastime was a visit to one of the many amusement parks in the state, such as Willow Grove Park on the outskirts of Philadelphia, Kennywood Park near Pittsburgh, and Carsonia Park outside Reading, many of which were at the end of a trolley or interurban rail line.

During the summer months those who could afford it might escape the heat by going off to Maine for a couple of months. Families not so well heeled could head for the New Jersey Shore or for wooded areas near Pennsylvania's many rivers, lakes, and streams. By the early twentieth century various resorts in the Pocono Mountains northeast of Philadelphia provided hotels and boardinghouses for inland vacations. Those with little disposable income cooled off behind an abandoned mill dam or stood before an opened fire hydrant. And on hot nights some city-dwellers dragged mattresses into small yards, or parks if there were any nearby—anything to escape oven-like row houses and apartment buildings in this age before home air conditioning.

For many children, baseball continued to be a favorite warm-weather pastime, with games played in vacant lots, back streets and alleys, and rural fields. In Pittsburgh and Philadelphia, baseball fans could attend Major League games in ballparks that stood in the midst of urban neighborhoods. Forbes Field in Pittsburgh, home of the Pirates, and Shibe Park in Philadelphia, where the Athletics played, were familiar and beloved places for several generations of baseball fans. During the earliest years of the century the Pittsburgh Pirates won several National League pennants with the help of their star shortstop, John "Honus" Wagner. In Philadelphia, Connie Mack's Athletics stirred the most excitement. The "A's" won several American League pennants under Mack, and two consecutive World Series victories, in 1929 and 1930, with the legendary pitching of Robert Moses "Lefty" Grove and the team's "million-dollar infield."

A strict color barrier forced blacks to create their own professional baseball teams, most notably the Hilldale Club of Philadelphia, whose president, Edward Bolden, formed the Eastern Colored League in 1923. In 1924 the first Negro World Series was played, pitting the Hilldale team, champion of the Eastern League, against the Kansas City Monarchs, champion of the Negro National League. During the 1930s the Pittsburgh Crawfords emerged as the elite team in the Negro National League with their Hall of Fame outfielder, James "Cool Papa" Bell. The end of the black major leagues came shortly after Jackie Robinson debuted with the Dodgers in 1947.

Sporting events brought people of different backgrounds together—for a moment. Although separated by class in box seats and bleachers, the fans cheered as one for the home team. They also avidly read the box scores and game summaries in the sports pages of the dailies, which were fast changing their formats to offer more sports for the men and home "features" for the women, to keep their readers. Organized sports, especially high school football games that were the big events in towns across the state on Saturdays, were one of the main ways that people retained their loyalty to place.

While popular culture found many expressions in the three decades after the turn of

A traveling Chautauqua meeting in Union County. Chautauquas brought lecturers, musicians, and entertainers to small towns during the summer months. Gathering crowds into large, circus-size tents, they typically featured educational fare in the afternoons and musical or theatrical performances in the evenings.

the century, a group of artists and writers were gravitating to rural Bucks County, northwest of Philadelphia and just a short train ride from New York City. Beginning about 1910 and continuing into the post–World War II period, these talented men and women were attracted to the rural scenery of the area and to the quaint farmhouses and village dwellings, such as those in New Hope, that could still be purchased for modest sums. Among those who flourished in Bucks County were painters Edward Redfield, who was known for his landscapes and particularly for his snow scenes, and Daniel Garber, also an accomplished landscape painter. Among the Bucks County writers were Dorothy Parker and Pearl S. Buck. Buck settled there after leaving China and publishing her trilogy about Chinese life, which won her the Nobel Prize in literature.

James Michener, a native of Bucks County who grew up in Doylestown, wrote more

than a dozen best-selling books, including *Tales of the South Pacific,* which was later made into an immensely successful Broadway play and movie. A recurrent theme in Michener's works was the waste and stupidity of racial and class prejudice. Although not from Bucks County, novelist John O'Hara, who grew up in and around Pottsville in Schuylkill County, likewise explored the personal and social costs of social prejudice.

Pennsylvania could also boast of two world-class symphony orchestras. The Pittsburgh Symphony, originally founded in 1896 and reestablished in 1927, gained fame under director Fritz Reiner. In Philadelphia its orchestra, founded in 1900, rose to great prominence under Leopold Stokowski, who took charge in 1912. Under both Stokowski and his successor, Eugene Ormandy, who became director in 1938, the Philadelphia Orchestra premiered a number of important twentieth-century compositions, including works by Mahler, Rachmaninoff, Stravinsky, Debussy, and Schoenberg. During the late 1930s and early 1940s, Philadelphians could also attend performances of the WPA Civic Symphony Orchestra, a depression-era group designed to give work to unemployed musicians. One of its distinctive characteristics was the playing of music by American composers, with native-born directors wielding the baton.

For Pennsylvanians of all backgrounds and walks of life, religion continued to play a large role in their lives. Some religious groups (especially Catholics and Quakers) provided education from elementary school through college, many offered assistance to the

The St. Peter Claver baseball team. St. Peter Claver was the first African American Roman Catholic church in Philadelphia.

TABLE 6.2 **REPRESENTATIVE RELIGIOUS AFFILIATIONS, PENNSYLVANIA, 1926**
(members as percentage of population)

	Pennsylvania	U.S.
Roman Catholic	22.93	15.85
Lutheran	6.09	3.38
Methodist	4.88	6.88
Presbyterian	4.85	2.24
Jewish	4.25	3.48
Baptist	2.43	7.19
German Reformed	2.33	0.31
Episcopal	2.06	1.58
Mennonite	0.28	0.07
Quaker	0.13	0.08
Moravian	0.08	0.03

SOURCE: David Cuff et al., eds., *The Atlas of Pennsylvania* (Philadelphia: Temple University Press, 1989).

needy, and most provided a place to socialize with other members of the faith. Churches also set up Bible camps and schools in the Poconos and elsewhere to provide a wholesome and healthful retreat from worldly diversions. For decades, Pennsylvania was the Bible camp capital of the nation. Churches, synagogues, and other houses of worship were also important vehicles for musical expression that ranged from gospel blues to classical pieces by Bach and Handel. Massive out-of-doors revival meetings, long a tradition in Pennsylvania, continued into the first half of the twentieth century. The most famous revival preacher was Billy Sunday, who appeared in many communities throughout the Commonwealth. Radio listeners during the 1920s could tune in to the nationwide broadcasts of Aimee Semple McPherson, known familiarly to her fans as Sister Aimee. She offered her Four-Square Gospel, of God, home, school, and religion. In pluralistic Pennsylvania the variety and scope of religious expression was truly impressive, even as radio and national publications began to break down local barriers and promote a more common religious—and consumer—culture.

Religious diversity also meant religious division. Not only were Catholics, Jews, Protestants, and others divided by faith, but differences in ethnicity, class, and other factors led to schisms and a continued discord within faiths, especially in the modernizing cities. Within the immigrant Catholic church, for example, Irish priests thought the Italians almost pagan for their effusive displays on feast days, and the Italians regarded

the Irish as spiritually sterile in their seemingly austere worship. Slovak Catholics had ideas about education that were quite different from those of Irish Catholics, with the former establishing their own schools whenever possible, to ensure that Slovak Catholic clergy would teach the catechism and not encourage American ways. Priests raised in the more authoritarian church culture of the Old World confronted laypersons in Pennsylvania who were demanding priests who spoke in their particular languages and who would be responsive to their particular economic and social needs. The success of some immigrants brought challenges to religious authority, while socialists, labor leaders, and political bosses competed with priests for immigrants' loyalties. In the early twentieth century, immigrant/ethnic churches remained vital institutions everywhere in the

Saturday-afternoon football games were common throughout Pennsylvania, offering an opportunity both to watch a sporting event and to socialize. This game was played on Bucknell University's first athletic field, Loomis Field, c. 1900.

Amid the grime of industrial cities, immigrant workers and their children built their churches, which stood as physical, cultural, and spiritual refuges from the smokestacked world ruled by the captains of industry. These immigrant churches reinforced immigrant/ethnic religious and social communities and sometimes became sources of social protest. Remarkable in that regard are the 1930s murals in St. Nicholas Church, Pittsburgh, the first Croatian Catholic church built in the United States. In this panel from one mural the Madonna of the Mon Valley mourns the Croatian American worker sacrificed on the altar of greed.

Commonwealth, and increased their importance as community centers by dispensing aid and comfort during the 1930s depression. However, immigrants' children became more Americanized and secularized, and even moved away from the "old" neighborhoods, especially during and after the 1940s. With this change, they also began to make new choices about where, with whom, and how often to worship.

COMPUTER OR SMOKESTACK

In the aftermath of World War II, Pennsylvanians remained proud of their industrial prowess and economic might. Less apparent was the fact that Pennsylvania, which remained second in manufacturing among the then forty-eight states, had stood only seventh in the value of war contracts awarded between 1941 and 1945. This was partly because the major automotive and aircraft industries were not concentrated in Pennsylvania. It was also not immediately obvious to the average citizen that the war had accelerated a shift in jobs to the western and southern states, where the winters were less severe—a trend that only intensified in the postwar years.

Yet during the war, researchers at the University of Pennsylvania in Philadelphia developed a promising new technology: the computer, which eventually went far in replacing the state's old smokestack industries with what became high-tech employment.

In 1946, under a contract between the university and the Army Ordnance Department, two researchers, J. Presper Eckert and John W. Mauchly, developed ENIAC, the world's first true computer.

A dramatic incident that illustrated the dangers and limitations of Pennsylvania's older industries and the need for something to replace them was the disaster that unfolded at Donora, a town of 14,000 people located about thirty miles south of Pittsburgh. There, in late October 1948, a deadly mix of sulfur dioxide, carbon monoxide, and metal dust, most of it from the massive Donora Zinc Works, a subsidiary of U.S. Steel, settled over the town, trapped by a warm layer of air above the narrow valley in which the community lay. Before the air currents changed four days later, 7,000 residents, half the town's population, were sickened, and twenty persons died from asphyxiation. The Donora Smog—or Donora Inversion, as it is also known—prompted the first serious investigations of air pollution by both state and federal authorities. Those actions eventually led to air-quality legislation on both the state and the national level, and helped to focus attention on environmental issues. One direct consequence was the landmark federal Clean Air Act of 1955.

In retrospect, the invention of the computer and the disaster at Donora, coming within two years of each other in Pennsylvania, seemed to offer an opportunity and a warning. It was unclear, as the fifth decade of the twentieth century drew to an end, whether the 10.5 million Pennsylvanians and their elected representatives in the ornate State Capitol at Harrisburg would make a smooth and successful transition to a new economy and its various demands.

Donora at noon on October 29, 1948, showing the deadly smog that enveloped the town. The investigation following this event marked the beginning of modern efforts to assess and confront the health threats from air pollution.

Baltzell, E. Digby. *Puritan Boston and Quaker Philadelphia.* New York: The Free Press, 1979.

Barton, Michael. *An Illustrated History of Greater Harrisburg.* Sun Valley, Calif.: American Historical Press, 1998.

Beers, Paul B. *Pennsylvania Politics Today and Yesterday.* University Park: The Pennsylvania State University Press, 1980.

Bodnar, John E., ed. *The Ethnic Experience in Pennsylvania.* Lewisburg, Pa.: Bucknell University Press, 1973.

Bodnar, John E., Roger Simon, and Michael P. Weber. *Lives of Their Own: Blacks, Italians, and Poles in Pittsburgh, 1900–1960.* Urbana: University of Illinois Press, 1982.

SOURCES *and* FURTHER READING

Brenner, Joel Glenn. *The Emperors of Chocolate: Inside the Secret World of Hershey and Mars.* New York: Random House, 1999.

Bush, George S., ed. *The Genius Belt: The Story of the Arts in Bucks County, Pennsylvania.* University Park: The Pennsylvania State University Press, 1996.

Contosta, David R. *A Philadelphia Family: The Houstons and Woodwards of Chestnut Hill.* Philadelphia: University of Pennsylvania Press, 1988.

———. *Philadelphia's Progressive Orphanage: The Carson Valley School.* University Park: The Pennsylvania State University Press, 1997.

———. *Suburb in the City: Chestnut Hill, Philadelphia, 1850–1990.* Columbus: Ohio State University Press, 1992.

Cupper, Dan. *The Pennsylvania Turnpike: A History.* Lebanon, Pa.: Applied Arts Publishers, 1995.

Downey, Dennis B., and Raymond M. Hyser. *No Crooked Death: Coatesville and the Lynching of Zachariah Walker.* Urbana: University of Illinois Press, 1991.

Franklin, Vincent P. *The Education of Black Philadelphia: The Social and Educational History of a Minority Community, 1900–1950.* Philadelphia: University of Pennsylvania Press, 1979.

Golab, Caroline. *Immigrant Destinations.* Philadelphia: Temple University Press, 1977.

Gottleib, Peter. *Making Their Own Way: Southern Blacks' Migration to Pittsburgh, 1916–1930.* Urbana: University of Illinois Press, 1987.

Greenwald, Maurine W., and Margo Anderson. *Pittsburgh Surveyed.* Pittsburgh: University of Pittsburgh Press, 1996.

Gregg, Robert. *Sparks from the Anvil of Oppression.* Philadelphia: Temple University Press, 1993.

Jenkins, Philip. *Hoods and Shirts: The Extreme Right in Pennsylvania, 1925–1950.* Chapel Hill: University of North Carolina Press, 1997.

Lorant, Stefan. *Pittsburgh: The Story of an American City.* Lenox, Mass.: Authors Edition Inc., 1975.

Lubove, Roy. *Twentieth-Century Pittsburgh.* Pittsburgh: University of Pittsburgh Press, 1995.

Lukacs, John. *Philadelphia: Patricians and Philistines, 1900–1950.* New York: Farrar, Straus, Giroux, 1981.

McCaffery, Peter. *When Bosses Ruled Philadelphia.* University Park: The Pennsylvania State University Press, 1993.

Morrison, Ernest. *J. Horace McFarland: A Thorn for Beauty.* Harrisburg: Pennsylvania Historical and Museum Commission, 1995.

Pinkett, Harold. *Gifford Pinchot and Public Forestry.* Urbana: University of Illinois Press, 1970.

Rose, James D. *Duquesne and the Rise of Steel Unionism.* Urbana: University of Illinois Press, 2001.

Squeri, Lawrence. *Better in the Poconos: The Story of Pennsylvania's Vacationland.* University Park: The Pennsylvania State University Press, 2002.

Stolarik, M. Mark. *Growing Up on the South Side: Three Generations of Slovaks in Bethlehem, Pennsylvania, 1880–1976.* Lewisburg, Pa.: Bucknell University Press, 1985.

Toker, Franklin. *Pittsburgh: An Urban Portrait.* Pittsburgh: University of Pittsburgh Press, 1994.

Warren, Kenneth. *Big Steel: The First Century of the United States Steel Corporation, 1901–2001.* Pittsburgh: University of Pittsburgh Press, 2001.

———. *Wealth, Waste, and Alienation: Growth and Decline in the Connellsville Coke Industry.* Pittsburgh: University of Pittsburgh Press, 2001.

Weigley, Russell, ed. *Philadelphia: A 300-Year History.* New York: W. W. Norton, 1982.

Wilson, William H. *The City Beautiful Movement.* Baltimore: Johns Hopkins University Press, 1989.

Wolensky, Kenneth, Nicole H. Wolensky, and Robert P. Wolensky. *Fighting for the Union Label: The Women's Garment Industry and the ILGWU in Pennsylvania.* University Park: The Pennsylvania State University Press, 2002.

The Postindustrial Age: 1950–2000

PHILIP JENKINS

I n 1950 travelers through Pennsylvania were still seeing a landscape marked by the familiar industrial stereotypes: the hellish steel mills, the mines and factories, and, hanging over all, the smoke and smog that residents regarded almost with affection as a badge of the state's prosperity. Over the next half-century much of the smoke cleared, but the new cleanliness was far from an unmixed blessing. It was achieved by the loss of many industries that had once given employment to millions of men and women and that over the decades had attracted millions of immigrants to the state. Hardest hit were the regions that at the beginning of the century had marked the frontiers of economic expansion: the boom communities of the anthracite and steel regions. Now that tide receded, leaving behind many deindustrialized valleys and villages like so many abandoned rock-pools cut off from the fleeing ocean. Also severed from their traditional importance were what had been the close-knit communities within the cities, which had been bound together by potent ties of work, religion, and ethnicity.

The new landscapes of prosperity were rather to be found around the older cities, in regions of suburbs and shopping malls, high-technology parks, and interstate highways—landscapes of a sort that had sprung up all over the United States. Although for many it was a time of unimagined prosperity, the second half of the twentieth century was for many other Pennsylvanians a painful and unsettling time. Probably no government could have succeeded in easing the trauma caused by these changes. And yet we

Workers leaving the Homestead Works by the Amity Street Gate, c. 1950. Blacks and whites worked in the same plant, but blacks usually held less-skilled and lower-paying jobs, and after work blacks and whites went their separate ways.

must emphasize that the process of deindustrialization was a transition, not a simple calamity. The changes the state underwent were part of a continuing process of economic and social development rather than a death knell.

CRISIS IN HOMESTEAD

The most important single change in Pennsylvania in the second half of the twentieth century was the decline of the traditional industries, a transformation that was at the heart of the other changes in social, economic, and political life. The scale of the tragedy appears in the steel cities of the Monongahela Valley, where the fate of the Homestead steelworks neatly encapsulates the story of many other heavy industrial plants in Pennsylvania. In the 1950s the city of Homestead was at its height, with 14,000 workers earning good wages at the local plant, and the Steelworkers Local boasted 10,000 members. Local stores flourished on the strength of the strong industrial economy, and the town's Eighth Avenue was a bustling commercial center. But like the other great steelworks, Homestead became increasingly uncompetitive, and even the profitable years of the Vietnam War only postponed the inevitable reckoning. Between 1940 and 1980 the city's resident population fell from 20,000 to 5,100. Worse was to come in the horrible years of the early 1980s. Homestead's open-hearth facility, OH5, closed in 1982, and the works itself followed in 1986. By 1990 the population had contracted to barely 4,000.

Realizing that the "Mon Valley," as it is known, was hovering on the edge of destruction, local grassroots activists now began a community organizing campaign that integrated the contributions of union rank-and-file leaders, ideological radicals, and clergy from local religious denominations. The movement remains a model of its type. These activists struggled to assist the unemployed workers, who faced conditions unparalleled since the years of Herbert Hoover; they also engaged in spectacular protests and stunts, challenging the steel owners in their plush residential areas and even in their churches. Still, the campaign could only delay the deterioration of the steel towns, where long-established businesses and stores were putting up their shutters—leaving downtown Homestead increasingly looking like a ghost town, and Eighth Avenue a commercial graveyard.

The town's physical appearance was made worse by a series of mysterious fires of the sort that affected many decaying towns in Pennsylvania, events that some explained in terms of desperate businesspeople seeking to grab insurance benefits through arson. Even the local paper, the *Homestead Daily Messenger,* suddenly ceased publication in 1979. With the economic base in ruins, local governments struggled for funds to pay for essential services, and cutbacks hit every area of life, including the schools, the police,

Homestead's open-hearth facility, OH5, closed in 1982. The rest of the Works closed in 1986. This photograph shows the mill partially demolished in the late 1990s.

and fire services. The steel closings tore the heart out of the community, which had to become accustomed to a long-term culture of chronic unemployment. When in 1992 the city of Homestead commemorated the centenary of the great industrial battle that had done so much to define American industrial conflicts, there was precious little of Homestead left to celebrate. By the end of the 1990s the neighboring community of West Homestead was literally prepared to give up its name, as it hit on the innovative fund-raising device of offering to change its name according to the wishes of the highest bidder or corporate sponsor; $1 million was suggested as an appropriate purchase price.

CREATING THE RUST BELT

The disaster that overtook the Mon Valley was all the more shocking because, in historical terms, it came relatively suddenly. In 1950 Pennsylvania's economy was still dominated by heavy industry. Giant corporations employed large armies of workers in vast productive complexes, and Pittsburgh was still in large measure the industrial capital of the United States. In 1951 journalist John Gunther saw Pittsburgh as "Gibraltar," "steel's own citadel: civilization based on industrial aggrandizement reaches here its blackest and most brilliant flower."

Pennsylvania's position was not unchallenged, as some older industries had been weakened between the two world wars by the depletion of natural resources or by the attractions of cheaper nonunion labor forces in other states. By the 1940s both the coal and the textile industries were facing difficulties, and the shift to road transportation steadily eroded the position of the railroads, which fought a desperate political rearguard action against the rival trucking firms. This change was bad news for older rail centers, such as Altoona and Johnstown. Meanwhile, the competing attractions of aircraft and automobiles made it likely that passenger-train service would not last long past the 1960s, or at least not as a profit-making concern.

In a partial offsetting of the losses from deindustrialization, Pennsylvania benefited from newer industries, such as heavy electrical manufacturing. Firms like Westinghouse and General Electric benefited from a cascade of military contracts during World War II, the Korean War, and the defense buildup of the 1950s. In 1950 almost half of U.S. Steel's business was devoted to defense work, as was more than one-third of Westinghouse's. The "Red Scare" raged so fiercely in Pennsylvania in the decade after 1945 precisely because the state's industries were so fundamental to the nation's defense effort, and thus so potentially vulnerable to sabotage. Though the specific products manufactured in the Commonwealth might change over time, there seemed no reason to believe that Pennsylvania would cease to be the economic powerhouse it had been for a century.

Yet the economic picture was becoming increasingly bleak, as Pennsylvania's industries declined in both absolute and relative terms. Between 1947 and 1958, Pennsylvania slipped from second to fifth place among manufacturing states, and it became apparent that the unemployment problem was very different from that of the cyclical depressions and downturns of past eras. Permanent layoffs in the coal, textile, and rail industries were leading to chronic unemployment in some regions. Taking anthracite and bituminous coal together, the number of miners in the state fell from 375,000 in 1914 to 52,000 in 1960, and to only 25,000 by the early 1990s. The industry was already experiencing serious difficulties by the early 1960s, when it was hit hard by new federal standards, including new clean-air legislation, and laws requiring higher health and safety standards, all of which raised production costs. Between 1979 and 1990, Pennsylvania's coal production fell by almost 25 percent. The collapse of the mineral industries was very marked in the anthracite region. The state produced more than 100,000,000 tons of anthracite in 1917, compared with barely 3 million annually by the 1990s. Other types of long-term decline hit the Philadelphia area, which lost two-thirds of its industrial jobs between 1925 and 1975.

Unemployment became a vital political issue for the state. From 1950 through 1962 Pennsylvania recorded unemployment rates that were 50 percent above the national average, and it had the nation's worst unemployment figures—behind only West Virginia. In 1956 Pennsylvania established an Industrial Development Authority to help rescue areas falling into semipermanent crisis, and the Authority did succeed in creating some new jobs. The booming economy of the mid-1960s lessened the crisis for a while—in fact, Governor William Scranton was even boasting in 1966 that the state faced a labor shortage. But the respite was only temporary, as coal employment continued to slide and the railroad industry entered ever-deeper difficulties. In 1958 the legendary Pennsylvania Railroad, once the nation's largest corporation, merged into the Penn Central Corporation, but that enterprise in turn declared bankruptcy in 1970, in the largest business failure in U.S. history up to that point. The nation's rail lines were reorganized into new ventures: Amtrak and Conrail. Corporate realignments were accompanied by drastic cuts in lines and services, and consequent

unemployment. Between 1974 and 1982 the rail industry in Pennsylvania shed one-quarter of its work force.

The problems with rail and coal were alarming enough, but in these cases the writing had been on the wall for several decades. In stark contrast, however, was the fate of the steel industry, which had long been the proud symbol of Pennsylvania's economic glory. "Pittsburgh Steel" was a byword for American toughness and resilience. When Steelworkers' Union official Harold J. Ruttenberg was asked "What is steel?" he replied simply "America!" In 1950 the major steel producers were recording the highest sales and profits ever. The following year, U.S. Steel initiated the largest steel expansion project in the nation's history at Morrisville: the Fairless Works. Still, in the early 1970s steel was regularly described as an American success story.

Signs of trouble began to accumulate in the late 1950s. The steel industry was hit hard by ruinous strikes in 1952 and 1959–60; the latter costing $6 billion in lost wages and production, and putting 200,000 Pennsylvanians out of work. American steel companies thought they were doing so well that they could ride out these disasters, and that they could afford to ignore a troubling amount of inefficiency and poor quality-control, aggravated by overstaffing, absenteeism, and theft. Gradually, though, these problems became more and more severe, at a time when other nations were investing in leaner and far more modern plants and were fighting hard to win export markets. These international rivals succeeded partly because they were starting from ground zero, having had their older industries destroyed in war, like Japan, or else were in the initial stages of industrialization, like Brazil and South Korea. These rival industries had new plants

It is no coincidence that the garment industry gained a foothold in Pennsylvania's hard-coal region at precisely the time mines were closing or reducing operations. "Runaway" garment factories, especially ones from Manhattan, set up sweatshops in mining towns where labor was plentiful and unions scarce. Throughout the 1940s and 1950s the International Ladies' Garment Workers' Union (ILGWU) gradually organized workers in the shops. Here ILGWU members picket Jenkins Sportswear during a 1958 strike on Main Street in Pittston.

U.S. Steel toppled the famous Dorothy Six blast furnace at the Duquesne Works in the summer of 1988, despite community protests to save it.

operating under innovative management and labor practices and did not suffer from the American burden of old habits, tradition, and the associated complacency.

From 1963 onward, Pennsylvania's steel industry began a period of sharp contraction, and by the 1970s the state's steel manufacturers and unions were allying to call for protective tariffs in order to save their industry. Though protectionism had long been the economic gospel for Pennsylvania's industrialists, in earlier days it had been justified by the need to defend fledgling industries. Now, however, the sense was that the American industry was frail, aging, and perhaps on the verge of extinction. By 1979 U.S. Steel was suffering massive losses (in 1980 the corporation lost $561 million in a single quarter). Major cutbacks and layoffs began in earnest, at legendary works like Youngstown and Homestead. By 1983 the cuts extended to such heroic names of Pennsylvania industry as McKeesport, Clairton, Braddock, and Duquesne. In the Pittsburgh area as a whole, the number of steelworkers fell from 90,000 in 1980 to only 44,000 by 1984. Wars have caused less economic damage than this.

By the 1970s the state had become decisively part of the "rust belt," characterized by decayed factories and mills surrounded by the remains of communities like Homestead, which had been called into existence to supply labor for those plants and thus lost their reason to exist. Pennsylvania's manufacturing sector recorded its highest level of employment ever in 1969, at 1.58 million workers, but by the early 1990s that figure had fallen by 40 percent, to less than one million. To put this in perspective, by the end of the century fewer Pennsylvanians were working in manufacturing than at any time since the middle of the Great Depression of the 1930s. Again indicating the parlous nature of the 1980s, the state lost one-quarter of its manufacturing jobs between 1979 and 1989 alone. Gibraltar had crumbled.

CITIES AND PEOPLE

The contraction of the state's industrial base naturally hit the cities and factory towns that had prospered in the opening years of the century. Some communities shrank in population, particularly in the anthracite regions and in the southwestern parts of the state (Table 7.2). Between 1930 and 2000, major cities losing a third or more of their people included Pittsburgh, Altoona, Johnstown, McKeesport, New Castle, Scranton, Wilkes-Barre, and Harrisburg; among smaller cities, declines of 50 percent or more occurred in

Nanticoke, Shamokin, and Monessen. The contraction amounted to 60 percent in Duquesne and Ambridge, 79 percent in Homestead. The population of the Greater Johnstown area fell from 112,000 in 1940 to 74,000 in 1990, down by one-third, and it was projected to sink below 50,000 by 2020. Even in Philadelphia, which had grown steadily since its founding in 1683 and which by 1950 exceeded 2,000,000 residents, a steady decline set in from the late 1950s. The city's population in the year 2000 was 30 percent below the mid-century figure.

After increasing steadily in almost every decade since the birth of the nation, the proportion of Pennsylvanians living in cities actually began to fall from the 1960s onward, and the percentage of urban-dwellers in the year 2000 was roughly what it was in 1930. Worst hit were the towns in the old heavy-industry regions. This was a far cry from the nineteenth-century boast that the soaring populations of complexes like Scranton–Wilkes-Barre would one day overtake Philadelphia.

The population of the state as a whole stagnated. From about 1770 to 1910 Pennsylvania had never recorded a single decade in which its population increased by less than 20 percent, and the rate sometimes approached twice that, but by the 1930s the population graphs flattened. Pennsylvania's population grew by only 12 percent between 1950 and 1970, and barely grew at all between 1970 and 2000. Though fertility remained high through the baby-boom years, the state was simply failing to retain many of its young people, who were joining the national drift to America's South and West. Although for much of the twentieth century Pennsylvania had been losing more migrants than it gained, the rate of out-migration became alarming from the late 1960s onward. Between 1990 and 2000 Pennsylvania's rate of population growth (3.4 percent) ranked it forty-eighth among all American states.

Like other northern and midwestern states, Pennsylvania's economic decline was reflected in a relative loss of political power. The state had thirty-six U.S. Representatives in the 1920s, but only twenty-seven by the 1960s and nineteen following the 2000 Census. The state's congressional representation shrank, while that of the southern and western states grew apace, and in the near future this trend is likely to continue. Pennsylvania's congressional seats were also, figuratively speaking, migrating south and west, to Arizona and Nevada, Georgia and Texas. The Commonwealth's population between 1990 and 2025 is projected to rise by only 7 percent, while that of

TABLE 7.1 **EMPLOYMENT IN THE PENNSYLVANIA STEEL INDUSTRY, 1974–1991**

District	1974	1991	Change (%)
Eastern Pennsylvania	35,301	21,521	–39.1
Johnstown	12,490	1,821	–85.4
Monongahela Valley	69,798	18,775	–73.1
Beaver Valley	29,874	9,321	–68.8
Total	147,463	51,438	–65.1

SOURCE: Adapted from Allan L. Rodgers, "The Rise and Decline of Pennsylvania's Steel Industry," in E. Willard Miller, ed., *A Geography of Pennsylvania* (University Park: The Pennsylvania State University Press, 1995), 293.

TABLE 7.2 **POPULATION CHANGE IN PENNSYLVANIA CITIES, 1930–2000**
(population numbers in thousands)

	1930	2000	Change (%)
Philadelphia	1,951	1,518	–22.2
Pittsburgh	670	335	–50.0
Scranton	143	76	–46.8
Erie	116	104	–10.0
Reading	111	81	–27.0
Allentown	93	107	+15.0
Wilkes-Barre	87	43	–50.5
Altoona	82	50	–39.0
Harrisburg	80	49	–38.0
Johnstown	67	24	–64.0
Lancaster	60	56	–7.0
Chester	59	37	–37.0
Bethlehem	58	71	+22.0
York	55	41	–25.0
McKeesport	55	24	–56.0
New Castle	49	26	–47.0
Williamsport	46	31	–32.0
Hazleton	37	23	–38.0
Norristown	36	31	–14.0
Easton	35	26	–24.0

SOURCES: Adapted from Paul D. Simkins, "Growth and Characteristics of Pennsylvania's Population," in E. Willard Miller, ed., *A Geography of Pennsylvania* (University Park: The Pennsylvania State University Press, 1995), 94; and from the online database on the 2000 U.S. Census provided by Mansfield University of Pennsylvania.

NOTE: Cities selected are those with populations in excess of 30,000 in 1930.

the entire United States will probably swell by more than one-third in the same period.

Pennsylvania's population growth since 1950 is by far the slowest of any of the largest states. The nation's second most populous state for most of the nineteenth century, after New York, Pennsylvania slipped into fifth place by the 1990s. The state's relative decline was epitomized by the fate of Philadelphia, the largest city in the earliest years of American nationhood and the second largest from 1800 through the 1880s. From 1890 to 1950 Philadelphia held third place behind New York and Chicago, but it fell to fourth position in 1960 and to fifth by 1990, as it was displaced by burgeoning Sun Belt cities like Los Angeles and Houston. If present trends continue, it will not be long before Philadelphia falls out of the nation's top ten urban centers altogether. Just as significant is the marked decline of Philadelphia's larger metropolitan region, which includes the suburbs and satellite towns; by this measure, the megalopolis known as Philadelphia-Wilmington-Trenton ranks only fifth in the nation.

The economic transformation could not fail to have social and demographic effects. Pennsylvania's population was steadily graying as the younger people left. By the 1990s the state stood second in the nation in the proportion of residents aged sixty-five or over (about 16 percent), and it had the second-highest median age, exceeded only by Florida. Just between 1990 and 2000 the state's median age rose, worryingly, from thirty-five to thirty-eight. Within the state, the oldest populations (that is, the highest median ages) are predictably found in the areas of most acute deindustrialization—in the anthracite country and the counties surrounding Pittsburgh.

This aging process reverberated through the state's social and political structures. The high proportion of nonemployed elderly clearly reduced the base of those eligible to pay state or local income taxes, and contributed to the impoverishment of government. At the same time, the presence of so many elderly people in the state made Pennsylvania very attractive to doctors dependent on Medicare payments and veterans' benefits. By the 1990s the state had significantly more doctors proportionate to the population than all but a handful of states, making the medical industries a major area of economic growth throughout the last quarter of the twentieth century (the state's important role in medical research and education also contributed to this preeminence). Conversely, young people are relatively scarce in the Commonwealth, with Pennsylvania forty-sixth in the nation in the proportion of people age eighteen or less. Related to this, the state ranks precisely last in the nation in the enrollment rate in public elementary and secondary schools. (Part of this low figure is due to the high enrollment in Catholic and private schools in the state, for Pennsylvania ranks among the most dependent on nonpublic sources of education.)

During the century after 1850, Pennsylvania had projected an image of raw, expansive economic power, but in later years the state acquired very different connotations, which were often exploited in popular culture treatments. Particularly during the 1980s,

OPPOSITE: Amish men at a barn raising. Even as suburban sprawl and tourists crowded into Lancaster County, the Amish persisted in holding onto the "old ways," which included a strong sense of community responsibility, as in coming together to raise a barn. But the Amish of today no longer rely on agriculture alone to make their way. In order to have enough income to keep their farms, many Amish use their carpentry and other skills in the off-season to earn extra money.

many films used Pennsylvania settings to symbolize a declining traditional America, an old industrial world of tight-knit ethnic communities rapidly falling into despair and poverty, and certainly no place for the young or ambitious. This image appeared in such films as *The Deer Hunter, That Championship Season, Flashdance,* and *All the Right Moves,* all of which implied to varying degrees that success was to be found only by clawing one's way out of this shabby, dying world; *Rocky* offered a similar theme. One curious counterexample here was the 1981 movie *Four Friends,* which actually depicted a man migrating *to* western Pennsylvania in order to work in a steel mill and to immerse himself into the folk customs and dances of the local Slavic community. The point of this quirky gesture, however, was that he was deliberately turning his back on modern America and returning to this older and more authentic world, however self-destructive his action would prove in the long run. Increasingly, industrial Pennsylvania seemed as detached from modern American trends and technologies as the world of the Amish.

Ironically, Pennsylvania communities succeeded in attracting some new investment by offering filmmakers access to their old industrial plants and streets, which so perfectly epitomized a bygone America. *The Deer Hunter* was the first in a long line. When in 1992 the makers of the film *Hoffa* wished to portray an early twentieth-century street scene, where better to film than in Pittsburgh's present-day Liberty Avenue? Pennsylvania's role as tragic museum piece was neatly captured in the music video of Billy Joel's song "Allentown," which argued that the American dream had been betrayed by mass unemployment and deindustrialization. Few argued with the song's basic thesis—though it was better suited to neighboring Bethlehem than to Allentown, which had not suffered from steel closures.

DEFENDING THE ENVIRONMENT

Although the shift away from the old world of mines and mills was in many ways a disaster for Pennsylvania, it did offer an opportunity for environmental changes that most observers view as positive. These changes remade the state's physical appearance more extensively than any event since the coming of industry in the mid-nineteenth century. In short, most of the state acquired far cleaner air and water and eliminated many of the noxious smells and health hazards that had been so fundamental a part of life.

A new postindustrial political consciousness was reflected in rising ecological and pro-environmental awareness in what had been a badly polluted state. The effort to defend and restore the natural environment dated back to the days of the pioneering conservationist Gifford Pinchot, and stream pollution and smoke control had been contentious issues in the legislatures of the mid-century. Even so, it seemed impossible that any administration could ever enact effective environmental laws in the face of opposition from both industrialists and unions. Coal industry representatives even argued that the choice was between having a viable coal industry and having fish in inland streams.

It was a bread-and-butter issue, and economically the choice was obvious. As the state Supreme Court ruled in 1886, the public good outweighed "the trifling inconvenience of particular persons" whose streams or air were poisoned. A general disregard for public health and comfort prevailed across the state. In 1951 John Gunther observed, "Philadelphia drinks its own sewage. The City of Brotherly Love is in fact the only one of similar rank in the nation where the quality of the drinking water is a compelling problem." (At this point the city was pumping 500 million gallons of raw sewage into the rivers that were the city's drinking supply.) Not until 1950 did Governor James Duff even succeed in passing a measure requiring communities along the Susquehanna to build sewage treatment plants, as opposed to simply pumping untreated wastes directly into the river.

In 1962 an old mining pit near the Odd Fellows Cemetery in Centralia, Columbia County, was converted into a landfill. When a fire broke out in the landfill that summer, it soon spread into the mines beneath, venting smoke and sulfur dioxide into the air above, and even seeping into the basements of local homes and businesses. A section of Route 61, shown here, cracked severely due to the fire, issuing smoke into the air. All efforts to contain the blaze have failed, and the fire continues to burn today.

Public opinion was galvanized by a series of traumatic events that suggested how far the environment had been degraded. By the 1960s, pollution was causing catastrophic fish-kills, which effectively signaled that the state's rivers were themselves dying. By 1962 the *Philadelphia Evening Bulletin* noted a fact obvious to anyone passing through the area: that the Susquehanna was "the color of a rotten orange" between Wilkes-Barre and Sunbury. One memorable symbol of the disastrous by-products of industry was the mine fire that began to rage underground in Centralia in 1962, issuing smoke and sulfur dioxide into the surrounding atmosphere and effectively killing the nearby town. The fire may yet burn for centuries to come.

The urgency of the environmental situation was recognized by visionary activists like Maurice Goddard, who served as the state's secretary of forests and waters and who carried on his campaign for clean air and water from 1956 until his retirement in 1979, through five administrations and under both parties. Also in the 1960s the political context in the Commonwealth was changing rapidly: the coal industry was losing much of its former clout, and the environmental movement began to have more influence, as evidenced by the nation's first Earth Day in 1970.

The defense of the environment became first politically possible and then essential. In 1965 a long-overdue law finally ended stream pollution exemptions for the coal industry, and at the end of the 1960s the Raymond P. Shafer administration began enforcing pollution laws with a dedication that was unprecedented in the state's history. In 1971 Maurice Goddard became the first secretary of the new Department of Environmental Resources and the state constitution was amended to include the ringing declaration that "the people have a right to clean air, pure water, and to the preservation of the natural, scenic and esthetic values of the environment. Pennsylvania's public natural resources are the common property of all the people, including generations yet to come" (article 1, section 27). Federal laws also had their effect, and notably the 1972 Clean Water Act,

"WE ALL LIVE IN PENNSYLVANIA": THREE MILE ISLAND

In 1979 American visitors to Europe were amazed to see the popularity of a slogan that seemed to blossom on banners and T-shirts across the Continent: "We all live in Pennsylvania." Far from being a highly successful promotion of the state's tourism agency, however, this message was deadly serious, for it was asserting the universal nature of the recent accident at Pennsylvania's Three Mile Island power plant, near Harrisburg.

On March 28, 1979, Three Mile Island (TMI) suffered an "event" that came perilously close to becoming a catastrophe. Maintenance workers accidentally shut off the water supply to the Unit Two reactor, which duly shut down as planned. Pressure built up rapidly, and a relief valve opened—but then stuck open, allowing thousands of gallons of radioactive coolant water to flood out and threatening to expose the nuclear core. About one-third of the core melted down, beginning a process that could ultimately have led to what was fancifully known as the "China Syndrome"—namely, that the core could burn through the earth with nothing to stop it until it arrived in China. In theory, such a total meltdown would have caused a vast release of radiation equivalent to the detonation of several hydrogen bombs in south-central Pennsylvania—and TMI came within an hour or less of such an event. It was a very, very close call.

The sense of threat was all the greater because the general public had become familiar with such incidents and their possible consequences from the recently popular film *The China Syndrome,* which had uncannily foreshadowed the details of the Three Mile Island accident. The situation was made worse by the early refusal of the power company, Metropolitan Edison, to acknowledge that a prob-

lem existed, so that rumors that contributed to the natural public panic spread rapidly. It did not help either that the federal Nuclear Regulatory Commission seemed not to know what had actually happened, or what it should do. In response, as many as 200,000 Pennsylvanians fled their homes.

Apart from the appalling publicity the event presented for the nuclear industry, Three Mile Island also raised troubling questions about the social dangers of technology and about whether issues of safety had been sacrificed for corporate profit. Three Mile Island offered a vital wake-up call about the nation's energy choices.

ABOVE: To protect the community around Three Mile Island during the threatened meltdown of the Unit Two reactor, Governor Dick Thornburgh ordered the evacuation of pregnant women and preschool children living within a five-mile radius.

which set forth standards that appeared unthinkably high. To a remarkable degree, though, these standards have been met on Pennsylvania rivers, which previously have been deemed beyond salvation. In turn, environmental improvement has contributed to other forms of economic growth, through tourism, outdoor recreation, and the leisure industries. And the state is not far from Goddard's declared goal of "a state park within twenty-five miles of every Pennsylvanian." Though many different motives take Pennsylvanians into the outdoors, the state still has a powerful hunting subculture; in a typical year, hunters kill about 350,000 deer and more than 2,500 bears.

The desire for a cleaner environment was one justification used for the shift away from coal as a source for generating electrical power. This left nuclear power as a major alternative, which at the time seemed a desirably clean high-technology solution. Pennsylvania played a pioneering role in the development of commercial nuclear power, as the nation's first operating plant went on line in Shippingport in 1957. By the 1990s, nuclear plants generated about one-third of the Commonwealth's electric power. However, the Three Mile Island accident of 1979 indicated that massive environmental and social damage was not only the preserve of the older industrial world. The accident, along with national energy crises in the 1970s, awakened the state to the need for conservation and a search for alternative sources of energy, but Pennsylvania remains largely dependent on fossil-fuel and nuclear power.

THE POLITICS OF INDUSTRY

Economic changes resonated through the political world. For most of the first half of the twentieth century, the most pressing issues in state politics involved the fate of heavy industry and were expressed largely in class terms, through controversies over strikes, the policing of labor disputes, and workers' rights to organize. These conflicts had culminated in the New Deal era, when the unions became a formidable force in the state's political system.

Largely due to the successes of the unions, the Democratic Party enjoyed a long period of hegemony, which is all the more remarkable because the Republicans had long operated virtually a one-party state in Pennsylvania, in the days when "political and industrial bossism merged." However, Pittsburgh had fallen to the Democrats in 1936, and Philadelphia likewise in 1951, and with these foundations the party's power at the state level could not be long delayed. After electing only one governor since 1891, Democrats now triumphed with George Leader in 1954 and David L. Lawrence in 1958, marking the first and, so far, the only occasion in Pennsylvania history in which one Democratic governor succeeded another. In 1956 the liberal Democrat Joe Clark began a twelve-year term in the U.S. Senate, defeating the popular Republican James Duff. In 1958 Pennsylvania Democrats elected more U.S. Representatives than the Republicans, for the first time since 1940. In contrast to the early years of the century, there was now

Civil defense preparations during the Cold War—such as "duck and cover" exercises for children, as portrayed here in the *Keystone Defender* in the mid-1950s—were promoted to the public as a means of protection, whereas their additional purpose was to instill fear of Communist attacks.

an authentic two-party system, in which Pennsylvania voters were quite willing to choose a Democratic U.S. President. In fact, the Commonwealth went for the winning candidate in every presidential election between 1952 and 1996, with the sole exception of 1968, when it bucked the trend by supporting Hubert Humphrey against Richard Nixon.

The continuing importance of the politics of class and industry is suggested by the events of the Red Scare in Pennsylvania, where anti-Communist rhetoric gained wide influence. The Communist Party had secured deep roots in the state during the 1930s, and at its height during World War II it commanded the loyalty of 4,000 to 5,000 Pennsylvanians. Naturally enough, the Communist presence infuriated the traditional bastions of the Right: the Republican Party, the Chambers of Commerce, the veterans' associations, and the conservative newspapers. However, anti-communism gained a bipartisan appeal because the Communist Party had gained a strong foothold in the unions and the ethnic societies, which were crucial to the success of the Democratic Party. Between about 1948 and 1954 a furious purge tried to expel Communists from the unions, especially from the United Electrical Workers union, which was so powerful in critical defense plants like Westinghouse. Democrats joined the Republicans in this campaign, as did the state's labor leaders. Pennsylvania experienced the full array of inquisitorial congressional hearings, which sought out Communists in schools and colleges no less than in the factories. The effort was supported by draconian state legislation; one statute banned the Communist Party from operating in the state, while the so-called Pechan Law demanded that all state employees take broadly worded loyalty oaths. The most sensational aspect of the anti-Red movement was the regiment of moles and informers who had penetrated the Communist Party on behalf of federal agencies. They later surfaced to tell fascinated media audiences about the dark deeds being plotted by Red spies and saboteurs. The best known was Matt Cvetic, whose "surfacing" in early 1950 ignited full-blown anti-Communist hysteria in Pittsburgh, a passion repeatedly stirred by Catholic activism.

Yet the great Red Scare can in retrospect be seen as the end of an era, the last manifestation of that decades-long terror that some radical group obeying a foreign state or international conspiracy would subvert Pennsylvania's vital industries. Matters changed

Matt Cvetic (*left*) and Harry Alan Sherman pose with literature and a "telephonic transmitting device" discovered in a raid on an alleged Communist meeting place.

In 1950 Pittsburgh was the scene of one of the great anti-Communist purges during what is sometimes called the McCarthy era, or "the Great Red Scare." The city had an active Communist Party that from 1948 was led by the charismatic Steve Nelson, and Communists had important footholds in local unions and ethnic societies. In February 1950 the extent of the party's power was exposed, disastrously, when former FBI informant Matt Cvetic appeared before a congressional committee and offered a sensational account of the structure, membership, and activities of the party. The exposé led to widespread persecutions of Communists named, but even worse was to come at the hands of local Judge Michael Angelo Musmanno, a fanatical Red-hunter who believed that "every Communist in the U.S. is a Soviet paratrooper already landed here." He also warned, "The steel city of America is reportedly listed in Moscow as the number-one target of Russian aerial invasion."

Infuriated by the recent outbreak of the war in Korea, Musmanno determined to root out the local "Reds" personally. In July the judge crossed the street from his Court of Common Pleas on Pittsburgh's Grant Street and entered the Communist Party bookstore to buy several classic Marxist texts, which he later used as damning evidence. Some weeks later, Musmanno, Cvetic, and some detectives raided Communist Party headquarters, which the judge described as "the equivalent of an advance post of the Red Army." Nelson and two other local party leaders were prosecuted for sedition, effectively for expressing Marxist views that called for the overthrow of American capitalism. The bizarre trial ran through 1952, and the proceedings epitomized the worst aspects of a kangaroo court:

Nelson was left without a lawyer for most of his trial, and in April 1951 he had to cope with the dreadful publicity from the film *I Was a Communist for the FBI*, then premiering only blocks away from the courthouse. The film was a scandalous fictionalized account of Cvetic's career among what were depicted as Communist spies and assassins. The case's final outcome was decided when the lone juror with doubts about Nelson's guilt was beaten by thugs who told him, "This'll teach you how to vote." Though the verdicts were later overturned, Musmanno parlayed his Red-baiting success into a prominent role in state politics: he served on the state Supreme Court and only narrowly lost the Democratic nomination for the U.S. Senate in 1964.

In the 1930s and 1940s Pittsburgh's multiethnic Hill District became increasingly African American as many whites moved to other neighborhoods. The *Pittsburgh Courier* was the main voice of the Hill's black residents. Founded in 1910 to complement the activities of the NAACP and the Urban League, the *Courier*'s reform agenda included working to defuse racial tensions in the city, as seen in this billboard.

fundamentally when those industries themselves lost their crucial role, and when the issue of assisting—or rather saving—the depressed areas took center stage in the state's political life, as it did from the 1950s onward. This effort also placed a new premium on the role of federal money in the state's economy and gave new importance to those politicians who showed themselves best able to win and distribute resources from Washington, D.C.

THE POLITICS OF CLASS AND RACE

From the 1960s onward the declining importance of heavy industry led to a redefinition of state politics, as traditional questions of class and economic power were supplanted by conflicts over race, gender, and interest group.

Pennsylvania politics were transformed by the shifting racial balance in the major cities, which brought black issues to the center stage of public life. The migration of African Americans into the cities reached new heights during World War II, while at the same time white residents were increasingly moving out of the city centers and into the swelling suburban communities. The urban black population thus increased both absolutely and relatively. Philadelphia had about 250,000 African Americans in 1940, representing about one-eighth of the population, but that figure had increased to 550,000 by 1963, or by more than one-quarter of the whole, and by 1990 it had reached 40 percent. By the last quarter of the twentieth century, Dauphin County (Harrisburg) was 15 percent black, and Allegheny County 11 percent.

These demographic changes were reflected in growing black political power. By the 1950s the Democratic Party in Philadelphia was under enormous pressure to ensure that black candidates were chosen for political office and judgeships, and the city's seventeen or so "Negro wards" represented a vital power-base that no party could afford to ignore. In 1958 African American Democrat Robert Nix was elected as U.S. Representative for Philadelphia's Fourth District; he later became the chief justice of the state Supreme Court. In 1969 Pittsburgh's K. Leroy Irvis became the first African American to serve as majority leader of the state House of Representatives, and the first black man to hold such a role in any state legislature in modern times; in 1977 he was elected Speaker of the House. Another African American who gained important office in this time was A. Leon Higginbotham, who served as president of the Philadelphia chapter of the NAACP before being appointed a District Court judge from 1964 to 1977; he subsequently became a judge on the U.S. Court of Appeals for the Third Circuit.

The 1960s marked a dramatic upsurge in militancy. During the 1950s the southern civil rights struggle attracted widespread bipartisan support in liberal northern states, but the issues raised about discrimination in jobs, housing, schools, and business opportunities were increasingly relevant to northern cities like Philadelphia and Pittsburgh. In particular, police forces were accused of racial brutality at least as severe as that prevailing in the segregationist South. Race questions came to pervade political life. In 1963 and 1964 the scale of civil rights demonstrations in Philadelphia swelled, and the number of violent confrontations accelerated, culminating in widespread rioting in North Philadelphia in August 1964. These events initiated a period of several years of sporadic riots and demonstrations, which for many observers became the most noticeable face of the social revolution in progress during those years.

Political violence with a powerful racial agenda now became a fact of urban life. For two decades after the terrifying 1964 riot on Columbia Avenue, the Philadelphia police force often found itself in physical conflict with political activists, usually African Americans. The most spectacular incidents involved a series of raids and gun battles in 1970, and the successive standoffs with the radical group MOVE. Between 1967 and 1971 few weeks passed without the local press reporting some riot or protest against racial injustice or police abuses, especially in the schools and colleges. In fairness, it should be said that although police officers misbehaved regularly, they were facing social unrest of startling breadth and severity, and it is difficult to imagine any force emerging from this situation with credit. Philadelphia's racial politics were echoed in other Pennsylvania cities, and urban rioting occurred in the mid-1960s in Harrisburg, York, Erie, and Chester. In Pittsburgh the riots following the assassination of Martin Luther King Jr. in April 1968 were the worst civil disorders the city had seen since the 1870s, and order was restored with the use of several thousand National Guard troops and the state police. Grievances of African Americans often mingled with the complaints of white liberals and radicals, whose protests were directed against the war in Vietnam.

"American Bandstand" grew up in Philadelphia in the 1950s, with Bob Horn (shown here in 1955) as its first host, and made its national debut in 1957 with Dick Clark as host. The show brought the "Philadelphia style" in music, dance, and dress to a national audience and for a time made Philadelphia the capital of broadcast rock and roll. Although almost all the dancers were white, and many were from local Catholic schools, "American Bandstand" booked black entertainers and provided a rare "integrated" setting on national television. In 1964 the show moved to California, as part of the exodus of Philadelphia-produced programs on national television to the West Coast that left Pennsylvania a broadcasting backwater by the mid-1970s.

Traditional divisions of left and right were now transformed, as the rise of Philadelphia's Frank Rizzo symbolized the redefinition of white ethnic politics. The expansion of blacks into previously white residential areas created severe resentment. One barometer of whites' disaffection was the success of George Wallace's third-party movement in white working-class areas of Pennsylvania cities in 1968. Though Wallace's appeal was multifaceted, appealing to those alarmed by economic change and the loss of local control, race was certainly his principal platform. His American Independent Party took 379,000 votes in Pennsylvania, about 8 percent of the whole, and Wallace took 80,000 votes in Allegheny County alone. Though the Wallace movement itself faded, the racial and social discontent that it reflected remained of lasting significance into the Reagan years and beyond.

Pennsylvania's major cities did indeed have grave social problems, to such an extent that many observers viewed these urban areas as being in a state of collapse. But the trend came to be seen largely, and misleadingly, in racial terms. Though the cities had been hit hard by economic changes and deindustrialization, it was all too easy to blame the changes on African Americans, who had come to play so crucial a role in urban affairs. In fact, as the cities became poorer and more violent, the blame for that poverty and violence fell on the residents, rather than on the disastrous economic conditions in which they found themselves. In reality, cities like Philadelphia had been in deep fiscal trouble long before the racial unrest of the 1960s, but the general economic decline hit particularly hard in some inner-city regions, which tended to have the highest proportions of African Americans. North Philadelphia, for instance, lost about half its population between 1950 and 1990, and much of Pittsburgh's Hill District was devastated in the 1960s and 1970s.

With shrinking tax bases, Philadelphia, Pittsburgh, and the other cities still found themselves in a grim fiscal situation. Attempts to raise real-estate and wage taxes on the remaining residents inevitably drove still more businesses and people beyond the city limits, creating a dreadful cycle of diminishing returns. Governments were thus forced to make cutbacks in services, thereby causing a steep decline in the quality of life, while financial austerity made it more likely that negotiations with city unions would end in

The Philadelphia Orchestra, as directed by Leopold Stokowski (1912–36) and Eugene Ormandy (1936–80), shown here, developed an equally famous "Philadelphia sound" in classical-music circles. Marian Anderson (1897–1993), whose studies and early career in Europe were financed by African American churches from her native Philadelphia, became world famous as a symbol of civil rights. In 1939 she sang before a crowd of more than 75,000 at the Lincoln Memorial in Washington, D.C., and in 1955 she became the first black singer to perform at the Metropolitan Opera in New York. She also served as the U.S. Representative for Human Rights to the United Nations.

damaging strikes. One turning point came in 1970 with the repeal of a state law prohibiting strikes by public employees. Labor chaos and public disorder ruled in the mid-1970s.

These turbulent events conceal the fundamental shifts in political power occurring in the state in this era, and the dramatic expansion of the African American role in politics and business. The rise of a new political elite was symbolized by the election of Philadelphia's first black mayor, W. Wilson Goode, in 1983, and blacks also advanced steadily into offices, such as state senator and state representative, city commissioner, and the judiciary. Other African Americans played a major role in national affairs, notably Philadelphia Congressman William Gray. Tragically, it was under Goode's regime that the long-simmering confrontation between the police and the radical group MOVE culminated in the 1985 police attack on the group's headquarters in West Philadelphia. The battle resulted in the deaths of eight MOVE members (including six children) and the destruction of many neighboring homes. Broadcast on national (and global) media, the MOVE disaster was appalling publicity for a Philadelphia seeking to erase the image of a violent and racially torn community.

Though racial conflicts declined dramatically at the end of the century, an uncomfortable reminder of earlier issues was provided by the case of Mumia Abu-Jamal. Cofounder of the Philadelphia chapter of the Black Panther Party, and later a supporter of MOVE, Abu-Jamal was tried and convicted for the 1981 murder of Philadelphia police officer Daniel Faulkner and sentenced to death. Legal anomalies in the trial, however, combined with Abu-Jamal's celebrity status as a writer, aroused controversy about the

ABOVE: Pope John Paul II arrived in Philadelphia in 1979, greeted by Mayor Frank Rizzo and John Cardinal Krol. The papal visit drew huge crowds to the city and, for a time, reinvigorated Catholics. The Polish pope and the city's Polish American archbishop also had a special affinity in their opposition to communism.

Many loved him, many hated him, but nobody ignored him. For better or worse, Frank Rizzo represented the soul of Philadelphia politics over a turbulent quarter-century. He was born in 1920, the child of a Calabrian family living in South Philadelphia. In 1943 he followed his father into the Philadelphia police force, of which he became commissioner in 1966. He became legendary for his determined resistance to minority protests during the days of rage in the 1960s, and he became a populist folk hero for many white residents, and especially for the city's ethnic blue-collar residents, who thoroughly identified with him.

Rizzo attracted countless memorable images in these years, often involving his well-armed officers forcefully raiding the premises of radical and black militant organizations. The crowning moment came in 1969 when Commissioner Rizzo, summoned from a banquet to confront a burgeoning riot, personally supervised his force's actions while stylishly attired in a tuxedo complete with a nightstick in his cummerbund. For his admirers, he epitomized a "Dirty Harry" image of the dedicated officer fighting for the decent people against criminals, terrorists, and rioters, and he did much to put the "law and order" theme in the center of American politics. For minorities and for liberals, he seemed unarguably to deserve words like "fascist" and "storm trooper." During the crisis year of 1970 he warned that to keep antiwar protesters and social radicals at bay "the only thing we can do now is to buy tanks and start mounting machine-guns." He continued:

"It is sedition. This is no longer a crime, but revolution. It must be stopped even if we have to change some of the laws to do it."

His self-dramatizing role as the Big Man laid the foundations for an enduring political career. Rizzo was elected mayor in 1971 and 1975, in contests that both exposed and aggravated the city's acute racial divisions. In his second campaign he promised, memorably, "to make Attila the Hun look like a faggot." His fanatical loyalty to his police force became ever more controversial at a time when protests were mounting about the corruption and violence of the city's officers, complaints that Rizzo conspicuously scorned. For almost twenty years, the politics of the state's largest city seemed almost to divide between the supporters and opponents of Frank Rizzo, for whom party labels were a matter of passing convenience. He ran again for the mayoralty, unsuccessfully, in 1983 and 1987, and he won the Republican primary for that office in 1991, shortly before his death.

In 1999 Philadelphia unveiled a statue of Frank Rizzo: it stands by the Municipal Services Building and faces the City Hall in which Rizzo had long played so enduring a role. A large mural of Rizzo greets visitors to the Italian Market in South Philadelphia, one of the white ethnic bastions of Rizzo's strength and, along with Rocky's gym nearby, a testimony to ethnic pride and a reminder that tough guys can make it in America.

ABOVE: Philadelphia Police Commissioner Frank Rizzo in 1969. Rizzo relished the "tough cop" image, parlaying it into two terms as mayor of Philadelphia.

By the 1970s African Americans in and from Pennsylvania were beginning to assume political power. In 1983 Philadelphia elected its first black mayor, W. Wilson Goode, and in 1985 Congressman William Gray became chairman of the House Budget Committee of the U.S. House of Representatives, making him one of the most influential power brokers in the nation. Goode, Gray, and Joseph Coleman, president of Philadelphia City Council (all pictured here in 1985, with Goode on the right and Coleman on the left flanking Gray), among other black politicians, came from church-based and civil rights social-activist backgrounds, on which they drew to build their political bases.

verdict. A "Free Mumia" campaign, which so powerfully recalls the radical rhetoric of the 1960s, has attracted worldwide attention, due in part to his own best-selling books. (The movement also became a major presence on the Internet.) For the political left in Europe as much as for North America, Abu-Jamal was a heroic symbol of the injustice inflicted on minority and Third World people. Celebrities who wrote on his behalf include Gwendolyn Brooks, Allen Ginsberg, Toni Morrison, Cornel West, John Edgar Wideman, and Alice Walker. However strange this concept would appear to most Pennsylvanians, at the turn of the millennium Abu-Jamal was in global terms perhaps the state's most famous resident.

In the city of York too, other ghosts of the 1960s were walking as the twentieth century drew to a close. During a long, hot summer in the city in 1969, black and white gangs often engaged in open warfare. Tensions reached dreadful heights that July. Following the shooting death of a white police officer, white militants gathered at a rally, where another officer was reportedly seen handing out ammunition to members of a white street gang and urging them to conduct "commando raids" against black neighborhoods. Shortly afterward, white extremists fired at a passing car, killing a black woman then visiting from her home in South Carolina. Rumors about the shootings circulated for years, but only in the 1990s did new facts come to light. In the year 2001, criminal charges were pressed against several participants in the case, including York's mayor, a former police officer, who was accused of leading the white power rally in 1969.

Urban rioting plagued a number of Pennsylvania cities during the mid- to late 1960s. Race relations were particularly volatile in York, where *Gazette & Daily* publisher Charles Gitt wrote, "They might as well proclaim this a city where race hatred reigns." Rioting broke out during the summers of 1968 and 1969, marked by incidents of rock-throwing, assaults, and arson. This photograph from July 1968 shows police using dogs at one riot scene. Many in the African American community charged that the police created the "K-9 Corps" especially to subdue black citizens in arrest situations.

Rioting recurred in York the following summer. Here the Pennsylvania National Guard rolls into town in July 1969.

CRIME AND JUSTICE

As the Frank Rizzo story indicates, racial tensions were often thinly concealed under the rhetorical cover of "law and order" politics. Soaring crime rates were a critical index of social decay: property-crime rates rocketed upward from the mid-1960s, reaching one peak around 1981 and another a decade later. This growth was particularly damaging to the public's sense of safety because it coincided with a contraction in the numbers of police officers, as cash-strapped cities sought to economize. In the 1970s the media

New prison construction in Pennsylvania absorbed an increasing proportion of state money in the late twentieth century. Facilities like this one in Indiana County—SCI Pine Grove—were part of a general trend toward tougher law enforcement, but poor communities also looked to new prisons as sources of economic development, bringing jobs.

dubbed Philadelphia (questionably) the "youth-gang capital of America." The soaring homicide rate of the 1970s and early 1980s also indicated the growing crisis. At the same time, the overburdened courts failed to deliver swift justice, and many lesser offenses were unofficially amnestied; by about 1990, Philadelphia had some 33,000 outstanding warrants, and only thirty officers to seek out and arrest the errant offenders. Matters deteriorated further in the decade after 1985, as new patterns of drug trafficking disrupted the long-established criminal networks, which for all their flaws at least had a vested interest in avoiding ostentatious violence. Philadelphia's murder total soared to more than 500 by the end of the decade, compared with about 120 annually in the late 1940s, and there was a dramatic rise in the proportion of murders involving young teenagers both as victims and as offenders. Similar rises were recorded in Pittsburgh and other major cities and were likewise generally blamed on the twin demon figures of crack cocaine and street gangs.

The reasons for increasing crime and violence are not hard to find, in that during the 1970s the large baby-boom generation was entering its most crime-prone age—its late teens—and the disastrous economic decline of the 1980s was inevitably going to have some spillover in terms of violence and substance abuse. Because blacks made up so large a share of the urban population, it is not surprising that news reports featured blacks as both the victims and the perpetrators of violence. Nevertheless, the images served to reinforce white stereotypes of black criminality.

In response, governments adopted ever-harsher penal policies, especially toward drug offenders. In keeping with national trends, every year from 1985 through the end of the century Pennsylvania added at least one new prison to its expanding range of facilities. Meanwhile, the state's corrections budget grew fivefold during the 1990s, to more than $1 billion. Taking state prisons and local jails together, Pennsylvania had some 14,000 inmates behind bars in the late 1970s, but this number rose to more than 35,000 by 1990, and to more than 60,000 at the end of the century. By this point about one-third of new prisoners were incarcerated for drug crimes. Including federal prisoners as well, the state had 77,000 inmates by the year 2000, a combined population equal in size to the city of Scranton. As happens so often in the United States, those sentenced to prison are disproportionately black and minority, so that a troublingly large proportion

John F. Kennedy came to Wilkes-Barre on October 28, 1960, just days before the presidential election, in which he won a closely contested campaign over Richard M. Nixon. Min Matheson, chairwoman of the ILGWU Local 22, spoke to the crowd at Public Square before Kennedy's arrival. At a time when few women held political office in Pennsylvania, Matheson was politically astute at lobbying state and federal officials on behalf of the working-class communities of the Wyoming Valley. Kennedy carried Pennsylvania in the 1960 election.

of that population found itself under the supervision of the criminal justice system, either incarcerated in adult or juvenile institutions, or subject to parole or probation. And the overcrowding in prisons did not ease as crime and violence rates fell steadily toward the end of the century.

Harsher attitudes toward crime are also evident in Pennsylvania's restoration of its death penalty law, which had remained inactive since 1962. The first of the new round of executions occurred in 1995. Symbolic of the state's shifting emphases in the last quarter of the century, Pennsylvania created two new major executive bureaus: the Department of Aging (1979) and the Department of Corrections (1984).

THE NEW POLITICS

Racial allegiances and concerns did much to replace class politics. Also contributing to this trend was the rise of moral issues in national affairs from the 1970s onward, in conflicts over abortion and homosexuality. These changes contributed to a growing conservatism in the state and opened the way to a major Republican revival. The state's changing demographics once more proved significant, as an aging population made the state conservative in areas of moral controversy and gender while remaining relatively liberal over issues of welfare and labor.

The African American civil rights movement inspired women, Indians, and gay and lesbian activists to follow in the same direction. Some of the earliest gay-rights protests occurred in Philadelphia, such as this demonstration outside Independence Hall on July 4, 1965. As with civil rights protesters at the time, marchers tried to look as respectable as possible to attract support. Gays and lesbians later faced the same dilemma as African Americans and feminists: Should they attempt to integrate into mainstream society, or militantly assert a "queer" identity that emphasized their special contributions to the greater culture?

The history of gender politics in Pennsylvania is paradoxical. It was marked by feminist successes in early years and by surprising setbacks later on. Traditionally, the state had produced a distinguished cohort of women political figures, including Genevieve Blatt, who was a perennial and popular candidate for state office in the 1950s and 1960s. Blatt's greatest triumph came in 1964, when she defeated the powerful Judge Michael Angelo Musmanno for the Democratic nomination for the U.S. Senate seat. Though she failed to win that seat, it was an impressive achievement, as she had in effect taken on the whole party organization. As early as 1962, women voters were out-registering men in Pennsylvania, and the gender gap grew steadily as the century progressed. In addition to their role in national and congressional elections, women played a decisive role in many community organizations and grassroots action groups.

During the 1960s and 1970s too, many of the state's women participated enthusiastically in the emerging women's movement, which grew out of the wider movement toward social liberation. In the long, historical perspective, the change in the role of women during these years will probably be remembered as one of the most important changes in American history, though most of the trends were not peculiar to Pennsylvania. As in the rest of the United States, women in Pennsylvania made sweeping gains in the professions from the 1970s on. But though not unique, Philadelphia deserves recognition as a vibrant center of the women's movement. Appropriately, this city was the setting for the epoch-making ordination of several women as Episcopal priests in 1974, an event that made news worldwide. Through the 1970s, feminist activism in Pennsylvania focused on securing passage of the federal Equal Rights Amendment, and such a law was added to the state constitution as early as 1971. Feminists also created a network of community institutions, including rape crisis centers and refuges for victims of domestic violence.

Changing attitudes toward gender and sexuality were also apparent from the growth of a visible gay and lesbian community in Pennsylvania. Before the 1960s, when homosexuality featured in the news it was usually in the context of a "vice raid" or a mass arrest of "perverts." One journalist recorded how in Pittsburgh "the prowling of sex deviates" around movie houses, public lavatories, and a downtown shopping arcade became so blatant in 1948 that the citizens rose up in arms. They told the Bureau of Police that their town virtually was being "taken over." In response, the police Morals Squad began a campaign against "the blatant prowlers, the ones who made quagmires out of public parks, the proselytizers of youth," which scored almost 500 "homosexual arrests" over a twenty-month period. Matters changed dramatically during the liberal 1960s, as protests against repression and discrimination increased, and Philadelphia in particular played a leading role in gay organization. On July 4, 1965, four years before New York's legendary Stonewall riot, some forty gay and lesbian demonstrators protested outside Independence Hall, under then-shocking slogans like "Homosexuals ask for the right to pursue happiness" and "End official persecution of homosexuals." Through the 1970s and 1980s, gay-rights issues became a familiar component of liberal rhetoric, and antihomosexual discrimination gained the kind of social stigma that had once befallen public displays of homosexuality. Conservative on many issues, Pennsylvania usually showed itself tolerant on matters of sexual expression.

More important than the political developments, though, were the changes in everyday life, which made it possible for ordinary people to follow alternative lifestyles and to restructure the whole notion of family. By the 1990s gay and lesbian couples in fourteen Pennsylvania counties were allowed to adopt children, though recent court decisions have cast doubt on the legality of the practice. By 2000 the U.S. Census counted more than 21,000 Pennsylvania households in which unrelated people of the same sex lived together in "a close personal relationship." Such households were especially numerous in Center City Philadelphia, Upper Darby in Delaware County, and New Hope, Bucks County, but they were widely scattered throughout the state. The numbers themselves are perhaps less startling than the fact that an official agency could ask about such a once-taboo subject, and that so many people would feel comfortable about responding.

In light of these achievements, it is remarkable just how unusually conservative Pennsylvania was in the latter years of the century compared with other large states. Throughout the 1990s the state had the dubious distinction of possessing an almost all-male congressional delegation—consisting of both U.S. Senators and (except for Marjorie Margolis-Mezvinsky, who was elected for one term in 1992) all twenty-one U.S. Representatives—and in 2000 only one woman was elected, making it 20–1 in the House. While the proportion of women in the state legislature grew steadily in the decade, it had reached only 12 percent of the whole by the year 2000. By this point, Pennsylvania stood forty-sixth among the states in terms of women's participation in state government, and Pennsylvania's women rank forty-fourth in voter registration. Presumably linked to this political weakness was the poor showing of women in many economic indicators, including wage equity with men.

The remarkable lack of women as political representatives reflected the influence of other factors beyond gender, particularly religion. Moral and cultural conservatism was most vigorously expressed in the debates over abortion and attempts by states to reverse the effects of the 1973 *Roe v. Wade* decision, in which the U.S. Supreme Court had legalized the procedure. The anti-abortion campaign was led especially by the Roman Catholic Church but was also taken up vociferously by conservative Protestant groups. The Catholic context gave the issue huge momentum in Pennsylvania, not only because of the numerical importance of that church in the state but also because of the over-

representation of Catholics in the political community. Although Catholics make up perhaps a one-third of Pennsylvania's population, in the 1990s they still represented almost 60 percent of its congressional delegation, and only somewhat less in the state legislature. Whatever changes have occurred in the electorate at large, the typical Pennsylvania legislator, whether at the state or the federal level, is still a white Catholic man, who is likely to lean toward Catholic positions on social issues.

By the 1980s, abortion became a critical litmus test, dividing liberals and conservatives, defining beliefs about morality and gender roles, and demonstrating just how far the old class politics had crumbled. Partly because of religious loyalties, anti-abortion attitudes were particularly likely to be found in traditional ethnic neighborhoods and in industrial towns and neighborhoods, as well as in conservative rural areas, while "pro-choice" ideas tended to characterize the major cities. Anti-abortion sentiment of the most uncompromising kind came to be a feature of state politics. This was the dominant motive in the third-party campaign of the Constitution Party, which ran Peg Luksik for governor in 1990, 1994, and 1998; in the last of those contests, she garnered an impressive 10 percent of the ballot. Throughout the 1980s and 1990s, abortion was perhaps the most contentious single issue in the state.

Although the most extreme activists wanted to prohibit abortion entirely, the federal courts prevented such drastic solutions, so an alternative strategy was implemented: to impose limitations that fell short of abolition. These measures culminated in the state's 1989 Abortion Control Act, which required a waiting period before an abortion and demanded that minor girls seek parental consent for the procedure. This law resulted in a

landmark case before the U.S. Supreme Court in 1992, *Planned Parenthood of South-Eastern Pennsylvania v. Casey,* which established the constitutional principle that restrictions like Pennsylvania's were permissible so long as they did not impose an "undue burden" on a woman seeking an abortion. Though nothing like the prohibition sought by the "pro-life" movement, the Pennsylvania case did give that movement a modest victory.

In the new political constellation many white urban and industrial voters found their attitudes redefined as politically conservative. Moreover, their overall influence declined relative to that of more traditionally conservative rural and suburban populations: the cities shrank, union memberships tumbled, and the disintegration of traditional party machines led to declining voter turnouts. Whereas in 1964, Philadelphia and Pittsburgh together accounted for about one-third of the state's votes, by the late 1990s that proportion had fallen to barely one-fifth. Many of the regions hit hardest by deindustrialization and population loss were the Democratic heartlands, such as Lackawanna County in the northeastern part of the state, and Fayette County in the southwest. The decline of the urban interest also placed a new premium on topics that carried weight in the countryside, such as the right to gun ownership. It is not surprising that Republican fortunes grew steadily from the late 1960s onward even though Democrats retained a sizable edge in voter registrations statewide.

This Republican revival has been apparent across the board in state and federal offices. In every election since 1968, the state has returned two Republicans as U.S. Senators, with the exception of the brief tenure of Democrat Harris Wofford from 1991 through 1994. Pennsylvania was classic territory for the conservative ethnic blue-collar voters defined as "Reagan Democrats." The picture has been more equally balanced in presidential votes. The state enthusiastically supported Ronald Reagan in the elections of 1980 and 1984 and went for George Bush in 1988. Pennsylvania went for Bill Clinton in 1992 and 1996, but in both cases the result was swayed by the potent third-party

The fundamental changes in national party politics and in Pennsylvania's place in national elections were framed between 1948, when Philadelphia was the site for the Republican, Democratic, and Progressive party conventions (all of which were pivotal in deciding on party nominations and courting the Pennsylvania vote), and 2000, when the Republican presidential candidate had been chosen even before the party gathered in Philadelphia for its convention. The primary system had taken the drama of nomination away from party conventions, and the wide television coverage led to carefully scripted performances at the events. In the year 2000 Philadelphia viewed the Republican convention as a tourism-building strategy that was a reflection of the city's inferiority complex in the shadow of New York City and Washington, D.C. But the conventions created their own dramas, as in the walkout of the "Dixiecrats" from the 1948 Democratic Convention, protesting nominee Truman's civil rights stand (*above left*), and in the demonstrations for all manner of causes during the Republican Convention in 2000 (*above right*).

candidacy of Ross Perot, who took as much as 18 percent of the state ballot in 1992. In 2000, however, Pennsylvania gave Democrat Albert J. Gore Jr. a slim margin of victory over Republican George W. Bush.

The party balance at the gubernatorial level was more mixed. The Democrats succeeded in holding their own through the 1970s and 1980s, but they did so by nominating figures like Robert Casey, the militantly anti-abortion and prolabor governor who held office from 1987 through 1995. Casey's stance on abortion made him a profoundly controversial figure in his own party. At the 1992 Democratic National Convention he was denied the right to address delegates, but his policies on such issues as protecting workers' compensation, improving the highway system, and creating jobs won him a devoted following in the state. After Casey, the Democratic Party was deeply divided and could attract only 30 percent of the vote in the 1998 gubernatorial contest, which resulted in the easy reelection of Tom Ridge. The Commonwealth ended the century very much as it had entered it, with Republican control at most levels of government.

PATRONAGE AND SCANDAL

Despite the sea change in political ideologies, some of the more controversial aspects of political life have changed all too little. Pennsylvania in the late twentieth century continued to have serious difficulties with political and official corruption; scandals often affected the outcome of electoral contests and seemed to be an enduring fact of life. It is an open question whether the state had an unusually corrupt political culture or whether the misbehavior that did occur was simply more likely to be exposed, given both the vigorous investigative journalism prevailing from the late 1960s onward and the activism of certain prosecutors. Richard Thornburgh, who served as governor from 1979 to 1987, was perhaps the most successful of many officials who built a career on the strength of his record in exposing the corruption of other officeholders.

Whatever the reason, the cities of Philadelphia and Pittsburgh had endemic corruption scandals involving their respective police forces, to the extent that senior police officers were repeatedly implicated in extorting money from criminal operations, or in actively organizing those operations, and similar events occurred in many smaller communities. It was a series of such corruption cases that, in 1951, ensured that Philadelphia would at long last fall to Democratic rule, ending a century of Republican hegemony, but the electoral revolution by no means ended the city's problem with structural graft. Still, in the 1950s the city employed 21,000 workers, all of whom were required to serve their partisan employers if they wanted to keep their jobs. And the traumatic scandals of the 1970s and the 1980s indicated the existence of systematic police corruption in Philadelphia, continuing a decades-long cycle of corruption and exposure that dated back to the days of Prohibition.

Repeatedly, corruption scandals determined political contests at the state level. One

THE ACTOR AS POLITICIAN:
DANIEL FLOOD

ABOVE: Congressman Daniel J. Flood of Wilkes-Barre, in typically flamboyant attire, with Miss Pennsylvania in 1971.

During the late 1970s, U.S. Congressman Daniel J. Flood was a memorable face in the traditional world of Pennsylvania pork-barrel politics, the old world of political machines lubricated by complex networks of favors and mutual back-scratching. Born in 1903, Flood spent his early career as a Shakespearean actor, which left its effects in the form of his florid dress and speaking style and his overall personal image, epitomized by a waxed mustache. He was first elected to the U.S. House of Representatives in 1944, and by the 1970s he was the firmly established congressman for the Eleventh Congressional District, mainly Luzerne County. Flood used his seniority on key committees to direct federal programs and funds to his district, and in 1972 in the wake of Hurricane Agnes he used his contacts with the Pentagon and the Nixon White House to get massive and immediate aid to flood-ravaged northeastern Pennsylvania.

In 1978 Congressman Flood became the center of controversy when an aide testified that he had demanded payments in exchange for using his political clout, and he was indicted for bribery and perjury in connection with influence-peddling. In addition, the state's Crime Commission suggested that Flood had used his influence to benefit a local contractor with powerful ties to the local Mafia family headed by Russell Bufalino. Nevertheless, with all these clouds hanging over his aging head, Flood ran for Congress in 1978 and trounced his Republican opponent. The only ill effect of the scandal seemed to be that his vote was reduced from its customary 70-plus percent of the ballot to a still-impressive 58 percent. Not for the last time, Pennsylvania voters demonstrated that they were more interested in whether politicians served the local community and "brought home the bacon" than in whether they were engaging in commonplace political corruption.

Congressman Flood went on to face other criminal charges and trials. He died in 1994, still a very popular figure in Luzerne County.

enduring problem involved the highly centralized structure of the executive branch, where all cabinet appointments were in the hands of the governor. There were abundant patronage appointments in the various state agencies, the Department of Transportation (PENNDOT) being the most notorious. As late as 1965 the governor had some 50,000 patronage appointments in his hands, most of which depended on the recommendation of the party apparatus at the county level. Throughout the 1970s and early 1980s, repeated patronage scandals had produced systematic evidence of use of the state payroll for the political benefit of Harrisburg officeholders and party officials. Many of the most notorious such instances occurred under Milton Shapp, who served as governor from 1971 to 1979 and whose second term was marred by charges of extortion, cronyism, and influence-peddling. The press reported with mingled awe and amusement on the large number of Pennsylvania public officials currently under investigation or facing criminal charges (though Shapp personally was not accused of benefiting from these activities). The state's political morality was perilously near to becoming a national joke.

Since the 1950s, reformers had attempted to reduce the vast discretionary power in the hands of the executive by increasing the number of elective officials in state agencies, and thus creating a system of checks and balances. The offices of treasurer and auditor general were made elective in 1950, while that of attorney general followed in 1980. These new positions did indeed have an effect, but not entirely in the ways foreseen by the reformers. For one thing, they actively expanded the field of party controversy, and they provided more springboards from which politicians could seek to launch political careers. In addition, the departments over which the newly elected officers presided were themselves often scandal-prone. Merely electing administrators failed to address the deeper underlying problem, that politicians desperately needed to raise funds for their political campaigns and that the legal avenues for doing so became severely constrained after the campaign finance reforms of the 1970s. The continuing economic decline may also have played a role, in drying up some legitimate forms of funding and in forcing individuals and parties to seek contributions from unorthodox sources. At the same time, Pennsylvania's constitution was revised in 1967–68 to permit future governors to run for two terms rather than one. This gave the office more power and prestige, but it also meant that governors spent their first term seeking funds for reelection campaigns.

During the 1980s, Pennsylvania politics suffered renewed scandals that reached high into the hierarchies of both political parties. One of the most corrosive involved CTA (Computer Technology Associates), which in 1983 was seeking a contract with state officials to undertake the reclamation of Social Security taxes that had been overpaid by the state. The contract negotiations, it was claimed, involved extensive graft, and between 1985 and 1987 a number of state and party officials were investigated and prosecuted. The affair reached a gruesome climax in January 1987 when Budd Dwyer, the Republican state treasurer, called a news conference before his sentencing on federal corruption charges. After delivering an irate speech about the injustice of his conviction, he

Governor Tom Ridge and Philadelphia Mayor Ed Rendell applaud Vice-President Al Gore at the groundbreaking ceremony for the Kvaerner Shipyard at the old Philadelphia Naval Shipyard in 1998. Alliances among state, local, and federal governments to attract foreign investment and new businesses characterized the 1990s. Such strategies sometimes worked, as in the Kvaerner deal, to find new uses for old industrial facilities and bring new technology and investment to the state. The mantra of such officials as the popular Ridge (a Republican, seated on the left) and Rendell (a Democrat, seated on the right) was partnership over partisanship to rebuild the state.

produced a revolver and committed suicide in front of the assembled journalists and television news cameras. The following year, Dwyer's main Democratic rival, Auditor General Al Benedict, was convicted of federal charges of racketeering, corruption, and influence peddling. The dual high-level scandals thus played a crucial role in determining the political line-up facing voters in the coming elections. It hardly helped when Attorney General Ernie Preate, a leading Democratic figure, was convicted in 1994 of violating election fund-raising laws. These goings-on served as an unpleasant reminder of some of the structural problems in the state's political life.

A NEW PENNSYLVANIA?

Through the late 1970s and 1980s Pennsylvania suffered a recurring problem with its national image. The disastrous publicity surrounding the Three Mile Island event of 1979 was followed by other undesirable news stories, including the MOVE siege and the

THE "GRAND EXPERIMENT": JOE PATERNO AND COLLEGE ATHLETICS

Penn State football coach Joe Paterno is one of the best-known figures in American sports and a widely recognized symbol of the Commonwealth of Pennsylvania. Born in Brooklyn, New York, in 1926, Paterno graduated from Brown University in 1950. Fully expecting that his next step would be law school, he moved later that year to State College, Pennsylvania, to accept what he thought would be a temporary position on the coaching staff of new Penn State head coach Rip Engle—and he never left town. In 1966 Paterno became the fourteenth head coach of the Nittany Lions and remains in that position to this day.

Paterno's professional life has been a story of records. As of the year 2002 he had the most wins of any coach in major college football. He had led Penn State teams to more bowl victories than any other college coach, and he was the only coach whose teams had won all four of the major New Year's Day games, namely, the Rose, Sugar, Cotton, and Orange Bowls. Among the greatest moments of his football career were five perfect seasons between 1968 and 1994 and two national championships, in 1982 and 1986.

Under Paterno's leadership, Penn State football gained a national following. In an age of showboating sports figures, the Nittany Lions with their white helmets and nameless blue jerseys exemplified the team approach and work ethic that had made Pennsylvania an industrial giant. Penn State regularly appeared on national television and prospered in the big business of college sports. Paterno's program also made the Nittany Lion logo a synonym for winning and one of the most recognized Pennsylvania images in the world.

Paterno was determined to prove that college sports was about more than just winning and losing and that "student" and "athlete" need not be contradictory terms. He called it the "Grand Experiment," and in his career (as of the year 2001) he produced twenty first-team Academic All-Americans, fourteen National Football Foundation and Hall of Fame Scholar-Athletes, and sixteen NCAA postgraduate scholarship winners.

Meanwhile, Paterno and his family have given millions of dollars back to the university, endowing faculty positions and scholarships in the College of Liberal Arts (including a scholarship in the classics to honor Paterno's high school Latin teacher), the School of Architecture and Landscape Architecture, and the University Libraries. He led the campaign to fund an addition to Penn State's Pattee Library that opened in 2000 and that attests to Paterno's primary dedication to academics over sports.

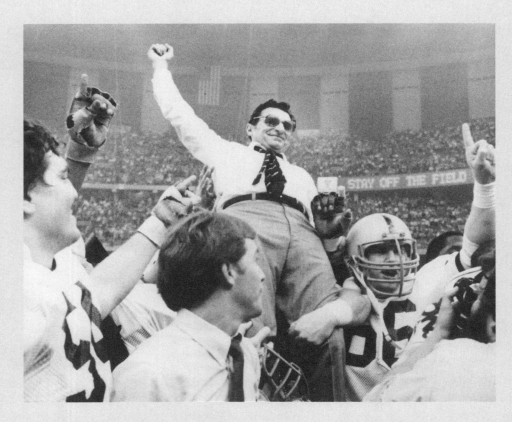

ABOVE: Joe Paterno is carried away by his team after the Sugar Bowl victory in January 1983 clinching Penn State's first national championship season.

Dwyer suicide, and at the same time the depressing industrial scene pervaded the motion pictures. Between 1980 and 1983 a news story datelined "Philadelphia" was likely to feature the sensational gang war in the city's Mafia "family" that claimed some twenty lives. A story from Pittsburgh, on the other hand, would likely focus on the collapse of the steel industry and the growing poverty of the Mon Valley. Even the 1985 film *Witness,* which reignited the long-standing popular romance with Amish life, offered a plot that assumed that the Philadelphia police force was violent, ruthless, and utterly corrupt. It also reiterated the bureaucratic legend that Philadelphia was "the 'speed' capital of the world," a national center for the manufacture and distribution of the illicit drug methamphetamine.

In Pennsylvania the post–World War II shift to the suburbs was most fully expressed in Levittown, a planned community of prefabricated houses (shown here) where the automobile was king. Government policies of providing mortgages for new home construction and underwriting highway construction spurred the move to the suburbs. The "cookie-cutter" housing and racial and ethnic exclusion of early postwar suburbia in time gave way to more variety as homeowners personalized their lawns and houses and new people moved in to claim the American dream. Nevertheless, the side effects of suburban sprawl—problems of water treatment, flood control, traffic management, and school funding—emerged as major political concerns in the late twentieth century.

Yet all these tales of woe concealed some major positive developments. Some had roots that went as far back as the 1950s but became particularly obvious from the mid-1980s onward. For all the weaknesses in Pennsylvania's economy, there were areas of major growth too, particularly in the service industries, as the state experienced the difficult transition to a mature postindustrial economy. By the early 1990s, while the state's largest employment category was manufacturing, with 950,000 jobs, there were major sectors in retail (862,000 jobs), services (797,000), finance (128,000), insurance (121,000), and real estate (43,000). The state gained 230,000 new jobs between 1995 and 1998 alone. There was particular growth in high-skill and high-technology occupations and in electronics, biotechnology, and pharmaceuticals, and both medicine and higher education were significant job-producers. Contrary to the worst fears of earlier years, there was indeed life after manufacturing.

The state's network of colleges and universities also provided expertise for rising industries, some of which found it convenient to relocate close to centers of higher education. One important innovation in this regard was the creation of Carnegie Mellon University, which was formed in 1967 by the merger of the Carnegie Institute of Technology and the Mellon Institute. By the 1980s barely 20 percent of Pittsburgh jobs were in manufacturing, and the city's third-largest employment sector was research and development. In the center of the state the rise of "knowledge industries" is suggested by the dramatic growth of the city of State College around the main campus of The Pennsylvania State University. For most of its history the town was a backwater dwarfed by the nearby Victorian town of Bellefonte, but by 1980 State College had

Lancaster's downtown businesses faced an uphill battle against the ever-growing suburban retail trade. Park City, a shopping mall northwest of downtown Lancaster, opened in 1971 in the midst of the city's redevelopment.

RIGHT: Like many American cities, large and small, Lancaster struggled to counter the effects of postwar suburbanization and the corresponding loss of jobs and services. City officials adopted an ambitious redevelopment plan designed to save the downtown business district. Historic buildings such as the Beaux Arts Hotel Brunswick, shown here, were demolished in the 1960s and replaced by modernist, concrete structures.

OPPOSITE: Advertisement from the *Sharon Herald*, December 2, 1967, promoting the opening of Interstate 80. The construction of the interstates, with federal matching funds, promised to revive the economy of the region, if also to alter its landscape significantly. The promise of this advertisement that I-80 would be the "Doorway to Your Driving Dreams" was not always realized, though, as the highway running across the state became more of a truck corridor for commercial vehicles passing through Pennsylvania than an avenue of wealth for the region. Still, I-80 opened up previously isolated mining and mountain communities to tourism, retirement living, and service industries.

become the core of a so-called metropolitan region, with more than 100,000 people. It has since enjoyed one of the highest rates of population growth in the state and is projected to become one of the Commonwealth's most important urban centers in the twenty-first century. State College also symbolizes another kind of potential wealth developing rapidly in the state: the vast leisure economy based on college football and other sporting events.

The State College example reminds us that not all Pennsylvania's cities were in decline, and in many cases shrinkage in the old urban cores was accompanied by expansion in booming suburbs. At least part of the change we are measuring here should be seen as a new kind of urbanism, rather than simply a story of decay. Suburban growth around Philadelphia flourished during the 1950s and has never really ceased. The story is neatly symbolized by the emergence of whole new communities like Levittown, the development begun in 1951–52 in lower Bucks County adjacent to the new Fairless Steel plant. Levittown was the prototype for many similar developments, which were also responding to the powerful demand for new homes for returning war veterans and their growing families. These schemes represented a powerful and expansive vision, and Levittown itself would include more than 17,000 single-family homes. Early writings on the community described it (wrongly) as the first large city in the United States to be preplanned since the creation of Washington, D.C., in the 1790s. Although derided by traditional elites as "little boxes" lacking character or individuality, the compact homes and gardens of Levittown and similar developments represented a utopian dream for couples who had grown up in the cramped traditional neighborhoods of the great cities. The new suburbs became immensely popular.

On the strength of such developments, the population of Bucks County grew by 112 percent between 1950 and 1960, Montgomery County grew by 46 percent, Delaware County by 34 percent, and Chester by 32 percent. Over the century as a whole, the largest increases in regional population occurred in these four counties around Philadelphia, which all form part of the larger Philadelphia Standard Metropolitan Statistical Area (SMSA), which also includes three counties in New Jersey. During the 1990s, Philadelphia proper experienced the sharpest population decline of any county in the nation, losing some 10 percent of its people, but this loss was made up in the surrounding counties of Bucks, Chester, and Montgomery. Consequently, a map of Pennsylvania at the start of the twenty-first century has an intriguing resemblance to the patterns of Franklin's era, in that both wealth and population are disproportionately concentrated in the southeastern corner of the state.

Also doing well in the last quarter of the twentieth century were York, Lancaster, and the urban complexes of Allentown-Bethlehem and Harrisburg-Lebanon-Carlisle. Harrisburg in particular owed its success to the substantial growth of state government from the 1960s onward, and its suburban expansion made neighboring Cumberland County grow at a rate rivaling that of the southeastern region. The populations of Lancaster, York, and Adams Counties all grew by about 8 percent during the 1990s alone.

To some extent, the contraction of urban populations reflected a fundamental shift in the economic role of cities. Cities became centers for financial services and retailing

rather than for industrial manufacturing, and the workers in the new office-blocks chose to commute from the suburbs rather than live in the immediate neighborhood. This development was made possible by the creation in the 1950s and 1960s of what were intended as high-speed access roads, such as Philadelphia's Schuylkill Expressway. However much the "Sure-Kill Crawlway" would be loathed by generations of later users, the road nevertheless represented a minor revolution in urban transportation. Already in 1951 John Gunther reported the opinion that "the automobile has killed Philadelphia by making it easier to flee from," and the escape routes proliferated in the next decade. The move away from the cities was accelerated by the growth of the Internet and other types of rapid electronic communication, which made it easier for people to work at home rather than venturing into the cities at all. Meanwhile, retail functions largely shifted to the suburban shopping malls, which could offer the parking facilities essential for a motorized population.

Across the state the proportion of residents living in downtown central cities declined, while that of the larger metropolitan region grew. In the Harrisburg-Lebanon-Carlisle region, for instance, the central city populations represented 36 percent of the larger region in 1940, but only 16 percent by 1990, a trend made possible only by the completion of local expressways, and especially the Harrisburg beltway. The comparable figures for Philadelphia were 65 percent in the central city in 1940, as against 35 percent for 1990; for Pittsburgh they were 32 percent and 19 percent, respectively.

Encouraging growth outside the old core cities was the development of the interstate system, following the federal Highway Reserve Act of 1956. Though the rail networks once dominated Pennsylvania's communications system, the key east-west axes were now the parallel interstates of I-76, the Turnpike, and the new I-80, which was incidentally one of the great feats of postwar engineering, in view of the very difficult terrain it traverses. I-79 and I-81 similarly serve north-south traffic, while I-476 created a direct route from Chester to Scranton. Access to interstates greatly increased the attraction of hitherto remote rural areas, which now offered locations for commuter dwellings, second homes and vacation homes, or retirement residences. Since the 1970s some of the most dramatic population growth has concentrated in the far northeastern part of the state—in the Pocono region, with its vibrant tourist economy. During the 1990s, Pike County's population grew by about 45 percent, Monroe's population by more than 30 percent, Wayne County's by 15 percent.

A CHANGING RELIGIOUS LANDSCAPE

Population shifts away from the urban cores had wrenching consequences for older neighborhoods, and particularly the ethnic communities that had once regarded those areas as their natural fortresses. Yet as in other aspects of urban development, decline in one sector was compensated for by growth elsewhere. Patterns of religious change offer

TABLE 7.3 RELIGIOUS AFFILIATIONS IN PENNSYLVANIA, 1990

	Number of Adherents (thousands)	Number of Churches
Roman Catholic	3,700	1,854
United Methodist	723	2,568
Evangelical Lutheran (ELCA)	682	1,390
Presbyterian Church (U.S.A.)	389	1,122
United Church of Christ	284	796
"Black Baptist" congregations	215	—
Episcopal	138	403
American Baptist	113	437
Assemblies of God	75	352
Church of the Brethren	57	NA
Mennonite	50	NA
Christian and Missionary Alliance	37	NA
Old Order Amish	31	NA
Evangelical Congregational	30	NA
AME Zion	28	NA
Church of the Nazarene	27	NA
Christian Church/Disciples of Christ	26	NA
Southern Baptist	25	NA
Latter-day Saints	25	NA
Jews	330	NA
Total religious adherents	7,300	

SOURCE: Martin B. Bradley, ed., *Churches and Church Membership in the United States, 1990: An Enumeration by Region, State, and County, Based on Data Reported for 133 Church Groupings* (Atlanta: Glenmary Research Center, 1992).

NOTE: Interpreting data for religious affiliations is notoriously difficult, because different communities employ such very different criteria in defining church membership and loyalties. I have here used the figures for "adherents" rather than for full members, which often appear in other sources. Religions other than Christianity and Judaism are not mentioned, mainly because of the difficulty in ascertaining membership figures. This particularly poses a problem for assessing the Muslim population; estimates of the number of Muslims in America, let alone in any single state, vary enormously.

some notable examples of these bittersweet trends. In Philadelphia proper the number of Catholics contracted by 25 percent between 1980 and 2000, but this decline was almost matched by growing numbers of the faithful in Montgomery, Chester, and Bucks. Church authorities responded by closing and merging downtown churches and schools while transferring resources to the swelling suburbs. This policy naturally ignited controversy among the older city parishes, which often had a close-knit ethnic identity. In the six counties of the Pittsburgh diocese, the number of Catholic parishes fell by one-third during a major reorganization between 1989 and 1994; there were ninety-two ethnic parishes at the start of this reform, and eighteen by its end. Consequently, it became very difficult for older residents to find churches that could offer services in languages like Slovak, reflecting the fragmentation of these once solid communities.

The Catholic experience was closely paralleled by the stories of other religious traditions, mainly Protestant and Jewish, which found new centers of growth in the expanding residential areas (Table 7.3). At first the religious profile of Pennsylvania seems very much what it has been for more than a century—a mixture of several major, long-established religious groups, such as Catholics, Lutherans, Methodists, Presbyterians, and Reformed/United Church of Christ members, among others. In 1990 these five groupings accounted for almost 60 percent of all Pennsylvania church members. But these figures

The continued vitality of religion in Pennsylvania can be seen in the many new evangelical churches that often serve suburban populations, as well as in older urban churches that are now home to new immigrant congregations. Shown here are the Spanish Assembly of God Church (*left*) in Lancaster and the State College Assembly of God Church (*right*).

can be misleading because the mainline Protestant denominations were stagnating or declining, partly for doctrinal reasons, partly through demographics. Also, these churches had in the past defined their efforts so much in terms of the traditional urban geography that they now found themselves saddled with a magnificent range of buildings stranded in the older urban landscape. Meanwhile, newer evangelical, Pentecostal, and fundamentalist religious groups targeted suburban and exurban populations and embarked on major programs of building and expansion. These churches were often successful precisely because they provided a sense of community for people living in the amorphous new housing developments. They have been particularly successful in directing their ministries at groups like children, singles, or the elderly.

For visiting Europeans, who in their own countries are used to seeing churches closed or decaying, one of the most astonishing elements of the American landscape is the number of churches built within the last decade or so, often grandly constructed. Many represent traditional churches—Methodist or Lutheran, for example—but increasingly common are the expanding evangelical denominations, like the Assemblies of God, Church of the Nazarene, and the Christian and Missionary Alliance, or one of the nondenominational community churches. The continued vigor of religious belief and practice represents one of the most potent continuities in Pennsylvania's history, and it shows no sign of diminishing in the new postindustrial society.

REVIVALS

Cities differed in how they responded to their changing economic roles. One great success story was Pittsburgh during its so-called urban Renaissance of the 1950s and 1960s, and the even more extensive "Renaissance II" of the 1980s. And though the central city lost a large share of its population, it also became a far cleaner and healthier community, finally free of the smoke and pollution that had made it one of the nation's most notoriously ugly and unhealthful major cities. Outside the center city, sections like Oakland, Shadyside, and Squirrel Hill became models of livable, cosmopolitan urban communities, with enviable access to cultural facilities. Some farsighted developments restored and made use of the city's plethora of old industrial facilities, with successful developments like the Station Square mall complex. By the 1980s Pittsburgh residents were trumpeting the findings of a Rand McNally survey that had anointed the city as the nation's "most livable." The classification would have amazed even the most enthusiastic civic boosters of an earlier generation, for whom Pittsburgh was prosperous, to be sure, but scarcely livable.

The Mummers Parade, starting from "Two Street" in South Philadelphia, became a Philadelphia New Year's Day tradition during the twentieth century, especially after World War II, when the costumes and productions became more spectacular and radio and television broadcasts dramatically enlarged the audience. The Mummers marched down Broad Street, as shown in this 1955 photograph of the Crescentville String Band, and strutted their stuff to appreciative crowds along the way and judges on the reviewing stand. The various clubs competing in the different divisions—string band, comic, and fancy brigades—kept alive ethnic and neighborhood ties in their membership and interests, which was part of their appeal in an age of growing anonymity.

In Philadelphia too, years of progressive decay from the 1960s through the early 1980s were finally reversed—with the success of massive gentrification, initially in Society Hill but later in many other areas, like the streets around Rittenhouse Square, in Queen Village, and Fairmount. Though the process was not without its critics, gentrification ensured that many of the nation's most historically and architecturally valuable streets would be preserved as thriving concerns, and that the central city region would not turn into the ghost town it had once threatened to become. "Gentrified" homes implied upscale stores and restaurants, as well as politically powerful and savvy communities that could not lightly be ignored when they demanded improvements in city services and police protection. In terms of urban history, the process saved the deeply humane institution of the "walking city." In the 1980s and 1990s, Philadelphia experienced a major spate of downtown building, particularly along Market Street, which often made ingenious use of historic buildings and storefronts. There was, however, controversy about the new skyscrapers that violated the traditional rule against building anything higher than the hat of the William Penn statue atop City Hall.

Neatly encapsulating the change in the Philadelphia's economic life was the fate of the magnificent old Reading Terminal building, which had symbolized the overwhelming

THE LAST OF THE PROGRESSIVES:
DAVID LAWRENCE

David Lawrence was a key figure in the political history of twentieth-century Pennsylvania who helped carry the ideals of the Progressive era and the New Deal into the second half of the century. He was part of the first generation of Democrats to dominate Pittsburgh after the electoral revolution of 1936, and he represented the Irish Catholic constituency that came to power through the revived Democratic organization.

Lawrence was born in Pittsburgh in 1889, in the tight-knit Irish neighborhood of "the Point." He rose through the Democratic Party, of which he became state chairman in 1934, and served as mayor of Pittsburgh from 1945 to 1959. His tenure as mayor was uniquely important for a city trying to deal with the ravages of unchecked industrialization, in terms of poor housing stock and dreadful pollution of air and water; it was described in 1944 as "the dirtiest pile of slag in the United States." Moreover, many of the industries on which the region's prosperity depended were entering a period of crisis.

With the powerful support of Richard King Mellon, Mayor Lawrence presided over the so-called Pittsburgh Renaissance project, which left its monuments in the Gateway Center, Mellon Square, and many new skyscrapers and culminated in the U.S. Steel Building of 1971. The aptly named Golden Triangle became an economic powerhouse well placed for the postindustrial age. Pittsburgh also acquired a new airport in 1951 and gained a crucial highway link to the Pennsylvania Turnpike. In the same years, the Lawrence regime declared war on smoke pollution and what had been the city's recurrent flood problem.

In many ways, what Lawrence helped achieve in the 1950s was what the Progres-sive reformers had been envisioning since the opening years of the century. Ironically, though, much of what he achieved was accomplished using the classic methods of an urban political boss, a type of authority he affected to despise. (Suspicious of these tendencies, Gifford Pinchot had once written: "There are times when Dave Lawrence / Fills me with abhawrence.")

In 1958 Lawrence became the first Catholic to sit in the governor's mansion, and within the Democratic Party he played a kingmaking role in the 1960 presidential campaign. In Pennsylvania his administration was as efficient and as fiscally responsible as the Pittsburgh years might have suggested, and his governorship was admirably scandal-free. However, reflecting the state's growing industrial crisis, much of his efforts focused on securing new sources of federal aid for the state's depressed and deindustrializing areas. At the time of his death in 1966 he held an elder-statesman role in Pennsylvania.

ABOVE: Governor David L. Lawrence beams while holding an issue of the *Pittsburgh Post-Gazette* proclaiming his hometown team, the Pirates, winners of the 1960 World Series.

Pittsburgh's "Point" under construction in 1951 (*top*), and a futuristic view of Pittsburgh by the *Pittsburgh Press* in 1959 (*bottom*). The remaking of "The Point" in Pittsburgh during the 1950s heralded the Pittsburgh Renaissance that transformed the Steel City's smoky, gritty downtown, parts of which are shown being demolished in this 1951 photo, into a modern corporate center of gleaming steel skyscrapers—the model for the city of the future as imagined by this 1959 front page.

The Pittsburgh Press

TWO CENTURIES OF PROGRESS · SUNDAY, JANUARY 18, 1959 · SECTION FOUR · BICENTENNIAL ISSUE

Next 200 Years... Renaissance To Quadricentennial

The annual Farm Show in Harrisburg is the largest of many agricultural expos held throughout Pennsylvania each year. With their competitions, displays of farm goods and animals, and sheer pageantry, these shows proclaim the continued vitality of agriculture.

power of the rail companies and was now handsomely restored. It was incorporated into the new Convention Center—a substantial investment that attracted much-needed tourist and convention business to the city. On a smaller scale, just as successful in re-creating a whole urban environment, is the Head House Square area, a highly effective use of eighteenth-century structures. Farther from the traditional center, moreover, a successful revival was in progress in what was once the industrial area of Manayunk. For older residents, the thought that Manayunk might be home to upmarket boutiques and chic restaurants was as amazing as the notion that Pittsburgh might ever be extolled for its "livable" conditions. The Philadelphia revival was symbolized by the city's achievement in becoming the venue for the 2000 Republican National Convention, which was all the more striking in view of the city's Democratic politics.

One sign of growth both in and around cities was the state's growing ethnic diversity, which reflected new waves of immigration. For most of the twentieth century the state had been characterized by a basic division between black and white residents, with very few "others"—Asians, Hispanics, or Native Americans. The turning point here was the Immigration Act of 1965, which removed the traditional obstacles placed in the way of migrants from Africa and Asia, and easier transportation from Latin America. By the year 2000 Pennsylvania's population was 86 percent white and 10 percent black, but 1.8 percent of residents were recorded as "Asian," and 3.2 percent were Latino or Hispanic, terms that can refer to either whites or blacks. "Other" categories made up about one percent. These figures suggest that Asians, Latinos, and others made up a total of only 5 percent—barely 600,000 people—though other estimates suggest considerably higher figures, particularly for Latinos. Whatever the reality, there is no question that these newer categories are growing rapidly and already exercise considerable influence in the major urban areas, particularly in cities like Philadelphia, Reading, Allentown, and Lancaster. Though Hispanic voters have historically been underrepresented in the formal political process, their significance is likely to grow in the near future. These groups have a far younger demographic profile than the state's white mainstream, and thus have a higher birth rate. As in each preceding generation, new voices will continue to make themselves heard in Pennsylvania's streets and workplaces.

AGRICULTURE

Pennsylvania's prosperity should not be seen entirely in urban terms. The Commonwealth has always had a rich agricultural foundation, which tends to be neglected in many popular accounts of the state when set beside the (once) more exciting stories of coal and steel. The proportion of land devoted to farming has declined, from some 14 million acres in 1950 to about 7.2 million at the end of the twentieth century, which represents roughly a drop from 50 percent of the state's total area to just 25 percent; in the same period, the number of farms fell from 147,000 to 46,000. Even so, Pennsylvania in the year 2000 had 5 million acres of harvested cropland, in addition to 2 million more in farm woodlands and pastures. Also, the decline in the absolute number of farms has been accompanied by a steady growth in farm size, from an average of 96 acres in 1950 to about 150 at the end of the century. Perhaps as many as 800,000 Pennsylvanians depend directly or indirectly on agriculture. Much of the best agricultural land is found in the south-central region, from Lehigh and Chester Counties in the east through Franklin and Cumberland in the west. That includes the counties slowest to lose farmland; counties such as Lancaster, York, Chester, and Berks are among the most important farming areas. The state Farm Show, held annually in

The Pocono vacation industry successfully reinvented itself in the latter decades of the twentieth century. As most of the old hotels closed, new "super resorts" stepped in to offer vacationers a full range of entertainment opportunities, including winter sports (thanks to the invention of artificial snow), golf, and nightclubs. Meanwhile, the honeymoon hotels of the postwar era gave way to so-called couples resorts that catered to unmarried and married guests alike. The "Champagne Glass Whirlpool Bath for Two," shown here, and the heart-shaped bathtub are both Pocono inventions.

Harrisburg, continues to be one of the great social events of the year for many Pennsylvanians.

Over the twentieth century, Pennsylvania agriculture experienced a shift from general farming to more specialized production. The state's farming wealth is particularly strong in areas like dairy-farming, which accounts for some 39 percent of total farm sales; Pennsylvania ranks one-fourth in the nation in dairy production. Other major sectors in the last quarter of the century included poultry (16 percent of sales) as well as cattle and calves (10 percent), nursery and greenhouse products (9 percent), and grains (8 percent). Much of this success has been based on exploiting new technologies, such as greater use of truck transportation, and improved fertilizers. Growth has been supported by close working relationships with academic programs in agriculture and agronomy—at Penn State University, for example.

The very success of Pennsylvania agriculture has intensified conflicts with other demands on the state's lands. During the great age of heavy industry, the chief complaint of the farming interest was that the mines and mills caused pollution that blighted the land, but in the last quarter of the twentieth century new and quite different conflicts emerged over the fate of that land itself. Across the state, land was much sought after, for new shopping malls and industrial parks, for suburban housing developments—and often for the retirement villages to house one of the new categories of migrants entering Pennsylvania. As the land is a finite resource, these additional demands led to soaring prices for land in some of the most desirable agricultural regions—in Lancaster County but also across much of the southern and central parts of the state. The enduring conflict over land use and "sprawl" is not one that can be resolved to the satisfaction of all parties, but the best that can be said is that it is clearly one of the consequences of success and growth. In the 1990s conservationists' efforts to save farm and other land from urban development, and planners' desire to limit "sprawl," led to a new political consciousness that in the year 2000 made possible the passage of one of the nation's most comprehensive land-development bills.

REINVENTING PENNSYLVANIA

Among the state's thriving industries in the late twentieth century was assuredly tourism, which already by the late 1960s had emerged as one of the state's largest industries and which would gain importance as the old heavy industries dissipated. However,

Independence Hall in the late 1940s (*top*) and again in 1957 (*bottom*). "Freeing" Independence Hall from its urban context became a goal of city planners in the 1950s, who envisioned a new public stage and a more inviting setting to show off the national symbol and promote cultural tourism. In the "urban renewal" phase of city planning during the 1950s and 1960s, many old buildings fell to the wrecking ball in an effort to create a broad vista. Today the mall in front of Independence Hall is again being recast to accommodate the new Constitution Center, a reminder that though the documents written by the founding fathers at Independence Hall might be enduring, cityscapes are not.

CORNPLANTER

Pennsylvania is unusual among eastern states in that it has no Indian reservation land. The last significant piece of Native American territory was the Cornplanter Grant, a small stretch on the west bank of the Allegheny along the New York State border. Named for the Seneca war-chief Cornplanter, the land was granted by the Pennsylvania legislature in 1791 in order to foster Cornplanter's friendship, and in 1794 Cornplanter played a critical role in securing a peace treaty with the United States.

The Cornplanter Grant, with its school and Presbyterian church, survived into the twentieth century, but most residents had moved away to larger reservations in New York State, leaving only a tiny Indian presence in Pennsylvania (most of the Delawares had long since moved to Oklahoma). By the late 1950s the Seneca lands were sought for the new federally funded Kinzua Dam, although taking the property meant revoking the Pickering Treaty of 1794, which had been signed by the administration of George Washington himself. The proposal was criticized as yet another trampling of Indian rights, and critic Edmund Wilson complained of "a particularly costly contrivance intended to serve the interests of a group of industrialists in Pittsburgh." (This was unfair, in that the dam did have sound motives in offering Pittsburgh vital protection from the seemingly endless danger of flooding.) Even Johnny Cash protested the scheme in a song that asked, "Cornplanter, can you swim?"

Nevertheless, the federal courts determined that treaty rights did not give Native Americans any immunity from the principle of eminent domain. Pennsylvania authorities agreed that the needs of modern urban communities far outweighed those of a people who were viewed only as relics of a distant age. The federal government appropriated $15 million to relocate the Senecas, and their lands were duly flooded. The dam opened in 1966. The cemetery, including the grave of Cornplanter, was moved to dry land.

ABOVE: Cornplanter mosaic in Heritage Park, Warren.

The Little League Baseball World Series, played annually in Williamsport, pumped money and enthusiasm into the once-dying former lumber capital of Pennsylvania. Little League became big business as crowds swelled and television brought the event to a worldwide audience. The growth and popularity of Little League baseball in the postwar era was due in large part to the population shift to the suburbs, where organized sporting activities for youths replaced the pickup-game sporting culture of urban life. Here Umpire-in-Chief Frank Rizzo works during a Little League World Series game in the early 1960s.

the soaring popularity of tourism deserves special consideration because of the questions it raises about the state's changing identity and self-image, and the ways in which an often troubled past is presented as a saleable commodity.

Tourism as such was scarcely a novelty. The discovery of the Pennsylvania German country dated back to the beginning of the century, and Philadelphia had long treasured, and even traded on, the monuments marking the birth of the American nation, above all Independence Hall and the Liberty Bell. Nevertheless, rather like the natural environment, historical monuments were to be preserved only as long as they did not stand in the way of economic development. As late as 1965 the area's rich historical connotations could not save the Cornplanter Grant, the last and most evocative link with the Commonwealth's Native American heritage. On a smaller scale, mid-century urban redevelopment across the state had rooted out much of the best Victorian architecture with no thought that it might be worth preserving, often to replace the older streetscapes with soulless car-parks.

In the mid-twentieth century, tourism became very big business, especially with the exploitation of the Amish in Lancaster County. The further city-dwellers drifted from

Filming a scene for the movie *Gettysburg* in 1992 on the grounds of Gettysburg Seminary. Director Ronald F. Maxwell based the movie on Michael Shaara's best-selling 1974 novel, *The Killer Angels.* Aggressive marketing of Pennsylvania as a venue for filmmaking has increased the number and variety of movies shot in the state and served to promote tourism.

any sense of rural roots, the more fascinating they found the Amish. Material goods that were commonplace in earlier eras were now reclassified as antiques, often of considerable value, that became the prized targets of forays by city-dwellers. Pennsylvania enjoyed particular success in repackaging its colonial sites for tourist consumption. Both Ephrata Cloister and the Hopewell iron furnaces are models of successful display and interpretation, and both gain much of their appeal by their evocation of an earlier and simpler America. The potential for tourist growth was all the greater given the easy proximity to the major population centers of the East Coast, and the development of the interstate highways. The same factors inspired other entrepreneurs to develop outlet malls, which attracted so much wealth to regions like Berks County. Now visitors could seamlessly combine their explorations of rural simplicity with the opportunity to make major consumer purchases.

Other parts of the state hoped to profit by presenting a historical ambience similar to that which had been so stunningly successful in the case of the Amish, and often the history on offer exploited events that at the time had been regarded as anything but picturesque. In the anthracite country, for instance, the affair of the Molly Maguires had left enduring bitter memories and ethnic divisions, but by the 1970s the story was retold as a heroic saga—and (ideally) an irresistible draw for tourists. The turning point was

the 1970 film *The Molly Maguires*, which laid the foundation for the emerging tourist sites at Eckley Miners' Village and in the community of Jim Thorpe. The county jail in which several Mollies were executed in 1877 was reopened as "The Old Jail Museum," which attracted more than 25,000 visitors in its first two years of operation. By the 1990s the Molly Maguire case had become the subject of historical reenactments, initially by local lawyers and antiquarians, and in 1998 the borough of Tamaqua dramatically reenacted the executions as part of the region's new "Molly Maguire Weekend."

If the idea of turning the terrorism of the Molly Maguires into romantic drama seemed bizarre, it was scarcely less surprising than the effort to appropriate the Johnstown Flood, that bloody monument to corporate greed and official malfeasance. The centenary of that catastrophe in 1989 was greeted with a striking public relations push and a major documentary film that attracted local rancor because it was seen as

America's love affair with railroads, especially "the Pennsy," has made sites like Altoona's famed Horseshoe Curve popular tourist attractions. This photograph was taken during a 1957 ceremony when PRR class K4 steam locomotive no. 1361 was placed on display at the Horseshoe Curve trackside park.

The city of Scranton has been particularly creative in marketing its coal heritage to tourists. Adjacent to the Pennsylvania Anthracite Heritage Museum, the Lackawanna Coal Mine Tour Company advertises its tours of the Lackawanna Coal Mine using this larger-than-life miner.

excessively gruesome in dwelling on the huge number of deaths. One day, Three Mile Island might acquire a similarly romantic cachet, perhaps with periodic reenactments of the disaster.

These major historical monuments represented the tip of a very large iceberg, as communities across the state tried to transform the detritus of the fading industrial society into commodified history for a newer postindustrial age. Promoters of tourism were realizing the potential of "industrial archaeology," a phrase that would have seemed almost comical to the entrepreneurs and workers who had originally developed these industries years before. In Altoona, a town overwhelmed by industrial contraction, hopes were pinned on the continued popular fascination with the railroads, an interest that grew as rapidly as the actual possibility of riding on trains diminished. The area cultivated the spectacular Horseshoe Curve, while a Railroaders' Memorial Museum was available in the city itself.

By the 1980s, sites from the industrial past were a major portion of the places commemorated in the Pennsylvania Trail of History—the sites and properties operated by the state's Historical and Museum Commission—a clear statement that Pennsylvania's past should no longer be viewed solely in terms of colonial glories and founding fathers. One of the more adventurous of such schemes involved the creation in 1989 of the State Heritage Parks, regional ensembles of sites that offered the opportunity to study industrial development in its wider geographical context, and permitting the visitor to understand the interdependence of industries and transportation facilities. Among the regions so far designated are the Allegheny Ridge Park, which focuses on the iron, steel, coal, rail, and canal industries of Blair, Cambria, and Somerset Counties, and the Lincoln Highway Heritage Corridor, which commemorates the nation's first transcontinental highway, the present Route 30. Such schemes were not confined to what were traditionally regarded as the industrial heartlands of the Commonwealth. Some important tourist development occurred in what is known as the Northern Tier, where the lumber industry was commemorated in a new museum in Potter County. In the nineteenth century, lumber had been one of the state's major enterprises, but as that industry faded, the trees returned, to re-create a new and greener Pennsylvania—which the uninformed wrongly took to be pristine wilderness. The boundary between industrial and "wilderness" tourism is not as firm as it may appear.

The marketing of industrial history was at its most ambitious in the northeastern anthracite country—inevitably perhaps given the region's modern-day economic plight. In a curious reversal of the state's past economic geography, the anthracite country now hoped to benefit by pulling in tourists from the flourishing tourist heartland of the Poconos. By the 1990s, tourists could re-create the wider world of the Molly Maguires by visiting sites like the Pennsylvania Anthracite Heritage Museum, and the adjacent Lackawanna Coal Mine, which offers tours of a coal mine that had closed for active operations in 1966. The tours are led by a former miner, a type that presumably will

Edmund M. Ashe, *Steel*, 1942. Ashe, who taught painting at the Carnegie Institute of Technology in the 1920s and 1930s, was one of many artists drawn to Pennsylvania's industrial might. This work and the three that follow are part of Penn State University's Steidle Collection in the College of Earth and Mineral Sciences, among the world's largest collections of art devoted to mining and industry.

ABOVE: Alan Thompson, *Company Row*, 1941.

RIGHT: Christian J. Walter, *Pittsburgh*, c. 1937.

Aaron Henry Gorson, *Pushing Coke from By-Product Oven*, n.d.

N. C. Wyeth, *Nightfall*, 1945. Wyeth, a world-famous member of the Brandywine "school" of artists and illustrators, presented the farmer as noble in character in this pastoral scene from southeastern Pennsylvania.

Dorothy Lauer Davids, *Duke Street Market*, c. 1944. Though she settled in Greensburg, Pennsylvania, in 1926 and lived there for the better part of her life, Davids found a kind of community in the daily personal exchanges of her native York, which she depicts in her painting of the Duke Street Market. The Market still operates today.

ABOVE: Horace Pippin, *Domino Players*, 1943.
Many of Pippin's paintings capture the daily
lives of blacks living in his native town of West
Chester in the mid-1930s.

LEFT: Francis Speight, *Beneath the Tracks,
Manayunk*, 1951.

Andrew Wyeth, *Tenant Farmer,* 1961. Wyeth,
a master of American realism, captures a scene
common throughout much of rural Pennsylvania during hunting season.

Story Quilt: Yo Blood Line, a quilt by Tina Williams Brewer, 1996. A Pittsburgh native, Brewer is noted for her contemporary story quilts, which draw richly on African symbolism to illuminate American history. Brewer is one of many Pennsylvanians who continue the commonwealth's rich tradition of quilting.

RIGHT: Jack Savitsky, *The William Penn Treaty*, 1982. A modern interpretation of Benjamin West's classic image, by Jack Savitsky, Pennsylvania's "primitive pop artist" of Carbon County.

BELOW *(from left to right)*: A sampling of Pennsylvania products: Mazza Vineyards, North East ■ Pfaltzgraff (The Pfaltzgraff Company), York ■ Martin Guitar (C. F. Martin & Co. Inc.), Nazareth ■ Slinky (James Industries), Hollidaysburg ■ Mr. Rogers Trolley (Holgate Toys), Kane ■ Berks Bologna (Berks Products), Reading ■ Boyd's Bears (The Boyd's Collection), Gettysburg ■ Crayola Crayons (Binney & Smith), Easton ■ Wos Wit Chow Chow (Grouse Hunt Farms), Tamaqua ■ Lucky Leaf Applesauce (Knouse Foods), Peach Glen ■ Heinz 57 Sauce (H. J. Heinz Company), Pittsburgh ■ Hershey bar (Hershey Foods), Hershey ■ Philadelphia Cream Cheese (Kraft), Allentown ■ Peeps (Just Born Inc.), Bethlehem ■ Wilbur Buds (Wilbur Chocolate Co.), Lititz ■ Mrs.T's Perogies (Ateeco), Shenandoah ■ Woolrich Stag Jacket (Woolrich, Inc.), Woolrich ■ Utz Potato Chips (Utz Quality Foods), Hanover ■ University Creamery Ice Cream (Penn State University), University Park ■ Iron City Beer (Pittsburgh Brewing Company), Pittsburgh ■ Yuengling Beer (Yuengling Brewery), Pottsville ■ Wilton Armetale, Mount Joy.

A coal barge shares the *Monongahela* with recreational boaters near Homestead. In years past, barges like this would have been a common sight, hauling the coal that fired Homestead's steel furnaces. Today barely a trace of the mills can be seen beyond the retail sprawl that dominates the shoreline, while the occasional barge delivers coal to power plants downstream.

soon be viewed as an exotic species. Visitors can also take in the houses of the coal-company owners and industrialists, such as the Asa Packer mansion in Jim Thorpe (the former Mauch Chunk). The residences of both the very rich and the working class are included in tours, but without much sense of the gulfs that separated the two classes in the past, divisions that were in fact often marked by profound suspicion and hostility. In the Scranton area, industrial facilities now redefined as historical monuments included the city's old iron furnaces, and a collection of rail memorabilia gathered in a national historical site advertised as "Steamtown USA," which incidentally makes excellent use of an impressive old roundhouse.

Collectively, these sites recalled what the tourist leaflets boasted as "Northeastern Pennsylvania's Industrial Golden Age." This "proud heritage" was evoked by "the heavy tools of an anthracite miner, railroad cars heaped with black diamonds, the humming textile mills, the patch homes of the miners and their families." Though it is in many ways a glorious story, a truly proud heritage, the epoch of Pennsylvania's industrial triumphs includes many moments of grief and horror that can be romanticized only by generations for whom the industrial past has become an utterly foreign country, another world.

Beers, Paul B. *Pennsylvania Politics Today and Yesterday.* University Park: The Pennsylvania State University Press, 1980.

Binzen, Peter. *Whitetown, U.S.A.* New York: Vintage Books, 1970.

Bowser, Charles. *Let the Bunker Burn: The Final Battle with MOVE.* Philadelphia: Camino Books, 1989.

Del Tredici, Robert. *The People of Three Mile Island.* San Francisco: Sierra Club Books, 1980.

Dublin, Thomas. *When the Mines Closed: Stories of Struggles in Hard Times.* Ithaca: Cornell University Press, 1998.

Ershkowitz, Miriam, and Joseph Zikmund, eds. *Black Politics in Philadelphia.* New York: Basic Books, 1973.

Ford, Daniel F. *Three Mile Island: Thirty Minutes to Meltdown.* New York: Viking Press, 1982.

Glasker, Wayne C. *Black Students in the Ivory Tower: African American Student Activism at the University of Pennsylvania, 1967–1990.* Amherst: University of Massachusetts Press, 2002.

Graham, Laurie. *Singing the City: The Bonds of Home in an Industrial Landscape.* Pittsburgh: University of Pittsburgh Press, 1998.

Hinshaw, John H. *Steel and Steelworkers: Race and Class Struggle in Twentieth-Century Pittsburgh.* Albany: State University of New York Press, 2002.

Hoerr, John P. *And the Wolf Finally Came: The Decline of the American Steel Industry.* Pittsburgh: University of Pittsburgh Press, 1988.

Jenkins, Philip. *The Cold War at Home: The Red Scare in Pennsylvania, 1945–1960.* Chapel Hill: University of North Carolina Press, 1999.

Labovitz, Sherman. *Being Red in Philadelphia.* Philadelphia: Camino Books, 1998.

Leab, Daniel J. *I Was a Communist for the F.B.I.: The Unhappy Life and Times of Matt Cvetic.* University Park: The Pennsylvania State University Press, 2000.

Lubove, Roy. *Twentieth-Century Pittsburgh: The Post-Steel Era.* Pittsburgh: University of Pittsburgh Press, 1996.

Luconi, Stefano. *From Paesani to White Ethnics: The Italian Experience in Philadelphia.* Albany: State University of New York Press, 2001.

Michener, James. *Report of the County Chairman.* New York: Random House, 1961.

Millennium Philadelphia: The Last 100 Years. Philadelphia: Camino Books, 1999.

Modell, Judith, and Charlee Brodsky. *A Town Without Steel: Envisioning Homestead.* Pittsburgh: University of Pittsburgh Press, 1998.

Nelson, Steve, James R. Barrett, and Rob Ruck. *Steve Nelson: American Radical.* Pittsburgh: University of Pittsburgh Press, 1981.

Paolantonio, S. A. *Frank Rizzo.* Philadelphia: Camino Books, 1993.

Popenoe, David. *The Suburban Environment.* Chicago: University of Chicago Press, 1977.

Schafer, Jim, and Mike Sajna. *The Allegheny River.* University Park: The Pennsylvania State University Press, 1992.

Serrin, William. *Homestead.* New York: Times Books, 1992.

Smith, W. Eugene, and Sam Stephenson, eds. *Dream Street: W. Eugene Smith's Pittsburgh Project, 1955–1958.* W. W. Norton, 2001.

Stein, Marc. *City of Sisterly and Brotherly Loves: Lesbian and Gay Philadelphia, 1945–1972.* Chicago: University of Chicago Press, 2000.

Stranahan, Susan Q. *Susquehanna—River of Dreams.* Baltimore: Johns Hopkins University Press, 1993.

Testa, Randy-Michael. *After the Fire: The Destruction of the Lancaster County Amish.* Hanover, N.H.: University Press of New England, 1993.

Toker, Franklin. *Pittsburgh.* University Park: The Pennsylvania State University Press, 1986.

Weber, Michael P. *Don't Call Me Boss.* Pittsburgh: University of Pittsburgh Press, 1988.

Wolensky, Robert P., Kenneth C. Wolensky, and Nicole H. Wolensky. *The Knox Mine Disaster, January 22, 1959: The Final Years of the Northern Anthracite Industry and the Effort to Rebuild a Regional Economy.* Harrisburg: Pennsylvania Historical and Museum Commission, 1999.

Wolf, George D. *William Warren Scranton.* University Park: The Pennsylvania State University Press, 1981.

The Making and Unmaking of the Pennsylvanian Empire

MICHAEL ZUCKERMAN

Their very names once defined the American dream. William Penn, who proclaimed religious liberty throughout his lands. Benjamin Franklin, who first told America's rags-to-riches story of self-made success. Tom Paine, who stirred its revolutionary Spirit of '76. Daniel Boone, who incarnated its westering ways. And those whose fortunes won them fame, like Stephen Girard, the nation's first celebrity millionaire; Nicholas Biddle, its most brilliant banker; Tom Scott, its first great corporate executive; and Andrew Carnegie, its greatest industrial genius. And those whose ideas and style gained them renown, like Edwin Forrest, the country's foremost Shakespearean actor; William Sellers, its most influential rationalist of industrial standardization; Henry George, its most original economic thinker; and Frederick Taylor, its theorist of workplace efficiency whose studies led the world to call the American system of mass production "Taylorism."

The roster went on and on. Merchant princes and robber barons, philosopher kings and political kingmakers and natural noblemen. William Bartram and Thaddeus Stevens. Benjamin Rush and "Pig Iron" Kelley. Charles Willson Peale and Lucretia Mott and Terence Powderly. Richard Allen and Edgar Allan Poe and Henry Clay Frick. Oliver Evans and Sarah Grimké and Thomas Eakins. Matthias Baldwin and David Wilmot and John Roebling and John Wanamaker. James Forten and Simon Cameron and Eadweard Muybridge and George Westinghouse. They innovated and dominated American commerce, industry, and finance. They shaped American science, technology, and culture.

They took the lead at the republic's every crisis. (Robert Morris financed the Revolution, Girard financed the War of 1812, and Jay Cooke financed the Civil War.) And more than all that, they—and legions like them—captured the country's imagination.

There are no Pennsylvanians of such eminence any more, and there have not been for years. The most distinguished son of the Commonwealth in the last half-century—athletes and entertainers aside—is probably Walter Annenberg. Despite his extraordinary accomplishments in the media and in philanthropy, his name is unknown to most Americans. The most famous—or, at any rate the most notorious—Pennsylvanian of the period is probably Philadelphia's Mayor Frank Rizzo. A recent survey of experts on municipal governance voted him one of the five worst mayors in all American history.

As with persons, so with places and things. In the years of the young republic, Pennsylvania provided the shrines of American nationhood. Independence Hall was, twice over, the birthplace of the United States. Valley Forge was the place of its testing, and Gettysburg was the place of the nation's preservation and reconsecration. In the late twentieth century the Commonwealth's contributions to the country's imagination of itself were primarily its vistas of devastation. The grim smokestacks and silent factories of the Monongahela Valley stood as the preeminent symbols of the national plague of deindustrialization. The stark chimneys of Three Mile Island emblemized the national disenchantment with technology. Until Chernobyl's explosion trumped TMI's near miss, Pennsylvania's greatest—and almost only—claim to world notice was the motto that popped up around the planet: "We all live in Pennsylvania."

To the end of the nineteenth century, the Commonwealth gave America the icons that bespoke its soul, such as the log cabin, the Conestoga wagon, and the Kentucky rifle, as it gave the nation the sinews that were its substance, like the first of its banks and insurance companies, the greatest of its railroads, the vast preponderance of its coal and iron and steel. At the end of the twentieth century, Pennsylvania led the nation in the production of mushrooms.

Just a century ago the astute Henry Adams "summed up the results of Pennsylvania influences" on American development. He "inclined to think that Pennsylvania set up the government in 1789; saved it in 1861; created the American system; developed its iron and coal power; and invented its great railways. . . . The Pennsylvania mind . . . was not complex; . . . but in practical matters it was the steadiest of all American types; perhaps the most efficient; certainly the safest." Who would say anything of the sort any more? A few years ago, the equally astute James Carville summed up what he learned in grueling political campaigns in the state. Without meaning to flatter Alabama, he said that Pennsylvania was Philadelphia at one end, Pittsburgh at the other, and Alabama in between.

In the twentieth century, Pennsylvania simply ceased to be the place it had been in the centuries before. From its founding, William Penn's province had been the fastest-growing colony in the New World. By the time of the Revolution, only Virginia could rival it, and Virginia was almost twice as old. Virginia had no city remotely to compare with Philadelphia, the biggest and richest port in British North America. And not even Virginia had agriculture as sophisticated, industry as advanced, or culture as cosmopolitan as Pennsylvania's.

It was no accident that the rebels made their revolution in Pennsylvania or that the young republic made its capital there. Pennsylvania was economically, politically, and militarily vital to the success of the Revolution and of the infant republic. More than that, it was the one place where delegates from all the diverse regions of the land could feel comfortable, or at least accepted. Penn's promotion of a robust religious, ethnic, and racial pluralism provided a legacy that lasted for generations.

There was symbolic significance in the fact that in 1776 Pennsylvania was the only place in the British colonies where Catholics could celebrate Mass openly. There was real practical significance in the fact that it was the epicenter of American Protestantism. All the religious groups of consequence in the colonies but the Anglicans and Congregationalists had their organizational center in Pennsylvania. Several had the larger part of their adherents in the province as well. Pennsylvania was the cockpit of colonial Baptists, Lutherans, Methodists, Presbyterians, Quakers, and Reformed. It was also the home of a host of radical sects—Amish, Dunkards, Mennonites, Moravians, and many more, and their still more radical offshoots, such as the Woman in the Wilderness and the Ephrata Cloister—which were unknown in most other colonies. After independence, the Commonwealth became the birthplace of American Episcopalianism and Unitarianism, and of every early independent African American denomination besides.

No state would ever again hold such a commanding place in the religious life of the land, or in its political, economic, and intellectual life either. But Pennsylvania did not slip from that pinnacle because it was in decline in the nineteenth century. On the contrary, it grew mightily, in population and in wealth. And its growth was indispensable to the growth of the nation.

In the seventeenth century the revolution that mattered most in the Western world was the religious revolution. New notions of religious freedom emerged, now here, now there, but nowhere else in the world as powerfully, as pervasively, and as prophetically as in Pennsylvania.

In the eighteenth century the decisive revolution was the democratic revolution. New ideas of popular participation in government appeared, now here, now there, but nowhere else in the world did they appear as resoundingly and as lastingly as in Pennsylvania.

In the nineteenth century, the revolution that shaped other revolutions was the industrial revolution. New sources of power and new forms of production and exchange developed, now here, now there, now everywhere, but nowhere else in the United States did they develop as intensively and extensively as in Pennsylvania. And nowhere was the Commonwealth's domination more decisive than in coal and iron.

All through the nineteenth century, Pennsylvania dominated American manufacture of glass, leather, machinery, railroad products, chemicals, oil, and natural gas. Off and on, it also led in shipbuilding, textiles, insurance, banking, cement, timber and wood products, and agriculture. All of that mattered. All of that made Pennsylvania, in all likelihood, the most prosperous state in the Union. But none of it mattered as coal and iron mattered. Coal and iron were prerequisite to national greatness in the nineteenth century. Countries that had coal and iron ruled the world. And the United States had them because Pennsylvania did. The Commonwealth had the vast preponderance of the nation's coal and, well into the century, of its known iron ore. Without Pennsylvania, industrialization in America would have been far more halting than it was, and the national economy might well have remained primarily agricultural.

All this was extraordinary. Pennsylvania was nearly the last of the original thirteen colonies to be established. Many, like New York, Massachusetts, Maryland, Connecticut, and Rhode Island, were founded fifty years before Charles II granted Penn his Woods. Virginia began fully three-quarters of a century earlier. The Quaker colony was a tiny outpost on the edge of the wilderness. And yet this marchland mote in the eye of the Old World mattered as none of England's older, better-established provinces did to the destiny of the West. From the first and for generations, it led Europe in much that was most momentous for European civilization. It forecast, if it did not cast, the shape of life in the Western world in centuries to come.

Willliam Penn himself made it all possible. He inaugurated a regime of religious toleration and pluralism—of separation of church and state—that had barely been imagined elsewhere. He promoted a polity of deliberate democracy that was inconceivable at home, a society of ethnic multiplicity that was unrivaled even in the New World, and a policy of multiracial amity with the Indians that was unique in Anglo-America and that endured for decades after his first treaties.

The Quakers who came with Penn and after him made actual what he made possible. They reformed the brutal criminal code of England, with its proliferative capital punishments, and instituted the most humane system of justice in all of Christendom; by the end of the eighteenth century, Pennsylvania allowed a death sentence only for first-degree murder. They accorded women positions of influence and leadership—even over men—that were unknown and almost unimagined in Europe and among other Euro-Americans; by the turn of the nineteenth century, most of the women who led the movement for woman's rights in the New World were Quakers or had been influenced by Quakers. They insisted that none who owned or traded slaves could continue as members of the Meeting at a time when few others even considered the commodification of Africans problematic; in 1780 they made Pennsylvania the first state in the world to pronounce the institution of slavery peculiar and to legislate its demise.

The fame of this remarkable little settlement ran far out of proportion to its numbers or its economic or military prowess. Pennsylvania was, to the commoners of Europe, "the best poor man's country" in the world. It was, to the elites of England and the Continent, something more. Voltaire and the philosophes hoped that Europe might one day emulate the Quaker colony. Abbé Raynal exempted only Pennsylvania from his influential theory of American Creole degeneration. Others went beyond words to deeds, uprooting themselves to migrate to Pennsylvania. Some, like Tom Paine, Alexander Wilson, and Benjamin Henry Latrobe, first found their voices in Pennsylvania. Others were already figures of fabulous stature before they came. Count Zinzendorf was the patron of the Moravians. Joseph Priestley was, with Lavoisier, the creator of the chemical revolution. Talleyrand was the greatest French diplomat of his day, and Joseph Bonaparte was the brother of Napoleon.

In the nineteenth century, Pennsylvania was still a tiny place. In 1850 it occupied less than 3 percent of the land area of the United States. But that tiny part of that fledgling nation played an astonishing part on the world stage. By mid-century, and in a single generation, Pennsylvania alone had funded more improvements in transportation than any nation on the planet excepting only France. Even before the beginning of the Civil War, Pittsburgh had established itself as the world center of iron and steel production. By 1880 the Pennsylvania Railroad, with its 30,000 employees, was the largest corporation in the world.

By 1980 the great forges of Pittsburgh and Bethlehem were increasingly being allowed to grow cold. The Pennsylvania Railroad was mostly a memory. And coal production was plummeting. Employment in the mines was less than one-tenth of what it had been before World War I. Anthracite extraction was down 95 percent over the same span of time. Both West Virginia and Kentucky had long since passed Pennsylvania in what had once been a veritable Pennsylvania monopoly.

The sharp contraction in coal production could be explained by extrinsic ecological and technological shifts. The fields and veins that were economically accessible were largely depleted, and coal was no longer the fuel of choice for domestic heating or industrial energy generation. The railroad's demise could be attributed, at least in some part, to changing consumer tastes and technological accident. People increasingly traveled by car rather than by train, and shippers increasingly sent their goods by truck over the interstate highway system. The Pennsy had been forced to merge with the New York Central in 1958, and the resultant Penn Central (with its headquarters in New York) had declared bankruptcy in 1970. In less than a century the biggest, richest, most powerful corporation in the cosmos had become the biggest business failure in history.

But the steel industry could not even rationalize its ruin by resource depletion, technological transformation, or changing consumption schedules. There was still abundant ore to be had, and sufficient fuel to fire the forges. There was more than enough demand for steel, at home and abroad. But production of steel shifted elsewhere, both within the United States and beyond. The precipitate collapse of the Pennsylvania industry was due, exactly as Philip Jenkins says, to hidebound mismanagement and complacency. Such mismanagement was as pervasive in Pennsylvania in the twentieth century as it had been uncharacteristic before. So was such bovine persistence in technologically exhausted soil, when entrepreneurs elsewhere were moving on to technologically greener pastures.

For centuries Pennsylvania was in the vanguard of every technological and ideational transformation. In the nineteenth century the Commonwealth led the nation in the development of the turnpikes, riverboats, canals, and railroads that constituted the transportation revolution. It likewise led in the production of mechanically controlled iron and steel machines and the creation of national markets based on banking and the railroad that were the core of the industrial revolution. It had enough of the traditional sources of energy—wood and water—to supply its own industries and to sell surpluses to other states to power theirs, and it had almost all the new sources of energy—coal and oil—besides.

In the twentieth century, Pennsylvania had every opportunity to perpetuate its imperial position. It had an unmatched cadre of industrial leaders, superbly trained engineers, and the best-paid and most-skilled working class in the world. It had immense wealth. And it had a head start on virtually every innovation that would be a decisive engine of economic development in the years to come.

The energy technologies that would supplant coal were oil, natural gas, and electricity. All of them had their origins in Pennsylvania, and all of them got away in the course of the twentieth century. Oil was first commercialized when Drake and Smith struck the black gold at Titusville in 1859. During the four decades that followed that discovery, the industry remained centered where it was centered from the first, in the oil fields of western Pennsylvania. As late as 1900 those fields still produced 60 percent of America's oil. Natural gas was captured soon after oil. Because it was a by-product of drilling for oil, it too was produced primarily in the Keystone State to the end of the nineteenth century. Electricity was theorized and applied in Pennsylvania as early as Franklin's experiments with kite and key. It was first elaborated in its modern form in Pennsylvania by George Westinghouse, who caught the wave of the industry's future by investing in the technology of alternating current while his competitors, including such formidable foes as Thomas Edison and J. P. Morgan, were still betting on direct current.

Pennsylvania prospered by producing, transporting, and refining all this energy to sell to others. As in the days of wood and water and in the time of steam and coal, so in the first generations of oil and gas and electricity. The state continued to attract a disproportionate share of the entrepreneurs of the world because it continued to have a disproportionate share of the strategic resources of the world. But over the course of the twentieth century its entrepreneurs managed to squander most of those advantages. The imperial Commonwealth that they inherited became just another place that imported its energy from afar and paid for it to the new lords of a new economic order.

There was only one energy technology in which Pennsylvania pioneered and did not lose its lead. The first operating plant in America for the nuclear generation of electric power went on line in the Keystone State in 1957. But while the rest of the nation grew skeptical of the promise of nuclear power, the Commonwealth kept the faith. As environmental criticism mounted and Wall Street lost interest, Pennsylvania utilities pressed on. By the 1990s, as Jenkins observes, nuclear plants generated one-third of the state's electricity. The state clung to this fading new technology with the same bulldog tenacity it had too long clung to fading old technologies, and its obstinacy left it a national leader by default, where few others followed.

If oil was the driving energy source of the modern age, the internal combustion engine was what it drove. And if oil's dominion was bound to be problematic for Pennsylvania once the great fields of the Southwest were opened, the hegemony of the automobile should have been God's gift to the Commonwealth. As David Contosta says, the automobile industry began in Pennsylvania and could easily have stayed there. The state had every element that success in automotive manufacturing required, except the wit and the will to capitalize on those advantages.

In much the same way, Pennsylvania pioneered the information and entertainment economies of the twentieth century but failed to follow up on its epochal innovations. Some, such as movies, might have been lost in the best of circumstances. Not even New York could compete with the sunny skies of southern California. But most could easily have stayed in the state. Like the auto industry, they went elsewhere for no discernible reasons other than failures of financing, nurturing, and nerve. The mass media commenced their career in Philadelphia long before the movie industry did. The first great popular magazine of America, *Godey's Lady's Book,* was published there, and the city remained a center of popular publishing for the next 100 years, until the demise of the Curtis Publishing empire and the dismantling of the Annenberg enterprises. Radio had its roots at KDKA in Pittsburgh, and television emerged in crucial part in the Delaware Valley. Both ended up based in New York and, later, in Los Angeles. The large-scale electronic digital computer was developed at the University of Pennsylvania, and its developers formed one of the first companies to exploit its commercial possibilities in the suburbs of Philadelphia. But the company floundered. Its inept managers were not replaced by markedly more competent ones, and its disgruntled employees did not remain in the region to start businesses of their own. An electronics industry that might have enriched Pennsylvania enriched other states instead. In information technology as in so many other spheres, the Commonwealth ceased to be a prime producer and began to be a consumer.

Though Pennsylvania is still the sixth most populous state in the nation, its demographics are disturbing. Its population has grown more slowly than all but five states since 1930. From its founding and for a quarter of a millennium, as a colony and as a commonwealth, Pennsylvania had never grown by less than 20 percent in a decade. But in the 1920s, its growth was barely half that. By the 1960s its increase was just 4 percent, or less than one-third the national average. In the 1990s it did not, for all practical purposes, grow at all.

Pennsylvania is also, as Jenkins points out, graying badly. It stands second only to

Florida in median age and percentage of population over sixty-five. It stands forty-sixth in percentage of population under the age of nineteen, and fiftieth—that is, last—in percentage enrolled in public elementary and secondary schools.

The state is not holding on to its young people, and it is not attracting outsiders to take their places, either. Eighteenth-century Pennsylvania was the chief destination for newcomers to the New World. Nineteenth-century Pennsylvania still surpassed every state save New York; from 1850 to the outbreak of World War I, one out of every six residents was an immigrant, and many more were migrants from other states. Four-fifths of the state's inhabitants were born in the Commonwealth, the highest percentage of native sons and daughters in the nation. Though Jenkins claims that the Immigration Act of 1965 opened a door to Africa, Asia, and Latin America through which new waves of immigrants streamed, his own data argue otherwise. According to the 2000 Census count, only 3 percent of the population is Hispanic and only 2 percent is Asian. The vibrant new migrations that Jenkins hails are indeed remaking America, but they are not remaking the Keystone State in any extensive way.

If Pennsylvania was the most radical place on the planet in the seventeenth century, and among the most revolutionary places in both the eighteenth and nineteenth centuries, it became a very conventional place in the twentieth century. If it was one of the most innovative and generous-spirited places in earlier times, it became a very conservative place in our time.

To the time of the Civil War, Pennsylvanians were instrumental in the inception of every essential reform impulse of their era. As often as not, they were almost alone in the endeavor. They fought at the forefront of the campaigns against slavery and for its abolition, for public education and for female education, for the protection of Native Americans and for humane care of the insane, for temperance and for prison reform, for woman's rights and for world peace.

After the turn of the twentieth century, however, Pennsylvania lagged where others led. As often as not, it stood outside the reform endeavor altogether. Progressivism affected the Commonwealth less than any other industrial state. The New Deal transformed the rest of the nation and left Pennsylvania almost untouched. Aside from one ineffectual relief law, the state legislature enacted no New Deal legislation before 1937. And the city of Philadelphia set itself so adamantly against Roosevelt's reforms that it even refused the federal money its unemployed needed so desperately.

Pennsylvania was not as backward in subsequent social movements, such as those for civil rights and against the war in Vietnam. But it was not forward, either. In the countercultural upheavals of the 1960s as in the Reagan revolution of the 1980s, it was stolidly in the middle. It moved when others moved, and not before. In its politics as in its economics, Pennsylvania's autonomy was at an end. In the nineteenth century its story was its own and could be told almost without reference to others. In the twentieth century its story was inseparable from—and dependent on—external developments.

Pennsylvania's drift from leadership toward the middle of the pack is evident everywhere. Its diminished dreams for the future are especially apparent in the state's shrinking commitment to education. In the nineteenth century, Pennsylvania was among the first states to establish a system of public education. It had the nation's first modern public high school and, as well, its first Roman Catholic high school. It had more colleges, universities, and other institutions of higher learning than any other state in the union.

At the end of the twentieth century, and excluding only Rhode Island, Pennsylvania had a smaller percentage of high school graduates than any state north of Virginia or east of the Dakotas. It also had a smaller percentage of college graduates than all but four of those eighteen northern states, and indeed a smaller percentage than a majority of the fifty states. It spent less per capita on elementary and secondary education than two-thirds of the states, and less per capita on higher education than three-quarters of them. On any analysis of its investment in education, it seemed more like a southern state, not a northern one.

On any measure of the opportunities it afforded its women, present-day Pennsylvania provided no better than it did for its youth. In the colonial era and well into the nineteenth century, the Quaker colony and its successor state taught the Western world. Compared with women in the rest of European America and in Europe itself, women in Pennsylvania had unrivaled privileges and power. By the late twentieth century, however, the state had quite forsaken its longtime leadership position. The most systematic recent attempt to canvass gender equality in the United States put the Commonwealth nineteenth on economic parity, twenty-eighth on legal parity, and fiftieth—dead last—on political parity.

The decay of creativity in the state was pervasive. And, at least as early as the onset of the twentieth century, the corruption that took the place of that creativity was pervasive too. Contosta tells the dismal tale of the building of the Capitol in Harrisburg, where the boodle cost the state twice as much as the actual construction and where high state officials as well as the Capitol architect had their snouts in the trough. He tells the even more dismal tale of the Kellogg survey in Pittsburgh, where researchers found that the "rampant greed" of the rich rulers of the city was literally poisoning its people and was altogether impervious to exposure. He might have extended his tale of two cities to a tale of three by including Philadelphia, which Lincoln Steffens famously called "corrupt and contented." All across the Commonwealth, citizens were coming to contentment with, or resignation to, corruption. A few generations later, those who came from other states would note with bemusement that, when politicians back home referred to their convictions, they spoke of their beliefs.

In 1776 Pennsylvanians played crucial parts in sparking a revolution that the rebels believed they could win because the British were corrupt and the Americans virtuous. In 1876 Pennsylvanians celebrated the 100th anniversary of the Revolution with an audacity and exuberance worthy of the founders. Visitors thronged to Philadelphia, where they thrilled to the promise of boundless technological progress and the intimation of manifest American destiny. In 1976 Pennsylvania marked the bicentennial of independence with a pointless party. Visitors stayed away in droves. In a city and a nation each five times more populous than it had been a century before, the bicentennial attracted barely as many attendees as the centennial celebration had. The tale of three '76s traces the same entropic trajectory as the tale of three cities.

By the end of the twentieth century, the state's economy was merely making the best of a bad thing. In this as in much else, Pennsylvania just lagged larger trends; it was a wagged tail where it had long been the wagging dog itself. High-pay industrial work slipped away and low-pay service work took its place. Union jobs vanished, and nonunion positions took their place. And little of it just happened to happen. The great preponderance was made to happen by management committed to downsizing and cheap wages. Tom Graham, appointed chief of steel operations at U.S. Steel in 1983, epitomized the shift. In his first four years he reduced a work force of almost 50,000 to one of less than 20,000. He dismissed nonunion hands without even giving them notice, issuing them pink slips at the end of their shift. He fired employees mere weeks before they were eligible for pension benefits. He contracted work out to cheaper nonunion labor. When organized laborers protested, he warned them not to "cling to a nostalgic past that is rapidly becoming irrelevant."

Pennsylvania had more than its share of such executives. Some, like Graham, were homegrown. Others, like Al Dunlap, were just passing through. Wall Street loved them all. The more they lowered labor costs, the more they raised the value of the stock that was almost their sole concern. But when they were done the steel companies and paper companies they managed still could not compete with their foreign rivals. And after they left, the human wreckage they had wrought remained behind. Indeed, it was evident in the very names by which they were known. Graham was "the people cutter." Dunlap was "Chainsaw Al."

Even when Pennsylvania did not trail national trends, its economic initiatives were in their own way disheartening. In the 1990s many of its communities tied their hopes of reversing decades of decline to the promotion of heritage tourism. And indeed they had exceptional attractions to promote. A study of Philadelphia commissioned by the Pew Foundation found that the Quaker City had a good deal more to offer heritage tourists than its competitors in Baltimore and Boston, even though those cities did more marketing and drew more tourists. But Philadelphia turned to heritage tourism by default rather than in recognition of its rich resources. City leaders knew well that tourism jobs paid much less than office work or manufacturing. They simply had no idea how to bring back the corporate headquarters or the industry that had once provided citizens much better jobs.

Though the data are, in the nature of the case, unavailable, there was a stunning suspicion that Philadelphia's leading export by tonnage in the 1990s was iron. This iron was not the kind that had once rolled forth from the state's majestic mills, but the ornamental iron that had for generations graced the city's homes, factories, and cemeteries. It was being stolen, by petty thieves with no more promising prospect of gainful work, for sale to dealers in more prosperous parts of the country. In an earlier period, Pennsylvania financiers and industrialists strip-mined the earth to build a nation. At the end of the millennium, grifters stripped the city to supply a niche market among new elites elsewhere.

All across a Commonwealth increasingly committed to the new mantra of heritage tourism, cities were similarly stripping themselves of their heritage. Exactly as Jenkins observes, they had redefined their material culture as antiques and sold it off. But the rewards they reaped were equivocal at best. The supply of artifacts was not inexhaustible. Like coal and oil and iron ore, it too could be depleted. And unlike such minerals, material culture was not just a natural resource. It was culture itself. The amenities that had made existence civilized in the past were drifting south and west as once they had drifted from Europe to Pennsylvania.

Decline, then, is the issue with which we have to deal. As scholars have noted, Pennsylvania once provided a pattern for America in both agriculture and manufacturing, but it once did too in transportation, religion, politics, settlement and land use, voluntary association, giant enterprise, science, medicine, finance, and advertising. For two centuries and more, this tiny patch of the planet nourished an astonishing cultural creativity. And then, in the twentieth century, it ceased to do so.

Americans do not deal comfortably with stories of decline. American history, as we like it, is a triumphal tale. Failure causes us acute discomfort. But American history, as we have lived it, is tinged with failure, and has been from the first. As Daniel Richter reminds us, European invasion of the Delaware Valley doomed its Indians to eventual decline and disappearance. As Susan Klepp adds, English invasion doomed the Dutch, the Swedes, and the French to decline too. As Pencak implies, the Revolution doomed the English to disappearance, and the Quakers to a kind of cultural inconsequence. Any account of Pennsylvania's first century must be a chronicle of losers as well as one of winners.

Indeed, in the deepest sense, it was bound to be. Beyond the military reckonings and the political castings of accounts, there was for the colony's founders a spiritual side of the settlement that was decaying from the first. No society in the world could ever have fulfilled the founder's soaring hopes of a Holy Experiment.

William Penn worked at the mystical confluence of early modern Europe's most radical ideas. He read the most visionary writers and corresponded with the most esoteric thinkers. Like them, he had a dream. His colony was conceived at once as a practical real-estate investment and an unabashed utopia. His capital, Philadelphia, was at once laid out in a geometric grid that maximized the money that could be made from city land, and named for the occult metropolis that symbolized the yearnings of the most advanced spiritual seers of the seventeenth century. As soon as his colony and his capital passed from vision to reality, they were fated to frustrate the sublime ambitions that gave them birth.

The ideal of religious liberty fired Anglican efforts to overthrow the Quakers, and Presbyterian efforts to overthrow them both. The ideal of a green country town gave way to an unbridled avarice that ended in helter-skelter subdivision of the great lots and dire environmental degradation. The ideal of interracial amity faded into the Walking Purchase, the French and Indian War, and the unpunished massacre of the Conestoga Indians by the Paxton Boys.

Yet the yearnings persisted. Pennsylvania in the eighteenth century was home to virtually every utopian religious sect on the continent. It was the seat of such antislavery sentiment as could be mustered in America, and of almost all the liberation of women as well. It provided people of many cultures with a safer haven than any other place in the New World. And it led the Old World as well as the New in working out the social logic of voluntary association and the political logic of pluralism, legitimate opposition, and partisan popular politics. It was the right place for raising the Revolution, for drafting the Declaration, for composing the Constitution, and for launching the great republic.

The nineteenth century too saw debasement of William Penn's dream. It was a time of declension. In less than 100 years the most radical democracy in America became a byword for the degradation of democracy. Popular jest had it that Rockefeller's Standard Oil Company could do anything with the state legislature but refine it. Popular jest did not know the half of it. Tom Scott had most members of the state legislature quite literally on the Pennsylvania Railroad payroll, at the ready to do his bidding.

Yet the yearnings still persisted. They shaped America's most formative efforts to rehabilitate the criminal, relieve the insane, redeem the slaves, and reform society. They informed the most sublime moments of the Civil War and the most large-hearted impulses of Reconstruction. They inspired, in men like Joseph Leidy and S. Weir Mitchell, the most innovative scientific and medical research and, in men like Thomas Eakins and Frank Furness, the most advanced artistic work of the century. Above all, they still led to the making of "the best poor man's country" on earth. Unskilled laborers poured into the mines and mills of the state, skilled workers into its shops. To the end of the nineteenth century, working people in Philadelphia had a standard of living that was unmatched anywhere else. While laboring families in other places filled fetid tenements and slums, ordinary workers in the Quaker City owned new three-bedroom houses and took vacations at the shore. It was not for nothing that journalists marveled at what they called a "city of homes," or that more than a dozen department stores lined Market Street to cater to the precocious consumerism of the working class. The American Dream had arrived in Philadelphia half a century early.

Only in the twentieth century were Pennsylvania's fadings and failings essentially unrelieved. Only then did the state attract less than a lion's share of doers and dreamers.

Only then did it lose the knack for parlaying past advantages into future ones. Only then did it cease to cherish cultural creativity. Only then did it no longer lead.

The causes of this decadence are confoundingly obscure. Did the decline and fall of Pennsylvania just happen to happen? No society stays on top forever. Or did others catch on, or catch up? Eventually, others always do. Or did changes from afar doom the Commonwealth's accustomed domination? Or did Pennsylvanians have a hand in their own undoing? There would be profit in pursuing such an inquest, for its own sake and for what it might suggest of what is still possible and what is not in time to come.

But it would be more rewarding to focus on the future. It would be better to ask whether there is for Pennsylvania any hope of recovery of its longtime leadership and dominance.

In the most insipid but by no means the most trivial sense, there is always such hope. Human communities themselves do renew. Even the South rose again. But such categorical responses do not get us far. They do not tell us what form the recovery might take, where it might occur, and how and when and why. They do not tell us whether there are any realistic prospects of such a renewal.

Recall Emma Lapsansky's invocation of Tocqueville. For that Frenchman, America was "an almost exclusively manufacturing and commercial association." And Pennsylvania was the epitome of that association. Its inhabitants, even more than most Americans, were restlessly ambitious. Their "principal object" was to explore a "boundless country" for "purposes of profit."

The very venturesomeness of the Commonwealth was also its vulnerability. Men and women went there because it was, with New York, the place to be for profit-seekers. They went not because they wanted to be *there* but because they wanted wealth. They would cease to go or stay when they could make more money elsewhere.

Daniel Boone and his family were typical of the migrations that made America. Early and easily they let go of their English Quaker roots and shed their Pennsylvanian identity. As Klepp suggests, their only essential loyalty was to the main chance.

The Pinchots were typical of the same unrooted pursuit of opportunity. As Lapsansky says, they too moved as the market beckoned: to New Jersey and New York almost from the first, to Michigan and Wisconsin soon enough. Their operations were never tied to their home in Pike County. Land, to them, was timber to be cut down and sold, not a place to settle.

And yet, after the founding generations of the family depleted the land, and left when there was no more wood to cut, some of those Pinchots stayed. Among their descendants was Gifford Pinchot, who reclaimed for loveliness and the promise of a richer life the forests that his ancestors had destroyed for money.

Much of that natural beauty remains in Pennsylvania. At the dawn of the twenty-first century, the state's landscape is still implausibly as it was when the first European colonists saw it in the seventeenth century. The vast majority of the state's inhabitants today live compacted in a dozen metropolitan areas. Outside those areas, the vast majority of the state resembles, more than almost any other eastern state, the way it was in the colonial era. The same mighty rivers still run. The same deep forests still stretch to the same endless mountains. Thanks to Gifford Pinchot and those who have followed his lead, state parks now preserve immense swaths of the state that have nearly reverted to their seventeenth-century appearance in the years since the first lumbering Pinchots logged them.

From the first, Penn invited settlers to come to those woods to stay. His promotional pamphlets warned away all who believed they would get rich quick in Pennsylvania. There was no gold or silver in the province, and early laws prohibited the cultivation of tobacco. But just as Penn promised, people who worked hard did find solid abundance. The people who took that promise most to heart, the Germans whom we now call the Pennsylvania Dutch, established a tradition of putting down roots. While farmers elsewhere exhausted the soil and moved on, the Germans fertilized and fallowed and evolved a sustainable economy that they follow to this day.

In the last decades of the nineteenth century, in the most widely celebrated sermon in American history, Russell Conwell was still promising enterprising Pennsylvanians that they could find all the wealth they wanted at home, that there were yet "acres of diamonds" in their natal place. But by then the bright lights were beckoning from afar. By then, Pennsylvanians were as ardent as other Americans for the grass that was greener.

Only in our own time are other Pennsylvanians beginning to learn the lessons that Penn and Conwell tried to teach and that the Pennsylvania Germans learned long ago. Only in the crucible of downsizing and deindustrialization have others decided to stay despite the decaying economy.

From the pathbreaking formation of a cordwainers' collective in the late eighteenth century, Pennsylvania pioneered in labor organization. As Pencak says, America's first unions and strikes all had their home in Pennsylvania. As Lapsansky adds, laborers' consciousness of being a separate constituency also arose first in the Keystone State in the first half of the nineteenth century. As Walter Licht adds further, almost all the major labor institutions of the modern age emerged in Pennsylvania, and under Pennsylvanian leadership, in the fifty years after that. The first of the two great national organizations, the Knights of Labor, was founded in Philadelphia and was led for its first decades by Philadelphians. The second of the two, the American Federation of Labor, traced its beginnings to New York but organized nationally on the call of a Philadelphia conference and had its first great test in Homestead. The other great labor movements of the era, the United Mine Workers and the notorious Molly Maguires, also had their bases and found their leaders in the Commonwealth.

Once working-class consciousness arose in America, it was always strongest in Pennsylvania. The organization of labor by working men and women—skilled and unskilled, craft and industrial, nonviolent and violent alike—was another aspect of the state's cultural creativity and leadership, and it lasted for more than a century. After the decline of the Quakers, working-class consciousness was in many ways the only distinctive consciousness of Pennsylvania.

Such consciousness, and the communal commitment it implied, was tested in the collapse of the industrial economy in the last decades of the twentieth century. And during the downturn a remarkable number of the people of the old industrial regions stayed. Much like New Englanders and southerners, the first regional losers of American history, Pennsylvanians discovered in themselves an un-American loyalty to place. They found, perhaps to their astonishment, that Bethlehem, Scranton, and the Mon Valley were home.

There may be nothing in this newfound attachment that augurs any economic upturn in the future. It was 100 long years before the South rose again, and then only because of fortuities like air-conditioning and the interstate highway system. It was 200 long years before places like New Hampshire became wealthy, and then only because of fortuities like the computer.

Like those southerners of the century between the Old South and the Sun Belt, and like those northern New Englanders before the emergence of Megalopolis, present-day Pennsylvanians live in the Mon Valley or in southeastern or northeastern Pennsylvania because they want to be there, more than because there is big money to be made there. This is not a negligible matter.

It is true that the Commonwealth has turned to promoting heritage tourism for lack of any better economic options. It is also true that the heritage tourism of Williamsport, or Jim Thorpe, or Philadelphia, arises out of authentic pride. In that sense, Jenkins may not be wrong to take the state's turn to history as an encouraging sign for the future. And the reminder in the Introduction to this book that Pennsylvanians are so preponderantly native-born may be a portent of promise.

Or, better, a portent of something subtly different. Focus on the future and its promise is the American pathology. Our story, as we have chosen to tell it to ourselves, in Pennsylvania as in the United States, has been a story of progress. It has been a story of the future more than of the past, of expectations more than of fulfillment. The Pennsylvanians who stayed in the Commonwealth after it was no longer the best poor man's country or the best rich man's country wanted connectedness and commitment more than they wanted the future. They wanted meaning more than they wanted promise. They wanted intrinsic gratifications, here and now, more than they wanted deferred gratifications in a better day to come.

There is an older, almost obsolete sense of revolution as a perennial revolving, an eternal return. In that older sense as well as in our more modern one, Pennsylvania may yet have another revolutionary meaning to offer America.

WAYS *to* PENNSYLVANIA'S PAST

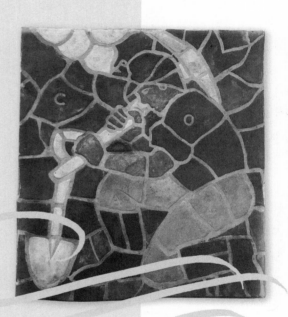

PART II

Geography

WILBUR ZELINSKY

History and geography are inseparable. They are best regarded as two alternative, complementary ways of studying a single ever-changing reality. Historians deal with all sorts of events—with the flow of things in time within our human world. Geographers study the attributes of *places* and the relationships among them. But places are also events. They are forever in flux, perhaps slowly and imperceptibly, perhaps swiftly and abruptly, or in fits and starts between spells of apparent stability. Similarly, events are all place-related, either directly and obviously, or in much subtler ways. Inevitably, a historical event or topic bears some relationship to a specific territory and generates a unique geography. We cannot do meaningful historical studies without appreciating geographical circumstances. Conversely, geography divorced from history and the flow of time becomes meaningless. Historians and geographers have too often ignored one another's approach. This chapter bridges the schism, nudging together the two perspectives, showing geography's mighty role in Pennsylvania's story.

THE PHYSICAL ENVIRONMENT IN MODERN PENNSYLVANIA'S HISTORY

Before treating the evolving interactions between human beings and their physical setting, it is essential to remember that the "natural" environment has never been and never can be fixed or static. Furthermore, it has long since ceased being natural. During more than 10,000 years of aboriginal occupancy, the territory now called Pennsylvania experienced substantial physical changes. Among them were major oscillations in climate and sea level, alterations in river flow, transformations of plant and animal communities, and some reshaping of landforms.

The European newcomers responded enthusiastically and with unprecedented speed to the area's potential. Over the four centuries of their presence, they reshaped the physical environment substantially, and especially to extract wealth. Pennsylvania may have been the twelfth of the thirteen British colonies to receive a substantial influx of European settlers, but of all the zones of settlement along the Atlantic Seaboard, it proved to be the most attractive for the colonists.

Take climate. No North American tract faithfully duplicates the weather patterns of Britain or northwestern Europe. But nowhere along the seaboard, or in the continental interior, is there closer resemblance to Europe than in Pennsylvania (and New Jersey) in terms of temperature and precipitation. Relatively infrequent are the prolonged frosts, heavy snows, and ice-blocked streams that make winters difficult in New England and upstate New York. Nor do Pennsylvanians have to endure the unbearable heat and humidity that residents of many parts of the South endure for much of the year. The Commonwealth suffers only rarely from tropical hurricanes, tornadoes, dust storms, blizzards, and other such meteorological events that bedevil much of the nation. Pennsylvania's climate may not be ideal (Philadelphia's summers can be sticky, and there are spells of arctic weather in the uplands), but nowhere else in colonial America would the European immigrant have experienced less physical and psychological trauma in adjusting to the weather.

Pennsylvania's natural attractions would not have been apparent before settlement. The science of meteorology had not yet developed, and scientific geography was in its infancy. Knowledge about climate regimes in North America was sketchy and often erroneous. More generally, the Commonwealth's physical geography remained unknown. Enlightenment came mostly with settlement.

The initial European foothold materialized in the colony's most agriculturally promising area: the narrow floodplain along the Delaware River and the wider, readily traversable Piedmont farther inland (see map of Topographic Zones of Pennsylvania in Chapter 1). This was an easily accessible tract. The Delaware River lacks those exceptional natural harbors that have been crucial to the prosperity of Boston, New York City, and Baltimore, but then as now, careful skippers of oceangoing and river craft could travel far upstream. To a lesser extent, the lower Susquehanna River offers navigational access to the Chesapeake Bay from the thriving farms of the Piedmont. The proximity of the most productive fields and pastures in colonial America to a series of ports along these two relatively placid waterways enabled Pennsylvania to become a major exporter of meat, grain, and other produce to distant markets by the eighteenth century. Later it became apparent that the city of Erie, sheltered by Presque Isle, was blessed with one of the rare decent natural harbors within the Great Lakes system.

The Commonwealth's landforms were less accommodating. Although the Triassic Lowland offered a wide, convenient aperture through an otherwise formidable Blue Ridge barrier (represented in Pennsylvania by the Reading Prong and South Mountain), what lay beyond were the difficult northeast-southwest–trending ridges and valleys of the "Endless Mountains." Farther inland, the traveler has to negotiate the challenging Allegheny Front, ascending to the Allegheny Plateau, and then traverse many deep gorges cut into the often rugged plateau country before reaching Lake Erie or the navigable Ohio River. Unlike New York's natural pathway across the Appalachian uplands through the Hudson Valley and the east-west trough that furnished the route for the Erie Canal, Pennsylvania could not be crossed by water. Well into the twentieth century, movement westward across Pennsylvania was frustrating and time-consuming. During the colonial period, settlers who might have opted for central or western Pennsylvania were deflected southwestward via the Piedmont or Great Valley into Virginia, the Carolinas, and other distant parts.

The topographic challenges of the Ridge and Valley region and the Allegheny Plateau retarded early road-building projects and contributed to serious construction problems and financial disappointments during the short-lived early nineteenth-century canal-building boom. As steam railroads began to dominate long-distance hauling of passengers and freight, great technical ingenuity and much heavy investment were required to lay rails across rugged terrain to connect Philadelphia and points between Pittsburgh and with destinations farther west. Similarly, only with the advent of powerful, advanced earth-moving equipment and other engineering innovations beginning in the 1930s did it become possible to build the Pennsylvania Turnpike and other limited-access, high-speed highways that could include tunnels where mountains were too steep to climb.

But the hillier sections of Pennsylvania were not altogether lacking in appeal for pioneer and later cultivators. Within certain valleys, coves, and basins, such as the Kishicoquillas (Mifflin County), the Nittany (Centre County), or the middle Susquehanna (Lycoming County), fertile soils and other resources permitted settlement to occur at the earliest opportunity, usually whenever the military situation allowed it and when land or water transport became feasible. Many of these pockets of agrarian enterprise were engulfed by urban or industrial expansion, but others survive intact, essentially unchanged because of relative isolation. Almost any valley in Fulton and Bedford Counties is a case in point.

Early Euro-Americans realized that Pennsylvania was indeed "the best poor man's country," and not only because of inviting soils and terrain in its southeastern quadrant. Luxuriant forests offered wild game, fish, and useful plants. To persons inured to the scarcity of good timber and limited access to wildlife in thickly occupied western Europe, the region must have seemed a veritable Eden. Forests were particularly critical in the colony's success. Clearing land for fields and pastures, and stripping forests in

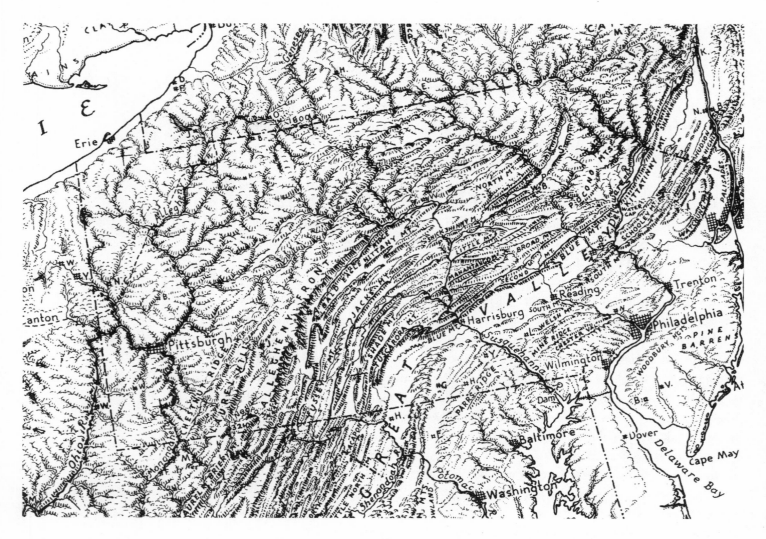

Landforms of Pennsylvania and neighboring areas. This classic topographic map illustrates several important points about the landscape of Pennsylvania: the state consists of a number of elongated regions parallel to the coast, the relief is lower closer to the ocean (where erosion has worked longer), and the texture of the landscape is finer in the southeast, where the rocks had been more deformed during mountain-building.

nearby uplands, furnished the wherewithal for forts, houses, barns, sheds, fences, mills, bridges, churches, vessels, and other structures and artifacts; provided fuel for cooking, heating, and industrial processes (especially making pig iron); and supplied lumber and other wood products for export to tree-starved Europe and the Caribbean.

After the territorial limits of profitable farming had been reached by the mid-1800s, a good many entrepreneurs, driven by an insatiable national and international demand for lumber, began denuding the wilder parts of Pennsylvania. Created thereby were some great personal fortunes and several cities, notably Williamsport. Only belatedly, after ruthless cutting and frequent fires had obliged lumbermen to migrate to the relatively undisturbed woodlands of the Great Lakes and the Southeast, did quiet return to nearly half the Commonwealth. Appearances to the contrary notwithstanding, Pennsylvania's forests today, now largely under the stewardship of federal, state, and local authorities, are almost entirely second, third, or fourth growth. Only in the most inaccessible recesses of the state, tracts too remote for the profitable hauling of logs, do we find a few hundred acres of what might pass for virgin woodland. Alan Seeger Natural Area offers the traveler who penetrates the near-wilderness of northeastern Hunting-don County a splendid sample of what much of primeval Pennsylvania must have looked like.

Pennsylvania's mineral wealth, unlike its lumber and fertile soils, was not visible to the first settlers. Much of southwestern Pennsylvania is underlain by thick, relatively accessible beds of high-quality soft, or bituminous, coal. The Commonwealth contains the northern segment of the world's largest deposits of the mineral, a series of fields running the length of the Appalachian Plateau from Pennsylvania to Alabama. Accessibility of coal, limestone, and, via river and lake transport, iron ore enabled Pittsburgh and such nearby communities as Homestead, Monessen, and McKeesport to become major producers of iron and steel and fabricated metal products by the late nineteenth century. On a lesser scale, modern iron and steel plants flourished in Bethlehem and other eastern and central sites favorably located with access to raw materials and markets. Even earlier, beginning in late colonial times, many small iron furnaces had exploited relatively modest pockets of iron ore and charcoal from neighboring forests.

Pennsylvania also boasts the world's greatest deposits of hard, or anthracite, coal in a northeastern region that was initially shunned because of its meager soils and difficult terrain. By the late 1800s the desirability of this fuel for home-heating and industrial use—and proximity to major population centers—resulted in intensive mining and dense occupation, mainly by an immigrant work force.

Another historically important mineral resource has been petroleum. The discovery of oil at Titusville in northwestern Pennsylvania in 1859 was the first in the Americas. Although subsequently overwhelmed by such states as Texas and Oklahoma, western Pennsylvania and eastern Ohio first developed the technology to extract and process oil and natural gas.

Europeans found other ways to transform Pennsylvania's preexisting environment. They deliberately or inadvertently introduced exotic species that brought about great changes in the landscape. In addition to Eurasian livestock, grains, root crops, fruits, and vegetables, which took over much of the land surface, many wild mammals and birds, weeds, grasses, insects, fungi, and micro-organisms smuggled themselves in and often enjoyed a competitive advantage over indigenous life-forms, causing the extinction of

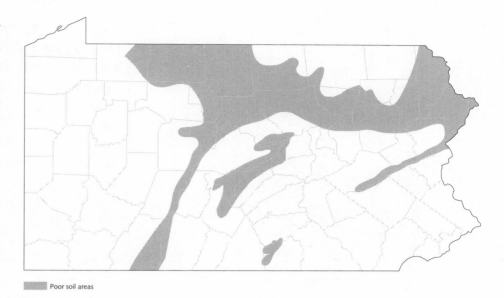

Poor soil areas

Areas of poor agricultural soil in Pennsylvania. By 1850, these areas of poor agricultural soil were the only portions of Pennsylvania that had not been occupied.

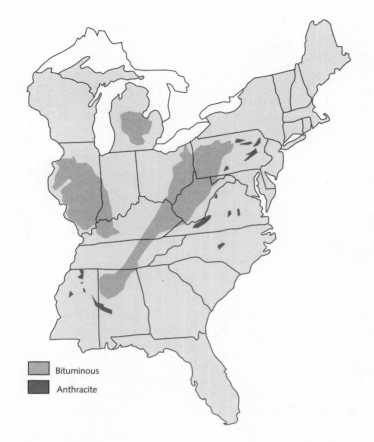

Eastern United States coalfields.

Bituminous
Anthracite

many. The gypsy moth and the blights that threaten the survival of elms and chestnuts are among the more notorious examples. Immigrants carried with them diseases, such as smallpox, measles, and diphtheria, to which they had developed at least partial immunity but which ravaged the aboriginal communities.

Modern Pennsylvanians have also energetically reshaped the surface of their land and modified its hydrology. Many streams have been reshaped, channelized, or realigned, and had their chemistry altered; damming has created scores of lakes and reservoirs; and much wetland has been drained and converted to new uses. Surface modification is most visible in the strip-mining carried out so extensively in the bituminous and anthracite coal regions. Countless quarries have left behind mountainous heaps of mine waste and slag. Despite recent efforts to render such lunar landscapes more attractive, the devastated tracts are still all too easy to find.

Less striking visually but greater in cumulative impact have been all the cuts and fills associated with road and railway construction, the building of dams, the repeated plowing of fields, and the scalping and reshaping of millions of acres so as to accommodate homes, factories, shops, streets, parking lots, and other facilities. Earth-moving and other human activities have altered natural drainage patterns, while runoff from pavements, fertilized fields and lawns, and other sources has resulted in water pollution. In many localities water tables have fallen dramatically.

Recent human activity has also adversely affected both air quality and local meteorological conditions. Pollutants from coal-burning plants in the Midwest drift with the wind into Pennsylvania. Locally generated are the "heat islands" that characterize every Pennsylvania city of any magnitude. These are zones of significantly elevated year-round temperatures with warmest peaks at or near city centers, the cause of which is the concentration of brick, stone, concrete, asphalt, and other heat-retaining surfaces. To some extent, these heat islands and all the varied kinds of combustion going on in Pennsylvania contribute to global warming.

BOUNDARIES AND THE ROLE OF POLITICS

All boundaries are artificial. Many, such as our interstate boundaries, are firmly fixed, presumably for eternity; others, such as those for congressional districts or telephone exchanges, are subject to change. Some, such as city limits or for state parks, can be quite visible, and, whether marked on the ground or not, the general public is aware of a good many. But many others appear only on maps and concern only administrators, businesspeople, and scholars. A minority of Pennsylvania's boundaries relate to physical geography, such as the Delaware River boundary with New Jersey or the county lines that follow ridgetops or streams. Most, however, are arbitrary straight lines or follow property lines. All have historical consequences.

Within a dense crazy-quilt of boundary lines, the political variety are the most conspicuous, consequential, and difficult to change. They are the products of historical and political happenstance, argument, diplomacy, and chicanery, not scientific deliberation. But once they have been documented with maps and signposts, there may be long-term, unanticipated problems that resist easy solution. This is most painfully the case with expanding metropolises throughout the United States.

The difficulty in reshaping or abolishing preexisting jurisdictions—usually dating from the eighteenth or nineteenth century when they may have made some sense—has led to no end of grief in the rational management of water, sewer, and traffic systems or in providing police, firefighting, and social services. Most distressing is the impotence of balkanized metropolitan areas in effecting plans to regulate growth and land use in some socially beneficial manner. We pay a high price for our outmoded geographies.

Fortunately, other inherited boundaries may be altered. They include the outer limits of military reservations, national and state forests and parks, highway right-of-ways, survey lines, and property lines. Less apparent and usually visible only on maps are a host of bounded areas generated in earlier years that can be rearranged periodically. These include utility service areas, zoning districts, church parishes, school districts, judicial, legislative, and business regions, and such intrastate administrative regions as those for the Bureau of Revenue or the state police.

Another important aspect of the Pennsylvania scene also has been shaped by political considerations: the siting of all manner of facilities. Consider the apparently irreversible shift of the state capital to Harrisburg or the planting of the immovable future Pennsylvania State University in a cornfield in Centre County. Think of the way that railroads were routed in the nineteenth century, the locating of state-supported hospitals, colleges, and prisons, or of military facilities, or the way that highways have been designed, or the choice of county seats. These were largely political decisions. If seldom optimal geographic decisions, they were indubitably geographic and in many instances have had decided, long-lasting effects.

THE HORIZONTAL LAYERING OF PENNSYLVANIA'S SOCIOCULTURAL SPACE

After geographers and other scholars observed, mapped, and analyzed a wide range of cultural and social items in Pennsylvania and adjacent areas, they noted certain connections among them. The Commonwealth has two interrelated sets of landscapes. The first might be considered horizontal: a layering, or regionalization, *in space,* of distinct sociocultural

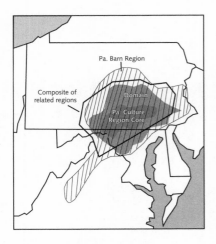

Structure of the Pennsylvania Culture Area.

areas that are also rooted in history. Their character has been determined by the timing of their occupation and the attributes of their settlers and their interaction with their environment and with other groups. For example, by the mid-eighteenth century Lancaster County was densely settled by a demographic mixture of English, Scots-Irish, and German immigrants whose cultural legacies produced a distinctive region. Utterly different is the "Northern Tier," where a relatively small band of settlers arrived a century later from upstate New York and implanted a fairly homogenous, attenuated version of New England culture.

A second set of landscapes might be regarded as a layering *over time,* a succession of material patterns and spatial arrangements produced by changing technologies, economies, mind-sets, and involvement with other places near and far. Although each historically imprinted landscape bespeaks a specific era, all are spatially embedded in particular locales.

The most readily mappable of our "horizontal" components of sociocultural tracts that comprise the Commonwealth is the Pennsylvania Culture Area (PCA). Despite its name, it does not coincide with the political state, covering as it does only a fraction of the state's surface and extending well into Maryland and small corners of Virginia and West Virginia. In contrast to the two other major colonial culture hearths of the Atlantic Seaboard—southern New England and the cradle of the South in the Chesapeake Bay area—the PCA's inhabitants remain oddly oblivious to the particularity of their turf. This ignorance may lie in the PCA's "middleness," in the absence of the marked regional peculiarity that sets a state such as Massachusetts or South Carolina off from the national norm. There is also the fact that Pennsylvanians have contributed so much to the molding and standardization of America's society and economy in the central portions of the country.

It is interesting to note a striking reversal in Pennsylvania's status vis-à-vis the cultural geography of North America since European occupation. In precontact times, it languished as a sort of backwater area well beyond the zones of livelier development. Advances in material and nonmaterial culture diffused in Pennsylvania's direction at a snail's pace from societies in the southern and southwestern sections of the future United States, and ultimately from Mexico.

The special personality of Pennsylvania, or rather of the PCA, emerged when several immigrant groups, primarily English, Welsh, Scots-Irish, and several varieties of Germans and a mixture of Protestants, converged in its southeastern corner during the eighteenth century. Their partial blending and cultural give-and-take, plus some inputs from the earlier Swedes, Finns, and Dutch, created whatever became distinctively "Pennsylvanian."

The uniqueness of the Pennsylvania Culture Area is most obvious in its settlement landscape, in its vernacular dwellings and celebrated barns, in the attributes of its farmsteads, and especially in the layout and appearance of its villages and cities. Large or

Characteristic streetscape in the town of West Chester.

small, the Pennsylvania town displays unique features: the exceptional tightness of construction (no gaps between buildings) and absence of front yards; the regionally distinctive house types; the predominance of brick buildings, sidewalks, and streets; the special geometry of streets and alleys, the importance of alleys, and the presence of a central "diamond"; the abundance of shade trees lining the streets; the formulaic set of street names (of trees in one direction, of numbers in the other); and the random intermixing of residential, commercial, and other functions. This special town-type flourished from the earliest days of British settlement through the 1850s. Thanks to Pennsylvania's social conservatism, these places still retain much of their regional character. These living museums, so to speak (Carlisle, Greencastle, and Ickesburg are fine examples), represent the urban ideals and styles of the North Sea countries (Great Britain, Germany, and the Low Countries) as of the early eighteenth century. They are history made tangible.

Other traits characterize the Pennsylvania Culture Area. The vocabulary, grammar, and pronunciation of American English, generic terms in place-names (such as "run" and "-burg"), and a particular mix of religious denominations as well as of ethnic groups distinguish the region. Much exploration of the PCA still remains to be done, especially in the realms of foodways, sport, and social customs, but some forays into the spatial aspects of political behavior (including, for example, dry laws and attitudes toward alcohol) strongly suggest the persistence of long-standing regional attitudes.

The shape and content of the Pennsylvania Culture Area matter beyond Pennsylvania. For much of early American history, Philadelphia and its hinterland served as a funnel through which immigrants and locals entered the major settlement streams

whereby the Middle West, the Upper South, and places beyond were settled. Because many of these settlers were Pennsylvania-born, local innovations and attitudes diffused throughout a broad swath of the continent. Historical geographers have thus far documented such items as the Conestoga wagon (named after its place of origin), log buildings, an important barn type, a distinctive courthouse square plan, and various advances in farming and mining technology and manufacturing processes.

The Pennsylvania Culture Area exists at various levels of intensity or purity. At its core, "Pennsylvanianess" exists in its strongest, most undiluted form, while in the zone denoted as the Domain this cultural system is still dominant but with less intensity. The Sphere is the zone of outer influence and peripheral acculturation. In its full extension, the PCA accounts for perhaps three-quarters of the Commonwealth's territory, especially if we include that ambiguous western tract where it shades into what becomes a different Middle Western Ohio or merges into the Upper South.

Other regional entities fall within Pennsylvania's political boundaries. Second in size is New England Extended, which embraces the Northern Tier and the Poconos. This tract has always been marginal to most of the state both geographically and historically because of difficulty of access, thinness of settlements, and relative economic insignificance. Its culture came from upstate New York, which in turn derived its character from the New Englanders who moved into that area.

Embedded within northeastern Pennsylvania is a small, starkly different, culture area: the Anthracite region. As the exploitation of hard coal became profitable in the late nineteenth century, a former near-wilderness, a jumble of ridges and valleys almost devoid of settlement, became thickly packed with the houses, churches, and shops of a highly diversified population drawn largely from central and eastern Europe. In every respect—vernacular architecture, ethnicity, religion, diet, and dialect, among others—the local scene reflects these immigrants whose cultural baggage differed sharply from other Pennsylvanians. Because the Anthracite region has fallen on hard times since the severe post–World War II decline in mining and associated enterprises, it has changed at a rate more sluggish than in the state's more prosperous areas. Because the built landscape remains largely unaltered from its heyday, this region, with its many old-fashioned ethnic churches and taverns and traditional wedding ceremonies, offers the outward impression of being fossilized.

Readers may be surprised when they note the absence of Appalachia in the Culture Areas of Pennsylvania map. "Appalachia" is a term of late nineteenth-century origin with a strong appeal to the American imagination. But even though we can define it physiographically, politically, and socio economically, its coherence as a culture area seems questionable. A number of Pennsylvania counties fall within the jurisdiction of the Appalachian Regional Commission, but the residents thereof are apparently unaware of, or indifferent to, any such regional designation.

Another regional entity of recent vintage is missing from the Culture Areas of Pennsylvania map: Megalopolis. This is the world's grandest conurbation, an uninterrupted stretch of urbanized territory connecting a group of once freestanding cities, that mass of city, suburb, and exurb reaching from southern Maine to Richmond, Virginia. Pennsylvania occupies the central section of this constantly expanding supermetropolis that has already begun to engulf Harrisburg and the fringes of the Anthracite. Even if there is no question that it is a demographic and economic phenomenon, Megalopolis fails utterly to qualify as a culture area.

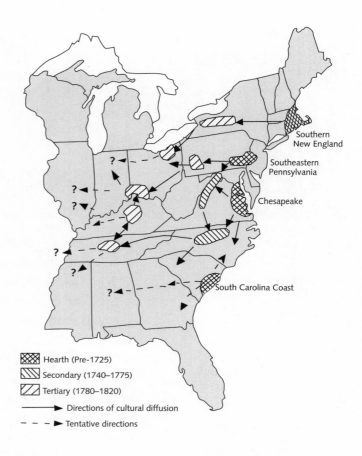

Hearth (Pre-1725)
Secondary (1740–1775)
Tertiary (1780–1820)
Directions of cultural diffusion
Tentative directions

Southern New England
Southeastern Pennsylvania
Chesapeake
South Carolina Coast

Cultural diffusion c. 1810. The southeastern Pennsylvania culture hearth played a pivotal role in the transmission of cultural traits from the Atlantic Seaboard into the continental interior, and thus in shaping the national cultural system.

THE VERTICAL TEMPORAL LAYERING OF PENNSYLVANIA'S SOCIOCULTURAL SPACE

In surveying the layering, or sandwiching, of Pennsylvania's landscapes over time, we find three distinct Euro-American episodes that all persist and coexist. To do full justice to a human presence that spans thousands of years, one should also reckon with the aboriginal landscape. Unfortunately, as we learn in Chapter 1, our knowledge of the geography of Pennsylvania's original inhabitants is fragmentary. Little of that early landscape has survived the European incursion. At best we can point to the many placenames derived from aboriginal languages but usually badly corrupted in spelling and pronunciation and mysterious as to meaning. The only other conspicuous traces of the

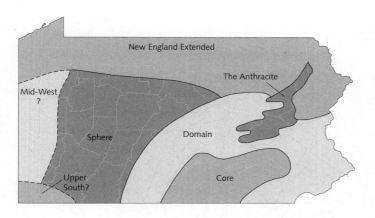

Culture areas of Pennsylvania.

pre-Columbian past are the ancient trails taken over by the newcomers that eventually became paved highways.

Landscape I, the earliest of the Euro-American strata, is also the most areally extensive. Essentially an earthbound, agrarian/mercantile, small-town world, it once comprised all those territories occupied and exploited by farming folk and associated merchants, artisans, and service workers from the early seventeenth century until the limits of arable land were reached in the 1850s. It still retains its integrity over most of its former expanse. Although never a pure subsistence economy, for most livelihoods ultimately depended on trade with distant communities, Landscape I involved much greater reliance on local resources and neighboring Pennsylvanians than has been the case for its successors.

This localized existence arose from the slowness, high cost, and unreliability of transport and communication, limited by the pace and hauling capacity of pedestrians, horses, oxen, and small rivercraft. The inhabitants of Landscape I were and are a varied lot, distinguished by ethnic origin, religious creeds, skills, social class, and their arrival via different routes at different times. Relative isolation and placeboundedness also contributed to diversity in the built landscape. Within each culture area, house, barn, bridge, and fence types, and farmstead and town layouts, may have adhered to a pervasive set of standards, but opportunity existed for variation, for expressing individuality. One diagnostic feature of Landscape I is the continuity of house styles between town and countryside.

Much of Landscape I has vanished, the victim of physical decay, abandonment, or preemption by the modern economy, but a surprising portion still exists. Many a small town or hamlet in the more isolated, economically sluggish tracts of Pennsylvania has scarcely altered in appearance since the mid-nineteenth century. Except for the power lines and telephone lines, the paved road, and an occasional advertising sign, there are many bucolic vistas that could pass for antebellum. Some localities like Kutztown, Punxsutawney, and Boalsburg have capitalized on their quaintness by arranging festivals and other devices to draw the tourist trade.

Even in less-stagnant locales the diligent observer can identify survivors from the pioneering period: old dwellings and inns that have been resurfaced or repainted, the vacant one-room schoolhouse, old gristmills and sawmills that may have been recycled into new uses, the old general store barely hanging on, worm fences, abandoned stone bridges, tottering log barns, and burial places where weathering has erased almost all inscriptions. More than half the built-up area of Pennsylvania remains Landscape I in essential anatomy and spirit, with only occasional modern accents such as the filling station, the traffic light, the video store, the pizza joint, billboards, and the factory-built silo. Landscape I remains the framework onto which two new generations of landscapes have been superimposed.

As the expression of a triumphant urban-industrial regime, Landscape II came into being in the late nineteenth century. Shaping it were the telegraph and the telephone, the steam railroad (after a brief spasm of canal-building), motor-driven ocean and lake craft, eventually automobiles, trucks, and paved highways, and all manner of new manufacturing and mining technologies. Supplanting a largely inward-gazing Landscape I, the transformed Pennsylvania, with its burgeoning cities, factories, mines, and lumber camps, became enmeshed within national and international markets in a large way and could not thrive or survive without them. But the new landscape was localized, a kind of archipelago with its standardized components scattered among strategic points.

Perhaps the most striking example of Landscape II stands along the banks of the Ohio, the Allegheny, and the Monongahela Rivers. The streamsides became lined, almost continuously, with steel mills and associated enterprises. Next to them were settlements for employees that, in terms of ethnic and religious composition or building styles, bore little resemblance to the bucolic Pennsylvania of earlier generations. Equally emblematic of the new order was the abrupt, intense "development" of the Anthracite region, previously noted. Scores of company towns, or "coal patches," usually with substandard housing and minimal amenities, dotted the bituminous fields of the Allegheny Plateau, and the oil fields in the northwest generated their own distinctive scene, while ephemeral logging camps came and went throughout vast stretches of upland Pennsylvania. But not all these new one-industry settlements were jerry-built. A few, such as Vandergrift (Westmoreland County) and Hershey (Dauphin County), were showplaces of benevolent capitalism.

All these new businesses and settlements had in common one thing, the lifeline on which they were utterly dependent: the railroad. It was intrusive wherever it appeared. The often architecturally pretentious depot was frequently the liveliest spot in town. In at least two instances, Altoona and Renovo, the entire city was the creature of the railroad industry.

In this period, Philadelphia, Pittsburgh, and many cities of middling size, such as Allentown or Pottstown, underwent major change, becoming ever more detached in appearance and function from the traditional countryside. Factories, warehouses, tenements, social facilities, signage, overhead wires, office buildings, and the occasional skyscraper filled the scene. But perhaps most noteworthy is the fact that, beginning in the 1850s with the subsequent absolute reliance on new modes of transport, communication, and commodity production, Pennsylvania had become strongly standardized, following nationwide patterns in the cultural and other human realms. Relatively little in Landscape II is distinctively Pennsylvanian.

If a Pennsylvania version of Rip Van Winkle had nodded off in the 1890s and then awakened 100 years later in, say, Levittown, King of Prussia, or Beaver Stadium, he would have found it difficult to believe he had not been abducted to a different state—or another planet. In actuality, he would have been transported to Landscape III. If Landscape I is earthbound, a panorama dominated by primary industries (the raising of crops and livestock, hunting, fishing, woodcutting, and quarrying mostly for local consumption), and Landscape II, so closely tied to modern manufacturing, is anchored in selected, economically advantageous sites, Landscape III has an entirely different spatial orientation, or lack thereof.

Landscape III is a modern—some would say postmodern—scene that is utterly dependent on the tertiary and quaternary industries, the enterprises that process and disseminate information and entertainment, that offer all manner of business and personal services, and that generally control and manipulate a complex economy and consumerist society. Consumption currently dominates life; production is merely taken for granted. Many business enterprises and residences can now be located virtually anywhere with scant recognition of classical spatial constraints. The homogenization of places and activities already under way in Landscape II has become ever more pronounced, as has the imprint of globalization.

Perhaps the generic, or diagnostic, feature of this current scene is the triumph of suburbia. These peripheral zones now girdle even the smallest urban places showing any sign of vitality. The grander examples are more than just clusters of single-family homes; they also contain apartment complexes, shopping malls, office parks, factories, hotels, and recreational attractions as well as schools and churches. The more elaborate suburbs, dubbed "edge cities," have become veritable freestanding cities in their own right with weakening ties to the old central city. No better example exists in Pennsylvania than the King of Prussia complex some seventeen miles northwest of downtown Philadelphia.

The so-called "galactic city" does not stop at the outer edge of the built-up suburbs. Extensive tracts of rural Pennsylvania are being "exurbanized." Dispersed new houses are occupied by people who do not earn their living from the soil but instead may be retired, commute long distances to work, or work at home. Closely related is the proliferation of seasonal second homes, many being weekend and vacation retreats alongside streams and lakes in forested areas.

Paradoxically, in this era of enhanced mobility, instantaneous communication, and widespread affluence, new varieties of specialized places have somehow materialized. The quest for pleasure and enriched lifestyles has spawned original localities or reshaped existing ones. Hordes of tourists have descended on, and thus substantially modified, the "Pennsylvania Dutch" countryside of Lancaster, Lebanon, and Berks Counties. A similar fate has befallen Central Philadelphia, Valley Forge, Gettysburg, and various historic villages with costumed performers and the annual festivals.

A sort of faux intimacy with earlier landscapes occurs when Landscape III folks recycle or gentrify certain old residential neighborhoods or turn defunct mills and abandoned stores into trendy boutiques, cafes, and pleasure havens, as with Pittsburgh's Southside. And a large new generation of millionaires has discovered the joys of gentleman farming and the equine life in portions of Westmoreland and Chester Counties. Motorists viewing the brilliant October hues of Pennsylvania's forests have enriched, and temporarily altered, many small towns, as have the seasonal hunters, skiers, and other winter sport enthusiasts. Perhaps the most intriguing example of the transformation of a once rather derelict area is the conversion of the Poconos into both a retreat for the elderly retired and a fashionable place for honeymooning.

Landscape III also features the mushrooming of new colleges and the expansion of preexisting institutions of higher learning. Their location is usually the result not of economic calculation but of historical happenstance or political whim. The growth of student bodies, staff, faculty, and ancillary activities, the influx of well-to-do retirees, and aggressive construction programs have transformed or revitalized many a town, while in the ultimate case of State College an entire metropolis was spawned solely by education and its offshoots. Furthermore, Penn State, like most other major multiversities, has generated clusters of "hi-tech" and research-and-development (R&D) enterprises nearby. But such industrial parks, so characteristic of Landscape III, do not always require a university for their germination. A case in point is the R&D corridor running northeast-southwest through suburban Montgomery and Chester Counties, a junior version of Silicon Valley, North Carolina's Research Triangle, or Boston's Route 128 corridor.

But all that is Landscape III does not glitter. Its seamier aspects include the junkyard and roadside litter, something much less pervasive in earlier, leaner times. In a prosperous society with a short attention span and an economy based on built-in obsolescence, we cast aside, preferably in tastefully screened yards, whatever becomes tiresome, unfashionable, or too much trouble or too costly to repair.

GEOGRAPHY AND HISTORY IN THE FIELD

There is more than one reason to urge the reader to venture forth into the field and to look around. In addition to the simple delight of travel, the truly observant traveler will quickly realize the connectedness of geography and history and begin to appreciate the role of the particular place and community within the encompassing matrix of time and space, to grasp the global via the local, and, at the personal scale, to perceive his or her locus within the larger scheme of things. Thus this experience can be a form of continuing self-education, a voyage of discovery that can become more meaningful with each repetition.

Just how the observer goes about this self-education depends on the time and means available. But one basic principle applies in all cases: locomotion should be slow. While much of both geography and history can be gleaned from an airplane window, the automobile or motorcycle, and perhaps small watercraft, make better sense, with frequent pauses and pedestrian digressions along the way. Except for specifically targeted sites, sterile, limited-access highways should be shunned. The optimum modus operandi is simply to drive or stroll along or near a preselected route. But serendipity should prevail. If an unexpected, unplanned path looks promising, explore it. Be alert to the possibility of chatting with locals who may carry in their heads much otherwise undocumented or invisible local geography and history.

Such excursions can be carried out by individuals but are much more rewarding if shared with others. Multiple pairs of eyes are better than one, and so too with different modes of curiosity and sensibility. But limit the size of the company to the number that can be comfortable within a single standard passenger vehicle.

For longer trips there is no end of worthwhile routes. The following are just a few of the possibilities. Cross-state journeys, occupying several days each, can be especially exciting. Perhaps the most intense juxtaposition of the geographic and historical, and of the three temporal landscapes, can be enjoyed by following north-south (or south-north) transects, especially in the eastern portions of the state. Begin, for instance, along the state border a few miles north of New Milford (Susquehanna County) in the Allegheny Plateau, then work southward into the Anthracite, either exploring or skirting Scranton, Wilkes-Barre, Hazleton, or Pottsville, before emerging into the utterly different world of Berks County and the rich geographic-historic tapestry that is Reading, and then finally reconnoitering the gentleman farming country of Chester County.

Or take a more westerly route. Begin at the great vista where the Susquehanna enters the state at Sayre (Bradford County), then venture south across plateau country to rejoin the river at Bloomsburg (Columbia County). Continue along or near the Susquehanna, then bear somewhat southeastward to take in the many sights of Lebanon and Lancaster Counties before reaching the Mason-Dixon Line. Along either transect Landscapes I, II, and III alternate, penetrate, and modify one another. These journeys would also traverse either two or three well-defined culture areas, the boundaries of which should be readily visible.

Those who prefer to experience a unidirectional passage through time should proceed westward from Philadelphia across the Commonwealth along or near U.S. 30, with occasional sidetrips. This would be equivalent to traveling from the late seventeenth century into the present day, but not without some abrupt time warps. The traveler would be passing across, and through gradations of, a culture area, in this instance the Pennsylvania Culture Area.

Single settlements, places that can be reconnoitered in a day or less, also can offer rewarding historical adventures, as demonstrated by Peirce Lewis in his account of Bellefonte (Centre County). For cities of any size I can do no better than urge careful reading of Grady Clay's uniquely helpful and charming *Close-Up: How to Read the American City*, which explains how to choose the most informative pathways and identify the most telling features of the city. Pennsylvania has scores, if not hundreds, of villages and hamlets that are worthy of scrutiny, some with only one or two streets and associated alleys.

A good example is Millheim (Centre County). As you amble the town's one-mile Main Street (Route 45) you have performed something analogous to a traverse by the geologist across an anticlinal valley (one in which the oldest strata of rocks lie at the center, with progressively younger ones upslope). There is a sprinkling of post–World War II items toward the edge, then, going inward, structures from the 1980s or 1990s

OPPOSITE: Buildings along Route 45, moving eastward from the Millheim Hotel to Aaronsburg, clockwise from top left.

followed by those from the 1890s and earlier, until, finally, the oldest, possibly late eighteenth-century buildings are revealed at or next to the town core. Then the whole sequence is reversed as the far side of town is approached. Much the same sort of time travel can be experienced in the smaller, equally venerable village of Aaronsburg a short distance down the highway from Millheim.

Whatever the amount of territory and time allotted for the excursion, the explorer should be equipped with a few essentials: camera, notebook, and/or tape recorder, the best possible map, and whatever good guide literature is available. The more serious, persevering individual might want to go about the photographic mission with the intent of creating an archival time series of sites especially vulnerable to change. Suburban sites ready for commercial or residential development, or old working-class neighborhoods on the verge of gentrification, would be likely examples. One would record location, subject, date, and time of day of each exposure. Then, two, five, ten, or whatever interval of years later, the photography could be repeated from the same spot at the same angle under similar weather, light, and season conditions.

What should one look at? Begin with the road or street itself and the artifacts directly associated with it. Then, looking beyond present-day design and features, seek clues that will help detect its earlier character and uses. Watch for traces of earlier pavements and surface markings, for possible abandoned streetcar or railroad tracks, for episodes of earlier grading or realignment, and for obsolete road-related signs and lighting apparatus. For guidance in such "above-ground archaeology," consult Thomas Schlereth's superlative *Reading the Road.*

Private dwellings have generated more interest and literature than any other artifacts and will yield the most immediate insights into local history and geography. Major and minor characteristics of vernacular, as well as more elegant, homes in the eastern United States from colonial times to the present have been studied in some detail. Even without painted or carved dates (or historical plaques), the observer can rather confidently assign a given house or neighborhood to a specific decade or cultural tradition. But the original date of construction is rarely enough. Most older dwellings have added or deleted porches, wings, and other features, altered styles, added new surfaces, changed functions, or altered their grounds and outbuildings. This is history at the intimate level.

Bridges and barns, of which Pennsylvania has so many historic examples, have also been much studied. Armed with the proper manual, the explorer can identify and date these items with relative ease. We are not so fortunate in other instances. Lacking are serious accounts of the history and styles of vernacular churches (which may have datestones) or of factories and mills (aside from early iron furnaces). Office buildings and shops have received scant notice even though they offer special insights into the past and an evolving present. In scouting older downtown blocks, the observer should not only note street-level features but also gaze upward. The second and third floors of the more venerable edifices usually nakedly reveal the initial architecture, whereas downstairs new modern materials, colors, and renovations, interesting in themselves, mask the original intent. Attention should also be paid, especially by the would-be photographic archivist, to our volatile strip malls and shopping centers. In the manner of an unstoppable epidemic, they have begun invading some Landscape I and II localities.

Perhaps the most rewarding moments the amateur historical geographer can spend in the field are those enjoyed in exploring cemeteries, whether in town or countryside. These come in a variety of forms and sizes: religious and secular; traditional and modern garden variety; public and commercial. Not to be ignored are the many small, scattered family burial grounds and the abandoned, overgrown plots. The amount of information these facilities contain about the locality and its inhabitants—their place and date of birth, ethnic and religious identity, occupations and military service, mode of death, their "when" as well as "where"—is virtually inexhaustible.

Other items of interest include past and present railroads (such as the ill-fated Allegheny Portage Railroad near Cresson, Cambria County), abandoned canals (such as those along the Juniata or the Delaware), old and new mines, quarries, and power lines. Be especially alert for deserted places and things: the neglected stone wall, the worm fence or hedgerow, collapsed millraces, fractured dams, orphaned orchards or flowerbeds near old house and barn foundations.

Verbal evidence of past geographies also abounds. Beside historical markers and gravestone inscriptions, note the patterns formed by street names in towns and what they say about the locality's history. Surnames on mailboxes may also tell a tale. Recording and mapping the incidence of the limited number of surnames in the Kishicoquillas Valley (Mifflin County) and then using the genealogical methods described elsewhere in this volume could yield a good deal of knowledge concerning the social geography and history of a particular place. As yet insoluble mysteries may be solved by surveying place-names, such as the cluster of central Pennsylvania communities bearing the generic term "Hall." Signs of all sort, but especially derelict advertising billboards and the like, can also provide windows into past times and vanishing geographies.

Maps are the most basic of documentary resources for the field researcher, and of Pennsylvania there are many thousands. Whether old or new, these items contain traces of the past, including many of the boundary lines discussed previously, layers of place-names, abandoned roads and trails, railroad right-of-ways, and extinct stations. When possible, consult the most detailed of maps covering the same locality over time and compare each with its successor(s).

The single most valuable map series for recent decades has been the U.S. Geological Survey's 1:24,000 (1 inch = 2,000 feet) series, one covering the entire state. Later editions (inspired by considerations of cost-containment) have used a purple overprint to show changes since the previous version. Such maps become four-dimensional, with brown contours expressing surface elevation and purple conveying changes during the specified time period.

CULTURE SHOCK ON THE FRONTIER

Among the many foreign visitors to an earlier America who published their impressions, few were more observant or readable than novelist Charles Dickens. Although he took special pains to gather information about penal institutions and other public buildings during his first encounter with the United States in 1842, he did not fail to notice whatever there was to be seen wherever he wandered. His one description of the landscape of a central Pennsylvania tract still in its pioneering phase is a priceless snapshot of a vanished scene. Seeing the landscape through an Englishman's eyes in the nineteenth century, and seeing it through one's own eyes today, provides a good comparison not only of landscape and change but also of perspective.

> Then there were new settlements and detached log-cabins and frame-houses, full of interest for strangers from an old country: cabins with simple ovens, outside, made of clay; and lodgings for the pigs nearly as good as many of the human quarters; broken windows, patched with worn-out hats, old clothes, old boards, fragments of blankets and paper; and home-made dressers standing in the open air without the door, whereon was ranged the household store, not hard to count, of earthen jars and pots. The eye was pained to see the stumps of great trees thickly strewn in every field of wheat, and seldom to lose the eternal swamp and dull morass, with hundreds of rotten trunks and twisted branches steeped in its unwholesome water. It was quite sad and oppressive, to come upon great tracts where settlers had been burning down the trees, and where their wounded bodies lay about, like those of murdered creatures, while here and there some charred and blackened giant reared aloft two withered arms, and seemed to call down curses on his foes.

American Notes (1842; reprint, London: Oxford University Press, 1957), 152–53.

Most Pennsylvania counties have acquired the commercially produced county atlases that flourished during the 1870s and 1880s. The handsome results include not only detailed property maps and much historical and biographical information, but also large-scale views of certain streets, public buildings, factories, and the homes and farms of leading citizens. At this climax of Victorian pride and optimism, many communities housed enough affluent residents to enable artists to earn a tidy profit creating and selling reasonably realistic perspective views of their towns. Comparisons between then and now, whether of atlas plates or perspective views, can be quite instructive.

Do not overlook property maps of various kinds, as well as other basic historical data, on file in each of the county courthouses and in historical libraries. Also helpful is the prodigious series of maps generated by the Sanborn Insurance Company from the late 1800s through the 1940s, depicting in full physical detail every structure in virtually every Pennsylvania city. Copies are accessible at the Library of Congress and a few major research libraries.

Photography has added a new dimension to geographic and historical scholarship dealing with the world of the past 150 years. Where pictures of older landscapes, single buildings, and other objects of interest are available, their utility is obvious, as, for example, antique picture postcards, often on sale at flea markets, with their images of older vistas and individual structures. A time series of photos of specific sites taken some years apart, as has been done with Philadelphia and Pittsburgh, reveals changes in their geography that is difficult to capture otherwise.

After vertical aerial photography began in the 1930s, Pennsylvania has been photographed more than once by federal and commercial agencies at relatively large scales. In recent years, highly sophisticated modes of remotely sensed satellite imagery, using a variety of bands in the electromagnetic spectrum, have provided both panoramic and microscopic views of places. Such types of remote sensing provide information about the past that is invisible on even the most detailed of maps or that eludes even the keenest of ground observers. Thus, in addition to abandoned roads, trails, canals, railroads, power lines, mine sites, house sites, and graveyards, aerial photos reveal boundaries of vanished farms and their fields and pastures and probable manner of cultivation, the extent of forest fires, various stages of forest exploitation, and shifts in drainage patterns. Variations in soil or vegetation color and texture may hint at previous land use, not just during the historical period but even earlier.

Geographers also use the printed word. Reasonably current descriptions of Pennsylvania or portions thereof are useful, but for historic-geographic insights older accounts are invaluable. Much can be learned by comparing Murphy and Murphy's 1937 geography text with what is observable today. A roughly contemporaneous WPA (Works Progress Administration) guide serves splendidly by highlighting what has survived from the depression decade and what has not.

Travel accounts by visitors from the eighteenth century onward, including Peter Kalm, John Bartram, Harriet Martineau, and Charles Dickens, among many others, have enriched us with important observations about an earlier Pennsylvania. If dates, itineraries, accuracy, and detail vary markedly from one writer to another, these early eyewitnesses can still furnish data that is not forthcoming from extant maps, drawings, or photos. So does the more realistic fiction dealing with Pennsylvania communities. John O'Hara's clinical description of a not-so-fictional Gibbsville (Pottsville), or the account of a steel-making town in Thomas Bell's *Out of This Furnace,* provide us with a solid base for understanding community change over the past several decades.

The places where one can lay hands on documentary aids are many and varied. The county courthouses and state agencies in Harrisburg have unique archival resources. Each of hundreds of municipal and college libraries has much to offer, as do the county historical museums and libraries and the collections of the many special-interest associations. Much material is now available on the Internet.

Geography has played a vital and intimate role in the history of Pennsylvania. The meaning, value, and history of any locality can be appreciated only by situating it in its social and physical environment, in its geographic linkages with places near and far, and in the ways in which these interrelationships have evolved over time. History and geography are matters too urgent and close to our lives to be left solely to the professionals. Clever amateurs can enrich their life and that of others by exploring some of the many ne-glected corners of Pennsylvania's geography and history.

SOURCES *and* FURTHER READING

Clay, Grady. *Close-Up: How to Read the American City.* New York: Praeger, 1980.

Cuff, David J., et al., eds. *The Atlas of Pennsylvania.* Philadelphia: Temple University Press, 1989.

Ensminger, Robert. *The Pennsylvania Barn: Its Origins, Evolution, and Distribution in North America.* Baltimore: Johns Hopkins University Press, 1992.

Finkel, Kenneth. *Philadelphia Then and Now: 60 Sites Photographed in the Past and Present.* New York: Dover, 1988.

Glass, Joseph W. *The Pennsylvania Culture Region: A View from the Barn.* Ann Arbor, Mich.: UMI Research Press, 1986.

Hansen, Judith W., comp. *Pennsylvania Prints from the Collection of John C. O'Connor and Ralph M. Yeager.* University Park: The Pennsylvania State University Museum of Art, 1980.

Lemon, James T. *The Best Poor Man's Country: A Geographical Study of Early Southeastern Pennsylvania.* Baltimore: Johns Hopkins University Press, 1972.

Lewis, Peirce F. "Small Town in Pennsylvania." *Annals of the Association of American Geographers* 62 (1972), 323–51.

Miller, E. Willard, ed. *A Geography of Pennsylvania.* University Park: The Pennsylvania State University Press, 1995.

Murphy, Raymond E., and Marion Murphy. *Pennsylvania: A Regional Geography.* Harrisburg: Pennsylvania Book Service, 1937.

Pennsylvania Atlas and Gazetteer. Yarmouth, Me.: DeLorme Mapping Company, 1996.

Pennsylvania Spatial Data Access System (PASDA). University Park: The Pennsylvania State University, Deasy Laboratory, 2002.

Reps, John W. *Bird's Eye Views: Historical Lithographs of North American Cities.* New York: Princeton Architectural Press, 1998.

Schlereth, Thomas J. *Reading the Road: U.S. 40 and the American Landscape.* Knoxville: University of Tennessee Press, 1997.

Smith, Arthur G. *Pittsburgh Then and Now.* Pittsburgh: University of Pittsburgh Press, 1990.

Toker, Franklin. *Pittsburgh: An Urban Portrait.* University Park: The Pennsylvania State University Press, 1986.

Warner, Sam Bass. *The Private City: Philadelphia in Three Periods of Its Growth.* Philadelphia: University of Pennsylvania Press, 1968.

Works Progress Administration (WPA) Writer's Program. *Pennsylvania: A Guide to the Keystone State.* New York: Oxford University Press, 1940.

Zelinsky, Wilbur. *The Cultural Geography of the United States.* Revised edition. Englewood Cliffs, N.J.: Prentice-Hall, 1992.

———. "Nationalism in the American Place-Name Cover." *Names* 30 (1983), 1–28.

———. "The Pennsylvania Town: An Overdue Geographical Account." *Geographical Review* 67 (1977), 127–47.

Architecture

RICHARD J. WEBSTER

For simplicity, architecture can be placed in two categories: cultivated and vernacular. Cultivated architecture is either designed by architects or influenced by their work. Architects, trained in the arts and techniques of building, design a building with a conscious idea of how it relates to architecture of the past and present, how it meets the client's needs and desires, and how it fits into its natural and built environments. The State Capitol in Harrisburg is a good example of cultivated architecture. Its architect, Joseph Huston, knew that the Commonwealth wanted a material expression of the state's greatness. At the time, the beginning of the twentieth century, Pennsylvania was at the height of its power and wealth. So Huston designed a building in a classical style that was then much in vogue, and he turned to great works of the past for the building's most imposing features. He modeled the dome after Michelangelo's dome on St. Peter's Basilica in Rome, and based the grand entrance lobby on the one in the 1874 Paris Opera. At the same time, the Capitol was located on a low hill overlooking the Susquehanna where a classical landscape plan would later be developed, enabling the Capitol to serve as a focal point for later office buildings.

Vernacular architecture consists of the buildings of the people, much as vernacular language is the people's language. The vernacular builder learned from ancestors and neighbors rather than from books or architects. He did not design, and he rarely put pencil to paper. He simply built with an innate sense of what was comfortable and

familiar for him and his community. As such, vernacular architecture is traditional and slow to change. A good example of vernacular architecture is the Hans Herr House in Lancaster County. Built in 1719 for a Mennonite bishop by his Swiss-born son, the stone house embodies almost every characteristic of Germanic farm dwellings of the time, from its squat proportions to its root cellar. Vernacular architecture is everyday architecture, the functional buildings of the farmstead and village, and can include such common structures as springhouses, corncribs, and livery stables. Vernacular architecture was much more common in the eighteenth-century countryside than in urban areas. It faded in the nineteenth century as the printing press and transportation systems broke down pockets of isolation, and today it is being sacrificed to the "gods of growth." Yet, vernacular architecture survives in many everyday structures, some as small as rabbit cages and birdhouses, which people build from memory or common sense rather than from a set of plans.

Log was perhaps colonial Pennsylvania's most common vernacular building material. Geographically and chronologically, log construction ranged from its Swedish origins along the Delaware River in the 1640s to America's western hinterlands into the twentieth century. Log remained the dominant building material in towns and countryside long after the American Revolution. On a trip from West Chester to Wilmington, Delaware, in 1798, one traveler noted that, except for five brick or stone examples, all the houses he encountered were log. Log houses were nearly as abundant in towns. As late as 1822, for example, approximately 90 percent of Huntingdon's buildings were log.

Scholars generally give Swedes and Finns credit for introducing log construction to the American colonies, but parts of Germany also have a log-building tradition. Increased German immigration in the second quarter of the eighteenth century altered and extended this building practice in Pennsylvania. Because its technology was relatively simple, its material abundant, and its construction quick, other immigrant groups, such as the Scots-Irish, easily adopted log construction. Log buildings were still being erected in rural areas into the early twentieth century.

When you encounter a log building, it almost certainly will not be Swedish, even though its builder may have been remotely influenced by the Swedes. Current academics argue that nearly all log construction techniques are Scandinavian, but these were easily copied by others. The key element in all log buildings is corner-notching, the means by which the logs are held together. If the corner-notching fails (from rot or poor construction), the walls collapse into a tumble of logs. The types of corner-notching are more numerous than we are able to address here. They range in complexity from simple saddle-notching, in which shallow recesses are cut into round logs, to sophisticated dovetailing of logs hewn on all four sides. Saddle-notched logs protrude from the corners of the house, like those on the once-popular toy Lincoln Log houses. Pennsylvania Germans appear to have developed one type of their own: the hewn, sharp-pointed flush-cornered V notch. The British, on the other hand, coming from a land without log construction, generally adopted corner-notching that required the least skill and time to erect: saddle-notching or the longer-lasting V-notch.

Hans Herr House, West Lampeter Township, Lancaster County, 1719. Large stone houses were uncommon on Pennsylvania's early eighteenth-century frontier but appropriate for socially prominent citizens, such as Hans Herr, a Mennonite leader. In this house he sheltered his family and stored his foodstuffs: grain in the upper loft, vegetables in the root cellar.

Beware of log construction, however. Just because a building is log does not mean that it is old. Logs are highly perishable. Old log houses, even those that have been well cared for, probably have few of their original logs, but an authentic eighteenth-century log house is rare. Most survivors today date from the nineteenth century and often are not the oldest buildings in their communities. Log houses are literally being uncovered almost yearly. Because early log-house owners recognized the material's perishability, they covered exterior walls with stucco or wood siding, and interior walls with plaster. When modern owners start to upgrade these houses, they discover—and often expose—the log walls. This practice may contribute to a neighborhood's charm and sense of primitive past, but it is historically inaccurate and is not good for the house's structural system, the logs. The more rustic the building—that is, the cruder its corner-notching—the younger the building probably is. As decades passed and different building practices were introduced, fewer people retained log-building skills, until by the turn of the twentieth century log construction was often quite primitive. Log houses have a cachet, so much so that today people build imitations. These houses only look like log; their construction and amenities are far removed from the vernacular real thing.

TOP: Log barn, near Coudersport, Potter County, 1900. Charles Bailey built his hay barn of round logs from cleared farmland. His saddle-notching, the simplest log-construction technique, and large hand-hewn shingles lent a rusticity to the barn, which was demolished in 1961.

BOTTOM: Moon-Williamson House, Fallsington, Bucks County, c. 1685. The Moon-Williamson House is among Pennsylvania's oldest log houses and has the most sophisticated log construction: squared logs and dovetail notching.

Log houses that have survived were built on stone foundations. Log and wood-frame buildings that sat directly on the ground fit another category of vernacular architecture: impermanent architecture. Many early Pennsylvanians built temporary shelters until they could erect a more permanent dwelling. The British often erected these wood-frame houses by dropping their corner posts into holes in the ground. These buildings rotted away long ago; archaeologists today find them in the form of dirt that has a different color and texture. Yet their materials—wood from Pennsylvania's abundant forests—and timber-frame construction with mortise-and-tenon joints characterized many, if not most, Pennsylvania buildings into the twentieth century. Balloon-frame construction with its two-by-four members cut by steam-driven circular saws and held together with machine-made nails became popular by the middle of the nineteenth century. Ever since, Pennsylvania's wood-frame houses have been built that way, whether for workers or farmers or as twentieth-century tract houses. Pennsylvania farmers, however, continued building barns with large timbers and wooden pegs well into the twentieth century.

A visit to the attic or basement of a house will reveal its construction technique and its approximate date of construction and alterations, if any. In addition to looking for straight up-and-down saw marks (early) or curved saw marks from circular saws (later), check the methods of joining the wooden members. An eighteenth-century house, for example, usually has no ridge pole, the horizontal beam that forms the roof's ridge.

Vernacular architecture is very much local architecture. Builders used local materials, which not only determined the building's appearance but also to a degree influenced its use. Wissahickon gneiss (sometimes called shist) with its sparkling flicks of mica, for example, is found almost exclusively in Philadelphia's Germantown and Chestnut Hill neighborhoods, while in Chester County many eighteenth- and nineteenth-century buildings are built of that county's unique green serpentine. Local stone continued to be used locally well into the twentieth century, but before the end of the nineteenth century transportation systems were carrying building stones quite far. The 1907 James V. Brown Library in Williamsport, Lycoming County, for example, is built of Chester County marble. An extravagant array of stone is found in Bryn Athyn, Montgomery County, on the Cathedral of the Church of the New Jerusalem. Its walls include not only local stone but also stone from Massachusetts, Rhode Island, Kentucky, Ohio, and Berks County, Pennsylvania.

Where good clays and sand were abundant, bricks were locally fired. Thomas Jefferson Wertenbaker, a Princeton University history professor, pointed out this geological distinction in the 1930s, giving rise to the so-called Wertenbaker Line, which runs southwestwardly from Trenton, New Jersey, to Wilmington, Delaware. Northwest of this elliptical line stand early stone structures; southeast of it brick is more common. Once canal and rail transportation developed in the nineteenth century, this pattern broke down, especially in towns where local entrepreneurs either manufactured brick or transported it from nearby brickyards.

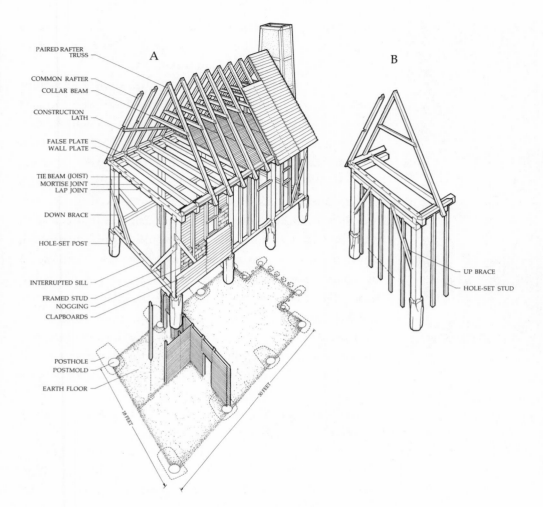

PAIRED RAFTER TRUSS
COMMON RAFTER
COLLAR BEAM
CONSTRUCTION LATH
FALSE PLATE
WALL PLATE
TIE BEAM (JOIST)
MORTISE JOINT
LAP JOINT
DOWN BRACE
HOLE-SET POST
INTERRUPTED SILL
FRAMED STUD
NOGGING
CLAPBOARDS
POSTHOLE
POSTMOLD
EARTH FLOOR

A

B

UP BRACE
HOLE-SET STUD

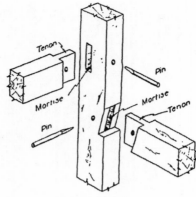

Mortise-and-tenon joints. Colonial timber-frame houses were held together with mortise-and-tenon joints, which required only an auger, a chisel, and a mallet to make. The tenon, or tongue, fits into the mortise, or slot; a hole is then bored through the joint, and a wooden pin is pounded through the hole to keep the joint in place.

LEFT: "Ordinary beginner's" house. This reconstruction drawing illustrates the framing and plan of the kind of dwelling recommended for Pennsylvania's settlers in a 1684 pamphlet distributed by William Penn. Nonpermanent architecture like this was common in the seventeenth-century English countryside.

Stonework varies widely. The simplest, rubble, is common for vernacular buildings, especially for barns and springhouses. Rubble, sometimes called fieldstone, is irregularly shaped and usually laid in a random manner. Because of its irregularity, it is difficult to lay coursed rubble walls, in which the stone is laid in courses, or roughly horizontal rows. Coursed stonework works best with dressed blocks of stone, and the most precise dressed stone is ashlar, finely finished stone laid with thin joints. Random rubble buildings were built almost from the beginnings of Pennsylvania's settlement and well into the nineteenth century, but ashlar buildings rarely date before the middle of the eighteenth century.

Colonial Pennsylvania Germans preferred stone for their distinctively different dwellings, which are characterized by squat proportions, an off-center chimney, and relatively steep roofs with two lofts above a single story. The most common ground-floor plan was three rooms (kitchen, sitting room, and bedroom). A four-room variant on this plan (the aforementioned Hans Herr House) included a pantry or workroom cut out of

Cathedral of the Church of the New Jerusalem, Bryn Athyn, Montgomery County, 1913–19. Gothic Revival architect Ralph Adams Cram, the Pitcairn family with its Pittsburgh Plate Glass fortune, and artisans following medieval techniques joined to create this mother church of the Swedenborgian faith. Although dedicated in 1919, the cathedral remains under construction.

the kitchen. At one time Germanic houses stood on the edges of present-day Philadelphia, but today they are found almost exclusively in the Great (or Cumberland) Valley.

Another significant Germanic contribution to our built environment is the distinctive Pennsylvania barn, whose origins rest in Switzerland. Characterized by its highly visible forebay or overhang and such secondary features as two interior levels and a banked ramp, the Pennsylvania barn proved extremely efficient, especially when it faced south to absorb the warmth of the winter sun. Its virtues did not go unnoticed. Early nineteenth-century agricultural writers praised the barn, and in 1865 the U.S. Commissioner of Agriculture published plans, elevations, and an essay explaining its advantages. The presence of a Pennsylvania barn is not proof of a Germanic family's residence, but it is a strong clue. Most of these barns have stone end walls with interior timber framing, but nineteenth-century barns were also built of brick or wood. The romantic hex signs that ornament many of these barns were not meant to ward off evil spirits but are only colorful folk decorations, sometimes added long after a barn's construction.

Brickwork in Pennsylvania falls into three primary, roughly chronological bonds (the pattern in which bricks are laid): English, Flemish, and American. English bond has alternating courses of headers (ends) and stretchers (long faces). It was most common in the seventeenth century and appears on a few early eighteenth-century Pennsylvania houses. Flemish bond, courses of alternating headers and stretchers, became very popular by the middle of the eighteenth century and was built well into the nineteenth century. Some houses, such as the 1696 Thomas Massey House in Broomall, Delaware County, have both bonds. American bond, which dominated nineteenth-century brickwork, has a course of headers once every third to sixth (occasionally eighth) course of stretchers. It is appropriately named because it reflects acknowledged American traits—speed and efficiency. It is the fastest and cheapest way to build a brick wall.

Unlike wood and stone, brick cannot be carved. Yet it lends itself to decorative work, especially when glazed headers contrast with the red brick. In early Pennsylvania, decoration could range from simple geometric patterns to something more personal, such as dates of construction or the original owner's initials. William Willis in York included both when he built his house in 1762, spelling out in glazed headers in the west gable "ww 1762." Datestones can perform the same service for stone buildings, but do not always believe what you see. Later owners have been known to add datestones or sometimes move them.

Joseph Collins House, West Goshen Township, Chester County, 1727; kitchen c. 1760. Collins and his family lived in an impermanent house for fourteen years before erecting this dwelling with a green serpentine ashlar front and rubble end walls and a pent roof between floors. The 1727 datestone is centered above the entrance. The rubble rear kitchen wing was added circa 1760.

Barn, Upper Pottsgrove Township, Montgomery County, 1852. The overhanging forebay is a central characteristic of the Pennsylvania barn. On the barn's opposite side, an incline leads to the threshing floor above the ground-level stables with their "Dutch" doors. The white-painted door and window surrounds and so-called hex signs contrast with the red-painted boards. X-pattern ventilators are visible on the stone end.

Nathaniel Irish House, Philadelphia, 1762–69. Like many eighteenth-century Philadelphians, house carpenter Nathaniel Irish built his dwelling in the fashion of postfire London houses, with two ground-story rooms. He demarcated the stories with a ground-story pent roof (demolished), a second-story string-course, and a third-story cornice. The arched passage to a rear yard was common for colonial Philadelphia houses.

RIGHT: Barnes-Brinton House, Pennsbury Township, Chester County, c. 1720. Flemish-bond walls and a double-diamond pattern in the gable demonstrate brick's expressive properties. Chadds Ford Historical Society has restored the building as a historic house museum.

By the time of Pennsylvania's founding, brick was the favored building material among affluent British subjects. Philadelphians, graced with good river clay and result-ant brickyards—and remembering London's disastrous fire of 1666—took the lead in developing Pennsylvania's brick architecture. Most of the city's earliest permanent build-ings were brick.

Understandably, Philadelphia also set the pattern for Pennsylvania's early urban architecture. As that eighteenth-century city quickly grew into one of the British Empire's great urban centers, master builders and bricklayers erected individual houses on long narrow lots. As other builders filled vacant lots, rows emerged with little or no open space. These rows enjoyed considerable variety. Houses rose to different heights, their back buildings had different configurations and extensions, and their fronts pushed toward or retreated from the curb lines. These houses produced an irregular streetscape, but one with front facades without terraces opening directly onto sidewalks. This pat-tern persisted well into the nineteenth century and can be seen in many Pennsylvania towns. Builders patterned the front facades of early Philadelphia houses, and often their plans, after the brick rows erected in London after its Great Fire. Pennsylvania's row houses, houses planned and built as rows of contiguous houses, are products of the industrial nineteenth century. Philadelphia took the lead here too, starting with Sansom Row in 1800. Thousands of these row houses, some built as cheap, low-rent housing and others with eclectic enhancements for middle-class clients, still stand in Pennsylvania's once-flourishing industrial towns and cities.

An architectural element found on early brick urban houses (and stone rural houses as well) is the pent roof. A pent roof is a small projection that usually extends along the length of a facade and is attached to projecting floor joists. This feature, not found on colonial architecture in New England, New York, or the Chesapeake, is a colonial Pennsylvania characteristic. Extensive debate has raged over whether the pent roof came from England or Germany. I have found many pent roofs in England but none in Germany. German settlers apparently adopted them from the English much as the English and Scots-Irish learned log construction from the Swedes and Germans. The pent roof afforded shelter from the elements, allowing residents to do handwork outside in daylight. Colonial Revival architects, aware of the pent roof's local uniqueness, contributed to its revival in the twentieth century. Skilled architects handled these new pent roofs appropriately, but many contemporary Pennsylvanians, in a naive attempt to make their buildings look traditional, have added pent roofs to buildings that never had them (and if one respects historical accuracy and architectural design never should have had them). Such buildings usually are quite evident. One of the more bizarre examples is the pent roof in the form of piano keys on Taylor's Music Store in West Chester, Chester County.

LEFT: Taylor's Music Store and Studios, West Chester, Chester County, nineteenth century; pent roof c. 1967. Pent roofs are so much a part of eastern Pennsylvania's built environment that they occasionally appear in unusual forms. Around 1967, piano keys were added to this music store, whose building dates from the nineteenth century.

RIGHT: Thatch pent roof, Barkway, Hertfordshire, England. This roof's location in an English village suggests the pent roof's national origins, and the kitchen chair indicates its historical function, providing an outdoor shelter for doing household chores in a time of poor illumination.

Cultivated architecture is most obviously characterized by style. Delineation of architectural styles can become an arcane study filled with intricacies and complexities. If you want to pursue this topic in detail, consult one of the many guides to architectural styles, but you need not invest a great deal of time and money in order to appreciate and enjoy Pennsylvania architecture. Each era has had its own dominant style, and that style tells much about the values and goals of its time. Simply observe the visual differences among these styles and you are well on your way to understanding how any particular building fits into a larger picture of Pennsylvania's history.

Pennsylvania's eighteenth-century cultivated architecture was in the English Renaissance style, which is commonly called Georgian. It is characterized by facade symmetry, a balance of horizontality and verticality, and Renaissance architectural details. Georgian architecture fit the values, social pretenses, and worldview of the British elite. Most literate citizens believed that Newton's laws of physics governed the universe,

Passage hall, Mount Pleasant, Philadelphia, 1765. Master builder Thomas Nevell designed Mount Pleasant with a wide passage hall that runs from the house's symmetrical landside to its nearly identical river front. A Doric frieze, a Renaissance classical detail, forms the hall's cornice. Its original owner, Captain John Macpherson, was a privateer during the French and Indian War, where he lost an arm but won a fortune, which he poured into this grand country seat.

RIGHT: William A. Todd House mantelpiece, Downingtown, Chester County, 1800. Todd's mantelpiece expresses the Federal style superbly. Its neoclassicism is evident both in details (for example, the urns and ribboned swags) and in techniques, such as the mantelpiece's delicate carving and the upper frame's punch-and-gouge work. Isolated ornament and slightly attenuated elements contribute to the style's delicacy.

making it balanced, mathematical, and to a great degree predictable. Into this worldview fit nearly every aspect of the arts and sciences: the U.S. Constitution of carefully calculated checks and balances, the highly structured minuet, and Georgian architecture, with its own balance and order. Independence Hall is a good example of the Georgian style, and if it were not famous for being central to our nation's founding, it would be famous as one of America's finest Georgian buildings.

The epitome of the domestic high style was the country house. The finest country houses, such as the 1765 Mount Pleasant in Philadelphia's Fairmount Park, have central passage hallways with staircases in the hallway or to the side (as in Mount Pleasant). Country houses were the mansions of their day. They were uncommon, but their central hallways became the standard interior plan for high-style houses until the Civil War period. Most of Pennsylvania's eighteenth-century architecture fell short of the Georgian style's design standards, but the Philadelphia region has many buildings with Renaissance proportions and details, especially moldings on door frames, windows, and chimney breasts. West of Lancaster and north of Easton, however, where settlement was thin, high-style Georgian design is rare.

Early nineteenth-century architecture, sometimes called the Federal style because it arrived from Britain about the time the new federal government began, is found more frequently than the colonial Georgian style and is the oldest surviving style in much of Pennsylvania. Others call it the Adamesque-Federal style because much of its ornament was derived from the Scottish-born architect and decorator, Robert Adam, who had

Independence Hall, Philadelphia, 1732–48; tower 1750–53. Built as the Pennsylvania State House, Independence Hall is better known for its historic gatherings than for its architecture. Nevertheless, it expresses English Renaissance principles well and is filled with richly carved details that many visitors fail to notice.

been inspired by Pompeii's Roman ruins unearthed in the last half of the eighteenth century. In Pennsylvania that delicate neoclassical (Adamesque) ornament is found on chimney breasts in particular. Master builders of the Federal style attenuated earlier classical proportions and smoothed surfaces to make buildings appear lighter. Such Renaissance details as columns or pilasters, for example, are thinner, exterior walls are stuccoed, and interior walls have chair rails lowered or removed altogether. The 1804 Isaac Meason

Pennsylvania State Capitol, East Wing, Harrisburg, Dauphin County, 1984–86. Although visually (and appropriately) subordinate to the older Capitol building, the East Wing (foreground), with its portico, dome, balustrades, and fountain, is a rare late twentieth-century expression of Renaissance classicism. The neoclassical North Office Building is at the far right.

House in Dunbar Township, Fayette County, designed by an English architect, demonstrates this cleaner, simpler treatment of eighteenth-century Renaissance classicism. Elsewhere in the countryside, builders put up unsophisticated but robust and creative expressions of the Federal style into the 1840s.

Meanwhile, by the 1820s, sophisticated builders and clients turned to a new Classical Revival, often called the Greek Revival. Its high-style keynote is the classical portico, which was applied to the fronts of all kinds of buildings, especially banks, churches, colleges, courthouses, and dwellings. The so-called Greek Revival, which often used Roman classical details in place of or in conjunction with Greek ones, became so popular in the United States between 1820 and the Civil War that it has been considered America's unofficial national style.

This second generation of Americans embraced the founding fathers' fascination with classicism and moved from reason to romance, from classical principles to classical reproductions. Literate citizens could see that columned buildings simulated ancient forms, and many argued that they also reflected ancient virtues and democratic principles. A Classical Revival building suggested that its occupants, whether they be legislators, bankers, or professors, possessed the same integrity and sensibilities as the leaders and philosophers of antiquity.

For public buildings, the Classical Revival has remained popular to the present day. Because ancient Greeks and Romans set the classical standard for the arts and public architecture, Pennsylvanians for nearly two centuries have built public buildings and museums in a broadly defined Classical Revival style. The 1906 State Capitol and the Philadelphia Museum of Art (opened in 1927) are perhaps our largest and best-known twentieth-century examples. The state's most explicit classical expression since the

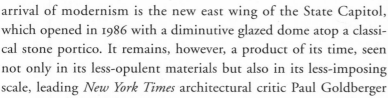

arrival of modernism is the new east wing of the State Capitol, which opened in 1986 with a diminutive glazed dome atop a classical stone portico. It remains, however, a product of its time, seen not only in its less-opulent materials but also in its less-imposing scale, leading *New York Times* architectural critic Paul Goldberger to suggest that it is less "a temple of democracy" than "a mall of democracy."

Antithetical to the Classical Revival is the Gothic Revival. Its pointed arches and soaring spires stand in opposition to the round arches and horizontality of classicism. Because the Gothic Revival grew out of the Middle Ages, when faith was ascendant, it has been the most common style for churches. Fortress Gothic was the favorite style for prisons, starting with the colossal Eastern State Penitentiary (1823–36) in Philadelphia and mimicked by county jails across Pennsylvania for the rest of the nineteenth century. Bleak stone walls and battlemented towers were designed not only to suggest the invincibility of justice but also to intimidate, to suggest suffering not unlike that endured in medieval dungeons.

Gothic Revival has also been a popular collegiate style. For more than a century the Gothic Revival was associated with monastic retreat and the harboring of knowledge during "dark" medieval centuries. Although Franklin and Marshall College's 1856 Main Hall in Lancaster is built of brick, a Renaissance material, its elongated corner pinnacles atop the tall central tower suggest the Christian educational values it aspired to teach. The Cathedral of Learning at the University of Pittsburgh suggests the same message in a more modern form. Built during the lean years of the Great Depression, an economic dark age of our own time, the Cathedral of Learning is a steel-frame skyscraper draped in stone Gothic form and details. In many respects it is eccentric, which is true of the

LEFT: Independent Congregational Church (Unitarian), Meadville, Crawford County, 1836. Not all Classical Revival buildings were designed equally well. Here architect George W. Cullum spaced the columns too widely and then placed two triglyphs (the vertical blocks in the frieze), instead of the customary one, between the columns. Regardless, the Greek Doric Order made the church an up-to-date Greek Revival work.

RIGHT: Clarion County Jail, Clarion, Clarion County, 1873–75. Like many jails across the state, Clarion County Jail features fortress Gothic details, in particular the castellated roofline and tower, which suggest harsh medieval incarceration. Until the building was vacated in 1995, the warden and his family lived in the picturesque brick front section and prisoners were housed in the stone rear cellblock. The architect, James McCullough Jr., was from Allegheny (now part of Pittsburgh).

Old Main, Franklin and Marshall College, Lancaster, 1854–56. Two modest 1857 Gothic Revival buildings flank Old Main, which was designed by Dixon, Balburnie & Dixon of Baltimore. Old Main expresses the romanticism and verticality of the Gothic Revival style, which is intensified by the building's site atop College Hill. Old Main today houses administrative offices and the Harold T. Miller Lecture and Recital Hall.

American Gothic Revival in general. For most American citizens, the Classical Revival rang more true to their secular democratic values than the English-based Gothic did.

Classical Revival was especially popular across the Northern Tier counties, where, without coincidence, we find such municipalities as Athens, Rome, Sparta, and Troy. Migration and location account for the style's concentration here. Settlers from New England in the second quarter of the nineteenth century, who at the turn of the nineteenth century had built clapboarded frame houses with New England plans, embraced the Classical Revival, which was popular in both New England and neighboring New York. A variety of expressions of the Classical Revival are found in this region. In addition to the easily recognized porticoed buildings are many expressions of naive architecture, an entertaining combination of high-style influences and traditional forms from the hands of local builders who had an incomplete knowledge of cultivated architecture.

Naive Classical Revival architecture grew out of builders' attempts to make traditional forms classical by applying classical details to simple frame houses. Because they did not understand classical proportions or design, their houses, while classical in intent, are awkward and pale imitations of porticoed classical buildings. A common naive Classical Revival house has its gable end facing the street, displaying a classical silhouette. Often the cornice is carried across the front, and sometimes pilasters at the front corners rise to an entablature below the cornice to form a two-dimensional portico. The strongest Classical Revival statement on these buildings is the frontispiece (or door surround), which consists of a simple broad entablature resting on wide vertical boards that resemble heavy classical pilasters. A variant is a five-bay Georgian farmhouse with Classical Revival details, such as a classical frontispiece marking the centered entrance and an entablature running across the front below the cornice.

At the other end of the state, ranging westward from Chester and Northampton Counties to beyond the western fringes of the Great Valley, is another form of naive architecture. Some scholars call it the Pennsylvania farmhouse. Characterized by two front doors, these nineteenth-century farmhouses were built by descendants of Pennsylvania's Germanic settlers. These scholars argue that the two front doors were the attempt by Pennsylvania Germans to give a socially accepted Georgian symmetry to the traditional Germanic house, which, with its three or four rooms clustered around the central chimney, had an asymmetrical front. In other words, these houses are material expressions of a people who were assimilating English aesthetics (the symmetrical facade) while practicing their traditional ways (the Germanic plan). Not everyone accepts this argument, contending instead that function—the use of the two front rooms as daily and special sitting rooms—determined the presence of two front doors. Perhaps future studies will show that both arguments have legitimacy. Regardless, the construction of so-called Pennsylvania farmhouses well after the Civil War era suggests the cultural, if not physical, isolation of much of rural Pennsylvania, because in the state's urban areas after 1850, Victorian architecture ruled.

"Victorian" is a dynastic term, referring to the reign of an English queen who took the throne in 1837, during the Classical Revival's heyday. A more descriptive and architecturally accurate term for this post-1850 architecture is "picturesque." The jumble of towers, overhangs, verandahs, bold cornices, and false fronts may seem cluttered to our eyes, but they are also picturesque. The lifeblood of that picturesque architecture was America's steam-powered industrialism, fueled in large part by the products of Pennsylvania's mines and forests. Industrial exploitation produced the wealth that financed and built the era's excessive and picturesque architecture. Picturesque styles are numerous and often mixed. Sorting them out takes practice and a guide book of architectural styles, but a style's name is less important than what it tells us about its time and place. One can enjoy a building's audacity and complexity without knowing its style.

Nowhere were those picturesque styles more superbly expressed than in Pennsylvania's two largest cities, where a burgeoning industrialism enriched local families and public treasuries. Politicians in Philadelphia and Pittsburgh used those fat treasuries to buy some of America's best architecture. Philadelphia City Hall is the nation's largest municipal building and its most flamboyant expression of the Second Empire (or French Renaissance) style in America. This style was imported from France on the eve of the Civil War and was much in fashion when City Hall's cornerstone was laid in 1871. Thirty years later, when the construction was declared finished, the style was old-fashioned. (The essential detail of this style is the mansard roof, which rises steeply from all four sides to create usable space in what ordinarily would be a cramped attic.) Philadelphia's City Hall is unique not only for its great size but also for its unequaled

Cathedral of Learning, University of Pittsburgh, 1926–37. Begun in 1926 under University President John Gabbert Bowman, who wanted to inspire the students, the building was dedicated in 1937. The architect, of Philadelphia, Charles Z. Klauder combined late nineteenth-century collegiate Gothic and the twentieth-century skyscraper to produce a visually successful edifice.

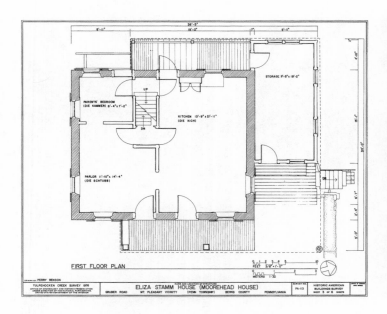

First-floor plan of the Eliza Stamm House, Penn Township, Berks County, c. 1865. As recorded by the Historic American Buildings Survey before demolition in 1977, the Eliza Stamm House had the same three-room plan as colonial Pennsylvania German houses. Stoves replaced the off-center fireplace, and the two front doors lent the facade symmetry, but the rooms' arrangements and functions remained unchanged.

RIGHT: Bell House, Mercer, Mercer County, before 1856. Residential Greek Revival style could be expressed inexpensively by turning a gable end to the street and trimming it with corner pilasters and an entablature to suggest a two-dimensional portico. Similar houses stand throughout the state, especially in the Northern Tier.

sculpture, which ranges from classical window trim to freestanding allegorical ensembles towering many stories above the street. Presiding at the very top of the marble-skinned iron-frame tower is the statue of William Penn that dominated center city's skyline for nearly a century, until skyscrapers began to rise above it after 1987.

Pittsburgh's Allegheny County Courthouse was begun later but finished sooner (1884–88) and in a different style. Its style, Richardsonian Romanesque, is named after the courthouse's architect, Henry Hobson Richardson, who was at the time perhaps America's leading architect. The distinguishing characteristic of this style is a massiveness usually expressed by heavy round arches. The Allegheny County Courthouse bristles with picturesqueness, from its rock-faced granite walls to the soaring 250-foot tower.

These features can be found on buildings of all kinds in nearly every city, town, village, and on many farms in the state. Some of those buildings—railroad depots, factories, opera houses, department stores—were creations of the nineteenth century and were erected on a scale unknown to earlier generations. Nineteenth-century Americans learned cultivated architecture primarily from architectural patternbooks and carpenters' manuals. These books discussed taste, illustrated buildings in various styles, and showed how to build complex elements, such as sweeping staircases. Books also nationalized America's architecture, making regional expressions increasingly rare—except among Pennsylvania Germans, who were slow to adopt the English language. In most cases, architects and builders used prints of elevations and plans as guides, as ideas for designing their clients' buildings. In rare cases, however, they appear to have copied (or ordered drawings of) a building directly from a book's pages. The William M. Allison House near Spring Mills, Centre County, for example, was drawn from A. J. Bicknell's 1873 *Detail, Cottage, and Constructive Architecture.*

Meanwhile, building suppliers distributed catalogs illustrating window frames, newel posts, mantelpieces, and other such items that could be ordered. So did architectural ironworks, advertising nearly every built element from porch trim to sidewalks. Iron shop-fronts became especially popular after 1850, and in urban areas entire facades were built of iron. Iron pilasters or cornices were cheaper and often more highly ornamented than carved stone examples, and were supposedly fireproof as well. Today, these mass-produced architectural elements are often covered with so many coats of paint that it is difficult to discern their material, although a streak of rust on a cornice, or testing a column with a magnet, will identify the iron. If lucky, you will find the maker's mark on the posts. Most of these iron fronts came from local foundries, but occasionally you will discover the mark of a distant ironmaker. Examples are widely dispersed across Pennsylvania. The cast-iron piers of the 1850s William Keen Building in Philadelphia, for example, bear the mark of Daniel D. Badger's New York architectural ironworks, and the front of the present school board offices in Wyalusing, Bradford County, is the work of the Mesker Brothers in St. Louis, Missouri, who patented their distinctive sheet-metal fronts in 1887.

By the 1880s another manufactured material, terra-cotta, had come into vogue. It can be traced to eighteenth-century England, but the late nineteenth-century affection for the material grew from the 1871 Great Fire of Chicago. While bricks and stone crumbled and cast iron melted or cracked in the holocaust's intense heat, terra-cotta emerged unscathed. Understandably, Chicago soon became the nation's center of terra-cotta production, but the name panel on the highly picturesque 1888 First Fire Company in West Chester, Chester County, came from Philadelphia. Early terra-cotta was buff-colored, but by the 1880s brick-red was the preferred color, as demonstrated by the West Chester fire hall and more fully by the 1890 University of Pennsylvania Library. As the dark, picturesque styles of the late nineteenth-century-brown decades gave way to academic classicism in the early twentieth century, manufacturers produced glazed terra-cotta, which remained popular for such commercial buildings as the three-story Eberhart Garage in Gettysburg, Adams County, and for classical details of which the largest and most imitative are the many-colored human figures in the one finished pediment of the Philadelphia Museum of Art.

In the late nineteenth century the building trades made a distinction between terracotta and artificial stone. Artificial stone was manufactured from a mixture of cement,

Philadelphia City Hall, 1871–1901. The mansard roof on the center and corner pavilions is the dominant characteristic of the gargantuan building's Second Empire style. The tower, capped by Alexander Milne Calder's statue of William Penn, is not representative of the style, but it lends a picturesque monumentality. John McArthur Jr. was City Hall's architect, assisted after construction began by the more prominent Thomas U. Walter.

Allegheny County Courthouse, Pittsburgh, 1884–88. This courthouse with attached jail is one of the best works of Henry H. Richardson, who died before its completion. It also was a model for courthouses throughout Pennsylvania. Modest imitations stand in Uniontown, Fayette County; Jim Thorpe, Carbon County; Bloomsburg, Columbia County; and Laporte, Sullivan County.

sand, water, and stone aggregate that was poured into molds. Like cast iron, its popularity lay largely in the cheapness of its complex forms. To hire stonecutters to carve stone with the same complexity would have been prohibitively expensive. Cast stone is still produced and takes experience to detect. The poster building for artificial materials is the 1898 Stroh Building in Jim Thorpe, Carbon County. Its Pompeiian brick front is trimmed with what appears to be cast-brownstone sills and lintels, ground-story iron piers with an infill of mid-twentieth-century artificial stone, and a sheet-metal cornice and parapet with a terra-cotta gable. Only the lack of concrete blocks prevents it from being a near-complete catalog of artificial materials.

Concrete block is an early twentieth-century material. In 1900 the number of concrete-block houses in the United States could be counted on two hands. Six years later thousands of firms were manufacturing a wide variety of concrete blocks emulating different stone facings. The most popular was the rock-faced block, which imitates roughly quarried stone. Houses built of this material are distinctive visually, not aesthetically, and still stand in small towns and old suburbs. These houses and commercial buildings often are "blockish" in form, and that and the uniformity of the rock-faced blocks make them appear rigid and naive today. In the first quarter of the twentieth century, however, a working middle class, enamored with manufactured products and looking for low cost,

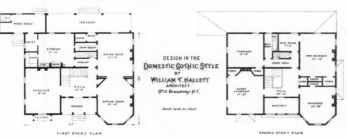

adopted the material. Mount Joy, Lancaster County, has an abundance of concrete-block structures, including the 1914 home of Jacob Y. Kline, who operated a nearby concrete-block works during the century's first two decades.

Contributing to the popularity of the concrete block were cheap, hand-operated machines that allowed thrifty home-builders to produce their own structural materials. Early concrete blocks had been large and heavy, sometimes weighing as much as 180 pounds, but by 1924 manufacturers had agreed on a more manageable standard size. The material's popularity was in decline, though, and the construction downturn, caused by the Great Depression of the 1930s and a growing preference for the smooth surfaces of modernism, contributed to the demise of the concrete block. It was replaced by the modern cinder block, a much lighter, smoother-surfaced hollow block that initially used coal cinders as an ingredient. An early cinder block was the "Straublox," manufactured by F. J. Straub in Lancaster, Lancaster County, beginning in 1919.

Related in form to many concrete-block houses is the foursquare house. The true foursquare is a cube, two to five bays across the front with an open porch and frequently a low dormer in its hipped roof. Pattern books and local builders offered various interpretations. The colonial foursquare incorporated classical porch columns and perhaps a squat Palladian window (an arched tripartite window like the one in Independence Hall's tower) and occasionally stained shingles wrapped around at least one of the stories. Many were prefabricated and sold through mail-order catalogs. Sears, Roebuck & Company was one of the largest of these house-manufacturing firms. The popularity of the foursquare peaked at the turn of the twentieth century and faded after World War I.

By then the bungalow was in ascendancy. Bungalows are low-slung, one-story or

LEFT: Architectural pattern book design for a house in domestic Gothic style. William Allison apparently ordered plans for his Centre County house from *Cottage and Constructive Architecture* (1873). The number of pattern books grew steadily in the last half of the nineteenth century; this particular one was aimed at experienced builders and their clients.

RIGHT: William M. Allison House, Spring Mills, Centre County, late 1870s. Allison owned a large farm and managed a woolen mill and gristmill that provided him with the income to build this Gothic Revival dwelling for his bride-to-be. Its Gothic features—tall proportions, flared eaves, and stick-style porch ornament— were drawn from a popular architectural pattern book.

Wyalusing Area School District Office, Wyalusing, Bradford County, c. 1900. After the Civil War, the railroad helped end local and regional architectural distinctiveness. Mesker Brothers, for example, distributed hundreds of iron storefronts throughout the nation from their facilities in St. Louis, Missouri. Their iron front on this otherwise brick building in the foreground was patented in 1887.

RIGHT: First West Chester Fire Company, West Chester, Chester County, 1887. Few buildings express late nineteenth-century picturesqueness better than this fire hall with its textured walls, diverse forms, and irregular silhouette. Architect T. Roney Williamson designed the tower to be both picturesque and functional; it housed an alarm bell and a drying rack for hoses.

story-and-a-half houses with overhanging roofs that sweep low over an open porch that blends indoor and outdoor space. Their natural materials, open and informal floor plans, and such distinctive details as exposed rafter ends and squat porch posts express their Americanization of the English Arts and Crafts style. They reflect the growing informality of American suburban life at the time, and the extension of that life to families of modest means.

Individual home builders purchased most of these prefabricated mail-order houses, but occasionally industrial firms erected scores of them for their workers. In 1920 the American Magnesium Company, for example, purchased from Sears, Roebuck & Company both foursquares and bungalows for its employees in Plymouth Meeting, Montgomery County, and three years earlier Inland Steel erected an entire town of workers' houses (in Indianola, Allegheny County) supplied by Sterling Homes in Bay City, Michigan.

Among the limited architectural styles of mail-order houses was the Colonial Revival style (sometimes called Georgian Revival in high-style applications). It proved to be the twentieth century's most durable and perhaps most popular architectural style. One of Pennsylvania's earliest sophisticated Colonial Revival buildings is Philadelphia's 1891 Germantown Cricket Club, which was cultivated in every sense, from membership to style. Colonial Revival, however, was not unique to Pennsylvania; it was a national phenomenon that in many respects is still with us. It touches almost every aspect of our world, from the built environment of house museums and garden design, to popular culture, where it ranges from the political (for example, ad hoc militia and Minute Man missiles) to the satirical ("Washington slept here"). The term "Colonial Revival" here is architecturally inclusive. It encompasses rustic early colonial forms, the sophisticated Georgian style, the elegant Federal style, and Spanish Colonial Revival expressions, such as stuccoed Mission-style houses, tiled patios, and Fiestaware.

Colonial Revival has been a remarkably flexible style, and until modernism's spread after World War II architects applied it to nearly every building type. Some designs were little more than colonial-detailed skins creatively grafted onto large-scale buildings with modern functions, as in the case of the 1929 Wawa Dairy creamery in Wawa, Delaware County. Others were more derivative. Lafayette College's 1950 Kirby House in Easton, Northampton County, for example, is a squat version of the reconstructed Virginia Governor's Palace in Colonial Williamsburg. Independence Hall, however, has been

TOP: Jacob Y. Kline House, Mount Joy, Lancaster County, 1914. Jacob Kline erected his foursquare house in 1914, showcasing such concrete details as rock-faced quoins and bold porch balusters manufactured in his concrete-block factory in Floria, which has since been incorporated into Mount Joy.

BOTTOM: Germantown Cricket Club, Philadelphia, 1890–91. Designed by one of America's most sophisticated architectural firms (McKim, Mead & White of New York), the building illustrates the creative design and large scale of the late nineteenth-century Georgian Revival variant of the Colonial Revival.

Borough Hall, Towanda, Bradford County, 1934. Local architect and former councilman Clarence M. Thompson patterned his design for Towanda's borough hall after Independence Hall in Philadelphia. He mimicked not only the tower of Independence Hall, with its Palladian window, but also the decked gable roof. The building's original means of summoning police (the old courthouse bell in the belfry) was less intentionally Colonial Revival. Borough Hall was a project of the Depression-era Public Works Administration.

Pennsylvanians' favorite colonial model. Buildings based on this historic landmark range from the diminutive 1934 Borough Hall in Towanda, Bradford County, to the sumptuous 1958 Erie Insurance Group headquarters in Erie, Erie County. The historical roots of other buildings are more subtle. The Cloisters, the 1928 Juniata College dormitory complex in Huntingdon, Huntingdon County, for example, is regarded to have been inspired by the Ephrata Cloister built by German Pietists in the 1740s in Ephrata, Lancaster County, but it much more closely resembles mid-eighteenth-century Moravian buildings in Bethlehem, Northampton County.

No one embraced the Colonial Revival more warmly than did middle-class homeowners. Beginning in the 1920s they found it the most pleasing veneer for their suburban dwellings, and often the most fashionable taste for their furnishings as well. Popular historical expressions included the Spanish Colonial and the Dutch Colonial, but most Pennsylvanians preferred versions drawn from colonial New England, the Chesapeake, and Pennsylvania. Since World War II every county has experienced tract developments filled with Colonial Revival houses; in some counties their numbers are legion. Colonial Revival remains the most popular residential stylistic finish, sometimes with only such details as pedimented doorcases or pent roofs alluding to the eighteenth century.

Even skyscrapers could be given Colonial Revival veneers, as Philadelphia's 1925 Insurance Company of North America (INA, now CIGNA) Building demonstrates. Pennsylvania architects did not pioneer skyscraper development. Until about 1930 they mimicked work in New York and Chicago. Within that emulative pattern, however, Pennsylvania skyscrapers were occasionally graced with styles or features appropriate for local firms. The INA Building's Colonial Revival details, for example, allude to the company's 1792 founding as America's oldest fire and marine insurance company.

Architects working in Pittsburgh have proven particularly clever in promoting their clients' images. The 1929 Koppers Building, for example, is capped with a copper chateauesque roof (which resembles a horizontally elongated pyramid), while across the street the 1932 Gulf Building for decades had atop its forty-four floors neon lights flashing primitive weather forecasts in corporate orange and blue colors (orange was good; blue was bad). In other cases, skyscrapers' building materials promote a corporation's product, an easier feat in Pittsburgh than elsewhere because of that city's many manufacturing industries. The 1953 and 1970 ALCOA buildings feature molded aluminum wall-and-window panels, the 1971 U.S. Steel building showcases its weathering Cor-Ten steel, and the postmodern 1984 PPG Place (Pittsburgh Plate Glass) resembles a glass cathedral.

Four successive styles dominated twentieth-century skyscraper design. A stripped

PPG Place, Pittsburgh, 1982–85. Designed by Johnson/Burgee Architects of New York, PPG Place is one of Pennsylvania's most interesting postmodern office buildings. It not only showcases the company's product (glass) but also alludes to the faith of the Pitcairn family, which founded the company. Compare this building with the Cathedral of the Church of the New Jerusalem in Bryn Athyn, Montgomery County, earlier in this chapter.

classicism was popular into the 1920s when taste shifted to the jazzy Art Deco, with its geometric ornament of chevrons, zigzags, and the like. Art Deco skyscrapers often climb in a series of setbacks, like those of the 1928 Pennsylvania Power & Light building in Allentown, Lehigh County, sometimes climaxing with a distinctive crowning element, such as the tiled dome atop Philadelphia's 1929 Drake Hotel. Others, such as the 1931 Hooker Fulton building in Bradford, McKean County, rise as towers directly to their Art Deco ornamented crests.

Hooker Fulton Building, Bradford, McKean County, 1930–31. The Art Deco (or Modernistic) style was a popular modern style that relied on geometric and abstract ornament, often in colored terra-cotta, seen here on the street-level piers and mint-green-and-black diamonds above the top story.

The International style, commonly considered "modern architecture," arrived in the United States from Europe about 1930. Just as World War I was believed to be the war to end all wars, the International style was to be the style to end all styles—so revolutionarily modern that it was free of all historical references. International-style buildings are characterized by an absence of ornament and an emphasis on enclosed geometrical volumes with smooth surfaces. In the hands of journeyman architects or penurious developers, the result can be facades that resemble graph paper and skyscrapers that look like piles of glass boxes. America's first skyscraper in this style, however, the 1932 Philadelphia Saving Fund Society (PSFS) building in Philadelphia's Center City, is an architectural masterpiece. Above the plate-glass ground-story shops and five polished-granite stories of banking rooms rises the twenty-seven-story office tower, cantilevered from the dark-brick spine housing the mechanical systems. The PSFS building has not even a hint of historical ornament. It was, and remains, thoroughly modern. The International style lost its revolutionary flair after World War II as it became the style of bureaucratic America, a no-nonsense style that reflected America's economic and military superpower status. For nearly four decades, corporate headquarters, office towers, and apartment buildings were erected in variants of this style. Representative of these buildings is Laurel Court, a 1968 Section 8 residence for the elderly in Pottsville, Schuylkill County.

In the 1980s major national corporations turned to a new style, Postmodernism. Robert Venturi, a Philadelphia architect, promoted this new style in the early 1960s as a visually and intellectually more complex style than the modernism it challenged. Postmodernism does not spurn history and ornament. It unabashedly incorporates historical architectural details, albeit in exaggerated forms and sometimes as architectural puns.

Two outstanding Pennsylvania postmodern works are the 1987 One Liberty Place in Philadelphia and the aforementioned PPG Place in Pittsburgh. Both exhibit an architectural richness in their unique silhouettes and make visual references to historical styles that were forbidden in the earlier International style. The Art Deco–style Chrysler Building, still one of the most distinctive features on New York's skyline, clearly inspired the design of One Liberty Place, especially its complex cap. On the other hand, PPG Place emulates Bryn Athyn's Cathedral of the Church of the New Jerusalem, a hand-crafted Gothic Revival work funded initially in 1913 by the Pitcairn family, which also

founded Pittsburgh Plate Glass. In addition to the glass pinnacles of PPG Place's forty-story glass-sheathed tower are the pleated reflective-glass walls whose reflections suggest Gothic tracery that varies with the hours of the day and the seasons of the year. By the end of the twentieth century, postmodernism had become the new orthodoxy; postmodern shopping centers and office parks with columns and pediments emulating classical porticoes erupted across the state.

Skyscrapers, like suspension bridges, are often best enjoyed from a distance, where one can appreciate their soaring grandeur. Up close the most interesting aspect is usually the lobby. Lobbies can range from pleasant and enticing to cold and uninviting.

Dutch Pantry, DuBois, Clearfield County, c. 1965. This restaurant building is regional roadside architecture at its best: colorful, self-consciously regional, and vaguely historical. Begun in Hummels Wharf, Snyder County, the small restaurant chain is now owned by a man who began his career as a teenage dishwasher in one of these restaurants.

Compare the lobby of Pittsburgh's Art Deco Koppers building with almost any office lobby built between 1950 and 1970 and you will understand why middle-class householders never warmed to modernism. Corporations appropriated the new modernism because it suggested power and newness, but most working people found it avant-garde, cold, even sterile. They preferred something warm and traditional like the Colonial Revival.

Some affluent Pennsylvanians, on the other hand, such as Philadelphia stockbroker William Wasserman and Pittsburgh department store magnate Edgar J. Kaufmann, were drawn to modernism. Wasserman in 1932 commissioned George Howe, architect of the famed PSFS building, to design a modern country house, Square Shadows, in Whitemarsh, Montgomery County. Although in the new modern style, "Square Shadows" uses local stone in its walls, allowing it to blend historically and visually into its landscape, so much so that it is all but forgotten today. Kaufmann also commissioned a famous architect, the brilliant but controversial Frank Lloyd Wright. Wright was sixty-nine years old and his career was in decline when Kaufmann in 1936 asked him to design a rural retreat along Bear Run near Ohiopyle, Fayette County. By January 1938 that house, "Fallingwater," was on the cover of *Time* magazine, Wright was entering arguably his most creative years, and Pennsylvania had acquired the most famous modern house in America, if not the world. Fallingwater is a bold blending of the modern and the natural. Anchored into the natural rock, cantilevered reinforced-concrete balconies float over Bear Run, becoming part of the waterfall. European modernists influenced Wright, but they did not sway him from his vision of what he called organic architecture. The democratic taste of his design is demonstrated by the great numbers who make the pilgrimage to remote Fallingwater (thirty-nine times as many), compared with those who visit Walter Gropius's 1938 International-style house in suburban Boston. In 2001 a $1 million project to permanently stabilize the structural system of Fallingwater and make other improvements was launched; although Fallingwater's distinctive balconies were built with more steel than code required, they have sagged over the decades and without intervention the house would have eventually toppled into Bear Run.

Public accommodations, enterprises that prosper by drawing the public through their doors, rejected modernism. Their roots rest in early inns and taverns, and their number grew with the automobile's popularity after World War I, especially alongside new, paved highways. Some early roadside eateries are unique and whimsical. The "coffee pot" restaurant on U.S. Route 30 in Bedford, Bedford County, assumed the shape of an old-fashioned coffee pot. In rural areas, the log cabin theme was popular, as seen in the 1932 Log Cabin Inn in Gaines Township, Tioga County, and in Limberlost in in Roystone, Warren County, both of which are in wooded areas along U.S. Route 6. More common were prefabricated diners, many of which have fallen to "progress." Still, a few such diners—the 1939 Wellsboro Diner in Wellsboro, Tioga County, for example—remain virtually untouched. Since about 1960, national chains and fast-food franchises have introduced an unfortunate blandness to their restaurants. They offer only distinctive silhouettes or vague historical references. A Pennsylvania chain, however, retains regional spunk. Dutch Pantry restaurants are a popular pastiche of gambrel roofs (perceived as Dutch Colonial since that style's promulgation by prefabricated home companies in the 1920s), hex signs (commonly accepted as Pennsylvania German folk art), cupolas (a colonial metaphor for importance), and a red-white-and-blue enamel finish (suggestive of cleanliness, modernism, and the U-S-A). Excellent examples stand near I-80 exits in DuBois and Clearfield, Clearfield County, where they serve the same function as inns and taverns did more than 150 years ago.

Pennsylvania's architectural treasury is richer than this short chapter suggests, but space constraints prevent much from being included. Churches, for example, receive little attention here, but they readily reflect a community's ethnicity, as the many onion domes built by Eastern European immigrants and their descendants in St. Clair, Schuylkill County, indicate. Workers' housing, especially in such coal-company towns as Colver, Cambria County, suggest the bitter old saying that Pennsylvania towns were built for working, not living, but they too get scant notice here. Regretful though such omissions may be, they leave patches of local architectural history to be discovered, or rediscovered, by Pennsylvanians who will continue to gain a greater understanding of their state's past through its architecture.

"Fallingwater," Ohiopyle, Fayette County, 1935–36. Named the best building of the twentieth century by the American Institute of Architects, this rural retreat is both romantic and modern. Instead of having the house overlook Bear Run, architect Frank Lloyd Wright virtually made it part of the stream. Today the Western Pennsylvania Conservancy operates the house as a museum.

SOURCES *and* FURTHER READING

Birchenall, Martha P., Sylvia Carson, and Gregory Ramsey. *Historic Buildings of Centre County, Pennsylvania*. University Park: The Pennsylvania State University Press, 1980.

Burns, Deborah Stephens, and Richard J. Webster, with Candace Reed Stern. *Pennsylvania Architecture: The Historic American Buildings Survey with Catalog Entries, 1993–1990*. Harrisburg: Pennsylvania Historical and Museum Commission, 2000.

Eisenhart, Luther P., ed. *Historic Philadelphia from the Founding Until the Early Nineteenth Century: Papers Dealing with Its People and Buildings, with an Illustrative Map*. Philadelphia: American Philosophical Society, 1953.

Ensminger, Robert F. *The Pennsylvania Barn: Its Origin, Evolution, and Distribution in North America*. Baltimore: Johns Hopkins University Press, 1992.

Jordan, Terry G. *American Log Buildings: An Old World Heritage*. Chapel Hill: University of North Carolina Press, 1985.

Lanier, Gabrielle M., and Bernard L. Herman. *Everyday Architecture of the Mid-Atlantic: Looking at Buildings and Landscapes*. Baltimore: Johns Hopkins University Press, 1997.

O'Gorman, James F., Jeffrey A. Cohen, George E. Thomas, and G. Holmes Perkins. *Drawing Towards Building: Philadelphia Architectural Graphics, 1732–1986*. Philadelphia: University of Pennsylvania Press, 1986.

Pendleton, Philip E. *Oley Valley Heritage: The Colonial Years, 1700–1775*. Birdsboro: Pennsylvania German Society and Oley Valley Heritage Association, 1994.

Sewell, Darrell L., ed. *Philadelphia: Three Centuries of American Art*. Philadelphia: Philadelphia Museum of Art, 1976.

Stotz, Charles Morse. *The Early Architecture of Western Pennsylvania*. New York: William Helburn, 1936. Reprinted as *The Architectural Heritage of Early Western Pennsylvania*. Pittsburgh: University of Pittsburgh Press, 1966.

Tatum, George B. *Penn's Great Town: 250 Years of Philadelphia Architecture Illustrated in Prints and Drawings*. Philadelphia: University of Pennsylvania Press, 1961.

———. *Philadelphia Georgian*. Middletown, Conn.: Wesleyan University Press, 1976.

Toker, Franklin. *Pittsburgh: An Urban Portrait*. University Park: The Pennsylvania State University Press, 1986.

Van Trump, James D., and Arthur P. Ziegler. *Landmark Architecture of Allegheny County, Pennsylvania*. Pittsburgh: Pittsburgh History & Landmarks Foundation, 1967.

Webster, Richard J. *Philadelphia Preserved: Historic American Buildings Survey Catalog*. Philadelphia: Temple University Press, 1976. Revised edition, 1981.

Archaeology

VERNA L. COWIN

Archaeology enhances and refines history. The discipline can be likened to a time machine—a vehicle by which bits and pieces of things lost or discarded in the past are used to build histories of events and peoples as far back as ancient times. For Pennsylvania this begins with likely the first people to enter the river valleys, 14,000 or more years ago. Because these and later Native American groups left no written accounts, archaeology is the only way to piece together a narrative about how these residents lived and moved about the land and waters of what is now Pennsylvania. What you read in Chapter 1 about the earliest Pennsylvanians sums the current status of the state's earliest history as formulated by archaeologists. But archaeology involves much more than examining peoples who did not leave records in writing; it encompasses all of our historic past as well. By finding and studying objects that were used by former residents, scholars can not only begin to reconstruct the lives of the original settlers, but also trace the comings and goings of subsequent Native Americans, Europeans, Africans, and others who followed in their footsteps, even up to the present day.

Whether down on hands and knees with a trowel and a paintbrush in hand, or standing aside to supervise a bulldozer that is removing soil from a large area, archaeologists look for places and things that can reveal something about any era. Sometimes the things lead to the identification of a person theretofore unknown to history. Archaeological investigations also can show changes in technology and even reveal lost

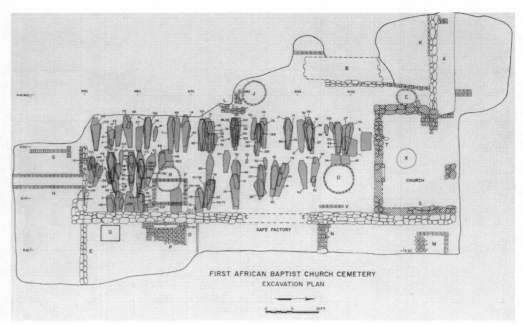

FIRST AFRICAN BAPTIST CHURCH CEMETERY
EXCAVATION PLAN

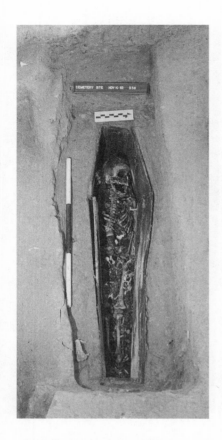

Intact coffin found in the First African Baptist Church cemetery, Philadelphia. The coffins at deeper levels were in most cases well preserved. At this site, gabled lids made of four pieces of wood were typical.

RIGHT: Recent excavation of urban sites has uncovered evidence of vibrant African American community life that is not so fully documented in other records. The excavation plan of the First African Baptist Church in Philadelphia shows the arrangement of burials relative to one another and to the walls. The 1984 dig in Center City recovered several well-preserved coffins with skeletal remains of blacks who were buried in the church cemetery sometime between the congregation's founding in 1809 and the closing of the cemetery in the mid-1840s. Examination of the site, the objects in the graves, and the bodies provided strong evidence of the persistence of West African burial practices and the incorporation of Christian traditions by black Baptists.

technologies. A lone artifact, when fully documented, can discover forgotten people, places, and things.

While Pennsylvania archaeologists tend to specialize in either the time before written records or historic time, there are many finer divisions of the discipline, such as geoarchaeology, industrial archaeology, and urban archaeology. Some practitioners focus their work on a single class of materials that are recovered from archaeological sites, such as identification of charred plant remains or the analysis of animal bones, fish bones and scales, or freshwater mussel shells. These specialists greatly assist other archaeologists in determining the activities that took place at an archaeological site, whether it is an old well on a city lot, or a fort, or a Native American settlement. Through multidisciplinary research, evidence found at any archaeological site, even if meager in terms of the types of materials that survive over time, enhances understanding of the past.

Archaeological sites within the Commonwealth are recorded in the Pennsylvania survey files maintained by the Pennsylvania Historical and Museum Commission in Harrisburg. The numbering system begins with 36, the alphabetical order of Pennsylvania among the states before the admission of Alaska and Hawaii. Next are two abbreviated letters to designate the county, followed by the number of the site within the county. For example, Meadowcroft Rockshelter is 36WH293, the 293rd site recorded in Washington County, and Sheep Rock Shelter is 36HU1, the first site recorded in Huntingdon County. More than 18,000 prehistoric and historic sites are listed in the files, and more are added each year.

Many of these sites are attributed to groups of American Indians who lived in what is now the Commonwealth for thousands of years before the arrival of Europeans. These

Archaeologists have been able to "reconstruct" Benjamin Franklin's house and court in Philadelphia. This photograph shows Franklin Court during the 1960 excavation. In the front is the privy pit, which was connected to the house and in which were found many items that had been thrown away during Franklin's day. Many objects recovered from the dig are on display today at the site arranged according to their likely use and location. The site and display are object lessons on how archaeology can help people understand the history of a person, a place, and a time.

places range from the elusive hunting camps used by the earliest of the hunting and gathering groups, to the stone outcrops and quarries that they and later people visited to obtain flint to replenish their toolkits.

Archaeologists discovered that European goods appeared on interior Indian sites before the newcomers themselves penetrated inland from the coast. Such nonnative artifacts as beads, trinkets, ornaments, and brass kettles moved along well-established trade routes and exchange networks. The routes across the landscape were footpaths, described by Paul A. W. Wallace in his *Indian Paths of Pennsylvania* as "dry, level, and direct." The trails were so efficient that many modern highways closely follow the original routes. Some of the paths have great antiquity, based on a study of the distribution of Paleo-Indian projectile points that were found years later by archaeologists as they searched along Catfish Path in Washington and Allegheny Counties. More than twenty Paleo-Indian sites are recorded in the Chartiers Creek drainage in Washington and Allegheny Counties. This and other Pennsylvania paths offered access to later Indian groups, traders, missionaries, soldiers, settlers, and immigrants who camped briefly or built settlements near them. Archaeologists call places where they find traces of human activities "sites," and the things discovered on them are known as "artifacts."

Native American sites are often discovered when plowing or some other disturbance of the upper soils brings artifacts to the surface. The open sites are found along river

Archaeologists processing soil samples through a flotation system to recover what they call "ecofacts," such items as minuscule charred seeds and fish scales. By fine-screening the lightweight materials that float to the surface, specialists in analysis of flora and fauna samples can determine diet, seasonality, and even climatic conditions present at the time the site was occupied.

BELOW: Concentration of Paleo-Indian sites located along Catfish Path in southwestern Pennsylvania.

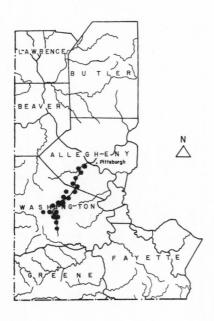

terraces, especially at or near a juncture with another stream; however, archaeological sites are spread widely across the landscape, from hilltops to valley floors. Archaeologists also look for former living areas beneath rock overhangs, called rock shelters, and sometimes even in caves. To interpret these sites properly, the investigators use special techniques to recover evidence for any plants and animals that were procured and used for food and clothing. Soil samples are processed through water flotation systems to recover charred seeds, vegetable fibers, tiny bones, and fish scales. Plant and animal remains contribute information that helps to determine the time of year a place was utilized and hold clues about the climatic conditions present at the time the site was occupied. Archaeologists also attempt to discover the sources of the raw materials used to make projectile points, knives, and other tools. By determining the source of the cherts and flints used to fashion chipped stone tools that are found at a site, one can determine the movement of raw materials and propose hypotheses about trade and exchange.

An "ideal" archaeological site would be completely undisturbed and contain either evidence of an incident that occurred sometime in the past or multiple layers of occupations stacked on top of each other. Unfortunately, such sites are rare. Wind, frost, water, plants, animals, insects, and human activities are just some of the factors that alter original deposits. Certain locations within Pennsylvania must have been especially attractive because places were chosen as living areas by different groups of people over and over again. Where conditions permit, these multiple activities create stratified sites that can contain evidence for both prehistoric and historic activities.

NATIVE AMERICAN SITES

The combination of knowledge gained from stratified sites, and the wealth of information gleaned from excavations at single occupations, contributes to the building of a chronological framework for the earliest settlements within Pennsylvania (Chapter 1). Perhaps the best way to appreciate archaeology as a way of understanding the past is to examine some of the major sites that provided new information. Meadowcroft Rockshelter, Washington County, and Sheep Rock Shelter, Huntingdon County, are among the state's most famous sites. Sheep Rock Shelter, located on the Raystown Branch of the Juniata River, was investigated by John E. Miller and members of the Society for Pennsylvania Archaeology during the summer of 1958. Staff from the State Museum of Pennsylvania directed work at the site over the next few years. Excavations were completed during field schools sponsored by Penn State University and Juniata College between 1958 and 1967.

It is often a challenge for archaeologists to separate one layer from another. To ensure proper interpretations, investigators must rely on the relationships among the types of artifacts found and on a variety of dating methods. The stratigraphy profile of one section of Sheep Rock Shelter, shown in the accompanying illustrations, shows that digging activities of later visitors to the shelter penetrated into earlier layers. In order to reveal each episode in the history of the site, archaeologists begin by removing objects and uncovering features that were buried and concealed by later deposits, but this is done by removing the levels in reverse order of the way they were originally laid down.

At Sheep Rock Shelter, wind, weather, and mostly dry conditions contributed to the preservation of normally perishable materials that included bone, antler, turtle shell, mussel shell, wood bark cordage, fabric, leather, fur, feathers, and vegetable remains. Such preservation is very rare except in the arid West. The uppermost deposits (Zone 1) dated from 1570 to 1960 contained recent debris, such as matchsticks, bottle caps, rifle and shotgun casings, a few buttons, and a 1903 penny. Also found were the remains of meals eaten by the hawks and owls that utilized the space beneath the rock overhang. The archaeologists carefully separated the animal deposits from those that were left by humans.

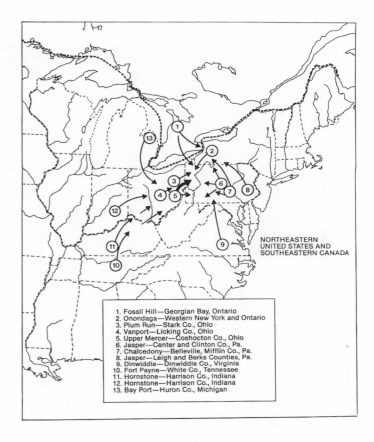

NORTHEASTERN
UNITED STATES AND
SOUTHEASTERN CANADA

1. Fossil Hill—Georgian Bay, Ontario
2. Onondaga—Western New York and Ontario
3. Plum Run—Stark Co., Ohio
4. Vanport—Licking Co., Ohio
5. Upper Mercer—Coshocton Co., Ohio
6. Jasper—Center and Clinton Co., Pa.
7. Chalcedony—Belleville, Mifflin Co., Pa.
8. Jasper—Leigh and Berks Counties, Pa.
9. Dinwiddle—Dinwiddle Co., Virginia
10. Fort Payne—White Co., Tennessee
11. Hornstone—Harrison Co., Indiana
12. Hornstone—Harrison Co., Indiana
13. Bay Port—Huron Co., Michigan

Movement of lithic materials into Pennsylvania. For making projectile points, Paleo-Indians sought out raw materials of the highest quality. The cherts and flints used to make tools were identified by Stanley W. Lantz, who also mapped the wide variety of places where they were found, at some of the earliest known sites in Pennsylvania.

Zone 2 of the shelter was almost entirely comprised of manure deposited in the 1860s by grazing domestic sheep that made their way down the steep slope to seek protection under the overhang. The presence of the sheep is commemorated in the site's name. Beneath the manure was a thin layer (Zone 3) of materials dating from 1570 to 1860. Lying below in Zone 4 was a Susquehannock level dating about 1560. In that zone archaeologists found an oval arrangement of pits, which they interpreted as a sleeping area because the pits were lined with bark, covered with mats fashioned from marsh grass, and sometimes covered further with forest leaves. Within the bedding materials were found grape stems, chestnuts, chestnut hulls, cobs of mature maize, gourd and pumpkin fragments, bean vines, ripe beans, and sunflower seeds. From the same area, the archaeologists excavated a bark container (see illustration in Chapter 1) filled with corncobs.

Because cord for spinning and small, dried human fecal deposits were found in the central portion of the sleeping area, the archaeologists concluded that women and children slept in the center of the oval while men slept in a protective circle around them. The Susquehannock group utilizing the shelter was likely comprised of no less than twenty adults, and the presence of so many cultigens and six stone hoe blades in Zone 4

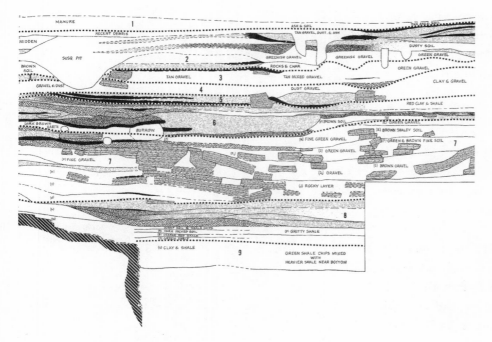

A section of the complex stratigraphy at Sheep Rock Shelter, zones 1–9.

TABLE 10.1 **SELECTED RADIOCARBON DATES FROM MEADOWCROFT ROCKSHELTER**

Radiocarbon Age	Date	Cultural Period
175±50	A.D. 1775	Historic
685±80	A.D. 1265	Late Prehistoric
925±65	A.D. 1025	Early Late Prehistoric
1880±65	A.D. 70	Middle Woodland
3090±115	1140 B.C.	Early Woodland
4005±85	3055 B.C.	Late Archaic
6630±70	4680 B.C.	Middle Archaic
8010±110	6060 B.C.	Early Archaic
14,925±620	12,975 B.C.	Paleo-Indian

SOURCE: J. M. Adovasio, A. T. Boldurian, and R. C. Carlisle, "Who Are Those Guys? Some Biased Thoughts on the Initial Peopling of the New World," in *Americans Before Columbus: Ice Age Origins* (Pittsburgh: University of Pittsburgh, 1988), which has a complete list of dates and the materials associated with them.

indicates that gardens were cultivated nearby. The Sheep Rock settlement appears to be similar to the pattern of scattered farming hamlets documented for the Susquehannock original homeland along the North Branch of the Susquehanna River north of Wyalusing and differs from Susquehannock settlements after European contact (Chapter 1).

Meadowcroft Rockshelter, located on the north bank of Cross Creek near the town of Avella in Washington County, was named the 1999 Commonwealth Treasure by the Pennsylvania Historical and Museum Commission. The site contains one of the longest archaeological sequences in the nation. It is also a candidate for one of the oldest sites in America because it contains evidence for what archaeologists call a "Pre-Clovis Occupation"—evidence that a culture was in place before the introduction of the classic fluted projectile points that are associated with the Paleo-Indians. Although there is controversy about some of the early dates, the total information package generated by research at Meadowcroft Rockshelter has greatly enhanced the state's archaeological record.

Artifacts found within the individual layers deposited beneath this massive rock overhang span the entire time that humans occupied Pennsylvania. Nearly 20,000 artifacts and more than 2 million flora and fauna remains were removed from the shelter during excavations that commenced in 1973. Samples for radiocarbon dating, which is based on the rate of decay or half-life of carbon 14, were taken from all levels where charcoal or charred basket fragments were encountered, and sixty-two of the samples yielded the dates that document the sequence of habitation in the shelter.

The excavated portions of Meadowcroft Rockshelter were subjected to rigorous study and resulted in an immense body of data. A portion of the site remains unexcavated; it is being preserved in order to retain a record for the prehistory of southwestern Pennsylvania, the upper Ohio Valley, and eastern North America. As new methods of analysis are developed in the future, the site will surely contribute even more data about the past. In the meantime, the cumulative knowledge gained through the analysis of the contents of each layer of each time period can be used to interpret all the other sites in the region.

The Shawnee-Minisink site, a fine example of an open stratified site, is located in the upper Delaware Valley at the intersection of Brodhead Creek with the Delaware River near the town of East Stroudsburg. About 15,000 years ago the last of the glacial advances began to retreat northward through the Delaware River valley, leaving behind a scoured-out U-shaped and mostly devegetated land surface. Filling of the valley began with alluvial outwash gravels from the retreating glacier, followed by depositions of loess, silt, and loam. Vegetation gradually returned, corre-

Meadowcroft Rockshelter's director of excavations, James Adovasio, looks over one of Meadowcroft's walls containing the longest continuous record of human occupation ever found in Pennsylvania.

lated with the shifts in the gradually warming climate. Data collected at this site clarify the subsistence strategies pursued by the Paleo-Indians. Carbonized seeds of grape, hawthorn, plum, hackberry, blackberry, copperleaf, chenopod, and amaranth were recovered from a Paleo-Indian hearth along with charred fish bone. Evidence from Shawnee-Minisink argues that these first people into the Delaware Valley were not primarily hunters of large game, but rather foragers who utilized this particular area in the late summer and early autumn to acquire a variety of food and other resources. The principal tools used by the foragers were endscrapers made of local black flint. Through study of the angles and the edges of these tools, the archaeologists concluded that bone and wood were being worked and that hide, sinew, and fibers were being processed. They deduced that the people who visited this campsite over a long span of time were subsisting on the flora resources available on the open riverbank. Fishing was an important seasonal activity. Pennsylvania's Shawnee-Minisink site is an important milestone in Paleo-Indian studies because it proved conclusively that a variety of subsistence resources were being utilized by Paleo-Indians and refuted the notion that Paleo-Indians were primarily hunters of big game animals.

After the Paleo-Indians lived at Shawnee-Minisink, there came a period when floods carried sand into the site and winds blew loamy deposits over the artifacts that the former residents had left behind. This was followed by a massive flood that buried the earliest deposits beneath about a meter or more of sterile sand, after which another group of people came to the site. These Early Archaic visitors used a wider variety of tools than the Paleo-Indians; the design of the new implements indicates that the utensils were used for cutting and drilling. Other Archaic populations followed and, as the forest vegetation shifted toward oak, hemlock, and chestnut, foraging groups came

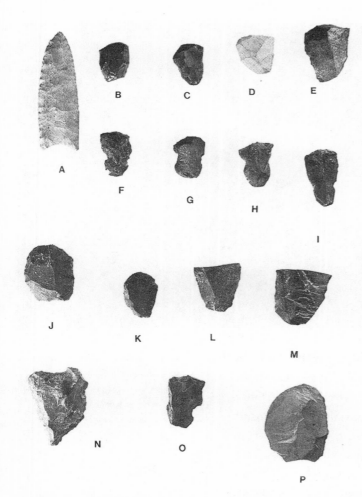

Paleo-Indian artifacts from the Shawnee-Minisink site: (A) classic Clovis fluted point; (B–E) endscrapers; (F–I) notched endscrapers; (J–K) full scrapers; (L and M) snapped-flake sidescrapers; (N) multiple-sided scraper; (O) spokeshave (for working arrow shafts); and (P) a flake knife.

more regularly and seasonally to collect ground-cherry, cheno-pod, and copperleaf.

Different groups came near the end of the Archaic period, and makers of Woodland pottery arrived even later. Use of the site spans nearly 11,000 years; one of the final episodes being the construction of a longhouse and the fashioning of Munsee (Minsi) pottery. The distinctive Munsee Incised pottery was associated with a triangular point, nutting stones, digging tools, and fire-cracked rock.

Perhaps the most dramatic American Indian sites are the villages that arose following the introduction of cultivated plants. The kinds of materials that are found include complete and broken ground-stone and chipped-stone tools; pottery vessels and sherds from broken pots; food-animal bones; mussel shells; and charred nut hulls and seeds. Wylie #3 is an example of villages built on top of each other. Archaeologists found evidence that four distinct Monongahela villages occupied this site periodically between around A.D. 1000 and A.D. 1500. Located on a farm in South Strabane Township, Washington County, Wylie #3 produced documentation about the types of fortifications and houses that were constructed there.

Wherever a post is sunk into the ground, a stain is left after the post decays. Archaeologists map these stains in order to reconstruct the form of any structure they locate. One of the houses dating to the first occupation at Wylie #3 had ninety-seven posts arranged in a circular pattern and an attached typical Monongahela house appendage with fifteen small sapling posts. Richard L. George, an archaeologist from Carnegie Museum of Natural History in Pittsburgh, theorizes that the appendages on the Monongahela houses were used for food storage and that these additions to the houses also might have been used to smoke otherwise perishable goods. He bases this theory on the fact that many of the house appendages show evidence of destruction by fire.

From village sites, archaeologists learn about the kinds of houses that were built, how they were placed in relation to other structures, and whether they were enclosed within a stockade. Archaeologists determine how the people lived and worked in the village by excavating carefully and mapping all the other things found at the settlement. Each pit, rock feature, post hole, whatever, is studied in order to discover where food was prepared and consumed, where the stone tools were chipped, where refuse was discarded, and whether any part of the village was set aside for community activities or rituals. The sum total of all this information, when coupled with analysis of the artifacts,

leads to the definition of the culture that left all this information behind. As knowledge accumulates, archaeologists are able to map the distribution of these cultures.

HISTORIC SITES

The state's historic-era sites include sixteenth- to eighteenth-century Indian settlements, European American frontier outposts, military fortifications, dwellings of many types (log cabins, farmsteads, single-family and multi-family homes, and mansions), religious communities, light and heavy industries, as well as institutions and public buildings. Like the cases cited above for Indians, individual archaeological sites add information about places, people, and things from the historical past. Some examples follow.

Beneath Pennsylvania's waters and offshore lie a variety of sunken craft. Archaeologists from the state's Archaeology Program recovered a dugout canoe from Curtis Pond, a small glacial lake near the headwaters of Lackawaxen River in Wayne

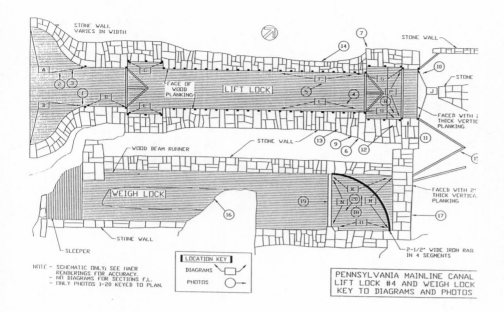

Diagram prepared by archaeologists and engineers during documentation of the Pennsylvania Mainline Canal Lift and Weigh Lock #4 in Pittsburgh. Note the preservation of the wooden gate sills in the lift lock, and the metal rail gate mechanism in the weigh lock.

County in 1998. The canoe underwent immediate conservation and is currently on display at the Robert D. Wilson Middle School in Waymart. The craft was made from a single log of either white pine or eastern hemlock; it has a rounded bow and a squared-off stern. Small decks or seats were carved into the canoe both fore and aft. Because the archaeologists determined that the canoe was fashioned by both fire and metal tools, it is probably not prehistoric and likely dates to either the Contact period or the Historic period.

Still buried beneath fill on the north side of Pittsburgh is a canal boat sealed in what was a turnaround basin of the western division of the Pennsylvania Canal. Two locks of the canal were uncovered during the construction of the East Street Expressway in Pittsburgh in 1987. Because of waterlogged conditions, wooden elements of the canal were preserved, leaving a gate, gate sills, quoins, and lining intact within the stone walls. Original engineering drawings of the Pittsburgh section of the canal no longer exist, so the archaeological work provided the first documentation of the nature of the canal locks on the city's north side. Of particular note was an anomalous iron rail that was associated with the gate in the weigh lock. Archaeologists believe that this rail is the only evidence for such a mechanism in the state canal system.

Fort Necessity

Archaeology can confirm, dispute, and even change the historical record. Take, for example, the site of the first skirmish of the French and Indian War when Lieutenant-Colonel George Washington fortified his camp at Great Meadows. Fort Necessity dates to 1754, but the first description of the structure did not appear until 1816, when it was described as being diamond-shaped in an account by Freeman Lewis, a professional surveyor. In 1931 the Fort Necessity Chapter of the Pennsylvania Sons of the American Revolution sponsored an archaeological investigation that located a diamond-shaped feature. Based on these findings and the 1816 account by Lewis, a replica of Fort Necessity was constructed.

Years later, however, researchers found two other references describing the fortification as being round with diamond-shaped breastworks. Subsequent archaeological excavations located remnants of the original stockade posts and proved that the fort was indeed small and round. As a result, the earlier diamond-shaped reconstruction was

demolished. The reconstruction that you see near the town of Farmington in Fayette County more truly represents Washington's hastily constructed fort. (The earlier excavations likely traced the breastworks and not the fort.) At Fort Necessity archaeology corrected both the historical record and archaeological record.

Hanna's Town

The original Hanna's Town no longer exists, but replicas of some of the original structures have been erected on the site, modern reconstructions based on the archaeology and history of the site. Archaeologists searched for documentation of events that occurred at Hanna's Town; they also looked for explanations that would reveal how the artifacts that they found came to the frontier settlement.

Hanna's Town became the first county seat west of the Allegheny Mountains, and its first court sessions were held in Hanna's Tavern on April 6, 1773. Robert Hanna came to western Pennsylvania as early as 1771 and served as a justice of the peace in what was then Bedford County. Before Westmoreland County was created out of Bedford on February 26, 1773, citizens from as far away as Pittsburgh had to travel to Bedford to settle legal matters. Hanna purchased a tract of land on either side of Forbes Road about eighteen miles west of Ligonier and built a tavern that later became the nucleus of the town.

A stockade was erected at the settlement in 1774 during Dunmore's War, a war waged by the British colonial governor of Virginia to clear the area of Indians. According to some sources, the stockade was rebuilt and even moved as the town developed. By 1775 Hanna's Town was as large as Pittsburgh, with thirty domestic structures, a jail, three taverns (run by Hanna, Charles Foreman, and Robert Orr), a blacksmith's shop, and a number of barns and outbuildings. During the Revolutionary War this frontier

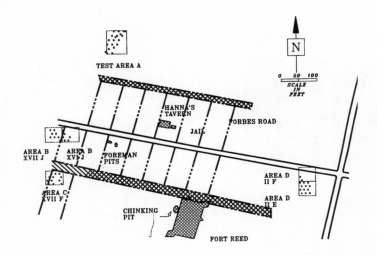

Map of the fort and other features at Hanna's Town.

town was a center of political, economic, and military activities. On July 13, 1782, a British and Indian force attacked and destroyed Hanna's Town.

Folklore and many of the Westmoreland County and western Pennsylvania histories named Guyasuta, a Seneca, as the instigator of the destruction. Following their archaeological work at Charles Foreman's tavern in Hanna's Town, James B. Richardson and Kirke Wilson launched historical inquiries in order to verify that Guyasuta was in the raiding party. The archaeologists located correspondence filed in the Haldimand Papers at the Public Archives of Canada, where they read: "On June 9, 1782, a force of 250 Seneca Indians, led by Sayengaraghta, a renowned Seneca war chief of the Turtle Clan, left his encampment at Buffalo Creek, south of Fort Niagara, to attack Hanna's Town."

This and other documentation found by the archaeologists suggest that it was Sayengaraghta, not Guyasuta, who led the raid that destroyed Hanna's Town. Although this answer came from written records rather than archaeology, the identification of Sayengaraghta by archaeologists pointed to the ways archaeologists rely on a variety of sources to corroborate accounts about any site.

Court was in session at the time of the raid, so the citizens gathered the court records and fled within the stockade. The town was almost completely burned; only two dwellings survived. Twelve houses were rebuilt, but the town never truly recovered from the devastation. When John Heckewelder traveled through the town in June 1789 he wrote in his journal: "This place consists of 20 wretched houses, all windowless, in a fertile but by no means beautiful region."

Before the Indian attack, the houses at Hanna's Town were no smaller than eighteen feet square and had shingle roofs and were in keeping with the general character of log architecture of the period. Archaeologists used the positions of log mold-stains in the subsoil to determine that the individual lots were probably sixty feet wide. Robert Fryman and John Eddins, as a result of their archaeological work in 1984, reported that the settlement pattern at Hanna's Town was typical of eighteenth-century urban and frontier communities—a rectangular arrangement of lots separated by streets running parallel to each other and connected by smaller perpendicular streets or alleys. This same pattern underlies Williamsburg and Fredericksburg, Virginia, and Bethabara and Brunswick Town, North Carolina.

The final blow to the existence of Hanna's Town came when a new road was built south of the settlement and when Greensborough (Greensburg) was named the new county seat in 1787. The settlement gradually decayed and ceased to be a town by the early 1800s, and by 1830 it was merely a one-family farm. The property was purchased by Westmoreland County in 1969; archaeological investigations were immediately launched and continue to the present. The first excavations attempted to locate the fort and Hanna's Tavern. Evidence of the fort (Fort Reed) was uncovered in 1971, and most of the investigators were surprised to learn that the spring that was so important to the town was located outside the fortification.

Hanna's Town artifacts are impressive and shed light about conditions in this frontier settlement. With the exception of locally manufactured redwares and a few porcelain sherds from the Bonnin and Morris factory (Philadelphia, 1770–72), most of the ceramics found at Foreman's Tavern were imports from England, and most were pieces from tea sets. After these objects arrived on the American shores, they had to be transported by wagon over the Allegheny Mountains to Hanna's Town, either on an original migration westward or with later shipments by merchants. Items of clothing adornment are of finer quality than expected, indicating that at least some of the settlers who came to this section of Westmoreland County possessed high-status personal belongings and household furnishings.

Thanks to the detective work done by Gene Burger, we know that a white metal (pewter or tombac) button recovered by archaeologists at Hanna's Town in 1970 was manufactured in Birmingham, England, probably by a man named John Rose. Burger found records in the Pennsylvania State Archives that documented that two casks of sundries belonging to Welsh, Wilkinson & Startin were taken by a carriage driver, Peter Hodgson, to London, where they were then shipped to Baynton, Wharton & Morgan in Philadelphia. Both casks had invoices listing buttons. Baynton, Wharton & Morgan were suppliers to Forts Pitt and Chartiers. Other records indicate that Michael Huffnagle and Joseph Irwin, Hanna's Town residents, purchased buttons in Pittsburgh. The Fort Pitt Day Book lists buttons as shipped to and through Pittsburgh from the end of the French and Indian War until the time of the American Revolution.

The documentary research conducted as part of the archaeological process tells us that the settlers in Hanna's Town had access to European goods; other artifacts found there reveal that this short-lived community was a frontier settlement that had links to a vigorous commercial trade. The trimmings from articles of clothing and the sherds of tea sets let us know that life in this short-term county seat was not mean and crude. A single archaeological object, like the Hanna's Town button, adds much to the interpretation of the site. The view of frontier colonial life in Pennsylvania is broadened when archaeologists are able to demonstrate the commercial and cultural connections between the Old World and a remote settlement on the then-far rim of the British North American empire.

A Pennsylvania Farm

Aware that Pennsylvania historians consider the nineteenth century as a time of significant economic and social transition, archaeologists went to the Livengood site in Somerset County to determine what they could learn about life on a farm during that period. The work was prompted by destruction of the site for construction of the U.S. Route 19 Bypass. Historic documentary research and archaeological investigations were launched, and results of the work were reported in 1998 by Danica Ziegler and colleagues.

The Livengood Farm site lies southwest of Meyersdale along the Casselman River. This area was settled in the late eighteenth century when predominantly German-speaking immigrants came and began to modify the local landscape to support their agrarian lifestyle. The landscape was further altered in the nineteenth century as a mix of farming enterprises and blossoming industries began to center around what was to become the Borough of Meyersdale.

Through deed searches, the archaeologists learned that this farmstead was occupied from 1815 to 1923 by successive generations of the Livengood family, beginning with Peter Livengood (1815–42) and followed by Christian P. and Catherine Livengood (1842–85) and Cyrus and Anna Hostetler (1885–1923). After 1923 the farm was held under various joint ownership arrangements. It was leased to tenants from the 1950s to the mid-1970s and, finally, demolished in 1977 to make way for the highway improvements.

The Livengoods were a Pennsylvania German family; the first generation was either Mennonite or Dunkard, the second generation attended the Mennonite church. The farm prospered under Christian Peter Livengood and operated on a higher-than-average scale than others in Somerset County, largely because of the production of butter (1,200 pounds in 1850 and 1,600 pounds in 1880). Commonly, the head male in the family tended the cows, while the work to produce dairy products was left to his wife. There was an extra female in the Livengood household, who perhaps served as a dairymaid because Mrs. Livengood's children were too young to assist with the churning of butter at the time when production became important in the household. Butter was more likely used as barter for needed goods rather than being sold for cash, but the enterprise was successful enough for the family to use the profits from their work to buy equipment and to make improvements on the property.

The buildings erected on the site represented Germanic vernacular architectural traditions modified by the incorporation of newer ideas. Archaeologists working at the site found two foundations, several areas with trash deposits, six postholes, a drainage ditch, three pipe trenches, three possible building trenches, and a burned area. The remaining structures represent a two-story brick bank house, a frame barn, a frame springhouse, a collapsed log structure, and two small frame sheds. Roads, fence lines, and fields were also present.

Because of the demolition to make way for the new road, most of the artifacts recovered from the Livengood farm were bricks, window glass, and cut nails. The domestic artifacts included earthenware, stoneware, creamware, pearlware, whiteware, porcelain, fiestaware, glassware and bottles, utensils, and furniture hardware. The distribution of redware containers at the Livengood farm suggests that food preparation and butter-making activities were associated with the basement kitchens at a frame and a brick structure at the site. The domestic artifacts indicate that the Livengoods were less interested in acquiring expensive table settings than in the outward appearance of their farm and its machinery. The analysis of the faunal assemblage revealed evidence of butchering; it is likely that livestock were being raised for family consumption rather than for market. The report states that "analysis of the faunal assemblage . . . reveals a subsistence based on self-sufficiency and community cooperation, an image in harmony with the Mennonite/Brethren faith to which these families adhered."

The archaeological and historical research about the Livengood site informs us that this Pennsylvania farm family chose to concentrate their efforts on the production of butter as a way to bolster earnings. This decision proved to be a wise one, because the income allowed them to purchase machinery and make improvements to their farm exceeding those of their neighbors. Before demolition, when the buildings and equipment were visible on the Somerset County landscape, they were the outward representations of the Livengood family's ethnic background and, even more important, marked the higher status of the family within their agrarian community. The household artifacts from the archaeological record affirm both the family's ethnic background and the importance of their churning enterprise.

The Livengood investigations disclose how a combination of digging both in the soil and in written records can reveal the vital character of people and places. Recognition of this family's reliance on butter-churning highlights the importance of this economic activity at a nineteenth-century Pennsylvania farm—something that hardly gains mention in traditional histories of the American economy.

Pittsburgh

Sometimes the information on just one artifact can re-create a bit of history. Such is the case with a broken bottle found in Pittsburgh. Recovered from one of the circular brick-shaft structures at the PPG site was a small, broken amber bottle embossed "Weyman & Bro., Pittsburgh, Pa." Once this item was identified as a snuff bottle, the researchers turned to advertisements, tax records, and deeds to determine the history behind the artifact. The results recalled Pittsburgh's great tobacco industry. The dominance of iron and steel production overshadowed many former important industries that also contributed to Pittsburgh's development. The Weyman bottle reminds us that the city's commercial development was strongly stimulated by a world of individual entrepreneurs who turned small businesses into profitable ventures.

Tobacco products were being manufactured in Pittsburgh as early as October 27, 1798, when Joseph McClurg & Company advertised their tobacco and snuff manufactory. While mostly remembered for his Pittsburgh Foundry, where he produced hollowware, utensils, plows, cannonballs, and machinery, McClurg had his beginnings in drygoods, groceries, spirits, and tobacco. George Weyman entered the tobacco business sometime between 1823 and 1827.

The 1826 city directory lists eleven tobacco manufacturers producing 4,833 kegs of tobacco and 4 million "segars" with a workforce of 140. By 1829 Turbit & Davidson had entered the business and W. and D. Rinehart opened their establishment in the city in 1838. The 1837 *Harris Business Directory* contains a picture of George Weyman's four-story factory, and the 1850 Manufacturers Census Schedule lists the value of his annual product at $30,198. The firm became Weyman & Son in 1857 when B. Frank Weyman entered the business. The Weyman & Brother logo appeared in 1867 when William Weyman became affiliated with the industry. By 1879 this firm had increased the worth of its annual product to $68,075.

In 1870 ten factories in Pittsburgh and Allegheny (now the North Side) were devoted exclusively to the manufacture of black chewing tobacco, and about 140 other establishments were engaged in other aspects of the trade. Six years later the city had 148 cigar factories employing 406 hands; Allegheny City had 102 firms with 408 employees. Contemporary accounts indicate that 22,266,044 cigars were sold from Allegheny, and 18,201,650 from Pittsburgh. Pittsburgh cigars were so famous that President Ulysses S. Grant had his own special brand made there, by a firm on Smithfield Street—a firm that could only have been Weyman & Brother, with offices at 409 Smithfield.

William Weyman died in 1877, but the firm continued its growth under B. Frank Weyman to the point that it employed thousands at a factory at the corner of Liberty and Union Streets. The factory and warehouse moved to Duquesne Way in 1886, and a branch was opened in New York City. Weyman brands became known nationally as *Weyman's No. 1 Cut and Dry, Weyman's Honest Weight,* and *Weyman's Hubble Bubble.*

The amber snuff bottle recovered at the PPG site most likely dates at or just after 1867, when the company first assumed the Weyman & Brother name. This single piece of material culture serves as a reminder of an important industry in Pittsburgh's past and helps us recall the importance of specialized commercial endeavors. The enterprising Joseph McClurg began with tobacco and eventually gained recognition through his foundry. Progressing from smoking tobacco and snuff to cigars, the Weymans, the Jenkinsons, the Rineharts, and other tobacco manufacturers made their own unique contributions to the growing economy of nineteenth-century Pittsburgh. After archaeologists unearthed and studied the Weyman bottle, the story was submitted to Pittsburgh newspapers and printed in *Carnegie Magazine.* Public reaction was one of surprise; indeed, the industry had been forgotten.

Another circular shaft structure at the PPG site contained a highly polished bone awl engraved "*Superfine, Paris,*" straight pins, wooden thread spools, and cloth pattern pieces. These items were traced through deed searches to Madame Margaret Bonnaffon. Her name and profession as a fancy French milliner and dressmaker are listed in the 1841 Pittsburgh city directory. She vanishes from city and county records after 1860.

Margaret, married to Anthony Bonnaffon, a dancing master who traveled about western Pennsylvania to conduct dancing schools and parties, appears to have achieved her own status in the city. Handwritten credit ratings found in a collection at Harvard's Baker Library portray her as a very superior woman, extremely well qualified for her business. By 1850 her millinery shop had a capital investment of $3,500, and she employed five female workers who earned an average of $44 each per month. Margaret was atypical of women employed in fashion commerce in the mid-1800s, in that she was not simply a seamstress or a dressmaker; a lone seamstress could earn a mere twenty-five cents for a long day working to hand-sew items that were pre-cut by a tailor. In contrast, Margaret was the proprietress of her own business and paid each of her workers $14 a month more than the national rate for similar services. Because considerable talent and skill were necessary to achieve ownership of a high-fashion shop, Margaret held a solid position within the community and the commerce of Pittsburgh. A chart showing the holders of pews in the First Presbyterian Church has Margaret's name on pew 10, fourth back on the right-hand side. She is one of only a few women who were listed as holding a pew.

In the 1980s Pittsburgh archaeologists found, buried beneath the modern city, historical artifacts that once belonged to nineteenth-century residents. The items had been sealed in by the repeated spreading of fill over the central business district in order to enlarge the restricted point of land between the Monongahela and Allegheny Rivers. This photo shows urban archaeologists working at the PPG site. Using heavy equipment, and employing the same principles that guide a hand trowel, they scrape away huge deposits of rubble to reveal the presence of old wells and privies. The circular shaft structures are believed to be water wells that were converted into disposal units following installation of a central water system in Pittsburgh.

Anthony died on March 26, 1859, while on tour in Washington, Pennsyl-vania, and newspaper accounts indicated that he was interred in Allegheny Cemetery in Pittsburgh. The archaeologists attempted several times to locate the grave but could find neither a record of the burial plot nor a headstone engraved "Bonnaffon" at Allegheny or any other city cemetery. Finally, an 1860 ledger book in the Allegheny Cemetery office disclosed that perhaps the last thing Margaret did before leaving Pittsburgh was to sell the burial plot and have Anthony's remains placed in an unmarked plot. The artifacts that led to discovering Margaret's identity cannot tell the rest of the story or disclose why she sold the plot, but the search for the identity of the person who owned and used the bone tool did provide insights into the entrepreneurial qualities of a woman who experienced success in a growing city. She faced the setbacks of two fires during her nearly twenty years of business and recovered each time. Her 1854 credit records, written after the second fire, indicate that she ran a large business and was making fashionable millinery for the upper "ten-dom" of the city.

Just as a few artifacts reminded us of the importance of tobacco and millinery/dressmaking in a developing urban center, the recovery of immense numbers of bottles and assorted other glassware at PPG and other Pittsburgh sites epitomizes the significance of the glass industries that once dominated Pittsburgh's ever-changing landscape.

Pittsburgh was once the nation's leading producer of glass bottles. Urban archaeological investigations at the Seventh Street site hint that the semiautomatic bottling machine may have been developed in Pittsburgh. The evidence came from "C & J Freel" soda pop bottles that only could have been manufactured between 1871 and 1872. That is at least nine years earlier than the standard dates cited for the introduction of semiautomatic bottling machines to the bottle manufacturing process. The semiautomatic machines were developed between 1880 and 1913, according to one author, and between 1892 and 1903 by another. The technology is recognized by the presence of a seam within a quarter-inch of the top of a bottle. Because Pittsburgh was a leading producer of glass bottles during this period, it is likely that innovations leading to the development of the semiautomatic machine had their beginnings in the Pittsburgh District as early as 1871. The seams on the "C & J Freel" bottles from the Seventh Street site, discarded in the 1870s and found by archaeologists in the 1980s site, provided the evidence about how these bottles were produced—a fitting reminder of the significance of glassmaking in Pittsburgh.

Archaeology and History

Archaeology can bring history alive. A few years ago a small group of archaeologists conducted a magnetometer survey (a ground geophysical survey using a portable instrument) across a portion of the Bushy Run Battlefield near Harrison City in Westmoreland County. The magnetometer readings detected a number of below-ground anomalies, and a single test trench in the area with the highest readings uncovered a section of the South Branch of Forbes Road. This was a route cut by Colonel Henry Bouquet in 1759. Buried beneath the grass and modern soils, the roadbed was intact with wagon ruts and seemingly even the footprints of the draft animals that traversed it.

History came alive that day as all those present realized that they had taken their archaeological time machine back to August 1763 and the battle that the park commemorates. That battle was a critical turning point in Pontiac's Rebellion, and the first British victory in the district of Pennsylvania, Maryland, Virginia, and the Carolinas. Bouquet's victory prevented Fort Pitt from being overrun and restored the communication links between the frontier and the settlements.

The archaeologists sat along the edge of their tiny trench, letting their feet rest ever so gently on the old land surface, and thought about the history of Bushy Run. Then the trench was lined with heavy plastic and backfilled in order to preserve that section of the ancient road intact. But now we know that this archaeological feature is within the park boundaries and that it can be interpreted for visitors who come to learn about what took place at Bushy Run. Until the magnetometer survey and testing, no one was really sure that the old road was still there, and because there are very few historic artifacts remaining from the battle, the presence of the road within the park's boundary is particularly important.

The old things that are buried all across the Commonwealth of Pennsylvania can add the kind of excitement to history that the archaeologists on Forbes Road felt. And the archaeological artifacts stored and studied at Pennsylvania's museums and historical societies represent the material culture of past peoples. These pieces, whether from the recent or distant past, all have stories to tell. Story is the foundation of history, and because history is a continuing process, archaeology will surely contribute more narratives in the future.

SOURCES *and* FURTHER READING

Adovasio, J. M., A. T. Boldurian, and R. C. Carlisle. "Who Are Those Guys? Some Biased Thoughts on the Initial Peopling of the New World." In *Americans Before Columbus: Ice Age Origins,* comp. and ed. Ronald C. Carlisle, 45–61. Ethnology Monographs 12, Department of Anthropology, University of Pittsburgh, 1988.

Bartlow, Judy, and Doug Plance. "Proton Magnetometer Testing at Bushy Run Battlefield, 36wm598." *Pennsylvania Archaeologist* 55 (102) (1985), 34–35.

Burger, Gene. "Button, Button, Who's Got the Button?" *Westmoreland History* (Newsletter of the Westmoreland County Historical Society, Greensburg, Pennsylvania), 1998.

Cotter, John L., Daniel G. Roberts, and Michael Parrington. *The Buried Past: An Archaeological History of Philadelphia.* Philadelphia: University of Pennsylvania Press, 1992.

Cowin, Verna L. "Archaeological Investigations at Bushy Run." Paper on file at the State Museum of Pennsylvania, Harrisburg, 1983.

———. "Archaeology and History: Hanna's Town Field Report." Publication 1, Westmoreland Archaeological Institute and the Continuing Education Division of Westmoreland County Community College, 1984.

Cowin, Verna L., and Deborah Casselberry. "Archaeology and History at the Seventh Street Site, Pittsburgh, Pennsylvania." Report prepared for the Pittsburgh Trust for Cultural Resources, Pittsburgh, by the Carnegie Museum of Natural History, Pittsburgh, and Greenhouse Consultants, New York, 1987.

Diess, Ronald W. "The Development and Application of a Chronology for American Glass." Midwestern Archeological Research Center, Illinois State University, Normal, 1981.

DiLiscia Construction Company and Parsons Brinkerhoff Construction Services Inc. "Stonemason's Record of Dismantling Portions of Lift Lock #4 and Weigh Lock, Pennsylvania Mainline Canal," Vol. 10 of "Series on Historical and Archaeological Investigations, I-279/I-579 Expressway Project, Allegheny County, Pennsylvania." Pennsylvania Department of Transportation, Federal Highway Administration, 1989.

Fryman, Robert J., and John T. Eddins. "Archaeological Testing Project: Settlement Boundaries and Lot Placement at Old Hanna's Town." Historical Heritage Institute, Westmoreland County Historical Society, Greensburg, 1985.

Grimm, Jacob L. "Hanna's Town." *Carnegie Magazine* 46, no. 6 (1984), 225–35.

Lantz, Stanley W. "Distribution of Paleo-Indian Projectile Points and Tools from Western Pennsylvania: Implications for Regional Differences." *Archaeology of Eastern North America* 12 (1984), 210–21.

McNett, Charles W., Jr. "Artifact Morphology and Chronology at the Shawnee Minisink Site." In *Shawnee Minisink: A Stratified Paleoindian-Archaic Site in the Upper Delaware Valley of Pennsylvania.* New York: Academic Press, 1985.

McNett, Charles W., Jr., ed. *Shawnee Minisink: A Stratified Paleoindian-Archaic Site in the Upper Delaware Valley of Pennsylvania,* ed. Charles W. McNett Jr. New York: Academic Press, 1985.

Michels, Joseph W., and James S. Duff. "Archaeological Investigations of Sheep Rock Shelter, Huntingdon County, Pennsylvania." Department of Anthropology, The Pennsylvania State University, University Park, 1968.

Richardson, James B., III. "Who Attacked Hanna's Town?" *SPAAC Speaks* (Newsletter of the Allegheny Chapter, Society for Pennsylvania Archaeology, Pittsburgh), 11, no. 1 (1975), 3–5.

Richardson, James B., III, and Kirke C. Wilson. "Hanna's Town and Charles Foreman: The Historical and Archaeological Record, 1770–1806." *Western Pennsylvania Historical Magazine* 59 (1975), 52–83.

Stackhouse, E. J., and M. W. Corl. "The Discovery of the Sheep Rock Shelter (Site 36HUI)." *Pennsylvania Archaeologist* 32, no. 1 (1962), 1–13.

Wallace, Paul A. W. *Indian Paths of Pennsylvania.* Harrisburg: Pennsylvania Historical and Museum Commission, 1971.

———. *Thirty Thousand Miles with John Heckewelder.* Pittsburgh: University of Pittsburgh Press, 1958.

Witthoft, John. "Sheep Rock Shelter: Reflections and Observations After Three Seasons of Excavation 1960–1962." In *Archaeological Investigations of Sheep Rock Shelter, Huntingdon County, Pennsylvania.* University Park: Department of Anthropology, The Pennsylvania State University, 1968.

Ziegler, Danica L., et al. "Phase II Investigation of the Livengood Farm Site (36SO219)." In volume 3: *Phase I and II Archaeological Investigations Along the Western Alternative of the U.S. 219 Meyersdale Bypass from the Southern Terminus to Elklick Creek.* Prepared for the Pennsylvania Department of Transportation District 9-0 by Greenhorne & O'Mara, Mechanicsburg, 1998.

Folklore and Folklife

SIMON J. BRONNER

Who hasn't told a story, invoked a proverb, or participated in a custom? Passing such things on is, after all, tradition. We all enact tradition, and in so doing make reference to and draw on the past. We know tradition has been around long before we were around, typically across many generations. We also associate it with particular groups—and those groups' basic values and beliefs. Inquiries into tradition therefore open up the experiences of groups, the attitudes they have had, and their everyday lives. The trouble is that expressions of tradition may be so basic to our lives that we don't take time to record them. We may take notice when the stories are not around anymore, or we find that our proverbs differ from someone else's, or that the customs persist while so much else changes in society.

Why at those moments of change, sometimes too late to recover traditions, do we especially appreciate their significance? As traditions fade, we may indeed see them more vividly as texts and performances revealing connections to society. We may comprehend the present as it has been shaped by, or broken from, the past. If tradition represents the continuity of the past with the present, we can and should "read" our narratives, speech, and customs for a special dimension of social life that informs history. Legends and songs often come to mind first, because they frequently contain references to historic events and heroes. America's tall-tale legacy of boisterous frontier folk heroes often begins across the Alleghenies of Pennsylvania with the legendary exploits of Daniel

Daniel Boone, one of America's earliest frontier folk heroes.

Boone (exalted in tall tales for his hunting and Indian-fighting), Simon Girty (known in lore as the "white savage"), and Mike Fink (the boastful "keelboatman"). More localized heroes preserved in story and song, such as "Madame Montour" (the "loyal" Indian interpreter for whom Montour County is named), Jennie Wade (the "heroine of the battle of Gettysburg"), Gib Morgan (the famed liar, or "Munchausen," and oilman), and "Cherry Tree" Joe McCreery (strongman of the lumber region [his name "Cherry Tree" comes from a locality in Indiana County]) are equally noteworthy for what they reveal of regional and occupational memory. Their stories also have been used to discuss the characteristics that Americans admired in the expansive nineteenth century—rugged, adventurous, boastful optimists on the move, often fighting elites and Indians.

The spirit of rebellion and democracy comes through in oral tradition of the "Fair Play Settlers" of the West Branch of the Susquehanna River, who declared independence from England at the same time that action was being taken in Philadelphia (a historic marker now designates the spot as the "Tiadaghton Elm" on the west bank of Pine Creek in Tioga County). No written record of the "Pine Creek Declaration of Independence," as it came to be known, has been found, but the names of the supposed signers have been passed down to the present. Couched in the rhetoric of frontier "outlaws," the narratives draw attention to the settlers' right of self-determination, which they had been exercising in fact since early in the 1770s. Removing themselves from colonial proprietary authority, they had established a "Fair Play" system of justice and a democratically elected tribunal. In effect, they formed a social compact deriving authority from the people. To be sure, official depositions can be found referring in detail to the Fair Play tribunal, and historians have also taken note of anecdotes handed down through the generations about disputes settled by the justice of the Fair Play system. An example, notable for its commentary on Indian-white relations, comes from a local history by John Meginness, which is not unusual in its recounting of anecdotes and traditions.

Joseph Antes, son of Colonel Henry Antes, used to tell this story: It seems that one Francis Clark, who lived just west of Jersey Shore in the Fair Play territory, gained possession of a dog which belonged to an Indian. Upon learning of this, the Indian appealed to the Fair Play men, who ordered Clark's arrest and trial for the alleged theft. Clark was convicted and sentenced to be lashed. The punishment was to be inflicted by a person decided by lot, the responsibility falling upon the man drawing the red grain of corn from a bag containing grains of corn for each man present. Philip Antes was the reluctant "winner." The Indian, seeing that the decision of the "court" was to be carried out immediately, magnanimously suggested that banishment would serve better than flogging. Clark agreed and left for the Nippenose Valley, where his settlement is a matter of record.

This example of folklore contains an account that is not part of the documentary record and that is valuable for the attitude expressed on behalf of a group or community. As in the case of the Tiadaghton Elm, the lore may be localized and tell what is memorable in a place's collective memory. It may express concerns that represent the spirit of the times. Especially significant is when narratives, sayings, and songs bring the values of the past into the present.

What do these legends, practices, and songs mean? How do they inform history? You can begin answering these questions by asking other people which activities they tell stories about, invoke, or participate in, or by checking reference works for versions in other locales, and from other times. Then you can reflect on the significance of what you found. In asking the question of meaning, you are engaged in folklore and folklife research. Folklore and folklife may be distinguished by the emphasis they place on tradition—on oral, customary, and material evidence, which are ironically called "nontraditional" in history books that narrowly use only written documents and often favoring "official" government records. The focus on "folk" typically reveals the practices of ordinary lives and the cultural, social, and ideological bases of different communities. Using "folk" invites questions of the process of creating community and continuity, sometimes in contrast to the emphasis on change or discontinuity in history. Folk studies can and should complement the "great events" of national history by providing in word, object, and deed symbolic testimonies of worldview at the most basic levels of our family, work, and community.

The "folk" modifying life and lore connotes a form of learning "by tradition"—that is, by word of mouth, demonstration and imitation, and custom. The folk can be any group, rural or urban, elite or poor. Some of the groups commonly using folklore to express identity and continuity are associated with region, ethnicity, religion, occupation, family, age, and sex. The "lore" refers to the narratives or knowledge—such as songs and legends—gained through the traditional learning process; the "life" describes everyday activity within a community. Lore may be thought of as the expressive, intellectual side of tradition, while life is its social and material basis. When someone passes on a story or song that is attached historically to a group, folklorists are wont to call the item a folkloric performance or text for the purposes of comparison and analysis. The folk item, like a story, invites repetition and variation and is usually connected to a social tradition. A "formal" or "official" item, like a novel or law, is fixed in time and is often attached to a single creator or institution. But when a carver makes a wooden chain based on the techniques or forms the artisan has seen previously, or when a child learns to cook a dish common to his or her heritage by watching a parent or elder do it, folklorists talk of tradition enacted by repeated demonstration and imitation. The importance of this learning can be traced to the kinds of values, beliefs, and symbols transmitted, and an understanding of the historical/cultural settings and groups in which they occur.

The tendency of folklore both to repeat and vary allows for tracing traditions across the landscape, and thereby locating paths of diffusion and cultural regions. It also permits reading different versions of traditions as keys to perceptions, biases, and beliefs in the content and performance of folklore and folklife. To be sure, a single text can be read for its symbolism, but more often folklore is gathered in aggregate, in order to make a case for the pervasiveness or complexity of beliefs within a culture and time transmitted through folklore. If folklore varies across space, it often remains stable in time, and therefore reflects the continuity of cultural values. When change, or discontinuity, is noted, such as in traditional floorplans or in rites of passage, this typically indicates dramatic historic shifts. For example, folklorists record stories and songs of the past heyday of mining in Pennsylvania to the present day not only to provide insight into the fears, hopes, and joys of miners' lives, but also to interpret the beliefs they held and the workers' attitudes toward the occupation and its communities at particular times. Furthermore, whether or not historians will ever uncover the facts of the secret society of the Molly Maguires, folklorists have recorded many legends and ballads that offer testimonies to attitudes toward mining conditions, references to the social hierarchy and ethnic complexity of the period, and commentaries on pivotal events that united and divided the communities.

One of the best-known narratives is about the indelible handprint in a Mauch Chunk jail that has fascinated curious onlookers for years. As one version goes, strapping Alex Campbell, charged with killing mine superintendent John P. Jones, went to the gallows on June 21, 1877, a date known in lore as "Black Thursday." Declaring his innocence to the sheriff who came to lead him to his death, he bent to the ground, gathered dust in his hand, and, dragging the iron ball and chain to the cell wall, clapped his hand high on the wall, crying, "There is the proof of my words. That mark will never be wiped out." Another version has Tom Fisher, who was executed in 1878, making the mark. His death proclamation was "My mark will stay here as long as this prison remains." Many texts are laced with Pennsylvania German elaborations of *hexerei* (magical belief) and the Irish Catholic belief in the miraculous. Historically traced, oral accounts give two opposing messages. Early anecdotes recorded between 1876 and 1880 cast the Mollies in the role of agitators and sadistic murderers loathed by God-fearing

Irish mining families. In the twentieth-century renderings of the Mollies, they appear heroically lashing out in the face of numerous indignities dispensed by mine operators, who trumped up conspiratorial plots to scare the mining communities. The significance of folklore, then, is the way it reveals the beliefs that people convey to one another and the images they create.

The history of Pennsylvania, if it tells the story of the peoples of Pennsylvania, is more than just a record of official state proclamations and a compilation of chronologies. History as narrative cannot be equated with truth, just as folklore does not translate to falsehood. Folklore is truthful as it expresses ideas and beliefs that affect social action. It is evidence that comes out in oral, customary, and material performance and is often not available from the documentary record. Traditional narratives, rituals, and buildings record experience of places and people that are left out of chronologies and that reveal their identity and function within broader contexts of region and nation. They can recount events not recorded elsewhere, many of which are passed down within families and communities, as with narratives of the Underground Railroad in Pennsylvania. In the case of the Underground Railroad, oral traditions detail buildings used for hiding and routes for escape. They also reveal themes of freedom and community self-help found in the narratives, African American symbols and codes found in spirituals and quilts, and the extent of runaway activity owing to an "organized" network. Often folklorists ask less "What really happened?" than "How was it perceived and expressed?" These questions lead to considerations of traditions as they arose in the past, transform in the present, and may emerge in the future.

The kinds of groups represented in Pennsylvania folklore and folklife research vary greatly. Still, it is true that the Pennsylvania "Dutch," or Pennsylvania Germans, may be the most famous group in the state known by its distinctive traditions. Their folk arts have persisted in isolated rural communities since the eighteenth century, and the decline of Pennsylvania German traditions in the face of mass culture is commonly discussed in the media. Folklorists since the nineteenth century, many associated with the Pennsylvania German Society founded in 1891, identified the special characteristics of Pennsylvania German experience by describing the ways that oral and material traditions combined in a regional folklife. The United States is usually regarded as possessing a common national culture, supposedly based on English inheritance. But traditions among the Pennsylvania Germans, such as bank-barn building, hex-sign making, Harvest Home and fastnacht celebrations, and ritual eating of pork and sauerkraut on New Year's Day, suggest that these Central Pennsylvanians hold a unique, important, and overlooked place in the American cultural landscape. Early folklorists countered an image of Pennsylvania Germans that had been brushed aside in the progress of civilization and promulgated by the forces of "English" dominance. They instigated a serious exploration into the function of these traditions in the persistence and diffusion of Pennsylvania German ideas in the region, state, and nation. References to repetition and

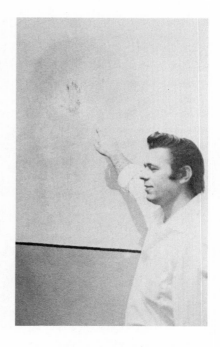

Legend has it that Alex Campbell of the Molly Maguires made this handprint on the Mauch Chunk jail wall on June 21, 1877, as he was being led to the gallows. Today the handprint is a popular tourist attraction in the town of Jim Thorpe. Here a prison trustee, Marvin Horn, shows the location and height of the print.

A Christmas celebration in the early 1800s, drawn by John Lewis Krimmel, a German painter who had emigrated to Philadelphia. Krimmel made this sketch, the first depiction of an American Christmas tree, while touring the Pennsylvania countryside. Trimming a Christmas tree was an old custom in Strasbourg, Alsace, and the popularity of the custom spread in early nineteenth-century Germany and the United States as Christmas became more child-centered. The original is at the Winterthur Museum, Winterthur, Delaware.

variation of Pennsylvania German folk arts not only showed the vibrancy of these communities within the life of the Commonwealth but also drew attention to the complexity, indeed the diversity, of these Pennsylvania German communities.

Isaac Stiehly (1800–1869) is a figure whose stories of the Pennsylvania Germans reveal much about the interplay of folklore and historical experience. His place in oral tradition, the folk arts, and religious life speak to a time of significant cultural historical transition in Pennsylvania. Especially during the period between 1840 and 1870, the isolation of rural, mid-state Pennsylvania German communities began to decrease because of state governmental influence, religious transformation brought by revivalism and the "Second Great Awakening," and cultural change in the wake of growing nationalization and "English" cultural settlement. Stiehly's legacy in folklore reminds us of an evolving meaning of Pennsylvania German identity. More than 130 years after his death, a cycle of Stiehly stories can still be collected from oral tradition in the Mahantango Valley in central Pennsylvania. Some of the stories first appeared in print in the first volume of the *Pennsylvania Dutchman* in 1950. William F. Yoder recounted Stiehly as a man who "achieved great renown over the whole Mahantango and Lykens (Hegins) Valley area." "All I know about him," he says, "is what tradition handed down to our day."

These stories emphasize Stiehly's role as a man of the people despite his lofty spiritual calling, his exceptional strength and stature, and his protectiveness of the "Dutch" communities. Possibly indicating secularizing influences on the Reformed Church, William Yoder offered the traditional story that one Sabbath morning Stiehly met a fisherman shooting pickerel, whereupon the minister said, "'Gebe mire das Gewehr' (Give me the gun)," and "took the gun, shot the fish, and went on to church!" The story can, in fact, be found elsewhere attached to other notable religious community leaders, but that does not diminish its historical impact. From a folkloristic viewpoint, it adds to the analysis of Stiehly as a legendary figure, a folk hero who became an emblem for his community. Another story further underscores Stiehly's status as local folk hero by bringing out his community-mindedness and his humble display of extraordinary strength—especially considering the stereotype of the minister as a literary type not engaging in taxing manual labor. Stiehly had helped a man hew heavy timbers for a building, but without other help available the problem of lifting the timber for hewing arose. Stiehly self-assuredly "lifted the log so his helper could put a block under the end." This is a story that reveals the equalizing tendencies in the tight-knit valley communities: everyone had to pitch in to get the work done.

Pennsylvania German dower chest, Mahantango Valley, from the early nineteenth century.

The Mahantango Valley's material traditions marked it as different, and they came to represent Pennsylvania German cultural identity to outsiders. The valley's gravestones appeared especially distinctive compared with the English tradition, which became more intrusive in the 1840s. As Stiehly's *Taufschein* (decorated baptismal certificates) recorded the beginning of life, so *Grabstein,* as Stiehly called his gravestones, marked the end of life. Unlike the *Taufschein,* the gravestone was a public statement recognizing the individual as a member of both a family and the Pennsylvania German community. Many of the designs around the baptismal text (Fraktur) surround the gravestone text: hearts, angels, stars, rosettes, tulips. Several stonecutters who advertised during the nineteenth century were also schoolteachers and preachers—community leaders—who produced Fraktur. The structure and content of *Taufscheine* and gravestones were essential links of tradition to the individual; they outlined the individual's relationships to the institutions within the folk culture—the church, the school, and the family, the three institutions that were the individual's triple focus in life. They emphasized the importance of maintaining tradition, particularly at moments of greatest social change, and disruption, within the family and community: birth and death.

The connection of Pennsylvania German gravestone design to *Taufschein* structure, however, was not originally clear. Eighteenth-century stones tend to be small and thick and have a rounded head; often made of sandstone, they have a restricted text and single illustrative motif, perhaps a heart or rosette. The elaboration of gravestones to resemble baptismal certificates became more apparent during the early nineteenth century. Pennsylvania German stonecutters switched to marble and used taller, thinner dimensions, thus achieving the look of a certificate: white, vertical, and literary. In keeping with the development of Pennsylvania German artistry during the 1830s in response to cultural intrusions, Pennsylvania German carvers used more text and decoration in their

gravestones, and at the same time standardized the form more. While we may expect traditional symbols to decline with cultural intrusions, in fact they increased to ward such intrusions off. Isaac Stiehly's role as a defender of his folk culture, documented in oral tradition, was to suggest these symbols to signify the vitality of the ethnic community.

In his work, Stiehly memorialized the pioneers of the valley, most of whom were born in the eighteenth century. In his first few years of production, Stiehly made fewer than fifteen stones annually, mostly for Salem Church near Klingerstown. Suddenly, in the early 1850s, his production jumped to more than twenty stones a year, and he placed stones in nineteen other churchyards. We can measure the extent of his community reach in the placement of stones—an area spanning twelve miles in the Mahantango and Hegins Valleys. Before he was through in 1869, he had carved more than 400 stones (309 still stand today). In their dimensions, Stiehly's stones are egalitarian, in that they make a distinction only between adults and children. They offer a strong visual reinforcement of joined religious and cultural place, and the span of years over which he worked conveys a sense of continuous cultural time. In several churchyards a few miles apart, Stiehly's stones stand one after another, making a case for the use of tradition to create community. His highly elaborated stones, like the decorated furniture that preceded them, were embellished expressions of regional identity sought out by residents. They presented an image of cultural strength through the emphatic reuse of old symbols, even as their intention suggested an imminent social weakening.

Although the Pennsylvania German dialect persisted in gathering places throughout the region, by World War II the younger generation was less likely to use the language. By then, the Pennsylvania Germans arguably had evolved into a "memory" culture, recalling the bonds of tradition from the past. In the 1940s and 1950s, vigorous folklore collection occurred in the area to record folk songs, spirituals, folktales, and legends representing the expressive performances of the culture. In the region's newspapers, Pennsylvania German-speaking columnists associated folklore with bygone days when the Pennsylvania Germans had no alternative lifeways. Folklife research meanwhile brought out crafts and skills that bridged the present and past. Basketmakers, furniture makers, quilters, hunters, and cooks expressed a continuing legacy. Into the twenty-first century in the region, annual meetings, called *Versommlinge* and featuring singing and folk dramas, signified organized "revivals" to recall the Pennsylvania German language as the symbol of a total community experience. Meanwhile, agricultural depression took farms and young people away from the Mahantango and Hegins Valleys, most of whom had given up the dialect. With Amish farmers and a religious commune moving into the region in the late twentieth century to take up some of the abandoned farms, and reintroducing Pennsylvania German language and culture, these valleys are facing yet another transition worthy of folklife attention.

Not far from Stiehly's valley, an emerging folk identity grew around the industrial development so integrally associated with Pennsylvania. The ethnically diverse communities that worked for the coal, lumber, and steel industries produced abundant examples of customs, speech, song, and legend that have been inadequately collected. This evidence fills out histories based on company documents and legislative records by giving voice to workers' views of industrial life through the nineteenth and twentieth centuries. Song was a powerful vehicle for communication among the workers, especially because they had little access to the company-controlled press. New words were put to many traditional airs known to Welsh, Irish, Cornish, Polish, and German workers. The songs circulated by oral tradition and were re-created and adapted in many local settings.

Consider "The Avondale Mine Disaster," probably the best-known mining ballad ever produced, which recounts the events of September 6, 1869, in Avondale, Pennsylvania, when a flue partition in a coal-mine shaft caught fire and sent 110 men to their death. It was the first large-scale tragedy in the Pennsylvania hard-coal fields. News of the event spread quickly and soon came to be reinterpreted in song and story. A rumor arose, for example, that the Molly Maguires had sabotaged the mine as a protest against mine owners. The story was critical of the Mollies for their reckless ways, and in some versions questioned the character of Irish miners.

Another theme was evident in a set of verses set to a traditional ballad form known in the British Isles and circulating shortly after the event in the coal region. The composer or composers are unknown, but the song soon appeared in oral tradition. Some enterprising printers made up cheap "broadside" sheets with different titles for the song. Setting a structure for mining ballads that followed, one type began by expressing pride

"The Avondale Mine Disaster" tells the story of the anthracite industry's first major tragedy in 1869. One of many variants of the song, this tune and wording was published in George Korson's *Pennsylvania Songs and Legends* (1949).

Moderately fast

1. Good Chris-tians all, both great and small, I pray you lend an ear, And list-en with at - ten-tion while The truth I will de - clare; When you hear this lam-en - ta - tion, 'Twill cause you to weep and wail, A - bout the suf-fo - ca - tion In the mines of Av-on-dale.

in the work, then shifts to horror at the disaster, then exalts the heroism of the would-be rescuers, and concludes with a morbid summary of the casualties. Another type blames the profit-hungry company for neglecting miners' safety.

Folklorist George Korson claimed that the ballads about Avondale were among the first songs he heard from miners when he began collecting in the 1920s, more than fifty years after the event. They were sung in barrooms, down in the mines, and in miners' homes. Singers often attached the Avondale words to different mine disasters through the years, and collectors recorded the song as far away as Newfoundland. Although the early collectors gave special attention to the words and music, it is also noteworthy to record the settings in which the song was sung, and the meanings given the song by singers and their audiences.

Compare the following two versions that appear in George Korson's collection, *Minstrels of the Mine Patch,* demonstrating both the repetition and the variation common in folk song:

> Good Christians all, both great and small,
>   I pray you lend an ear,
> And listen with attention while
>   The truth I will declare;

When you hear this lamentation,
    It will cause you to weep and wail,
About the suffocation
    In the mines of Avondale.

On the sixth day of September,
    Eighteen hundred and sixty nine,
Those miners all then got a call
    To go work in the mine;
But little did they think that day
    That death would gloom the vale
Before they would return again from
    The mines of Avondale.

                            ("Avondale Mine Disaster")

Come, friends and fellow Christians, and listen to my tale,
And as I sing, pray drop a tear for the dead of Avondale;
The sixth day of September, in eighteen sixty-nine
We shall never forget the day until the end of time.

One hundred and eight men went in the mine as I am told,
Not thinking that before the eve in death they'd all lie cold.
And some there were with snowy locks and others in their prime
And children in their tender youth were working in the mine.

                            ("Avondale Disaster")

The dangers of the mine, the insensitivity of management, and the effect of mining on families resound through other songs based on the Avondale disaster, such as "The Sugar Notch Entombment" and "The Mines of Locust Dale."

Ethnic appeals enter into several versions, such as "Charley Hill's Old Slope," which begins: "Come all ye true born Irishmen Wherever you may be, I hope you'll attention pay And listen unto me. It's of those true-born Irishmen That left their native clay, To seek their destination Here in Americ-a." The Avondale song was often accompanied by cautionary tales of moaning ghosts in the shaft who served to underscore the suffering in the mines. Two volunteers who valiantly attempted rescue were made heroes and were identified by their ethnicity in song: "Two Welshmen brave, without dismay, And courage without fail, Went down the shaft without delay, In the mines of Avondale."

To underscore the terror of the event, the images in song were often gruesome. Several songs appeal to "brother miners" to respond: "The news of the sad accident the valley soon went round, And quick their brother miners came flocking to the ground, Where the miners' little children, Their darling wives likewise, The hills all around they

Two depictions of the Avondale mine disaster, published in *Frank Leslie's Illustrated Newspaper* in 1869.

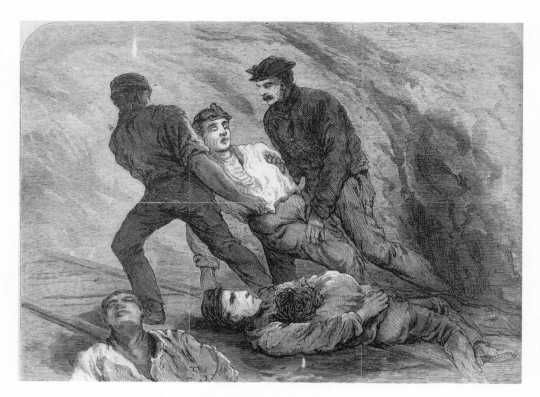

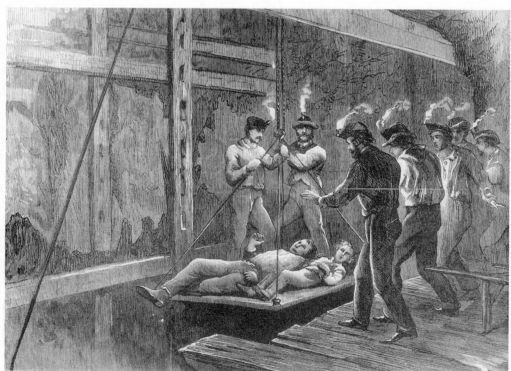

did resound With sad and mournful cries." Besides the impact of the folk poetry immediately after the disaster to encourage legislative reforms, the songs and legends resurfaced around other disasters to remind workers that there was a pattern to the dangers. Indeed, the song became part of political campaigns to force restrictions on child labor, impose safety standards, and demand inspections.

Another example of a Pennsylvania folk tradition that became a center of political debate is the Hegins Pigeon Shoot. In most states today, the pigeon shoot would be illegal, although forms of it were once widespread in early America. But it carried on legally in Pennsylvania and was a regular feature of many private hunting and fishing clubs until 1999. It was part of hunting-related practices, including turkey shoots and snake hunts that were common in Pennsylvania. Rural Pennsylvania has been a haven for hunting traditions, as indicated by the fact that Pennsylvania usually leads the nation in the number of hunting and fishing licenses issued. The beginning of hunting season is a major event, and the opening of deer season is a school holiday in many parts of the state. Hunters extol their union with nature, initiate novices and recognize seasoned veterans, engage in long rounds of storytelling at primitive lodges, and don earthy dress and body appearance to separate the activity from modern life. In their talk, they often speak of the days of yore in the primitive wilderness and imagine themselves as part of a classic American story of triumphing in the woods.

Amid this hunting heritage, Hegins held the nation's largest pigeon-shooting public contest until it was discontinued in 1999. Begun in the 1930s as part of a homecoming festival held during the Labor Day weekend, it announced the end of summer and the foregrounding of the fall recreational hunting season around which the lives of many families in the Hegins Valley are structured. Into the 1980s the Hegins Park publicized the event as a tradition because it had been active for almost fifty years and evoked occupational hunting activities that were once part of the seasonal cycle dating back to the beginning of settlement of the central Pennsylvania valleys in the eighteenth century.

Beginning in 1989, animal rights protesters sought to end the tradition. They derided the event as a "blood sport" and referred to shooters as barbarians rather than tradition-bearers. When protesters appeared on the scene, supporters viewed their demonstrations as not so much an objection to the event but more as an attack on a way of life that had been handed down through generations. Indeed, the use of youngsters, called "trapper boys," to help the men who shot the birds became hotly disputed. While families watched adults take aim and shoot, the trapper boys gathered the downed birds in sacks and unceremoniously disposed of them. If the shot birds were not dead when they were picked up, the boys finished the job. Protesters saw this division of roles as initiating the boys into the acceptability of violence. The boys understood it as an appropriate task before they would be allowed to shoot the birds themselves; being in the shoot was a maturation rite. The boys willingly took on responsibility in the social struc-

Two scenes from the Hegins Pigeon Shoot in 1991, the largest such event in the nation until it was discontinued in 1999.

ture of the community. Their views of labor in an agricultural valley centered on human dominance over land and beast; many could cite Bible passages to underscore the idea of human dominion over nature. The townspeople of Hegins loudly retaliated against protesters because they felt that an urban authority and moral system had eroded the foundation of their rural society.

Media attention to Hegins during the 1990s sparked a nationwide debate on the value of this traditional custom to a community. The discourse can be examined historically for its late-twentieth-century reflection on the extent of "rights" and associated social movements in America. In the wake of the civil rights and woman's rights movements, social advocates claimed rights for animals, and in so doing came into conflict with many traditions associated with Pennsylvania community life. Another twentieth-century issue was the advance of mass culture, and what it meant for community authority to maintain folklife. The shouts and signs during the historic confrontation at Hegins divided between the protesters' rhetoric of "rights" for the animals, and supporters' messages of respect for tradition and community. Although the protests did not shut the shoot down, decisions in the courts did. Nevertheless, shoots continue in private clubs, and hunting rituals persist.

In the Hegins pigeon shoot, a social custom closely associated with Pennsylvania heritage that might be categorized under recreational or community folklife came under public scrutiny for its political as well as historical impact. Along with the Avondale mine disaster songs' meanings for coal miners, and the coal region and the symbolism of stone expressed by Isaac Stiehly, who became a folk hero for his ethnic culture, we behold here folklore and folklife at the center of social and cultural questioning. These instances involve more than collecting texts from the past; they emphasize the need for historians to record attitudes that are apparent from traditions *about* the past as well as *of* the past as they are enacted over time. These examples refer to the power of tradition to keep memory alive through shared expressions and to suggest an outlook on, a consciousness of, a perception of the past related to the present. The problem of tradition in American history brought out by folklore and folklife research puts into focus the unsettled issue of locating America's cultural continuity with a past, *some* past, and often a *contested, plural* past, not revealed easily by recording of events and biographies.

Folklorists use four basic approaches to interpret traditions and their historical role: (1) archival and artifactual compilation, (2) field collection, (3) ethnography, and (4) lifestory recording or interview. The approaches do not have to be mutually exclusive and may be chosen depending on the questions to be answered.

Documentary records and printed sources can be well mined for evidence of folklore and folklife. Researchers look to these records particularly to answer questions about the everyday life and traditions of historic communities. Diaries, calendars, almanacs, account books, scrapbooks, recipe books, documents of rites of passage, and letters often contain records of local customs, beliefs, speech, stories, and crafts. Local historical societies often collect these documents to record family and community life. For instance, child-rearing practices, seasonal chores, pastimes and games, and community festivals, as well as major storms and disasters, are often recorded in diaries. Such information is incorporated in the design of exhibitions focused on traditional activities in a typical year for the miner at Eckley Miners' Village near Hazleton and the farmer at the Landis Valley Museum near Lancaster. By inventorying folk items within the context of their historical and social backgrounds, folklorists construct a picture of everyday practices that can portray the structure of time, leisure, and work in the life of the past. Artifactual evidence complements this research into everyday life. Craft products such as baskets, pottery, and ironwork show the skills, symbols, and demands of past lives, while paintings and photographs document a community's environment and its traditional celebrations.

The kinds of social historical questions answered by compiling inventories of folkloric references in documents and artifacts may include the significant shifts in language, ethnicity, and technology revealed in patterns of everyday life. Other questions concern identity. Many historical societies record place-name legends and heroic narratives that suggest sources of identity to a community. The legendary material kept in diaries and newspapers can be read for how a community relates regional and national events. Mac Barrick's study of David Lewis (1790?–1820), known fondly in central Pennsylvania legend as "Lewis the Robber," a Robin Hood–type of character, made extensive use of newspaper accounts that often circulated legends about Lewis. Barrick also used printed

"First Communion" remains a major milestone in the lives of young girls and boys in the ethnic churches of Pennsylvania. This photo commemorates a Mt. Carmel Polish Catholic First Communion in the early 1900s.

pamphlets recounting oral elaborations of Lewis's crime, an account of his life, and his confession. The vending of these pamphlets circulating legendary material was popular at public executions, a long-standing custom in England and apparently imported to the New World. Records that document interactions such as court cases are especially useful to view a discourse on customs, and testimony often relates accounts of crime as they were reported in oral tradition. For example, Pennsylvania has had its share of cases where the ethnic-religious beliefs held by such groups as the Amish have come up against the interests of the state. Furthermore, testimonies in fugitive-slave cases have been invaluable in analyzing the narrative tradition of the Underground Railroad.

The field collection differs from the archival and artifactual record because it is compiled from living sources, but it shares an emphasis on accumulating texts toward the goal of identifying patterns. By collecting information in the present from informants, preferably from active tradition-bearers, researchers become aware of the continuity of traditions from the past into the present. The researcher analyzes the content and distribution of the items and evaluates them against the social background of the tradition-bearers and communities. The texts can be oral in the words of stories or songs, social in the order of games and rituals, and material in the forms of crafts and buildings. The arrangement of the collection may be geographical, as in the inventory and classification of traditional barns, foods, and speech to question the cultural boundaries of a region. It can also be thematic according to matters of age, nature, or community. It can be social, to question the forms of expression common to or about, coal miners, children, or Jews. It is difficult to say how many versions have to be collected or how many informants are needed to come up with a "comprehensive" collection. The test of representativeness applies equally to the texts of the past as well as those of the present. The collection needs to be a sample that does a good job of signifying a place or people. It is "annotated" and compared with reference to other collections, often to hypothesize origin, function, and diffusion of the items. For instance, major indexed collections have been published on beliefs arranged by types in North Carolina, Utah, and Ohio. Although no statewide survey on that magnitude has been published for Pennsylvania, field collections on beliefs, speech, and customs have been deposited in various archives, including those of Ursinus College, Penn State–Harrisburg, and the University of Pennsylvania.

UNDERGROUND RAILROAD

In the 1850s this area known as Tanner's Alley, was important on the Underground Railroad. Fugitive slaves hid at Joseph Bustill's & William Jones's houses, a block apart. Frederick Douglass & William Lloyd Garrison spoke at Wesley Union AME Zion Church nearby.

Dedication of an Underground Railroad historical marker, Harrisburg, April 28, 2000. Oral traditions point to black churches throughout Pennsylvania that served as stations on the Underground Railroad. One such station, Old Bethel African Methodist Episcopal Church in Reading, is now a museum of African American history.

The ethnography is more an observation of a context than a collection of texts. The researcher identifies a bounded cultural scene, such as a ritual or service, and records the behavior, objects, and speech within the setting. The purpose of the observation is to analyze the distinctive symbolic uses of behavior, objects, and speech within that scene in order to evaluate the social significance of the scene as a communicative system. Examples of ethnographies in Pennsylvania include the use of bocce-playing by Italian American men in Philadelphia, to connect socially; and the use of Yiddish storytelling

by elderly Jews from eastern Europe in a community center, to designate their value system within the larger Jewish community. The ethnography is usually more limited, and arguably less comparative, in its scope than the field collection or documentary record, but it can be used effectively to interpret the meaning of symbols and performances of community life. It adds a behavioral component to historical analysis and questions the meanings and functions of scenes for various groups. It often operates on the assumption that people most reveal themselves in community performances, such as rituals, customs, and celebrations. When comparable ethnographies are available for the same scenes over time or across space, specific associations can be made about change or persistence of traditions in performance.

The life story or interview records the narratives of individual lives. It has been especially valuable in folklore and folklife research to draw biographies of outstanding tradition-bearers, particularly within ethnic-religious groups, but it also has been used commonly to trace the social uses of tradition in ordinary lives. It therefore is not only applied to the elderly but also used with youth to evaluate family and local legacies. I distinguish between life story and interview because the latter is intended to extract information about traditions, whereas the life story is the dramatic rendering of one's life as a coherent narrative with a plot and a moral. The life story reminds us of the way that we narrate our identities, our connections to the past and to place, in the form of story. Frequently collected examples of the "personal narrative" in life stories are mothers' birthing accounts, immigrants' sagas of the trip to America, and reminiscences of engagements and weddings. There can be substantial overlap between the "oral history"

To Save Lives, Strengthen Israel, Aid Democracy

פֶּסַח
חַג הַמַצּוֹת

intended to obtain reflections about the past and the "life story" narrating it. The folk-loristic perspective on the life story questions the way the narrative was composed, structured, and performed, as well as the details and reflections revealed.

Approaches using folklore and folklife can help us construct a folk history, a history that represents the narratives of people about their past in family, work, play, and community. This history consists of ever-emerging sagas worthy of consideration in any assessment of American experience. A sense of place, identity, or connection can be heard in the ways in which people express themselves with reference to tradition. The traditions may be in the form of speech, story, song, or craft, and they adapt to new

Model Passover Seder at Harrisburg Hebrew School, 1951. The banner above reads "To Save Lives, Strengthen Israel, Aid Democracy." It refers to efforts by American Jews after World War II to resettle Holocaust survivors and establish the State of Israel. Remembering the Holocaust is central to maintaining Jewish identity in America, as elsewhere.

Needlework by Pang Xiong Sirarathasuk, Upper Darby, Pennsylvania, January 1990. A member of the Hmong people from Xieng Khouang Province in central Laos who became refugees after years of war in Southeast Asia, Pang settled in the Philadelphia area in 1979. Here she shows the intricate textile art known as *paj taub* (flower cloth, or story cloth), which depicts the unwritten history and oral tales of the Hmong heritage. She has been active in encouraging the continuation of this folk art and in maintaining Hmong celebrations of the New Year and marriage. She has also demonstrated Hmong singing and crafts at the Smithsonian Folklife Festival and many Pennsylvania folklife exhibitions.

RIGHT: Members of the Owen family at a "quilting bee" near Lancaster, 1995. Quilting remains a tradition, an art, and a source of income for many Pennsylvanians.

environments and times. Whereas much of Pennsylvania folklore and folklife research in the twentieth century focused on ethnic, regional, and occupational groups, historians can use the evidence of folklore and folklife to assess the cultural historical experiences of an expanded range of groups and experiences that characterize Pennsylvania. Beyond industrial occupations, are there emergent traditions within the service and information economy? Beyond the settlement community, are there rituals, legends, and material symbols for such institutions as schools, colleges, hunting lodges, resorts, and military installations? How does Pennsylvania figure in the historical identity of such groups of high-schoolers as the Goths, Wiccans, and Raves of the 1990s, with their intentional construction of lore and ritual? Beyond the traditions of gender, will historians record the active lore of sexuality and sexual preference? If there is a folklore of identity that expresses through traditions Pennsylvanians' connections to, or constructions of, a legacy, there is also a folklore about legacies. Rather than dismiss "Indian legends" told by nonnatives, belief narratives about William Penn and the Walking Purchase uttered by children, or even ethnic and racial slurs, historians can compile them to gain insights into varieties of memory and outlook in and about Pennsylvania.

My suggestion of topics and approaches still begs the question of history's relationship to folklore and folklife that opened this chapter. I have made a case that folklore and folklife provide an inside-out view of history. There is a dualism to this view. From one perspective, folklore and folklife offer a social and cultural autobiography by which lives and ideas of people in community, past and present, are recorded. In another, folklore and folklife provide a symbolic biography of others that is revealed in narratives and beliefs—those of others, not of ourselves. We therefore have materials that portray both the continuities and the discontinuities within a legacy, and the relationships among neighbors, groups, and communities. By expressing ideas in the creative form of folklore with reference to tradition, there is an implication that the values and attitudes conveyed are deep-seated, and perhaps difficult to express otherwise in documents and even in conversation. William Penn understood these points as early as 1683 when he referred to "the stories of our necessity being either the fears of our friends, or the scare-crows of our enemies." A century and a half later, Isaac Stiehly, hardly as famous but nonetheless greatly influential in his social world, also realized the power of folklore when he inspired his community by elaborating symbols of their cultural legacy. Songs and legends responding to the Avondale mine disaster remind us of adaptations of tradition with the rise of industry and its various communities. In the twenty-first century, we can look back to recover these legacies even as we can look around to view emerging stories and new identities.

SOURCES *and* FURTHER READING

Abrahams, Roger D. *Deep Down in the Jungle . . . : Negro Narrative Folklore from the Streets of Philadelphia.* Chicago: Aldine, 1970.

Barrick, Mac E. *Lewis the Robber: A Pennsylvania Folk Hero in Life and Legend.* Special issue of *Midwestern Folklore* 20 (Fall 1994), 69–138.

Beam, C. Richard. *The Thomas R. Brendle Collection of Pennsylvania German Folklore.* Volume 1. Schaefferstown, Pa.: Historic Schaefferstown, 1995.

Boyer, Walter, Albert Buffington, and Don Yoder. *Songs Along the Mahantongo: Pennsylvania Dutch Folksongs.* Lancaster: Pennsylvania Dutch Folklore Center, 1951.

Brendle, Thomas R., and William Troxell. *Pennsylvania German Folk Tales, Legends, Once-Upon-a-Time Stories, Maxims, and Sayings Spoken in the Dialect Popularly Known as Pennsylvania Dutch.* Norristown: Pennsylvania German Society, 1944.

Bronner, Simon J. "Elaborating Tradition: A Pennsylvania German Folk Artist Ministers to His Community." In *Creativity and Tradition in Folklore,* ed. Simon J. Bronner, 277–325. Logan: Utah State University Press, 1992.

———. *Following Tradition: Folklore in the Discourse of American Culture.* Logan: Utah State University Press, 1998.

———. *Popularizing Pennsylvania: Henry Shoemaker and the Progressive Uses of Folklore and History.* University Park: The Pennsylvania State University Press, 1996.

Buffington, Albert F. *Pennsylvania German Secular Folksongs.* Breinigsville: Pennsylvania German Society, 1974.

Dorson, Richard M. *American in Legend: Folklore from the Colonial Period to the Present.* New York: Pantheon, 1973.

Gillespie, Angus K. *Folklorist of the Coal Fields: George Korson's Life and Work.* University Park: The Pennsylvania State University Press, 1980.

Glimm, James York. *Flatlanders and Ridgerunners: Folktales from the Mountains of Northern Pennsylvania.* Pittsburgh: University of Pittsburgh Press, 1983.

Goldstein, Kenneth S., and Robert H. Byington, eds. *Two Penny Ballads and Four Dollar Whiskey: A Pennsylvania Folklore Miscellany.* Hatboro, Pa.: Folklore Associates, 1966.

Korson, George, ed. *Black Rock: Mining Folklore of the Pennsylvania Dutch.* Baltimore: Johns Hopkins University Press, 1960.

———. *Minstrels of the Mine Patch: Songs and Stories of the Anthracite Industry.* Philadelphia: University of Pennsylvania Press, 1938.

———. *Pennsylvania Songs and Legends.* Philadelphia: University of Pennsylvania Press, 1949.

Leach, MacEdward, and Henry Glassie. *A Guide for Collectors of Oral Traditions and Folk Cultural Material in Pennsylvania.* Harrisburg: Pennsylvania Historical and Museum Commission, 1968.

Macneal, Patricia M., Bonelyn L. Kyofski, and Kenneth A. Thigpen, eds. *Headwaters and Hardwoods: The Folklore, Cultural History, and Traditional Arts of the Pennsylvania Northern Tier.* Mansfield, Pa.: Northern Tier Cultural Alliance, 1997.

Meginness, John. *Otzinachson: A History of the West Branch Valley of the Susquehanna.* Williamsport, Pa.: Gazette & Bulletin Printing House, 1889. Page 470.

Noyes, Dorothy. *Uses of Tradition: Arts of Italian Americans in Philadelphia.* Philadelphia: Philadelphia Folklore Project, 1989.

Reed, Henry M. *Decorated Furniture of the Mahantongo Valley.* Lewisburg, Pa.: Bucknell University Press, 1987.

Rosenberger, Homer Tope. *Mountain Folks: Fragments of Central Pennsylvania Lore.* Lock Haven, Pa.: Annie Halenbake Ross Library, 1974.

Shoemaker, Alfred L. *Christmas in Pennsylvania: A Folk Cultural Study.* 1959. Reprint, Harrisburg: Stackpole Books, 1999.

———. *Eastertide in Pennsylvania: A Folk Cultural Study.* 1960. Reprint, Harrisburg: Stackpole Books, 2000.

Staub, Shalom, ed. *Craft and Community: Traditional Arts in Contemporary Society.* Philadelphia: Balch Institute for Ethnic Studies and Pennsylvania Heritage Affairs Commission, 1988.

Wallace, Anthony F. C. *St. Clair: A Nineteenth-Century Coal Town's Experience with a Disaster-Prone Industry.* New York: Alfred A. Knopf, 1987.

Yoder, Don. *Discovering American Folklife: Essays on Folk Culture and the Pennsylvania Dutch.* Harrisburg: Stackpole Books, 2001.

———. *Pennsylvania Spirituals.* Lancaster: Pennsylvania Folklife Society, 1961.

Yoder, Don, and Thomas Graves. *Hex Signs: Pennsylvania Dutch Barn Symbols and Their Meaning.* 1989. Reprint, Harrisburg: Stackpole Books, 2000.

Genealogy

JAMES M. BEIDLER

Genealogy, the study of the blood linkages between parents and children as well as less-direct relationships, gives people a personal stake in history. It wraps individual identities in the context of historical events. Pennsylvanians researching family histories can find Quakers such as Thomas Coates of Philadelphia, colonial-era Germans such as Martin Eisenhauer from Berks County, nineteenth-century Austrians such as Katharina Schumpp of Carbondale, or twentieth-century Croatian Americans such as John Tucec of Duquesne. Because of the Commonwealth's long-standing mix of cultures and the multiple ethnic origins of its people, any individual Pennsylvanian stands the chance of finding ancestors from Pennsylvania who spoke different languages and lived through diverse experiences.

How to research and tell the family story depends on the time period, the place of residence in Pennsylvania and elsewhere, and to some degree the ethnic origins of the particular ancestral family. Those who attempt research on family history find that there are many quirks, idiosyncrasies, and seeming roadblocks. But they also find that the study of genealogy can be extraordinarily rewarding, because it provides a family with a unique opportunity to personalize Pennsylvania's history by learning about the family's forebears. As new generations have learned this process, it is more than a happy coincidence that they have produced and preserved records of historical significance about the "Everymen" of bygone eras, and as a consequence have in turn provided fodder for historians.

Detailed tombstone. A nineteenth-century marker that goes into much more detail than today's memorials.

Although studies of bloodlines have taken place since colonial times, the first great coming of Pennsylvania genealogy as an organized discipline occurred in the last quarter of the nineteenth century. Beginning roughly about the time of the centennial of the Declaration of Independence in 1876, pride in ancestry and the nation's history led to the formation or revitalization of many patriotic societies—for example, the National Society of the Daughters of the American Revolution (1890) and Sons of the American Revolution (1876, formally organized 1889). Another motivating factor was surely the increasing flood of immigrants as the nineteenth century closed, at a time when Americans were acutely conscious of "race" and concerned about preserving the character of the "founding fathers" in culture. Native-born Americans, whose lineage went back to the "old immigration" to the United States (from northern Europe and the British Isles) insulated themselves from the "corruptions" of the new wealth and new people by establishing societies that not everyone—especially "new immigrants" from southern, central, and eastern Europe—could join. This burst in interest also led to the publication of many county histories and some family surname books.

The genealogies compiled during this "first coming" potentially had certain advantages. While eyewitnesses to the American Revolution were dead, there were many people who had talked with men and women or heard stories from the generation who remembered the revolutionary era and days of the early republic. Whatever the accuracy and reliability of such memories, the stories linked the late nineteenth century to the nation's beginnings in human terms and no doubt quickened interest in genealogy and history. Compared with today, a century ago fewer records had been lost to time, neglect, and natural disaster, though it is significant that back then most family records remained in private hands instead of being deposited in public archives for general use; in addition, 100 years ago more of the tombstones were legible.

Despite this potential, much of the genealogy done at the end of the nineteenth century was of poor research quality. County histories were typically compiled from circuits of the countryside that were two parts sales mission (promise to buy a book, get a biography; buy a book and pay an extra fee, get a photograph with your biography) and one part research. (A glaring example of the genre is Morton L. Montgomery's *Historical and Biographical Annals of Berks County, Pennsylvania,* 2 vols. [1909], an oft-cited and oft-incorrect source for information on Berks County families.) Daughters of the American Revolution applications were reviewed more on the basis of then-current social stature than on soundness of revolutionary pedigree. Family surname histories were published without the footnotes and primary source citations that are essential for future researchers who seek to "track back" information about ancestors to original records. Primarily because of the slipshod approach to genealogy by many of those practicing it a century ago, genealogists as a group acquired a "black sheep" reputation with many historians that never has been fully erased. In addition, a number of sources (such as the U.S. Census returns profiled later) were not available to researchers.

Many Pennsylvanians are currently involved in the great "second coming" of genealogy. Since the nineteenth century there has been steady interest and a gradual rise in the quality of genealogy, assisted by microfilming programs and the collection of records by such groups and institutions as county historical societies and the Pennsylvania State Archives. Alex Haley's book and the television miniseries *Roots* are often credited with supplying the spark that ignited research among the masses, but the explosion in genealogical interest was fueled by the melding of two crucial forces: an increase in the sheer number of people with retirement leisure time and the ability of home computers to bring instant communication and sources of information to the desktop through the Internet. The availability of such a means to accomplish a good deal of research without leaving the house has had much to do with the popularity of genealogy at the most recent turn of the century.

Leading the way has been the Church of Jesus Christ of Latter-day Saints (the Mormons). Its members collect genealogical information as part of the group's teaching that deceased relatives of church members can be rebaptized, but they have made the databases they have compiled available to nonmembers as well as to Mormons. These databases and millions of rolls of microfilm of church and other records from around the world were traditionally available only at the Mormons' Family History Library in Salt Lake City, Utah, but in 1999 the Mormons made them available on an Internet website. All this has changed the traditional protocol of genealogical communication, from placing a "query" in a genealogical society's quarterly publication seeking information about a particular ancestor or family, to electronic mail that has compressed the amount of time one must wait for information from months into days, hours, minutes, or even seconds. But despite these profound changes, such as the increase in technology and the decrease in waiting time, the challenge of genealogy done well has become no less arduous. If anything, the larger amount of information made available by the computer age means that there are even more undocumented and inaccurate pedigrees to snare novice or careless family historians.

GENEALOGISTS AS DETECTIVES

Something that has not changed about genealogists is the need for

The major databases of the Church of Jesus Christ of Latter-day Saints, which are collectively known as "FamilySearch," are the Ancestral File, the International Genealogical Index (IGI), and the Family History Library Catalog.

The Ancestral File is a compilation of genealogies contributed by thousands of people, including patrons of the church's Family History Centers, and the information is mostly about deceased people. The only problem with using the Ancestral File is that the information is only as good as the documentation used by the submitter, and the quality of that documentation varies greatly.

The International Genealogical Index lists dates and places of births, christenings, and marriages of millions of deceased people who lived from the early 1500s to the early 1900s. These data have been extracted from thousands of original records. Millions of names appear in the IGI and can often be the springboards for finding ancestors in a previously unknown locale. The IGI is only an incomplete abstract of information from original records; for example, in baptisms that have been extracted into the IGI, only the child's and the parents' names are listed, while the original record probably shows baptismal sponsors, who were often family members and sometimes recorded as such.

The Family History Library Catalog lists the holdings of the Family History Library in Salt Lake City, Utah, which include more than 2 million microfilms and 400,000 books. Copies of the microfilms can be rented for use at local Family History Centers.

GENEALOGY AND THE PHILADELPHIA SOCIAL HISTORY PROJECT

Historians have been using genealogical materials for a long time, but the new interest in community studies and family history since World War II has led a new generation of historians to cross the aisle from "traditional history" to the "new social history," which emphasizes history "from the bottom up." The "new social history" sent historians to census, court, church, and family records to search out the "common" people, who left few written accounts of their own lives. One of the many tasks such historians set for themselves was to chart the movement of people into and out of places, work, and social conditions over time.

Perhaps the largest and most ambitious such effort was the Philadelphia Social History Project (PSHP), a collaborative enterprise that between 1969 and 1981 brought historians, sociologists, economists, demographers, and genealogists together to map everything from occupational structure and work patterns to residential mobility and family formation among immigrant, black, and working-class people in Philadelphia between 1850 and 1880. The studies emanating from the PSHP revealed a Philadelphia in motion, as "lower-class" people sought work in an industrial metropolis that was expanding outward spatially while also becoming divided internally according to job, race, and wealth. Computers made the processing of immense data possible, but the "new social history" perspective and shared methodologies of the investigators made possible the most extensive and integrated portrait of an urban population to date. The PSHP was both multidisciplinary and interdisciplinary, and its machine-readable database, now archived at the University of Pennsylvania, remains a trove of vital information that genealogists and historians might mine for many years to come.

them to be detectives. As with private eyes from fictional thrillers, good researchers of family histories thrive on the acquisition of information. To do this most efficiently, both groups use logic to forge ahead from known facts (however scanty those facts might be), formulate hypotheses on where additional information will be found, test those hypotheses against actual data, and then go through the process again depending on what is found in the actual data.

Genealogists often have an advantage over detectives, of course, when they are researching their own ancestry, because a family history search is usually greeted more warmly than a visit from a private eye. And, indeed, the best genealogy usually begins with the individual who is doing the search and works backward in time. Too often researchers have wasted an inordinate amount of time by visiting a research facility like the State Library of Pennsylvania in Harrisburg, plucking one of its thousands of family surname history books from the shelf simply because it bears the researcher's surname, and treating it as if the Holy Grail had been found. The unfortunate reality is that, even for less-common names, the chance of such a surname history containing a given individual's line is much less than a sure bet. A researcher who begins by critically examining what he or she knows about parents, grandparents, great-grandparents, and so on, and then adds to that knowledge by interviewing family elders will be much more focused when making that first research foray into printed and other sources. Interviews with family elders are often fine oral histories that are worth preserving for more than just the family data they yield, because interviewees' stories may be rich in providing the context of a family's history in a way that no document will. (For example, where other than an oral history interview can one learn how two "average" individuals met and fell in love?) Beginning genealogists should also attempt to inventory and abstract any family documents—for example, Bibles with filled-in family pages, diaries, scrapbooks, photograph albums, and privately held birth certificates—that are in their or another's possession. These are sources of premium value.

A beginning researcher might be disconcerted to find that at times information gleaned from family interviews contradicts conventional wisdom. A good example is the Anthony Tobin (circa 1871–April 25, 1923) family based in southern Schuylkill County. A once-over-lightly look at the area's records made it seem likely that this family would be of either Welsh or Irish descent, but family legend had it that a mid-1800s immigrant forebear was a Polish Jew named Tobinsky. More focused research in Schuylkill County records uncovered a marriage license of Anthony Tobin under the name Anthony Dubinski, a native of Germany. U.S. Census records found the family recorded under the name Hobin as well as Tobin, and placed Anthony Tobin/Dubinski's birthplace as either Pennsylvania or Germany; his parents' birthplaces as either Germany or Russia; and his parents' mother tongue as Polish. While there was no confirmation on the immigrant's religion, the attempt to verify a family anecdote that seemed absurd at least proved an eastern European origin, rather than the original hypothesis of the British Isles.

TIME AND PLACE: THE CROSSHAIRS OF RESEARCH

Crucial to any genealogical search is the ability of the researcher to look at the world of an ancestor at the time and in the place that individual lived. This is important both for efficient use of records and for placement of an ancestor in context. Time and place to a genealogist are like a set of crosshairs—at the intersection of which nearly always is found the most information about an ancestor.

In searching for records and documents relating to ancestors, genealogists need to get a sense of what records are most valuable in a particular time period or geographic area. Otherwise they risk looking for needles that don't even exist in a particular haystack. The example of Leo Ohnmacht, a German immigrant who lived in present-day Lackawanna County during the 1800s, illustrates the principles of time and place. In seeking marriage data on this individual (who married around 1866, according to census data), a researcher need not spend time looking for a marriage license because most parts of Pennsylvania (including Lackawanna County) did not record such licenses until 1885. The researcher must also be cognizant of shifts in county and municipal boundary lines, since records created in a particular time period will be found under the county or municipality of which a place was a part during that time. In Leo Ohnmacht's case, this means that until 1878, when Lackawanna County was created out of Luzerne County, records such as the U.S. Census will be found under the Luzerne heading. In addition, records created by counties, such as wills and deeds, do not move to a new courthouse when a new county is split off. As this applies to Leo Ohnmacht, records relating to people who resided in the new Lackawanna County did not follow; the records remained in the Luzerne County Courthouse in Wilkes-Barre.

Placing an ancestor in context has many uses. For researchers interested in fleshing out an ancestor's biography, newspapers and other documents of the time period can be of much use. Context also helps winnow out unnecessary record groups; for example, if a German immigrant ancestor in the colonial period is known to have come from a village in the Electorate of Hanover, it will be almost impossible to find this immigrant in the Philadelphia ship lists that are such a gold-mine for finding German immigrants from that era. The reason for this "omission" is a simple historical fact: the ship listings only recorded "foreigners" who owed no allegiance to the British Crown, and Hanover's "Elector" (its title for the ruler) was simultaneously King of England during most of the eighteenth century. Hence, Hanoverians were already subjects of the king in his role as elector.

A SOURCE IS A SOURCE—UNLESS IT'S SECONDARY

It is an unfortunate and somewhat ironic fact of genealogical life that those doing family research in the "first wave" a century ago often failed to use primary sources, even though they surely had access to documents that now no longer exist. The total amount of information available to the "second wave" genealogists of today dwarfs that of a century ago (including access to such crucial items as the manuscript U.S. Census schedules), but much of the increase in that information is attributable to the march of time and the ability to record and sort research on a computer—quantity rather than quality.

The terms "primary source" and "secondary source" as used by trained genealogists deserve definition, because knowing the difference between the two is critical in determining the believability of an individual's research. Primary sources are documents or records created around the time of the event in question by or with the help of someone in the position to have participated in or observed the events and ideas in the document or record. The definition for secondary sources is easier. Secondary sources are any records or documents that are not primary. Examples, as usual, will help turn words into learning. The original will of an individual on file in a county courthouse is a primary source. A compilation of abstracts from that original will and others, possibly rearranged and usually indexed, is a secondary source. The convenience of secondary sources often makes them a seductive substitute for primary sources in genealogists' eyes. But good genealogists never rely on that secondary source unless the primary data is literally no longer available (as opposed to merely difficult or inconvenient to access); instead, they use the secondary source as a gateway to finding the primary source, and then use the primary source as their evidence.

This is not to say that primary sources do not contain errors. Death records such as obituaries, death certificates, and tombstones are regarded as the least reliable of primary sources because such records, while classified as primary because they pass the test of "someone in the position to know the facts of the assertion," come from someone who often is not in the "*best* position to know"—that is, the deceased. When confronted with contradictory recordings in two different sources, the rule that proves true most often is that the record closest in time to the event will be correct. For example, if different dates of birth are found in an infant baptism and tombstone record, go with the baptism. The accuracy of records kept and produced by a family are often subject to the perils of fading memories (especially regarding dates), while those on file in public repositories that were the work of "third parties" such as courthouse clerks and census takers—or even circuit-riding ministers—most often show their inadequacies when recording the names of people they did not know well. Precisely because there are so many errors in records, redundancy is a virtue in genealogy; if possible, researchers should find two recordings of every vital event.

But the errors found in primary sources pale before the mistakes that often litter such secondary sources as family surname books and nineteenth- and early twentieth-century county histories. Even when compilers were diligent in their tasks, the sheer volume of names and dates makes it more likely that many a wrong fact was incorporated into the long half-life accorded errors in print. And unfortunately compilers often were not diligent. An excellent example of a secondary source gone amiss is the history of the Kreiser family found in the *Biographical Annals of Lebanon County* (1904). From its mistake-to-end-all-mistakes of calling the Kreiser immigrant Frederick instead of Caspar (the immigrant did at least have a son Friedrich, or Frederick), to errors regarding the timing and location of the family homestead (they are placed in Lebanon County at least seventy years too soon), primary data—ship lists, tax records, church records, a will, and so on—prove that the yarn spun in the *Biographical Annals* is false. Yet some members of this family still believe in the undocumented secondary source naming an immigrant Frederick, instead of the plethora of primary documentation stacked squarely behind an immigrant named Caspar. This is a case of genealogy misinforming history; when new works by well-meaning amateurs cite county biographical histories, the result is that such errors in print are given further credence.

Another aspect of genealogical sources is that they are most often born as something other than a record to be used in genealogy. The U.S. Census, for example, is required by law—as an enumeration—yet has come to be a valuable resource for genealogists. Other sources are as relevant for historians as for genealogists—for example, tax lists, which the historian can use as statistics to document economic status. In addition, an emerging trend among genealogists is the expansion of the use to which they put the data they have found. This trend includes the cross-referencing of

KATE DAUB WILL

This early twentieth-century will of Kate Daub entertains as well as informs. The information about the son Rolandus was partially corroborated by his descendants.

I, Kate Daub, widow, residing at 344 N. 12th Street, in the city of Lebanon, Pa., do make and publish my last will and testament, as follows:

To my youngest child, Mary, wife of Levi Keller, I give nothing, because she never tried to please me and was not obedient to my wishes. To my oldest son, Rolandus, I give nothing, because, some years ago, I have good reason to believe he made an unsuccessful attempt to kill me. Jere Gamber is to have his home in my house as long as he lives, rent free, and in case he needs help Adam Bombergers is hereby directed and ordered to give him cash whenever necessary and charge the same against my estate. At the death of said Jere Gamber it is my wish that my two other children, Lizzie and Harry, shall give him a decent burial. All my just debts are to be paid, and the remainder of my whole estate, real and personal, I give, devise and bequeath unto my two children Lizzie and Harry, executors of this my last will and testament. I give unto my grandchild, Carrie Allwein, my white sewing machine. In testimony whereof, I have hereunto set my hand and seal, this tenth day of March A.D. 1902.

Kate Daub

Witnesses:
Aaron Sattezahn
Robt. L. Miller

The will of Kate Daub is found in *Lebanon County Wills*, 1:229. Lebanon Register of Wills Office, Lebanon.

ancestors' health data to create a "medical family tree" that can help individuals understand the risks they may face from inherited diseases and conditions.

CHRONOLOGY USING THE "BIG 3" DATES AND OTHER SOURCES

There is usually much more to a person's life than birth, marriage, and death, yet the dates of those events are often the shorthand that represents an ancestor to the genealogist. The "Big 3" dates are the ones that appear on most types of pedigree charts. There is a "why" behind this that goes far beyond birth, marriage, and death as mere dates; the logic attached to the acquisition of these particular landmarks relating to ancestors' lives is that, simply, they point to clusters of genealogical records, sometimes in less than obvious ways. "Obvious" records regarding a marriage date are a license, a private certificate, and a newspaper notice; more subtle records are the greater likelihood (especially in the twentieth century and beyond) that a married couple will buy a home, generating a deed record and changes in tax status (as often reflected in eighteenth- and nineteenth-century Pennsylvania tax records). In some cases, in the time period before all counties in Pennsylvania began to record licenses in 1885, the only evidence of a man's marriage will be his shift in tax status from the "single freeman" category to the "inmate" (meaning a renter heading a household in this context) or "freeholder" (an owner of real estate).

Which sources are best for finding Pennsylvania vital records depends on the time period of the search. Except for sporadic records of marriages, the Commonwealth's first such records that have survived date from 1852 to 1855, when birth and death registers were kept on the county level. Philadelphia began registration of births, marriages, and deaths in 1860 and several of Pennsylvania's larger cities began registration in the 1870s. For the rest of Pennsylvania, marriage licenses were recorded continuously beginning in 1885. The counties were also responsible for registering births and deaths from 1893 to 1905. From 1906 to the present, birth and death certificates have been required and kept on the state level.

For the roughly two centuries before Pennsylvania enforced civil registration of vital records, researchers often find church records to be the most useful recordings of these events. In Christian denominations with a belief in infant baptism, registers of baptismal records are an excellent substitute for true birth records. Privately made birth or baptismal certificates also can be found for individuals in the seventeenth, eighteenth, and nineteenth centuries with some frequency. Marriage registers were often kept by ministers, sometimes in the form of a private pastoral register if a minister served more than one congregation concurrently, as was common in some denominations into the twentieth century. Newspaper reporting of marriages also became common in the early 1800s. Church burial records are also useful because in many cases tombstones erected in earlier centuries have become illegible due to acid rain. In other cases no memorial marker was ever erected for a deceased. Newspaper obituaries are also a source of death records, though in most cases they do not become detailed until after civil registration was in vogue.

Among the most useful genealogical records are the U.S. Census returns. The census, begun in 1790, has been taken every ten years since with increasing sophistication and value to researchers. Returns are kept private for seventy-two years after the census. From 1790 to 1840, only the names of heads of households appear in the census, with other family members represented by tick marks within age ranges. Beginning with 1850, each individual's name, gender, race, and age appears, but relationships between members of the household and its head can be only implied until the 1880 census, when that information was first recorded. Nearly all the 1890 manuscript census returns, including those for Pennsylvania, were lost to a fire in 1921. Depending on the particular year, certain questions were posed, such as the value of real estate owned, the amount of schooling, home ownership, the birthplace of parents, and mother tongue. The early censuses have been indexed in paper form; for part of the 1880 census and all of the 1900, 1910, and 1920 censuses, a "Soundex" that groups sound-alike surnames to form an index recorded on microfilm is available.

Pennsylvania also conducted a census of sorts, known as the Septennial Census because it was taken every seven years from 1779 to 1863, in order to apportion representatives in the Pennsylvania legislature. The amount of information is more reminiscent of a tax list than the federal census, and many of the returns have been lost.

Municipalities and other local governments sometimes conducted censuses, though infrequently and often erratically. A valuable source for black genealogy and history is the 1837 census of blacks in Philadelphia that the Society of Friends organized to show the value of blacks to the city and the Commonwealth. A source less likely to invite inquiry by individuals in search of ancestors is the census of prostitutes in Philadelphia attempted before the Civil War.

The first cousins of censuses are county tax lists. While these lists too do not show nearly as much information as the U.S. Census, they are valuable for tracking ancestors' residences between censuses, as are the city and county directories put out for businesses in many parts of Pennsylvania, many of which date to early in the nineteenth century. A type of tax record that has survived for few other states except Pennsylvania is the 1798 U.S. Direct Tax, nicknamed the "Window Tax" because one of the questions used to determine assessment was the dwelling's number of windows; not all Pennsylvania's returns are extant, but the ones we do have give a great amount of detail on the types and size of late eighteenth-century dwellings.

Several types of records filed in Pennsylvania's county courthouses are essential to genealogists. Estate records—which include wills, administrations, and Orphan's Court proceedings—almost always open the door to learning about family relationships. If an individual dies having made a will, which shows exactly how he or she wants possessions to be distributed, that will must be probated (recorded) in the county Register of Wills

TABLE 12.1 **MAJOR RECORD GROUPS TO SEARCH**

Record	Use of This Type of Record	For This Time Period	Where Found
Birth	Private certificates	Any	Private and museum collections
	Christian baptismal registry	Any, especially to mid-1800s	Individual churches, denominational archives
	Birth registers	1852–55, 1893–1905	County register of wills
	Pennsylvania birth certificates	1906+	Pennsylvania Department of Health
	Newspaper notices	1900s	State Library of Pennsylvania
Marriage	Private certificates	Any	Private and museum collections
	Marriage registers	Any	Individual churches, denominational archives
	Newspaper notices	Mostly 1800s+	State Library of Pennsylvania
	Marriage licenses	1885+	County register of wills
Death	Burial records	Any	Individual churches, denominational archives
	Tombstones	Any	Field work, listings in historical societies
	Cemetery lot listings	Mostly 1800s+	Less common for church graveyards
	Newspaper obituaries	Any	State Library of Pennsylvania
	Death registers	1852–55, 1893–1905	County register of wills
	State death certificates	1906+	Pennsylvania Department of Health
	Estate records	Any	County register of wills
Residence	U.S. Census	1790–1920 (every 10 years)	National Archives
	Pennsylvania Septennial Census	1779–1863	Pennsylvania State Archives
	County tax records	Any	County tax assessors
	State land records	Any, especially to mid-1800s	Pennsylvania State Archives
	County deeds, assignments	Any	County recorder of deeds
	City and county directories	Any	Local historical societies
Military service	Compiled service record	Any	National Archives
	Pension records	Any	Pennsylvania State Archives, National Archives
Immigration	Passenger lists	Any	National Archives
	Naturalization records	Any	County, federal, and special courts

office for it to be put into force. Should an individual die without a will, someone (generally a family member) will file to administer the deceased person's estate. In some cases the record of an administrator being appointed is the only estate document about an individual who dies without a will. More often, however, petitions needed to be made to the county's Orphan's Court, which handled all actions relating to estates. These petitions are valuable because they usually name all the deceased's heirs—widow, children, and grandchildren (in the case of deceased children). Older documents usually also

THE JOHANNES KREMER FRAUD

Sometimes the best examples of genealogical research and where it can lead are from your own experiences. This was the case with my first attempt to join the Society of the War of 1812. I had decided to seek admission to the society mostly as a research challenge, but little did I realize at the time how challenging this task would become. I consulted my personal genealogical chart and came up with about a dozen men from the proper time (born before 1795, still alive in the 1810s), and found records of four men in the published *Pennsylvania Archives* volumes on War of 1812 soldiers (found in the Second Series) who either were my ancestors or bore the same name. I zeroed-in on John Kremer (in German, Johannes Kremer) of Bern Township, Berks County, because I knew I had excellent documentation on my descent from him in the form of a family Bible that covered several generations, as well as other primary records.

To prove that the John Kremer listed in the published *Pennsylvania Archives* was not just any John Kremer but indeed my ancestor, I took a trip to the National Archives in Washington, D.C., to look at John Kremer's federal pension file. And here my initial try at finding an 1812er went down the tubes. First of all, it took about five hours for the pension file to be paged to the National Archives reading room (as a note to others: the more popular Revolutionary War pension files have all been microfilmed, and Civil War files are paged much faster), and I was then fighting the clock to get back home. So I decided to just photocopy the whole file—a very thick file of dozens and dozens of sheets—and digest it once I left. This I did, but what I found left me laughing at the futility of my attempt. I still believe it is true that my ancestor John Kremer was a War of 1812 soldier; however, after examining the papers in the pension file, it became obvious to me that these papers related to the attempt by the son John of my ancestor also named John

to impersonate his father and gain a pension based on the father's service. Why the fact that the son was born in 1807—and clearly states this in his pension application—did not immediately alert the examiners to the scam is a question I can't answer. (Let me point out, for the record, that I am a descendant of one of the elder John's daughters, not of the impersonator.)

There are two outcomes to this story. First, the son's pension file did yield some dates and information on collateral family members, and because it wasn't being stated for monetary gain I give it a certain credence. Second, I started over with another ancestor, Johann Peter Etschberger of Tulpehocken Township, Berks County, and that proof of service was unquestioned. Because Etschberger was a sergeant whereas the elder Kremer was a corporal, I even moved up a rank in the process!

The National Archives pension file numbers are OW34947 (John Kremer) and WO30590 / WC21817 (Peter Etschberger).

name the husbands of daughters. At times, genealogists warmly welcome finding evidence of family discord in estate matters, because that can lead to more paperwork regarding an estate, and hence to more detailed disclosure of family names and relationships. Probate records also provide much historical information. For instance, inventories taken of the deceased's personal estate list every item the individual owned. Much information about social standing can be gleaned from this listing of possessions, which often includes a listing of money owed to the deceased along with the names of those who owed it. Such documents allow historians to conclude that, contrary to the current assessment of physicians around the top of the American income heap, doctors in the nineteenth century were distinctly middle class.

Land records are found on two levels in Pennsylvania. Documents concerning the original purchase of land from the proprietaries (in the colonial era) and later the Commonwealth are in the custody of the state; transactions other than the original purchase are found in county courthouses. Researchers must be warned, however, that the transfer of land in Pennsylvania was not always done according to the theory. Since the sale of land from the Commonwealth was a process involving several steps, some people stopped at an early step, then willed or deeded the land (with these transactions being recorded on the county level), and only much later did a subsequent holder of the land take the final step or steps to gain true title to the land from Pennsylvania.

In addition to showing residence, deeds can be valuable to genealogists for the family relationships they show. Transfers of land could also be accomplished by "assigning" the deed from the previous sale of land to a new owner, and hence are called "assignments" when recorded on the county level. The problem with deeds and land research, however, is that deeds did not need to be recorded at the county courthouse to be valid—they were just as useful in a hip pocket or between floorboards—and therefore many chains of ownership are interrupted by such documents that have been lost after years in private hands. Once again, records of landownership allow the gleaning of a generous number of historical conclusions. When it comes to land, genealogists are probably most fascinated with the ebb and flow of family land fortunes, while historians can use the land records to reconstruct rural communities and show how they changed over time. Both genealogists and historians use land records to trace the "genealogy" of a particular house or piece of land.

Another category of record that can be a boon to genealogists is an ancestor's military pension record. In nearly all cases, some type of affidavit needed to be filed to secure a pension, and such affidavits are often chock-full of genealogical information on the veteran or widow seeking the pension, their children, dates and places of birth and marriage, and details about the veteran's military service. Where to find records of service and pensions associated with those records depends on the specific war. The Civil War is a turning point; for earlier wars, up to and including the Civil War, more records are found on the state level (especially concerning service) than the federal level. This is mostly because in conflicts before the Civil War the individual state militias were far more important (from a manpower standpoint) than the tiny U.S. Army. From the Civil War onward, this began to change as the U.S. Army became a larger organization on a permanent basis, and as a consequence there are more federal records for later wars and fewer in the custody of the state.

Once a genealogist has an idea of the full gamut of records that can be helpful in research, an exercise that can be helpful in organizing this search is to compile a chronology of records regarding an ancestor—with the goal of finding records to fill in the gaps in the ancestor's life. For example, if all that is known about a particular ancestor is that she and her husband had children in 1901 and 1904, the chronology (when combined with knowledge of records) should spur the researcher to look for a 1900 U.S. Census record, which asks married persons how long they were married. Based on the census information, county marriage licenses should then be checked for a license that would yield, among other things, names of the bride's and groom's parents.

ETHNIC GENEALOGY

Ethnicity and religion also have an impact on what records are available about Pennsylvania ancestors. Determining ethnicity often helps a researcher decide which religion's records to investigate regarding an ancestor. Ethnicity also provides clues as to the time period that an ancestor probably came to America. In addition to immigration, migration patterns within Pennsylvania and the nation help researchers form hypotheses on where to find an ancestor in a particular time period.

Pennsylvania's earliest non-Indian settlers—before the colony was founded by the Penns—were Swedes who populated both sides of the Delaware River valley in the mid-1600s. Once Pennsylvania was established, the next settlers were primarily Quakers, and other English and Welsh, though the first Germans were not far behind. Scots-Irish emigrants and a huge influx of Germans began populating the frontier by the 1730s. There were black Pennsylvanians almost from the Commonwealth's beginning, but they remained a tiny minority until the South-to-urban migrations of the early and mid-twentieth century. As a consequence, the great majority of blacks face the same problems with genealogy as other African Americans: how to penetrate the deep shroud placed upon information by slavery.

What all this means to the genealogist is a treasure hunt for ethnicity as an entry-point to vital records about each group, kept primarily by churches. Quakers kept methodical records of births and therefore are a prized find to many genealogists. Among the English, the Anglican Church evolved into today's Episcopal Church, while dissenters were first known as Methodist Episcopal (now part of the United Methodist Church). Scots-Irish were usually Presbyterian. Germans included Lutherans, Reformed (now part of the United Church of Christ), Mennonites and Amish, Catholics, Unitas

Church register page in German. Some of the most useful records will be in another language, such as this baptismal register from Zion Union Church, Madisonburg, Centre County. A researcher might need to learn a foreign language as well as a different cursive script in order to decipher records.

Fratrum (nicknamed Moravians), Jews, and others. Some of these groups kept excellent registers; others may have started registers that have not survived. In the cases of German Lutherans and Reformed, a shortage of clergy in the eighteenth and early nineteenth centuries forced their pastors to minister to many congregations at once, often resulting either in records kept at one congregation for several (leading to incorrect assumptions about residences of parishioners) or in private pastoral registers being kept instead of congregational ones. Many of the extant records have been transcribed and published, yet some remain in the hands of the original congregations or even private individuals. Pennsylvanians with Mennonite ancestry often have difficulty finding birth records for their kin from previous centuries, for the reason that Mennonites do not perform infant baptism and therefore keep fewer records of genealogical value than many other Christian churches.

The largest migrations of the first two-thirds of the nineteenth century to Pennsylvania were of the so-called "second wave" Germans (mostly from the northern and eastern German states, unlike their eighteenth-century compatriots, more of whom hailed from central and southern Germany) as well as great numbers of Irish. Most Irish were Roman Catholics, especially those arriving from the mid-nineteenth century and later, and it is unfortunate (from a genealogist's standpoint) that many Catholic dioceses treat the records they keep such as births and marriages as "private sacramental records" that should not be accessible to public use. Policies vary by diocese, but for the most part Catholic records can be accessed only with difficulty.

Starting with the final third of the nineteenth century and continuing for the rest of the great era of immigration to the United States (that is, up to the early 1920s), the focus of immigration shifted away from the traditional northern European areas to the southern and eastern portions of the Continent. Among the more prominent groups of this "new immigration" were the Italians, Poles, Russians, Jews, Slovaks, Serbs, Croatians, and Greeks. In general, fewer of these groups' church records have been published, although quite a few have been microfilmed by the Mormon church or others. On the other hand, because these groups immigrated closer to the present day, genealogists researching them have a larger array of civil records than those seeking seventeenth- and eighteenth-century ancestors. In such cases as Italy, where civil registration of births, marriages, and deaths began in 1809, it is quite possible for the genealogist to get several generations deep into Europe using civil records, before turning to church records.

Immigration and naturalization records are a crucial category of documents because they can often help link the Old World with the New. Once again, time and place are all-important. Philadelphia was the major port of immigration in the colonial era and into the 1800s, before being eclipsed by New York City. Many ship lists from both ports have been microfilmed by the National Archives, but not nearly as many have been indexed. Naturalization documents were generated if and when aliens became U.S. citizens. The problem with accessing naturalization documents is that local, state, and federal courts all had jurisdiction over this process, which could commence in one court and be concluded in another court years later and counties away from the first one—and not necessarily in the county of residence of the immigrant.

NAMES AND SPELLINGS

Poor spelling is a special affliction to good genealogy. In the case of surnames, many a pedigree connection has been lost (at least temporarily) by a researcher who simply could not fathom the degree to which an ancestor's name was misspelled. Odd or archaic nicknames have created a similar type of confusion regarding first names. Once again, researchers need to put themselves in the times and places of their ancestors, the first rule being that standardization of spelling is the function of a highly literate society communicating in one language. Even today this is not always the case; it was less so in a bygone age when literacy for many meant signing their own names, not necessarily reading enough to see whether the courthouse clerk or census taker was recording those names anywhere close to the same way they themselves would have supposed the names to be spelled. Pennsylvanians have illustrated this principle from the very genesis of the Commonwealth. Beginning with the changes made to names of the German minority in colonial times and continuing into the twentieth century with surnames from southern and eastern Europe as well as other continents, surname spellings have been more variable than most people understand. The common refrain "Our names are spelled differently so we must not be related" is found to be not necessarily true as pedigrees are examined closely.

Almost all surnames fall into one of four categories, according to the surname authority Elsdon Smith. Patronymics, which are those surnames derived from father's given names, such as Johnson, make up about one-third of all surnames; names taken from occupations, such as Smith, are found about 15 percent of the time; nicknames indicating actions or characteristics, such as Small, about 10 percent of the time; and place names, for example England or London, account for better than two-fifths of all surnames. Elsdon Smith also puts forth eight ways in which surnames change: respelling, translation, transliteration (between different alphabets), abbreviation, extension (adding letters), conversion (which closely overlaps translation), dropping diacritical marks, and substitution (a complete change in name). If a researcher already knows or suspects what nationality the name comes from, then he or she should go to a dictionary of that language in an attempt to define the name, which might also reveal a spelling variant or two of this surname. Finding out an ancestor's nationality can pay off in other ways too. Researching Pennsylvanians who

TABLE 12.2 **EVOLUTION OF A SURNAME**

In Original European Records	In Colonial Pennsylvania Church and Civil Records	In Twentieth-Century Records
Krück or Krueck (pronounced "Kruh-eek")	Grig Grik Krig Kreek Creek	Krick Crick Creek

came from Wales can be made difficult by the group's comparatively small number of surnames—just thirty-nine make up 95 percent of all surnames—but another facet of the Welsh is a naming pattern that aids genealogists. Sons were named, in order, for paternal grandfather, maternal grandfather, paternal great-grandfather, and father's maternal grandfather; daughters were named in a similar fashion. Other ethnic groups offer naming patterns that assist in identifying likely given names.

First or given names at times prove difficult for researchers when the diminutive forms (nicknames) appear to have a tenuous connection to the longer form. Diminutives that clip the second syllable of a name—such as Sam for Samuel or Don for Donald or Cathy for Catherine—seldom cause a problem. Confusion becomes likely, however, among certain ethnic groups, especially when the first syllable of a name is clipped. Good examples from ethnic German names are Klaus for Niklaus, Bastian for Sebastian, Stina for Christina, Trina for Katrina. Another naming custom, particularly found among French and Germans, that perplexes researchers is the use of a single first name (Jean or Johann for males, Marie or Maria for females) common to many or all of a family's children that is followed by a distinctive middle name—the one used by the individual throughout his or her life. For example, an infant baptized as "Johann Peter" typically would be known throughout the rest of his life as "Peter." The additional complication is that there might be a spotty reference later on as "John Peter," and if this is how the man's will was recorded, then he might be indexed as "John P."

The use of suffixes such as "Senior," "Junior," or "the Third" after names offers an interesting lesson on how genealogy and historical context are inseparable. An illustration from the Daub family of Lebanon County is helpful. There is a tombstone for a Henry Daub Jr. in Myerstown, Lebanon County. The natural assumption that he was the son of a Henry Daub Sr. was made and disproven in the course of research. In fact, he was the son of a Peter Daub but the *son-in-law* of a Henry Daub. Up to and through the nineteenth century, "Senior" and "Junior" often were used in the sense that we would use "the Elder" or "the Younger" today, with no definite implication of relationship indicated. Since the styling "the Third" often was not used at all until the twentieth century, there are instances in which the middle individual of

MARGARETHA AND REBECCA: THE SAME PERSON

A perplexing problem for novice genealogists with Pennsylvania German ancestry has been the relationship between the two women's names "Margaretha" and "Rebecca" as used in the 1800s. There are quite a few documented instances of women born with the first name Margaretha (the German form of "Margaret"), who are found in later life with the name Rebecca.

For these women, Rebecca does not appear to have been a nickname, but rather a confusion between the nicknames for Margaret (Peggy) and Rebecca (Becky). The theory behind this bewilderment is that the two nicknames are not easy to distinguish when spoken with a Pennsylvania German accent, and especially because the German pronunciation of P's and B's is quite similar.

The conclusions for researchers are twofold. First, when what appears to be separate daughters named Margaretha (or Margaret) and Rebecca are found, take a look at whether they might actually be the same woman. Second, in searching for birth, confirmation, marriage, or other early data for a woman who died in the 1800s with the name Rebecca, realize that records from her early life will probably be found under "Margaretha." A discussion of this and other Pennsylvania German naming quirks can be found in "Pitfalls of Pennsylvania German Names," published in the *Journal of the Berks County Genealogical Society* (Reading, Pa.), 8 (September–October 1987), 24.

With the dawning of a new century and as families split up in search of work in neighboring communities, family reunions became opportunities to get reconnected. This picture is from the 1904 Baker-Fuller Reunion, held near Tunkhannock. (This photograph is in the possession of Robert L. Baker, who is president of the Baker-Fuller Families and whose grandfather and great-grandparents are in the photo.) Descendants still gather on the second Sunday in August each year. The family's 97th reunion was held at Francis Slocum State Park near Dallas on August 13, 2000. Reunion events are still common in Pennsylvania. In Centre County alone, more than sixty family groups had reunions in the summer of 2000.

three namesake generations began his life as "Junior" and graduated to "Senior" after his father's death and son's birth.

As Pennsylvania genealogists ride the "second wave" of family history research, which is unlikely to crest for some time, one trend of continuity transcends the greatly enlarged amount of information available to researchers on the Internet and the supposed "breakdown of family" in American culture. Despite the high divorce rate of the last half of the twentieth century, the dramatic rise in illegitimacy, and increased mobility that denies many Pennsylvanians a sense of place, families—nuclear (husband, wife, and children) and extended—are still important. One way this importance manifests itself is through events dubbed "family reunions." While many suppose that family reunions are going out of style, anecdotal evidence supports the notion that while some reunions indeed have been discontinued, others are started that take their places.

Family reunions, historically, have lasted an average of three generations (roughly sixty years) because that is usually how long it takes for a family to lose its sense of common identity. Genealogical projects, which provide a way of salvaging that common identity, are a key way for family reunions to continue. Pennsylvania's many family reunions therefore offer an opportunity for researchers not only to share and add to their stores of information, but also to preserve family ties for the future generations.

Genealogical records are the records of history and other disciplines. In its most basic form, genealogy is nothing more than adding layers of ancestors to an individual's identity in the hope that those layers enlighten and inform the sense of identity of the descendant. And while it might be possible to create a family tree without the context of history—a correct theory but an impracticable practice—it is squarely impossible to master an understanding of history without some sense of the people involved in that history. And without the contextual identity that genealogy adds to these historical people, it might as well be no history at all.

SOURCES *and* FURTHER READING

Crandall, Ralph. *Shaking Your Family Tree: A Basic Guide to Tracing Your Family's Genealogy.* Dublin, N.H.: Yankee Books, 1986.

Crichton, Jennifer. *Family Reunion.* New York: Workman Publishing Company, 1998.

Crist, Robert Grant, ed. *Penn's Example to the Nations: 300 Years of the Holy Experiment.* Harrisburg: Pennsylvania Council of Churches, 1987.

Dructor, Robert M. *A Guide to Genealogical Sources at the Pennsylvania State Archives.* Second edition. Harrisburg: Pennsylvania Historical and Museum Commission, 1998.

Guiseppe, M. S. *Naturalizations of Foreign Protestants in the American and West Indian Colonies.* Baltimore: Genealogical Publishing Company, 1979.

The Handybook for Genealogists. Ninth edition. Logan, Utah: Everton Publishers, 1999.

Heisey, John W. *Pennsylvania Genealogical Library Guide.* Morgantown, Pa.: Masthof Press, 1997.

Helm, Matthew L., and April Leigh Helm. *Genealogy Online for Dummies.* Second edition. Foster City, Calif.: IDG Books Worldwide, 1999.

Hodge, Ruth E. *Guide to African American Resources in the Pennsylvania State Archives.* Harrisburg: Pennsylvania Historical and Museum Commission, 2000.

Hoenstine, Floyd G. *Guide to Genealogical Searching in Pennsylvania.* Hollidaysburg, Pa.: Floyd G. Hoenstine, 1978.

Iscrupe, William L., and Shirley G. M. Iscrupe. *Pennsylvania Line: A Research Guide to Pennsylvania Genealogy and Local History.* Fourth edition. Laughlintown, Pa.: Castle Press, 1990.

Lackey, Richard S. *Cite Your Sources: A Manual for Documenting Family Histories and Genealogical Records.* Jackson: University Press of Mississippi, 1980.

Meynen, Emil. *Bibliography on the Colonial Germans of North America.* Baltimore: Genealogical Publishing Company, 1982.

Munger, Donna Bingham. *Pennsylvania Land Records: A History and Guide for Research.* Wilmington, Del.: Scholarly Resources Inc., 1991.

My History Is America's History: 15 Things You Can Do to Save America's Stories. Washington, D.C.: National Endowment for the Humanities, 1999.

Nelson, Lynn. *A Genealogist's Guide to Discovering Your Italian Ancestors.* Cincinnati, Ohio: Betterway Books, 1997.

Ninkovich, Thomas. *Family Reunion Handbook.* San Francisco: Reunion Research, 1998.

Renick, Barbara, and Richard S. Wilson. *The Internet for Genealogists: A Beginner's Guide.* Fourth edition. La Habra, Calif.: Compuology, 1998.

Schaeffer, Christina K. *Genealogical Encyclopedia of the Colonial Americas.* Baltimore: Genealogical Publishing Company, 1998.

———. *Guide to Naturalization Records of the United States.* Baltimore: Genealogical Publishing Company, 1997.

Smith, Elsdon C. *American Surnames.* Baltimore: Genealogical Publishing Company, 1995.

Strassburger, Ralph Beaver, and William John Hinke. *Pennsylvania German Pioneers.* 2 vols. Baltimore: Genealogical Publishing Company, 1980.

Stratton, Eugene A. *Applied Genealogy.* Salt Lake City: Ancestry Inc., 1988.

Wolfman, Ira. *Do People Grow on Family Trees? Genealogy for Kids and Other Beginners.* New York: Workman Publishing Company, 1991.

Woodroofe, Helen Hutchison. *A Genealogist's Guide to Pennsylvania Records.* Philadelphia: Genealogical Society of Pennsylvania, 1995.

Woodtor, Dee Parmer. *Finding a Place Called Home: A Guide to African American Genealogy and Historical Identity.* New York: Random House, 1999.

Photography

LINDA RIES

The announcement in January 1839 by Frenchman Louis Jacques Mandé Daguerre, that he had perfected a means of permanently fixing a reflected image on a metal plate, forever changed the way human beings perceive themselves and their world. People could now re-create the universe through mechanics, chemistry, and the sun. Photography joined cave paintings, clay tablets, papyrus, ink-and-paper, and printing, as a tool, a method of creating a record, and therefore of keeping history.

Photography's special usefulness to history lies in its ability to collect information graphically and retain it for serving a later purpose, such as reconnaissance, study, or pleasure. A photograph is a reflected image captured on a light-sensitized medium (the word comes from two Greek words that mean, literally, "light writing"). This was accomplished through the use of a camera, basically a small, lightproof chamber with a covered hole at one end. The medium was most often a sheet of plate glass, metal, film, or paper coated with various chemicals, among them crystals of silver, to render it light-sensitive. Thus prepared in darkness, the medium would be inserted into the camera facing the covered hole. The camera would be pointed at its subject, the cover removed, and the sensitized plate exposed to light for a specified length of time. The cover would be replaced, and the plate then removed from the camera, again in darkness, and put through a bath of chemicals to "fix" the subject on it permanently. For much of photography's history, this is essentially how images were made, though

Joseph Saxton's daguerreotype of Central High School for Boys, Philadelphia, probably September 25, 1839. The oldest surviving photograph in the western hemisphere.

recent technologies, especially electronic and digitized media, have begun to alter this basic method.

Images, no matter how created, can demonstrate changes to people and places over time: the transition from newborn to adult; or the construction, use, and razing of buildings; even such cataclysmic events as the Battle of Gettysburg or the Johnstown Flood. Cameras can be sent to record remote landscapes that we cannot physically visit or have easy access to: Mount Everest, the planet Mars, the nucleus of a cell, or the wreckage of the *Titanic*.

Photographs today are accepted as part of daily life. A world without them is difficult to contemplate. Billions are made daily, for commercial, industrial, scientific, and personal use—from ubiquitous driver's license portraits to the sophisticated imagery of quark motions. Before photography, scientific inquiry was flawed by the subjectivity of written observation. Appreciation of one's own visage was fleeting or nonexistent, limited to a mirror reflection or to those with economic means to have portraits created. The effect of the photograph on mid-nineteenth-century sensibilities was to shatter these limitations, expanding and altering life by bestowing increased powers of access and observation. Photography democratized portraiture, making it easily and inexpensively accessible to all. It helped to objectify scientific investigation and to promote and catalyze the sharing of new discoveries and inventions.

The objectivity and truthfulness of information presented by a photographic image was considered a revelation. Indeed, the idea that an image represented actual fact was innocently accepted for many years after photography's assimilation into society in the 1840s. With more sophisticated equipment and more savvy audiences it was eventually realized that photography's ability to depict an objective "truth" is more complex. We see in the image what the photographer wants us to see, and uncaptioned or misrepresented photographs can lead to false ideas and interpretation. Historians, who seek truth about the past, must be mindful of this aspect of historical images as they conduct research.

Significant technical and artistic developments in the medium occurred in Pennsylvania. Perhaps because of this, pioneering research into the history of photography occurred here as well. A brief accounting of some of these developments, and a discussion of different types and formats and how they were used, will be useful in determining where and how to conduct research with historical photographs. Though

Daguerre announced his findings early in 1839, his actual method was not revealed until a meeting of the Academy of Sciences in Paris that August 19. In exchange for a lifetime pension from the French government, Daguerre eschewed a patent and freely presented his process to most of the world. Almost immediately, scientists and entrepreneurs everywhere attempted to replicate his results. In the United States, one month later, D. W. Seagar of New York City was credited with successfully making a daguerreotype on September 16, 1839, but this image has not survived. In Philadelphia, Joseph Saxton, a native of Huntingdon County and an engineer at the U.S. Mint, fashioned a camera out of a cigar box and a crude lens and inserted in it a metal plate coated with light-sensitive chemicals. On or about September 25, 1839, he pointed this apparatus out the second floor window of the Mint and made a faint but discernible image of the Central High School for Boys. This, the earliest surviving photographic image made in the western hemisphere, is now housed at the Historical Society of Pennsylvania.

In the weeks and months that followed, others attempted to modify and improve Daguerre's work, notably brass-founder Robert Cornelius and chemist Dr. Paul Beck Goddard of Philadelphia. Dr. Goddard realized that the addition of bromine to the sensitized chemicals shortened exposure times from minutes to seconds, making portraiture feasible. In October 1839, using himself as a subject, Cornelius made an experimental image this way, and produced one of the first photographic portraits of a human being. Later, in May 1840, Cornelius opened what is possibly the world's first commercial studio at South Eighth and Lodge Streets. John McAllister Jr. ran an optical business on nearby Chestnut Street, providing Cornelius and other daguerreians with lenses for their cameras. An advocate of the medium though not a photographer himself, McAllister had his portrait made by Cornelius. McAllister's son William became an early amateur photographer and often daguerreotyped members of his family, creating in essence the first family photograph album.

Cornelius taught daguerreotypy to many, notably Marcus Aurelius Root, originally a miniature portrait painter by trade and an early champion of photography as a fine art. Root excelled in photographic portraiture. People desiring their likenesses, and those desiring training in the new medium, visited his popular Chestnut Street gallery in Philadelphia and a gallery he operated in New York with his brother Samuel. Root taught other early practitioners, who in turn moved across Pennsylvania and elsewhere, disseminating photography throughout the young nation.

Robert Cornelius, self-portrait, c. October–November 1839. A handwritten note with the image states "The first light picture ever taken."

"Dancing (fancy)." Series of timed still photographs of a woman dancing, by Eadweard Muybridge.

The British photographer and early experimenter in motion picture studies Eadweard Muybridge, found sponsorship from the University of Pennsylvania to advance his work. Between 1882 and 1887, at the university's Veterinary Department, he conducted some of his world-renowned time-and-motion studies of humans and animals. Through synchronization of cameras placed at consecutive intervals, and fast shutter speeds tripped by electromagnets, he was able to create a series of timed still photographs demonstrating the mechanics of people walking and dancing, a bird in flight, a horse trotting, and even the gait of an elephant. He published this study as the monumental eleven-volume *Animal Locomotion: An Electrophotographic Investigation of the Consecutive Phases of Animal Movements, 1872–1885* (1887), containing 781 plates and more than 100,000 individual images. It is unsurpassed as the most comprehensive work of its kind and is still consulted today by artists as a source of reference. Thomas Edison keenly followed Muybridge's work during his development of motion pictures.

Philadelphia painter Thomas Eakins had an ongoing professional relationship with Muybridge. He had worked briefly in conjunction with him during Muybridge's locomotion studies at Penn. As an instructor at the Pennsylvania Academy of the Fine Arts, Eakins was interested in the illustration of movement in painting, especially the depiction of human and animal forms, and body and muscle action. He used photography for this purpose, and the influence of many of his images can be seen in his paintings. Likewise, Lloyd Mifflin, a Lancaster County painter, employed his own photographs for the same purpose regarding natural forces: the action of waves on the Susquehanna River, the subtle movements of clouds, or the stance of cows in a field.

An accounting of photography endeavors in the Commonwealth of Pennsylvania

COMMON TYPES OF PHOTOGRAPHIC IMAGES AND FORMATS

Daguerreotype: 1839 to c. 1860. A silver-plated sheet of copper commonly found in miniature cases. Because it has a mirror-like effect, the image must be viewed at an oblique angle. Supplanted commercially by paper processes. Its heyday was the 1840s and 1850s.

Ambrotype: c. 1855 to c. 1860. A negative on glass placed against a black background, often made of paper or paint, to produce a positive image. Usually has a dull, flat finish. Commonly found in miniature cases. Its heyday was the 1850s and was largely supplanted by paper processes.

Tintype or ferrotype: First introduced in the United States in 1856, used well into the early 1900s. Has a dark, flat finish made by "japaning," or coating a piece of iron with a black lacquer. Placed in miniature cases, later adapted to the carte-de-visite and other formats.

Carte-de-visite: Late 1850s to c. 1910. The first mass-produced paper image, produced using the negative/positive process. The same negative could be printed over and over, potentially producing many prints from one image. Wildly popular for portraiture during 1860s, cartes-de-visite were less expensive to make and sell than the above processes. Commonly 4¼" x 2½", printed on a thin albumenized paper, and pasted on a heavy card stock. Albumenized paper usually ages to a sepia color.

Cabinet card: Mid-1870s to c. 1910. Another popular mass-produced paper image, commonly 6½" x 4½", printed on a thin paper and mounted on heavy card stock.

Stereograph: 1850s to c. 1940s. A pair of matching positive images mounted on heavy card stock, usually measuring 3½" x 7", and creating a three-dimensional image when both images are viewed through a stereoscope. Early stereocard stock is flat; later (c. 1880s) it is curved to enhance the 3-D effect. These were popular as parlor entertainment in the late nineteenth and early twentieth century.

Lantern slide: 1870 to c. 1950. A 3¼" x 4" positive transparency on glass, black and white, tinted, or hand-colored. The first form of photography intended for projection on a screen before an audience. Supplanted by the 35 mm film slide.

Picture postcard: Postal cards were used in the last half of the nineteenth century, but picture postcards were first introduced at the 1893 World's Columbian Exposition in Chicago. Divided-back cards were introduced in 1906. One of the most popular and prolific forms of photographic reproduction in the twentieth century.

Silver gelatin process: Early 1900s to the present. Replacing the albumen process and utilizing silver crystals suspended in a gelatin emulsion. Became the dominant process for use in black-and-white photography. The silver tarnishes, creating an iridescent effect, and the paper and gelatin will yellow with age.

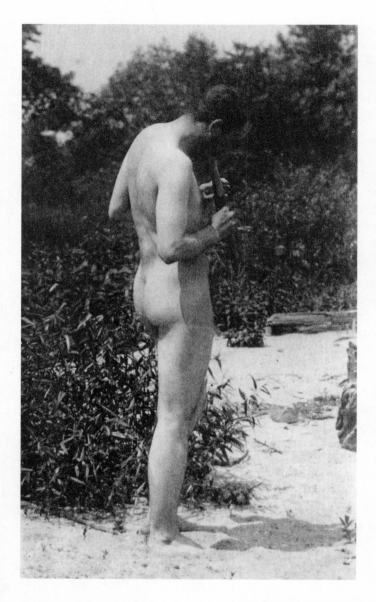

"Thomas Eakins nude, playing pipes, facing right," by circle of Eakins, c. 1883.

must include the proliferation of professional and amateur camera clubs and photography associations such as the Photographic Society of Philadelphia and the Pennsylvania Photographers Association. Trade periodicals produced by these organizations, such as *The Philadelphia Photographer*, were avidly read. The groups also frequently banded together with others out of state to create joint exhibitions. In Philadelphia the Sixth Annual Joint Exhibition held at the Pennsylvania Academy of the Fine Arts in 1893 helped introduce pictorialism in America.

Notable photographic achievements in Pennsylvania influenced motion pictures as well. Early film mogul Siegmund Lubin began his career as an optician, by coincidence, at the same site where Robert Cornelius opened his photography studio some sixty years earlier at Eighth and Lodge (now Ranstead) Streets in Philadelphia. He created, produced, and distributed films at "Lubinville" at Twenty-Second and Indiana Streets, and later "Betzwood," an estate near Valley Forge. His empire largely collapsed after a devastating nitrate film fire in 1913, and a series of financial woes that plagued him until his death in 1923. Another film pioneer, Edwin S. Porter of Connellsville, learned still photography at a relative's commercial studio and later worked with Thomas Edison in New Jersey during the 1890s on some of the first motion pictures ever made. Porter is credited with the idea of the "screenplay," or a story written especially for a motion picture that included dramatic narrative and sequenced pacing of simultaneous action, the forerunner of the feature film. His most important works include *The Life of an American Fireman* (1903) and *The Great Train Robbery* (1903). The movie theater industry began on Smithfield Street in Pittsburgh in June 1905, when Harry Davis established a storefront theater for the exclusive showing of films and illustrated song slides. His "Nickelodeon" idea quickly caught on all over the United States. In New Castle, the mighty Warner Brothers empire got its start in 1906 when members of this immigrant family from eastern Europe showed *The Great Train Robbery* and other films at a makeshift theater with chairs borrowed from a funeral home next door.

Different processes, formats, and equipment influenced the way images were made and how they looked. The process for the daguerreotype and its later cousins the ambrotype and tintype involved no negative, meaning each image was unique and could not be reproduced without rephotographing. By the early 1860s, the positive/negative

The film studio "Lubinville," North Philadelphia, 1911.

process had come to dominate commercial photography. One negative could be created and printed on sensitized paper to produce many original positive images, each the same as the other. Likenesses and landscapes could then be mass-produced, sold cheaply, and widely distributed, thus accelerating photography's ability to share information over time and space. It therefore became even easier for people to obtain their own portraits.

The early positive/negative technique was somewhat complicated and tricky—part science, part finesse. To create a negative, the photographer had to mix appropriate amounts of toxic chemicals to create collodion, and coat plates of clear glass with this viscous solution. The sitter or subject was then arranged within the image frame, and the plate was loaded in the camera and exposed while still wet. Exposure times were judged according to available light, then the plate was removed from the camera and developed. Creation of the positive was accomplished through a contact process, where developing paper would be placed in a holder against the negative and exposed to light, usually sunlight. This was manageable in the photographer's darkroom laboratory when doing portraiture, but landscape images heightened the degree of difficulty. Heavy wooden cameras, jars of chemicals, and glass plates had to be transported by train, wagon, or simple man-hauling to the desired exposure sites—not an easy task given Pennsylvania's rolling topography.

The positive paper print was available in several extremely popular formats in the mid- to late nineteenth century, among them the carte-de-visite, the stereograph, and

INTERPRETING AND DATING A HISTORICAL PHOTOGRAPH

Though the subject in the accompanying image is not identified by name, individual pieces of evidence can help us interpret and date the photograph:

1. Format: A carte-de-visite, not widely used commercially in central Pennsylvania until after about 1860.

2. Focal length: Full-body portraits were more common in the early 1860s, before improved lenses for close-ups.

3. Dress: Wearing a summer dress, probably calico, consisting of a short-sleeved blouse and skirt with a geometric design. Young girls such as this one generally wore heavily starched petticoats rather than hoop skirts in the early 1860s.

4. Background: Studio chairs were popular throughout nineteenth-century photography.

5. Photographer's imprint: Often gives name and location of studio. Researching these marks combined with city directories or newspaper advertisements can help narrow the date the image was taken. From newspaper advertisements, it is known that Lochman was at the Marion Hall location in Carlisle and using this particular imprint between November 1862 and January 1865.

6. Negative number: Though most nineteenth-century commercial photograph negatives have not survived, comparing the negative number against others from the same studio, or other evidence such as directories or newspaper ads, may give an idea of the date of the image.

We can tell that the young lady posed for her portrait at Charles Lochman's gallery probably between November 1862 and January 1865. Because she is wearing a light, short-sleeved dress, the image was probably taken in the warm-weather months, further narrowing possible dates to between Spring 1863 and Fall 1865. The tax stamp, issued between 1864 and 1866, further refines the date to between 1864 and 1865.

C. L. LOCHMAN,
ARTIST,
Main St., opposite Marion Hall,
Carlisle, Penn.
———
Negatives preserved.

ABOVE LEFT: Unidentified girl, carte-de-visite by Charles L. Lochman, Carlisle, c. 1860–65.

ABOVE RIGHT: Reverse of previous image showing Lochman's imprint.

LEFT: Typical stereograph card issued by the Keystone View Company of Meadville, #75-20049: "Miners going into the slope, Hazleton, Pa.," c. 1915.

BELOW: Typical carte-de-visite of a Civil War soldier, Lieutenant Bruce Rice of the Bucktail Regiment.

later the cabinet card. These were commonly printed, using albumen, or egg whites, as the emulsifier, on a thin photographic developing paper. The print was then glued to a paper card, often with identification on front or reverse as to subject and photographer. German immigrants to Philadelphia, brothers Frederick and William Langenheim, introduced the stereograph to America in 1854. This was a means of creating a three-dimensional image with the aid of a viewing device. The mass-produced stereograph, also called stereoview, became an inexpensive and popular form of home entertainment by the end of the nineteenth century. It was also used as an educational tool by schools, churches, and civic organizations. Usually sold in sets, or as a series showing a sequence of events on any given topic, stereograph images could take viewers around the nation or the world, to strange and exotic places, or illustrate certain events, such as President James Garfield's assassination or World War I actions. By 1900 the Keystone View Company, owned and operated by B. L. Singley of Meadville, was one of the world's largest purveyors of stereo images.

The Civil War boosted the popularity of the carte-de-visite format. Portraits of soldiers in uniform to send to wives, sweethearts, and families were in high demand. The carte-de-visite was small, usually 2¼ by 4 inches, and easily carried or sent through the mail. For example, Lieutenant Bruce A. Rice from McKean County joined in May 1861 Company I, First Rifles, known as the Bucktail Regiment. Rice had a carte-de-visite

John Benninghoff Run, Oil Creek, 1865.

image made by the Washington, D.C., gallery of R. W. Addis, probably while his unit was moving through Virginia, and likely sent it home to his family. The value of his portrait certainly became more poignant for friends and relations after Rice was killed at Strasburg, Virginia, in June 1862. Cabinet cards, introduced in the 1870s, eventually replaced the carte-de-visite in popularity and were common until about 1910. These came in a standard size, usually 4 by 6 inches, and were usually placed on dressers and cabinets in Victorian parlors.

At the height of the industrial revolution, railroad, coal, oil, and other commercial and manufacturing interests often hired professional photographers to create landscape images of their products and facilities for promotional purposes. Pennsylvania corporations were no exception. Among others, the Pennsylvania and the Lehigh Valley Railroads employed William T. Purviance, and later William H. Rau. William T. Clarke worked for companies in the lumber region, and John A. Mather in the northwestern oil fields. These practitioners excelled in the difficult process of landscape photography. Their photographs were dominated by mighty steam locomotives, forests not of trees

The Horseshoe Curve. From "Horse Shoe, Photographic Views on the Penn'a Central Rail Road," by William T. Purviance, c. 1860.

but of oil derricks, yawning mine shafts and tunnels, and coke ovens and blooming and steel works stretching in long perspectives to the horizon. Humans appear tiny, off to the side, in awe of their own technological creations for the conquering and subduing of natural forces. This kind of photography exemplified progress: improvements in communication, transportation, and daily life.

Another technical revolution in photography occurred at the end of the nineteenth century. Smaller, lighter cameras became commercially available, along with prepared "dry" negative glass plates in the 1870s and cellulose film negatives marketed by George Eastman in the 1880s. Gelatin eventually replaced albumen and collodion as an emulsifier for developing and printing. The burden of mixing chemicals and developing was essentially eliminated, and negatives could be loaded into the camera quickly and easily. The addition of a flash permitted night and mining photography for industrial use, and sophisticated lenses enabled close-ups. The camera could now move about with greater ease, to places it had not been before, and could be operated by people who were photographers not by vocation, but by avocation only. No longer was photography the exclusive realm of the professional. Eastman's motto for his popular Kodak camera was "You push the button, and we do the rest." Again, the democratizing effect of photography was extended. People became their own visual diarists of the world about them, recording what interested and pleased them. Many amateurs, such as Francis Cooper of Spruce Hill, Juniata County, contentedly used the camera to record family members and friends, events, and places, giving rise to an informal and personalized photography.

"Charlie and Lil [Milliken] in stand in grove. Summer, 1898," photograph by Francis Cooper.

Social and industrial reformers, however, seized the new kind of image-making as an instrument for social change. As photography could demonstrate technological advancements, it also could reveal the price paid for the "progress" of the industrial revolution. Coal and iron fields were not limitless; forests took time to grow; land needed time to heal. There was also a human cost: the health and safety of those toiling in heavy industry or simply living nearby. Laborers, usually the most recently arrived and therefore lowest-paid immigrants, often lived in squalor. These new subjects for images, often matched with heartrending captions and alarming statistics, were created to convince government authorities, politicians, and the general citizenry of the need for improvement of social conditions. Designed to invoke pathos and sympathy for the subject, humans now loom large in such photographs, which were often characterized by close-ups of workers' haggard faces gritty from an honest day's work. Landscapes that formerly emphasized the domination of humanity over nature now showed humankind's

cruelty toward nature and the resulting misery: industrial polluters pouring chemical wastes into the air or into streams; lack
of safety conditions for workers; and poor living conditions for
working families. The use of photography in this type of investigative reporting eventually became known as "documentary"
photography and, later, photojournalism.

The Pittsburgh Survey, published between 1909 and 1914,
was an innovative and exhaustive six-volume research effort
funded by a group of concerned urban reformers and writers
from New York. Edited by Paul Underwood Kellogg, it revealed
poor and unhealthy living conditions in and around Pittsburgh.
One notable edition of this survey, Margaret Byington's
Homestead: The Households of a Mill Town, used statistics and
narrative to make its point, but it was the denuded landscapes
and portraits of immigrant laborers by Lewis Wickes Hine that
readers found compelling. Hine is also known for his work with
the National Child Labor Committee to reform child labor
laws. His haunting images of dirty breaker boys in
Pennsylvania's anthracite region, old before their time, helped
influence the enactment of legislation in this regard.

Others in Pennsylvania also carried the banner of
Progressive Era civic reform. In Harrisburg, Mira Lloyd Dock

Immigrant housing in Munhall Hollow, Homestead, a photograph by Lewis Wickes Hine
captioned "Where Rents Are Cheap: In the
Crowded Section: Three Families Share the
House and Seven the Yard." From The
Pittsburgh Survey.

and J. Horace McFarland proposed, among many other projects, to pave open sewers
and muddy streets, beautify rivers and roadsides, and, in short, bring about more healthful living environments. They were also skilled amateur photographers who made liberal
use of lantern-slide images of what they found, when they delivered their forceful traveling lectures to many audiences all over the nation in a plea for change. The lantern-slide
show, an early form of group entertainment and education using transparent glass
images projected on a wall or screen, was popular at the turn of the twentieth century,
only to be supplanted by motion pictures. Dock, and especially McFarland, effectively
convinced their audiences of the need for clean and paved streets, urban planting and
parks, and city beautification in general. Methods employed during the lectures included
the use of before-and-after slides indicating how blighted areas could be changed. A
community's "good" qualities threatened by "bad" influences were contrasted, such as a
garbage dump juxtaposed in the same image frame with a school, or unsightly billboards
next to a church. Children were depicted engaged in poor, unproductive behavior versus
healthful play. Like social reformers Jacob Riis and Lewis Hine, Dock and McFarland
also recognized the mass-communications potential of the medium when they published
images alongside their articles in the popular magazines of the day, such as McCall's,
Collier's, and Ladies' Home Journal.

A STREET TREE AS GOD MADE IT | A STREET TREE AS MAN IMPROVES IT

WITH MUNICIPAL CONTROL THE TREES MAY STAY AS GOD MADE THEM
WITHOUT MUNICIPAL CONTROL MAN MUTILATES THEM

TOP LEFT: Lincoln School, Harrisburg, and surroundings, June 2, 1906, by J. Horace McFarland Company.

TOP RIGHT: McFarland lantern slide contrasting treatment of city trees and including dramatically worded captions.

BOTTOM: Old shacks and dump facing the new Carnegie Library, Pittsburgh, April 19, 1906, by J. Horace McFarland Company.

Government also utilized photography's potential for its own far-ranging needs. Different agencies and units would hire staff photographers or contract with professionals to record and promote the services they perform according to their public mandate. For example, the Pennsylvania Department of Highways (now the Department of Transportation), created in 1903, began photographing road construction for its own internal use to demonstrate improvements to highways. Later, to promote travel and tourism on its road system, it created scenic highway images directed toward the public. Images were also created for staff education, safety, and legal or record-keeping purposes. Other agencies, such as Health, Public Welfare, Police, and Justice, made photographs for similar internal and external reasons.

During the 1930s, federal documentary photographers passed through Pennsylvania, and most notable were those working for the U.S. Farm Security Administration (FSA), including Ben Shahn, Arthur Rothstein, and Walker Evans. Though their mission was primarily to record images for Congress to study the living conditions of America's depression-era poor in rural regions, they also recorded urban workers and their families, many out of work and on government relief. In Pennsylvania the photographers chiefly visited Allentown, Bethlehem, Pittsburgh, Johnstown, and places like the government town of Norvelt in Westmoreland County built for depressed miners and their families. These photographs, in Hine's tradition, tended to be straightforward mid- to close-up range portraits of careworn, hardworking

folks down on their luck. Landscapes, often stark and dreary, showed exhausted mill towns and bleak cities. These kinds of images helped convey the need for government assistance in social and economic reform.

Another technological revolution in photography occurred during the mid- to late twentieth century. With post–World War II prosperity came the development and proliferation of photography and motion-picture products for home use. These included color film, lighter cameras increasingly made of plastic parts, improved apertures and shutters for faster film speeds, and the disposable flashbulb. Edwin Land invented "instant" black-and-white photography with the Polaroid camera in 1947 and the color Polaroid in 1963. The home movie industry was heralded with the introduction of eight-millimeter and super-eight-millimeter films and projectors, led by Bell & Howell during the 1950s. Not only could people record themselves, but they now could record the novelty of themselves in motion. The family's still or movie camera went wherever the family did: to birthday parties, weddings, banquets, vacations, holiday celebrations, or any

"Cooperstown Road After Improvement. Northwestern Construction Company. Jackson Township, Venango County." Undated c. 1914, recording work done by a contractor for the Department of Highways.

Workers in Dauphin County, Route 34, posing for a photograph, April 20, 1933. Made to demonstrate to employees the importance of safety on the job: "Every man must wear goggles."

other events, even popular fads thought to be worth recording for posterity or for fun.

Perhaps because of these significant achievements, the study of photographic history has likewise been a pioneering activity in Pennsylvania. Marcus Root wrote *The Camera and the Pencil* (1864), one of the earliest recountings of daguerreian times. For the publication, Root interviewed many of the pioneers, including Saxton, Cornelius, McAllister, and Goddard. At the dawn of the twentieth century, historian Julius Frederick Sachse was one of the first to realize the importance of preserving the now-rare records and materials relating to early American photography. His father, John Henry Frederick Sachse, worked for a time with the Cornelius & Baker Company brass foundry and had sat for his portrait by Robert Cornelius in February 1840. Likely because of this family relationship, the younger Sachse grew up with an appreciation for photography. A man

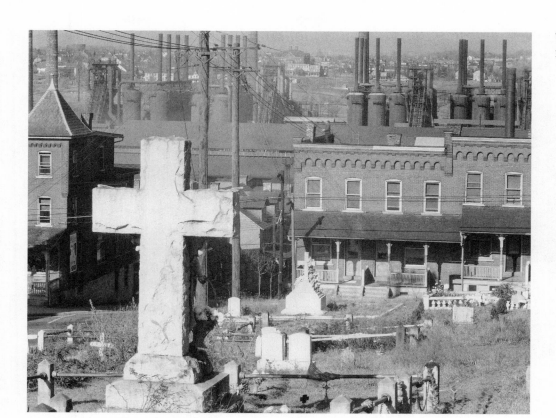

Walker Evans photograph of Bethlehem grave-yard and steel mill, November 1935.

of broad historical interests, he also helped save precious early manuscripts and imprints of the Ephrata Cloister, was a co-founder of the Chester County Historical Society in 1888, and helped organize the Pennsylvania Federation of Historical Societies in 1905. He remained active in a myriad of history-related organizations in southeastern Pennsylvania and was friend and colleague to Governor Samuel W. Pennypacker, himself once president of the Historical Society of Pennsylvania. Sachse, also involved as the Historical Society's first staff photographer, copied many of their early daguerreotypes.

Sachse was also editor of the *American Journal of Photography* between 1890 and 1897 and contributed numerous articles, including many of the earliest monographs on the history of the medium. He recognized the historical significance of many important early images and took pains to acquire them, such as Marcus Root's display at the 1876 U.S. Centennial of forty daguerreotypes by some of the pioneers noted above.

Sachse's granddaughter, Marian S. Carson, shared his love of history and inherited much of his personal collection, which included Robert Cornelius's 1839 self-portrait. Like her forebear, Marian Carson had broad historical interests and especially advocated the preservation and study of Pennsylvania's early photography. In the 1930s she acquired the John McAllister Jr. Family papers and photographs, including the many daguerreotypes William McAllister made of his family. The collection is now at the Library of Congress.

"Mug shot" of prisoner, Eastern State Penitentiary, 1915. Created as part of prisoner's file.

Pennsylvania was also the site of the nation's first museum and scholarly journal devoted entirely to the history of photography. In 1940 Louis Walton Sipley founded the American Museum of Photography on South Fifteenth Street in Philadelphia. The museum closed upon Sipley's death in 1968, and its contents eventually went to the International Museum of Photography in Rochester, New York. The publishing of the scholarly journal, *History of Photography,* was initiated in 1976 by Heinz Henisch of The Pennsylvania State University.

By the 1970s other historians had recognized the value of photography as evidence for the study of history. William C. Darrah of Gettysburg College during this time wrote definitive works on two nineteenth-century formats: the carte-de-visite and the stereograph. He advocated incorporating the study of images as part of interpretation of a particular historical subject, for "the whole field of photographic documentation is still in its infancy." Darrah's work showed that large amounts of information can be gleaned from a single photograph. Such details as the approximate age of the subject, and the clothing, hairstyle, background properties and furniture, weather, building signs, photographer's imprints, format, and provenance, among several other clues, can make seemingly unidentified portraits and landscapes yield information to narrow down or precisely fit identities and time frames. Studying large groupings or aggregates of these photographs can likewise produce significant data about historical persons, places, or events. As the archaeologist uses artifacts to recreate a vanished culture, so too can the historian re-create the past by analyzing collected images. Integrating this study with use of such written records as the federal census, city directories, newspapers, and family records can help complete the historical method applied to any given topic.

William A. Frassanito's *Gettysburg: A Journey in Time* (1975) is considered a landmark of this kind of photographic detective work, adding considerable knowledge to the already large body of scholarly information about the famous 1863 Civil War encounter in the small south-central Pennsylvania town. As Frassanito describes, Alexander Gardner and his crew from Washington, D.C., were the first photographers to arrive on the aftermath of the battlefield, probably on July 5, 1863. They found and photographed dead soldiers that burial details had not yet reached. Gardner used these images after the war in his 1866 publication, *Photographic Sketch Book of the Civil War.* The *Sketch Book* shocked, horrified, and thrilled audiences at the time. Gardner dramatized his images with such captions as "A Harvest of Death" for a group identified as Confederates; and "The Field Where General Reynolds Fell" for a group of Union soldiers. He labeled two others "A Sharpshooter's Last Sleep" and "The Home of a Rebel Sharpshooter" to

"A Harvest of Death," Plate 36 in Alexander Gardner's *Photographic Sketch Book of the Civil War*. Identified in Gardner's text as Confederate soldiers.

"The Field Where General Reynolds Fell," Plate 37 in Alexander Gardner's *Photographic Sketch Book of the Civil War*. The same bodies as in Plate 36, photographed from a different angle and identified in Gardner's text as Union soldiers.

"A Sharpshooter's Last Sleep," a dead Confederate soldier at Devil's Den, Gettysburg, Plate 40 in Alexander Gardner's *Photographic Sketch Book of the Civil War.*

"The Home of a Rebel Sharpshooter," Plate 41 in Alexander Gardner's *Photographic Sketch Book of the Civil War.* The same soldier as in Plate 40, moved several yards from the original location on a blanket by Gardner and his crew.

describe a dead Confederate soldier at Devil's Den. The photographs and captions were unquestioned well into the twentieth century as true depictions of the great battle. However, Frassanito noticed inconsistencies in the images. Photographs published and presented by Gardner as completely different subjects had many similarities in detail of clothing, body position, and landscape features. Frassanito compared the prints presented in Gardner's publication with the original negatives and prints at the National Archives, the Library of Congress, and other institutions. Among many other revelations, he discovered that the corpses in "A Harvest of Death" and "The Field Where General Reynolds Fell" were actually the same group of bodies photographed from two different angles. The second image was also not made near the place where General John Reynolds had died on the first day, but rather at the opposite end of the field after the action of the third day. Furthermore, the unfortunate Confederate soldier of "A Sharpshooter's Last Sleep" and "The Home of a Rebel Sharpshooter" was the same corpse dragged from its original position and posed several times by Gardner and his crew for more "dramatic" interpretation of the scene. Frassanito concluded that Gardner had deliberately manipulated these images and captions to construct and espouse his own views on the horrors of war, and also to offer a publication that would sell. Because of Frassanito's efforts, we now have a clearer interpretation not just of photography and the Battle of Gettysburg, but also of the nature of depicting truth.

Historians during the mid- to late twentieth century began turning from traditional "great man" studies and increasingly advocated the significance and contributions of previously unrecognized groups and cultures to history. Likewise, they began turning away from traditional textual sources to new alternatives for insights to the past, among them oral history, archaeology, and historical photography. Pennsylvania studies relying heavily on historical photographs include the publications *Still Philadelphia: A Photographic History, 1890–1940* (1983) and *Philadelphia Stories: A Photographic History, 1920–1960* (1988), both by Fredric Miller, Morris Vogel, and Allen Davis, and *Work Sights: Industrial Philadelphia, 1890–1950* (1986) by Philip Scranton and Walter Licht. These works deliberately avoided traditional historical-document analysis in favor of using photo "essays" to tell the story of life in Philadelphia in the early to mid-twentieth century. The results evoked a feeling and understanding for the city that would be difficult to render in a written text. For *Philadelphia Stories,* the authors employed the family snapshot as a novel device to further personalize Philadelphia's collective memory. These informal family images of weddings, birthdays, confirmations, and other events revealed not only how people saw themselves but also what they considered significant enough to record.

Scholars have also realized that the very men and women who made the historical images are themselves understudied resources. Analysis of the life of a "typical" commercial photographer can give new or broader perspectives on the town in which he or she plied their trade, and on nineteenth-century lifestyles and entrepreneurship in general.

Ben Shahn photograph of Hungarian miner (and wife), October 1935, Calumet: "Worked in the mines for thirty-four years, now sixty-three with no pension and no work."

For example, *Enterprising Images: The Goodridge Brothers, African American Photographers, 1847–1922* (2000) by John V. Jezierski, dramatically demonstrates how photographer Glenalvin Goodridge and his extended family lived and conducted their trade within the sphere of racism as free men in antebellum York. Their struggles and triumphs can be considered analogous to the lives of other free blacks living in the Commonwealth and in the United States.

Where can the historian find such collections relating to Pennsylvania? This of course depends on the subject under scrutiny. With time, images, after initial use by their creators for reconnaissance, business, scientific, legal, or other immediate purposes, take on historical value for new audiences, just like written records. And as with written records, they are housed in public and private institutions all over the world, not just in Pennsylvania, and not just at institutions related to history. While specific locations of collections are too vast to enumerate here, it is useful to consider examples on a local, statewide, and national level. Finding images may be as simple as checking within one's own personal or family history materials, and moving outward from there. A good starting point is a county or local historical society, or any library or museum with connections to the vicinity's people, places, and events. Many such organizations maintain images created by commercial photograph businesses. For example, the Historical Society of Dauphin County holds the Allied Pix Collection, relating to political and social events in the Harrisburg area between 1973 and 1996; and the Cumberland County Historical Society houses the negatives of A. A. Line, a Carlisle commercial photographer active during the late nineteenth century. Individual families often donate personal materials to such institutions as well. Collectively, all these sources can be used to create a historical portrait of the region and community to be studied and appreciated.

College and university libraries also acquire photography collections. The

"Drinking Olde Frothingslosh and wearing Davy Crockett hats," a family photograph, December 1955, by Evelyn Ries, at the Ries home in the South Hills section of Pittsburgh.

Archives of Industrial Society, part of the Hillman Library of the University of Pittsburgh, maintains the City Photographer of Pittsburgh Collection. The Pattee Library of The Pennsylvania State University acquired William C. Darrah's collection of 57,000 cartes-de-visite upon his death in 1989. The Theater Collection of the Free Library of Philadelphia houses Siegmund Lubin material, and the Pennsylvania Academy of the Fine Arts has the photography of Thomas Eakins. Religious organizations, from dioceses to synods to each individual church and synagogue, maintain photograph archives. Private corporations and businesses in the Commonwealth, from the Heinz Food Corporation to Slinky, all maintain business records, many including photographs originally made for promotional or technical purposes.

On a larger public level, many city and county governments also maintain their own archives, such as the Philadelphia City Archives and the Counties of Delaware, Chester, Lehigh, and Westmoreland. The Pennsylvania State Archives primarily holds records of state agencies operating under the governor's jurisdiction, including an inheritance of photographs made by and for various departments of their operations all over the Commonwealth. It also maintains the photographs of J. Horace McFarland, Mira Lloyd Dock, and the Pennsylvania Railroad.

Pennsylvania images can also be found on a national, and international, level.

Government institutions such as the Library of Congress hold, for example, the collections of Marian Carson, the Civil War negatives of Alexander Gardner, and photographs made for the Farm Security Administration (FSA); the National Archives also holds Civil War and FSA images. The National Agricultural Library, part of the U.S. Department of Agriculture, also maintains McFarland photographs. Private institutions include the Hagley Museum in Delaware, housing the corporate archives of several out-of-existence Pennsylvania companies, such as Midvale Steel, the Vulcan Iron Works, and others; and the International Museum of Photography in Rochester, New York, maintains Lewis Hine's images and the holdings of the Sipley Museum. The Keystone View Company stereoviews are now known as the Keystone-Mast Collection at the California Museum of Photography at the University of California at Riverside. Though the University of Pennsylvania Archives maintains some records and images created by Eadweard Muybridge, most of his holdings were bequeathed to the Kingston Museum at his native Kingston-on-Thames, England.

The Internet has enabled researchers to locate photography collections around the world quickly and easily. For research regarding photographers, the International Museum of Photography in Rochester, New York, maintains an online database filled with biographical and statistical information. Many institutions have online databases permitting item-specific searches, some including scanned copies of their images. The Library of Congress, for example, has digital versions of Alexander Gardner's Gettysburg images available for research. It also maintains the American Memory website, containing digital photograph collections from institutions all over the United States.

Use of historical images requires the same professional courtesy, ethics, and standards as for documentary citations. Yet the same historians who provide minutely detailed footnotes and citations for their textual sources are often guilty of neglecting the same for the images they use. We have learned that an uncaptioned image is only half the story, something to decorate the text block rather than reinforce historical analysis. Providing the original caption, or if there is none, an explanatory one, respects the integrity of the original image and the intended audience. By the same token, providing the negative or master print number, collection title, and the institution provides clear, specific data for future scholars. Good stewardship of historical resources is important no matter what they are.

Photography reached yet another technological crossroads at the dawning of the twenty-first century. Magnetic, electronic, and digital means of creating photographs have become commercially available and are enormously popular with public and professional alike. Photographs can be sent into the atmosphere as electronic impulses and rearranged as a digitized image on viewing screens almost instantaneously around the globe. These sophisticated formats promise to continue photography's role as a tool for recording history, yet at the same time the task for the historian in extracting usable data from these kinds of records proves daunting. These are machine-readable, rather than human-readable, formats. One must have more than the naked eye; one needs the proper equipment: a projector, a computer, a videotape or compact disc player, in order to understand and interpret what has been recorded. Though faster and more efficient at recordation, these formats are also the most fragile in terms of extended preservation. Electricity is needed to run machinery, models become obsolete, magnetized tape degrades. To properly utilize them, one must visit specialized archives outfitted with proper environmental conditions, appropriate playback equipment, and preservation techniques. Also, as photography becomes more sophisticated, so does the difficulty in searching for the truth in it. Images can easily be manipulated with home computer equipment to disguise or alter what is presented to the viewer. People and features can be removed or replaced, and fictional landscapes can be conjured up from the mind of the creator. Deciding the nuances between truth and fiction in photography will continue to be a dilemma for the viewer. The potential for research, however, remains the same as when Daguerre introduced his method in 1839. It is the historian's task to recognize and realize that potential.

SOURCES *and* FURTHER READING

Brugioni, Dino A. *Photo-Fakery: A History of Deception and Manipulation.* London: Brassey's, 1999.

Crawford, William. *The Keepers of Light: A History and Working Guide to Early Photographic Processes.* New York: Morgan & Morgan, 1979.

Danly, Susan, and Cheryl Leibold. *Eakins and the Photograph.* Philadelphia: Smithsonian Institution Press for the Pennsylvania Academy of the Fine Arts, 1994.

Darrah, William C. *Cartes-de-Visite in Nineteenth-Century Photography.* Gettysburg, Pa.: William C. Darrah, 1981.

———. *The World of Stereographs.* Gettysburg, Pa.: William C. Darrah, 1983.

Day, Sarah, ed. *Gathering History: The Marian S. Carson Collection of Americana.* Washington, D.C.: Library of Congress, 1999.

Eckhardt, Joseph P. *The King of the Movies: Film Pioneer Siegmund Lubin.* London: Associated University Presses, 1997.

Eskind, Andrew, and Greg Drake. *Index to American Photographic Collections* (International Museum of Photography). Third edition, revised and updated. Boston: G. K. Hall, 1995. Also available on-line.

Finkel, Kenneth C. *Legacy in Light: Photographic Treasures from Philadelphia Area Public Collections.* Philadelphia: Photography Sesquicentennial Project, 1990.

———. *Nineteenth-Century Photography in Philadelphia.* New York: Dover Publications, 1980.

Fleischauer, Carl, and Beverly W. Brannan, eds. *Documenting America, 1935–1943.* Berkeley and Los Angeles: University of California Press in association with the Library of Congress, 1988.

Frassanito, William A. *Early Photography at Gettysburg.* Gettysburg, Pa.: Thomas Publications, 1995.

———. *Gettysburg: A Journey in Time.* New York: Scribner's, 1975.

Gardner, Alexander. *Photographic Sketch Book of the Civil War.* New York: Dover Publications, 1986 reprint.

Jezierski, John V. *Enterprising Images: The Goodridge Brothers, African American Photographers, 1847–1922.* Detroit: Wayne State University Press, 2000.

Miller, Fredric M., Morris J. Vogel, and Allen F. Davis. *Still Philadelphia: A Photographic History, 1890–1940.* Philadelphia: Temple University Press, 1983.

———. *Philadelphia Stories: A Photographic History, 1920–1960.* Philadelphia: Temple University Press, 1988.

Muybridge, Eadweard. *Animal Locomotion: An Electro-Photographic Investigation of Consecutive Phases of Animal Movements, 1872–1885.* Philadelphia: J. B. Lippincott, 1887.

Reilly, James M. *Care and Identification of Nineteenth-Century Photographic Prints.* Kodak Publication No. G-2S. Rochester, N.Y.: Eastman Kodak Company, 1986.

Ries, Linda A., guest ed. "Special Issue: History of Photography in Pennsylvania." *Pennsylvania History* 64 (Spring 1997), 169–356.

Ries, Linda A., and Jay W. Ruby, comp. and ed. *Directory of Pennsylvania Photographers, 1839–1900.* Harrisburg: Pennsylvania Historical and Museum Commission, 1999.

Root, Marcus A. *The Camera and the Pencil; or, the Heliographic Art.* Introduction by Beaumont Newhall. 1864. Reprint, Pawlet, Vt.: Helios Press, 1971.

Rudisill, Richard. *Photographers: A Sourcebook for Historical Research.* Brownsville, Calif.: Carl Mautz Publishing, 1991.

Scranton, Philip, and Walter Licht. *Work Sights: Industrial Philadelphia, 1890–1950.* Philadelphia: Temple University Press, 1986.

Severa, Joan. *Dressed for the Photographer: Ordinary Americans and Fashion, 1840–1900.* Kent, Ohio: Kent State University Press, 1995.

Stapp, William F. *Robert Cornelius: Portraits from the Dawn of Photography.* Washington, D.C.: Smithsonian Institution Press, 1983.

Welling, William. *Photography in America: The Formative Years, 1839–1900.* New York: Thomas Y. Crowell, 1978.

Art

RANDALL M. MILLER AND WILLIAM PENCAK

History and art have always been fellow travelers. Preliterate people looked to art for instruction as well as for inspiration, and in the age of literacy the culture-shaping power of art has increased as mass-mediated visual images bombard the senses. This process sometimes takes the form of public art, commissioned and directed by governmental entities, but it mostly includes private expression through painting, sculpture, and other art forms. As such, art promises a way into a people's past.

Art that memorializes history can stir the soul to consider the meaning of patriotism and the sacrifices it has involved. At first, many Americans considered the Vietnam War Memorial in Washington, D.C., insufficiently heroic: sunk in a landscape, it is almost invisible until you are literally in it—much like the Vietnam issue in American history. By putting the name of every American known to have died in the conflict on the wall, however, artist Maya Lin turned the memorial into an ever-evolving creative work, where people add mementos to honor those they knew. As you walk the length of the wall, your face reflected in the black stone, you are forced to look at yourself and question your own feelings about the war and the men and women who died in that faraway country. So too can other artistic expressions cause, even compel, viewers to consider their place in history.

Even art that is not historical can provide insights into history. For example, the Andy Warhol Museum in Pittsburgh, where the huge works require entire walls or rooms, gives a glimpse into the thought and times of this Pittsburgh-born artist. Warhol's most famous works use Campbell's Soup cans in various formats to comment on how the modern world has come to depend on bland, commercially packaged goods. At the other end of Pennsylvania, in Chadd's Ford, the values of rural Americans emerge with eloquence from the paintings of the Wyeth family. The rustic wood along Brandywine Creek is the perfect setting for contemplating the world we have lost.

This chapter approaches art as a way to finding Pennsylvania's past. It focuses on representational art—primarily paintings—by trained artists who sought to exhibit and sell their work. This focus does slight other important art forms, such as sculpture and monuments. Indeed, the grand Alexander Milne Calder statue of William Penn atop City Hall in Philadelphia, and the statue of mayor, union leader, and temperance advocate Terence Powderly in front of City Hall in Scranton (to name only two), reveal much about public interest in those Pennsylvania places. Also excluded is folk art, which functions within the context of folklore and folk culture (see Chapter 11). But in the short compass allotted for this chapter, we propose a more limited, though colorful, sampling by looking at Pennsylvania subjects as depicted in paintings, murals, glass, and tiles. With only a few exceptions, these works can be seen in museums, galleries, historical societies, and public buildings throughout Pennsylvania. Our hope is that this first taste might encourage readers to make their own forays into Pennsylvania's rich artistic heritage and to consider the ways in which art and history intersect.

Probably no artistic representation of a Pennsylvania event is better known than Benjamin West's *William Penn's Treaty with the Indians* (1771), first exhibited at the Royal Academy of Art in London in 1772 and then reproduced as an engraving for sale to the public. West completed his painting on commission from Thomas Penn, who was angling to silence critics of his proprietorship of Pennsylvania by trading on the memory of his father. West eagerly accepted the commission to paint a subject he knew well— and that ensured him an exhibition in London where the aspiring American artist hoped to throw off his provincialism and win fame and fortune. West worked quickly to complete the painting. For his "sources" on the 1682 meeting of Penn and the Lenape, he drew on the oral tradition of the treaty that was common coin among Pennsylvanians, likenesses of Quakers dead and alive, images of Natives' look and dress as recalled from his youth and as copied from costumes brought to him from the Penn family collection in London, and the attire of prosperous eighteenth-century London Quakers. His purpose, he later wrote, was to "express savages brought into harmony and piece [*sic*] by justice and benevolence" rather than to present a documentary record. But viewers of his work did not see it that way.

The painting achieved almost instant fame and soon came to represent the way generations would remember Penn and relations with the Indians. That Benjamin West cast the Natives as noble figures added to the power and appeal the painting had for

Benjamin West, *William Penn's Treaty with the Indians*, 1771.

European and later American audiences, for whom "the noble savage" became the symbol of innocence lost. West's interpretation of the treaty transcended history to become the great "truth" of Pennsylvania's beginnings and promise as a "Holy Experiment" where peace and toleration would bring harmony and prosperity. Whether such a meeting between Penn and the Lenape ever occurred under the elm tree at Shackamaxon in November 1682 soon became irrelevant; the painting emblazoned the event as historical reality on the minds of generations of Americans.

West's painting has been copied in various forms almost from the time of its first engraving to the present day and gained much currency among artists during the nineteenth century. Around 1830 the Quaker Edward Hicks began working West's treaty scene into his own image of peace and harmony, *The Peaceable Kingdom,* perhaps the second-most recognized symbol of Pennsylvania art. In each subsequent rendering of *The Peaceable Kingdom,* the figures of Penn and the Indians at the supposed treaty meeting grew larger. Hicks had his own uses for the Penn treaty scene, and in one version he

Emanuel Gottlieb Leutze, *George Washington Crossing the Delaware*, 1851.

substituted the likenesses of prominent Quakers and George Washington for the nameless Quakers of West's painting, and converted the message from peace with Indians to peace among the feuding Quakers of his day.

By the mid-nineteenth century, as Americans marched westward to conquer a continent, interest in the treaty scene began to fade. The image came to be associated more with Pennsylvania and less as a national symbol. The image was revived later in the century, and by peace advocates during times of national crisis, and it continued to serve as a symbol in popular culture through the twentieth century—and sometimes to mock American pretensions of tolerance and justice. Artistic representations of the Penn Treaty can tell us much about art as history. In the case of West's powerful work, its constant reproduction in lithographs, in illustrations for books, in quilts, on china, on tablecloths, and in so many other expressions have embedded the image deep in the American psyche and seemingly revalidated it with each depiction—so much so that it has become almost impossible to imagine the event, and the people, any other way. Like other grand "historical paintings"—especially John Trumbull's *Declaration of Independence, 4 July 1776* (1787–1820), Emanuel Leutze's *George Washington Crossing the Delaware* (1851), and Peter Frederick Rothermel's *The Battle of Gettysburg: Pickett's Charge* (1867–70)—it functions to create a historical reality. And the grand scale of the art and its prominent exhibition in public places add to its "truth."

In the case of Leutze's painting showing Washington standing in a Durham boat while his men row across an ice-choked Delaware River, the visual power of that work of art blinds the viewer to the fact that in the real crossing the general had not been so foolish or arrogant as to stand in an overloaded boat. Today, crowds clog the banks of the Delaware on Christmas Day to witness the annual reenactment of Washington's famous crossing, which the "living history" actors play out almost in accord with Leutze's visual script. A large photographic reproduction of Leutze's painting can be seen in the visitors center of Washington Crossing Historic Park, and many people expect to see that historical "reality" when they assemble on the Pennsylvania side of the river to relive the historical moment. Such is the power of art to dictate "history."

The desire to see people and events draws us to art, especially when other visual representations are not available. We tend to accept the image at face value, not much questioning the accuracy of the details. Lacking other visual evidence, how is one to know what so-and-so looked like, for example? During the nineteenth century, when "history painting" was still in vogue, the artists' heroic presentations of events were readily accepted by a people eager to find a past worthy of its ambitions. Artists chose great events that instilled patriotism—and, not incidentally, that sold prints. The story of America, and of Pennsylvania, became the story of great men and great deeds seen and recorded. Art figured prominently in creating that narrative, and as such it was (and is) a historical source.

Portraiture is an important and immensely popular art form for "documenting" the past. Painted portraits were the principal art form during the colonial period and remained important into the twentieth century. Portraits of prominent people hanging on the walls of virtually every historical society and museum in the state also provide a lens through which to see Pennsylvania life and culture, albeit largely from the perspective and in the interests of the upper class, who could afford such likenesses. Sometimes a portrait is the only, or at least the principal, record we have of an individual. Quakers in early Pennsylvania, however, generally abjured the vanity of portraits and invested their money in silver, furniture, and other fine goods that quietly bespoke their wealth and had ready uses.

The lack of patronage and the newness of the colony discouraged artists from settling in Pennsylvania. The first artist to live and work in Pennsylvania for any time was Gustavus Hesselius, a Swedish-born ship and house painter who came to Philadelphia in 1712 or 1713. Among his better-known works is a portrait of Penn's confidant and secretary James Logan, done in straightforward style with no reference to Logan's great wealth, library, or mansion.

Students of history find much of interest in the portraits of the Delaware Indian chiefs Lapowinsa and Tishcohan by Hesselius, which he painted on a commission from John and Thomas Penn in 1735. The artist probably completed the two works before the famous Walking Purchase Treaty of 1737, by which the Penns cheated the Delawares out of a large chunk of land. Hesselius was not part of the land swindle, and he cast the two

Robert Feke, *Benjamin Franklin*, 1746.

RIGHT: Charles Willson Peale, *Benjamin Franklin*, 1785.

chiefs as "noble savages." The paintings have ethnographic value in that they are among the few likenesses of individual Indians in Pennsylvania or anywhere in colonial America. Ironically, however, they have been so often reproduced in history books to represent "the colonial Indian" that they have almost lost their particular history. Whether the paintings reveal any sympathy on the part of Hesselius toward the Natives' plight or speak to Pennsylvanians' attitudes toward the Natives is more conjectural.

Portraits of prominent Pennsylvanians became more common as the eighteenth century wore on. Free of Quaker inhibitions, wealthy Anglicans and other Pennsylvanians wanted to advertise their increasing status, so they willingly sat for portraits. Wealth and station demanded no less, and so did important events in one's life, or in the birth of a new nation. Thus, gentlemen sat for their portraits in military garb to show their rank and to claim their rightful place as defenders of their people. During and after the American Revolutionary War, men asserted their patriotic bona fides through portraiture. The portraits of revolutionary generation patriots on display in the Second Bank of the United States building on Chestnut Street in Philadelphia amply make the point.

Portraits also can be a means of controlling history. A comparison of the many portraits of Benjamin Franklin shows how. Franklin once observed that in presenting himself to the public, as in his autobiography, he was careful to "dress for the ball." So what are we to make of Franklin posing as an English gentleman in a 1746 portrait by Robert Feke—this from an apprentice-turned-printer who once scolded his wife for affectation after she bought silverplate for the breakfast service? Or of a 1777 likeness of Franklin in a fur cap playing the part of the backwoods savant, a print that circulated widely in France and served him well in pleading America's cause? Or of the 1785 portrait by an admiring Charles Willson Peale showing Franklin without wig and peering pensively through his bifocals?

All the portraits were of Franklin, but they were more than mere likenesses. The different ways Franklin "dressed" for his portraits reveal much about the uses of portraiture to establish a social and political "self." In portraits for which he sat, and thus exercised some control over his own image, Franklin's earlier elegant attire gave way to a simpler look, a change of attire that coincided with Franklin's move from ambitious English provincial to American patriot and self-made man. And lest anyone forget who "Dr. Franklin" was, several portraits included Franklin's useful inventions, especially the lightning rod by which he "tamed" electricity and safeguarded people's property. Surely Americans could trust a scientist who had such impressive credentials to help in the "experiment" of building the young republic.

Over time, portraiture became more "democratic"; more people could afford to sit for a portrait—and wanted to do so, whether as a statement about their status or simply as a way of recording their existence. Consider one of the most famous portraits of a "common man," John Neagle's *Pat Lyon at the Forge* (1829). In this very large painting, Neagle presents the ruddy-faced, muscular blacksmith at work in his shop, an artisan whose size, direct gaze, and confident stance assert that he is the measure of any man. The portrait mocks pretensions of the upper classes, for the Irish-born Lyon had commissioned it to pronounce his stature as a self-made man. The cupola in the background is of the old Walnut Street prison in Philadelphia, where a younger Lyon had once been locked away by his betters on a false charge of bank robbery. After Neagle's full-length portrait of Pat Lyon was hung near portraits of George Washington (by Gilbert Stuart) and other American statesmen in the Pennsylvania Academy of the Fine Arts (where they remain juxtaposed), tourist guidebooks from the antebellum period onward pointed to the Washington and the Lyon portraits as emblematic of the early republic's sense of history and the promise that upstanding men could get ahead.

Depictions of "the common man" gained increasing currency during the days of Jefferson and Jackson, when the politics of universal (white) manhood suffrage and direct appeals to the masses for votes made farmers and workers objects of artistic and literary attention. Portraits of political and military leaders continued to fill the national pantheon and promote patriotism, but civic painting increasingly turned to celebrations of historical events and American places, as well as to recording public ceremonies and culture in which ordinary people took center stage. In art, as in literature, "the people"

entered the national narrative as true bearers of American character. To know them was to know America. Pennsylvania scenes and events figured prominently in this new narrative.

Philadelphia was often the setting for genre painters, who made the city stand for the rise of "the common man" in a host of works depicting civic events and everyday life. Philadelphia's economic and political prominence naturally invited such interest, but the presence of an art school and a clientele for artists ensured that the burgeoning city of workers would get its place in the artistic imagination.

Among the most prolific and successful genre painters in Pennsylvania was John Lewis Krimmel, a German immigrant trained in Europe who worked in Philadelphia from 1809 to 1822. Krimmel painted many subjects, but he was especially interested in scenes of people assembling in public spaces. Most famous is his painting *Fourth of July in Centre Square* (1812), in which he brought together a host of urban types, including a stylish African American couple, several fashionable young ladies and gentlemen, playful (and pestering) children, sober Quakers, and besotted dandies at the voting table. Benjamin Henry Latrobe's new pumping station and William Rush's sculpture and fountain stand in the background in a scene that is at once a useful index of contemporary styles and artistic and architectural achievement, and a parody of social pretensions at the dawning of democracy.

In 1819 Krimmel painted another Fourth of July celebration, this one a watercolor showing "republican ladies" selling songsheets and fruit, conversing, and enjoying a feast with their menfolk, and men parading in military units, talking politics, entertaining the company, and sharing in the feast. Black children and white children are playing games, including one lad brandishing a pistol and another under a table who is apparently up to no good. It is significant that in both paintings of the patriotic gathering, Krimmel mixed men and women as participants in the public sphere—an image that is somewhat at odds with the common historical assumption that women remained on the sidelines of public life during that period.

Krimmel was not the only artist drawn to the busy mix of everyday urban life. Many artists were fascinated by the way cities brought together people from all walks of life. Their views were not always favorable: caricatures of blacks, immigrant Irish and Germans, and working-class men and women abounded. In part, such caricatures reflected Americans' ambivalence about city life, where jostling for place and hustling for a living made "democracy" appear crude and disruptive, and where the new "penny press" daily newspapers fed readers a steady round of lurid stories of crime and corruption. The new and different people crowding into towns and cities threatened to overturn established religious, racial, and social hierarchies—or so the worried middle- and upper-class critics warned. For all the popular rhetoric about Americans being one people bound together by history and culture, the antebellum era pointed to differences, distinctions, and divisions. Artists and writers joined the fray, typing particular peoples as a way to make sense of them and to impose a sense of order on a society aswirl.

M. E. D. Brown, *The Gold & Silver Artificers in
Civic Procession 22 Feb 1832.*

Artists did not shy away from addressing, however obliquely, the political and social
issues of the day. For instance, M. E. D. Brown in his *Gold and Silver Artificers in Civic
Procession, 22 Feb 1832,* made political capital with the ironic juxtaposition of workers
involved in refining gold and silver passing before the reviewing stand at the Second
Bank of the United States. The Bank was the symbol of concentrated wealth, and therefore a political bogeyman. Perhaps unintentionally, Brown added a new level of irony,
for both the artificers and the Bank were living on borrowed time in 1832. Technology
threatened the autonomy of artisans, while Jacksonian politics soon undid the Bank and
any claim Philadelphia still might have had as the financial center of the nation.

As the century wore on, artists surveyed the ever more varied worlds of the city.
Upper- and middle-class life received most attention, especially through family portraits
and scenes of domestic harmony, but lower-class life also gained notice. Journalists and
reformers led the way into the world of immigrants and the working classes, and "reform
photographers" made the case for social action. By the turn of the century, some
Pennsylvania artists used paintings to crusade for city beautification and civic improvement. Others fell under the spell of the "Ashcan School" from New York in painting city
scenes in ways that simultaneously caught the gaslit glow of cities that never slept and
protested the grim darkness shrouding tenement lives. They all painted with a purpose,
which should never be ignored in assessing the meaning of their work and using it as a
historical record.

Many such painters worked in western Pennsylvania, where they found an ample panorama of the new industrial and urban order to observe and record. Notable among them was David Gilmour Blythe, a carpenter and itinerant painter who settled in Pittsburgh in 1855 and began recording the dark side of the fast-rising industrial city before he turned to paintings on political subjects. In a series of paintings, Blythe presented his "street gallery" of moneygrubbing, contemptible, and seemingly incorrigible hustlers, crooks, and ruffians. The Pittsburgh that Blythe knew and depicted in the 1850s contrasted sharply with the bucolic scenes landscape artists had made of the city. Blythe's interest was in describing the place and its people, not promoting it. Pittsburgh was in fact at that time plagued by epidemic disease, sunk in dirt and squalor, teeming with unemployed and underemployed immigrants, and wracked by crime and violence.

Blythe's view of "the common man" was often contemptuous, as best revealed in his painting *The Post Office* (1860–63), in which Blythe shows the backs of a group of men and women, of varying contemporary costume, cramming into the general delivery window, while off to one side a boy picks the pocket of a man reading a sheet of some kind. On the other side stands a man oblivious to the tumult, reading a paper as another man looks over his shoulder. The classical bust over the window looks down on the mayhem. Was this a premonition of a new fall of Rome? Was the "new" industrial Pittsburgh the harbinger of the republic's moral collapse? Perhaps not, if one contrasts the painting with Blythe's *In the Pittsburgh Post Office* (1859–62), which shows properly attired "gentlemen" sending and getting their mail and keeping up with the news by reading the papers. Which view of the post office most fully expressed Blythe's true estimate of the political and social prospects of his city and his country is a question the historian must consider. Perhaps both did, and it is significant that, in Hogarthian fashion, Blythe left two images for contemporaries to ponder.

In Pennsylvania, railroads had a special place, for the state's prosperity hinged on their growth, and Pennsylvanians' love affair with trains never ended, despite the cries about monopoly and abuses. In art too the railroad enjoyed favor among Pennsylvanians, who preferred scenes of locomotives thrusting forward and of such engineering marvels as Altoona's Horseshoe Curve, over images of trains despoiling the landscape. Hardly a Pennsylvania historical society or museum lacks a paean to railroads in its collection, and in 1998 the Pennsylvania Historical and Museum Commission and the state Department of Transportation unveiled a special railroad heritage license plate featuring Grif Teller's 1928 painting *When the Broad Way Meets the Dawn*.

Some Pennsylvania artists entered the national debate on the meaning of industrial progress with works that reveal the conflicted views contemporaries had about the new industrial age. A profusion of landscapes painted during the nineteenth century conveyed the redemptive powers of contemplating nature. The Westmoreland Museum of American Art in Greensburg, perhaps best known for its industrial art, has an impressive collection of southwestern Pennsylvania landscapes showing vistas beloved by nine-

David Gilmour Blythe, *In the Pittsburgh Post Office*, 1859–62.

teenth-century artists and their public, an increasingly urban public that found such tranquillity increasingly harder to come by. George Hetzel's *Two Young Fishermen in a Summer Landscape* (1867) is typical of the genre. Two small figures are surrounded by an abundant, sublime natural area awaiting exploration, but with a fence and meadow hinting that humans had already found a way to enter nature. In many such landscapes human figures, towns, and railroads appear as small elements amid an overwhelming and apparently indestructible natural grandeur, suggesting that man and the machine might live compatibly with nature. But a closer look at many such scenes reveals that nature did not remain inviolate and that the machine was already coming into fuller view, even as a central focal point.

George Inness, a painter of poetic landscapes who once dismissed realism in painting as "pudding twaddle," had his say about "the machine in the garden" when he was hired by the Delaware, Lackawanna & Western Railroad to paint a landscape showing

David Gilmour Blythe, *The Post Office*, 1860–63.

its new roundhouse. His famous landscape *The Lackawanna Valley* (1855) seems to make the case for the railroad as consonant with nature, even as it conveys the power and energy that enabled the railroad to conquer time and space. The railroad buildings and tracks are part of the pastoral setting, and the smoke of the locomotive billows up like a puff of cloud. Another reading might elicit a more insidious view, for the tree stumps in the foreground and the centrality of the oncoming train cutting into the landscape suggest that the bucolic valley is about to yield to industry's advance. Or perhaps Inness preferred a middle ground, a cultivated landscape—rather than a wilderness—as the path to progress and happiness. Inness left it to the viewer to make the choice. The

painting—then and now—forces the viewer to consider the direction in which the machine was taking America. That question especially vexed Pennsylvanians at that time.

Whatever their own thinking about the railroad's proper place in the landscape, artists learned to ride the rails as they looked around the state for subjects to paint. Perhaps more than anywhere else in America, in Pennsylvania the industrial landscape became a field of interest to artists. The ubiquity of Pennsylvania industrial landscapes in art collections across the state attests to the constant tug of the subject for artists and provides a rare example of sustained artistic inquiry into that world. The industrial landscapes the artists discovered and represented were generally darker and less congenial than Inness's view of the Lackawanna Valley, but artists sometimes found beauty in them. Even industrial blight could possess a certain majesty.

A useful exercise for the student of Pennsylvania history is comparing painterly and photographic images of common industrial landscapes and workplaces to observe the ways the medium influenced the message. This exercise becomes more important when considering the post–Civil War rush toward realism, when many painters eschewed the antebellum emphasis on the sublime, allegory, and historical subjects in favor of close depictions of familiar scenes and everyday objects. Such realist painters often worked in still lifes, but they also ventured into scenes of daily life. Despite their reach for "realism," most such painters preferred what novelist Henry James called the "smiling aspects of life." They lavished attention and detail on the portraits and possessions of the genteel classes, rather than visit and "document" urban slums, factory-town warrens, and ravaged landscapes. Among the major realists, only Philadelphia's Thomas Eakins, a close

Thomas Eakins, *The Champion Single Sculls (Max Schmitt in a Single Scull)*, 1871.

student of anatomy and photography, dared show the callouses and blemishes of working people, as in his paintings of scullers rowing on the Schuylkill River and boxers fatigued in the ring.

Artists rarely went inside Pennsylvania's forges and ironworks, or any factories, in search of labor as subjects for their work. Machines more than men caught their eye. From the mid-nineteenth century into the 1930s, the sheer size of steelmaking machinery awed the artists, as it did all observers, and on canvas the pouring of molten steel from the giant Bessemer crucible became a leitmotif for the industrial might of Pennsylvania—and of America. Here was the forge of progress, the artists announced in what became perhaps the most common artistic expression of the new industrial order.

Pennsylvanians worked in a variety of industrial landscapes. Artists captured many of them, but perhaps none was so compelling as coal mining. A stunning variety of coal-related paintings can be found in the Steidle Collection at The Pennsylvania State University, the largest collection of late nineteenth- through mid-twentieth-century American industrial art anywhere. There one can see Carrie Pattison's blue-gray painting

Edmund M. Ashe, *The Cast*, 1939.

of a large bituminous coal mine and plant snaking its way across the Indiana County landscape like a giant anaconda. In the same collection is Lawrence Whitaker's more benign view of the entrance to a small Pennsylvania coal mine, in which man- and donkey-power are the chief means of grubbing coal from hills as yet only pockmarked with mines and not dominated by them. Lest anyone think that the mine ruled the man, Roy Hilton's classic painting *The Miner* (c. 1936) portrays the miner as master of his world. Grimy as he is, Hilton's steel-helmeted and leather-jacketed miner has the light and tools to make his own way.

During the 1930s especially, the world of work was the subject of public concern and artistic expression. New Deal arts programs left a rich legacy of American scenes and

Carrie Pattison, *Bituminous Coal Plant*, c. 1935.

regional historical images in post offices, public buildings, courthouses, and schools throughout the state. Although often polemical, murals and bas-reliefs of muscular men in field and factory cast farmers and industrial workers as noble figures in the march of progress and, like New Deal politics, seemingly shifted authority from big business to brawny labor.

Roy Hilton, *The Miner*, c. 1936.

Public art sponsored by federal programs, such as the Treasury Department's Section of Painting and Sculpture and the better-known and more amply supported Federal Arts Project of the Works Progress Administration (WPA), usually required that artists consult with local citizens in choosing the subjects and venues for the art. Local citizen groups insisted on accuracy in details and integrity of subject, on their terms. The federal agencies' opposition to abstraction, and preference for "regionalist" art, and their policy of employing artists who were themselves natives or residents of the regions in which they would work, further weighted the public art toward recognizable and acceptable images of local folkways, places, people, and history. The resulting art, displayed in public buildings, often served as an index of social values and political interest in particular communities.

An example is Christian J. Walter's *Pittsburgh* (1937), which he did while working for the WPA. It reveals more about steel-mill life than social scientists and other observers presented in statistical profiles of workers' wages and conditions in the factories. The factory complex looms large, with the blue-gray pallor of smoke choking the background color and clouding out the lines of the buildings, but in the foreground the green of trees and bushes contrasts with the drab housing and, more important, children play and women go about their business. Walter, who had been painting scenes of western Pennsylvania oil derricks, glassworks, dredging, and steel mills, knew the territory and placed people in the context of mill communities rather than merely as cogs in a wheel. He thus offered a larger panorama of experience than an "outsider" might see. The many examples of such New Deal and other public art from the period show students of history how particular people idealized certain aspects of the past and sought to express an appreciation for their communities.

Visitors to Pennsylvania's State Capitol cannot escape history. In fact, the works of art throughout the Capitol building provide excellent examples of how public art tells

the story of Pennsylvania's people and progress from many points of view. Within the Capitol building are both explicitly historical artworks and works depicting natural scenes and landscapes. Over the years, new works were added or replaced others, but the result has been that, over time, the building has provided visitors and historians with a window through which they can see and experience the ever-changing ways that law-makers, public officials and custodians, museum professionals, and artists have viewed Pennsylvania's history. Close examination, however, reveals that the views of so many different people and interests are not always coherent or even compatible. Yet certain common themes regarding Pennsylvania's past recur again and again.

Whose history will visitors to the State Capitol find in the building? The thousands of works of art there convey varying interpretations of Pennsylvania's past, and of which Pennsylvanians have been significant. In keeping with the standard view of history at the time the Capitol was constructed, "great men" and the celebration of the state's great resources in the late nineteenth century received the most attention. The state also commissioned artworks reflecting the Commonwealth's diversity of people, principles, and places. The history of "ordinary" people, of the environment, and of ideals realized and betrayed is present as well. To find some of that history, one can literally look beneath one's feet to discover the images of nature and of Native Americans, soldiers, immigrants, workers, and women—on which the feet of legislators and lobbyists and many others have trod for a century—all in the nearly 400 Moravian tiles Henry Mercer laid into the ground floor of the Capitol. More than thirty of the tiles are no longer visible because they were covered by other things built over them, but today one can do history from the bottom up by turning the Pennsylvania State Capitol upside down and inside out.

Jared French's mural *Meal Time with the Early Coal Miners*, completed in 1938 for the U.S. Treasury Department's Section of Painting and Sculpture, can be seen in the Plymouth post office. Like many "American Scene" artists of the day, French believed that public art should speak to and for the common people by celebrating work and depicting the laboring class in heroic poses.

Two of the twenty-four stained-glass windows by William B. Van Ingen that adorn the House and Senate chambers of the Pennsylvania State Capitol. These depict Justice and Bridge Building.

And what a Capitol it is. When on October 4, 1906, President Theodore Roosevelt dedicated the building, he declared: "It's the handsomest building I ever saw." Nearly a century later, after painstaking restoration that began in 1982 and is still in progress, the building still strikes visitors with awe. They gaze upward at the magnificent dome that rises 272 feet and is modeled on the domes of St. Peter's in Rome and of the U.S. Capitol in Washington, D.C., or marvel at the marble staircase and well-appointed legislative chambers, which resemble the Paris Opera House built under Napoleon III. Pennsylvania's achievements, the Capitol seems to say, rank with those of the cultures that erected those distinguished models.

The State Capitol, which took nine years to build at the cost of $13 million, seems like the bargain of the century. In reality, however, it was the steal of the century. Its architect, the state treasurer, the state auditor general, the superintendent of construction, and the chief contractor were convicted of inflating the real cost of the building by $4 million and pocketing the difference. Much of the take came from the culprits' billing the state for every piece of wood, bronze, and paneling either by the foot or by the pound, and then inflating the number of pieces purchased. In addition, brass was passed off as bronze, and plaster as mahogany, and chandeliers were weighed down with base metals. Yet this very corruption permitted the Capitol to express Pennsylvania's hidden history. The officials were so concerned with padding the bills that they allowed artists to fill many of those nooks and crannies with true works of art, enabling visitors to look beyond the opulence and find the Capitol's other marvels.

For example, at the top of both the House and the Senate chambers, almost invisible to the legislators on the floor but at a level with the public galleries, are Philadelphia artist William Van Ingen's twenty-four individual stained-glass windows in which women represent "Weaving," "Glass Blowing," "Commerce," and other endeavors, as well as such laudable subjects as "Temperance" (in consumption of alcohol), "Peace," "Education," and "Liberty." Yet even from the galleries these noble goals are half-hidden in recessed frames off to the sides. The electorate has to look hard, beyond the virtuoso political maneuverings below that threaten to dazzle them, to discover what Pennsylvania has stood for.

Also hidden in nooks, and visible only to those who look upward to see them as they walk through the corridors of power, are fourteen small semicircular murals (lunettes) also by Van Ingen. Here the religious diversity and importance of Pennsylvania's spiritual heritage may be recovered. Each mural represents a religious denomination important in the state's history: the Ephrata Cloister, the Moravians, the Dunkards, the Rosicrucians, the Mennonites, and the Quakers are given pride of place over Episcopalians and Roman Catholics, to emphasize Pennsylvania's acceptance of those whom others had persecuted. At the start of the twenty-first century, the Capitol seems to suggest that the higher reaches of the human mind and spirit are not completely inaccessible, but that one must struggle to discern them in the face of all the paraphernalia of a society that prefers to extol and exhibit its wealth.

In contrast, and prominent among the art the Capitol's designers wanted us to see, is the work of Edwin Austin Abbey. His thirty-five-foot-wide mural, *The Apotheosis of Pennsylvania,* dominates the House chamber, presenting an imposing if conventional view of the state and its history. The only woman in the painting is "The Genius of State" (a seated representation of the Goddess of Liberty), and beneath her are arrayed twenty-eight great white men: pioneers, explorers, statesmen, businessmen, scientists, generals, inventors. Closest to ordinary people are two outsiders who made Pennsylvania their home: the radical revolutionary Thomas Paine (an English immigrant who lived in Pennsylvania for seventeen years, moved to Revolutionary France, and died in poverty in New York) and John Fitch (a native of Pennsylvania who invented the steamboat twenty-two years before Robert Fulton but failed as a businessman and committed suicide in Kentucky). Paine and Fitch symbolize a commonwealth of people who moved into the state, but also the people who leave for lack of opportunity.

Abbey's vision of history also appears in the two murals flanking the *Apotheosis.* On the left, an elegant William Penn surrounded by equally genteel Quakers shakes hands with an Indian warrior of noble bearing, while some of the latter's followers—unlike Penn's, who are standing and looking forward—squat and look backward: Indians are inferior and backward-looking, lacking in energy, while the erect whites are poised to seize control of the future, albeit peacefully, and tower over them. On the right of the *Apotheosis,* the Declaration of Independence is read from a balcony to a group of middle- or upper-class men, while a man with a sword bars a woman with children (who are being signaled to be quiet) from the political arena. Meanwhile, a skeptic scratches his head. The woman and the skeptic cannot make their voices heard in the same public space where adult male patriots respond vociferously to doctrines read to them.

Unlike Abbey's work, there is no doubt at all that Violet Oakley, who finished Abbey's work after his death in 1911, consciously intended to highlight the historical roles of women, minorities, and the poor. Whereas the most notable feature of Abbey's House chamber mural is the female "Genius of State" bearing an oversized sword (ironic for Pennsylvania, founded as a pacifist haven), Oakley, herself a pacifist, directs our eyes in the Senate toward a kneeling woman figure representing "Unity." She presides over the end of all warfare that so many Americans briefly believed would come with the Allied victory in World War I. Kings give up their crowns, a Red Cross worker joins a soldier in washing the blood off his hands, a black woman cleanses her baby in water to symbolize the end of slavery. Women, one of them pacifist Jane Addams and most of them women of color, join workers in framing a painting from which the wealthy and powerful are absent.

Oakley's paintings of great scenes from American history reflect her commitment to the peace movement and her reformist ideas. The questioning, despairing, and angry faces of the revolutionary soldiers and populace make as much of an impression in *Washington Marching to Philadelphia* as the general himself does sitting proudly on a white horse, his confidence about to be belied by his defeat at Brandywine, which Oakley mentions in her caption. She emphasizes that the American Revolution inaugurated a perpetual revolution: "The Declaration of Independence . . . gave liberty not alone to this country but hope to all the world for all future time." To drive home the point that a conservative revolution that merely threw off the British yoke was not enough, her painting of the Constitutional Convention has an African American servant or slave piling up the massive tomes of political theory about which the statesmen are so vigorously debating.

Moving to the Civil War, Oakley has both Abraham Lincoln, in her mural of Gettysburg, and Pennsylvania's General George Gordon Meade, with his troops, looking downward. Lincoln is ignoring the tiny political figures in the background while casting sorrowful eyes on a crippled soldier and grieving family who dominate the foreground as the real heroes of the war. Similarly, Meade shows no joy or pride as he reviews his troops, whom, like those in Washington's ranks, Oakley accurately depicts as mostly youths, and handsome ones at that, to emphasize who bears the brunt of battle. The caption for the Gettysburg piece, taken from an address Lincoln made at Independence Hall, reads in part: "In due time the weights would be lifted from the shoulders of all men and that all should have an equal chance." Oakley's murals, unlike Abbey's, subtly undercut the message of the building in which they are situated. The real glory of Pennsylvania is the people who have tried, sometimes in vain, for a better life, under-

Violet Oakley's *International Unity and Understanding* graces the Pennsylvania Senate. Oakley devoted this frieze to her mystical vision of a united world.

mined by their leaders' wars and political corruption. Like so many historians writing in the late twentieth century, Oakley insisted that the history of the common folk is vital to that of the Commonwealth.

On the floor, Henry Mercer's tiles echo Oakley's vision. Number 303, "Reading the Declaration of Independence," depicts a skeptical soldier with working-class features looking away from the document toward a confident bewigged figure. According to Mercer, who described each of his tiles in detail in a small book, the image represents "the rival claims of war and statecraft to the founding of the nation, and the soldier's denial, that in the revolution of 1776, the pen was mightier than the sword." Mercer characterizes the Battle of Gettysburg using a single, sturdy Northern soldier triumphing over his Southern rival. In "Washington Crossing the Delaware," the general is only one figure of many and stands on the extreme right, not dominating the painting. His expression is thoughtful, troubled, as it must have been in the dark night before the victory at Trenton, rather than the proud victor aware of the outcome in advance in Emanuel Leutze's more famous painting.

Mercer's comment on his "Penn's Treaty"—in which three Indians and two Quakers meet on equal terms, unlike in Abbey's romanticized version or those of Benjamin West and the many artists who drew on West's painting—in many ways encapsulates both Pennsylvania's history and the way to study it most effectively. Said Mercer: "In the midst of wharves, factories, ware-houses, and a few ancient smoke-blackened dwellings, a small marble monument now [1909] marks the site where the 'treaty tree,' protected by the British garrison in 1776 as a venerable relic, blew down in 1810." In Mercer's version, Indians stand on the side of the new town of Philadelphia, and the Quakers are on the wilderness side of the tile, so that true reciprocity characterizes the event. Like the thirty-nine of Mercer's tiles that are now no longer visible (mostly depicting nature and Native Americans), the history of Pennsylvania has too often been hidden or obscured, as its people's collective achievements both as individuals and through public power have been lost in emphasis on famous men and quaint customs of bygone days.

As of the year 2002, however, the Capitol was still an impressive edifice, although it had become part of what is known as the "Capitol Complex." The city of Harrisburg boasted even taller office buildings and hotels, a sign that visiting lobbyists and permanent bureaucrats complemented and supplemented the formal branches of the legislature in much of the actual business of making law and defining policy. Thus, the Capitol was still a reflection of the society around it. Wealth and formal authority still had great visibility and influence, but their power rested both on citizens whose stories are rarely told and on the work of equally anonymous special-interest groups and civil servants whose number and functions were expanding as the traditional three branches of government superficially remained the same. In 1997 the Capitol Preservation Committee turned its attention to Mercer's tiles fifteen years after it began refurbishing the grand staircase and legislative chambers. With that, the Capitol was starting to catch up to those historians and others who have increasingly written about the communal triumphs and trials of "ordinary" Pennsylvanians, who, from the perspective of looking at history from the bottom up, are really most extraordinary people.

This overview of art and the history of Pennsylvania must end with an invitation to see more art—and to linger longer in viewing it—in public buildings, historical societies, museums, and elsewhere, as a way to find the many Pennsylvanias and Pennsylvanians that have existed in imagination and in reality. In doing so, we ought to consider what Charles Willson Peale understood when he opened his museum in Philadelphia two centuries ago. Peale, who was at once artist, educator, scientist, museum curator, and entrepreneur, believed that knowledge was not segregated into compartments, and in setting up his museum he stocked the cabinets with natural-history specimens and filled the walls with portraits, all in his effort to bring representations of "America" to the public. His famous painting *The Artist in His Museum* (1822), in which he pulls aside the curtain to reveal the wonders of man and nature within, thus asserted the validity of the visual arts as essential to relating and understanding a people's past, and thereby in helping that people imagine its future. Let the image of that painting stand as the invitation to consider the ways art might point to Pennsylvania's past as well as its present.

Chambers, Bruce W. *The World of David Gilmour Blythe.* Washington, D.C.: Smithsonian Institution Press, for the National Collection of Fine Arts, 1980.

Ford, Alice. *Edward Hicks: His Life and Art.* New York: Abbeville Press, 1985.

Harding, Anneliese. *John Lewis Krimmel: Genre Artist of the Early Republic.* Winterthur, Del.: Winterthur Museum, 1994.

Johns, Elizabeth. *American Genre Painting: The Politics of Everyday Life.* New Haven: Yale University Press, 1991.

Lindsey, Jack L. *Worldly Goods: The Arts of Early Pennsylvania, 1680–1758.* Philadelphia: Philadelphia Museum of Art, 1999.

Marling, Karal Ann. *Wall-to-Wall America: A Cultural History of Post-Office Murals in the Great Depression.* Minneapolis: University of Minnesota Press, 1982.

Mercer, Henry Chapman. *Guide Book to the Tiled Pavement in the Capitol of Pennsylvania.* 1908. Reprint, Harrisburg: Capitol Preservation Committee, 1997.

Novak, Barbara. *Nature and Culture: American Landscape and Painting, 1825–1875.* New York: Oxford University Press, 1980.

Park, Marlene, and Gerald E. Markowitz. *Democratic Vistas: Post Offices and Public Art in the New Deal.* Philadelphia: Temple University Press, 1984.

Pennsylvania Capitol Preservation Committee. *A Comprehensive Preservation Plan of the Pennsylvania Capitol.* 2 vols. Harrisburg: Capitol Preservation Committee, 1996.

Richman, Irwin. *Pennsylvania's Painters.* University Park: Pennsylvania Historical Association, 1983.

Sellers, Charles Coleman, and Anthony N. B. Garvan. *Symbols of Peace: William Penn's Treaty with the Indians.* Philadelphia: Pennsylvania Academy of the Fine Arts, 1976.

Sewell, Thomas, ed. *Thomas Eakins.* Philadelphia: Philadelphia Museum of Art, 2001.

Torchia, Robert. *John Neagle, Philadelphia Portrait Painter.* Philadelphia: Historical Society of Pennsylvania, 1989.

Vogel, Morris J. *Cultural Connections: Museums and Libraries of Philadelphia and the Delaware Valley.* Philadelphia: Temple University Press, 1991.

Oral History

LINDA SHOPES

In the mid-1990s, health educator Patricia Fabiano conducted a series of interviews with Dolores Bordas Kosko of McKees Rocks, Pennsylvania, as part of her study of the First Thursday Girls' Club, a group of working-class women from McKees Rocks who have met socially on the first Thursday of the month for more than forty years. During the interviews, Kosko spoke about her experiences working at Dravo Corporation, an industrial manufacturing plant established in the 1930s and located on Neville Island in the Ohio River, just offshore from McKees Rocks. As she tells it:

> I went to work for Dravo [in June 1972]. I didn't want to progress, all I wanted to do was go back and help supplement [my husband's] income, because we were struggling. It was just too hard on one salary. We had zip. We lived from one pay to the other. There were no extras. And we never went on vacation, we couldn't afford it. . . . By that time Valerie was twelve, Diane was nine, and I went to work part-time, which was fine. But then, you know, you work three days, and then the next thing you know, they want you to work four days, and then before you know it you're working five days, with no benefits, no nothing. No paid vacation. Then they offered me the full-time job, and I thought, "Well, I'm working five days anyways, and it seems to be working." I was right there on [Neville] Island so it was very convenient, so I did go as a full-time employee.

Over the years, her work life continued to change:

> And I did that for maybe about three years, and then I was offered . . . a job as a supervisor. What did I know about being a supervisor? I took it, and I think to myself, "How did I ever do it?" Without any formal training. I did not have a college degree. They gave me the job of supervisor of stenographic services. I had ten girls reporting to me. Responsible for a co-op program of students going to business school and working at Dravo. Setting that program up. Interviewing. I never had any formal instruction on how to interview people. I was interviewing people. I had to do performance reviews. Writing procedure manuals. Maybe part of it is my sense of organization. Do you develop a sense of organization, or is that ingrained in you, a part of your personality?
>
> And then after that, as I look back now, it seems like every four years I made a change. I was transferred over to Automation Systems, responsible for office automation, testing software, making recommendations. I still very much wanted to go to college, to get a college degree. I didn't think I was going to be able to go for the four years, but I definitely wanted to have an associate's degree. And Dravo had the tuition refund program. You have to pay for it first, and then they reimbursed you for it. And I started with classes. It took me twelve years. But I have my associate's degree in Business Administration. I'm not bragging, but I just feel very proud of myself that I was able to do it, working full-time, raising a family, working overtime also when projects needed it or demanded it.

Then in 1988 Kosko lost her job. This disrupted her life and challenged her to reassess certain assumptions and choices:

> After sixteen years at Dravo my job was eliminated because they were downsizing. Always in the back of your mind you think, "Oh, I wish I could get laid off and I'll sit at home." And no one really knows what happens to them when there really is a layoff. But my job was eliminated, I was laid off. And I had two weeks, they gave me a two-week notice. And a lot of people reacted with anger when they were laid off. They just picked up their stuff and they left their office. I got laid off, I came out of the office, and I went back to my office, and I went back to work. And people were walking past my office because they put two and two together, so they figured I got laid off, but they couldn't figure out why I was still working. But I never thought I should do it any other way. I had a job, I had a project to finish. And I finished it in the two weeks, and then when the two weeks were over, then I packed up my stuff and I left. Why? Dravo was good to me. I got my education. They paid me. That was the contract

with them. My contract was to finish that project. And I did. And I wouldn't do it any other way.

But the day I had to walk out of there, it was the most horrible feeling. I felt as though I was in limbo. Like I wasn't anywhere, and I thought to myself, "I should be enjoying this time off." But I had out-placement services, and I went to work at that. But I didn't start at eight o'clock. I started at eight-thirty, because I really didn't want to bump into the people in the elevators. So I went in a little bit later, and I left like four o'clock because my job was to get a job. I felt like I was in limbo. Like I didn't have an identity. I didn't have an identity. I wasn't. I was Dolores Kosko, but yet I wasn't Steve's wife, I wasn't Valerie's mother, or Diane's mother, or Julia Bordas's daughter. I felt in limbo, that I had no identity. That's the only way that I can describe it. I was collecting unemployment. Steve was working. And I had severance pay 'til the end of the year. What drove me [to find another job]? I don't know. [My friend] Joanne would say to me, "You're crazy. Stay home!" But I don't know. I still don't know what it was.

Should I go to do something different? And I looked at that, but I'm not good at sales, because I can't sell a product I don't believe in. I can't lie to anyone. So I knew sales wasn't for me. The position I really liked the best at Dravo was where I was responsible for office automation, and then I was responsible for the voicemail and I did training sessions. And then, I realized then, that I missed my calling. I should have gone to school to be a teacher. That's my one regret, that I didn't go to college. But, at the time, I don't think I was mature enough, or I didn't know what I wanted to do. My parents wanted to send me to college, but I felt that I didn't want to burden my parents because my parents really couldn't afford it. So I just went to Robert Morris [School of Business] for a six-month course, but after my layoff, that's when I realized that I missed my calling. But I didn't know that when I was eighteen.

This lengthy excerpt from Fabiano's interviews with Dolores Kosko suggests the value and power of oral history as a source for Pennsylvania history. Kosko's experience embodies two major themes of both Pennsylvania and U.S. history during the second half of the twentieth century—the entry of increasing numbers of women into the paid labor force and the massive loss of jobs resulting from capital flight—and her narrative gives life to the generalizations of standard historical accounts. It exemplifies the particular trajectory of many women's work history, from part-time jobs to supplement husbands' wages when children have reached school age to gradually increasing responsibility and a growing sense of professionalism; and it describes the way one person responded to the shock of losing a job, reminding us that women office workers, as well as the prototypical male steelworkers and miners, have been victims of deindustrialization. In a more subtle way, it suggests how economic constraints and the lack of per-

Members of the First Thursday Girls' Club, 1996. *Back, left to right:* Carole Wickert Hunkle, Joanne Fabiano Alder, Betty Leone Borden, Dolores Bordas Kosko. *Front, left to right:* Donna Hufnagel Muha, Anna Dellemonache Tapler, Patti Fedyshen Borden.

ceived options inhibited the aspirations of working-class women at mid-century. And it does this in language that is concrete, lively, and accessible. Kosko's narrative is at once a source of information and insight and a good story. It illustrates ways in which oral history can be used to broaden and deepen our understanding of the past.

ORIGINS OF ORAL HISTORY

Oral history, understood in the broadest sense as the transmission of knowledge about the past through the spoken word, is probably the oldest way humans have learned about history. Family stories told and retold around the holiday table, recollections of a town's past invoked in community meetings, informal knowledge of an institution passed down from employee to employee are all, in a way, oral history. Similarly, historians, social scientists, and writers have long drawn on orally transmitted material for their work. Both the Iroquois history codified in the Constitution of Five Nations (see Chapter 1), and the early twentieth-century survey of social conditions in Pittsburgh (see Chapter 6), relied on oral sources. In the former, oral tradition formed the basis of a political document; in the latter, interviews with working-class Pittsburghers provided essential information about their living and working conditions. Likewise, for generations history-conscious individuals have worked to preserve others' firsthand accounts of the past for the record, often precisely at the moment when the historical actors themselves, and with them their memories, were about to pass from the scene. During the eighteenth and early nineteenth centuries, for example, as the eastern United States became increasingly settled, scribes recorded accounts from Native Americans and frontier people about life in early Pennsylvania and elsewhere. Similarly, shortly after Abraham Lincoln's death in 1865, his secretary, John G. Nicolay, and law partner, William Herndon, gathered recollections of Lincoln, including some from interviews, from people who had known and worked with him.

Among the most notable of these early collecting efforts are the thousands of life histories recorded by writers and other white-collar workers employed by the Federal Writers Project (FWP) of the Works Progress Administration (WPA) during the late 1930s and early 1940s. Deeply populist in intent and orientation, these narratives aimed to document the diversity of the American experience and the ways ordinary people were coping with the hardships of the Great Depression. Plans for publication fell victim to federal budget cuts and a reorientation of government priorities as World War II drew near; most of the life histories remain in manuscript form at the Library of Congress and other repositories around the country. The best known of these FWP life histories are the "slave narratives" elicited from elderly former slaves living in the South; other narratives were collected from a variety of regional, occupational, and ethnic groups. In Pennsylvania, FWP workers conducted field interviews, including some life histories, as part of their research for sixteen (never published) local and regional ethnic studies, as well as for *Pennsylvania: A Guide to the Keystone State,* published in 1940 as one of a series of state touring guides produced by the WPA.

For all of their considerable value, these early efforts to record firsthand accounts of the past can be termed "oral history" by only the most generous of definitions. While methods of eliciting and recording these narratives were more or less rigorous in any given case, the absence of audiotape and videotape recorders, and the reliance on human note-takers, raises questions about their reliability and veracity. Many early interviews were also idiosyncratic or extemporaneous efforts, done with little intention of developing a permanent archival collection; interviews for the Pittsburgh survey (1909–14), for example, were not preserved for the record. Thus, historians generally consider oral history as beginning with the work of Allan Nevins at Columbia University in the 1940s. It was Nevins who first initiated a systematic and disciplined effort to record on tape, preserve, and make available for future research recollections deemed to be of historical significance. He had been working on a biography of President Grover Cleveland and found that Cleveland's associates had left few of the kinds of personal records—letters, diaries, memoirs—biographers generally rely on. Moreover, the increasing bureaucratization of public affairs was standardizing the paper trail, and the telephone was replacing personal correspondence. Nevins came up then with the idea of interviewing participants in recent history as a supplement to the written record. He conducted his first interview in 1948, with New York civic leader George McAneny, and both the Columbia Oral History Research Office—the largest archival collection of oral history interviews in the world—and the contemporary oral history movement were born. No similar apocryphal moment exists for oral history in Pennsylvania, though it is likely that the first tape-recorded interview in the state self-consciously defined as oral history and preserved for the historical record is a 1953 interview with Francis Perrine of Mercer County, conducted by Mae Beringer. Mr. Perrine was 104 years old at the time of the interview; and his recollections extend back to the mid-nineteenth century.

Early interviewing projects at Columbia and elsewhere tended to focus on the lives of the "elite," leaders in business, the professions, politics, and social life. But oral history's scope widened in the 1960s and 1970s, in response both to the social movements of the period and to historians' growing interest in the experiences of "non-elites." Interviews have been conducted with blue-collar workers, with racial and ethnic minorities, with women, with labor and political activists, and with a variety of local people whose experiences typify a given social experience. Similar in intent to the WPA interviews of the previous generation, this latter work especially has helped realize oral history's potential for restoring to the record the voices of the historiographically—if not

FROM PEASANT FARMER TO MILL FOREMAN

Among the sixteen local studies planned by the Federal Writers' Project in Pennsylvania was a multiethnic study of New Castle, a town dominated by the Carnegie Steel Company and called "Tin Plate Town" by project workers. On January 20, 1939, Steven Kantes was interviewed for this study by project worker John Slizeski, a local writer and member of New Castle's Slovak community. Warren V. Massaro, supervisor of the study, edited Slizeski's field notes for publication in the projected (and never completed) "Tin Plate Town" volume. The text below shows both Slizeski's original version of Kantes's account and Massaro's editorial changes; deletions from the original are crossed out, additions are in brackets. In addition to correcting grammatical errors and tightening Slizeski's prose, Massaro's editorial interventions emphasized Kantes as an immigrant success story, most notably concluding with his purported promotion to foreman—a fact not recorded in Slizeski's field notes. Perhaps more important, however, as with all the WPA life histories, the language here is the writer's and the editor's, not the speaker's.

In my interview with one of the [This story of a New Castle] Slovak[,] men in New Castle who is at the present time head foreman [in the tin house] at the Shenango tin m[M]ill, in the tinning department, he tells of his childhood days in his native country [is an illustration of the ambition and will to succeed which possessed many of the Slovak immigrants]. When he [this man] was a boy of twelve[,] he would go out [worked] in the fields [of his native land] and work for [often putting in] twelve and [to] fourteen hours a day without anything to eat while working [any food]. The horse [He would work with his father hauling timber from the forests,] and [the] wagon which they used to haul timber from the forest would sometimes stick [would be stuck] in the muddy roads two or three [four or five] times a day. When this occurred he would [Each time this happened, the timber would] have to [be] unload[ed, and reloaded when] the wagon before getting out of the mud, after freeing the wagon from the mud he would again load it with the timber [was free again]. When the [At the end of the]days work was over his father gave him the job of leading [the boy would have to take] the horses to their stables, which were a good distance [miles] away from his [their] home. He tells of [Often he would] sleeping near [in] the stables over night because the nights were too dark and the fields too muddy to travel home for a evenings rest.

One day when he had went to the [visited a nearby] city he [and] met a Jewish bartender whose son had a blacksmithshop. This man took a great interest in this [The boy wanted to learn a] trade and went about seeking the blacksmith shop [get away from the farm]. When he finally contacted the master of the shop, he was informed that his parents would have to sign a contract which gave the master of the shop all the power over the youngster for [The blacksmith agreed to take him on as an apprentice for] four years, he was to receive no [without] pay for his work during this length of time. In those four years he would become a skilled blacksmith and machinest. The boy's father did not [approve], want to sign the contract, the boy pleaded with his father to sign the contract for he knew he would like the blacksmith work better than working in the muddy fields all day without anything to eat. The father [but finally] signed the contract [papers releasing his son to the blacksmith.] and the boy worked very hard for [After] four years ~~to become a~~ [he had learned the trade of] blacksmith and a machine[ist]. ~~Becoming a good blacksmith and machinest he was offered a job which payed him~~ [and was employed at] a dollar and fifty cents ~~a~~ [per] week. When he ~~had reached the age of~~ [was] eighteen [years old], [he received a letter from] a friend ~~of his~~ in America ~~wrote him a letter stating~~ [which had told him] that he could [easily] earn a dollar a day ~~in America~~ [there]. ~~He set about~~ [The boy] borrow[ed]~~ing~~ money from ~~his~~ friends and ~~neighbors~~ [relatives] to ~~finance his way~~ [come] to America. ~~.~~ ~~It did not take him long to secure~~ [and soon found] a job ~~after his arrival in the new land of opportunity. His first job was in a glass factory where his daily wage was~~ [here which paid him] a dollar and twenty-five cents [a day].

One day ~~as~~ [when] he was passing ~~a~~ [the] tin mill ~~in order to get to a grocery store, a~~ [the] watchman ~~of the mill happened to see him pass and inquired~~ [on duty asked him] if he wanted a job [in the mill]. ~~This Slovak did~~ [The young man could] not understand ~~what he was saying he~~ [English and] thought ~~the man was~~ [he was being accosted by] a policeman because ~~he wore a~~ [the watchman was wearing a cap and] badge. One of ~~the men from his native~~ [his] country[men] explained ~~to him that the watchman had asked if he wanted a job. He~~ [things and the Slovak boy] took the job ~~because the tin mill was paying their laborers a dollar and forty cents a day~~ which [paid him fifteen cents a day more] ~~was a better wage~~ than he ~~was earning in the glass factory~~ [had been receiving]. [One day, a short time ~~A~~[a]fter [he had started] working in the [tin] mill[,] ~~for a short time~~ one of the machines broke. ~~and no one was around who could fix it.~~ A[nother] Slovak [workman] ~~who was working at this time~~ told the boss that a man from his ~~native~~ country could [do the] repair [work, since there was, at that time, no one else around to do it] ~~the machine if they would give him the required tools.~~ ~~Our informant~~ [The man] could not ~~speak~~ [as yet manage] the English language[,] so he drew pictures of the tools which he [would] need~~ed~~ ~~to fix the machine.~~ [When] ~~T~~[t]hese ~~tools~~ were ~~given~~ [brought] to him ~~and soon~~ [he repaired] the machine ~~was in running order.~~ ~~This led to his~~ [L]ater [he was] promot~~ion~~[ed to]~~and he was given a position as~~ millwright [and still later was made a foreman].

The author is indebted to James Abrams, whose "Composite Pennsylvania: Cultural Pluralism and WPA Folklife Programming in the Keystone State, 1936-1941" (Master's thesis, University of North Carolina at Chapel Hill, 1988) provided this example.

historically—silent. An oral history program brochure from the University of Pittsburgh in the 1970s expresses a point of view that has governed much of the oral history generated over the past three decades:

> Textbook history has frequently overlooked the stories of the working people who were the history—your parents and grandparents—people who had not time to write books. . . . Through tape-recorded interviews, we can begin to understand events through the life histories of those who were there. We can gather together an accurate history of all people, not merely the wealthy and powerful. Through oral history, our history becomes richer, documenting the struggles of ordinary people to build a nation. . . . History becomes our story.

Like President Cleveland's associates, few people leave self-conscious records of their lives for the benefit of future historians; some are illiterate, some too busy; some don't think of it; some simply don't know how. And many think—erroneously, to be sure—that they have little to say that would be of historical value. Although most people do show up in the public record, in the sorts of documents used by genealogists and described in Chapter 12, these records provide only the chronological skeleton of a life, with few details and little depth. By recording the firsthand accounts of an enormous variety of narrators, oral history has, over the past half-century, helped democratize the historical record.

PENNSYLVANIA COLLECTIONS

Even a cursory survey of existing oral history collections in Pennsylvania suggests something of its range. Early projects included a Bryn Mawr College initiative to document the history of the college as well as the achievements of distinguished alumnae; the United Steelworkers of America Project at Penn State, including almost 300 interviews with both union leaders and rank-and-file members; and a series of interviews conducted by the Pittsburgh Section of the National Council of Jewish Women to record the immigrant Jewish experience in that city. While the number of existing interviews with Pennsylvanians speaking on topics broadly related to the state's history is impossible to gauge accurately, it surely runs to several thousand. Appropriately enough given the state's history, many—perhaps the majority—focus on industrial and ethnic history. Major collections include those developed by the Ethnic Studies Program at the Pennsylvania Historical and Museum Commission under the leadership of John Bodnar during the 1970s and early 1980s and now maintained at the Pennsylvania State Archives; documentation projects conducted under the auspices of the Folklife Division of America's Industrial Heritage Project (more recently, the Southwestern Pennsylvania Heritage Preservation Commission) during the 1990s and available in the Special

Collections Division of the Stapleton Library at Indiana University of Pennsylvania; and several collections generated by individuals and institutions and preserved at the Archives of Industrial Society at the University of Pittsburgh.

Another important group of Pennsylvania collections focuses on community history. Housed at dozens of libraries, historical societies, and other local institutions around the state, these interviews typically recount stories of people, places, and activities that defined everyday life in a particular locale during the twentieth century. Many of these community collections have been developed by local groups seeking to document their own history, suggesting how oral history can democratize the process of doing history as well as the content of the history produced. Several colleges and religious orders in the state also have oral history collections documenting their institutional histories; Pennsylvania political history is the focus of several collections; the fiftieth anniversary of World War II stimulated a number of interviewing projects; and there are other collections too numerous to list, focusing on various, specific topics. It's anybody's guess how many interviews remain in private hands: the fruit of classroom assignments, family history projects, and independent research efforts. Indeed, researchers interested in *any* topic related to Pennsylvania's twentieth-century history would be well advised to search for relevant oral history collections, as well as to consider conducting a series of interviews with key individuals themselves.

Miner's wife preparing a bath for her husband, 1946.

ORAL HISTORY AND THE TELLING OF PENNSYLVANIA'S HISTORY

As the lengthy quotation that opens this chapter suggests, oral history affords the historian new information and fresh insights into the past, sometimes with visceral force. Mildred Allen Beik's *The Miners of Windber,* a study of community life and labor struggles in a Pennsylvania coal company town, relies on interviews for its detailed discussion of women's contributions to the family economy—no accident, given the scarcity of written sources on the subject. Consider the poignancy of the following interview excerpt quoted in Beik's work: "[The miners] came home, and [the wives] would get the big tub out, see. Then my Dad would wash up, down to his waist, and then they had

CONDUCTING AN ORAL HISTORY INTERVIEW

Conducting an oral history interview would appear to be a simple activity: after all, anyone can put a tape recorder in front of someone and ask that person to talk about his or her life. But appearances are deceiving. Doing a good interview, one that has historical merit and is useful to others, requires careful preparation, skillful interviewing, and conscientious follow-up. Several manuals providing guidance on everything from conducting a single interview to managing a multi-interview project are listed among the resources at the end of this chapter. Here are some guidelines to get you started interviewing.

Before the interview:

1. Develop a clear focus for the interview, a set of historical questions and topics you want to pursue. Too many interviews wander aimlessly from topic to topic with no apparent underlying purpose. Ask yourself the "So what?" question: Why is the topic of the interview important?

2. Learn all you can about the subject matter of the interview—the more you know, the more informed your interviewing will be, and the richer the resulting oral history. Read relevant secondary sources and review available primary sources.

3. Develop an outline for the interview. This should not be a set of specific questions, which can inhibit a free-flowing inquiry, but rather a road map, a list of topics and subtopics to guide the interview.

4. Contact the potential narrator in advance of the interview by letter or by telephone to secure his or her permission for an interview. Explain the purpose of the interview, the subjects you'd like to discuss, the uses to which the interview will be put, where the tapes and any other material will be located after the interview, and who will have access to the interview.

5. Once a person has agreed to an interview, conduct what oral historians call a "pre-interview." This is an informal conversation aimed at getting a feel for what the person knows about the topic at hand and finding out the basic biographical details of the person's life—when and where the person was born, who his or her parents were, what the person's educational, occupational, and residential history is, and so on—so that you have a framework for the interview.

6. Consider what personal biases you may bring to the interview and adjust your methodology accordingly.

7. Become familiar and comfortable with your recording equipment. Put an introduction on the tape, including your name and the narrator's name, the subjects of the interview, and the place and date of the interview.

During the Interview:

8. Structure the interview as a series of topical inquiries. Begin with broad, general questions: "Tell me something about . . ." "What is your understanding of . . . ?" Then gradually ask more specific questions to fill in the picture.

9. Stick to the narrator's firsthand experience. Don't ask the narrator for *the history* of some historical period or event; take him or her through a more-or-less chronological account of his or her own experience.

10. Ask open-ended questions that give the narrator lots of room to respond from his or her own perspective. Ask one question at a time. And don't ask leading questions—that is, questions that imply the answer you want.

11. Give the narrator time to answer a question, to gather thoughts and consider what he or she wants to say. Don't interrupt a narrator or jump in with another question when the narrator pauses.

12. Stay focused on the interviewee's narrative. Don't swap stories, respond with anecdotes of your own, or turn the entire interview into a pleasant little chat.

13. Don't be afraid of difficult and challenging questions. However, start with questions that will likely be easy for the narrator to answer and then move gradually into more sensitive topics. Ask difficult questions in a spirit of open inquiry. If the narrator seems to be avoiding a critical issue, refer to a third party ("I have read that . . . ," "Others have told me . . ."). Be judicious with adversarial questions.

After the Interview:

14. Have the narrator sign a release form, at minimum allowing you to use the interviews. Most narrators sign over copyright and ownership of the tape to the interviewer or sponsoring institution.

15. Label both the cassette tape or audio disk and its storage box with the names of the narrator and interviewer and the date and topics of the interview.

16. As a courtesy, give the narrator a copy of the interview tape or disk.

17. Consider transcribing the interview. If you don't have the time to transcribe or the money to pay someone else to do it, at least develop a running summary of topics discussed on the tape to facilitate access at a later time.

18. Consider ways to use the interview, to share what's on tape—or on a group of tapes—with others, through a publication, a media production, or some other means.

19. Place the interview or group of interviews in an archives or other public repository so others can have access to them.

what they call a *csutak*—Hungarian for a big soap rag. And my Dad would fold it up. It would be like a big pancake, yah, and [he'd] slap it on his back. That was the signal for my mother to scrub his back."

The new knowledge gained from oral history doesn't find its way only into books. Motivated by the absence of African American men in most accounts of the steel industry, as well as popular ignorance about black steelworkers' long and bitter struggle against discrimination in the mills, filmmakers Ray Henderson and Tony Buba interviewed dozens of African American steelworkers in Pittsburgh, Baltimore, Maryland, and Birmingham, Alabama. Their film, *Struggles in Steel,* is comprised almost entirely of excerpts from these interviews. Although some of what these narrators said can be gleaned from the written record, their deeply affecting stories of both individual and collective efforts to overcome racial barriers could not have been, nor could their particular perspective on work in an industry and in a society deeply divided by race.

Museums also have relied on oral history to amplify the record. For example, in the 1980s staff at the Kemerer Museum of Decorative Arts in Bethlehem interviewed people who had known and worked with its founding donor, Annie Susen Grim Kemerer. The goal was to learn more about Kemerer's life and collecting habits. Based on information gleaned from these interviews, the museum revised its tours to present a more accurate picture of Mrs. Kemerer. Gone was the wealthy connoisseur, replaced by a woman of comfortable means with eclectic, unschooled tastes; gone too were the anecdotal, and unsubstantiated, stories about specific objects.

The cumulative evidence of a body of interviews can also provide the basis for new interpretations of the past. The writing of history, like all intellectual work, is driven not only by the discovery of new information, new facts about the past, but also by new ways of thinking about that information, new ways of putting the facts together. For example, two books published in the mid-1980s, both drawing extensively on the evidence of oral history, vigorously disputed prevailing notions of early twentieth-century rural migrants and foreign immigrants to Pennsylvania as uprooted and alienated victims of circumstance, forever strangers in an unfamiliar world. This perspective perhaps quite logically derived from the sources traditionally used to write the history of these groups: public records chronicling individuals' encounters with established institutions—schools, courts, hospitals, welfare agencies—often as troublemakers or supplicants, and accounts of outside observers with little access to the interior life of the group.

Yet Peter Gottlieb, in his aptly titled study of black migrants from the South to Pittsburgh, *Making Their Own Way,* demonstrates how African Americans negotiated a harsh industrial system and actively transformed themselves from rural agricultural workers to members of the urban working class. Dispossessed from the land in the South, relegated to unskilled laboring jobs in the North, subjected to discrimination in housing and other areas of social life, the sixty-five African Americans he interviewed nonetheless talked about making choices that allowed them to create meaningful lives,

"Colored Men at Checkers, 17th Street above South Street, Philadelphia, September 28, 1938." Like Peter Gottlieb's interviews with Pittsburgh African Americans in the 1970s, this photograph, taken for the Pennsylvania Federal Writers' Project never-published study, "The Negro in Philadelphia," provides an intimate glimpse into the dense community life of Pennsylvania's urban blacks.

achieve dignity within their communities, pursue opportunity, and seek justice. Similarly, John Bodnar's *The Transplanted,* drawing in part on dozens of interviews conducted under the auspices of the Ethnic Studies Program of the Pennsylvania Historical and Museum Commission, argues that immigrants creatively adapted Old World culture to New World realities, working hard, relying on kin networks, and thereby fashioning a way of life and a place for themselves in the United States.

It is not difficult to understand how oral history opened Gottlieb and Bodnar to these new views of the past. In an interview, the voice of the narrator literally contends with that of the historian for control of the story. Recounting details of everyday life and making sense of personal experiences, narrators turn history inside out, demanding to be understood as purposeful actors in the past, not easily fitting into preexisting categories of analysis. Chapter 6, for example, describes the oppressive working conditions and constrained opportunities of young breaker boys in Pennsylvania's mines and the efforts of Progressive reformers to ameliorate the hard realities of the industrial system—for example, by working to abolish child labor. Yet child laborers understood their work somewhat differently—not as a social problem that needed to be solved, but as the accepted first step in a lifetime of labor. Their families likewise recognized the importance of establishing good work habits at an early age. Here is how Monsignor Joseph Miliauskas, who had worked as a breaker boy as a child, put it in a 1973 interview:

When . . . I got a job, I didn't tell my father and mother until I come home after . . . I was hired. The second day I came home from the breaker—you see, . . . when they unload that coal from the cars in the breaker, . . . you'll always find some rock mixed in with the coal. It's up to slate pickers . . . there'd be four, five slate pickers . . . to watch and get the slate out, pick it out of the shoot, throw it to the side there and let the clean coal go down. . . . It was our job to pick out all the slate because slate won't burn. And when you get slate in a ton of coal, . . . that one piece of slate will outweigh three or four or five pieces of coal the same size. And you're gypped . . . [and] people won't buy from you any more. And the boss is there right behind everybody with a broom. And if he catches you slipping up, letting some slate come down, boy, you'll get it in the back with a broom. Oh, he'll sock you—come right up if you're the first one and if you don't throw much slate. He'll come up there, let you have it. . . .

So, the second day, my fingers are all cut up, bleeding. I asked the boss if I could go home. He hit me with a broom: "You stay here." Twelve o'clock came, the whistle blew. I took my lunch pail and I go home. I come home and I said to my mother, "Mom, I'm not going back tomorrow to work any more." I says my fingers are all bloody. "Oh, yes, you are. We didn't tell you to get this job. You got it on your own. You started, you're gonna stay with it." So, I stayed home that afternoon, put some—I don't know what stuff—on my fingers. But I went back. And when you're there about two or three weeks, your fingers get hardened up. No more blood. And you get used to that. Some fellows get gloves, you know. And if you could spot the pieces of slate, you know, and pick them out with your gloves, okay, the boss will let you wear the gloves. But after you're there three or four weeks, your fingers get hardened up to that.

Furthermore, as Monsignor Miliauskas goes on to explain, work around the mines did not destroy the boys' rambunctious sense of fun:

You worked from seven o'clock until twelve, and then you had a half an hour to eat and back to work you go, [from] twelve-thirty, I think it was, [to] four-thirty. Yet in the breaker, you know, you'd eat your sandwich in no time, and you'd start playing tag and, honest to god, we knew every hole in that breaker. We'd hide and go through in complete darkness. The machinery, we'd be over it, around it, and everything else. You get to know it, you know, because everything stops during lunch hour, see. And you get to know all those holes and everything else. You're like a bunch of rats in that breaker.

Without denying the real abuses of child labor in an industrial system or questioning the motives of the reformers, oral history thus helps us understand the drive to abolish child labor as emblematic of broader social tensions over the proper role of children and the nature of childhood. Indeed, by opening up opportunities for all parties in any given historical situation literally "to speak their mind," oral history helps us understand how deeply conflicted our history has been.

Oral history can inform our understanding of Pennsylvania's history in yet another way. An interview is not simply a series of facts recalled about the past, but a structured story, an act of memory shaped as much by the moment of telling as by the history being told. Compressing years of living into a few hours of talk, a narrator selects, consciously and unconsciously, what to say and how to say it. The resulting narrative is unavoidably interpretive, an effort to impose order on experience, and hence an expression of identity and consciousness, culture and worldview. Interviews, for example, often include "moral tales," anecdotes of righteous action that suggest what narrators value. "One thing I'd like to tell about my grandmother," reminisced Louise Rhoads Dewees when queried in 1976 about her growing-up years, "she was not a very expressive person, but one time she heard of a family with three daughters about the same age as her own three daughters, who were in pretty hard straits. And she had just finished making three elegant, new costumes for her daughters, in the days when a dress . . . took a great deal of labor. And, instead of giving the three girls the discarded ones of her daughters, she gave them the three brand-new ones, which I've always liked to remember." In addition to expressing the value the narrator places on charity and self-denial, this story illustrates the way ancestors frequently figure as role models in our imagination. Similarly, several narrators, interviewed as part of a project to document the Society of Friends in Chester County, proudly describe ancestors' encounters with William Penn and other colonial Quaker worthies. Whether these stories are true or not is not the point; what is important is the way a family connection with Penn and his contemporaries supports the narrators' deep sense of Quaker identity.

Despite the specificity of these examples, it is impossible to identify anything uniquely "Pennsylvanian" in the hundreds of interviews conducted with state residents: existing interview collections are too idiosyncratic, the state's population is too diverse, the similarities to interviews done elsewhere in the United States are too obvious. Yet because so many oral history projects in Pennsylvania focus on blue-collar workers, these interviews can provide insight into the ways memories of the past become interpretations in the present, and thereby offer insight into some of the ways a reasonably broad swath of the state's population understands its world. If there is a single theme running through the interviews, it is the importance of "hard work" in the shaping of people's lives and identities. "Our people, . . . they're the ones who built the steel mills to what they are today," union activist Adam Janowski stated proudly and emphatically in a 1976 interview with historian James Barrett for the Homestead Album Oral History Project. "They took everything in stride, I tell you," he continued. "I seen them myself. I was a young man and I seen how hard those fellows used to work."

This observation is repeated in one way or another in interview after interview, and narrators' consciousness of "our people," in Adam Janowski's words, as hardworking undoubtedly reflects the material conditions of their lives. Yet Janowski, more explicitly than most, reveals a racial dimension to his understanding of "our people," whom he defined this way: "After the [1919 steel] strike they wanted to lay [African American strikebreakers] all off. At least they laid off ninety percent because the [white] men was experienced in their jobs and the foremen could call the white man a goddamn hunky and tell him to get that goddamn thing moving! But they couldn't say that to a black man. He would pick up a bar and hit him over the head, you know? Our people took that all the time. They're the ones who built the steel mills. . . ." Perhaps still bitter about black strikebreakers more than half a century later, undoubtedly mindful of the way "his people" indeed "took that all the time," perhaps reading black militance of the 1970s back a half-century, Janowski reveals the profound sense of alienation and difference that white Pennsylvanians have felt from black Pennsylvanians.

Almost twenty years later, Theresa Pavlocak, an elderly resident of eastern Pennsylvania, struck a similar theme when interviewed for historian Thomas Dublin's study of deindustrialization in the region. She remembered the Depression this way: "If you didn't have a job in the colliery, the men had no work. So they had WPA. They worked on the roads. You didn't get welfare. We never got the welfare. We did it the hard way." Further into the interview, she reflected on her generation's lifetime of labor: "People were proud; they didn't want no welfare. Not like now; people look for it. In those days, people were proud; they didn't want it." And toward the conclusion she commented on the success of her own and her friends' children and contrasted that with the circumstances of some "newcomers," often a euphemistic way of referring to recent African American and Latino migrants to the region: "It seems like [our] children are all [moved] away from here and it's just a new generation coming in here—different people. We have quite a bit of welfare. There's a lot of new people moving in on welfare—in order to help them, for them to pay the rent. They get their rent and a few dollars, whatever they get. If they're happy on welfare, I guess they stay there. Most of them don't want to, though. No. Like all my friends' children, they're all educated or they're away, they all have good jobs. My son, he has a good job."

Like Janowski, Pavlocak reveals both an identity grounded in a generation of people who indeed worked hard, and a sense of difference from "newcomers," who are sometimes not white and who presumably do not work as hard as they themselves have. For her, as Dublin has observed, the WPA of the 1930s, as well as the Social Security and Black Lung benefits that have more recently sustained many older people in northeastern Pennsylvania, are not understood as "welfare"; nor is the difficulty of obtaining work

in an era of deindustrialization understood as an explanation for "newcomers'" apparent lack of ambition. If we take Janowski's and Pavlocak's ways of viewing the past as fairly typical of their race, generation, and class, their interviews become a means of understanding how identity and memory are implicated in the racial politics and moral conservatism described in Chapter 7 as dominating state politics in the late twentieth century.

Reading a broad sampling of interview transcripts from oral history collections around the state also helps explain the localism that, if not uniquely Pennsylvanian, is certainly characteristic of much of the state's culture. In addition to focusing on hard work, narrators consistently formulate their stories of the past in terms of specific places. Memories are rooted in some place; interviews are replete with references to streams, hills, homes, streets, stores, churches, theaters, farms. In some interviews, local history is defined almost entirely in terms of specific places, quite independent of interviewers' questions. One interview, for example, began with the interviewer asking, "What do you remember about Middletown at that time [1912, when the narrator moved to the town]?" leaving the narrator ample room to define the way he would remember his community. His response: "I just don't know how to express it. It looked very much like it does now. We went to housekeeping at 329 North Union Street and lived there about eight years and then we moved here in this house at 37 Union Street and lived here ever since." He doesn't know how to respond, but then immediately orients his memories around the specific homes in which he has lived. Another narrator, when asked at the end of the interview to identify "three of your most memorable experiences in Hershey [the community under discussion]," responded by linking memories to specific places: marrying her husband at the First United Methodist Church, attending the groundbreaking for the Hershey Medical Center, and attending events at the Hershey Theater. More typically, talk on any subject is interlaced with place references, often resulting in lengthy catalogs of "what was where when" and "what was there then," and in painstaking efforts to identify the local coordinates of a specific site. Recollections of specific places often also lead to a chain of human associations, again suggesting narrators' need to place memories someplace. "When we moved back home at the hill from the Bard farm, I was eight years old," one narrator began. He continued:

> My mother raised turkeys. We used to carry them all the way from that hill, down across the old covered bridge to East Middletown and she sold them for eight cents a pound. . . . We'd cut back by Sam Seiders' farm and then we'd cut across old Ev Booser's farm in back of where Detweilers lived to the dam. . . . The Sam Demy farm later became Sam Seiders' farm and is now Simon Grubb's, Seiders' grandson's farm. Mrs. Seiders had a retarded brother. When [Sam] Hess [her father] sold to old man Bard, there was a $2,000 dowry set aside for this boy and the interest used for his keep. Sam Hess, before he died, had the stone house where Matt Seiders lived built for this boy. This was his home and the old mother's after the father died. When the mother died and he got worse, the relatives took turns with him, and Matt bought his house.

Here information about a woman's contribution to the family economy, the transmission of property, and the care of the disabled in a turn-of-the-century community are all embedded in a chain of associations about a specific piece of property. Whether as cause or effect, the profound attachment to place revealed in interviews helps explain the localism evidenced by the division of the state into more than 5,000 separate local jurisdictions in the Commonwealth, the difficulties bedeviling efforts at regional planning, and the strand of parochialism in Pennsylvania culture.

ISSUES IN ORAL HISTORY

For all its considerable value in deepening our knowledge and understanding of Pennsylvania's history, oral history is not an unproblematic enterprise, nor is it a source that "speaks for itself." In Pennsylvania, as elsewhere in the world, those who want to put oral history to its best use need to consider a number of archival, methodological, and interpretive issues. Archival concerns cluster around issues of access. Within the Commonwealth, as elsewhere, hundreds of oral history interviews conducted by individuals for their own research projects remain in private hands, simply inaccessible to others.

OPPOSITE: During the 1980s and 1990s, anthropologist Judith Modell and photographer Charlee Brodsky used photographs as a way to elicit memories of Homestead, a town hit hard by the demise of the steel industry in those years. Responses were varied and often paradoxical. Brodsky's contemporary photo of a town down on its luck (*top left*) sometimes evoked fond memories of better times, sometimes a chain of intimate associations, sometimes anger at the United States Steel Corporation for abandoning Homestead. Residents looking at older pictures of a grim and grimy place (*bottom left*) recalled the once vivid sense of community then. And those who grew up in Homestead and looked at formal family portraits (*top right*) recalled parents as hardworking, and working most of the time.

Insofar as this prevents others from examining the sources from which a historical account has been constructed, it violates the principle of equal access to sources that is fundamental to historical inquiry in a democratic society. It also prevents others from building on these sources and can lead to duplication of efforts. Other interviews, conducted under institutional auspices and nominally available to others, nonetheless languish in file cabinets and on shelves, unindexed, uncataloged, untranscribed—and hence unnoticed and unused. Here the development of even minimal procedures for gaining intellectual control over the interviews and rudimentary finding aids is called for.

Most oral history specialists recommend transcribing interviews—that is, creating a verbatim written version of the taped conversation—to enhance accessibility, for it is much more efficient to read a transcript than to listen to a tape. However, a transcript only approximates what is on the tape: while it may get the words right (although a surprising number of transcripts do not), it fails to convey meaning that is expressed by tone of voice, the pacing of speech, and other sonic but not verbal information. Irony, for example, is often communicated in speech by inflecting certain words or phrases, and thus can be lost as these words are translated into writing. Increasing use of the Internet to present the taped as well as transcribed versions of an interview may help restore oral history to its aural origins, though oral historians are legitimately concerned about the potential for embarrassment and misuse arising from unrestricted web access to interviews.

A final issue raised by the aural nature of oral history is sound quality. Project planners have tended to slight the importance of good equipment and technical skill in the actual recording of an interview, and as a result many existing interviews are difficult to hear, thereby inhibiting access. As new technologies increasingly allow for the presentation of the recorded voice, attention to the quality of the recording itself is becoming an important element of oral history.

Interviews, both collectively and individually, are only as good as the methodology employed in gathering them. While there is no such thing as a perfect interview, the best interviews are intellectually focused inquiries conducted by informed, perceptive interviewers. Unfortunately, much oral history, including some in Pennsylvania collections, is needlessly mediocre, the result of faulty project design and flawed interviewing strategies. An interview project—that is, a collection of interviews on a given topic—can be defined too narrowly, on specific questions of interest to an individual researcher, or, as is more often the case, too broadly, with no clear set of historical questions driving the inquiry. A narrowly defined project may serve a specific research agenda, but it is a missed opportunity to enhance the historical record. The individual interviews in such a project also tend to be interpretively thin. By failing to place recollections of specific events within the broader trajectory of a narrator's life, we lose proportion, context, and an understanding of how subsequent events shape the narrator's current understanding of the past. Political interviews are especially prone to these problems: a person is interviewed about participation in a political event or movement, or because of a relationship to a political figure, but how this episode or person figures into the narrator's life over time is ignored.

More typical, however, are oral history projects that are diffused, even random, inquiries. In these cases, project planners did not first identify just what they wanted to learn about the past from the interviews, and so did not think through what questions to ask. Most especially, they ignored the "So what?" question—that is, why are the topics under discussion important in the first place? Community-based oral history projects are frequently plagued by such problems. Local history is often defined as a series of mundane facts about the past in a given locale, and rather than as key relationships and issues that have shaped and defined life in that place. Furthermore, all too often narrators are selected from among the people who have lived longest in the area rather than for the variety of perspectives they can bring to the topic at hand. The interviews themselves tend to wander from topic to topic, replete with details of everyday life in the past but with little clear sense of what those details add up to.

Alice Hoffman, at the time coordinator of Penn State University's Steelworkers' Oral History Project, interviews two members of the United Steelworkers of America. Hoffman has reflected on how her father's position as director of social insurance activities for the American Federation of Labor (and, after 1955, the AFL-CIO) from 1944 to 1956 helped open doors as she began interviewing steelworkers: "The labor movement . . . is rather like an extended family, that is, for the people who were on the staff and the people who were organizing. . . . They were trade union activists, and their allegiance was to some kind of concept of collective action. They called each other 'Brother' and 'Sister.' When I first started this project one of the advantages that I had was that wherever I went with trade union activists, I was a universal daughter, and that's because most of the people knew who my father was, and admired him. That enabled me to get information that I think another researcher would not have access to."

While careful planning can avoid many of these problems at the outset, skillful interviewing is also an important component of good oral history methodology. An interview is always a dialogue: the questions of the interviewer elicit certain responses from the narrator, which in turn shape the interviewer's subsequent questions, and on and on. But an interview is always something of an improvisation. The interviewer can—and should—be both knowledgeable about the subject under discussion and well prepared for each interview. The subtleties of the interpersonal exchange (a certain phrase might evoke a particular response, or a certain tone of voice set up a particular dynamic) and the overall context of the interview (such as the narrator's general frame of mind or the interviewer's level of anxiety about probing the past) also contribute to the overall outcome of an interview. The best interviews have a measured, thinking-out-loud quality, as perceptive questions work and rework a particular topic, encouraging the narrator to remember details, seeking to clarify that which is muddled, making connections among seemingly disparate recollections, challenging contradictions, evoking assessments of what it all meant in the past and what it means now. The best interviewers listen carefully between the lines of what is said for what the narrator is trying to get at, and then have the presence of mind, and sometimes the courage, to ask the hard questions. Yet too often out of inattention or ignorance or discomfort the interviewer avoids critical inquiry, seemingly satisfied with superficial, self-justifying, nostalgic, or simply incomplete responses.

Consider the following excerpt from an oral history project documenting twentieth-century life in a town in central Pennsylvania. The narrator, a lifetime resident of the town and owner of a small business started by his father, is recounting his mental map of the community at an undetermined time in the past. He begins with topography and physical features and then moves into social geography and observations about ethnicity:

> INTERVIEWER: You just talked about neighborhoods. Were there a lot of ethnic neighborhoods?
> NARRATOR: Yes—
> INTERVIEWER: Was there an Irish enclave?
> NARRATOR: Yeah. Let me put it this way. St. Catherine's Church was out, which is now out on East Lincoln Street, way out, that's Lincoln and Cedar, they had all the Italian people. The oldest Catholic church was St. Mary's down on Green Street. . . . 1741, that was the oldest Catholic church in the city and the county. St. Mary's—that's the one with the cemetery up the street there. They were all Irish, in the beginning they were all Irish.
> INTERVIEWER: Was there ever an Oriental population?
> NARRATOR: No.

The interviewer then asks, "Mostly European?" and the narrator offers the following unsolicited commentary:

> Yes. This is what happened in the city today. We never had anything, problems that they have today. I don't know why people are down on Puerto Ricans, but they are in this city.

Clearly, he, like many, is troubled by contemporary ethnic relations and, also like many, recalls a past when social life seemed less stressful. This is on his mind, and it comes out without anyone asking. But then in a classic example of avoiding difficult lines of inquiry, the interviewer's next question is a complete non sequitor: "How about the fire brigades?" The narrator responds obligingly with appropriate information, and the discussion quickly shifts to a less difficult topic. Similar failures to listen carefully and ask the hard questions mar too many interviews.

Finally, those interested in a fuller understanding of interviews as a historical source might appropriately consider a range of interpretive issues. As suggested in the discussion about the contributions of oral history to Pennsylvania's history, interviews are increasingly understood not so much as exercises in fact-finding, to be evaluated for their accuracy as measured against some external standard, but as interpretive, or subjective, documents, to be analyzed for their meaning. There is a growing literature on the interpretive complexities of oral history interviews, some of it listed among the sources at the end of this chapter. Much of this literature begins with certain premises: that an interview is, above all, a storied account of the past recounted in the present; that it is a response to a particular person and to that person's questions, as well as to the narrator's inner needs to make sense of experience; and that what is said draws on the narrator's linguistic conventions and cultural assumptions. A good way to begin to analyze an interview, or group of interviews, then, is to consider who is saying what, to whom, and for what purpose.

Let us end where we began and subject Patricia Fabiano's interview with Dolores Bordas Kosko to critical analysis. Recall that Kosko's account of her family and work history is excerpted from interviews that focused on her participation in a club of women who have met informally every month for more than four decades. It is one of several interviews Fabiano conducted with the club's seven members for a study of the relationship between informal support systems and health, understood as a sense of coherence and well-being. Fabiano is a good interviewer. She is prepared and has prepared Kosko for the interview by explaining the purpose of her study. Long acquainted with Kosko and knowledgeable about but not part of her world, she is deeply respectful and appreciative of the club. She assumes its value for its members and wants to understand how it works to enhance health. She also wants to situate the story of the club in broad biographical and social—that is, historical—context. These preconditions to the interview create enormous rapport and set the stage for creative inquiry.

Much of the richness of Kosko's account comes from her effort to address Fabiano's questions (regrettably not included in the edited transcript) thoughtfully and honestly. The framing questions Fabiano brings to the study also provide a way for Kosko to draw on an interesting repertoire of both personal and social explanations as she puts her life into words. Like most people speaking within the individualizing framework of an interview, Kosko presents herself as the hero of her own story, a sturdy survivor and ethical person who will finish a job even when laid off and who cannot lie in a way that she feels would be necessary for a career in sales.

The assumptions of the study also work to create a self-consciously progressive narrative shaped around the theme of growing confidence and autonomy. Not incidentally, this theme resonates with contemporary feminism, which has validated women's aspirations, and the right of married women to work outside the home. Though Kosko would not likely identify herself as a feminist, the assumptions and language of feminism inflect her account. And when Kosko's very identity is challenged by the loss of her job, she explains the limited options and missed opportunities in her life in terms of both personal limits ("I don't think I was mature enough [to go to college at eighteen]") and the constraints imposed by her family's class position ("My parents really couldn't afford it").

To assess the interview in this way does not reduce it to an exercise in good feeling or in telling the interviewer what she wants to hear. Nor does it suggest that it is in any way untruthful, or that all interviews are equal; some are richer, more thoughtful, more insightful than others, offering up more for historical analysis. Rather, it helps us understand how deeply situated, contingent, and subjective oral history is as a source for Pennsylvania history.

SOURCES *and* FURTHER READING

Abrams, James Francis. "Composite Pennsylvania: Cultural Pluralism and WPA Folklife Programming in the Keystone State, 1936–1941." Master's thesis, University of North Carolina at Chapel Hill, 1988.

Beik, Mildred Allen. *The Miners of Windber: The Struggles of New Immigrants for Unionization, 1890s–1930s.* University Park: The Pennsylvania State University Press, 1996.

Bodnar, John. *The Transplanted: A History of Immigrants in Urban America.* Bloomington: Indiana University Press, 1985.

Coles, Robert. *Doing Documentary Work.* New York: Oxford University Press, 1997.

Dublin, Thomas. *When the Mines Closed: Stories of Struggles in Hard Times.* Photographs by George Harvan. Ithaca: Cornell University Press, 1998.

Fabiano, Patricia. "The First Thursday Girls' Club: A Narrative Study of Health and Social Support in a Working-Class Community." Ph.D. dissertation, Graduate School of the Union Institute, 1999.

Frisch, Michael. *A Shared Authority: Essays on the Craft and Meaning of Oral and Public History.* Albany: State University of New York Press, 1991.

Gottlieb, Peter. *Making Their Own Way: Southern Blacks' Migration to Pittsburgh, 1916–1930.* Urbana: University of Illinois Press, 1987.

Henderson, Ray, and Tony Buba, producers. *Struggles in Steel: The Fight for Equal Opportunity* (film). San Francisco: California Newsreel, 1996.

Kuhn, Cliff, and Marjorie L. McLellan, eds. *Magazine of History* 11 (Spring 1997). Special issue on oral history for secondary and undergraduate teachers.

Mercier, Laurie, and Madeline Buckendorf. *Using Oral History in Community History Projects.* Los Angeles: Oral History Association, 1992.

Modell, Judith. *A Town Without Steel: Envisioning Homestead.* Photographs by Charlee Brodsky. Pittsburgh: University of Pittsburgh Press, 1998.

Oblinger, Carl. *Interviewing the People of Pennsylvania.* Harrisburg: Pennsylvania Historical and Museum Commission, 1978.

Pennsylvania History 60 (October 1993). Special theme issue on oral history in Pennsylvania, edited by Linda Shopes.

Perks, Robert, and Alistair Thomson. *The Oral History Reader.* New York: Routledge, 1998.

Portelli, Alessandro. *The Battle of Valle Giulia: Oral History and the Art of Dialogue.* Madison: University of Wisconsin Press, 1997.

———. *The Death of Luigi Trastulli and Other Stories: Form and Meaning in Oral History.* Albany: State University of New York Press, 1991.

Ritchie, Donald A. *Doing Oral History.* New York: Twayne Publishers, 1995.

Thompson, Paul. *The Voices of the Past: Oral History.* Second edition. New York: Oxford University Press, 1988.

Yow, Valerie Raleigh. *Recording Oral History: A Practical Guide for Social Scientists.* Thousand Oaks, Calif.: Sage Publications, 1994.

Literature

DAVID DEMAREST

WORKERS, WORKPLACES

In *Patches of Fire* (1997), his powerful memoir about the Vietnam War and its impact on his later life, Pittsburgh writer Albert French describes his first night's battlefield duty: posted alone to man a hilltop lookout near Chu Lai.

> I could hear the sounds of ammo belts shaking and the sudden sound of some-one rolling or climbing. Then I could see ahead, I could see the hole in the ground. It looked like a small circle of darker blackness. I could see Wiggins and someone with him as I neared the hole.
>
> "Okay, it's your watch," Wiggins was whispering back to me.
>
> "Okay," I whispered.
>
> I was there now, still on my knees, peering down into the hole. I could not see the bottom of it. I eased myself into it and found I could stand; it was chest deep.
>
> "See ya at chow," Wiggins whispered as they began crawling away. I watched them crawl until I couldn't see them. Then I listened to their sounds until I could no longer hear them. . . .
>
> I stood, staring and looking around, trying to see into the black shapes, trying to take them apart and put them back together in my mind so I could

I was grown tired of London, remembered with pleasure the happy months I had spent in Pennsylvania, and wished again to see it. (c. 1725)

—BENJAMIN FRANKLIN, *The Autobiography*

tell what they were. Without knowing, remembering when, at what moment, I had pointed the rifle into the dark and gripped it tightly. Now, very slowly and without taking my eyes from the dark, I eased my hand from the foregrip of the rifle and very slowly reached in my pockets and gently pulled the grenades out, one by one, remembering that I had not taped them. I placed them on the edge of the hole and quietly put my hand back on the rifle.

Something moved and was moving toward me, in me. It moved slowly, but I could feel it. I steadied myself and kept my eyes on the night.

French's style is startling in its unrelenting simplicity, in the exactness of its physical detail. The reader, with the actor, is thrust against a frightening problem. The ever-so-careful gestures spell out the fierce control, never to be relaxed for a moment, that French knows he must exert if he is to get himself and his squad through this night alive—and then the days and weeks ahead.

Is this memoir, about war in a far-off place, "Pennsylvania literature" in any particular way? I would argue, yes. French is a native Pittsburgher, and the state's young people, especially those from working-class and/or minority families, served in large numbers in Vietnam, as well as in other U.S. wars. But in *Patches of Fire* it is above all the pressured concentration on "facts," on a world of physical problems that must be mastered by skill and endurance, that recalls the worlds of other Pennsylvanians—for example, William Z. Foster's 1890s apprenticeship in Philadelphia's harrowing workplaces described in *Pages from a Worker's Life* (1939), or Michael Musmanno's account in his novel *Black Fury* (1966) of a boy's initiation into underground mining. Or Thomas Bell's vision.

In a brilliant short story, "Zinc Works Craneman to Wed" (*Story*, May–June 1939), Thomas Bell follows the automobile ride of two couples up the Monongahela River, from Braddock to Donora, in the late 1930s. As they near their destination, their casual chatter turns more and more to the groom-to-be's job as overhead crane operator.

"I'll tell you what gets me," Dave said. "I can stand the dust and the smoke and the wet days, but what gets me is when something goes wrong and I have to walk that rail. The damn crane never breaks down near a ladder. So I have to get out and walk that rail. It ain't a foot wide and it's easy thirty feet above ground. I'm no iron worker and I'm telling you my knees are shakin' when I reach the ground."

"I'll have to come down and watch you sometime," Johnny said. "It ought to be good."

"Then I have to walk it again with the electrician or the millwright, and if he decides he needs something who goes for it? Me. I come back with my hands full, which just makes it that much better. If it's cold weather there's just enough frost on the rail to make the goin' good. . . ."

Johnny laughed.

Sitting in the front seat, the men joke nervously, with a touch of bravado. This is work they can deal with, though Dave needs something better, safer—soon. The women, in the back seat, are fearful and angry. "You get out of the zinc works altogether," the bride-to-be, Mary, calls out. "That's all I ask."

In the story's last paragraph, Bell abruptly shifts from the male point of view and looks through Mary's eyes: "During the day I'll think of him in that crane, working; and late in the afternoon, with the house smelling of supper, I'll stand behind the curtains in the front room, watching the street, waiting for him to come around the corner." Moral of story: Women too pay a price for these physically punishing traditional male jobs.

The fatality that drives French's style in *Patches of Fire* also hangs over Bell's story. These are classic twentieth-century workplaces—battlefields, heavy industry—with their risky topographies, dangerous machines, and remote and often adversarial managers. (Bell's cousin, Ray Shedlock, whom Bell incautiously mentions by name in the story, was summoned by Donora's real-life zinc mill superintendent and warned against "talking to writers"—if he wanted to keep his job.)

Both French and Bell characterize job choices made in their generations by many Pennsylvanians. Often there was little choice. Jobs were tight in a town like Donora in the 1930s. The mill was the main opportunity; after all, a dangerous job in the zinc works was—a job. In the early 1960s, when French came of age, skilled work in steel was still not likely for African Americans. As a seventeen- or eighteen-year-old, French saw few opportunities: "June 1962, graduation time, and what? The mills, the service, the streets—fuck school, I was too dumb and poor anyway." He joined the Marines.

Literary accounts suggest that a kind of stoic work ethic took over in those who endured in industrial blue-collar jobs. In her book *Singing the City* (1998), Laurie Graham sums up by quoting a Pittsburgh steelworker: "'The point of this place,' he said, 'is that this is what life is and you just do it. It's what your dad does, your neighbor does, it's just the deal. No one whined and cried.'" Graham admires this no-nonsense view that she finds in blue-collar Pittsburghers, as well as the skills called forth by some industrial work.

The poet Peter Blair, perhaps a decade younger than French—young enough to be a grandson of Bell—presumably had more career choices than many who came of age before the 1960s. But his family roots were blue-collar: one of his grandparents worked in the zinc mill at Slovan in Washington County. His book *Last Heat* (2000) is a meditation on blue-collar inheritance, why its work ethic and workplaces must be explored critically, but honored. In the last two-thirds of a seventy-line narrative poem titled "Changing Rolls on the Universal Mill," Blair describes his delicate, frightening task inside a steel-rolling machine.

> I crawl on boards laid over the rolls,
> ease my ankles into dark spaces.

Above me, the cable hook swings
lower, closer. Inside
the stand's sweltering chamber,
I worm to the sawed-off, barrel-round chunk,
touch its fire-cracks with a glove,
feel its warm breath.

Between vertical rolls
that could labor me like a hot ingot
into one dimension,
I inch my shoulders up. Bearings
ooze grease. Water drips.
Chains cling tense to gears.
On my belly, I grab the hook,
yell to the crane. No one hears.
Nowhere to look but up
into the steep well of the machine shafts,
past girders and darkness
to the halogen stars.

Inside the universal mill
I fit my body to the curves and teeth
its operators never see.
That machine turns us all
in its cogs & gears. I feel its loneliness,
wonder how I'll go back on break
to my chipped ham sandwich,
and warm Coke black as grease,
the men joking & complaining.

Lower it! The cable coils.
I bring it under, graze my back
on the roll's moist girth.
I wriggle, stand, hook it, and squirm out
onto the cool mill floor,
back among men.
The broken pillar arcs above me,
sways on its cable,
trailing splintered shadows.

I don't know yet what I'm seeing
when they set it down in sunlight

near the mill door for inspection,
analysis, and scrap, or what impressions
the roll is making on my body,
still wet and warm with its touch.

Blair's experience is evoked in details that present a real—a detailed, physical—workplace. But his language enlarges the experience. This is engorgement by a giant machine ("inside / the stand's sweltering chamber / I worm") that can crush him in his puny isolation ("vertical rolls / that could labor me like a hot ingot / into one dimension"). In this guise the mill becomes a machine of fate (a "*deus ex machina*"?): "Inside the universal mill / . . . That machine turns us all in its cogs & gears. I feel its loneliness." There's no heaven to appeal to here: "No one hears. / Nowhere to look but up / into the steep well of the machine shafts, / past girders and darkness / to the halogen stars" (not *heavenly* stars).

Still, the machine, as Blair imagines it, is also a woman—a mother or a lover. As the men approach to start the job, an earlier stanza notes, "*First we undress her,*" and sexual, anthropomorphic suggestions follow: the machine's "warm breath," "curves and teeth," "moist girth," "wet, warm . . . touch," etc. When the narrator finally emerges into the light, it's almost like birth: "I don't know yet what I'm seeing."

The overall effect of this poem's very up-close workplace report—in the context of Blair's book as a whole—is to suggest a kind of love / fear / fascination in the workers' regard for these giant machines. The poem is a tribute to the monumentality of industrial work and the pressures its workers dealt with daily: a tribute from a postindustrial son and grandson to his forebears' world. And Blair makes it amply clear that his family left him no choice: he *had* to work in the mill during off-months in his higher education, because otherwise his father and brother would taunt him mercilessly. In a poem titled "Beneficiation," set in a sinter plant, Blair recalls: "That spring, / I'd graduated high school. My father insisted / the mill would make me a man." The epigraph for "Beneficiation"—underscoring the metaphor—is a quotation from *The Making, Shaping, and Treating of Steel:* "Beneficiation: controlled burning of iron ore to make it desirable feed for a blast furnace."

Part of this workplace scene is the anger of class. Sorting through the topography of the steel mill, Blair suggests the fissures of class division. When the top roll of the universal mill breaks, "the white hats / come down from the pulpit" and hover over the job. One by one, the crew all make their excuses to avoid crawling into the hot machine; finally they get to low man on the totem pole—"Okay Blair, you're it." Ultimately, Blair understands that this workplace will always make him choose sides. In another poem ("Coke Man"), when a white hat calls him off the job for a moment and starts a friendly conversation, he feels fear—"fear, orange / as my hard hat, that I'll [have to] spend each morning / alone with him: informant, suck-up, boyfriend." In "Furnace Greens," about working at the blast furnace complex in Rankin, Blair sums up—

I drove home with explosions
ringing in my ears, my lips blackened by soot,
eyebrows and nose hairs singed.
Army vets would fit right in. They knew the slang,
the smoldered deference to authority,
the snicker and snort as the foreman left
the room. They knew it was war.

Another western Pennsylvania poet of Blair's generation, Jan Beatty, reports her experience as a woman from a blue-collar background who also is moving toward middle-class roles. In her case, she kept herself going early on with such jobs as waitressing. Like the mill, the restaurant in the poem "Awake in a Strange Landscape," in *Mad River* (1995), is a geography of class differences:

I work with people too young to remember
Vietnam, or even Watergate.
They speak in airy voices of becoming
accountants, going into advertising.
They say it must have been neat
to live in the sixties.
   The black cooks rap to L. L. Cool J in the kitchen.

The fat woman wants to order half of a grilled sandwich.
I tell her we will have to throw the other half away.
She says that's okay, waving her diamond hands,
her Talbot's bag at her side.
   I am heaping trash on the dishwasher.
   He is still singing under piles of remains,
   wet cigarettes soaked with coffee,
   everything that is used.
   With strong black arms, he scrapes the blood-
   colored lipstick from wine glasses
   for three dollars an hour.

The waitresses are talking about how fat they are,
about working out, about spring break,
about the real job they will get.

In the "service" economy too, the unbeautiful hierarchy of the American workplace unfurls.

The hierarchies of work—in factories, offices and eating-places—are structured across the residential landscape in topographies of class, race, and ethnicity. The geography of home life—its boundaries, segregations, and exclusiveness—is one of literature's great subjects. Novels and stories about Pennsylvania bristle with insistence that readers step across borders and experience places they would never in real life enter, be invited to—or perhaps dare to go.

The work of John Edgar Wideman is an example, meditating as it does in an ongoing series of fictions and memoirs, on race and racism in both Pittsburgh and Philadelphia. The first chapter of Wideman's *Two Cities* (1998) conjures up the legendary MOVE leader John Africa walking on Philadelphia's Spring Garden Street Bridge, near Powelton Village—a route that's "a no-man's-land shortcut to cross the river into center city" passing over "vacant lots, abandoned warehouses, long, low sheds like airplane hangars, barbed-wire-topped Cyclone fences guarding acres of rusting junk." Sometimes a cop car slows to a crawl, scoping out African American walkers: "If they say you are in the wrong place, you're in the wrong place. Doesn't matter how old and harmless you are, if they want to teach a lesson you'll never forget, the ground opens up, people fall through and keep on falling and who knows where you'll land." The narrator (here a photographer named Martin Mallory who joins John Africa on his walks) recalls that "before they built the high-rise dormitories for the tech college you could walk north from Powelton Village to the zoo or east to the art museum and not be bothered." Now it was a dangerous crossing, "walking through that hive of buildings where students live, a black man with no business except passing through where he's not supposed to be anyway." A MOVE home in Powelton Village was the target of a police attack in 1978. Later John Africa would be killed (presumably) with ten others in the 1985 police firebombing of MOVE's house on Osage Avenue—an act of official terror to which Wideman has repeatedly returned in his fictions. In Mallory's words: "Just got to let people know a war's on. Gotta let folks in the Village, the whole city see for themselves what we're all up against."

In the Pittsburgh Wideman depicts in his fiction, the "Village" in effect becomes Homewood, another real-life, inner-city neighborhood: a mile long, a half-mile wide, bounded on the south by the main line of the Pennsylvania Railroad, on the north by steep hills that look down on their wooded far side into the Allegheny Valley. The grid of blocks highlighted by Wideman retains actual names: Finance, Susquehanna, Tioga, Cassina—small streets and alleys that are intersected by larger, north-south avenues: Homewood, Braddock, Brushton.

The key marker, the boundary, is the railroad tracks: a high embankment—a wall— that runs west and southeast as far as the eye can see. The tracks signal a safety zone to a pedestrian black man. A memorable vignette in *Sent for You Yesterday* (1983) shows Albert Wilkes returning home: the jazzman, the dandy, the fugitive who had shot a cop (evidently in self-defense) seven years ago and fled. Now, in 1934, on Homewood Avenue, Wilkes crosses "through the deep shadow under the railroad bridge and he knew he was in Homewood again. Sure he had made it back. This was the exact place, this daylight after the dark tunnel, this door you pushed through to get into Homewood, this line you stepped over." Crossing into Homewood—where people know, respect, and are a bit afraid of him—Wilkes may find a degree of safety: camaraderie and even protection from an old friend like John French, who when they were younger shared his taste for women and wine.

What the novel makes quickly clear, however, is that Wilkes brings danger with him; he does not want to play it safe. His image demands that he dress conspicuously, that he resume his piano-playing, that he cross the tracks in the opposite direction to restart an affair with a white woman up on Thomas Boulevard. French counsels caution but knows better: "You never could tell Albert Wilkes nothing. . . . John French stings the gray pavement exactly where he was aiming. Wine color, blood color . . . that be all that's left of Albert when they catch him up on Thomas Boulevard." Wilkes is a foil to French, who now, in middle age, is a conservative family man. For French the pressing boundaries are economic. To support his family, he is a craftsman, a plasterer, who in this segregated system works as a day-laborer, doomed to wait every morning "on the corner of Frankstown and Homewood where the white men drive up in their trucks with that little piece of work you might get if you're lucky, if you're early and smile and act like Jesus hisself behind the wheel of them pickups. Grin like the white man gon carry you to Great Glory but you knowing all the time he gon take you to some piece of job and pay you half what he pays his own kind." Wilkes, who has seen pictures of medieval torture, tells his friend: "They got us on a rack, John French. They gon keep turning till ain't nothing connected where it's supposed to be."

Despite these racist pressures, in *Sent for You Yesterday* Wideman finds great strength in the families of Homewood before World War II. The Campbells, the Tates, and centrally Freeda and John French are strong, loving couples and parents. Freeda watches the neighborhood for potential threats to her husband and her four children, especially the boy Carl—"Told him a million times to stay off those tracks." Now that Wilkes is back, her overriding anxiety is that Wilkes will lead John French into trouble. In a long sentimental exchange at the end of the first half of the novel, Freeda pleads with her husband to stay home, not to respond when Wilkes tempts him. French defends Wilkes, but agrees. He thinks of the sunset he's just watched from the porch. "I'll stay," he tells her, and they sit down together, listening for the children.

In the first half of *Sent for You Yesterday,* Wideman sees segregation as both a curse and a blessing:

I think of my grandmother and grandfather and the children they were raising in that house on Cassina and I see islands, arks, life teeming but enclosed or surrounded or exiled to arbitrary boundaries. And the city around them which defined and delimited, which threatened but also buoyed and ferried them to whatever unknown destination, this city which trapped and saved them, for better or worse, never quite breached Cassina's walls.

By contrast, in the second half of the novel, ranging from the 1940s to the early 1970s, Homewood is shown unraveling from the impact of a variety of factors: hardcore drugs; the erosion of local, mainstreet shopping; the new availability of some public facilities (for example, institutionalization of old-age and mental patients), which ironically seem to undercut the neighborhood's collective sense of responsibility. Above all, there is the continuing failure of real economic opportunity in the larger society. The career of Carl French, John's son, is symbolic. As a returned veteran of World War II, he decides to become an art student at Carnegie Tech, but his white professor warns him away: "'Companies don't hire colored artists.' He didn't say nigger artists but that's what he meant." Carl drops his effort to make it in the mainstream.

The three major characters in the last half of the novel—Carl and his best friends Brother and Lucy Tate (who's also his lover)—are attractive figures, but all are unable to cope with the slow deterioration of their inner-city neighborhood. Brother Tate, in effect, commits suicide, repeating as an adult a fatal version of the game he and Carl played as children: jumping across the tracks at the last possible second in front of an oncoming train. Carl and Lucy's long love for each other is a hopeful note, but unlike the extended families they descend from, they live separately and have no children. In the early 1970s, Lucy's sense of the inner-city village harks back to their parents' generation: "They made these streets. That's why Homewood was real once. Cause they were real. And we gave it all up. Us middle people. You and me, Carl. We got scared and gave up too easy and now it's gone. Just sad songs left."

While Wideman's Homewood was eroding in the 1950s and 1960s, just a few blocks south (across the tracks) a grid of all-white, middle-class streets was mostly prospering. Annie Dillard's memoir, *An American Childhood* (1987), written about the small Pittsburgh neighborhood of Point Breeze, is a counterpoint to Wideman's work. Dillard is the same generation as Wideman, and like him a child of the inner city who eventually left the region to make her own career. But the contrast between the neighborhoods they write about is stark. Observed on the map, the carry-through of north-south street names perversely underscores the abruptness of class and race differentials. Richland Street north of the tracks—in Homewood—cuts across blocks of small frame or brick row-houses; two blocks south of the tracks, Richland reemerges as Richland Lane, a private, dead-end street of middle-class homes that become quite stately at the far end (one of the locations where Dillard's well-off family—inheritors of corporate wealth—lived when she was a child).

An American Childhood is episodic, and many of its small events and situations invite juxtaposition to *Sent for You Yesterday*. Dillard opens with the men going off to work in the morning—to banks and corporate offices. She stresses their cars: "The men left in a rush; they flung on their coats, they slid kisses at everybody's cheeks, they slammed house doors; they ground their cars' starters till the motors caught with a jump." In a telling metaphor, she notes that after the men drive off "every woman stayed alone in her house in those days, like a coin in a safe"—a far cry from Wideman's emphasis on the women of Cassina Way "stationed" in their windows, watching for problems, while their men wait on street corners hoping for day-jobs. In Homewood, the neighborhood bars are recreational gathering places; by contrast Dillard remembers: "Bars were so far from our experience that I . . . assumed, in my [make-believe] detective work, that their customers were ipso facto crooks." The Dillard family drove to a country club, at an unspecified location, for recreation. In Dillard's careful world, the official route for disciplining the sexuality of growing kids was "dancing school . . . Friday after Friday, for many years until the distant and seemingly unrelated country clubs took over the great work of providing music for us later and later into the night until the time came when we should all have married each other up, at last."

Like children on the other side of the tracks, Dillard explored her neighborhood. "Walking was my project before reading," she says. "The text I read was the town; the book I made up was a map." As a tomboy full of athletic energy and eagerness, Dillard avidly claimed her territory: pelting cars with snowballs, joining boys' sandlot baseball games, roaming Frick Park by herself, though her father tells her not to because "bums lived there under the bridges." Her vigorous child's-life-on-foot takes her in every direction but one: she doesn't wander across the tracks into Homewood.

An American Childhood regards Homewood diffidently. It is not posed as a threat, or as a community damaged by discrimination. Homewood is someone else's space, its residents noted neutrally, rather distantly, as "the people of Homewood, some of whom lived in visible poverty, on crowded streets among burned-out houses." Dillard remembers how for years her mother drove her to the public library in Homewood. There, in the library, in "the last and darkest and most obscure of the tall nonfiction stacks," she notices *Negro History,* shelved alongside *Natural History*—the latter is what she's looking for. In this incidental way, Dillard's memoir reminds us of the irrelevance at best, to which segregation assigned blacks in the 1950s, before the civil rights movement was well under way. Crossed from either side, the rail tracks between Homewood and Point Breeze were clearly a boundary, though for whites not yet a challenging signifier.

One scene in particular in *An American Childhood*—depicting a neighbor girl ice-skating after a storm—evokes especially well the ambiance of the middle-class home in the 1950s.

The night Jo Ann Sheehy skated on the street, it was dark inside our house. We were having dinner in the dining room—my mother, my father, my sister Amy, who was two, and I. There were lighted ivory candles on the table. The only other light inside was the blue fluorescent lamp over the fish tank, on a sideboard. Inside the tank, neon tetras, black mollies, and angelfish circled, illumined, through the lightshot water. . . .

We sat in the dark dining room, hushed. . . . The world outside was dangerously cold, and the big snow held the houses down and the people in.

Behind me, tall chilled windows gave out onto the narrow front yard and the street. A motion must have caught my mother's eye; she rose and moved to the windows, and Father and I followed. There we saw the young girl, the transfigured Jo Ann Sheehy, skating alone under the streetlight.

She was turning on ice skates inside the streetlight's yellow cone of light—illumined and silent. She tilted and spun. She wore a short skirt, as if Edgerton Avenue's asphalt had been the ice of an Olympic arena. . . . Under her skates the street's packed snow shone; it illumined her from below, the cold light striking her under her chin. . . .

This was for many years the center of the maze, this still, frozen evening inside, the family's watching through glass the Irish girl skating outside on the street. Here were beauty and mystery outside the house, and peace and safety within.

This image of safety yet transparency—of risking, reaching out for an expanded expression of self, even transcending in imagination ethnic borders (Jo Anne Sheehy's Irish Catholicism is underscored)—all of this manages to suggest the point and privilege of middle-class life. In the context of neighborhood boundaries, this dream of beauty and risk, enjoyed in safety, is what it means to live on the right side of the tracks.

Any number of fictional representations depict Pennsylvania's divided landscapes and separated neighborhoods. Early in the twentieth century Willa Cather—always a writer to commemorate place—mapped Pittsburgh's class divisions in such classic stories as "Paul's Case" and "Double Birthday." In the latter she shows different classes and ethnicities mingling in the shops and on the sidewalks of inner-city neighborhoods—South Side, Old Allegheny—while new suburbs like Squirrel Hill loom pretentiously, with their "big, turreted stone houses" and "iron-bound security." In "Paul's Case," a teenager from a drab section of East Liberty who worships the glitter of high-art as escape watches a diva leave a concert and enter a posh hotel, disappearing behind "swinging glass doors, which were opened by a negro in a tall hat and a long coat. . . . He seemed to feel himself go after her up the steps, into the warm lighted building, into an exotic, a tropical world of shiny, glistening surfaces and basking ease." In reality, of course, the windows are a taunting class barrier. Paul is still outside in the slush of the driveway standing in the rain—left to the disillusion that will end in suicide.

Back east across the state, John O'Hara anatomized class geographies in his fictions—for example, in his fine short story "The Doctor's Son" (1935), set in "Gibbsville" (Pottsville) and surrounding anthracite patch towns during the great influenza epidemic of 1918. In this story Dr. Malloy's fifteen-year-old son, James, chauffeurs a young medical student who is substituting for the father, who is worn out from his workload of cases. The locations move from Gibbsville, the regional center, to a moderately large coal town, Collieryville, to a small patch town identified only as "Kelly's Patch" after the owner of the local saloon. In the process, a very precise social hierarchy—a class map—is established. The doctor, like his student substitute, is a "university man"—"which meant the University of Pennsylvania." The bona fides of the doctor's good friend David Evans, a resident of Collieryville, are displayed like a resumé:

> Mr. Evans was district superintendent of one of the largest mining corporations, and therefore Collieryville's third citizen . . . ranked with the leading doctor and the leading lawyer. After him came the Irish priest, the cashier of the larger bank (of which the doctor or the lawyer or the superintendent of the mines is president), the brewer, and the leading merchant. David Evans had been born in Collieryville, the son of a superintendent, and was popular, a thirty-second degree Mason, a graduate of Lehigh, and a friend of my father's.

The wives of the doctor and Evans—as characterized by the son, James Malloy—describe the step down, socially, that constitutes the world of Collieryville: "When my mother had large parties she would invite Mrs. Evans, but the two women were not close friends. Mrs. Evans was a Collieryville girl, half Polish, and my mother had gone to an expensive school and spoke French, and played bridge long before Mrs. Evans had learned to play '500.'" The world of the patches is a step further down still: Catholic, Irish, and—at the very bottom—"Hunkie." Here "the practice of medicine was wholesale"—mostly wives and mothers coming in to a central place, such as Kelly's Saloon, to pick up medicine "for absent patients."

O'Hara shows us these several interconnected communities under great duress: everyone exhausted, fearful, irritable. Everyone's prejudices are visible. Still, even though medical attention is meted out according to an ethnic and class pecking order, there is a sense of common humanity—some effort to reach as many of the infected people as possible. When a disheveled "Hunkie woman" cannot explain in English who's sick in her family, Kelly advises the doctor's son and the medical student that they'll have to go and look for themselves. An Irish neighbor woman intervenes:

> "To be sure, and ain't that nice? Dya hear that, everybody? Payin' a personal visit to the likes of that but the decent people take what they get. A fine how-do-ya-do."

"You'll take what you get in the shape of a puck in the nose," said Mr. Kelly. "A fine way you do be talkin' wid the poor dumb Hunkie not knowing how to talk good enough to say what's the matter wid her gang. So keep your two cents out of this, Mame Brannigan, and get back into line."

When the doctor's son and "Doctor" Myers go to the woman's house, her five-year-old daughter dies while they are there. "The woman [took] the dead girl in her arms. She did not need the English language to know that the child was dead. She was rocking her back and forth and kissing her and looking up at us with fat streams of tears running from her eyes." They find her husband, dead some hours already, in another room. The lives and deaths in this miner's family are rendered shockingly brutal in O'Hara's blunt reportage. *This is the way it was, this is the way it always is,* the tone seems to say.

PROMISED LAND: A SENSE OF PLACE

> Sometimes my affection for this place wavers.
> I am poised between a vague ambition
> and loyalty to what I've always loved,
> kedged along inside my slow boat
> by warp and anchor drag. But if I imagine
> seeing this for the last time,
> this scruff of the borders of West Virginia,
> Pennsylvania, and Ohio, shaped by hills
> and rivers, by poverty and coal,
> then I think I could not bear to go,
> would grab any stump or tree limb
> and hold on for dear life.
>
> I keep trying to say what I notice here
> that's beautiful. There's the evening star
> riding the purple selvage of the ridges,
> and the flat shine of the Ohio where men
> in folding chairs cast their lines out
> toward the backwash of the barges.
> There are the river names: the Allegheny,
> the Monongahela, and the names of the tributaries,
> Fish Creek, Little Beaver; the towns
> named for function, Bridgeport, Martins Ferry,
> or for what the early settlers must have
> dreamed of, Prosperity and Amity.

Why can't we hold this landscape in our arms?
The nettle-tangled orchards given up on,
the broken fence posts with their tags
of wire, burdock taking over uncut fields,
the rusted tipples and the mills.
Sometimes I think it's possible
to wash the slag dust from the leaves
of sycamores and make them green, the way
as a child, after lesson and punishment,
I used to begin my life again. . . .

Maggie Anderson is a poet of landscapes (and sometimes of vegetable-gardening) who has written about many areas of the country, evidently following the perigrinations of her own life and career. In her poems from the 1980s and early 1990s, her strongest attachment is clearly to the hills and river valleys of West Virginia and western Pennsylvania. The poem excerpted above—"A Place with Promise" (from Anderson's 1992 collection *A Space Filled with Moving*)—is typical in raising scenes and themes familiar in the region. "Promise" hangs over the poem, the idea of the "Promised Land" made explicit in namings of this landscape: "what the early settlers must have dreamed of, Prosperity and Amity." "Promise" in a different sense—as an alternative to life in this region—is also invoked in the narrator's opening confession: "Sometimes my affection for this place wavers. / I am poised between a vague ambition / and loyalty to what I've always loved." The lines suggest that the narrator herself may want to search for something different, a better life someplace else. In its miniature way, the poem thus opens the all-American—and Pennsylvanian—theme of "moving on," if it becomes necessary or alluring to do so. (*A Space Filled with Moving* turns out to be another name for the United States and for the American experience.)

Notably, the landscape depicted in "A Place with Promise" is a *used* landscape: shaped by "poverty and coal" (as well as "hills and rivers"), its orchards "nettle-tangled," "given up on"; its fence posts "broken." In these environs, the good life is leaning back in your folding chair and casting your line out—"toward the backwash of the barges." As the poem implies, the *used* quality of this landscape is not only its signature but also part of its appeal. It is a landscape with a visible history in which human presence and struggle are invested. An air of elegy clings to these little farms now abandoned by workers. The poet embraces these places with affection: "I could live beyond damage and reproach, / in a place with such promise, / like any of the small farms among the wooded hills, / like any of the small towns starting up along the rivers."

In a larger context, Anderson evokes in a poem like this a recurrent look of rural landscape throughout much of the eastern United States. As family farms become uneconomical, small homesteads were abandoned, their barns and houses left to rot, their fields to return to nature (or occasionally to be reinvested by agribusiness in single crops). In another poem, "Abandoned Farm, Central Pennsylvania" in *Windfall* (2000), narrating a trip back through her genealogy into the Susquehanna River Valley, Anderson discovers a once-rich abandoned farm and wanders through the house and barn appreciatively, noting tools ("the floor / cluttered with pitchforks / and wheelbarrows, feed pails"), the "fine workings / of white oak beams, and a loft / of piled locust, cut and saved / for fence rail and door peg." In imagination, the exploration of this abandoned farm becomes a return "home"—union with ancestral family and historic place:

> In the southwest corner, field stones
> are piled against the windbreak.
> An old potato digger leans, like a fussy child,
> against crumpled wire fence.
> I mount the sun-warmed grooves of seat
> and lean onto the handles, just as if
> I have known this movement all my life.
>
> Who knows what the body can remember
> from far back, through the blood
> traces of habit and sweat? . . .

This search for a home place, in a used (hence valued) landscape plays out familiarly in Pennsylvania: a place people came to originally in search of economic sufficiency, then left behind, moving on, often west, to other promises as options here gave out.

South of Reading, in and around towns named variously in different stories throughout a long career, John Updike has explored a "thickly German county" fifty miles west of Philadelphia. Meditating on his personal home place in "A Soft Spring Night in Shillington" (in his memoiristic *Self-Consciousness* [1989]), he sums up: "I loved Shillington not as one loves Capri or New York, because they are special, but as one loves one's own body and consciousness, because they are synonymous with being. . . . If there was a meaning to existence, I was closest to it here." Indeed, in *Self-Consciousness* Updike walks us through a block-by-block, building-by-building remembrance of this place where he began life, a fortunate child: "The pavement squares, the housefronts, the remaining trees. . . . I loved this plain street, where for thirteen years no great harm had been allowed to befall me." Nonetheless, Updike became, and has stayed, an "expatriate"—going off to Harvard for college, then settling for many years north of Boston in the new postwar suburbia, where "my wife and I found ourselves in a kind of 'swim' of equally young married couples. . . . As a group, we had a lovely time being young adults in Ipswich."

Despite his warm, remembered regard for Shillington, Updike's writing has often commented on the need to leave such a place of origin. In the short story, "The Happiest I've Been," the narrator is a boy returning to college in the Midwest with a friend, Neil Hovey, who is driving from "Olinger" as far as Chicago. Hovey and the narrator both have ancestral roots in Olinger, which gives them, the narrator suggests, a certain westering optimism: "He and I lived with grandparents. This improved both our backward and forward vistas; . . . we had a sense of childhoods before 1900, when the farmer ruled the land and America faced west." Thus this story orients westward (*Go west, young man!*). The boys stop first in Olinger to party with friends, then drive toward the Pennsylvania Turnpike, as "red dawn light touched the clouds above the black slate roofs." They cross the Susquehanna "on a long smooth bridge below Harrisburg," come into the "tunnel country," then make the "long irregular descent toward Pittsburgh." Cautionary notes are in the background: the Korean War is going on (and Neil hopes to be drafted), the roads are icy in the mountains. But driving west—in a life-opening direction—feels overwhelmingly good. "There were many reasons for my feeling so happy. We were on our way. I had seen a dawn. . . . Ahead, a girl waited who, if I asked, would marry me, but first there was a vast trip: many hours and towns interceded between me and that encounter. . . . There was the quality of the 10 A.M. sunlight as it existed in the air ahead of the windshield, filtered by the thin overcast, blessing irresponsibility."

The young people in "The Happiest I've Been" are securely middle-class (in his foreword to *The Olinger Stories* Updike notes: "Olinger, if it is like Shillington, is a square mile of middle-class homes"). A darker reading of the region—and of recurrent efforts to escape it—is created in the long-running *Rabbit* saga. The famous first book of the series, *Rabbit, Run,* powerfully depicts a low-skilled, unmotivated former high school basketball player in his mid-twenties. Harry Angstrom—nicknamed "Rabbit"—feels trapped, most directly by his unhappy sexual liaisons: his too early, thoughtless marriage to Janice, and their scarcely wished for offspring; his extramarital relationship with Ruth and a new pregnancy to deal with. The basic issue, however, is the constricted world of a small Pennsylvania town, which seems to doom his life to dull repetition, his most vivid moments—on the high school basketball court—fading forever behind him.

The novel is effectively bookended by two extended attempts at flight. The first, by car, occurs in the early pages of *Rabbit, Run.* Harry's destination is vague, but he is heading south: "Down, down the map into the orange groves and smoking rivers and barefoot women." As he drives out of town (leaving "that flowerpot city"), the popular music on the radio seems to mock him: "'Secret Love,' 'Autumn Leaves' . . . Supper music, music to cook by." He struggles to suppress a "vision of Janice's meal sizzling in the pan, chops probably, the grease-tinted water bubbling disconsolately." He crosses into Maryland on Route 222, listening to the mélange of radio commercials and popular songs, stopping at a gas station with its clutter of icons: a Coke machine, stacked cans of liquid wax. Late in the evening, in a roadside cafe, Rabbit suddenly feels he is different from the other customers: " . . . the young men sitting in zippered jackets in booths three to a girl, the girls with orange hair hanging like seaweed or loosely bound with gold barrettes like pirate treasure. . . . He had thought, he had read, that from shore to shore all America was the same. He wonders, Is it just these people I'm outside, or is it all America?" The commercial popular culture of the United States is the primary language Rabbit knows, and painfully he's learning that he has no means to project himself beyond it. He turns around and heads back home. (Rabbit is a descendant of O'Hara's Julian English [*Appointment in Samarra*], an earlier victim of Pennsylvania small-city angst who also briefly contemplates flight by auto.)

In the final pages of the novel, Rabbit tries escape again—this time, leaving the burial of his infant daughter, on foot, running, climbing up the mountain at the edge of town, through the woods he'd played in as a boy, which now become a kind of dark night of the soul. Old pine trees throw dense shadows and "rocks jut up through the blanket of needles, scabby with lichen; collapsed trunks hold intricate claws across the path."

> He stops, stunned, on the edge of a precipitate hollow whose near bank is strewn with the hairy bodies of dead trees locked against trunks that have managed to cling erect to the steep soil and that cast into the hollow a shadow as deep as the last stage of twilight. Something rectangular troubles this gloom; it dawns on him that on the floor of the hollow lie the cellarhole and the crumbled sandstone walls of a forgotten house.

Ghosts!—an abandoned home left in this battered landscape by some early settler who moved on. By the time Rabbit emerges near the summit, within sight of "Pinnacle Hotel," he is ready to slink back into town, to one of his women.

After this Rabbit's tale, a reader may wish to revisit one of the great political visions of the promised land nurtured in Pennsylvania. Mike Dobrejcak, Thomas Bell's idealistic Slovak steelworker in *Out of This Furnace,* is another figure trapped in a relatively small Pennsylvania town—this time, Braddock, in the early years of the twentieth century, putting in eighty-four-hour weeks at the blast furnaces. At a climactic moment in his character's career (shortly before he dies in a mill accident in 1914), Bell lets Mike articulate his ideals. As he and his buddy Steve Bodnar leave a bar in the First Ward (beyond the wall "the mill rumbled on, efficient and sober and not to be swerved from its tasks"), Mike harangues Bodnar: "I used to ask myself, Is this what the good God put me on earth for, to work my life away in Carnegie's blast furnaces, to live and die in Braddock's alleys? I couldn't believe it." When he realizes that Steve is too drunk to listen, Mike subsides into a set of personal reflections:

> He had felt that no human being need go without his portion of comfort and beauty and quietness; the world held enough for all and if some had less than others it was because men had ordered it so and it lay in men's hands to order

differently. It had seemed to him that men needed only to have this explained to them and they'd rise and do what was necessary; and when they didn't he felt angry and bewildered. . . .

Unless this was so he felt there was no use going on. Unless this could be proved true here and now, today, in the teeming alleys and courtyards and kitchens of the First Ward, it was true nowhere, never. And unless it was true there was no hope.

It would be another quarter-century before Big Steel recognized the Steel Workers Organizing Committee. Finally, in 1937, Mike's son Dobie, lifting "his eyes to the dark sky," can declare in triumph: "We've come a long way, hey Pop?" Looking out from his house high on a hill above the steel valley, Dobie thinks of the union triumph as a realization of the American promise:

[B]ecause Dobie had been born and raised in a steel town, where the word [American] meant people who were white, Protestant, middle-class Anglo-Saxons, it hadn't occurred to him that the C.I.O. men were thinking and talking like Americans.

"Maybe not the kind of American that came over on the Mayflower," he reflected, "or the kind that's always shooting off their mouths about Americanism and patriotism, including some of the God-damnedest heels you'd ever want to see, but the kind that's got *Made in U.S.A.* stamped all over them. . . .

Made in the U.S.A., [Dobie] thought, made in the First Ward. . . . It wasn't where you were born or how you spelled your name or where your father had come from. It was the way you thought and felt about certain things. About freedom of speech and the equality of men and the importance of having one law—the same law—for rich and poor, for the people you liked and the people you didn't like.

Bell's now-famous novel about immigrant labor stops on this triumphant note—looking toward the future but remembering the past.

It is fitting to end this highly selective survey of literary texts of Pennsylvania with a passage that alludes to the state's most celebrated text: the Declaration of Independence. Dobie's passionate appeal to American values brings together two of the great liberation struggles—nationhood and labor—that define Pennsylvania's centrality as a historic place.

Anderson, Maggie. *A Space Filled with Moving.* Pittsburgh: University of Pittsburgh Press, 1992. Quotations from pages 19–20. © 1992, reprinted by permission of the University of Pittsburgh Press.

———. *Windfall: New and Selected Poems.* Pittsburgh: University of Pittsburgh Press, 2000. Quotations from pages 66–68. © 2002, reprinted by permission of the University of Pittsburgh Press.

Beatty, Jan. *Mad River.* Pittsburgh: University of Pittsburgh Press, 1995. Quotations from pages 27–28. © 1995, reprinted by permission of the University of Pennsylvania Press.

Bell, Thomas. *Out of This Furnace.* 1941. Originally published by Little, Brown. Reprint, Pittsburgh: University of Pittsburgh Press, 1976. Quotations from pages 191–92, 197, 199, 404, and 410–11.

———. "Zinc Works Craneman to Wed." *Story,* May–June 1939, 91–95. Quotation from page 95.

Blair, Peter. *Last Heat.* Washington, D.C.: Word Works, 2000. Quotations from pages 13, 31, and 40–41, reprinted by permission of The Word Works Washington Prize Collection, Washington, D.C.

Cather, Willa. "Double Birthday" (1929). Originally published in *Forum* magazine. References here are to *From These Hills, From These Valleys,* ed. David Demarest, 145–62. Pittsburgh: University of Pittsburgh Press, 1976. Quotation from page 156.

———. "Paul's Case" (1905). Originally published in the Willa Cather short-story collection *The Troll Garde.* References here are to *Youth and the Bright Medusa* (a Cather short-story collection), 181–212. New York: Alfred A. Knopf, 1920. Quotations from pages 188–89.

Dillard, Annie. *An American Childhood.* New York: Harper & Row, 1987. Quotations from pages 15, 16, 30–31, 43, 44, 51, 81, 83, and 88.

Foster, William Z. *Pages from a Worker's Life.* New York: International Publishers, 1939.

French, Albert. *Patches of Fire: A Story of War and Redemption.* New York: Anchor Books, Doubleday, 1997. Quotations from pages 16 and 25–26.

Graham, Laurie. *Singing the City.* Pittsburgh: University of Pittsburgh Press, 1998. Quotations from page 140.

Musmanno, Michael. *Black Fury.* New York: Fountainhead Publishers, 1966.

O'Hara, John. "The Doctor's Son" (1935). Originally published in *"The Doctor's Son" and Other Stories* (New York: Harcourt Brace). References here are to *Gibbsville, Pa.: The Classic Stories,* 38–64. New York: Carroll & Graf, 1992. Quotations from pages 40, 41, 45, 47, and 50.

Updike, John. "The Happiest I've Been" (1954). Originally published in the *New Yorker.* References here are to *The Olinger Stories,* 101–21. New York: Vintage Books, Random House, 1964. Quotations from pages 104 and 121.

———. "Home." In *Pigeon Feathers,* 151–68. New York: Alfred A. Knopf, 1962. Quotations from pages 51–52 and 157.

———. *Rabbit, Run* (1960). New York: Alfred A. Knopf. References here are to the collected volume *Rabbit Run, Rabbit Redux, Rabbit Is Rich.* New York: Alfred A. Knopf, 1981. Quotations from pages 24–25, 33, 297 and 299.

———. *Self-Consciousness.* New York: Alfred A. Knopf, 1989. Quotation from page 30.

Wideman, John Edgar. *Sent for You Yesterday.* Boston: Houghton Mifflin Company, 1983. Quotations from pages 20–21, 55, 61–62, 85, 86, 150, and 198.

———. *Two Cities.* Boston: Houghton Mifflin Company, 1998. Quotations from pages 1–3, 5, and 21.

During the colonial period, governors were appointed by authorities in Sweden, Holland, or England. Under the Penn proprietorship, which began in 1682, members of the Penn family always governed technically but usually lived in England and delegated their responsibilities in Pennsylvania to a deputy.

From 1776 to 1800, political parties were relatively unformed and allegiances shifted frequently. Franklin in 1776/77, Wharton, and Reed supported the Constitution of 1776 and were called Constitutionalists. Moore and Dickinson opposed the Constitution and were called Republicans, although by the mid-1780s the term "Federalist" was coming into vogue. Franklin from 1785 to 1788 and Mifflin from 1788 to 1799 commanded widespread nonpartisan support both from Federalists and from their opponents, who were at first called Anti-Federalists then later Jeffersonians, Republicans, Democrats, or some combination thereof (Jeffersonian Democrats, Democratic-Republicans, Jeffersonian Republicans). Mifflin's opponents were Federalists, but, except in 1793, most Federalists also supported him.

YEAR	GOVERNOR

Under the Swedes:

1638	Peter Minuit
1641	Peter Hollandaer
1643	John Printz
1653	John Pappegoya (Printz's son-in-law)
1654	Johan Claudius Rysingh

Under the Dutch (Swedish colony captured by Peter Stuyvesant, 1655; colony divided into city and company, 1657–62; colony united, 1662):

1655	Deryck Schmidt (pro tem)
1655	John Paul Jacquet
1657	Jacob Alricks (city)
1659	Alex. D'Hinoyossa (city)

All candidates garnering less than 1,000 votes in an election are excluded from this listing.

YEAR	GOVERNOR
1657	Goeran Van Dyke (company)
1658	William Beekman (company)
1662	William Beekman
1663	Alex. D'Hinoyossa

Under the British (Dutch colony captured by the British, 1664):

1664	Col. Richard Nicolls, governor
1664	Robert Carr, deputy governor
1667	Col. Francis Lovelace

Under the Dutch (British colony recaptured by the Dutch, 1673):

1673	Anthony Colve, governor
1673	Peter Alricks, governor

Under the British (colony recaptured by the British, 1674):

1674	Sir Edmund Andros

Under the Proprietary Government:

1681	William Markham, deputy governor
1682	William Penn, proprietor
1684	The Council, Thomas Lloyd, president
1688	Five commissioners appointed by Penn
1688	John Blackwell, deputy governor
1690	The Council, Thomas Lloyd, president
1691	Thomas Lloyd, deputy governor of province
1691	William Markham, deputy governor of lower counties
1693	Benjamin Fletcher (governor of New York), governor
1693	William Markham, lieutenant governor
1695	William Markham, deputy governor
1699	William Penn, proprietor
1701	Andrew Hamilton, deputy governor
1703	The Council, Edward Shippen, president
1704	John Evans, deputy governor
1709	Charles Gookin, deputy governor
1717	Sir William Keith, deputy governor
1726	Patrick Gordon, deputy governor
1736	The Council, James Logan, president
1738	George Thomas, deputy governor
1747	The Council, Anthony Palmer, president
1748	James Hamilton, deputy governor
1754	Robert Hunter Morris, deputy governor
1756	William Denny, deputy governor
1759	James Hamilton, deputy governor
1763	John Penn, lieutenant governor
1771	The Council, James Hamilton, president
1771	Richard Penn, lieutenant governor
1776	John Penn, lieutenant governor

During the Revolution:

The Committee of Safety, Benjamin Franklin, chairman (September 1776–March 1777), Constitutional

Presidents of the Supreme Executive Council (1777–1788):

1777	Thomas Wharton Jr.
1778	George Bryan (acting president)
1778	Joseph Reed, Constitutional
1781	William Moore, Federal
1782	John Dickinson

1785   Benjamin Franklin, Federal
1788   Thomas Mifflin, Federal

YEAR	GOVERNOR	VOTE

Governors After 1788:

YEAR	GOVERNOR	VOTE
1790	Thomas Mifflin, Democrat/nonpartisan	27,725
	Arthur St. Clair, Federal	2,802
1793	Thomas Mifflin, Democrat/nonpartisan	18,590
	F. A. Muhlenberg, Federal	10,706
1796	Thomas Mifflin, Democrat/nonpartisan	30,020
	F. A. Muhlenberg, Federal	1,011
1799	Thomas McKean, Democrat	38,036
	James Ross, Federal	32,641
1802	Thomas McKean, Democrat	47,879
	James Ross (of Pittsburgh), Federal	9,499
	James Ross, Federal	7,538
1805	Thomas McKean, Independent Democrat	43,644
	Simon Snyder, Democrat	38,438
1808	Simon Snyder, Democrat	67,975
	James Ross, Federal	39,575
	John Spayd, Federal	4,006
1811	Simon Snyder, Democrat	52,319
	William Tilghman, Federal	3,609
1814	Simon Snyder, Democrat	51,099
	Isaac Wayne, Federal	29,566
1817	William Findlay, Democrat	66,331
	Joseph Hiester, Federal	59,272
1820	Joseph Hiester, Federal	67,905
	William Findlay, Democrat	66,300
1823	J. Andrew Schulze, Democrat	89,928
	Andrew Gregg, Federal	64,211
1826	J. Andrew Schulze, Democrat	72,710
	John Sergeant, Federal	1,175
1829	George Wolf, Democrat	78,219
	Joseph Ritner, Anti-Mason	61,776
1832	George Wolf, Democrat	91,335
	Joseph Ritner, Anti-Mason	88,165
1835	Joseph Ritner, Anti-Mason	94,023
	George Wolf, Independent Democrat	65,804
	Henry A. Muhlenberg, Democrat	40,586
1838	David R. Porter, Democrat	127,825
	Joseph Ritner, Anti-Mason	122,321
1841	David R. Porter, Democrat	136,504
	John Banks, Whig	113,473
1844	Francis R. Shunk, Democrat	160,322
	Joseph Markle, Whig	156,040
	F. J. Lamoyne, Abolition	2,566
1847	Francis R. Shunk, Democrat	146,081
	James Irvin, Whig	128,148
	E. G. Reigart, Native American	11,247
	F. J. Lamoyne, Abolition	1,861
1848	William F. Johnston, Whig	168,522
	Morris Longstreth, Democrat	168,225
1851	William Bigler, Democrat	186,489
	William F. Johnson, Whig	178,034
	Kimber Cleaver, Native American	1,850
1854	James Pollock, Whig and American	203,822
	William Bigler, Democrat	166,991
	B. Rush Bradford, Free Soil	2,194
1857	William F. Packer, Democrat	188,846

YEAR	GOVERNOR	VOTE
1857	David Wilmot, Free Soil	146,139
	Isaac Hazelhurst, American	28,168
1860	Andrew G. Curtin, Republican	262,346
	Henry D. Foster, Democrat	230,230
1863	Andrew G. Curtin, Republican	269,506
	George W. Woodward, Democrat	254,171
1866	John W. Geary, Republican	307,274
	Hiester Clymer, Democrat	290,096
1869	John W. Geary, Republican	290,552
	Asa Packer, Democrat	285,956
1872	John F. Hartranft, Republican	353,287
	Charles R. Buckalew, Democrat	317,760
	S. B. Chase, Prohibition	1,259
1875	John F. Hartranft, Republican	304,175
	Cyrus L. Pershing, Democrat	292,145
	R. Audley Brown, Prohibition	13,244
1878	Henry M. Hoyt, Republican	319,567
	Andrew H. Dill, Democrat	297,060
	Samuel R. Mason, National Greenback	81,758
	Franklin H. Lane, Prohibition	3,653
1882	Robert E. Pattison, Democrat	355,791
	James A. Beaver, Republican	315,589
	John Stewart, Independent Republican	43,743
	Thomas A. Armstrong, Greenback-Labor	23,484
	Alfred C. Pettit, Temperance	5,196
1886	James A. Beaver, Republican	412,285
	Chauncey F. Black, Democrat	369,634
	Charles S. Wolf, Prohibition	32,458
	Robert J. Houston, Greenback	4,835
1890	Robert E. Pattison, Democrat	464,209
	George E. Delamater, Republican	447,655
	John D. Gill, Prohibition	16,108
1894	Daniel H. Hastings, Republican	574,801
	William M. Singerly, Democrat	333,404
	Charles L. Hawley, Prohibition	23,433
	Jerome T. Ailman, People's	19,464
	Thomas H. Grundy, Socialist Labor	1,733
1898	William A. Stone, Republican	476,206
	George A. Jenks, Democrat	358,300
	Silas C. Swallow, Prohibition	132,931
	J. Mahlon Barnes, Socialist Labor	4,278
1902	Samuel W. Pennypacker, Republican	593,328
	Robert E. Pattison, Democrat	450,978
	Silas C. Swallow, Prohibition	23,327
	William Adams, Socialist Labor	5,155
	J. W. Slayton, Socialist	21,910
1906	Edwin S. Stuart, Republican	506,418
	Lewis Emery, Jr., Democrat	458,054
	Homer L. Castle, Prohibition	24,793
	James A. Maurer, Socialist	15,169
	John Desmond, Socialist Labor	2,109
1910	John K. Tener, Republican	415,614
	William H. Berry, Keystone	382,127
	Webster Grim, Democrat	129,395
	John W. Slayton, Socialist	53,055
	Madison F. Larkin, Prohibition	17,445
1914	Martin G. Brumbaugh, Republican	588,705
	Vance C. McCormick, Democrat	453,380
	Joseph B. Allen, Socialist	40,115
	Matthew H. Stevenson, Prohibition	17,467
	William Draper Lewis, Roosevelt-Progressive	6,503
	Charles N. Brumm, Bull Moose	4,031

YEAR	GOVERNOR	VOTE
1918	William C. Sproul, Republican	552,537
	Eugene C. Bonniwell, Democrat	305,315
	E. J. Fithian, Prohibition	27,359
	Charles Sehl, Socialist	18,714
	Robert C. Macauley, Single Tax	1,077
1922	Gifford Pinchot, Republican	831,696
	John A. McSparran, Democrat	581,625
	Lilith Martin Wilson, Socialist	31,748
	William Repp, Prohibition	4,151
	William H. Thomas, Industrial	3,137
	John W. Dix, Single Tax	2,246
1926	John S. Fisher, Republican	1,102,823
	Eugene C. Bonniwell, Democrat	365,280
	George E. Pennock, Prohibition	19,524
	John W. Slayton, Socialist	11,795
	H. W. Hicks, Workers	3,256
1930	Gifford Pinchot, Republican	1,068,874
	John M. Hemphill, Democrat	1,010,204
	James H. Maurer, Socialist	21,036
	Frank Mozer, Communist	5,267
1934	George H. Earle, Democrat	1,476,467
	Wm. A. Schnader, Republican	1,410,138
	Jesse H. Holmes, Socialist	42,417
	Herbert T. Ames, Prohibition	13,521
	Emmett Patrick Cush, Communist	5,584
	Bess Gyekis, Industrial Labor	2,272
1938	Arthur H. James, Republican	2,035,340
	Charles Alvin Jones, Democrat	1,756,192
	Jesse H. Holmes, Socialist	12,635
	Robert G. Burnham, Prohibition	6,438
1942	Edward Martin, Republican	1,367,531
	F. Clair Ross, Democrat	1,149,897
	Dale H. Learn, Prohibition	17,385
	Joseph Pirincin, Socialist Labor	5,310
	John J. Haluska, United Pension	7,911
1946	James H. Duff, Republican	1,828,462
	John S. Rice, Democrat	1,270,947
	James A. W. Killip, Prohibition	13,838
	George S. Taylor, Socialist Labor	10,747
1950	John S. Fine, Republican	1,796,119
	Richardson Dilworth, Democrat	1,710,355
	Richard R. Blews, Prohibition	12,282
	Reginald B. Naugle, G.I.'s Against Communism	7,715
	Thomas J. Fitzpatrick, Progressive	6,097
	Robert Z. Wilson, Socialist	5,005
	George S. Taylor, Industrial Government	1,645
1954	George M. Leader, Democrat	1,996,266
	Lloyd H. Wood, Republican	1,717,070
	Henry Beitscher, Progressive	4,471
	Louis Dirle, Socialist Labor	2,650
1958	David L. Lawrence, Democrat	2,024,852
	Arthur T. McGonigle, Republican	1,948,769
	Herman A. Johnson, Socialist Labor	8,677
	Eloise Fickland, Workers	4,556
1962	William W. Scranton, Republican	2,424,918
	Richardson Dilworth, Democrat	1,938,627
	George S. Taylor, Socialist Labor	14,340
1966	Raymond P. Shafer, Republican	2,110,349
	Milton J. Shapp, Democrat	1,868,719
	Edward S. Swartz, Constitution	57,073
	George S. Taylor, Socialist Labor	14,527
1970	Milton J. Shapp, Democrat	2,043,029

YEAR	GOVERNOR	VOTE
1970	Raymond Broderick, Republican	1,542,854
	A. J. Watson, Constitution	83,406
	Francis McGeever, American Independent	21,647
	George S. Taylor, Socialist Labor	3,588
1974	Milton J. Shapp, Democrat	1,878,252
	Drew Lewis, Republican	1,578,917
	Stephen Depue, Constitution	33,691
1978	Richard Thornburgh, Republican	1,966,042
	Peter Flaherty, Democrat	1,737,888
	Mark Zola, Independent	20,062
	Lee Frissell, Independent	17,593
1982	Richard Thornburgh, Republican	1,872,784
	Allen E. Ertel, Democrat	1,772,353
	Mark Zola, Socialist Worker	15,495
	Lee Frissell, Consumer	13,101
	Richard D. Fuerle, Libertarian	10,252
1986	Robert P. Casey, Democrat	1,717,484
	William W. Scranton III, Republican	1,638,268
	Heidi J. Hoover, Consumer	32,523
1990	Robert P. Casey, Democrat	2,065,281
	Barbara Hafer, Republican	987,463
1994	Thomas Ridge, Republican	1,627,976
	Mark S. Singel, Democrat	1,430,099
	Peg Luksik, Constitutional	460,269
	Patrick Fallon, Libertarian	33,602
	Timothy E. Holloway, Patriot	33,235
1998	Thomas Ridge, Republican	1,736,844
	Ivan Itkin, Democrat	938,745
	Peg Luksik, Constitutional	314,761
	Ken Krawchuk, Libertarian	33,591

SOURCES: 1633–1788 from *Smull's Legislative Handbook 1872* (Harrisburg: Benjamin Singerly, State Printer of Pennsylvania, 1872); 1790–1898 from *Smull's Legislative Handbook 1904,* comp. Thomas B. Cochran and Herman P. Miller (Harrisburg: William Stanley Ray, State Printer of Pennsylvania, 1904); 1902–94 from *The Pennsylvania Manual,* vol. 113 (December 1997); 1998 from *The Pennsylvania Manual* (2000).

This Select Bibliography suggests ways to Pennsylvania's past, with an emphasis on finding aids for and general treatments of Pennsylvania history. It is suggestive rather than comprehensive in coverage. The suggestions for further reading at the end of each chapter provide listings of the critical works for their respective time periods and the topics discussed in each chapter. Although the citations therein are mostly books, and favor recent titles to reflect the most current scholarship, the chapter bibliographies taken together constitute an important overall bibliography on Pennsylvania history and historical methods. This Select Bibliography complements such work and extends it by pointing to ways to go deeper into the past through the use of primary and other sources.

This bibliography also reminds students that no single approach or source speaks for the whole of the past. Historians must consult a variety of sources, for only in doing so is it possible to see an individual, institution, idea, or event in its many facets. Perspective informs content, and context informs text. Also important to note is that the authors of the "history" of Pennsylvania chapters in Part I of this book relied on a great range and diversity of sources, many of which are "invisible" and "silent" in the reading because no special attention was called to them as unusual sources in Part II, which discusses "nontraditional" sources.

The lack of any special discussion of such sources should in no way diminish their significance. Far from it. The historians writing the chapters in Part I drew much from the secondary literature on their topics in defining historical categories, posing questions, understanding context, and finding information. But they also mined so-called traditional primary sources that long have been the "stuff" of historical research—especially government records and reports of all kinds (for example, written charters and constitutions, treaties, laws and court decisions, land records, agency and special commission reports, census data, and the personal and public records of governors, lawmakers, and other public officials), the personal papers of individuals (for example, diaries, letters, memoirs), institutional records (for example, business accounts and reports, minutes and reports of civic and reform organizations), and newspapers and journals of all kinds reporting the events and interests of their day. Without such sources it would be impossible to know, even to find, Pennsylvania's history. A history of the people of the Commonwealth is necessarily revealed in the seemingly dry bones of written records as much as it is in their folklore, art, oral history and other accounts of themselves. Helping students of Pennsylvania's past to locate and use such sources is one of the principal purposes of this Select Bibliography.

The literature on Pennsylvania is vast, though often uneven in coverage. Historically, the colonial period through the nineteenth century has received the most study from scholars, and still does even as important new work on twentieth-century topics has become available during the last quarter of that century and the beginning of the twenty-first century. Until the 1960s, political, economic, religious, and military history dominated writing on Pennsylvania, but since the advent of "the new social history" in the 1960s, with its emphasis on writing history "from the bottom up," students of Pennsylvania's past have devoted much attention to the lives and interests of women, immigrant/ethnic groups, African Americans, and the working class. Studying the everyday lives of "ordinary people" poses its own problems of (and offers new prospects for) sources, as discussed in the Part II chapters in this book.

So too, even traditional topics, such as politics, have demanded new approaches. A new emphasis on studying political culture rather than just the history of elections, political parties, and political jockeying in the capital has redefined the ways historians approach questions of political power and policy-making, inside and outside the normal channels of political participation and practice, from voter mobilization to boycotts, rallies, and even riots as expressions of political beliefs and interests. Politics seems to be everywhere in "the new political history" that includes struggles for power in the family, in the workplace, and in the schools in definitions of politics. Such interest that moves politics beyond the stump and the statehouse requires more than just tallying votes at elections and tracking executive, legislative, and judicial decisions to understand "politics."

Like the new social history, and all the other "new histories" that have expanded the universe of historical inquiry, the history of the Commonwealth demands new sources and new ways of reading sources already at hand. Much of such inquiry, though, rests on careful readings of written documents, some long in use, such as the so-called traditional sources noted above. And many old questions that perennially need reexamination—such as who ruled the statehouse and what those in power did with the public trust—can be answered primarily by turning again to those traditional sources. New perspectives also invite new readings of traditional primary sources just as they point to the use of new kinds of sources. Good history demands no less.

The historians' new perspectives on a host of topics, and interest in getting "the people" into the historical narrative, have led to an increasing reliance on anthropology, archaeology, folklore, linguistics, oral history, photography, and more—as reflected in this book. So too have such perspectives and interest recast the content and character of historical inquiry. Making sense of these and other changes in the ways scholars have revised and rewritten Pennsylvania history can be a daunting task. Happily, guides to resources, bibliographies, and general works exist to make it possible to find necessary sources for all manner of topics and to chart the ways scholars have used such materials to discover and present Pennsylvania's past.

The essential introduction to the historical literature on Pennsylvania is Dennis B. Downey and Francis J. Bremer, eds., *A Guide to the History of Pennsylvania* (1993), which consists of historiographical essays emphasizing recent literature arranged chronologically from "Indian Pennsylvania" to "Modern Pennsylvania, 1919–1990" and including a general description of thirty-three archival and manuscript repositories in the state. Indispensable for lists of secondary works are the bibliographies sponsored by the Pennsylvania Historical and Museum Commission (PHMC) and/or the Pennsylvania Historical Association (PHA). They include Arthur C. Bining, Robert L. Brunhouse, and Norman B. Wilkinson, eds., *Writings on Pennsylvania History: A Bibliography* (1946); Norman B. Wilkinson, comp., and S. K. Stevens and Donald H. Kent, eds., *Bibliography of Pennsylvania History* (2nd ed., 1957); and Carol Wall, ed., *Bibliography of Pennsylvania History: A Supplement* (1976). The PHMC published six consecutive supplements to the Wilkinson, Wall and other bibliographies. They covered titles through 1985, and then two more supplements, for 1986 and 1987, were published in issues of *Pennsylvania History.* Comprehensive annual, or even topical, bibliographies slackened during the 1980s and 1990s, but the PHMC and the PHA together revived the annual bibliography of Pennsylvania history for the year 2001, with the bibliography available on the PHMC and PHA websites and the promise of continued annual bibliographies to come thereafter. Also useful is the State Library of Pennsylvania's annual bibliography, *Year's Work in Pennsylvania Studies,* which began in 1965 and continued to 1974/1975.

The aforementioned bibliographies principally identify books and articles on Pennsylvania history and subjects. For recent work, students should consult *America: History and Life,* published annually since 1960, which provides abstracts as well as citations to the periodical literature and listings of book reviews. In searching for Pennsylvania topics in this or any bibliographical aid, the student should look for particular subject headings and also references to the Middle Atlantic region when considering broader issues. Both *The Pennsylvania Magazine of History and Biography* and *Pennsylvania History* regularly publish book reviews of key new works directly focusing on or related to Pennsylvania subjects; and *Pennsylvania Heritage* likewise reviews three to five books on Pennsylvania in each issue. Roland M. Baumann, comp., *Dissertations on Pennsylvania History, 1886–1976: A Bibliography* (1978), lists more than 700 dissertations, many of them unpublished. A similar effort to identify the large number of dissertations completed since 1976 is much needed. Nothing of such scope exists for the many master's theses on Pennsylvania history for any period.

Specialized bibliographies are also useful, though few exist that cover the literature from the 1980s and after. Among the several topical bibliographies are John E. Bodnar, ed., *Ethnic History in Pennsylvania: A Selected Bibliography* (1974); Elizabeth Haller and Florence Jean Wright, comps., *New Perspectives: A Bibliography of Racial, Ethnic, and Feminist Resources* (1977); and Charles W. Lenz, comp., *A Selective Bibliography to Industrial, Socioeconomic, and General History Materials for Pennsylvania's 67 Counties* (1974). An instructive introduction to the issues and literature on African Americans in Pennsylvania is Joe William Trotter Jr. and Eric Ledell Smith, eds., *African Americans in Pennsylvania: Shifting Historical Perspectives* (1997). No other group has received such extensive and careful historiographical treatment. Several county historical societies have published bibliographies pointing to both printed and manuscript resources for studying their respective counties. A good example is Robert E. Carlson, ed., *Delaware County (Pennsylvania) Bibliography* (1989).

Newspapers are essential sources for local, regional, and state history. The only general listing for the state is Glenora Russell, ed., *Pennsylvania Newspapers: A Bibliography and Union List* (1978), but the State Library of Pennsylvania in Harrisburg, the Carnegie Library in Pittsburgh, the Free Library of Philadelphia, the Historical Society of Pennsylvania, and the Historical Society of Western Pennsylvania all have important newspaper collections. So do many local and county historical societies and public libraries. For a listing of museums and historical societies, many with runs of local newspapers, see Jean H. Cutler, ed., *Keystone Treasures: A Guide to Museums and Historical Societies in Pennsylvania* (2000). For information about newspaper holdings and special collections relating to local and regional history, consult the particular library entry in the *American Library Directory, 2001–2002* (2001), an indispensable source, published annually, giving much information on the location and interests of public, private, special, and college and university libraries.

Every close student of Pennsylvania's past will want to use the rich and extensive research materials held by The Pennsylvania Historical and Museum Commission. The Commission's collections cover virtually every aspect of life and history in Pennsylvania, but the PHMC has developed special strengths in the following areas: agricultural history, community and domestic life, industrial history, military history, Native American and ethnic history, politics and public policy, religion and communal societies, and rural and agricultural life. For a good, brief overview of the research collections and facilities at the PHMC, consult the PHMC booklet *Research Collections at the Pennsylvania Historical and Museum Commission* (1999). And for more detailed information and updates on collections, see the PHMC website at www.phmc.state.pa.us (and click on the appropriate link—for example, "Pennsylvania State Archives"). The PHMC brochure and website noted above, and the several guides to collections noted below, supersede the *Preliminary Guide to the Research Materials of the Pennsylvania Historical and Museum Commission* (1959) and other State Archives guides published in the 1970s and 1980s. The PHMC collections are administered and located in one of four bureaus: the Bureau of Archives and History, The State Museum, the Bureau for Historic Preservation, and the Bureau of Historic Sites and Museums. Within the State Archives, The State Museum, and the Bureau for Historic Preservation—all in Harrisburg—the collections are organized and administered by discipline. The Bureau of Historic Sites and Museums maintains twenty-five properties across the state, many of which have document and artifact collections pertinent to their particular subject and interpretive mission. Addresses and descriptions of the historic properties are available on the PHMC website and in the PHMC brochure listed above.

The PHMC has published topical guides to its collections at the State Archives, the most recent of which provide useful detailed descriptions of individual collections and subject indexes. Among them are Robert M. Dructor, *Guide to Genealogical Sources at the Pennsylvania State Archives* (1998); Ruth E. Hodge, *Guide to African American Resources at the Pennsylvania State Archives* (2000), which builds on and supersedes David McBride, *The Afro-American in Pennsylvania: A Critical Guide to Sources in the Pennsylvania State Archives* (1979); Donna B. Munger, *Pennsylvania Land Records: A History and Guide for Research* (1991); and Linda A. Ries, *Guide to Photographs at the Pennsylvania State Archives* (1993). All these guides are most valuable when supplemented by the finding aids in the State Archives pages of the PHMC website, which provides the researcher with the most up-to-date and comprehensive list of the collections. In addition, the State Library's Government Documents Section has runs of state agencies' publications, which are linked to the agency record groups found in the Archives.

Also essential to the study of the state's history are the extensive collections at the Historical Society of Pennsylvania (HSP) in Philadelphia. The HSP has a large collection of books and other printed materials on state, regional, and national history, an important newspaper collection with special strength in eighteenth- and nineteenth-century newspapers, and an almost unparalleled manuscript collection for the colonial period through the nineteenth century. The HSP's collections have been enriched by its merger with the Balch Institute for Ethnic Studies, which brought numerous ethnic and foreign-language newspapers, records of immigrant and ethnic group organizations, and artifacts to its collections, many of those materials documenting late nineteenth- through twentieth-century life and institutions. The HSP's manuscript materials are most fully described in its *Guide to the Manuscript Collections of the Historical Society of Pennsylvania* (3rd ed., 1991). The Balch's collections are described in Monique Bourque and R. Joseph Anderson, eds., *A Guide to Manuscript and Microfilm Collections of the*

Research Library of the Balch Institute for Ethnic Studies (1992). The Library Company of Philadelphia, next door to the HSP, complements the HSP holdings with its renowned collection of printed works (e.g., books, pamphlets, broadsides, lithographs, photographs) from the colonial era through the late nineteenth century, with many materials pertinent to state and regional history. The Senator John Heinz Pittsburgh Regional History Center of the Historical Society of Western Pennsylvania holds significant runs of newspapers, documents, and manuscripts on western Pennsylvania, with special strengths in Pittsburgh-area subjects.

Local and county historical societies are a vital resource, often for more than the particular histories of the locality or county. Many have significant holdings in local or county newspapers, government reports, personal papers, institutional records, photographs, and artifacts. Jean Cutler, ed., *Keystone Treasures* (cited above) identifies such societies, and the *American Library Directory* (cited above) briefly describes their collections. County and local governments retain records on land and other property holdings and transfers, vital statistics, taxes, civil and criminal actions, and more. Although badly in need of updating, a first step in identifying such materials is Sylvester K. Stevens and Donald H. Kent, eds., *County Government and Archives in Pennsylvania* (1947). In addition, many local public libraries collect and maintain printed works, newspapers, and other materials on the history of the town(s) or county they serve. Also important are libraries and museums devoted to special topics that are also relevant to Pennsylvania's past—for example, the Military History Institute at the U.S. Army War College in Carlisle, the Civil War Library and Museum in Philadelphia, the German Society of Pennsylvania in Philadelphia, the Railroad Museum of Pennsylvania in Strasburg, the Pennsylvania Anthracite Heritage Museum in Scranton, the Moravian Archives in Bethlehem, the Presbyterian Historical Society in Philadelphia, the Quaker Collection at Haverford College in Haverford, and the Hagley Museum and Library in Wilmington, Delaware (which has valuable collections of Pennsylvania and regional businesses). Seminaries of religious groups often have printed and other materials important to Pennsylvania history. No comprehensive bibliographical listing of the holdings of the special-interest libraries and museums in the state exists, so it is necessary to consult the particular institution directly for finding aids. Also worth visiting are college and university libraries in the state, most of which have basic collections in Pennsylvania history and related subjects and several of which have important documentary, archival, and artifact collections. The Pennsylvania State University at University Park holds large collections of insurance maps, railroad records, newspapers, and business and labor materials for Pennsylvania places and organizations.

Pennsylvania's many historical and history-related journals offer various mixes of current research on virtually every aspect of Pennsylvania history, book and exhibit reviews, and documents. The four most important such journals are the venerable *Pennsylvania Magazine of History and Biography* (published since 1877 and the oldest continuously published historical journal in the nation), *Pennsylvania History, Pennsylvania Heritage,* and *Western Pennsylvania History* (formerly *Pittsburgh History* and the *Western Pennsylvania Historical Magazine*). The newest magazine (2001) is *Pennsylvania Legacies,* published by the Historical Society of Pennsylvania. Local and county historical magazines vary in coverage and quality, but offer access to local materials and often include photographic and other illustrative material from the societies' holdings. The most complete collections of local and county historical journals are at the State Library in Harrisburg, but the HSP also has many such journals dating back to their first issue. Also worth consulting for historical topics and documents are special-interest journals with an explicit Pennsylvania interest—the *Pennsylvania Genealogical Magazine, Pennsylvania Archaeologist, Keystone Folklore,* and *Der Reggeboge* (of the Pennsylvania German Society), among others—or with a related interest: such as *Quaker History* or the *William and Mary Quarterly* (for the colonial/Revolutionary eras), to cite two. The best single index to the periodical literature from 1960 to today is *America: History and Life* (cited above), although the *Pennsylvania Magazine of History and Biography* has two comprehensive indexes that cover volumes 1 through 123 (1877 to 1999 inclusive) and *Pennsylvania History* has an index for its earlier volumes.

For so large and significant a state, Pennsylvania has not generated many general histories, and most of those written have emphasized political and economic history rather than social, cultural, and intellectual developments. The standard history of the commonwealth was Philip S. Klein and Ari Hoogenboom, *A History of Pennsylvania* (2nd and enlarged edition, 1980), now out of print. Klein and Hoogenboom focus largely on political and economic matters, but they also offer a wide panorama on Pennsylvania's past. The book lacks a general bibliography, but chapter bibliographies provide helpful introductions to the basic literature. The best short treatments of Pennsylvania are Thomas C. Cochran, *Pennsylvania: A Bicentennial History* (1978); Sylvester K. Stevens, *Pennsylvania: Birthplace of a Nation* (1964); and Paul A. W. Wallace, *Pennsylvania: Seed of a Nation* (1962)—all of which are strongest on the colonial period through the nineteenth century. Sylvester K. Stevens, *Pennsylvania: The Heritage of a Commonwealth* (4 vols., 1968), has much detail and includes biographies of prominent Pennsylvanians. *Our Pennsylvania Heritage* by William A. Cornell and Millard Altland has been used in many schools since it was introduced in 1959. The *Pennsylvania Manual,* published every other year by the Commonwealth of Pennsylvania's Department of General Services, includes a brief historical overview of the state, the text of the state's constitution, and historical statistics and listings on elections, officeholders, and local government, in addition to current information on government, education, media, and nonprofit organizations.

It is not surprising that Pennsylvania's earlier history has claimed the most attention from historians, anthropologists, archaeologists, and others plumbing Pennsylvania's past. General works of note are Joseph E. Illick, *Colonial Pennsylvania: A History* (1976), which remains probing and prescient; and Joseph J. Kelley Jr., *Pennsylvania: The Colonial Years, 1681–1776* (1980), which contains much information and many vignettes. Still useful is Howard M. Jenkins, ed., *Pennsylvania, Colonial and Federal: A History, 1608–1903* (3 vols., 1903).

The public issues marking later periods in Pennsylvania history have benefited from a series of books published by the PHMC. Although the books concentrate on political and economic concerns overall, and do not extend to the twentieth century in coverage, each work still stands as the first step toward understanding the public interests of the period under review. To date, they include Theodore Thayer, *Pennsylvania Politics and the Growth of Democracy, 1740–1776* (1953); Robert L. Brunhouse, *The Counter-Revolution in Pennsylvania, 1776–1790* (1971); Harry M. Tinkcom, *The Republicans and Federalists in Pennsylvania, 1790–1801* (1950); Sanford B. Higginbotham, *The Keystone in the Democratic Arch: Pennsylvania Politics, 1800–1816* (1952); Charles M. Snyder, *The Jacksonian Heritage: Pennsylvania Politics, 1833–1848* (1958); John F. Coleman, *The Disruption of the Pennsylvania Democracy, 1848–1860* (1975); and Frank B. Evans, *Pennsylvania Politics, 1872–1877: A Study in Political Leadership* (1966). Also in the series, but published by the Historical Society of Pennsylvania and the University of Pennsylvania Press, respectively, are Philip S. Klein, *Pennsylvania Politics: A Game Without Rules, 1817–1832* (1940); and Erwin S. Bradley, *The Triumph of Militant Republicanism: A Study of Pennsylvania and Presidential Politics, 1860–1872* (1964). The best overview of Pennsylvania politics from the 1930s to 1980 is Paul B. Beers, *Pennsylvania Politics Today and Yesterday: The Tolerable Accommodation* (1980).

The Pennsylvania Historical Association (108 Weaver Building, Pennsylvania State University, University Park, PA 16802) has published, and continues to commission, fifty- to eighty-page monographs on a host of subjects, intended for school use and general readership. They include an "Ethnic Studies" series with pamphlets on African Americans, Irish, Jews, Pennsylvania Germans, Poles, and Scots-Irish to date, and works on such varied topics as architecture, decorative arts, painters, constitutions, reformers, religious leaders, the Quakers, the iron industry, and transportation, among others.

County and city/town histories offer much information, but their reliability is uneven. Between the nation's centennial and the mid-1890s, encyclopedic histories published for many counties contain detailed information not easily found elsewhere, especially about the social origins of the communities where much of Pennsylvania's population lives today. Many such county histories, though, must be used with caution. Too many skew the story uncritically to emphasize the "great men" of the county (some of whom commissioned the work or paid subscriptions to it for publication) and give others (especially workers, minorities, and women) short shrift. More recent county and city/town histories are not necessarily more critical in perspective, but often have more up-to-date information and a wider range of inquiry and representation (including photographic illustrations). Especially useful city histories are Russell F. Weigley, ed.,

Philadelphia: A 300-Year History (1982); Edwin Wolf II, *Philadelphia: Portrait of an American City* (1975); Stefan Lorant, *Pittsburgh: The Story of an American City* (1964); Roy Lubove, ed., *Pittsburgh* (1976); and Franklin Toker, *Pittsburgh: An Urban Portrait* (1986).

For a wider canvass of the state, and much valuable historical information, see E. Willard Miller, ed., *A Geography of Pennsylvania* (1995); David J. Cuff, William J. Young, Edward K. Muller, Wilbur Zelinsky, and Ronald Abler, *The Atlas of Pennsylvania* (1989); and Deborah Stephens Burns and Richard J. Webster, with Candace Reed Stern, *Pennsylvania Architecture: The Historic American Buildings Survey with Catalog Entries, 1933–1990* (2000). One good, and fun, way to get started surveying Pennsylvania's varied past is by tracking the historical markers across the state. George R. Beyer, *Guide to the State Historical Markers of Pennsylvania* (2000), which arranges the markers by county and includes the text of each marker, makes it possible to do so.

A wag once quipped, "Real people don't read footnotes." Perhaps not, but they ought to do so. That's where the proof is. Absent footnotes, as in this book, "people" would do well to consider and examine the sources historians used and recommended. Then they too might become not only readers of Pennsylvania's past but also students of it.

CONTRIBUTORS

JAMES M. BEIDLER is Executive Director of the Genealogical Society of Pennsylvania. He writes "Roots & Branches," a weekly newspaper column that appears in *The Patriot-News* of Harrisburg, Pennsylvania, is genealogy columnist for *German Life* magazine, and publishes regularly in professional journals. In addition to writing on genealogical concerns, he sits on the State Historic Records Advisory Board.

SIMON J. BRONNER is Distinguished University Professor of American Studies and Folklore at The Pennsylvania State University, Harrisburg. He is the author or editor of more than eighteen books, including *Following Tradition: Folklore in the Discourse of American Culture; Lafcadio Hearn's America;* and *Popularizing Pennsylvania: Henry W. Shoemaker and the Progressive Uses of Folklore and History.* He is also series editor for the Pennsylvania German History and Culture Series for Penn State Press.

DAVID R. CONTOSTA is Professor of History at Chestnut Hill College in Philadelphia. He is the author of more than a dozen books on such subjects as urban and suburban history, architecture and landscape, orphanages, higher education, and various topics in social, cultural, and intellectual history. Among his books are *Henry Adams and the American Experiment; Suburb in the City: Chestnut Hill, Philadelphia;* and *Philadelphia's Progressive Orphanage: The Carson Valley School.* He is currently writing a history of Philadelphia's Main Line suburbs.

VERNA L. COWIN is Research Associate, Section of Anthropology, Carnegie Museum of Natural History. Until her retirement from her position in March 2001, she was Associate Curator of Anthropology at the Carnegie Museum of Natural History, where she headed the museum's archaeological investigations of prehistoric and historic sites in the Upper Ohio Valley. She has published articles and reports on Pittsburgh archaeological resources, the excavation and interpretation of the Pennsylvania Canal, shell ornaments from New York, and other topics.

DAVID DEMAREST is an emeritus professor of English at Carnegie Mellon University, where he has devised and taught a number of courses on the culture of industrialism: working-class literature, documentary photography, oral history, and reading the built landscape. Among his works are two anthologies about regional topics, *From These Hills, From These Valleys: Selected Fiction About Western Pennsylvania* and *The River Ran Red: Homestead 1892*.

PHILIP JENKINS is Distinguished Professor of History and Religious Studies at The Pennsylvania State University. Born in Wales, he has lived in Pennsylvania since 1980. He has published sixteen books, several of which treat twentieth-century Pennsylvania subjects. Among his most recent works are *The Next Christendom: The Coming of Global Christianity; The Cold War at Home: The Red Scare in Pennsylvania, 1945–1960;* and *Hoods and Shirts: The Extreme Right in Pennsylvania, 1925–1950*.

SUSAN E. KLEPP is Professor of History and Affiliated Professor of Women's Studies and African-American Studies at Temple University and Senior Research Associate at the McNeil Center for Early American Studies. Her books include *The Infortunate: The Voyage and Adventures of William Moraley* and *The Demographic History of the Philadelphia Region*. She has published widely on women, race, demographics, and social history, including recent articles in the *Journal of American History* and the *William and Mary Quarterly*. She also has several studies on eighteenth-century Pennsylvania women forthcoming.

EMMA LAPSANSKY is Professor of History and Curator of Special Collections at Haverford College, where she teaches courses on Quaker history, American social history, and material culture. She is widely published on Quaker, African American, and regional history and the history of community formation, and she has forthcoming volumes on Quaker and material culture and on the correspondence between a nineteenth-century Quaker colonizationist and a number of black and white abolitionists.

WALTER LICHT is Associate Dean and Professor of History at the University of Pennsylvania. His books include *Working for the Railroad: The Organization of Work in the Nineteenth Century; Work Sights: Industrial Philadelphia, 1890–1950; Getting Work: Philadelphia, 1840–1950;* and *Industrializing America: The Nineteenth Century*. He is currently completing a study of the economic decline of the anthracite coal region of eastern Pennsylvania.

RANDALL M. MILLER is William Dirk Warren '50 Sesquicentennial Chair and Professor of History at Saint Joseph's University and president of the Pennsylvania Historical Association. He also is a former editor of the *Pennsylvania Magazine of History and Biography*. He is the author or editor of twenty books on such topics as the American Civil War, slavery and the Old South, urban history, immigration and ethnicity, religion, social reform, the American Revolution, Germans in America, film and television, and American diaries. His most recent book, co-edited with Robert Engs, is *The Birth of the Grand Old Party: The Republicans' First Generation*.

WILLIAM PENCAK is Professor of History at The Pennsylvania State University and edited *Pennsylvania History* from 1994 to 2002. He also is founding editor of *Explorations in Early American Culture*, a publication of the McNeil Center for Early American Studies. He has published books on topics as varied as Thomas Hutchinson and loyalism during the American Revolutionary era, the American Legion, and Icelandic runic literature. Among his publications on Pennsylvania are several co-edited collections published by Penn State Press, including *Beyond Philadelphia: The American Revolution in the Pennsylvania Hinterland; Making and Remaking Pennsylvania's Civil War; Riot and Revelry in Early America;* and the forthcoming *Friends and Enemies in Penn's Woods*.

DANIEL K. RICHTER is the Richard S. Dunn Director of the McNeil Center for Early American Studies and Professor of History at the University of Pennsylvania, where he teaches and writes on colonial North America and Native American history before 1800. His books include *Facing East from Indian Country: A Native History of Early America*, finalist for the Pulitzer Prize in History; *The Ordeal of the Longhouse: The Peoples of the Iroquois League in the Era of European Colonization;* and, as co-editor, *Beyond the Covenant Chain: The Iroquois and Their Neighbors in Indian North America, 1600–1800*.

LINDA RIES is an archivist with the Pennsylvania State Archives and Editor of *Susquehanna Heritage: A Journal of the Historical Society of Dauphin County*. She is the author of the *Guide to Photographs at the Pennsylvania State Archives* and co-author of the *Directory of Pennsylvania Photographers, 1839–1900*. She has written numerous articles on the history of Pennsylvania photography and edited a special issue, "The History of Photography in Pennsylvania," for *Pennsylvania History* (1997), which won the Hamer Award of the Society of American Archivists for the best work published in the United States presenting archival materials for 1997.

LINDA SHOPES is a historian at the Pennsylvania Historical and Museum Commission and former president of the Oral History Association. She is co-editor of *The Baltimore Book: New Views of Local History;* guest editor of the special issue of *Pennsylvania History* "Oral History in Pennsylvania" (1993); and author of "Making Sense of Evidence: Oral

History," an on-line publication of History Matters website. Her most recent work is "Oral History and the Study of Communities," published in the *Journal of American History* (2002).

RICHARD J. WEBSTER is Professor of History and American Studies at West Chester University. His books include *Philadelphia Preserved: Catalog of the Historic American Buildings Survey* and (with Deborah Stephens Burns and Candace Reed Stern) *Pennsylvania Architecture: The Historic American Buildings Survey with Catalog Entries, 1933–1990.* His current project is a book on eastern Pennsylvania for the "Buildings of the United States" series.

WILBUR ZELINSKY is Professor Emeritus of Geography at The Pennsylvania State University and former president of the Association of American Geographers. At Penn State, his teaching and writing focused mainly on the cultural and social geography of North America, and he developed his special passion for Pennsylvania. The recipient of the Cullum medal from the American Geographical Society in 2001, he is the author of several books, including *The Cultural Geography of the United States* and most recently *The Enigma of Ethnicity.*

MICHAEL ZUCKERMAN is Professor of History at the University of Pennsylvania, where he teaches a wide range of courses from early America to the modern day. He has written *Peaceable Kingdoms: New England Towns in the Eighteenth Century* and *Almost Chosen People: Oblique Biographies in the American Grain;* edited *Friends and Neighbors: Group Life in America's First Plural Society;* and co-edited *Beyond the Century of the Child: Crossroads of Cultural History and Developmental Psychology.*

ILLUSTRATION CREDITS

Abbreviations for frequently cited sources:

FLP   The Free Library of Philadelphia
HABS Historic American Buildings Survey, Library of Congress, Washington, D.C.
HSP   Historical Society of Pennsylvania, Philadelphia
LCP   The Library Company of Philadelphia
PHMC The Pennsylvania Historical and Museum Commission, Harrisburg
PSUP The Pennsylvania State University Press, University Park

MERCER TILES

The names and numbers of the Mercer tiles that decorate the opening page of each component of this book are listed below. The images are provided courtesy of the Capitol Preservation Committee, Harrisburg.

Title Page/Cover, Keystone 139; *Foreword,* Liberty Bell 127; *Preface,* Blowing the Dinner Horn 29; *Introduction,* The Arms of Pennsylvania 375; *Part I Title Page,* Frying in the Open Fire 68; *Chapter 1,* Indian Rock Picture 344; *Chapter 2,* Penn's Treaty 97; *Chapter 3,* Reading the Declaration of Independence 303; *Chapter 4,* Conestoga Wagon 134; *Chapter 5,* Gettysburg 389; *Chapter 6,* Automobile 353; *Chapter 7,* The House of Steel 204; *Epilogue,* The Hawk or Eagle 329; *Part II Title Page,* Coal Miner 131; *Chapter 8* (Geography), Mason and Dixon's Line 300; *Chapter 9* (Architecture), The Log House 4; *Chapter 10* (Archaeology), Arrowhead 248; *Chapter 11* (Folklore and Folklife), White Children Rescued by Indians 335; *Chapter 12* (Genealogy), Oak Leaves 86; *Chapter 13* (Photography), Camera and Photographer 305; *Chapter 14* (Art), Indian Picture of the Rattlesnake 256; *Chapter 15* (Oral History), The Telephone 307; *Chapter 16* (Literature), Typewriter 388; *Appendix,* Cherries 110; *Select Bibliography,* Screech Owl 51; *Contributors,* Bee-Hive 16; *Credits,* The Dog 148; *Index,* Pine Cones 292.

MAPS

Page numbers in the Maps section are in boldface type. On a page with more than one illustration, the credits correspond to illustrations clockwise from top left.

Chapter 1: **xxiv** PSUP map. **5** PSUP map. **8** PSUP map. **9** PSUP map. **20** PSUP map. Source: *1960 Soil Classification: A Comprehensive System* (Washington, D.C.: Soil Survey Staff, 7th Approximation, 1960). **22** PSUP map. Source: Barry C. Kent, *Discovering Pennsylvania's Archaeological Heritage* (Harrisburg: PHMC,

1980), 31. **32** Courtesy of the Smithsonian Institution. Source: William C. Sturtevant, gen. ed., *Handbook of North American Indians,* vol. 15: *Northeast,* ed. Bruce G. Trigger (Washington, D.C.: Smithsonian Institution Press, 1978), 214. **36** Courtesy of Daniel K. Richter.

Chapter 2: **51** Courtesy of the National Archives (the Netherlands), Archives of the Dutch East India Company, 1602–1795 (1.04.02). **56** Courtesy of Terry T. Jordan and the University of Texas Cartography Lab. Source: Terry T. Jordan and Matti Kaups, *The American Backwoods Frontier: An Ethnic and Ecological Interpretation* (Baltimore: Johns Hopkins University Press, 1989), 241. **66** Copyright © 1982 by University of Pennsylvania Press. Reprinted with permission. Source: Richard S. Dunn and Mary Maples Dunn, eds., *The Papers of William Penn,* vol. 2: 1680–1684 (Philadelphia: University of Pennsylvania Press, 1982), 491. **77** PSUP map. **96** Source: David Humphreys, *An Historical Account of the Incorporated Society for the Propagation of the Gospel in Foreign Parts* (London: Downing, 1730), endpiece.

Chapter 3: **113** PSUP map. **135** PSUP maps modified from maps in David J. Cuff, William J. Young, Edward K. Muller, Wilbur Zelinsky, and Ronald F. Abler, eds., *The Atlas of Pennsylvania* (Philadelphia: Temple University Press, 1989), 88. **145** Courtesy Pennsylvania State Archives, Harrisburg. **146** PSUP map modified from map in David J. Cuff, William J. Young, Edward K. Muller, Wilbur Zelinsky, and Ronald F. Abler, eds., *The Atlas of Pennsylvania* (Philadelphia: Temple University Press, 1989), 81.

Chapter 4: **179** PSUP map. **180** PSUP map.

Chapter 5: **223** PSUP map. Source: *Report of the Department of Forestry, 1914–1915* (Harrisburg: Department of Forestry, 1916). **230** PSUP map. Source: Richard G. Healey, Trem Stamp, Paul Carter, and David Kidd, *Historical GIS of the North-Eastern United States* (1999) http://www.envf.port.ac.uk/geo/geo.htm (follow links to on-line resources). **233** PSUP map.

Chapter 6: **271** PSUP map. Source: Bureau of the Census, *U.S. Census of Population* (Washington, D.C.: GPO): *1880* (1883), 883; *1920* (1922), 525; *1940* (1943), 2, pt. 6: 31.

Chapter 8: **392** Copyright © 1957 Erwin Raisz. Reprinted with permission from Raisz Landform Maps, Brookline, Massachusetts. **393** PSUP map. **394** PSUP map. Source: U.S. Department of Energy, *Outlook for U.S. Coal* (Washington, D.C.: Department of Energy, 1982). **396** PSUP map. Source: J. W. Glass, *The Pennsylvania Culture Region: A View from the Barn* (Ann Arbor, Mich.: UMI Research Press, 1986). **399** PSUP map. Source: J. R. Gibson, ed., *European Settlement and Development in North America* (Toronto: University of Toronto Press, 1978), 75. **400** PSUP map. Source: Wilbur Zelinsky's original compilation (1987).

BLACK AND WHITE ILLUSTRATIONS
Page numbers in the Black and White Illustration section are in boldface type. On a page with more than one illustration, the credits correspond to illustrations clockwise from top left.

Chapter 1: **7** PHMC. **11** PHMC. **13** PHMC. **14** PHMC. **15** PHMC. **16** PHMC. **17** PHMC. **21** PHMC. **26** Detail from *Plan du Fort Frontenac ou Cataraouy* (c. 1720) courtesy of the Newberry Library, Chicago. **27** Detail from John Bartram, *Observations on . . . His Travels from Pensilvania to Onondago . . .* (London, 1751). **28** PHMC. **29** PHMC. **31** PHMC. **34** The State Museum of Pennsylvania, Harrisburg. **35** PHMC. **37** PHMC. ▪ Courtesy of James Bradley. **38** PHMC. **39** Archives Nationales, Paris. ▪ Retouched by Matthew C. Robbins. Courtesy of the Robert Dechert Collection, Department of Special Collections, Van Pelt/Dietrich Library Center, University of Pennsylvania, Philadelphia. **40** PHMC. **41** PHMC. **43** Annenberg Rare Book and Manuscript Library, University of Pennsylvania, Philadelphia.

Chapter 2: **48** LCP. **52** LCP. **54** American Swedish Historical Museum, Philadelphia. **55** Courtesy Allison-

Shelley Collection, Rare Books and Manuscripts, Special Collections Library, The Pennsylvania State University Libraries, University Park. **57** Photo by George Ambrose, Friends of the Swedish Cabin, Drexel Hill. **59** From Benson John Lossing, *Harper's Encyclopædia of United States History* . . . (New York: Harper, 1905), 115. **60** American Swedish Historical Museum, Philadelphia. **62** Copyright of the Library of the Religious Society of Friends, London. **64** HSP, Atwater Kent Museum, Philadelphia. ▪ HSP. **68** Independence National Historical Park, Philadelphia. **70** Courtesy Provost and Fellows of Worcester College, Oxford. **71** The York County Heritage Trust, York. **72** Gift of the Heirs of J. Stogdell Stokes, 1952, Philadelphia Museum of Art. **72** Purchased with the Joseph E. Temple Fund, 1926, Philadelphia Museum of Art. ▪ Gift of Mr. and Mrs. Robert L. Raley, 1997, Philadelphia Museum of Art. **73** LCP. **76** Pennsylvania State Archives, Harrisburg. **79** HSP. **80** From "[Mother Maria's Music Book]," manuscript music book with illustrations for *Zionitischer WeyrauchsHügel* ("Schwester Maria," Ephrata, 1751). Courtesy of Guy Oldham, London, England. **81** Moravian Historical Society, Nazareth. **82** LCP. **85** Courtesy Rare Book Department, FLP. **86** LCP. **87** Courtesy Winterthur Museum, Winterthur, Delaware. **88** HSP. **89** Independence National Historical Park, Philadelphia. **93** LCP. **95** LCP. **98** Quaker Collection, Haverford College Library, Haverford.

Chapter 3: **102** National Portrait Gallery, Smithsonian Institution, Washington, D.C. ▪ Yale University Art Gallery, New Haven, Connecticut. **105** HSP. **106** PHMC. **107** © The Right Hon. The Earl of Derby. **108** LCP. **110** LCP. **111** Public Record Office, London. **114** LCP. **115** LCP. **116** From *The Pennsylvania Journal,* 1765. **117** Independence National Historical Park, Philadelphia. **119** Courtesy University of Pennsylvania Art Collection, Philadelphia. **120** LCP. **122** Courtesy Lancaster County Historical Society, Lancaster. **124** Courtesy of the American Revolution Center, Valley Forge. **125** Chicago Historical Society, Chicago. **126** Bequest of Charles Allen Munn, 1924, The Metropolitan Museum of Art, New York. **128** HSP. ▪ Henry Hope Reed Collection, Frick Art Reference Library, New York. **129** Courtesy John Carter Brown Library at Brown University, Providence, Rhode Island. **130** The State Museum of Pennsylvania, Harrisburg. **131** Collection of The New-York Historical Society, New York. **132** Independence National Historical Park, Philadelphia. **134** LCP. **137** Pennsylvania Hospital Historic Collections, Philadelphia. **138** LCP. **139** LCP. **141** Urban Archives, Temple University Libraries, Philadelphia. ▪ Delaware Art Museum, Wilmington, Delaware. **143** LCP. **144** LCP. **147** Washington and Jefferson College Historical Collection, Washington. **149** The York County Heritage Trust, York.

Chapter 4: **155** Pennsylvania State Archives, Harrisburg. **156** Historical Society of Western Pennsylvania, Pittsburgh. **158** Grey Towers Collection, USDA Forest Service, Milford. **159** Grey Towers Collection, USDA Forest Service, Milford. **160** Courtesy Hagley Museum and Library, Wilmington, Delaware. **162** Beverly R. Robinson Collection, United States Naval Academy Archives, Annapolis, Maryland. ▪ Courtesy Erie County Historical Society and Museums, Erie. **164** Pennsylvania Academy purchase from the estate of Paul Beck Jr., Pennsylvania Academy of the Fine Arts, Philadelphia. **165** Rogers Fund, 1942, All rights reserved, The Metropolitan Museum of Art, New York. **166** Reproduced with the permission of Rare Books and Manuscripts, Special Collections Library, The Pennsylvania State University Libraries, University Park. **167** Courtesy Landis Valley Museum, Lancaster. **169** Courtesy Lancaster County Historical Society, Lancaster. **170** Courtesy Lancaster County Historical Society, Lancaster. **174** LCP. **175** Friends Historical Library, Swarthmore College, Swarthmore. ▪ LCP. **176** LCP. **177** "Walking Dresses of the Thirties," from *Godey's Lady's Book,* October 1835. ▪ LCP. **181** Pennsylvania Canal Society Collection, National Canal Museum, Easton. **182** Wayne County Historical Society, Honesdale. ▪ Pennsylvania State Archives, Harrisburg. **183** PHMC. **184** Historical Society of Western Pennsylvania, Pittsburgh. **187** Palmer Museum of Art, The Pennsylvania State University, University Park. **188** Courtesy Print Department, Boston Public Library, Boston. **190** LCP. **191** Dreer Collection, HSP. **192** LCP. **193** From William Still, *The Underground Railroad,* 1872. **194** National Archives, College Park, Maryland. **195** LCP. **196** HSP, Atwater Kent Museum, Philadelphia. **198** LCP. ▪ Carnegie Library of Pittsburgh. **200** Historical Society of Western Pennsylvania, Pittsburgh. ▪ Courtesy La Salle University Art Museum, Philadelphia. ▪ LCP.

Chapter 5: **204** Photo by Mark Thistlethwaite, The State Museum of Pennsylvania, Harrisburg. ■ Carnegie Library of Pittsburgh. **205** *Police Gazette,* August 13, 1892. **208** National Archives, College Park, Maryland. ■ Courtesy Bradley R. Hoch. ■ Samuel Bates Papers, Pennsylvania State Archives, Harrisburg. ■ Library of Congress, Washington, D.C. **210** Courtesy Print and Picture Collection, FLP. **212** LCP. **213** Carnegie Library of Pittsburgh. **214** LCP. **215** Cumberland County Historical Society, Carlisle. **218** Pennsylvania State Archives, Harrisburg. **220** Courtesy Hagley Museum and Library, Wilmington, Delaware. **221** Courtesy Hagley Museum and Library, Wilmington, Delaware. **222** Courtesy Print and Picture Collection, FLP. **224** Photo by John Horgan Jr., Anthracite Heritage Museum, PHMC, Scranton. **225** Pennsylvania State Archives, Harrisburg. **226** Pennsylvania State Archives, Harrisburg. **227** Carnegie Library of Pittsburgh. **228** Carnegie Library of Pittsburgh. **231** Frederick Winslow Taylor Collection, Stevens Institute of Technology, Hoboken, New Jersey. **232** LCP. **233** Historical and Genealogical Society of Somerset County, Somerset. **234** Pennsylvania State Archives, Harrisburg. ■ Private collection. **235** Pennsylvania State Archives. **236** Drake Well Museum, PHMC, Titusville. **237** Drake Well Museum, PHMC, Titusville. **238** Photography Collections, University of Maryland, Baltimore County, Maryland. **239** Collections of the Lehigh County Historical Society, Allentown. **240** Historical Society of Western Pennsylvania, Pittsburgh. **243** Independence Seaport Museum, Philadelphia. **244** PHMC. **245** Pennsylvania State Archives, Harrisburg. **247** Courtesy Print and Picture Collection, FLP. **248** Huntingdon County Historical Society, Huntingdon. **249** Courtesy National Museum of American Jewish History, Philadelphia. **250** Courtesy Erie County Historical Society and Museums, Erie. **251** From *Solid for Mulhooly: A Political Satire by Rufus E. Shapley,* 2nd ed. (Philadelphia, 1889), 70. **252** Pennsylvania State Archives, Harrisburg. **254** American Cities Collection, National Archives, College Park, Maryland.

Chapter 6: **258** Pennsylvania State Archives, Harrisburg. **261** Violet Oakley papers 1841–1981, Archives of American Art, Smithsonian Institution, Washington, D.C. **262** Carnegie Library of Pittsburgh. **263** From *Radio Broadcasting News,* March 26, 1922, Carnegie Library of Pittsburgh. **264** Anthracite Heritage Museum, PHMC, Scranton. **265** Burg Collection, Pennsylvania State Archives, Harrisburg. **266** Photo by John Horgan Jr., Anthracite Heritage Museum, PHMC, Scranton. **267** Pennsylvania State Police. **268** Pennsylvania State Archives, Harrisburg. **270** Courtesy Mária Stefania Slošiarová, Literary and Art Archives of the Slovak National Library, Martin, Slovak Republic. **272** Gift of the Burdnak and Koval families, Johnstown Area Heritage Association, Johnstown. **273** Urban Archives, Temple University Libraries, Philadelphia. **274** From the collection of Delphia Shirk, Union County Historical Society, Lewisburg. **275** From the collection of Cherry Will, Union County Historical Society, Lewisburg. ■ Union County Historical Society, Lewisburg. ■ Reproduced with the permission of The Pennsylvania State University Archives / Penn State Room, University Park. **276** Drake Well Museum, PHMC, Titusville. **278** Historical Society of Western Pennsylvania, Pittsburgh. **279** Annenberg Rare Book and Manuscript Library, University of Pennsylvania, Philadelphia. **280** Pennsylvania State Archives, Harrisburg. **281** Courtesy Anne Dzamba, Chester County Historical Society, West Chester. **282** Photo by Daise Keichline, courtesy Nancy J. Perkins, Archives of John T. Keichline, Mountain View, California. ■ Carnegie Library of Pittsburgh. **283** Pennsylvania State Archives, Harrisburg. **287** Pennsylvania State Archives, Harrisburg. **288** Historical Society of Western Pennsylvania, Pittsburgh. **289** Chester County Historical Society, West Chester. **291** Urban Archives, Temple University Libraries, Philadelphia. **295** Carnegie Library of Pittsburgh. **296** James R. Cox Collection, 1923–1950, AIS 69:5, Archives Service Center, University of Pittsburgh, Pittsburgh. **297** Carnegie Library of Pittsburgh. **299** Pennsylvania State Archives, Harrisburg. **300** National Archives, College Park, Maryland. **301** Records of the Pennsylvania Turnpike Commission, Pennsylvania State Archives, Harrisburg. **302** Courtesy Carnegie Library of Pittsburgh. **303** PHMC. **304** Courtesy Eric Leif Davin. **305** Centre County Historical Society Collections, State College. **306** Urban Archives, Temple University Libraries, Philadelphia. **308** Courtesy American Heritage Center, University of Wyoming, Laramie, Wyoming. **310** From the collection of Katherine Roush, Union County Historical Society, Lewisburg. **311** UNITE Archives, Kheel Center, Cornell University, Ithaca, New York. **312** Courtesy HSP, The Balch Institute for Ethnic Studies, Philadelphia. **313** Union County Historical Society, Lewisburg. **314** Photo by Theresa Heineman. **315** Copyright © 2000 *Pittsburgh Post-Gazette.*

Chapter 7: **318** United States Steel Corporation photo. Reproduction by Randolph Harris. **319** Photo by Charlee Brodsky. **321** Courtesy Stephen N. Lukasik, Lukasik Studio, Dupont. **322** Historical Society of Western Pennsylvania, Pittsburgh. **324** Photo by Karl G. Rath, PHMC. **327** Photo by Myke Scholtes. **328** Historical Society of Dauphin County, Harrisburg. **331** Courtesy *Pittsburgh Post-Gazette* Archives. **332** Reprinted by permission of GRM Associates Inc., Agents for the *Pittsburgh Courier*. Copyright © 1951 by the *Pittsburgh Courier*; copyright renewed 1979 by the *Pittsburgh Courier*. Photo courtesy Library and Archives Division, Historical Society of Western Pennsylvania, Pittsburgh. **334** Urban Archives, Temple University Libraries, Philadelphia. **335** Marian Anderson Collection of Photographs, Annenberg Rare Book and Manuscript Library, University of Pennsylvania, Philadelphia. **336** Photo by Michael Viola. Courtesy *Philadelphia Inquirer*. **337** Urban Archives, Temple University Libraries, Philadelphia. **338** *Philadelphia Daily News* / Michael Mercanti. **339** The York County Heritage Trust, York. **340** Courtesy *Indiana Gazette*. **341** Courtesy Stephen N. Lukasik, Lukasik Studio, Dupont. **342** Urban Archives, Temple University Libraries, Philadelphia. **344** AP/WIDE WORLD PHOTOS. **345** Urban Archives, Temple University Libraries, Philadelphia. ▪ AP/WIDE WORLD PHOTOS. **347** Urban Archives, Temple University Libraries, Philadelphia. **349** AP/WIDE WORLD PHOTOS. **350** Courtesy Sports Information Department, The Pennsylvania State University, University Park. **351** Urban Archives, Temple University Libraries, Philadelphia. **352** Lancaster Newspapers Inc. **353** Mercer County Historical Society, Mercer. **356** Photo by David Schuyler. ▪ PSUP photo. **357** Urban Archives, Temple University Libraries, Philadelphia. **358** Pennsylvania State Archives, Harrisburg. **359** Carnegie Library of Pittsburgh. **360** Pennsylvania State Archives, Harrisburg. **362** Courtesy Caesars Pocono Resorts, Scotrun. **363** Urban Archives, Temple University Libraries, Philadelphia. **364** Photo copyright © 2002 Jim Schafer. **365** Little League Baseball Incorporated. **366** Courtesy Pennsylvania Film Office. **367** Altoona Railroaders Memorial Museum, Altoona. **368** Artwork by Marijo DePaola. **369** PSUP photo.

Chapter 8: **397** Photo by Wilbur Zelinsky. **398** Photo by Wilbur Zelinsky. **405** PSUP photos.

Chapter 9: **412** Pennsylvania State Archives, Harrisburg. **413** Photo by George Eisenman, 1971, HABS. **414** Photo by William J. Bulger, 1936, HABS. ▪ Photo by Jack E. Boucher, 1985, HABS. **415** Drawing by Cary Carson and Chinh Hoang, 1981, courtesy Cary Carson. ▪ Drawing by Stevenson Flemer. **416** Photo by Richard Webster, 2000. **417** Photo by Ned Goode, 1958, HABS. ▪ Photo by Charles H. Dornbusch, 1941, HABS. **418** HABS. **419** Photo by Richard Webster, 2000. ▪ Photo by Richard Webster, 1994. **420** Photo by Jack E. Boucher, 1960, HABS. ▪ Photo by Ned Goode, 1962, HABS. **421** Pennsylvania State Archives, Harrisburg. **422** Photograph copyright © Thorney Lieberman, courtesy CelliFlynnBrennan Architects & Planners, Pittsburgh. **423** Photo by William J. Bulger, 1936, HABS. ▪ Courtesy Clarion County Historical Society, Clarion. **424** Courtesy Archives and Special Collections, Franklin and Marshall College, Lancaster. **425** Photo c. 1998, Courtesy Department of University Relations, Graphics, Marketing, and Printing, University of Pittsburgh, Pittsburgh. **426** Drawing by Perry Benson, 1976, HABS. ▪ Photo by J. Bulger, 1936, HABS. **427** HABS. **428** HABS. **429** From *Cottage and Constructive Architecture* (New York: Bicknell, 1873). ▪ Photo by Alison Taggart, Historic Registration Project of the Centre County Library. **430** Photo by Richard Webster, 1994. ▪ Photo by J. Max Mueller, c. 1890, Chester County Historical Society, West Chester. **431** Photo by Richard Webster, 2000. ▪ Photo by Jack E. Boucher, 1972, HABS. **432** Photo by Richard Webster, 1981. **433** Courtesy PPG Industries. **434** Photo by Richard Webster, 1993. **435** Drawing by D. E. Sutton, c. 1930, HABS. ▪ Photo by Richard Webster, 1994. **436** Photo by Harold J. Webster, 2001. **437** Photo by Jack E. Boucher, 1985, HABS.

Chapter 10: **440** Courtesy Redevelopment Authority of the City of Philadelphia and John Milner Associates. **441** Independence National Historical Park, Philadelphia. **442** Photo by Steve Warfel, 1995, The State Museum of Pennsylvania, PHMC, Harrisburg. ▪ Adapted from Stanley Lantz, "Distribution of Paleo-Indian Projectile Points and Tools from Western Pennsylvania," *Archaeology of Eastern North America* 12 (1984), 210–21. **443** From Stanley Lantz, "Distribution of Paleo-Indian Projectile Points and Tools from Western Pennsylvania," *Archaeology of Eastern North America* 12 (1984), 225. **444** From Carl A. Bebrich and Lorraine

M. Willey, "The Stratigraphy of the Sheep Rock Shelter," in *Archaeological Investigations of Sheep Rock Shelter,* vol. 3 (Department of Anthropology, Pennsylvania State University, May 1968), Appendix I. **445** Photo by James B. Richardson III. **446** From Charles W. McNett Jr., ed., *Shawnee Minisink: A Stratified Paleoindian-Archaic Site in the Upper Delaware Valley of Pennsylvania* (New York: Academic Press, 1985), 90. **447** Courtesy of Verna Cowin. **448** From "Stonemason's Report of Dismantling Portions of Lift Lock #4 and Weigh Lock, Pennsylvania Mainline Canal," prepared by Parsons Brinckerhoff Construction Services Inc. **449** The State Museum of Pennsylvania, PHMC, Harrisburg. **450** Prepared by Robert J. Fryman and John T. Eddins, 1985. **455** Photo by Verna Cowin.

Chapter 11: **460** From E. G. Cattermole, *Famous Frontiersmen, Pioneers, and Scouts: The Vanguards of American Civilization* (Chicago: Donohue Brothers, 1888), 24. **463** From Rosemary Scanlon, "The Handprint: The Biography of a Pennsylvania Legend," *Keystone Folklore* 16 (Summer 1971), 105. **464** Courtesy Joseph Downs Collection of Manuscripts and Printed Ephemera, The Winterthur Library, Winterthur, Delaware. **465** Photo by Simon Bronner, private collection. **466** Photos by Simon Bronner. **468** From George Korson, ed., *Pennsylvania Songs and Legends* (1949), 386. **472** Photos by Simon Bronner. **474** Collection of Simon Bronner. **475** Photo by Simon Bronner. **476** Courtesy George Caba and Simon Bronner. **477** Photo by Arnold Zuckerman, Historical Society of Dauphin County, Harrisburg. **478** Photos by Simon Bronner.

Chapter 12: **482** Photo by James Beidler. **498** Courtesy Robert L. Baker.

Chapter 13: **502** HSP. **503** Marian S. Carson Collection, Prints and Photographs Division, Library of Congress, Washington, D.C. **504** From Eadweard Muybridge, *Animal Locomotion: An Electro-Photographic Investigation of Consecutive Phases of Animal Movements, 1872–1885,* vol. 6: *Females and Children* (Philadelphia: J. B. Lippincott, 1887), plate 187. **506** Charles Bregler's Thomas Eakins Collection, purchased with the partial support of the Pew Memorial Trust, Pennsylvania Academy of the Fine Arts, Philadelphia. **507** Courtesy Theater Collection, FLP. **508** A. A. Line Collection, Cumberland County Historical Society, Carlisle. **509** Photograph Collection, MG-218, Stereoviews, Pennsylvania State Archives, Harrisburg. ▪ Rowland Stebbins Photograph Collection, MG-218, Pennsylvania State Archives, Harrisburg. **510** Photo by John Mather, Mather Collection, DW 498, Drake Well Museum, Titusville. **511** Cecil Fulton Photograph Collection, MG-218, Pennsylvania State Archives, Harrisburg. **512** Francis Cooper Collection, MG-464, Pennsylvania State Archives, Harrisburg. **513** From Margaret Byington, *Homestead: The Households of a Mill Town* (1910). **514** J. Horace McFarland Collection, Neg. 746, MG-85, Pennsylvania State Archives, Harrisburg. ▪ J. Horace McFarland Collection, LS 3051, MG-85, Pennsylvania State Archives, Harrisburg. ▪ J. Horace McFarland Collection, Neg. 844, MG-85, Pennsylvania State Archives, Harrisburg. **515** Department of Highways, #360, Record Group 12, Pennsylvania State Archives, Harrisburg. **516** Department of Highways, #6803, Record Group 12, Pennsylvania State Archives, Harrisburg. **517** U.S. Farm Security Administration / Office of War Information, LC-USF342-001167-A, Prints and Photographs Division, Library of Congress, Washington, D.C. **518** Department of Justice, Record Group 15, Pennsylvania State Archives, Harrisburg. **519** E468.7.G19, Prints and Photographs Division, Library of Congress, Washington, D.C. ▪ LC-B811-0234, Prints and Photographs Division, Library of Congress, Washington, D.C. **520** LC-B811-0277, Prints and Photographs Division, Library of Congress, Washington, D.C. ▪ LC-B817-7942, Prints and Photographs Division, Library of Congress, Washington, D.C. **522** Library of Congress, Prints and Photographs Division, U.S. Farm Security Administration / Office of War Information, LC-USF33-006007-M5. **523** Courtesy Linda A. Ries.

Chapter 14: **529** Gift of Mrs. Sarah Harrison, The Joseph Harrison Jr. Collection, Pennsylvania Academy of the Fine Arts, Philadelphia. **530** Gift of John Stewart Kennedy, 1897, The Metropolitan Museum of Art, New York. **532** Bequest of Dr. John Collins Warren, 1856, Harvard University Portrait Collection, Harvard University Art Museums, Cambridge, Massachusetts. ▪ Gift of Mrs. Sarah Harrison, The Joseph Harrison Jr.

Collection, Pennsylvania Academy of the Fine Arts, Philadelphia. **534** Gift of the Lyon Family, Pennsylvania Academy of the Fine Arts, Philadelphia. **536** LCP. **538** Gift of Martha C. Karolik for the M. and M. Karolik Collection of American Paintings, 1815–1865, © 2002 Museum of Fine Arts, Boston. All rights reserved, Reproduced with permission, Courtesy Museum of Fine Arts, Boston. **539** The Carnegie Museum of Art, Pittsburgh. **540** Railroad Museum of Pennsylvania, PHMC, Strasburg. **541** Purchase, The Alfred N. Punnett Endowment Fund and George D. Pratt Gift, 1934, The Metropolitan Museum of Art, New York. **542** Steidle Collection, College of Earth and Mineral Sciences Museum and Art Gallery, The Pennsylvania State University, University Park. **543** Steidle Collection, College of Earth and Mineral Sciences Museum and Art Gallery, The Pennsylvania State University, University Park. **544** Gift of Mr. and Mrs. Edmund G. Fox, class of 1925, Steidle Collection, College of Earth and Mineral Sciences Museum and Art Gallery, The Pennsylvania State University, University Park. **545** Copyright Smithsonian American Art Museum, Washington, D.C. / Art Resource, New York. **546** Capitol Preservation Committee, Harrisburg. **549** Pennsylvania House of Representatives Commonwealth Media Services, Harrisburg. **550** Capitol Preservation Committee, Harrisburg.

Chapter 15: **556** Collection of Patricia Fabiano. **561** Photo 245-2515, National Archives, College Park, Maryland. **564** Pennsylvania State Archives, Harrisburg. **568** Photo by Charlee Brodsky. ▪ Photo by Charlee Brodsky. ▪ Photo by Charlee Brodsky, Lake Erie Collection, University of Pittsburgh, Pittsburgh. **571** Labor Archives, The Pennsylvania State University Libraries, University Park.

COLOR ILLUSTRATIONS

Peale, *Artist:* Gift of Mrs. Sarah Harrison, The Joseph Harrison Jr. Collection, Pennsylvania Academy of the Fine Arts, Philadelphia. ▪ Cooper, *South East Prospect:* LCP. ▪ Hicks, *Peaceable Kingdom:* Bequest of Charles C. Willis, Philadelphia Museum of Art. ▪ Charter: Pennsylvania State Archives, Harrisburg. ▪ Haidt, *First Fruits:* Moravian Archives, Bethlehem. ▪ Hesselius, *Tishcohan:* HSP, Atwater Kent Museum, Philadelphia. ▪Hesselius, *Lapowinsa:* HSP, Atwater Kent Museum, Philadelphia. ▪ Copley, *Mr. and Mrs. Mifflin:* Bequest of Mrs. Esther B. Wistar to the Historical Society of Pennsylvania in 1900 and acquired by the Philadelphia Museum of Art by mutual agreement with the Society through the generosity of Mr. and Mrs. Fitz Eugene Dixon Jr., and significant contributions from Mrs. Myer Eglin, and other donors, as well as the George W. Elkins Fund and the W. P. Wilstach Fund, 1999, Philadelphia Museum of Art. ▪ Trumbull, *Declaration:* Architect of the Capitol, Washington, D.C. ▪ Krimmel, *Election Day:* Henry Francis du Pont Winterthur Museum, Winterthur, Delaware. ▪ Broadside: Gift of Georgianna Hartzel in honor of Charles W. Mann Jr., Ammon Stapleton Collection, Rare Books and Manuscripts, Paterno Library, The Pennsylvania State University, University Park. ▪ Park, *Flax Scutching Bee:* Gift of Edgar William and Bernice Chrysler Garbisch, Photograph © 2002 Board of Trustees, National Gallery of Art, Washington, D.C. ▪ Inness, *Lackawanna Valley:* Gift of Mrs. Huttleston Rogers, Photograph © 2002 Board of Trustees, National Gallery of Art, Washington, D.C. ▪ Hetzel, *Fishermen:* Gift of the Westmoreland Society, Collection of the Westmoreland Museum of American Art, Greensburg. ▪ Eakins, *Gross Clinic:* Jefferson Medical College of Thomas Jefferson University, Philadelphia. ▪ Fowler, Wilkes-Barre: Photo by Scott E. Kriner, The Pennsylvania State Archives, Harrisburg. ▪ Van Ingen windows: Capitol Preservation Committee, Harrisburg. ▪ Abbey, *Camp:* Capitol Preservation Committee, Harrisburg. ▪ Oakley, *Penn's Vision:* Capitol Preservation Committee, Harrisburg. ▪ Oakley, *General Meade and Troops:* Capitol Preservation Committee, Harrisburg. ▪ Cassatt, *Mother and Two Children*: Anonymous Gift #1979.1, Collection of the Westmoreland Museum of American Art, Greensburg. ▪ Lawrence, *Migration:* The Phillips Collection, Washington, D.C. ▪ Demuth, *Lancaster:* The Louise and Walter Arensberg Collection, Philadelphia Museum of Art. ▪ Ashe, *Steel:* Steidle Collection, College of Earth and Mineral Sciences Museum and Art Gallery, The Pennsylvania State University, University Park. ▪ Thompson, *Company Row:* Steidle Collection, College of Earth and Mineral Sciences Museum and Art Gallery, The Pennsylvania State University, University Park. ▪ Walter, *Pittsburgh:* Steidle Collection, College of Earth and Mineral Sciences Museum and Art Gallery, The

Pennsylvania State University, University Park. ■ Gorson, *Pushing Coke:* Steidle Collection, College of Earth and Mineral Sciences Museum and Art Gallery, The Pennsylvania State University, University Park. ■ Wyeth, *Nightfall:* Private Collection, courtesy of Brandywine River Museum, Chadds Ford. ■ Davids, *Duke Street Market:* Gift of Mr. Paul Davids, Collection of the Westmoreland Museum of American Art, Greensburg. ■ Pippin, *Domino Players:* The Phillips Collection, Washington, D.C. ■ Speight, *Manayunk:* Collection of the Greenville Museum of Art, Greenville, North Carolina. ■ Wyeth, *Tenant Farmer:* Gift of Mr. and Mrs. William E. Phelps, Delaware Art Museum, Wilmington, Delaware. ■ Brewer, *Yo Blood Line:* Gift of Tina Williams Brewer, The State Museum of Pennsylvania, Harrisburg. ■ Savitsky, *Penn Treaty:* Gift of Jack and Mary Lou Savitt, The State Museum of Pennsylvania, Harrisburg.

COVER ART

Charles C. Hofmann, *View of Henry Z. Van Reed's Farm, Papermill, and Surroundings,* 1872, detail. Abby Aldrich Rockefeller Folk Art Museum, Colonial Williamsburg Foundation, Williamsburg, Virginia.

BACK COVER ART

Christian J. Walter, *Pittsburgh,* c. 1937, detail. Steidle Collection, College of Earth and Mineral Sciences Museum and Art Gallery, The Pennsylvania State University, University Park.

INDEX

Asian immigrants, *478*
Assemblies of God, 356, *356*
Assembly. *See also* Pennsylvania State Legislature
    under Constitution of 1776, 121, 123
    fishing laws, 86
    French and Indian War and, 112
    laws, 69
    overthrow in 1776, 117, 119, 120
    powers, 67
    Quaker influence, 66, 67, 74, 83
    ratification of U.S. Constitution, 142
    during Revolution, 115
astrology, 84, *110*
astronomy, 30, *85*, *119*
Atlantic Coastal Plain, 8, 29, 33
Atlantic Monthly, 273
atlatls (spear-throwers), 11, *13*
automobiles. *See also* roads
    effects on cities, 354
    license plates, 537
    manufacturing, 293, 303, 377
Avella (Washington County), 444
"The Avondale Mine Disaster," 467–71, *468*
Avondale mine fire, 224, 467–71, *470*
"Awake in a Strange Landscape" (Beatty), 580
Azilum, 144

B

Bache, Benjamin Franklin, 144, 146, 148
Badger, Daniel D., 427
Baer, George F., 264–65
Bailey, Charles, *414*
Baker, Robert L., *498*
Baker-Fuller Reunion, *498*
Baldi, Charles C., 268
Baldwin, Matthias, 154, 185, 221, 371
Baldwin Locomotive Works, 185, 221, *221*, 304
Ball, John, 199
Baltimore (Maryland), 180, 185, 187
Baltzell, E. Digby, 169, 293
banking
    African Americans in, 287
    buildings, *165*, 197
    during Civil War, 212
    development, 117, 133–35, 136, 164–66
    in Philadelphia, 164–66, 287
    in Pittsburgh, 230, 262
Bank of North America, 117, 123, 133–35, 136
Bank of Pennsylvania, 133–35, 164–65, *165*
Bank of Philadelphia, 165
Bank of the United States, 164, 165, 186, 188
Bank War, *188*
Bantam Car Company, 303
Baptists, 80, 81–83, *82*, 136, 172, 373

Barker, Joe, 172–73
Barkway (Hertfordshire, England), *419*
Barnes-Brinton House, *418*
barns
    log, *414*
    Pennsylvania style, 416, *417*
    raising, *275*, *325*
    timber-frame, 414
Barrett, James, 567
Barrick, Mac, 473–74
Bartoli, F., *131*
Bartram, Alexander, 138
Bartram, Jane, 138
Bartram, John, 85, *107*, 409
Bartram, William, 85, 371
baseball, 309, *312*, *365*
Bates Union, 176
The Battle of Gettysburg: Pickett's Charge
    (Rothermel), *204*, 530
Baynton, Wharton & Morgan, 451
beads, *37*
beans, 17–18, 22, 23, 27, 55
Beard, Charles A., 6
Beatty, Jan, 580
Beaver County
    iron and steel industries, 260, *304*
    nuclear power plant, 329
    population declines, 323
    union leaders in politics, 298
beavers, *47*, *49*, 58
Beaver Stadium (Centre County), 401
Beaver Wars, 65
Becker, Carl, 116
Bedford (Bedford County), 436
Bedford County, 449
    agriculture, 391
    architecture, 436
    religious groups, 79
    tourism, 366
Beik, Mildred Allen, 561–63
Beissel, Conrad, 79
Bell, Alexander Graham, 222
Bell, James, 309
Bell, Thomas, 409, 576–77, 591–92
Bell & Howell, 515
Bellefonte (Centre County), *282*, 351, 404
Bellevue Hotel (Philadelphia), 307
Bell House, *426*
Benedict, Al, 349
"Beneficiation" (Blair), 579
Benevolent Protective Order of the Elks, 307
Benezet, Anthony, 85, 95, 139
Beringer, Mae, 557
Beringia, 5

Berks County, 404. *See also* Reading
    agriculture, 361
    Boone family in, 73
    Fries's Rebellion, 103, 147, 148
    genealogical research, 482, 491
    German immigrants, 70–71
    housing, *426*
    outlet malls, 366
    during Revolution, 118, 129
    tourism, 400, 402
Bern Township (Berks County), 491
Bethel Church (Philadelphia), *139*, 141, 286
Bethlehem (Northampton County)
    architecture, 432
    founding, 79
    growth, 171
    museums, 563
    photographs of, 514, *517*
    population growth, 353
    prisoners of war, 122
    refugees from Indian raids, 112
    steel industry, 236, 326, 375, 393
    strikes, *267*
    Sun Tavern, 148
Bethlehem Steel Corporation, 231, *267*, 285, 302
Bettering House, 108
Bicknell, A. J., 426
Biddle, Nicholas, 186–88, *188*, 197, 371
Bingham, Anne Willing, 144
Bingham, William, 136, 144
Biographical Annals of Lebanon County, 487
Birch, William, *139*
birds, hunting, 86
birdstone, *15*
Bituminous Coal Plant (Pattison), *543*
bituminous coal region, 236. *See also* coal mining
    accessibility of coal, 393
    canals, 182–83
    during Civil War, 212
    company towns, 401
    deindustrialization, 320
    maps, *223*, *394*
    production, 262
    unions, 245
Black Fury (Musmanno), 576
Black Panther Party, 335
Blair, Peter, 577–80
Blair County. *See also* Altoona
    industrial history, 368
    railroads, 165
Blatt, Genevieve, 342
Bloomsburg (Columbia County), 404, *428*
Blue Ridge mountains, 8, 391
Blythe, David Gilmour, 537, *538*, *539*

photography studios, *508*, 523
population, 353, 354
railroads, 187
Carlisle Indian Industrial School, *283*
Carnegie, Andrew, 234, 371
bankers, 229, 230
life, 92, 229, 233
philanthropy, 260, *262*
Carnegie (Allegheny County), 290
Carnegie Institute of Technology, 351
Carnegie Library (Pittsburgh), *514*
Carnegie Mellon University, 351
Carnegie Museum of Natural History, 446
Carnegie Steel Company, 204, 205, *227*, 229, 260, 558–59. *See also* Homestead; United States Steel Corporation
Carpenters Hall (Philadelphia), 118
Carson, Marian S., 517, 524
Carson College for Orphan Girls, 283–84
Carsonia Park, 309
Carson Valley School, 283
Carville, James, 372
Casey, Robert, 345, 346
Cash, Johnny, 364
Cassatt, Alexander J., 251
Cassatt, Mary, 251
The Cast (Ashe), *542*
Catfish Path, 441, *442*
Cathedral of Learning (University of Pittsburgh), 423–24, *425*
Cathedral of the Church of the New Jerusalem (Bryn Athyn), 414, *416*, 434
Cather, Willa, 585
Catholic Church. *See* Roman Catholics
cattle, 185. *See also* dairy farming
Catto, Octavius V., 251, 252, *252*
Cayuga people, 20, 23
CCC. *See* Civilian Conservation Corps
cemeteries, 177, *177*, 406, *440*. *See also* graves and burials
Census, Septennial, 489
Census, U.S., 485, 487, 489
Centennial Exposition of 1876, 221, 222, *222*, 247, 379–80, 517
Central High School for Boys (Philadelphia), *502*, 503
Centralia (Columbia County), 327, *327*
Centre County. *See also* State College
churches, *494*
family reunions, *498*
houses, 426, *429*
salvage drives, *305*
settlement, 391
suffragette marches, *282*

towns, 400, 404–6, *404*
Chadd's Ford (Delaware County), 528
chairs, *72*
Chamberlain, Mason, *102*
Chambersburg (Franklin County)
Civil War battle, 214–15, *215*
railroads, 187
The Champion Single Sculls (Max Schmitt in a Single Scull) (Eakins), *541*
"Changing Rolls on the Universal Mill" (Blair), 577–79
Chapter of Perfection, 79
charitable activities
of business leaders, 169
of Carnegie, 260, *262*
during Civil War, 213–14, 250
during Depression, 294–95, *296*
following Johnstown Flood, 234
of religious groups, 78, *296*
Charles II, King of England, 64, 374
Charleston (South Carolina), 210–11, 307
"Charley Hill's Old Slope," 469
Charter of Privileges, 66–67, 132
Chartiers Creek, 441
Chatham Village (Pittsburgh), 297, *297*
Chautauqua meetings, *310*
Chesapeake & Delaware Canal, 169
Chesapeake Bay, 34, 35, 38, 390
Chester County
agriculture, 88–90, 361
architecture, 419, *419*, 420
archives, 523
artists, 528
building materials, 414, *417*, *418*, 427, *430*
Catholics, 355
high-technology companies, 403
horse farms, 402, 404
immigrants, 269–70
labor force, 94
loyalists in, 123, 126
lynching, 289, *289*
marble, 414
population growth, 353
Quakers, 82, 566
representatives in Assembly, 123
slaves, 94
Swedish Lutherans, 83
textile industry, 269–70
Chester County Historical Society, 517
Chester (Delaware County)
highways, 354
riots, 333
shipbuilding, 236
Swedish settlement, 54, 60

topographic region, 8
Chestnut Hill (Philadelphia), 414
Chew, Benjamin, 125
Chew mansion, *124*, 125
Chicago
Columbian Exposition, 257, 505
Great Fire, 427
child labor, 239–40
breaker boys, 262–63, *264*, 513, 564–66
efforts to end, 280, 513, 564–66
in Philadelphia, 221, 240
textile industry, 136, 221
children. *See also* education
adoptions, 343
African American, 242
Jewish, *249*
leisure activities, 309
orphans, *249*, 250, 266, 283
Quaker view of, 63
Roman Catholics, *474*
Chingas, Chief, 112
Chiton, 50
Christ Church (Philadelphia), 95, 106, *106*, 117
Christiana (Lancaster County), 193–94
Christian and Missionary Alliance, 356
Christiana Riot, 194
Christmas, 84, *464*
Chrysler Building, 434
churches. *See also* African American churches; religions
architecture, 406, *416*, 423, *423*, 434, 437
art in, *314*
Bible camps, 312
building materials, 414, *416*
charitable activities, *296*
in colonies, 106, *106*
ethnic, 269, *272*, 312–14, *314*, 355, 399, 437, 495
records used in genealogical research, 488, 493–95, *494*
suburban, 355, 356, *356*
Church of England. *See* Anglicans
Church of Jesus Christ of Latter-day Saints. *See* Mormon Church
Church of Scotland. *See* Presbyterians
Church of the Nazarene, 356
cigars, 453–54
CIGNA, 432
CIO. *See* Congress of Industrial Organizations
cities. *See* Philadelphia; Pittsburgh; urban areas
Citizens & Southern Bank & Trust Company, 287
City Beautiful movement, 257–59, 513, 536
Civic Club of Harrisburg, 259
Civilian Conservation Corps (CCC), *300*
civil service, 280

Great Depression (cont'd)
    impact on Pennsylvania, 292, 293–94, 300,
        378, 429, 567
    photography, 514–15, *517*, *522*
Great Lakes, 9, 131, 162. *See also* Erie, Lake
Great Lakes Coastal Plain, 20, 35
Great Lakes Lowlands, 23
Great Valley, 8
Greek immigrants, *272*
Greek Revival architecture, 197, 411, 422–23, *423*,
    424, *426*
Greeley, Horace, 199
Greencastle (Franklin County), 397
Greene County, agriculture, 166
Greensburg (Westmoreland County), 450, 537–38
Grey Towers, 279
Griffitts, Hannah, 105, 127
Grimké, Sarah, 371
Gropius, Walter, 436
Grove, Robert Moses, 309
Grundy, Joseph R., 279
Guffey, Joseph F., 296
Gulf Building, 432
Gulf Oil, 262
Gunther, John, 319, 327, 354
Guyasuta, 450

H
Hagley Museum, 524
Haldeman, Jacob, 170
Haley, Alex, 483
Hall, Charles M., 230
Hamilton, Alexander, 135, 136, 148, 150
Hancock, Winfield S., 212
Handsome Lake (Skaniadariyo), 131
Hanna, Robert, 449
Hanna's Town (Washington County), 132, 449–51,
    450
Hans Herr House, 412, *413*, 415
"The Happiest I've Been" (Updike), 590
Harding, Warren G., 262
Harkum, Hannah, 81
Harper's Weekly, 211, 227
Harris, Woogie, *288*
Harrisburg Bridge Company, 154
Harrisburg (Dauphin County). *See also* State
    Capitol Building
    African Americans, 171
    banks, 164, 165
    bridges, 154, *155*
    Capitol Complex, 550–51
    city beautification, 257–59, *513*
    civic leaders, 170
    ethnic groups, *476*

Farm Show, *360*, 361–62
floods, *302*
growth, 156
industries, 236
metropolitan area, 353, 354
military camps in Civil War, *211*
Paxton Boys, 114
photographs of, *514*
population, 187, 189, 322, 353, 354
railroads, 187
riots, 333
schools, *514*
slaughterhouses, 185
as state capital, 150, 161, 395
State Library of Pennsylvania, 484
Underground Railroad, 193, *475*
Harrisburg Hebrew School, *477*
Harrison, H., *190*
Harrison City (Westmoreland County), 456
Hartranft, John F., 212
Haviland, John, 197
Havre de Grace (Maryland), 180
Hayes, Rutherford B., 233
Hazleton (Luzerne County), *225*, *265*, 404, 473, *509*
Head House Square (Philadelphia), *269*, 360
health. *See also* diseases; medicine
    conditions in early twentieth century, 274
    effects of pollution, 327
    mental, *137*
    research, 84–85
health care industry, 325, 351
Heckewelder, John, 42, 74, 450
Heemskeerk, Egbert van, *62*
Hegins Pigeon Shoot, 471–72, *472*
Hegins Valley, 464, 466, 467, 471
Heinz, Henry J., 262
Heinz, John, III, 262
Heinz Company, 226, 262, 523
Henderson, Ray, 563
Hendricks, Garret, 97
Hendricksen, Cornelius, 49, *50*
Henisch, Heinz, 518
Heritage Park (Warren), *364*
heritage tourism. *See* historic sites
Herndon, William, 556
Herr, Hans, 412, *413*, 415
Hershey, Catherine Sweeney, 266
Hershey, Milton S., 265–67
Hershey Chocolate Company, 265–67, 303
Hershey (Dauphin County), 265–67, 401, 569
Hesselius, Gustavus, 531–32
Hessian soldiers, 122, *122*, 124
Hetzel, George, 538
Hicks, Edward, 529–30

Higginbotham, A. Leon, 333
Highspire (Dauphin County), *182*
Highway Reserve Act of 1956, 354
highways. *See* roads
Hilldale Club, 309
Hilton, Roy, 542, *544*
Hine, Lewis Wickes, 513, *513*, 524
Historical and Biographical Annals of Berks County,
    Pennsylvania (Montgomery), 482
historical societies, 196, 483, 517, 561
Historical Society of Dauphin County, 523
Historical Society of Pennsylvania, 196, 517
historic sites
    Gettysburg battlefield, 218
    in Philadelphia, 196, *363*, 365, 380, 385, 402
    surveys, 294
    tourism, 196, 365, 366–68, 380, 385, 400, 402
    Valley Forge, 195–96, 199
H. J. Heinz Company. *See* Heinz Company
Hmong people, *478*
Hodgson, Peter, 451
Hoffman, Alice, *571*
Hog Island Shipyard, 285, *287*
holidays
    Christmas, 84, *464*
    ethnic celebrations, 268
    Fourth of July, *164*, 195, 535
    New Year's Day, *357*
Hollidaysburg (Blair County), 165
Holmesburg, 117
Homestead Album Oral History Project, 567
Homestead (Allegheny County)
    economy, 318–19
    housing, *513*
    local government, 298
    photographs of, *369*, 513, *513*, *569*
    population, 318, 323
    steel strike, 204–5, *205*, 229, 242, 319
    steelworks, 260, 318, *318*, *319*, 322, 393, *569*
Homestead Daily Messenger, 318
homosexuals. *See* gays and lesbians
Honesdale (Wayne County), 183
Hooker Fulton Building, 433, *434*
Hoover, Herbert, 262, 295, *295*
Hopewell (Bedford County), 366
Hopewell civilization, 13, 15, 16, 42
Hopkinson, Francis, *105*
Horgan, John, Jr., *264*
Horn, Bob, *334*
Horn, Marvin, *463*
Horseshoe Curve, *367*, 368, *511*, 537
Horstmann, William, 221
Hostetler, Anna, 452
Hostetler, Cyrus, 452

Netherlands
    settlements in America, 38, 39, 41, 49
    trappers, 49
Nevell, Thomas, *420*
Neville, John, 147, *147*, 148
Nevins, Allan, 557
New Castle (Lawrence County), 322, 506, 558–59
New Deal, 295–96, 298, 299, 300, *300*, 358, 378, 542–44
New England, settlers from, 103, 130–32, 398, 424
New England Extended culture area, 398
New Hanover Township (Montgomery County), 84
New Hope (Bucks County), 310, 343
New Milford (Susquehanna County), 404
New Netherlands, 58–59
New Orleans, 157
new social history, 484
newspapers. *See also* mass media
    African American, 189, 286–87
    in Civil War, *213*
    Italian, 268
    in Philadelphia, 144
    records used in genealogical research, 488–89
    sedition arrests, 148
    sports news, 309
New Sweden, 50–58
    agriculture, 53, 54–55
    descendants of settlers, 56, *57*, 493
    Dutch conquest, 58, 60
    epidemics, 58
    establishment, 50–52
    Fort Christina, 38, 50, 53, 57, 58
    governors, 50, 52, 54, *54*, 56, 58, 60
    log buildings, 53, 55, *57*
    relations with Indians, 41, 50–52
    settlers, 53, 54, 56–57, 59
    slaves, 54, 56–57
    women, 60
New Sweden Company, 38
Newton, Isaac, 419–20
New Year's Day, *357*
New York Central, 375
New York Charity Organization Society, 273
New York City
    architecture, 434
    Coney Island, *234*
    manufacturing, 219
    population growth, 150
    port, 185, 186
    transportation to, *86*
Nicolay, John G., 556
NIRA. *See* National Industrial Recovery Act
Nittany Lions. *See* The Pennsylvania State University

Nix, Robert, 333
Nixon, Richard M., 330, *341*, 347
NLU. *See* National Labor Union
Noble and Holy Order of the Knights of Labor. *See* Knights of Labor
nominating conventions, 163, 196, 209, 361
Nones, Benjamin, 146
Non-Importation Agreements, 116
normal schools, 249
Normile, Paul, 298
Norristown (Montgomery County), 183
Northampton County. *See also* Bethlehem
    architecture, 431
    banks, 164
    Committee of Associators, 122
    Fries's Rebellion, 103, 147, 148
    immigrants, 70–71, 144
    Indian attacks on settlers, 77
    Moravian communities, 79, *81*
    support for Revolution, 129
Northern Tier, 368, 396, 398, 424
North Philadelphia, 333, 334
Northumberland County, population declines, 323
Norvelt (Westmoreland County), 514
novels. *See* literature
nuclear power, 328, 329, 349, 372, 376–77
Nuclear Regulatory Commission, 328
Nutimas, *76*, 77

O

Oakland (Susquehanna County), 174
Oakley, Violet, 261, *261*, 548–50, *550*
Oestreicher, David M., 42
O'Hara, John, 311, 409, 586–87, 591
Ohiopyle (Fayette County), 436, *437*
Ohio River, 9, 157
Ohio Valley, 10
    agriculture, 15–16, 18
    British forces in, 113–14
    competing claims to, 110
    industrialization, 401
Ohnmacht, Leo, 485
Oil Creek, *510*
Oil Creek Furnace, 176–78
oil industry
    boom, *236*, 237
    company towns, 401
    competition from Southwest, 377
    development, 176–78, 237–38, 376, 393
    financing, 230
    photography, 510, *510*
    power of Standard Oil, 237–38, 276, 382
    railroad transportation, 237–38

Old Bethel African Methodist Episcopal Church (Reading), 475
Old Economy Village, 199
Old State House (Philadelphia), 196. *See also* Independence Hall
The Olinger Stories (Updike), 590
Olyphant Colliery, *266*
Onandaga people, 20, 23, 37–38
Oneida Community, 199
One Liberty Place, 434
Operation Rescue, *344*
L'Opinione, 268
oral history
    collections, 556–57, 560–61, 569–70
    conducting interviews, 562, 571–72
    editing, 558–59
    interpretations, 572–73
    interviews, 553–56, 558–59, 565, 566–68
    issues, 569–73
    memories of places, 568–69
    methods, 557, 570–71
    origins, 556–57
    as source for history, 555–56, 560, 561–66
    university programs, 557, 560
    use in folklore and folklife research, 476–77
    use in genealogical research, 484
Order of the Star-Spangled Banner, 209
Ormandy, Eugene, 311, *335*
Orphan's Court, 489, 490
Orr, Robert, 449
orreries, *119*
Ottawa people, 112–13
Otto, Bodo, 126
Out of This Furnace (Bell), 409, 591–92
Overpeck complex, 29, *29*
Owasco culture, 20–23, 25
Owen family, *478*

P

Packer, Asa, 369
Pages from a Worker's Life (Foster), 576
Paine, Thomas, 117, 128, 371, 375
    Common Sense, 119–20
    portraits, 547
    protests against British rule, 118
    view of Test Oath, 123
Paleo-Indian period, 3
    archaeological sites, 441, 445
    climate, 10
    hunting, 3, 7–8
    spearheads, 7, *7*, 441
    tools, *443*, 445, *446*
Panic of 1819, 165
Panic of 1837, 189

Purviance, William T., 510
PWA. *See* Public Works Administration

Q

"The Quaker Meeting" (Heemskeerk), *62*
Quaker Party, 115, 116, 118, 120, 142
Quakers
    in Assembly, 67, 68–69
    beliefs, 63, 84
    birth records, 493
    Capitol murals depicting, 547
    census of blacks in Philadelphia, 489
    in colonial era, 81, 373, 374, 382
    criticism of, *114*, 115
    declining membership, 136, 172
    in England, 63
    involved in Revolution, 117, 121
    meetings, *62*, *175*
    opponents of slavery, 97, 139, 174, 190, 191,
        374
    oral histories, 566
    origins, 62–63
    pacifism, 63, 112, 119, 120, 127, 128, 138
    in Philadelphia, 106, *108*
    playing cards depicting, *70*
    in political cartoons, *114*, *115*
    political power, 66, 74, 83
    refusal to take oaths, 123
    slave owners, 63, 94–95
    social reformers, 169
    voting rights, 120, 123, 142
    wealth, *68*, 88, 221, 531
    women's roles, *62*, 63, 82, 195, 374
Quasi-War, 146
Quay, Matthew, 247, 253, 254, 255
quilts, *68*, *478*

R

Rabbit, Run (Updike), 590–91
raccoons, *55*
race. *See also* African Americans; Philadelphia,
        racial tensions in; whites
    anti-discrimination laws, 296
    differences in colonial era, 93, 95
    legal distinctions, 69
    in literature, 581–82
    political issues, 332–34
    racism, 80, 173, 190, 285
    riots, 333, 338, *339*
    segregation, *212*, 217, 252, 285, 288, 582–83, 584
    tensions, 190–92, 567
radio, 262, *263*, 309, 312, 377
Rafinesque, Constantine Samuel, 42
Railroaders' Memorial Museum, 368

railroads. *See also* Pennsylvania Railroad
    abandoned, 406
    advertisements, *183*
    bridges, 159
    built by state government, 178, 183
    during Civil War, 212, 233
    coal transported on, 183
    competition from trucks, 320
    construction, 165, 183–85, 232, 394
    dangers of, *194*
    decline, 321, 375
    depots, 401
    financing, 185, 188, 212, 223
    impact, 185, 187
    locomotives, 185, 212, 221, *221*, 260
    map, *230*
    networks, 183, *230*
    obstacles, 301, 391
    paintings of, 537, 538–40
    passenger trains, 183, *249*, 320
    photography, 510, *511*, 523
    racial discrimination in, 251
    steam power, 183
    strikes, 203–4, *204*, 217, 233, 242
    technology, 229
    tourism and, *249*, 367, 368, 369
Rambo, Britta Mattsdotter, 56
Rambo, Peter Gunnarsson, 56, *57*, 90
Rapp, George, 199
Rau, William H., 510
Raynal, Abbé, 375
Reading (Berks County), 404
    amusement parks, 309
    automobile industry, 293
    banks, 164
    canals, 180
    industries, 179, 236
    iron forges, 91
    prisoners of war, 122
    railroads, 183–85
    refugees from Indian raids, 112
    support of Revolution, 126
    Underground Railroad in, *475*
Reading Terminal building (Philadelphia), 357,
        360
Reagan, Ronald, 345, 378
Reconstruction, 210, 216, 217, 251
Reconstruction Finance Corporation (RFC), 301
redemptioners, 93
Redfield, Edward, 310
Red Scare, 320, 330, 331
Reed, Esther DeBerdt, *128*
Reed, Joseph, 127, 133
Reed, Sarah, 250, *250*

Reformed Church
    church records, 495
    in colonial era, 78, 373
    German immigrants, 72, 493
    members' support of Revolution, 126
    in twentieth century, 355
reformers. *See* Progressive Movement; social
        reformers
Reiner, Fritz, 311
religions. *See also* churches; *and specific religious
        groups*
    abortion issue, 343–45
    after Revolution, 136–37
    in Britain, 62, 63
    Capitol murals depicting, 547
    charitable activities, 78, *296*
    in colonial era, 78–84, 136
    divisions within cities, 172, 194
    European, 49
    evangelical, 356, *356*
    evolution of practices, 83–84
    Great Awakening, 80, 81, *82*
    of immigrants, 70
    of Indians, 27, 30, 36, 39, 49, 131
    mystics, 79, *79*
    national organizations, 136–37, 373
    proportion of population, 173, 174
    racism in, 80
    revival meetings, *174*, *175*, 312, 464
    schools affiliated with, 311, 313, 325
    science and, 84–85, *85*
    Second Great Awakening, 464
    of slaves, 74, 80, 81–83
    in twentieth century, 311–14, 354–56
religious freedom, 67, 83, 174, 373, 374, 382
Rendell, Ed, *349*
Renovo (Clinton County), 401
republican mothers, 137, *138*
Republican Party. *See also* Federalists
    bosses, 247, 255, 277–79, 292
    dominance of state, 253–55, 270–71, 277–79
    in 1850s, 206, 207, 209–10
    in eighteenth century, 103, 117, 121, 123, 133
    founding in 1856, 209
    governors, 253, 298–300, 346
    nominating conventions, 209, *345*, 361
    Pennsylvanians in national government, 142,
        262
    in Philadelphia, 292, 298
    progressives, 271, 279, 299
    in state politics, 341, 345, 346
    view of Reconstruction, 216
    women in, 250
Republic Steel, 302

establishment, 132, 449
highways, 301
horse farms, 402
iron industry, 161
tax resisters, 130
Whiskey Rebellion, 103, 147–48, 150
Westmoreland Museum of American Art, 537–38
West Philadelphia, 56, *107*, 335, 581
Weyman, B. Frank, 454
Weyman, George, 453, 454
Weyman, William, 454
Weyman & Brother, 453, 454
When the Broad Way Meets the Dawn (Teller), 537, *540*
Whig Party, 116, 206, 207–9
Whipper, William, 190
Whiskey Rebellion, 103, 147–48, 150
Whitaker, Lawrence, 542
White, William, 136–37
Whitefield, George, 81
Whitemarsh (Montgomery County), 436
whites. *See also* Europeans; immigrants; race
ethnic politics, 334, 337
movement out of cities, 332
racial identity, 74–75
Whitsett Mine, *240*
Wickham, Mary Fanning, 307
Wideman, John Edgar, 338, 581–83, 584
Wilkes-Barre (Luzerne County), 404
banks, 165
courthouse, 485
immigrant miners, 224
Kennedy's visit, *341*
population, 322, 323
railroads, 183
soldiers from, 306
telegraph system, *270*
topographic region, 8
William A. Todd House, *420*
William Cramp & Sons, *232*
William Keen Building, 427
William M. Allison House, 426, *429*
William Penn's Treaty with the Indians (West), *66*, 528–29, *529*, 530
Williams, G. Grant, 286–87
Williamson, T. Roney, *430*
Williamsport (Lycoming County)
library, 414
Little League Baseball World Series, *365*
lumber industry, 182, 237, 392
tourism, 385
Willing, Thomas, 135, 136
Willis, William, 416
Willow Grove Park, 309

wills, 487, 489–92
Wilmington (Delaware), Fort Christina, 38, 50, 53, 57, 58
Wilmot, David, 168, 169, 207, *208*, 209, 371
Wilmot Proviso, 207
Wilson, Alexander, 375
Wilson, Edmund, 364
Wilson, James, 133, 142
Wilson, Kirke, 450
Windfall (Anderson), 589
window tax, 489
Winner, William E., *196*
Wissahickon Creek, 79
Wissahickon gneiss, 414
Wister, Owen, 308, *308*
witches, 84, 109
Wofford, Harris, 345
Wollstonecraft, Mary, 128, *138*
wolves, 58
Woman in the Wilderness, 373
Woman's Suffrage Association, 280
women. *See also* gender
abolitionists, 191
African American, 195, 241
artists, 251, 261, 548–50
clergy, 342
clothing, 290
debutantes, 306–7
education of, 137–39, 246, 249, 283–84
flappers, 290
immigrants, 269–70
legal rights, 93
magazines, 177, *177*, 377
middle class, 249, 250, 270
moral responsibilities, 137–38
in New Sweden, 60
organizations, 250, 251
pavilion at Centennial Exposition, 222
in Pennsylvania colony, 70
Pennsylvania German names, 497
photographers, 199
political activists, 342, 343, 535
prostitutes, 489
Quakers, *62*, 63, 82, 195, 374
during Revolution, 127, 128, 138
rights of, 128, *138*, 194–95, 342, 379
roles, 49, 137–39, *138*, 177, 250, 342, 561–63
social organizations, 307
social reformers, 217, 250, 259, 276, 280–84
support for French Revolution, 139
union leaders, *341*
unpaid labor in homes, 241, 561–63
upper-class, 104–5
volunteers in Civil War relief efforts, 213–14, 250

voting rights, 168, 249, 250, 280, 281, *281*, 282, 284
work in colonial era, *71*, *90*
writers, 86, 307, 580, 583–85
women, Indian
agriculture, 15, 18, 26
cultural roles, 48
gathering by, 16
matrilineal cultures, 24, 44, 48
pottery, 15
women in labor force. *See also* workers
African Americans, 241
clerical workers, 246, 249
domestic servants, 241
immigrants, 269–70
milliners, *90*, 454–55
oral histories, 553–55, 573
in Pittsburgh, 240–41
sales clerks, 247
textile industry, 136, 221, *239*, 240, 269–70
unemployment, 294
wages, 274, 280
during World War II, 304
women's movement, 194–95, 342
Wood, G., *87*
Woodland period, 3. *See also* Late Woodland period
agriculture, 15–16, 446
archaeological sites, 446
burial mounds, 13
Early, 13–15, *15*, *16*
foods, 15–16, 17–18
hunter-gatherers, 3–4, 16, 18, 20
material cultures, 13
Middle, 12, 13, 15–16, 20
pottery, 15, *16*, 21, 446
Woodmen of the World, 307
Woodson, Lewis, 189–90
Woodward, George, 299
Woodward, George W., 299
workers. *See also* child labor; strikes; unions; women in labor force
apprentices, 93, 108–9
churches, 136
in cities, 170–72
class consciousness, 384–85
in colonial era, *90*, 92–94, 116
Democratic Party and, 206
effects of industrialization, 172, 173
entertainment, 307–9
housing, 401, 431, 437
immigrants, 171–72, 176, 178, 220, 221–23, 228, 267, 273
in literature, 576–80, 591–92